TRAVELER'S GUIDE TO

MEXICAN CAMPING

Explore Mexico and Belize With Your RV or Tent

Second Edition

Mike and Terri
Church

ROLLING HOMES PRESS

Published by
Rolling Homes Press
161 Rainbow Dr., #6157
Livingston, TX 77399-1061

www.rollinghomes.com

Printed in the United States of America
First Printing 2001

Publisher's Cataloging in Publication

Church, Mike, 1951-
Traveler's guide to Mexican camping : explore Mexico and Belize
 with your RV or tent / Mike and Terri Church–Second Edition
 p.cm.
 Includes index.
 Library of Congress Control Number: 2001130820
 ISBN 0-9652968-6-5

1. Camp sites, facilities, etc.–Mexico–Guidebooks. 2. Camping–Mexico–Guide-books. 3. Mexico–Guidebooks. I. Church, Terri. II. Title. III. Mexican Camping

GV191.48.M6 C58 2001
917.2'4'836–dc21   2001 130820

DEDICATION

As always this book is dedicated to Joyce and her family (Mike, Jon, Jeremy, Julie, and Jace), our support team back in Redmond, WA.

ACKNOWLEDGEMENTS

Much of the information in this book came from conversations, letters, e-mails and tips passed along by other Mexican RV travelers. Many thanks to all of you. The following is a partial list of the people who have taken the time to share their knowledge. Please forgive us if we've inadvertently left your name off the list.

Sue and Bill Abbott, Bess and Chuck Alexander, Anne and Ed Barrett, Marshall Becker, Julia and Volker Biebesheimer, Lucette and Dirk Bogaert, Juanita and Roy Boorman, Becky and Garrett Bosch, Michelíne Bourbeau, Jean and Jerry Bradbury, John Bryant, Becki and Bob Burr, Rosie and Russ Burrows, Judy and Rush Busbee , Mary and Don Busick, Mary and Hal Cairns, Brenna Chaloupka, Dan Clarke, Audrey and Chris Costello, Rob Craig, Sandra and Bart Cross, Jane and Earl Cruser, Kay and Don Damkaer, William Darrow, Daubie Daubenberger, EllaBeth and Bruce Deitle, Jane and Bill Edwards, David Eidell, Bernice and Harry Eldon, Carole and Joe Ellis, Ed Emerick, Kay and Chuck Fishburn, Jeanine Flury, Bill Forgie, George Foster and Louise, John Geyer, Marlene and Bill Gibbon, Barbara Gilliam, Dorothy and Bob Gilreath, Jeanne and Don Glass, Filipa and Nigel Gow, Ron Gregory, Carol Grimmer, Marilyn Gutgsell, Deanna Hampton, Beth and Harlan Hansen, Bob Hawes, Kathey and Vern Heaney, Irene and Rudy Herman, Gloria and Ed Helmuth, Peggy and Bob Herlocker, Lane Hernandez, John Holod, Dee and Bill Holt, Tom Horovatin, Yvonne and Bruce Horton, Diane and Lorne Houston, James Hruska, Jeanne and Dick Hurley, Vicki and Gerry Jacobs, Edie and Dan James, Paul Jenkins, Walt Jenkins, Lorri Jones, Marilyn and Loren Kaufman, Anne Kiehl, Linda and Juergen Klauke, Marilyn and Larry Knight, Juanita and Ron Kohn, Erika and Hans Krauklis, Dave Krieg, Fernand Labonté, Steve Lacey, Louis Lampe, André Langevin, Kate Lansdown, Gwen and Lowell Larsen, Dorothy and Jim Lear, Leonard, Gilles Lesage, Tony Lozano, Margie and Gaylord Maxwell, Pat McGrath, Elizabeth MacCormack, Shirley and Bob Mackin, Shirley and Mal MacDonald, Juanita and Roy Majusaki, Tom Marlatt, Elaine and Dick Marshall, Peachy and Sandie McGeachy, Vonnie and Ken McIntyre, Helen and Henry Mitchell, Robert Moore, Eddie and Rob Nagels, Bonnie and Gary Neighorn, Marilyn and Brodie Nimmo, Karen and John Nickel, O.B. O'Brian, David Orozco, Cece and Al Osterling, Claudette and André Paquette, Carole and Nolan Parrett, Louise Patenaude, Ann and Harold Peabody, Doris and Don Pearson, Rich Peterson, Liz and John Plaxton, Sheelah and Bob Pomerleau, Tina Poole, Chuck Potter, Rhonda Powell, Joy and Jim Prentice, Rosa and Bud Richardson, Dorita and Parker Roe, Nicole Rousseau, Ida and Lobo Saar, Ginger and Jim Schlote, Renata and Heinz Scholz, Fred Schweizer, Iris and Tom Sharpe, Pat Shea, Barbara Sherman, Les Shoemaker, Marilyn and William Shumate, Grietje and Jan Slot, Gisela and Jim Spires, Karen and Tony Steflik, Carolyn and Jim Strom, Gloria and Bill Thompson, Bob Todd, Bill Trimble, Riet and Ted Vandenmeiracker, Joe Vinson, Cathy and Ed Volt, Marcia Waggoner and Martin, Judy and Jerry Wagoner, Lee and Tom Walker, Virginia and Ralph Wiggers, Shirley and Don Willard, Barbara and Jerry Wilson, Dianne and Brett Wolfe, Floyd Woods, Dorothy and George Young, Meg and Pete Zearbaugh, Juan Manual Zepeda, Lee Zieger, Sandie and Jim Zwart.

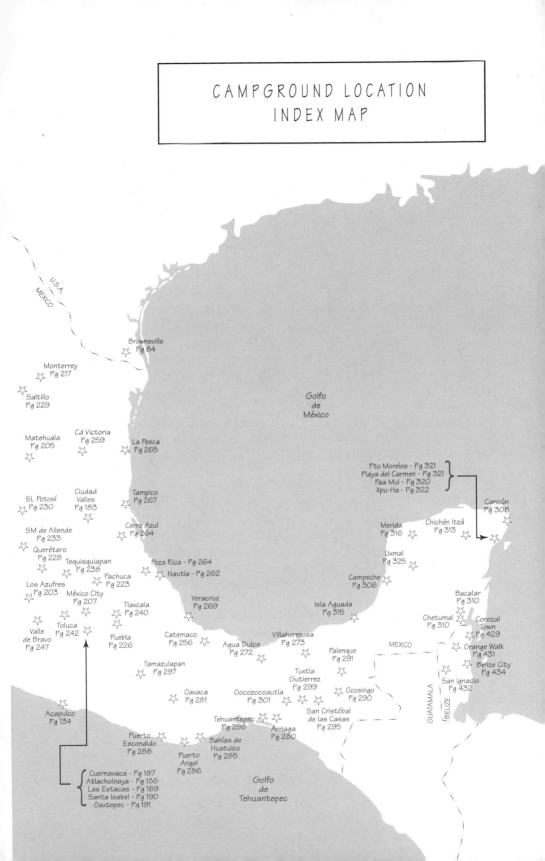

CAMPGROUND LOCATION INDEX MAP

Brownsville
Pg 84

Monterrey
Pg 217

Saltillo
Pg 229

Golfo
de
México

Matehuala
Pg 205

Cd Victoria
Pg 259

La Pesca
Pg 265

Pto Morelos - Pg 321
Playa del Carmen - Pg 321
Paa Mul - Pg 320
Xpu-Ha - Pg 322

Cancún
Pg 308

SL Potosí
Pg 230

Ciudad
Valles
Pg 183

Tampico
Pg 267

Merida
Pg 316

Chichén Itzá
Pg 313

SM de Allende
Pg 233

Cerro Azul
Pg 264

Querétaro
Pg 228

Tequisquiapan
Pg 238

Poza Rica - Pg 264

Nautla - Pg 262

Uxmal
Pg 325

Los Azufres
Pg 203

Pachuca
Pg 223

México City
Pg 207

Campeche
Pg 306

Bacalar
Pg 310

Tlaxcala
Pg 240

Veracruz
Pg 269

Isla Aguada
Pg 315

Chetumal
Pg 310

Corozal
Town
Pg 429

Valle
de Bravo
Pg 247

Toluca
Pg 242

Puebla
Pg 226

Catemaco
Pg 256

Agua Dulce
Pg 272

Villahermosa
Pg 273

MEXICO

Orange Walk
Pg 431

Tamazulapan
Pg 297

Palenque
Pg 291

Belize City
Pg 434

Tuxtla
Gutierrez
Pg 299

Ocosingo
Pg 290

San Ignacio
Pg 432

GUATAMALA

BELIZE

Acapulco
Pg 134

Oaxaca
Pg 281

Oocozocoautla
Pg 301

San Cristóbal
de las Casas
Pg 295

Tehuantepec
Pg 298

Arriaga
Pg 280

Puerto
Escondido
Pg 288

Bahías de
Huatulco
Pg 285

Puerto
Angel
Pg 286

Golfo
de
Tehuantepec

Cuernavaca - Pg 187
Atlacholoaya - Pg 188
Las Estacas - Pg 189
Santa Isabel - Pg 190
Oaxtepec - Pg 191

U.S.A.

MEXICO

WARNING, DISCLOSURE, AND COMMUNICATION WITH THE AUTHORS AND PUBLISHERS

Half the fun of travel is the unexpected, and self-guided camping travel can produce much in the way of unexpected pleasures, and also complications and problems. This book is designed to increase the pleasures of Mexican camping and reduce the number of unexpected problems you may encounter. You can help ensure a smooth trip by doing additional advance research, planning ahead, and exercising caution when appropriate. There can be no guarantee that your trip will be trouble free.

Although the authors and publisher have done their best to ensure that the information presented in this book was correct at the time of publication they do not assume and hereby disclaim any liability to any party for any loss or damage caused by errors, omissions, or any other cause.

In a book like this it is inevitable that there will be omissions or mistakes, especially as things do change over time. If you find inaccuracies we would like to hear about them so that they can be corrected in future editions. We would also like to hear about your enjoyable experiences. If you come upon an outstanding campground or destination please let us know, those kinds of things may also find their way to future versions of the guide or to our internet site. You can reach us by mail at:

Rolling Homes Press
161 Rainbow Dr., #6157
Livingston, TX 77399-1061

You can also communicate with us by sending an e-mail through our web site at:

www.rollinghomes.com

TABLE OF CONTENTS

PREFACE

Traveler's Guide to Mexican Camping is one of five guidebooks for campers that we have written and publish. The titles of the others are *Traveler's Guide to European Camping, Traveler's Guide to Alaskan Camping, Traveler's Guide to Camping Mexico's Baja* and *RV Adventures in the Pacific Northwest*.

Like all of our books this one is a guidebook written specifically for camping travelers. As a camper you don't need the same information as a fly-in visitor. You don't care much about hotels, pricey restaurants, and airline schedules, but you need to know which campgrounds are near, how to drive right to them without making wrong turns, and where to buy supplies. We want our book to be the one you keep up front where it's handy, the one you refer to over and over because it contains what you need to know in a convenient format.

We hope that RV travelers to Mexico will find this second edition of *Traveler's Guide to Mexican Camping* to be even more helpful than the first. We've been amazed and very pleased at the enthusiastic reception of the first edition by the RVing community in Mexico. We hope you all like this one even better!

In researching this new edition we were surprised at the number of changes that we found. If you are worried that RVing is dying out in Mexico you will be encouraged to hear that we have included over sixty new campgrounds and discovered only ten or so that have closed. We admit that a few of the new campgrounds were places we just missed last time, but many of them were new too. Fact is, there are so many campgrounds that we've actually published a new book that covers the Baja Peninsula, we felt we had to do that in order to do the Baja Peninsula justice. Baja campgrounds are still included in *Traveler's Guide to Mexican Camping* but there are more of them and a lot of extra information in the new book which is titled *Traveler's Guide to Camping Mexico's Baja*.

We're excited by some of the new things to be found in this book. Here are just a few of them:

• There seems to be a lot of interest in visiting Belize. We've included a full chapter about visiting that country in an RV.

• We had a GPS receiver for the entire research trip this time so you'll find GPS coordinates for almost every campground.

• The book never seems confusing to us, but a few readers complained that they sometimes have trouble quickly finding campgrounds. We've included a new index map in the first few pages of the book to help out.

- First-timers or veteran travelers crossing into Mexico at a new place needed more information so we've greatly expanded the *Crossing the Border* chapter.

- Sometimes it's hard to get through the big towns. In the last book we told how to bypass Mexico City, this time we've added bypass routes for Tampico and Veracruz to make driving up or down the east coast much easier.

- You'll find new campgrounds and information to make visiting the following destinations in your RV much easier: Nuevo Casas Grandes and the Paquimé archeological site and museum, Creel and El Fuerte and the Copper Canyon, the Monarch butterfly reserves, Paricutín volcano, San Luis Potosí, Villahermosa, Playa del Carmen, Ocosingo and the Toniná archeological site, and the Teotihuacán archeological site near Mexico City.

All of this talk of the new things to be found in this edition obscures the one thing we are really most proud of. We really believe that *Travelers Guide to Mexican Camping* is making Mexico much more accessible to first-time RV visitors. More and more we meet first-timers carrying a copy of this book while making lengthy visits deep into Mexico, and doing so with little problem.

We tried to keep these people in mind during the past year as we revisited virtually all of the campgrounds listed in this book. We used our own instructions to find each one, and we tried to watch for ways to make our instructions and maps clearer and more accurate. Veteran travelers may feel that we've gone a little overboard in places, just try to remember that the camping public isn't at all uniform. What seems overkill to one may be just right to another. We've tried to strike a balance while keeping in mind that it's no fun to find yourself in a cul-de-sac driving a big rig at the end of a long day with no room to turn it around and no real idea where you will spend the night. We've all been there.

We had a wonderful time traveling throughout Mexico again to update this book. Each time we visit we find new things to do, see, and experience. It's a fact that the more you get to know Mexico the more you enjoy it. After this last trip we are even more anxious to return than before, there are so many things we want to see and do! With any luck at all we'll meet you along the way.

MEXICO

Top Row Left: 5th-Wheel Near Cataviña On The Baja
Top Row Right: Flowers In The Market At Tonalá
Bottom Row Left: Boats At The Floating Gardens At
                 Xochimilco Near Mexico City
Bottom Row Right: RVs Parking Along The Water In Chetumal

CHAPTER

· · · · · · · · · · · · · 1

WHY CAMP MEXICO?

The U.S. – Mexico border is like no other border on earth. Between the two countries there are huge contrasts in culture, language, wealth, lifestyle, political systems, topography, and climate. All of this means that Mexico is a fascinating place to visit. Best of all, you can do it in your own RV.

Mexico Is a Land of Amazing Variety

Most people who visit Mexico climb on a jet and spend a week or two at one of five or six Mexican beach resorts. These places are all world-famous—who hasn't heard of **Cancún, Acapulco, Puerto Vallarta, Ixtapa/Zihuatenejo,** and **Cabo San Lucas.** These are great places to visit—but the best way to do so is in your own vehicle. They all offer good campgrounds and have their own sections in this book. But there are lots of other attractions in this fascinating country. The vacation traveler who only visits the tourist cities misses almost all of the best Mexico has to offer. Here's a very incomplete listing of some of the things you can see and do in Mexico.

The beach resorts are on the coast, of course. But there is lots more coastline in Mexico that the travel agents don't even know about. Mexico's beaches are beautiful, mostly empty, and generally sport truly superior weather. Some of the best free camping you'll ever see is along the **beaches of Mexico's Baja and west coasts**. You could write a entire book just about Mexico's beaches, in fact, it's been done.

If beaches aren't your thing don't despair. The interior of Mexico is full of attractions. Many *norteamericanos* (Mexican term for Canadian and U.S. citizens, also known as *gringos*) are drawn to the superior climate and cultural attractions of **Guadalajara, Lake Chapala, San Miguel de Allende, Álamos, Guanajuato,** and **Cuernavaca.** All have populations of permanent residents from the United States and Canada.

Bustling **Mexico City** is now or will soon be the largest city in the world, it is easy to visit from nearby campgrounds. Less well known colonial or neoclassical cities like **Querétaro, San Luis Potosí, Zacatecas, Aguascalientes** and **Oaxaca** also make fascinating destinations.

Perhaps you want to explore, to get off the beaten path. There are enough remote rugged byways in Mexico to keep you busy for years. Consider the desert roads of the **Baja Peninsula**, the hiking trails of the **Copper Canyon**, and the often impassable jungle tracks of Lacandón **Chiapas** and the **Yucatán**. The campgrounds listed in this book aren't remote, but some make good bases or jumping-off points for more rugged locales.

Probably most of us have limited contact with the Mexican people who have settled into the United States and Canada. Traveling in your own vehicle and living off the normal non-tourist economy will give you lots of chances to meet people from all social classes. Many of these folks will have had little contact with norteamericanos. We're confident that you will be amazed by the attitudes and abilities of these people who many of us would consider disadvantaged and downtrodden. As a whole you'll find the Mexican people to be friendly, cheerful, helpful and very family oriented. The chance to meet and understand the people of Mexico, who comprise a growing segment of the population of our own countries, is one of the best reasons of all to visit Mexico.

Pre-Columbian Mesoamerican city sites are scattered throughout the country. If you are fascinated by history you'll love Palenque (everyone's favorite), Teotihuacán, Monte Albán, Chichén Itzá, Uxmal and photogenic Tulúm. These sites are only an introduction, there must be at least a hundred major archeological attractions in various stages of preservation and reconstruction in Mexico. In fact, there are so many sites that you may even discover one yourself.

The Catholic religion has been important in Mexico since the very beginning of the Spanish conquest. For this reason you will find lots of religious buildings throughout the county. Probably most interesting are the churches, cathedrals, and monasteries of what are often called the "colonial cities" and the missions of the Baja Peninsula and northwestern Mexico. It can be rewarding to visit the remote missions of the Baja or study the architecture of Mexican churches.

Mexico is well known as a shopping paradise, particularly for crafts. Well represented in the municipal markets, *tianguis* (open-air markets), and shops are pottery, clothes, furniture, metalwork, rugs, hammocks, baskets, masks, alebrijes (fantastic wooden or papier-mâché animals), and lots more. You'll find that it is much easier to bring your treasures home in your own vehicle than in a suitcase.

For outdoors-oriented sports types the Baja Peninsula and west coast offer some of the best deep-sea fishing in the world. Scuba and skin divers love the Cancún coast, particularly Cozumel. Sailborders congregate on the Baja. Bird watchers will find interesting places to explore throughout the country. The entire Baja west coast is a surfing paradise. Ocean kayakers travel the length of the Baja east coast. Hikers join the Tarahumaras in the remote Copper Canyon. Bird hunting has long been popular in Sonora and Sinaloa. These are just a sampling of the available outdoor pleasures.

Mexico is Easy to Visit

There can be no foreign country that is easier to visit than Mexico. You need simply drive your rig to one of many border towns, spend an afternoon securing Mexican insurance and doing last-minute shopping, and then cross the border the next morning. Within a few hours you'll be far from the hectic border area and will reach your first night's stop well before dark.

For your visit to Mexico you'll find there are few formalities and little documentation needed. You'll need little more than the camping vehicle you use at home and some rudimentary documentation showing that you are a U.S. or Canadian resident. There are now procedures in place when you cross the border to insure that you bring your vehicles back out of Mexico, they don't want you to sell it without paying the proper taxes. All together border formalities seldom take over a half-hour, the details are covered in *Chapter 3 - Crossing The Border*.

Mexico is Inexpensive

In past years Mexico was truly a bargain. Today that is not quite so much the case. The actual costs vary from year to year, they depend upon the value of the peso in relation to the U.S. and Canadian dollars.

When camping you live off a different economy than jet-flying tourists. You'll shop with Mexican citizens for food and gasoline. About the only thing you'll buy that is priced for norteamericanos is your campsite. Even these tend to be less expensive than those outside Mexico, and certainly they are in much more attractive and exotic locations.

Mexico Has All of the Services You Need

Modern Mexico is a far cry from what it was just 15 years ago. There has been massive consumer-oriented investment. In larger towns almost everyone shops at modern supermarkets. Gasoline stations are popping up everywhere, they have unleaded gasoline and diesel. Campgrounds are located conveniently in most localities where you'll want to stay, and with this book you'll have no problem finding them. Most have full hookups so you can be very comfortable.

Mexico Has Good Roads, And They Get Better Each Year

During the last 15 years there has been a massive road-building effort undertaken in Mexico. Modern superhighways now link most sections of the country. Many of these, unfortunately, are toll highways but there are usually free alternatives. Take a look at the *Toll Roads* section of the *Details, Details, Details* chapter. Certainly you'll never have to drive on a gravel road unless you want to get way off the beaten path.

Mexico Has Wonderful Weather

Mexico's weather is the main reason many people head south. During the winter you can easily find tropical weather in Mexico. If hot weather doesn't appeal just head for the highlands. Guadalajara and Cuernavaca are both said to have springtime weather year-round.

Mexico can also be a good summer destination. If you want to get away from the sweltering humidity of the central United States just head for Colonial Mexico. There you'll find little humidity and warm but comfortable summer temperatures.

Mexico is a Land of Adventure

Has traveling the freeways of the U.S. and Canada begun to bore you? Would you like to actually use that four-wheel-drive on your new rig? Do you dream of a campsite with no one else around? If you answer yes to any of these questions then Mexico is the place for you.

This is not to say that you will find adventure if you are not looking for it. Travelers sticking to the beaten path of Mex 15 down the west coast will hardly know they're not in the U.S. But venture off the beaten track and Mexico can indeed be a land of adventure.

Consider the following. The people speak a different language than you do, often it is not Spanish. There may be freeways but there are also thousands of miles of jeep tracks. Much of the population in remote areas is composed of Indians living in near stone-age conditions. Certainly many of the people you will meet off the beaten track are almost entirely isolated from modern culture.

The truth is that even if you stick to major roads and camp only in formal camp-grounds your visit to Mexico will be an adventure you'll never forget.

Safety and Political Stability

Probably the main reason that Mexican campgrounds aren't overrun with folks from north of the border is that people have fears about their safety in Mexico. Remember that the unfamiliar is often scary. For example, people from Europe think that the United States is one of the most violent places in the world, yet most U.S. citizens have little contact with any kind of violence.

We are convinced that Mexico is no more dangerous than the United States or Canada. During our travels we have never been the victims of any kind of violence. Nor have we ever had anything stolen from us (except perhaps some change at gas stations). We've talked to many people and few of them have ever had any problems either.

Just like in your own home country you must take certain precautions. We talk about some of these in the *Safety and Security* section of our Chapter 2.

Another perceived problem in Mexico is lack of political stability. We often hear on the news that there has been political violence or that there are demonstrators on the streets of Mexico City. The truth is that Mexican politics are different than the ones we are accustomed to. As a traveler you can easily avoid this type of political unrest if you want to. After all, your home is on wheels and any type of political violence is front page news so you should usually have plenty of warning.

MEXICO OFFERS LOTS TO DO - SOME POSSIBLE ITINERARIES

Probably the best way to actually show you what Mexico has to offer is to outline a few popular expeditions. Thousands of people each year follow itineraries similar to the *Down the West Coast* and *Baja Peninsula* ones outlined below. The *Grand Coastal Tour* is popular with experienced Mexico travelers who have the time to visit both the Yucatán Peninsula and the west coast. If you are interested in Mexican history and culture you'll love the *Colonial Mexico* itinerary. The time given for each itinerary is the bare minimum required to do the entire trip, but each can be shortened by turning back north before reaching the southernmost point. Each can also be easily stretched to three or four months by adding days in the destinations mentioned or by making side trips. It's also easy to combine parts of these itineraries for a great trip that is either shorter or longer than the ones outlined. As you review the itineraries you should use our index at the back of the book to find more detailed information.

DOWN THE WEST COAST (24 DAYS)

The popularity of this tour is due to excellent roads and lots of good RV parks in a variety of ocean-side cities, towns, and beach-side locations. Mex 15 from Nogales is a reasonably priced four-lane toll road almost all the way to Mazatlán, farther south the roads are two-lane but not bad. From the first day there are excellent campgrounds with modern hookups. If you would like a taste of Mexico with little in the way of inconvenience, this is the tour for you. It's the perfect introduction to Mexico, we think even better than the Baja. We've allowed at least one layover day at almost every stop to make this a leisurely tour.

Day 1 - Nogales to Bahía Kino - 239 miles (391 km), 7 hours - You can now pick up both your tourist card and vehicle permit at the Km 21 checkpoint south of Nogales. Plan on about an hour to accomplish both, then drive south on four-lane Mex 15 to Hermosillo. Follow signs through town for Bahía Kino, Hermosillo's traffic is busy but its boulevards are for the most part not difficult to drive even in a big rig. There is a long bypass around the southern edge of the city, it is the best route if you are headed south directly to Guaymas, but when bound for Kino Bay we prefer to follow signs that direct you around a northern bypass route. Bahía Kino offers many campgrounds and is a popular destination for fishermen and campers who are looking for a quiet beach not far from the border.

Day 3 - Bahía Kino to Guaymas/San Carlos - 153 miles (250 km), 4 hours - Retrace your steps to Hermosillo and then turn south to Mex 15 and the twin towns of Guaymas and San Carlos. You might stay at the historic Hotel Playa de Cortés at Miramar beach or the new El Mirador outside San Carlos.

Day 5 - Guaymas/San Carlos to Álamos - 157 miles (257 km), 4 hours - Álamos will be your only chance on this itinerary to visit an old colonial mining town. They're more common in the interior. Drive south on Mex 15 until you reach Navojoa, then turn inland. Álamos has been adopted by many norteamericano residents, it offers good restaurants and tours of restored colonial homes.

Day 7 - Álamos to Los Mochis - 127 miles (208 km), 3.5 hours - South again on Mex 15 is Los Mochis or perhaps El Fuerte. From either town you can take a two-day ride on the Chihuahua-Pacific Railroad to see the Copper Canyon.

Day 10 - Los Mochis to Mazatlán - 259 miles (423 km), 6.5 hours - Follow the toll highway south only as far as Culiacán. Drive right by the entrance to the very expensive Maxipista toll road and follow Mex 15 Libre south to Mazatlán. Mazatlán is many folk's idea of the perfect destination with all of the advantages of a major city and many good RV parks as well.

THE MIRADOR IN SAN CARLOS

Day 13 - Mazatlán to San Blas - 180 miles (294 km), 6 hours - From Mazatlán south you are on two-lane free roads. Just before the highway begins climbing toward Tepic follow the small highway toward the ocean and San Blas. Here you'll probably first start to feel like you are in the tropics, you can make an expedition in a small boat to see tropical birds and crocodiles.

Day 14 - San Blas to Puerto Vallarta - 107 miles (175 km), 4 hours - From San Blas south to Puerto Vallarta you have a huge choice of campgrounds suitable for a short stop or months-long sojourn. Most are in very small towns. The road south from San Blas through Miramar and Zacualpan is small and slow until it reaches the main coastal road, Mex 200, at Las Varas. Puerto Vallarta itself has two excellent campgrounds conveniently located for enjoying this popular resort.

Day 17 - Puerto Vallarta to Manzanillo - 173 miles (282 km), 5 hours - Like the coast north of Puerto Vallarta, that north of Manzanillo offers many camping possibilities. Most of these are less formal and don't offer the same quality facilities as those farther north. On the other hand the pace is even more relaxed and the beaches even less crowded.

Farther south along the coast the campgrounds are much more scarce and the distances longer. Take a look at the *Grand Coastal Tour* to see what lies farther south.

Day 20 through Day 24 - Return to Nogales - 1,173 miles (1, 914 km), 35 driving hours - In returning to Nogales we do less sightseeing. Overnight stops on the way north are at one of the campgrounds north of Puerto Vallarta, then Mazatlán, Los Mochis, and Guaymas.

If you enjoyed this tour you're ready for a much longer one next year. How about a coastal tour?

GRAND COASTAL TOUR (ALSO CHIAPAS AND OAXACA) (45 DAYS)

The Grand Coastal Tour is a fascinating way to spend the winter. You travel down Mexico's eastern Gulf Coast, spend some time on the Yucatán Peninsula near Cancún, penetrate the fascinating Indian regions of Chiapas and Oaxaca, and then finish by tracing the popular west coast of Mexico.

Make no mistake, this is a **long trip**. Forty-five days is barely adequate but a full two to three months would be much more fun. A forty-five day schedule gives one day layovers for relaxing or sightseeing on the Costa Esmeralda and at Uxmal, Mérida, Cancún, Palenque, San Cristóbal de las Casas, Oaxaca, Puerto Escondido, Acapulco, Manzanillo, and Puerto Vallarta. Six days are set aside to relax along the Caribbean coast south of Cancún. This isn't really much because on many days you will drive long hours and on layover days there is lots of sightseeing to do. In all you will drive more than 4,600 miles (7,500 km) inside Mexico.

It is easy to modify this itinerary to make it shorter or longer. One easy modification would be to cut out the Yucatán, Chiapas and Oaxaca by cutting across the Isthmus of Tehuantepec on Mex 185. This would cut the trip down to 22 days, but it would also mean that you wouldn't visit three of the most interesting regions of Mexico. Better would be to drive directly to Palenque from Villahermosa and bypass only the Yucatán, reducing the trip to 27 days. Also popular is combining a route down through the interior to Oaxaca and then heading for Chiapas and the Yucatán or back up the west coast. Other modifications will be obvious to you, they would include numerous opportunities to head inland and visit colonial cities.

Day 1 - Brownsville to Ciudad Victoria - 197 miles (322 km), 6 hours - The first day's drive to Ciudad Victoria is conveniently short. The best crossing from the U.S. is probably the new Veteran's Memorial Bridge near Brownsville, Texas. It doesn't open until 8 a.m. Get a fairly early start so that you have plenty of time to get to Ciudad Victoria before dark. Border formalities shouldn't take more than an hour. From near the border follow a short bypass around the edge of Matamoros and then follow Mex 180 and Mex 101 south to Ciudad Victoria. These are excellent two and four-lane free roads. Ciudad Victoria and the Victoria Trailer Park are a good, comfortable introduction to Mexico.

Day 2 - Ciudad Victoria to Tampico - 148 miles (242 km), 4 hours - This is a short driving day. Make a late departure from Ciudad Victoria and travel down Mex 85 to Tampico. You'll cross the Tropic of Cancer not long after your start. Follow the instructions we give for finding the Campestre Altamira and using the bypass to avoid driving in busy downtown Tampico.

🚐 Day 3 - Tampico to Costa Esmeralda - 209 miles (342 km), 7 hours - You may doubt that it will take you 7 hours to drive only 209 miles, and it may not! The roads in this section of Mexico are heavily traveled by trucks and need lots of repairs. If you happen to catch them after their almost-annual reconstruction you may cruise right through in a much shorter time, but don't count on it.

Once again you are on mostly two-lane free roads as you bypass Tampico and then follow Mex 180 south. Make sure to bypass Tuxpan on the shortcut through Alamo. You'll probably find unavoidable heavy traffic through Poza Rica but it won't last long and soon you'll arrive at the much slower-paced Emerald Coast north of Nautla. If you are like us you'll decide you've earned at least one day's layover here. A good way to occupy your time if you tire of the beach is a visit to the famous El Tajín archeological site with its Pyramid of the Niches.

🚐 Day 5 - Costa Esmeralda to Veracruz - 100 miles (164 km), 3 hours - This is a short drive down an increasingly tropical coast to Veracruz, one of Mexico's most historical cities. You'll pass Mexico's only nuclear reactor at Laguna Verde. North of Veracruz you could make a decision that would cut at least two days off this trip. There is now a new very nice toll road that bypasses Veracruz and Catemaco. Many people now rip right on through to Rancho Hermanos Graham RV Park north of Villahermosa. If you plan to do this make sure you make an early start and bring lots of money, the toll road is very expensive.

🚐 Day 6 - Veracruz to Catemaco - 105 miles (171 km), 3 hours - A short drive south on old Mex 180 will bring you to the hill village of Catemaco. The short driving day will give you lots of time to wander this interesting little town, perhaps take a boat ride, and enjoy a good sleep in the cool mountain night air.

🚐 Day 7 - Catemaco to Villahermosa - 109 miles (178 km), 3 hours - The distance given for this day's drive is actually only to Rancho Hermanos Graham RV Park. You may want to drive on to visit the La Venta Museum in Villahermosa. You can stay in Villahermosa or return to the RV park in the evening.

🚐 Day 8 - Villahermosa to Isla Aguada - 209 miles (341 km), 8 hours - We've added two hours to this day's driving time to account for a stop at the La Venta Museum in Villahermosa. The road into Villahermosa is almost all four-lane parkway, but after leaving town on Mex 180 to the coast you'll find that the road narrows and the driving is much slower. Recently some bypasses have been constructed around a few of the villages on this route which does help some, but in others the road passes right through the center of the village. There's plenty of room and few vehicles but you must drive slowly and watch for kids, turkeys and pigs. There are now toll bridges across the lagoon mouths on this route, no ferry travel is required. Isla Aguada is another very small village, many people decide to spend several days enjoying the laid-back pace and walking along the beaches looking for shells.

🚐 Day 9 - Isla Aguada to Campeche - 104 miles (170 km), 3 hours - Follow Mex 180 along a mostly deserted coastline to the old city of Campeche. Avoid the toll road that starts south of Campeche, it is expensive and won't save much time at all, our directions for finding the campground assume that you will arrive on the free road.

🚐 Day 10 - Campeche to Uxmal - 105 miles (171 km), 3 hours - Our favorite route between Campeche and Uxmal follows small back roads to the Edzná archeological site and then north on Mex 261 to Camping Sacbe some 9 miles (15 km) south of Uxmal. In the evening attend the Sound and Light show in Uxmal, it is a great introduction to one of the most interesting Yucatán sites. You can spend the next day at Uxmal and at other nearby sites like Kabah and the Loltún Caves. Once again, you could easily spend several more days and still not see everything.

Day 12 - Uxmal to Mérida - 48 miles (79 km), 2 hours - Another short driving day will take you north to Mérida. Use the ring road to easily pass around to the north end of town and the Rainbow RV Park. Visits to central Mérida for sightseeing and shopping, to Celestún to see the flamingos, or perhaps to Progreso and the north coast will easily fill the next non-driving day.

Day 14 - Mérida to Chichén Itzá - 70 miles (115 km), 2.5 hours - After a short day's drive to Pisté you have all afternoon to explore the Chichén Itzá site. Once again you have a choice of free or toll roads, we prefer the free road, it is much more interesting.

Day 15 - Chichén Itzá to Cancún - 122 miles (200 km), 3.5 hours - Follow the free road to Cancún (or the toll road if you're in a hurry). Consider touring Valladolid or the Balankanche Caves en route. Once you reach Cancún base yourself at Trailer Park Mecoloco. It is convenient to the Isla Mujeres ferries and, if you don't have a small vehicle, to busses into Ciudad Cancún town and on out to the Hotel Zone.

CHAC-MOOL AT CHICHÉN ITZÁ

Day 17 - Cancún to Paa Mul - 50 miles (82 km), 1.25 hours - When you've had your fill of Cancún head out to a campsite on the long tropical coast to the south. For hookups take a look at Cabañas Paa Mul. After a night or two there you may decide to move to one of the smaller places to the north or south.

Day 24 - Paa Mul to Chetumal - 183 miles (298 km), 5 hours - Well rested from at least a week on the coast it is time to move on. The Cenote Azul Trailer Park is a popular stop for those interested in making an early start the next day. Take a swim in the huge Cenote Azul across from the campground.

Day 25 - Chetumal to Palenque - 298 miles (487 km), 8.5 hours - This is a long day's drive on virtually empty two-lane roads. Escárcega is the only town of any size along the way. Make sure to get an early start. Don't be surprised if you are stopped several times during the day by army patrols wanting to check your papers. You are very close to the Guatemala border. In Palenque many people like to stay at the Mayabell because it is so close to the ruins and is a good place to hear the howler monkeys during the night, but if you have a large rig you might find more maneuvering room at Los Leones Trailer Park.

Day 27 - Palenque to San Cristóbal de las Casas - 108 miles (177 km), 4.5 hours - The small and sometimes steep paved highway between Palenque and San Cristóbal should be adequate for any size rig under normal conditions. We've driven it in a large motorhome pulling a tow vehicle. Just take it slow and easy. The route passes through many mountain Indian towns, you'll see Indians along the road gathering firewood or on their way to the market towns. In San Cristóbal large rigs will want to stay at the Bonampak, but travelers with smaller vehicles will probably prefer the Rancho San Nicholás since it is a slightly shorter walk from the center of town.

Day 29 - San Cristóbal de las Casas to Tehuantepec - 232 miles (379 km), 7 hours - Another long day's drive on two-lane roads will bring you to Tehuantepec. En route you'll pass through Tuxtla Gutiérrez, a bypass will let you avoid the worst of the traffic. If you don't mind a hike you can walk in to town from the Hotel Calle.

Day 30 - Tehuantepec to Oaxaca - 154 miles (251 km), 5 hours - The drive today involves a long climb on hot two-lane roads. Watch your engine temperature and don't hesitate to give your rig an occasional rest. Don't expect much traffic. Oaxaca itself is one of Mexico's most enchanting large cities. There's the Monte Albán archeological site just outside town, the surrounding crafts villages, and the old and attractive central area.

Day 32 - Oaxaca to Puerto Escondido - 190 miles (310 km), 7 hours - This route follows Mex 175 as it climbs up and over the coastal range, don't take it unless you are certain that your rig can handle some pretty extreme grades, both up and down. If you have any doubts backtrack to Tehuantepec and then follow the coast north. Once you reach the Oaxaca coast you have a choice of seaside resort towns, east for Bahías de Huatulco, straight for Puerto Angel, or west to Puerto Escondido. All have very different personalities and all have RV parking areas of one kind or another. They're close enough together that you can easily take a look at all three.

Day 34 - Puerto Escondido to Acapulco - 246 miles (402 km), 7 hours - Two-lane Mex 200 along the coast between Puerto Escondido and Acapulco varies in quality, but it won't seem bad after all you've been over. Acapulco is a huge place and you have a large variety of decent campgrounds available to you.

Day 36 - Acapulco to Playa Azul - 231 miles (377 km), 7 hours - The section of road between Acapulco and Manzanillo is pretty remote, they don't see a lot of campers. Many people bound for Acapulco actually come through the interior. There is really only one formal campground along this long stretch of beautiful beaches, Playa Azul. Many sources warn against free camping on one of the many tempting beaches, we recommend using formal campgrounds.

Day 37 - Playa Azul to Manzanillo - 221 miles (362 km), 7 hours - Once again this is a fairly long segment through country that doesn't get many tourists. At Tecomán, south of Manzanillo, you'll find a toll road that leads past Manzanillo. We don't use it because the free road is fine, and we like to drive through Manzanillo because the supermarket north of town is a good place to pick up supplies. You probably won't want to camp in Manzanillo itself, the good campgrounds lie along the coast to the north. Mileage for this day is calculated to Melaque, 39 miles (64 km) north of Manzanillo.

Day 39 - Manzanillo to Puerto Vallarta - 134 miles (218 km), 4.5 hours - Mex 200 north to Puerto Vallarta runs inland for much of the distance, then you descend out of the mountains and find yourself on the steep coast just south of town. Watch carefully as you make the final descent toward central PV, the bypass goes right and is easy to miss. PV itself has two good campgrounds and there are many more along the coast to the north.

Day 41 - Puerto Vallarta to Mazatlán - 287 miles (469 km), 9 hours - Not long ago traffic had to climb into the mountains and pass through Tepic on this segment, now there is a near-sea level route running near San Blas from Las Varas through Zacualpan, Platanitos, and Miramar which connects with Mex 15 north of Tepic. Mex 15 north to Mazatlán continues to be mostly two-lane although it is bound to be widened soon. Mazatlán offers many RV parks, this is one of the most popular RV destinations in Mexico.

Day 43 - Mazatlán to Los Mochis - 259 miles (423 km), 6 hours - There is four-lane road all the way to the border from Mazatlán. We recommend using the toll road for the entire distance, except the section between Mazatlán and Culiacán. The alternate Mex 15 Libre is fine, it will take you an hour to an hour and a half longer, and it will save you a ton of money. The Culiacán-Mazatlán Maxipista is one of the most expensive roads in Mexico. North of Culiacán rates are less expensive and the toll road is the way to go. You might consider leaving your rig in Los Mochis for a few days while you ride the Chihuahua-Pacific Railroad along the Copper Canyon.

Day 44 Los Mochis to Guaymas/San Carlos - 220 miles (359 km), 5 hours - You'll make good time on this section of road, there are just a few places (Navojoa, Ciudad Obregón) where you'll have to slow as you pass through town. Guaymas/San Carlos is a fishing port with several RV parks, many people stop here and don't go any farther south.

Day 45 - Guaymas/San Carlos to Nogales - 257 miles (419 km), 7 hours - Your final day on the road should be a breeze. Drop your vehicle papers at the station that is on the highway about 19 miles (31 km) south of Nogales. After turning them in follow signs to the truck crossing west of Nogales. You may have up to an hour wait at the border, lines going into the U.S. tend to be much longer than those coming out. You won't believe how smooth the roads in the U.S. will feel after 45 days and 4,500 miles in Mexico, but things will seem so sterile!

COLONIAL MEXICO
(27 DAYS)

This is an unusual tour, relatively few campers spend much time touring the interior. On the other hand, if you are interested in the Mexican culture this route will give you an amazingly complete look at the country's historical cities. In 27 days you will cover 2,150 miles (3,500 km) and visit 13 important cities. The interior is one of our favorite parts of Mexico.

You will probably quickly notice that the route does not touch the coast even one time. If you are addicted to sun and sand this can be easily remedied. From many points on this route; particularly Puebla, Cuernavaca, Pátzcuaro and Guadalajara; the coast can be reached in one reasonably comfortable day of driving.

Day 1 - Nuevo Laredo to Saltillo - 193 miles (315 km), 6 hours - After spending an hour or so crossing the border head south toward Monterrey. We recommend the free road, it won't slow you down much on this relatively short day. When in doubt just follow the trucks, they are well aware of which toll routes are economically practical. When you reach Monterrey drive on past the new toll ring road and take the older free one, it too is a comparative bargain. From Monterrey to Saltillo the road is a free highway with at least four lanes at all times, one of the best free roads in Mexico. The campground in Saltillo is conveniently located near a major supermarket and buses to central Saltillo pass right out front. Go into town and see your first cathedral and central square, Saltillo's is considered the best in northern Mexico.

Day 2 - Saltillo to Matehuala - 157 miles (257 km), 3.5 hours - Head south on Mex 54 toward Matehuala and San Luis Potosí. You'll find mostly free roads. Where there is no alternative free road the toll road rates tend to be reasonable. Matehuala doesn't have much to offer except a decent campground in a convenient location. The 19th-century silver town of Real de Catorce makes an interesting side trip from Matehuala but takes most of a day to accomplish.

Day 3 - Matehuala to San Miguel de Allende - 255 miles (416 km), 6 hours Once again you drive south on good roads that let you make excellent time, the highways are four lane now all the way to the cut-off to San Miguel de Allende. Mex 54 easily bypasses San Luis Potosí, again follow the trucks for the best route. You'll leave Mex 54 on a much smaller but still paved and adequate side road to reach San Miguel. As you approach from the east make sure to watch for the bypass, it is signed for Celaya. Both San Miguel campgrounds lie to the south of town, you don't want to try to navigate central San Miguel's streets in even a small vehicle.

San Miguel is a favorite town of norteamericanos living in Mexico. It is also conveniently located for day trips to Guanajuato and Dolores Hidalgo. We've given you two free days to explore here, they will probably not be enough.

Day 6 - San Miguel de Allende to Querétaro - 38 miles (62 km), 1.5 hours - Make an early start so that you arrive early enough to explore town. Big rigs should stay at the Azteca Parador Hotel, smaller ones will enjoy Querétaro's Flamingo Hotel

19TH-CENTURY SILVER TOWN OF REAL DE CATORCE

because they can walk in to town. Querétaro is one of Mexico's most attractive and historic cities.

Day 7 - Querétaro to Mexico City - 132 miles (215 km), 3 hours - From Querétaro to Mexico City you will be on four to six lane toll road the entire distance. This is a government-operated toll road with a reasonable price so enjoy yourself. Catch the Tepotzotlán off-ramp just past the last toll booth for Pepe's RV Park. You can stay here and easily catch a bus to the nearest subway station. The three-hour round trip can be tiring, we recommend that you spend a couple of days in a reasonably-priced Mexico City hotel. Check at the campground for recommendations. Don't forget to tour Tepotzotlán itself, the museum here is one of the best colonial period museums in Mexico.

Day 11 - Mexico City to Puebla - 98 miles (160 km), 3.5 hours - Don't forget to pick the right day for your transit around northeast Mexico City, take a look at the license plate rules and driving instructions for this route in our Mexico City section. Once you are established on Mex 150 heading east to Puebla the toughest part of your day is over. This excellent toll road sweeps you up and out of the Mexico City plateau and right into Puebla. Spend several days in Puebla expanding your Talavera dish collection and enjoying the best food Mexico has to offer.

Day 13 - Puebla to Cuernavaca - 109 miles (178 km) - 3 hours - From Puebla head west on Mex 150 toward Mexico City, but catch Mex 15 south to Cuautla past Ixtaccíhuatl and Popocatépetl volcanoes. From Cuautla to Cuernavaca there are several routes and also several excellent campgrounds. This area is called the Morelos Valley and is something of a playground for Mexico City residents, it also has great historical importance. Morelos is filled with spas and balnearios, archeological sites, and colonial buildings. Taxco, the silver town, is an easy day trip from Cuernavaca.

Day 16 - Cuernavaca to Valle de Bravo - 144 miles (235 km), 5 hours - Rather than heading north through Mexico City to reach Valle de Bravo it is easier to take a more roundabout route. Drive south on Mex 95 (either the toll road or the free road) toward Taxco. Then cut north on Mex 55 through Ixtapan de la Sal to Toluca. Bypass Toluca on the ring route (actually surface streets in the outskirts of the city but not too bad) to Mex 15 headed west toward Morelia. Just past Villa Victoria follow the road south to the holiday town of Valle de Bravo.

Day 17 - Valle de Bravo to Pátzcuaro - 181 miles (296 km), 7 hours - Getting an early start head north again to Mex 15 and follow this twisting but extremely scenic road west to Morelia. Follow the bypass south around Morelia to catch the excellent free highway southwest to Pátzcuaro. Pátzcuaro is an enchanting town, well known for its crafts but also an excellent base for touring one of the most interesting and scenic regions of Mexico.

Day 20 - Pátzcuaro to Guadalajara - 200 miles (326 km), 6 hours - From Pátzcuaro drive north to Quiroga and then continue your journey along Mex 15 to Guadalajara. Rather than driving on in to Guadalajara when you near the city consider

LAS ESTECAS RIVER PARK NEAR CUERNAVACA

spending the night in more relaxed Villa Corona or Chapala.

Day 23 - Guadalajara to Aguascalientes - 153 miles (250 km), 4 hours - From Guadalajara the itinerary begins to trace its way back northward. There are a variety of routes north to Aguascalientes including a toll road. For smaller rigs with good power and brakes we recommend the very scenic (and free) Mex 54 to Jalpa and then Mex 70 to Aguascalientes. Otherwise use Mex 80 or Mex 45. If you base yourself at the Hotel Medrano in Aguascalientes you can easily explore the central district of the city.

Day 24 - Aguascalientes to Zacatecas - 80 miles (130 km), 2 hours - Zacatecas is a short day's drive north on a combination of toll and free roads. Zacatecas is a relatively small city, and is almost undiscovered by tourists although it rivals Guanajuato in attractions. We like to stay at the Motel del Bosque which is conveniently located for a stroll into town or a ride on the overhead tram.

Day 25 - Zacatecas to Saltillo - 228 miles (373 km), 5.5 hours - Mex 54 will take you north to Saltillo and your last night before returning to the U.S.

Day 26 - Saltillo to Nuevo Laredo - 193 miles (315 km), 6 hours - Don't forget to turn in your vehicle documents when you cross at Columbia or in Nuevo Laredo.

THE BAJA PENINSULA
(17 DAYS)

The 1,060 mile (1,731 km) long Mex 1 stretches the entire length of the Baja Peninsula, from Tijuana in the north to Cabo San Lucas at the far southern cape. The two-lane highway gives access to some of the most remote and interesting country in the world including lots of desert and miles and miles of deserted beaches. Outdoorsmen love this country for four-wheeling, boating, fishing, beachcombing, and just plain enjoying the sunshine.

This proposed itinerary takes 17 days and allows you to see the entire length of the peninsula. There are layover days at Guerrero Negro, Bahía Concepción, La Paz, and Cabo San Lucas. Many travel days require only a morning of driving leaving lots of time to relax and explore.

The most tempting modification to this itinerary will be to spend more time at each stop. There are also many additional stopover points along this route, just take a look at the campground map at the beginning of each one of our campground chapters. Finally, it is possible to take a ferry from either La Paz or Santa Rosalía to the Mexican west coast where you can head north for home or head south for more fun.

Day 1- Tijuana to Ensenada, 67 miles (109 km), 2 hours - This first day you cross the border at Tijuana. You probably won't even have to stop when entering Mexico because vehicle permits aren't required on the Baja. There's a four-lane toll road that follows the coast all the way to Ensenada. Once you arrive you will park and visit the *Migración* (Immigration) office near the entrance to town to get the tourist permits that are required since you will be in Mexico over 72 hours. You completed the drive to Ensenada before noon so there's plenty of time to look around town and pick up some groceries at one of the large modern supermarkets. Instead of spending the night at a campground in town you decide to stay at the beautiful Estero Beach Hotel/Resort campground beside the ocean a few miles south of Ensenada. You can celebrate by having dinner at the excellent hotel restaurant.

Day 2 - Ensenada to San Quintín, 116 miles (190 km), 3 hours - This will be another short day so there's really no hurry to get started. You'll pass through rolling hills with the countryside getting dryer as you head south. At San Quintín you have a choice of campgrounds, try the Old Mill Trailer Park if you want full hookups and a restaurant or maybe the El Pabellón to sample a simple ejido-run campground with miles of windswept beach out front.

Day 3 - San Quintín to Bahía de los Ángeles - 219 miles (358 km), 7 hours - This is a longer day's drive so get a fairly early start. You'll want to stop and explore the cactus and rock fields in the Cataviña area before leaving Mex 1 and driving east on a paved but worn road to Bahía de los Ángeles for your first glimpse of the Gulf of California. There's not a lot to the town itself, perhaps this is a good opportunity to head north of town and free camp along the water. If you have a small boat you might give the fishing a try. This is also great kayaking water.

Day 4 - Bahía de los Ángeles to Guerrero Negro - 121 miles (198 km), 3.5 hours - Today's destination is back on the other side of the peninsula, the salt-producing company town of Guerrero Negro. You'll spend two nights here because you want to visit the gray whale nursery lagoon (Scammon's Lagoon) south of town. Spend the first night at the Malarrimo RV Park and visit their well-known restaurant. The second night you can spend at the primitive camping area right next to the lagoon after a day on the lagoon with the whales.

Day 6 - Guerrero Negro to San Ignacio - 89 miles (145 km), 2.5 hours - San Ignacio is a true date-palm oasis in the middle of desert country. A good place to stay is the Rice and Beans Oasis, another campground with a good restaurant. Before dark drive your tow car down to the plaza at the center of town to do some people watching and take a look at the old mission church and rock-art museum.

Day 7 - San Ignacio to Bahía Concepción - 95 miles (155 km), 3 hours - Today, once again, you return to the Sea of Cortez side of the peninsula. You'll pass two interesting towns en route, Santa Rosalía and Mulegé. Neither has much room for big rigs so don't drive into either of these little towns. At Santa Rosalía you might leave your rig along the highway and take a stroll to see Eiffel's church. You'll probably have a chance to explore Mulegé later since it is quite close to the evening's destination at Bahía Concepción. Many people decide to end their journey at this point go no further since the ocean-side camping along beautiful Bahía Concepción is many folk's idea of camping paradise. We'll assume that you decide to only stay for two nights. Hah!

Day 9 - Bahía Concepción to La Paz - 291 miles (470 km), 8 hours - Since you are all rested up after that time along the bahía you decide get an early start and blast on through all the way to La Paz. Don't forget to drive into Loreto for a quick look around, this was the first permanent Spanish settlement on the peninsula. You'll have to ignore the golf course too, even though you'll see people teeing off as you pass.

You will find your progress along the coast to be quite scenic but slow, especially as

FISHING IS A FAVORITE PASTIME ON THE BAJA

you climb up and over the Sierra Gigante, but once on the plains to the west the roads are flat and straight allowing you to make good time. A late arrival in Pa Paz is not a problem because there are lots of campgrounds to choose from. You can take it easy the next day and explore this most typically Mexican of Baja cities.

Day 11- La Paz to Cabo San Lucas - 145 miles (236 km), 4 hours - Today you will arrive in the true tourist's Baja. Take the long route to the Cape area by following Mex 1 around the east side of the Sierra de la Laguna. You'll have made reservations at one of the campgrounds near Cabo San Lucas to ensure a place to base yourself. Consider yourself pre-warned that the Cape area probably won't appeal as a place to spend much time after all you've seen on the way south.

Day 13 - Cabo San Lucas to Todos Santos - 50 miles (81 km), 1.5 hours - A short drive north along the west coast on Mex 19 will bring you to San Pedrito RV Park on the coast south of Todos Santos. This is an excellent place to spend several weeks along a beautiful Pacific beach or to prepare yourself for the trip north.

Day 14 through 17 Todos Santos to Tijuana - 963 miles (1,572 km), 28 hours driving time - You really have two choices for the return to the border. Many folks catch a ferry from La Paz to Topolobampo near Los Mochis and then drive north on four-lane Mex 15 to cross the border at Nogales near Tucson, Arizona. Others simply drive back the way they've come. By putting in decently long days of driving you could make the trip in four days with overnight stops at Ciudad Constitución (254 miles), San Ignacio (255 miles), and El Rosario (304 miles).

CHAPTER

. . . . 2

DETAILS, DETAILS, DETAILS

Budget

For most travelers the important budget items will be insurance, campground fees, gasoline, tolls, food, and entertainment expenses. The amount of money you spend really depends upon how you live so we will not attempt to set out a standard budget. Most people who spend time in Mexico find that it is much less expensive than a similar stay in the United States or Canada, however, this is only true if you limit the amount of time you spend on the road.

See the *Insurance* section of Chapter 3 for information about how to get an insurance quote. Your U.S. or Canadian automobile insurance will not adequately cover you in Mexico.

Campground fees vary with region. Prices on the Baja and along the west coast, in Guaymas, Mazatlán, and Puerto Vallarta, are high by Mexican standards because the traffic will bear it. In the interior and southern Mexico prices are lower. Each campground listing in this guide gives a price range for the campground, see Chapter 4 for more information about this. During the winter of 2000/2001 we spent six months traveling throughout Mexico in a van-type RV (19 feet long) staying in a different campground each night always using full hookups, we averaged $13.46 U.S. per day. It is often possible to negotiate a lower rate for longer stays.

Gasoline prices in Mexico are higher than those in the U.S. For several years they have increased several cents at the first of each month although just recently Pemex announced that such increases would stop. In April 2001 they were as follows: Magna-Sin $2.18 (medium-octane unleaded), Premium Unleaded $2.44, Diesel $1.80. See the *Fuel and Gas Stations* section below for more information.

Tolls are a cost of driving in Mexico that most of us are not accustomed to. You can choose to avoid toll roads if you like. This is a complicated subject so see the detailed discussion below under *Toll Roads*.

We find that our grocery bills in Mexico run about 85% of what they would in the U.S. This will vary considerably depending upon what you eat and where you buy your food. Fruits and vegetables are a bargain, meat and fish tend to be cheaper than in the U.S. and Canada, canned and processed foods more expensive. See the *Groceries* section below for more information. Eating out can be economical in Mexico unless you happen to be in a resort area.

Campgrounds

Mexican campgrounds vary a great deal. In the interior and less traveled areas you will often consider yourself fortunate to find a hookup behind a hotel. The nicest campgrounds tend to be nearer the border and in popular areas of the Baja Peninsula and the west coast.

Bathroom facilities in Mexican campgrounds are often not up to the standards of Canadian and U.S. private campgrounds. Cleanliness and condition vary widely, each of our campground descriptions tries to cover this important subject. Campers in larger rigs probably won't care since they carry their own bathrooms along with them. Other campers might keep in mind that many of the campgrounds they frequent in the U.S. and Canada, especially in national, state, or provincial parks, have pit toilets and no shower facilities. The majority of Mexican campgrounds in this guide provide at least flush toilets and some kind of shower.

In rural Mexico it is usually not acceptable to put used toilet tissue in the toilet bowl, a waste-paper basket is provided. Toilet tissue creates problems for marginal plumbing and septic systems, it plugs them up. Travelers who have visited other third-world countries have probably run into this custom before. You will have to bring along your own toilet tissue, few places in Mexico provide it.

On the Yucatán Peninsula and in southern Mexico campgrounds usually have cold showers. Air temperatures are often so warm that a cold shower actually feels pretty good. If you absolutely HATE cold showers try this: take along a wash cloth and give yourself a sponge bath, only stick your head under the shower to wash your hair. It is actually bearable.

Most of the larger campgrounds in Mexico, especially in the areas that are well traveled by RVers, have hookups for electricity, water and sewer. Almost all of the primary campgrounds covered in this book have them but the actual condition of the outlets, faucets, and sewer connections may not be very good. We find that in many campgrounds the hardware wasn't great when installed, and maintenance doesn't get done unless absolutely necessary. It is often a good idea to take a look at the connections on a parking pad before pulling in, you may want to move to another one.

Mexico uses the same 110 volt service that we use in the U.S. and Canada so your RV won't have to be modified for Mexico. Many campgrounds only have small two-slot household-type outlets so be sure that you have an adapter that lets you use these smaller sockets. Most sockets do not have a ground, either because the plug is the two-slot variety without the ground slot, or because the ground slot is not wired. Test the electricity at your site before plugging in. You can buy a tester at your camping supply store that will quickly indicate the voltage and any faults of the outlet. This is cheap insurance. Make yourself a two-prong adaptor that can be reversed to achieve correct polarity and that has a wire and alligator clip so you can provide your own ground.

Even if the voltage in a campground appears to be OK when you hook up it may not stay that way. Voltage usually fluctuates in Mexican campgrounds during the day.

Many accessories and appliances in modern RVs are sensitive to this and can be damaged by very high or low voltages. Most experts say you are safe between 104 and 128 volts. You should monitor voltage to see if this is a problem. Many people with modern RVs have large battery banks and solar panels, consider using these instead of electrical hookups in problem campgrounds.

We've used laptop computers extensively and had no problems with the electrical current in Mexican campgrounds. Full-size desktop computers might be a different story. Currency fluctuations, spikes, and grounding problems are likely to affect them more.

Air conditioner use is often a problem in Mexico. Don't count on using one except along the west coast, the northern Gulf of California, and some Baja campgrounds. Even if 50-amp service is offered by the campground heavy air conditioner use can cause voltage drops because most campgrounds do not have adequately sized transformers.

Water connections are common, but you may not want to trust the quality of the water even if the campground manager assures you that it is good. See the *Drinking Water* section of this chapter for details on how to cope with this.

Sewer connections in Mexican campgrounds are usually located at the rear of the site. You should make sure that you have enough hose to reach several feet past the rear bumper of your rig before you come south. You probably won't be able to buy any sewer hose or holding tank chemicals south of the border.

Caravans

An excellent way to get your introduction to Mexico is to take an escorted caravan tour. Many companies offer these tours, by our count there are about 200 caravans into Mexico each year. These range from luxury tours taking several months and costing multiple thousands of dollars to tours of less than a week for a fraction of that price.

A typical caravan tour is composed of approximately 20 rigs. The price paid includes a knowledgeable caravan leader in his own RV, a tail-gunner or caboose RV with an experienced mechanic, campground fees, many meals and tours at stops along the way, and lots of camaraderie. Many people love RV tours because someone else does all the planning, there is security in numbers, and a good caravan can be a very memorable experience. Others hate caravans, and do so for approximately the same reasons.

Remember that there will be a lot of costs in addition to those covered by the fee paid to the caravan company including fuel, insurance, maintenance, tolls, and groceries. We hear lots of good things about caravans, but also many complaints. Common problems include caravans that do not spend enough time at interesting places, delays due to mechanical problems with other rigs in the caravan, and poor caravan leaders who do not really know the territory or speak the language. A badly run caravan can be a disaster.

We've given the names, addresses and phone numbers below of some of the leading caravan companies. Give them a call or write a letter to get information about the tours they will be offering for the coming year. Most also have web sites, you can find links to them on our web site: www.rollinghomes.com. Once you have received the information do not hesitate to call back and ask questions. Ask for the names and phone numbers of people who have recently taken tours with the same caravan leader scheduled to be in charge of the tour you are considering. Call these references and find out what they liked and what they didn't like. They are likely to have some strong feelings about these things.

Adventure Caravans, 124 Rainbow Dr. # 2434, Livingston, TX 77399-1024 (800 872-7897 or 936 327-3428).

Adventuretours, 305 W. Nolana, Suite 2, McAllen, TX 78504 (800 455-8687 and 956 630-0341).

Aztec Trails RV Tours, 131 Rainbow Drive #3182, Livingston, TX 77399-1031 (e-mail: aztec@mail.udg.mx).

Baja Winters RV Tours, 3760 Market St. NE, PMB #615, Salem, OR 97301 (800 383-6787).

Camping World President's Club Tours, P.O. Box 161, Osceola, IN 46561 (800 626-0042).

Eldorado Tours, P.O. Box 1145, Alma, Arkansas 72921 (800 852-2500 or 501 632-6282).

Fantasy RV Tours, Inc., P.O. Box 97605, Las Vegas, NV 89193-5605 (800 952-8496).

Good Sam Caraventures, P.O. Box 247, Greenville, MI 48838 (800 664-9146).

Meadowlark Tours, Box 25, Mossbank, SK, Canada, S0H 3G0 (306 354-2434).

Point South RV Tours, 11313 Edmonson Ave., Moreno Valley, CA 92555 (800 421-1394 or 909 247-1222).

Tracks to Adventure, 2811 Jackson Ave., El Paso, TX 79930 (800 351-6053).

Vagabundos del Mar Boat and Travel Club, Adventure Tours, 190 Main St., Rio Vista, CA 94571 (800 474-2252).

You might also check with the owner association of the type of rig you drive, we've run into caravans composed of Airstreams, Bounders, Road-Treks, and others.

Cash and Credit Cards

Mexico, of course, has its own currency, called the peso. During the 2000/2001 season there were about 9.5 pesos per U.S. dollar. The currency has been relatively stable since a large devaluation in 1994. Some visitors, particularly on the Baja Peninsula, never seem to have any pesos and use dollars for most purchases. They pay for the privilege, prices in dollars tend to be higher than if you pay in pesos. Outside of border areas and the Baja dollars are not readily accepted.

Cash machines are now widespread in Mexico and represent the best way to obtain cash. If you don't already have a debit card you should take the trouble to get one before heading south, make sure it has a four-digit international number. Both Cirrus (Visa) and Plus (MasterCard) networks are in place, not all machines accept both. Given a choice we would choose Cirrus, it seems to be more widely accepted. Don't be surprised if a machine inexplicably refuses your card, bank operations and phone lines are both subject to unexpected interruptions. If you can't get the card to work try a machine belonging to another bank or just go directly to a teller inside the bank. You should consider bringing a backup card in case the electronic strip stops working on the one you normally use. Most cards have a maximum daily withdrawal limit, usually about $400 U.S. In Mexico this limit is sometimes lower than it is in the U.S.

Traveler's checks are a decent way to carry money for emergencies. You never know when your debit card will inexplicably stop working.

Visa and MasterCard credit cards are useful in Mexico. Restaurants and shops, particularly in tourist areas, accept them. Outside metropolitan and tourist areas their acceptance is limited. A few Pemex stations are beginning to accept credit cards but they charge a significant fee for doing so, almost all large supermarkets now accept Visa and MasterCard. It is also possible to get cash advances against these credit cards in Mexican banks but the fees tend to be high.

Children

Children love camping, and Mexico has great beaches and other recreational possibilities. Mexicans love children so they certainly won't feel unwelcome. Each year during the winter we meet more families who are traveling while home-schooling, during the summer there have always been a lot of kids. Can you think of a better place to learn Spanish?

It is entirely possible to travel with children during the school year. Home-schooling is now quite popular and most school districts will allow it, especially if it is only for a year or so and the object is to travel in an educational place like Mexico. Policies vary, you may find that the school district will provide a lesson plan, give you assistance with your own, or require the use of a correspondence school. Check with your state department of education about the legalities and procedures. Don't forget about the advantages of a laptop computer with CD ROM drive. There is more and more reference and educational material available in a compact format on disk. Home-schooling requires discipline but can be very rewarding.

Drinking Water and Vegetables

Don't take a chance when it comes to drinking Mexican water. Even water considered potable by the locals is likely to cause problems for you. It is no fun to be sick, especially when you are far from the border in an unfamiliar environment. There are several strategies for handling the water question. Many people drink nothing but bottled water. Others filter or purify it in various ways. There are reverse-osmosis and ionization systems being marketed for use in RVs that work well, or you can use bleach and a filter as we do.

We purify all of the water that goes into our rig's storage tank with common bleach. Then we use a filter to remove the bleach taste, the microorganisms in the water have already been killed by the bleach. This means that we never hook up permanently to the local water supply, we always use the stored water in our rig. The advantage of this system is that you do not need to keep a separate supply of drinking water underfoot. The proof is in the results. We are almost never sick, and if we are it is usually possible to trace the problem to something we ate or drank while away from the RV. The filter we use is commonly offered as standard equipment on many RV's, it is manufactured by Everpure. Other charcoal filters probably work equally well to remove the taste of the bleach.

The system we use is called superclorination. Add 1/6 ounce (1 teaspoon) of bleach (5.25% sodium hypochlorite) per each 10 gallons of water. The easiest way to do this is to measure it into the same end of your fill hose that will attach to or into your rig. That way you purify the hose too. Do not use bleach that has scents or other additions. Also, some bleach sold now is concentrated, that would change the dosage if there was a significant change in the normal 5.25% concentration of sodium hypochlorite. Fortunately, much bleach sold in Mexico has water purification instructions right on the label, if it does it should be safe to use.

If you don't want to bleach your water the easiest alternative is to drink bottled water. Everywhere in Mexico you can buy large 19 liter (approximately five-gallon) bottles of water. They are available at supermarkets, purified water shops, or from vendors who visit campgrounds. These are very inexpensive, you can either keep one of the large bottles by paying a small deposit or actually empty them into your own water tank.

Occasionally, even if you bleach your water and use a filter, you will pick up a load of water that doesn't taste too good. This is usually because it contains salt. A filter won't take this out. You can avoid the problem by asking other RVers at the campground about water quality before filling up.

Another source of potential stomach problems is fruit and vegetables. It is essential that you peel all fruit and vegetables or soak them in a purification solution before eating them. Bleach can also be used for this, the directions are right on the label of most bleach sold in Mexico. You can also purchase special drops to add to water for this purpose, the drops are stocked in the fruit and vegetable department of most supermarkets in Mexico.

Driving in Mexico

If there were only one thing that could be impressed upon the traveler heading south to drive in Mexico for the first time it would be "drive slowly and carefully". The last thing you want in Mexico is an accident or a breakdown, driving slowly and carefully is the best way to avoid both of these undesirable experiences.

Mexico's roads are getting better. There are now long stretches of superhighway, the quality and engineering of some of these highways will amaze you. On the other hand, many Mexican roads are of a lower standard than we are accustomed to. Surfaces are poorly maintained, potholes are common, roads are narrow, signage is often poor or lacking. Cautious driving will mean fewer flat tires and broken springs.

The quality of Mexican drivers varies, of course. We think that on average, as a group and with lots of exceptions, they tend to be more aggressive than they should be considering the quality of the vehicles and roads. Many Mexican vehicles would not be allowed on the roads in the U.S. or Canada. They are slow, have poor brakes, lights that don't work, and bald tires. It is very common for tires to blow out, often because they have been run to the cord.

As you travel cross-country on two-lane roads you will probably be astounded by the aggressiveness of bus and truck drivers. Here's a piece of advice, never get into a race with a bus driver, their rigs are powerful and drivers fearless to a fault. They will not give up and commonly are involved in accidents, don't contribute to the problem.

Do not drive at night. There are several reasons for this. Animals are common on roads in Mexico, even in daylight hours you'll find cows, horses, burros, goats, pigs and sheep on the road. At night there are even more of them, they're attracted by the warm road surface and they don't have reflectors. Truckers like to travel at night because they can make good time in the light traffic. Some of these guys are maniacs, in the morning you'll often see a fleet of tow trucks lined up along the edge of a highway trying to retrieve one from a gully. Truckers also often leave rocks on the road at night, this is done to keep someone from hitting them when they break down, or to block the wheels when stopped on a hill. Often these rocks aren't removed, they're very difficult to see in time at night. Finally, driving at night means that if you have a breakdown you're going to be in an unsafe position. Mexican roads are good places to avoid after dark.

No discussion of driving in Mexico is complete without a discussion of traffic cops and bribes. Traffic cops (and many other government functionaries) are underpaid, they make up for it by collecting from those who break the law. This is not condoned by the government, but it is a fact of life. Norteamericanos usually feel uncomfortable with this custom and as a result they are difficult targets for cops with a *mordida* habit. Unfortunately some cops do not yet know this.

The best way to avoid the mordida trap is to scrupulously follow all traffic laws. Even if everyone around you is breaking the law you should follow it. If only one person in a line of cars gets ticketed for not stopping at a railroad crossing you can be sure that

MEXICAN PARKING LAW ENFORCEMENT

it will be you. Here are a few of the many pitfalls. Obey all speed limits, especially easy to miss are those at schools and small towns along a highway. Stop at the stop sign at railroad crossings even though no one else will. In many towns the heavy traffic is directed to stay on the laterals or follow a special route marked "tráffico pesado" (heavy traffic) or "tráffico pasado" (through traffic). Watch for these signs because if you are in an RV these truck routes probably can be interpreted as applying to you. Do as the trucks do. Usually any rig with duals on the back is considered a heavy vehicle.

In the event that you do get stopped we recommend against offering a bribe. It is possible that you might get yourself in even worse trouble than you are already in. If you can't talk your way out of a fine the normal practice is to accompany the officer back to his headquarters (bringing your vehicle) to pay the fine. Most fines are quite reasonable by norteamericano standards. Occasionally a police officer will suggest that such a trip can be avoided by paying a reasonable fee to him on the spot, let your conscience be your guide. If you do run into a totally unreasonable police officer it is possible to report him to the government through the tourist information hot line, (5) 250-0123. To do this you must have the officer's name, badge number, and vehicle number. Without these you will get nowhere.

If you park in a town and city and find your license plates gone when you return you will probably be able to find them at the local police office. Police routinely remove plates of illegally parked vehicles to make sure that the owner comes in to pay the fine. If the curb is painted red it is a no parking zone, yellow means parking during "off" hours, and white means its OK to park at all times.

Everyone's least favorite thing is to get involved in an accident. In Mexico there are special rules. First and most important is that you had better have insurance. See the *Insurance* section in Chapter 3 – *Crossing the Border*. Your insurance carrier will give you written instructions about the procedure to follow if you get into an accident. Take a look at them and discuss questions with your agent before you cross the border to make sure you understand exactly how to handle an accident before it happens.

Road signs in Mexico are usually not hard to understand. International-style signs are used for stops, parking, one way roads and many other things. However, we often meet folks with questions about one or another sign they have been seeing during their travels. Nearby you'll find our signpost forest, pictures of signs you're likely to see along the road and their translations.

Drugs, Guns, and Roadblocks

Visitors to Mexico are not allowed to possess either non-prescription narcotics or guns (except those properly imported for hunting). Do not take either in to Mexico, they can result in big problems and probably time spent in a Mexican jail.

Roadblocks and vehicle checks are common in Mexico. Often the roadblocks are staffed by military personnel. These stops can be a little intimidating, the soldiers carry automatic weapons and bring them right in to your rig when doing an inspection. English, other than a few words, is usually not spoken at the checkpoints but not much communication is really necessary, we have never had a problem. In general you will probably be asked where you came from (today), where are you going, do you have drugs or guns, and perhaps why you are in Mexico. It seems like every third rig or so gets inspected so don't get paranoid if yours is chosen. Accompany the person inspecting the rig as they walk through to answer any questions they might have, sometimes they have trouble figuring out how to open unfamiliar cabinets and storage areas. We generally discourage offering a beverage or anything else to officials at checkpoints, this might be considered a suspicious bribe, or might get the inspecting soldier in trouble with his superiors.

English-Language Bookstores and Magazines

We recommend that you do your shopping for both travel guides and recreational reading before you cross the border. Stores with good selections of English-language books are virtually nonexistent in Mexico. We've included a list of recommended travel guides under *Travel Library* below.

There is a much better situation with regard to English-language newspapers. Kiosks in most cities carry *USA Today* and other major U.S. newspapers. There is an English-language newspaper published in Mexico City called *The News*. It also is available in larger cities. News magazines like *Time* and *Newsweek* publish Latin American editions in English, they also are available in larger cities and tourist towns.

Ferries

The company Sematur Transbordadores runs ferries between the Baja Peninsula and the mainland of Mexico. The routes are between Santa Rosalía and Guaymas, between Pichilingue (just outside La Paz) and Topolobampo (near Los Mochis) and between Pichilingue and Mazatlán. If you do not want to drive the Baja Peninsula highway both ways this is a great way to turn your Mexican trip into a loop trip and see some of the mainland.

The runs take between 6 and 17 hours. Most vehicles on the routes are trucks. A lot of the provisions for the southern Baja come across on these boats. These ferries are work boats, don't expect much in the way of amenities. Cabins are available on some but not all runs.

If you plan to take your vehicle from the peninsula to the mainland you will need a vehicle permit. See the *Crossing the Border* section for more information about this. You will need a reservation for the ferry, you can call the main reservation office in Mazatlán by dialing 01-800-696-9600. They say you need to make reservations at least three days in advance but we recommend that you make your reservation at least two weeks before you want to travel. They also have a very useful web site with rates, schedules, and reservations at www.ferrysematur.com.mx. The phone number for the ticket office in La Paz is (1) 125-2346 and the one in Santa Rosalía is (1) 152-0014.

Free Camping or Boondocking

By free camping we mean camping outside an organized campground. In Mexico the term is really a misnomer, often there are costs involved in free camping. You often have to pay a "tip" or buy a meal to really feel comfortable in a free camping spot.

A grizzled old-timer we met in Pátzcuaro explained Mexican free camping pretty well in just a few words. When we asked him if there was a campground where he'd just spent the night before he said "What? A campground in Mexico? We just find a wide street with a streetlight to park under and ask the first person to come along if it is OK to park there. They always say yes." Once you have permission it is a good idea to get to know your neighbors, that way they might watch out for you.

Security is a real issue when you camp outside formal campgrounds. RVs, and to a lesser extent, vans, stand out. You will be noticed and an RV is uniquely vulnerable. Any thief knows you have lots of valuable stuff in that vehicle. The best free camping spots are patrolled in some way. Several rigs traveling together are much safer than one alone. Most importantly, however, never park alongside the highway.

Here are a few possibilities for free camping: balnearios, gas stations, restaurant parking lots, tourist attraction parking lots, streets near police stations (ask for permission at the station, they may have a better suggestion), city squares, front and back yards of houses, ranchos and farms, and beach areas. One popular guide even suggests garbage dumps, we think he's kidding. You'll find others as you spend more time in Mexico.

Big Pemex stations along the major highways deserve special mention. During the past few years these big truck stops have become popular places to overnight. If you purchase gas when you spend the night in one it will make RVers much more welcome.

Fuel and Gas Stations

Choosing the brand of gas you're going to buy is easy in Mexico. All of the gas stations are Pemex stations. Pemex is the national oil company, it is responsible for everything from exploring for oil to pumping it into your car. Gas is usually sold for cash although a few stations now accept cards. There are usually two kinds of gas, Magna Sin in green pumps and higher octane Premium in red pumps. The old leaded Nova (blue pumps) has disappeared. You'll probably be using Magna Sin, with a nominal octane rating of 87 you may or may not find that it is acceptable. If you get a lot of pinging you will probably want to step up to the more expensive premium.

Diesel is carried at many stations, particularly along truck routes.

Gas sells for the same price at all Pemex stations throughout the country except that a few states have lower tax rates (both Baja states and Quintana Roo) so their gas is a few cents cheaper. An exception to the uniform price rule is very small stations in very remote places. Gas in these establishments is often pumped out of drums and can cost many times the Pemex price. With proper planning you won't ever use one of these places.

Gas stations are not as common in Mexico as they are in the U.S. and Canada. Some towns have no station, others only a few. In general it seems that there is one station for every 10,000 people in an area. That isn't as few as it seems since car ownership in Mexico is not widespread.

The rule of thumb in Mexico used to be that you should fill your tank whenever you burned half a tank. Stations were scarce and sometimes they wouldn't have gas when you reached them. This is still a good idea on the Baja and in more remote places. Even though most stations now have a Magna Sin pump they are sometimes out of gas. If an unexpected RV caravan decides to stop for gas in a remote station it can drain the tanks dry until more arrives.

Almost everyone you meet in Mexico has stories about how a gas station attendant cheated them. These stories are true. The attendants don't make much money and American tourists are easy prey. You can avoid problems if you know what to expect.

The reason that the attendants are able to cheat people is that there are no cash registers or central cashiers in these stations. Each attendant carries a big wad of cash and collects what is displayed on the pump. Don't expect a receipt. Until the stations install a control system with a separate cashier there will continue to be lots of opportunities for attendants to make money off unwary customers.

VERIFIQUE
MARQUE CEROS

VERIFY ZERO MARK

The favorite ploy is to start pumping gas without zeroing the pump. This way you have to pay for the gas that the previous customer received in addition to your own. The attendant pockets the double payment. The practice is so widespread that at many stations attendants will point to the zeroed pump before they start pumping. Signs at most stations tell you to check this yourself.

There are several things you can do to avoid this problem. First, get a locking gas cap. That way the attendant can't start pumping until you get out of the rig and unlock the cap. Second, check the zeroed meter carefully. Do not get distracted. If several people try to talk to you they are probably trying to distract you. They'll ask questions about the rig or point out some imaginary problem. Meanwhile the pump doesn't get zeroed properly.

While the gas is being pumped stand right there and pay attention. Another trick is to "accidentally" zero the pump and then try to collect for an inflated reading. If you watch carefully you will know the true reading and won't fall for this. Sometimes the pump gets zeroed before the tank is full, so don't just assume that you can chat because you have a big tank.

The process of making change presents big opportunities to confuse you. If you are paying in dollars, which is common on the Baja, have your own calculator handy and make sure you know the exchange rate before the gas is pumped. When paying do not just give the attendant your money. He'll fold it onto his big wad of bills and then you'll never be able to prove how much you gave him. We've also seen attendants quickly turn their backs and stuff bills in a pocket. Hold out the money or lay it out on the pump, don't let him have it until you can see your change and know that it is the correct amount.

All attendants will not try to cheat you of course. You'll probably feel bad about watching like a hawk every time you fill up with gas. The problem is that when you let down your guard someone will eventually take advantage of you, probably soon and not later. It is also customary to tip attendants a peso or two, we think honest attendants deserve to be tipped more.

Green Angels

The Mexican government maintains a large fleet of green pickups that patrol all major highways searching for motorists with mechanical problems. Usually there are two men in the truck, they have radios to call for help, limited supplies, and quite a bit of mechanical aptitude. Most of them speak at least limited English. The service is free except for a charge for the cost of supplies used. The trucks patrol most highways two times each day, once in the morning and once in the afternoon. You can call for help from the Green Angels, the nationwide telephone number is (5) 250-8221 or (5) 250-8555.

Groceries

Don't load your rig with groceries when you head south across the border. There is no longer any point in doing so. Some Mexican border stations are checking RVs to see that they don't bring in more than a reasonable amount of food. Also, there are sometimes checkpoints along the highways where things like chicken, pork, or fruits are confiscated in an effort to control insect pests and animal diseases. You could lose a lot of groceries if you've overstocked.

Modern supermarkets in all of the large and medium-sized Mexican cities have almost anything you are looking for, often in familiar brand names. You can supplement your purchases in the supermarkets with shopping in markets and in small stores called *abarrotes, panaderías, tortillarias,* and *carnecerías* (canned goods stores, bakeries, tortilla shops, and butcher shops).

Mexican supermarkets are much like French hypermarkets (or a modern Wal-Mart). Names to remember are Comercial Mexicana, Gigante, Ley, Soriana, and yes, even Wal-Mart. In addition to all kinds of groceries they carry clothing, hard goods, electronics, hardware, and almost everything else. To get to the groceries you must push your cart past lots of other temptations.

Compiling a list of things that are hard to find in a Mexican supermarket gets more difficult every year. About the only things we have difficulty finding now are good dill pickles, canned tomatoes, decent peanut butter and any type of carbonated soda

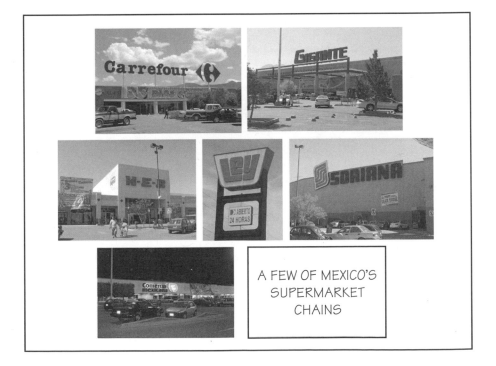

A FEW OF MEXICO'S SUPERMARKET CHAINS

not manufactured by the Coca-Cola Company (Coke has an amazing Mexican distribution system and the president was an executive with the company) or Pepsi.

Almost any population center, from the largest city to the small regional market towns, has a market building with stalls selling fruits, vegetables, meats, and even fully cooked meals. Surrounding the market building may be even more temporary stalls. The sights, sounds and especially smells will both attract and repel you. Most of us would hesitate to purchase anything from the butcher stalls, even if the butcher has a clue about the cuts sold north of the border. Fruits and vegetables are another story. Those available in supermarkets cannot usually compare with the quality and selection available in the markets. Besides, dickering in the market is one of the real pleasures of Mexican living.

Health Matters

The health hazards of traveling in Mexico are not particularly intimidating. You might want to take a look at the section of this chapter titled *Insects and Other Pests*. Two other things you'll want to be aware of are the extremely warm temperatures in the summer, particularly in the south, and the high altitudes of the interior. Give yourself time to acclimatize before pushing yourself.

Health care south of the border is readily available and quite good. Many doctors practicing in the U.S. were trained in Mexico, the standards are high. Language is seldom a problem. Mexico has socialized medicine, the government health organization is called the IMSS. Many norteamericanos who live in Mexico have joined the IMSS and use it for all of their health care, the price is quite reasonable by U.S. or Canadian standards. These IMSS facilities are not supposed to treat non-members but we often hear about travelers getting excellent emergency treatment in remote places where the IMSS may be the only alternative. There are also many private doctors and hospitals throughout the country and their prices are very reasonable. For recommendations check with long-term residents in trailer parks, with hotels, or with tourist offices.

Prescription medicines are also readily available in Mexico. Many things that require a doctor's prescription north of the border do not require one in Mexico but this does not apply to narcotics of any kind. Costs are said to average about 20% of that in the U.S. Many residents from north of the border shop for their medicine in Mexico.

Getting insurance reimbursement for costs in Mexico is sometimes problematic. Medicare from the U.S. will not reimburse Mexican expenses. Some private insurance does pay or reimburse Mexican expenses, check with your broker or carrier. If your insurance does not cover you in Mexico you should check into supplemental coverage. We are told that Canadians are better served by their government health coverage, it will cover Mexican expenses but not those incurred in the U.S. You'll want to check into this if it applies to you.

Another popular insurance is coverage for air transportation out of Mexico in the case of major medical problems. Often this coverage is offered as an add-on to your automobile insurance.

Holidays

Mexicans love holidays, most mean at least a minor fiesta. Some of the major ones result in big migrations to the ocean and mean full campgrounds. Most national holidays are celebrated almost everywhere with street fairs and firecrackers. Individual towns have their own fiesta days, we've tried to mention some of these in our individual city descriptions.

The two long winter holidays are the Christmas holidays and Semana Santa or Holy Week. The Christmas Holidays run for about a week on each side of the new year. You can expect significant numbers of Mexican families in the campgrounds, especially along the ocean, during this week. Semana Santa is the Easter holiday. Even more people seem to celebrate this one at the beach. Be prepared for a lively and interesting week.

Hotels

While you are traveling in Mexico, even if you are in an RV, don't forget that you are not limited spending the night camping. Mexican hotels and motels can be inexpensive and convenient alternatives to campgrounds. In many parts of the country campgrounds are scarce, especially along the east coast and in the interior. Hotel prices are reasonable when compared to those in the U.S., particularly if you stay in places oriented toward Mexican customers. Many hotels and motels outside central urban centers have enough parking space for larger rigs and good security. You may even be able to park on the hotel or motel grounds and stay in your own rig. Often management will string an electric cord. Travelers driving smaller RVs and cars have the advantage, they can stop for the night at virtually any hotel. All RV drivers should exercise caution when visiting hotels because overhead clearance is often restricted at entry gates and parking areas. Park out front and walk in to scout the situation. There is often an alternate entrance for larger rigs.

Insects and Other Pests

Large areas of Mexico are covered with desert and jungle, if you live outdoors you're bound to run into some unfamiliar bugs. Most aren't a problem but you should be alert. Tent campers in particular should be on constant watch for scorpions, tarantulas, and other poisonous spiders. Mosquitoes and small biting flies can also be a problem. Probably the best insurance is a good insect-tight tent. Always check shoes and clothes for stinging insects and tarantulas before putting them on. Campers, especially tent campers, who are planning to camp in tropical areas should consider malaria pills. Your personal physician at home can prescribe them and they are inexpensive in Mexico.

For RVers the largest problem is usually ants. You shouldn't be surprised if your rig gets invaded. You can help avoid this by not leaving food and water out. Fix small water leaks so they don't become a magnet for ants in dry desert climates. When parked you should make sure that your rig isn't being brushed by branches and leaves. Many people also put ant powder around their tires. If you do find yourself with an ant problem don't panic, they are easy to get rid of if you have the right tool. We've been extremely pleased with the effectiveness of the small ant baits sold in many U.S. supermarkets. Ants go into these little plastic stick-ons and pick up insecticide which they take back to the nest, within a day or so the ants start disappearing, within a week they're gone. We've not seen these in Mexico even though they may be available, make sure to take some with you when you go south.

Insurance

See Chapter 3 – *Crossing the Border*.

Internet

The internet has become a wonderful tool for research. There are a great number of web sites with information about Mexico. Rather than trying to list them all here we have set up our own web site: **www.rollinghomes.com.** On it you will find current links to other web sites with good information about Mexico.

We have another use for our web site. As a small publisher we can only afford to update our travel guides on a three to five year cycle. In order to keep the books more current we publish updated information on the web. Our site has pages for each of our books with updates to our books referenced by page number. We gather information for these updates ourselves and also depend upon information sent in by our readers. This information is only posted until we put out a new edition, once the new edition comes out we zero out the page and post updates only for the new book.

The internet is also a useful tool for communicating from Mexico. Internet cafes are common in Mexico. Few homes have computers and good telephone connections so Mexicans commonly go to these cafes to use computers. You'll find them in any city.

Laundry

Getting your laundry done in Mexico shouldn't present much of a problem, unless you want to do it yourself. There are laundromats in most larger towns and cities, ask at the campground for directions. In most places you leave your laundry and pick it up the next day, prices are very reasonable. Only on the Baja and on the west coast will you find campgrounds with coin-operated machines that you can use yourself, we've indicated their presence in the campground descriptions.

Mail

Mail service to and from Mexico is not great. We find that letters from Mexico often take several weeks to reach their destination in the U.S. or Canada.

To receive mail in Mexico there are really two options: have it addressed to the campground or to general delivery at the local post office, known as *Lista de Correos*. We recommend that you use the post office method unless you are very sure (actually discuss the issue with the campground manager) that you have a good campground address, these change often and some campgrounds are not set up to reliably receive mail for their guests.

Here's a tip for addressing mail to Mexico. Mexico uses zip codes that look just like those in the U.S. If you are not careful your mail will go to the U.S. zip code instead of to Mexico. Always put the zip code on Mexican mail in front of the city name and precede the number with the letters CP. This will alert postal machines and workers and should reduce the problem.

Mexican post office boxes are addressed as Apdo. or Apdo. Postal. Many of the campground addresses in this guide include Apdo. numbers. If they do, you do not need to include street address information when sending mail to them, it is only included here to help in finding the campground.

Maps

The American Automobile Association (AAA) publishes the best easy-to-find road map available in the states. It is a one-sheet map but is relatively up-to-date and accurate. It even shows some of the toll road toll plazas, something no other map we've seen does.

In 1997 a new road atlas of Mexico began appearing in Mexican stores. Called the *Guia Roji Atlas de Carreteras* it is updated every year. This red-colored atlas is widely available in book stores and at newsstands in larger cities in Mexico. A similar guide called the Guia Verdi (green-colored) also is available at some newsstands, the maps are the same but the Guia Verdi does not have city maps. These atlases are almost up to date and almost accurate, they're the best thing to be available in Mexico for some time. The Amazon internet bookstore carries this book although it sells it for a much higher price than stores in Mexico, you'll find a link to the book on their site from our web site at www.rollinghomes.com.

Guia Roji also publishes a larger 17 by 11 inch format *Gran Atlas de Carreteras* that has one state on each page. For the most part it seems to be drawn with the same accuracy as the *Atlas de Carreteras* mentioned above except that small states are shown in amazing detail. There is a smaller but similar atlas called the *Atlas de los Estados de la Repúbilica Mexicana* and published by HFET, S.A. de CV but it is very difficult to find.

The Secretaría de Comunicaciónes y Transportes and Secretaría de Turismo have published a Tourist Road Map that is not bad. It has a lot of detail and shows most of the new toll roads. You may receive a copy if you send for information from the tourist offices. If not you can probably flag down a green angel and buy one from him, we did.

Topographical maps produced by the Mexican government are available in Mexico from offices of the INEGI (Instituto Nacional de Estadistica, Geografía, y Informatica) in each state capital in the county. Not all offices have all available maps at all times however. These come in both 1:50,000 and 1:250,000 scales.

Hikers and explorer types love the 1:1,000,000 maps produced by International Travel Maps (ITMB) 245 West Broadway, Vancouver, B.C., Canada V5Y 1P8; 604-687-3320). They cover the Baja Peninsula, the Yucatán, the Gulf Coast and Southern Mexico. ITMB also publishes a 1:3,300,000 scale map of all of Mexico.

It is also possible to order maps by mail, both highway and topographical, from several outlets in the U.S. Three that we like are Seattle's Wide World Books & Maps (4411A Wallingford Ave., Seattle, WA 98103), Tucson's Map and Flag Center (3239 North First Ave., Tucson, AZ 85719, 800-473-1204 or 520-887-4234) and Map Link (25 East Mason Street, Santa Barbara, CA 93101; 800-627-7768 or 805-965-4402).

Propane

Either propane or butane is available near most larger town or cities. The LP Gas storage yards are usually outside central area of town. Ask at your campground for the best way to get a fill-up, in many locations trucks will deliver to the campground. We've also seen people stop a truck on the street and get a fill-up.

We're accustomed to seeing only propane in much of the U.S. and Canada because butane won't work at low temperatures, it freezes. In parts of the southern U.S. and the warmer areas in Mexico butane is common and propane not available. This probably won't be a problem, most propane appliances in RVs will also run on butane. Make sure you use all the butane before you take your RV back into the cold country, however.

The fact is that you may never need to fill up with LP Gas at all. We find that if we fill up before crossing the border we have no problem getting our gas to last four months because we only use it for cooking. Some people run their refrigerators only on gas as a way to protect sensitive electronics panels in modern refrigerators from the fluctuating electrical voltage common to Mexican campgrounds. You may want to check into this, it is virtually impossible to get an RV refrigerator fixed in Mexico.

Public Transportation

Much of the population of Mexico depends upon public transportation, they just don't have automobiles. Public transportation usually means busses, but taxis are usually available and sometimes reasonably priced, and Mexico City even has an extensive (and cheap) subway system.

Between cities bus travel is extremely inexpensive and convenient. First class buses run frequently, you'll see hundreds of them on the road. Second class busses run the same routes but aren't nearly as convenient, they stop constantly. You'll see lots of these too. Try taking advantage of the busses to do a little sightseeing. For example, we think busses from Puebla, Cuernavaca, Querétaro or even San Miguel de Allende are a good way to visit Mexico City.

Inside cities busses make a great way to get around if you don't want to drive or haven't brought along a tow car. Leave the rig safe in the campground and catch a bus. These can take several forms. They may be normal city busses (often a converted school bus) or they may be collectivos (Volkswagen combis). In a normal bus you just pay the driver as you board. It is a good idea to ask if the bus really goes where you think it does. For example, if you are going to the city center say "¿ a centro?" (to the center?). Collectivos are much the same except that you often climb aboard and then pass your money through the hands of other passengers after pulling away from the stop. Bus and collectivo stops often aren't marked but you'll see groups of people standing waiting. Often you have to wave the bus down or it won't stop.

Reservations

You may want to make campground reservations before leaving Canada or the U.S. Many popular destinations do fill up during the months of December, January, February, March and early April. Travelers who definitely want to stay in one particular campground or want to have a particular location in a campground (like on the water) should make the attempt. We say "make the attempt" because reservation-making is often a matter of luck. Our campground descriptions indicate those where reservations are suggested and give the reservation phone number. The process is not generally simple. Usually it involves a phone call and then a letter with check or money order. We recommend that you not just send a letter or check without talking to someone at the campground. Often the most reliable way (or only way) to make a reservation is to make arrangements in the spring when you leave the campground for your stay the next year. Snowbirds who always go back to the same place usually do this, they'll arrange to be in the same slot year after year.

Now the other side of the coin. We **never** make reservations and seldom have a problem getting into a campground. During the busy season (January through the end of March) we often have to settle for a less-desirable slot or campground when traveling the popular Baja or the west coast. There is also one campground on the Yucatán where reservations are recommended, that is Paa Mul. Occasionally you will find a campground to be full in other places because a caravan happens to be in town, but our experience is that there is usually room to squeeze one more rig in for the day or so that the caravan is in town.

Safety and Security

Mexico would be full of camping visitors from the U.S. and Canada if there was no security issue. Fear is the factor that crowds RVers into campgrounds just north of the border but leaves those a hundred miles south pleasantly uncrowded. People in those border campgrounds will warn you not to cross into Mexico because there are bandidos, dishonest cops, terrible roads, and language and water problems. The one thing you can be sure of when you get one of these warnings is that that person has not tried Mexican camping him/herself.

First-time camping visitors are almost always amazed at how trouble-free Mexican camping is. Few ever meet a bandido or get sick from the water. The general feeling is that Mexico is safer than much of the U.S., especially U.S. urban areas. After you've been in Mexico a few years you will hear about the occasional problem, just as you do north of the border. Most problems could have been easily avoided if the person involved had just observed a few common-sense safety precautions. Here are the ones we follow and feel comfortable with.

Never drive at night. Night driving is dangerous because Mexican roads are completely different at night. There are unexpected and hard-to-avoid road hazards, there are aggressive truck drivers, and there is little in the way of formal security patrols. If there are really any bandidos in the area they are most likely to be active after dark.

Don't free camp alone except in a place you are very sure of. Individual free campers are uniquely vulnerable. Many folks don't follow this rule and have no problems, it is up to you.

Don't open the door to a knock after dark. First crack a window to find out who is knocking. Why take chances. We've talked to a number of people who wish they'd followed this rule, even in campgrounds.

Don't leave your rig unguarded on the street if you can avoid it. Any petty crook knows your rig is full of good stuff, it is a great target. We like to leave ours in the campground while we explore. Use public transportation, it's lots of fun.

There are a couple of security precautions that you can take before leaving home, you probably have already taken them if you do much traveling in your rig. Add a deadbolt to your entrance door, some insurance policies in the states actually require this. If possible install an alarm in your vehicle, it can take a load off your mind when you must leave it on the street.

If you do find that you need some help the Mexican Ministry of Tourism has a 24-hour help hot line. The number is (5) 250-0123.

A final tip—don't park under any coconuts, they make a big dent if they fall on your rig or your head!

Signs

Sometimes it is a little difficult to interpret the signs along the road. We've taken pictures and put together the graphic on the following two pages to provide a little help.

Spanish Language

You certainly don't need to be able to speak Spanish to get along just fine in Mexico. All of the people working in campgrounds, gas stations and stores are accustomed to dealing with non-Spanish speakers. Even if you can't really talk to them you'll be able to transact business.

On the other hand Mexico is a great place to learn Spanish. In many campgrounds you'll find groups of people who bring in a tutor and study on a regular schedule. There are also lots of Spanish schools scattered around the country. Best-known as good places to study Spanish are San Miguel de Allende, Guadalajara, Mexico City and Oaxaca but most larger cities have language institutes. A less formal arrangement with a Spanish speaker also works well, you can teach English and learn Spanish.

Telephones

Telephone service is rapidly improving in Mexico but is still expensive. Almost all cities now have Telmex phones on the street that you can use to call home for a reasonable fee, if you know how. Other companies, like AT&T, have started competing with Telmex so the improvement should continue. Cell phones are becoming more and more popular although rates are high.

It seems like every country has a different system of area codes and telephone numbers. Mexico is no exception. The country is modernizing and this year things are in flux. Formerly each number had a one, two or three digit area code and a 5, 6, or 7 digit individual local number for a total of eight digits. A new system is now being adopted. It too will have eight digits, but now there is a one digit area code and then a seven digit local individual number. It means that local callers must now dial seven numbers instead of the 5, 6, or seven that they were able to dial before. The new system is being put in place at different times in different areas, but that's not a problem for us because you can use the new system everywhere now, you'll just be dialing an extra number or two for local calls that you really don't yet need to dial. All of the phone numbers in this book are written using the new system.

To call into Mexico from the U.S. or Canada you must first dial a 011 for international access, then the Mexico country code which is 52, then the Mexican area code and number. Often businesses will advertise in the U.S. with a number which includes some or all of these prefixes. Now that you know what they are you should have no problems dialing a Mexican number.

To call the U.S. or Canada out of Mexico you dial 00, then the country code which is 1, then the area code and individual number. You can do this from most Telmex streetside phones (often labeled as Ladatel). To dial a Mexican number from these phones (in the same city) you only dial the local number with no area code, if you are calling another city you dial 01, then the area code, then the local number. Street-side phones take coins or special Ladatel prepaid cards, the cards are available in drug stores and other places. You will be able to watch your money drain away by watching the readout on the front of the phone, actually these cards are a reasonably inexpensive way to make long-distance calls. During the 2000/2001 season the rate was about $1.00 per minute for calling the states from most of Mexico.

During the winter of 2000/2001 the best deal we heard about for calling the states was a Sam's Club pre-paid AT&T card. These cards could only be purchased in Sam's Clubs north of the border, not the Mexican stores. The rate was about $.45 per minute from most of Mexico. The cards are handy because you can add money to them over the phone by giving a credit card number, even from Mexico. At the beginning of the season the rate was even lower, but it was increased. This just emphasizes that telephone rates in Mexico are changing rapidly, next year is hard to predict.

Another way to call out of Mexico is to use a special access telephone number which will connect you with AT&T, MCI, Sprint, or other service provider. Our experience is that this is more expensive than using either a pre-paid card from the states or one of the Telmex/Ladatal cards from a Mexican drug store. Make arrangements for doing this before leaving home, your long distance provider probably offers the service and can give you a special card, security code, and instructions for making these calls. The same system is used for making calls throughout the world. You don't have to insert money into the phone to make this type of call except perhaps a small coin to get things started. The AT&T access number is 001-800-288-2872, MCI is 001-800-674-7000, Sprint is 001-800-243-0000, AT&T Canada is 001-800-123-0201 and Bell Canada is 001-800-010-1990.

In the past the least expensive way to call home has been to call collect. Collect is now one of the most expensive ways to call. To make a collect call to the U.S. or Canada

TELEPHONE AND
INTERNET ACCESS

Right Turn
Allowed
With Caution

Immigration
Customs

Clearance
5.8 Meters

Stop

Falling Rocks
(Derumbe)

Speed Bump
(Topes)

Heavy Traffic
Stay Right

Left Lane Only For Passing

Laterals Only For
Light Vehicles

Toll Booth In 250 Meters

Bicycle Path

In Fog Turn On Lights

Dim Your Lights For
Approaching Traffic

Keep Quintana Roo Clean

Keep Your Distance

Dangerous Curve
in 400 Meters

No Right
Turn

Slow

Reduce Your Speed

In Baja California South
Seatbelts are Mandatory

Truck Entrance And Exit

Dangerous Intersection
In 400 Meters

This Is Not A High
Speed Road

Avoid Accidents - 50 KM/H

Happy Travels
Pass With Caution

Thanks For Using Your
Seatbelt

Stay Right

The Best Part Of Your
Vacation Is A Healthy
Return Home

Drive With Caution

Drive With Caution
Your Family Waits For You

Viewpoint of Mill

No Driving On the Shoulder

Do Not Leave Rocks
On The Pavement

NO FRENE
CON MOTOR

No Braking With Engine

NO MALTRATE
LAS SEÑALES

Don't Mistreat The Signs

NO MANEJE
CANSADO

Don't Drive Tired

NO REBASE CON RAYA
CONTINUA

No Passing When
Continuous Line

No Passing On the Shoulder

Obey The Signs

For Turning Left
Wait For The Light

Bus Stop 300 Meters

Pavement Slippery When Wet

Allow Passing
Utilize The Extreme Right

Toll Booth In 500 Meters

Town Near

Caution Pedestrian Crossing

Precaucion Wind Zone

Highway Under
Repair in 500 Meters

Caution Livestock Zone

Throwing Trash Prohibited

Reduction Of Shoulder
In 200 Meters

Tope

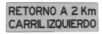

Respect The Speed Limit

U-Turn In 2 Kilometers
Left Lane

PGR Stop 500 Meters

Exit in 150 Meters For
Vehicles Without Brakes

If You Drink Don't Drive

No Passing

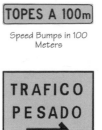

Heavy Traffic Go Right

Slow Traffic Right Lane

Light Vehicles Turn
Left For Tajin

Heavy Vehicles Turn
Left For Tajin

Tropic Of Cancer

One Lane in
500 Meters

Urban Zone Slow Down

First Aid Station   Km
Marker

No Parking

Use Your
Seatbelt

No Passing

Livestock on
The Road

Water On The
Road (Vado)

Level Of
Water
Over Road

from a street-side phone dial 090 and an English-speaking operator will come on and help you. You can also make these calls using the access numbers given directly above.

If a town does not yet have the street-side phones it usually has a phone office. You go in and the operator will dial for you and send you to a booth. When you are finished she'll get the charge and you pay her with cash.

The latest scourge to hit the telephone-starved traveler to Mexico is credit card-accepting phones placed conveniently in most tourist areas. Many Mexican businesses have allowed these things to be installed as a convenience to their customers since a normal phone is almost impossible to obtain. Unfortunately they are a real problem, the rate charged is often in excess of $10 per minute for calls to numbers outside Mexico. We have talked to several unsuspecting users who found charges of several hundred dollars on their credit card statements when they returned home. You can pick up any of these phones and ask the English-speaking operator for the initial and per-minute fee. If you are asked for a credit card number on any long-distance call you should be suspicious. Hopefully these rates will go down as people wise up and learn to ask.

Toll Roads

During the last fifteen years or so Mexico has built many fine roads. These new highways are loved and hated. They're loved in part because they make virtually the entire country easily accessible to visitors. They're hated because they are toll roads, and the tolls are some of the highest in the world.

The new toll roads are typically beautiful four-lane superhighways. Also typically there is a perfectly free alternate route. Unfortunately the alternate is often in very poor condition and full of trucks. It will often take you at least twice and often three times as long to travel a given distance on the free road. You'll use lots more gas, you'll have a much higher chance of having mechanical trouble or an accident, and the wear on your rig will be significantly higher.

It has been the government's policy to have a free road alternate whenever a toll road is built. Sometimes the free road is the best route and sometimes the toll road is best. If there is no alternate route the toll road is often more reasonably priced than if there is one. All of this makes choosing a route very complicated. When we are driving a big rig (usually a motorhome with tow car) we follow the trucks. They are knowledgeable and generally do a pretty good job of making the convenience/cost trade-off decision to our satisfaction. In a smaller vehicle like our 19-foot van we almost always choose the toll roads. You will have to determine your own tolerance for grinding up grades behind slow trucks and bouncing over potholes.

Typically tolls are charged based upon the number of axles (*ejes*) on your vehicle. There will be a rate for automobiles (and vans and pickups without duals), one for two-axle rigs (that's you if you have duals), and then rates for 3, 4, 5 and so on. There are twists to the rates in different areas, one you often see in poorer agricultural areas is that a pickup without duals and pulling a trailer pays much less than one with duals and the same trailer. A typical rate structure for 50 miles on a new toll road with a free alternate (the most expensive type) is as follows: autos - $3.75 U.S., 2 axles - $6.25 U.S., 3 axles - $9.50 U.S., 4 axles - $12 U.S., 5 axles - $15.25 U.S. These rates are of course converted from pesos. You can see that traveling by toll road can be a significant cost especially in an RV with lots of axles.

As you whiz along on the toll roads with no traffic (everyone else is on the free road) you'll wonder why the toll road operators don't lower their rates to get more traffic. It seems obvious that they would make more money charging more cars smaller fees. This is a constant topic of conversation around the evening cocktail table in RV parks. Although many of the new toll roads were built by private companies and originally operated by them they are now almost all run by the federal or state governments. We note that rates have not come down since the governments took over operations from the bankrupt toll road operators.

Travel Library

Don't go to Mexico without a general tourist guide with information about the places you'll visit. Even if you're in Mexico for the sun and fun you'll have questions that no one seems to be able to answer. Our current favorite is **Lonely Planet Mexico** *(7th Edition)* published by Lonely Planet Publications in 2000, ISBN 1-86450-089-1.

Another very good guide is **Mexico Handbook** *(2nd Edition)* by Joe Cummings and Chichi Mallen, published by Moon Publications Inc. in 1998, ISBN 1-56691-123-0. It covers cities and towns, ruins, and even a surprising number of trailer parks and camping spots.

A cult favorite in the travel guide genre is **The People's Guide to Mexico** by Carl Franz, published by Avalon Travel Publishing, ISBN 1-56261-419-3). This book has been around since 1972, it's frequently updated, and it's filled with an encyclopedic mix of information about pretty much everything Mexican that you will wonder about during your visit. It's also so well written that it is hard to put down.

In guidebooks as in maps the American Automobile Association is an excellent source of information. Their **Mexico Travel Book**, updated annually, covers only the cities they think worth a visitor's time. It is so well organized that we use it when we travel to make sure we aren't missing anything. In the back there's even a decent campground directory.

For background information about Mexican history, culture and politics you should read Alan Riding's book **Distant Neighbors**. The book was originally published in 1984. It is somewhat outdated but you will be amazed at how it explains many of the things that are happening in Mexico today. The book is still in print and paperback editions are not difficult to find.

There are many more excellent Mexico books. See our internet site at www.rollinghomes.com for links to many at internet bookstores.

A visit to Mexico is a great way to study Spanish. Make sure to bring along a good Spanish-English dictionary. Also consider bringing a Spanish textbook, you might just decide to do a little studying.

Traveling in Groups

Many people feel more secure traveling with several other rigs in Mexico, especially if this is a first visit. In fact they are more secure. Several rigs free camping together on a beach are much less likely to be bothered than a single camper. Likewise, if one rig has mechanical problems the others can provide help, or at least help to get help. When it comes to figuring out the unfamiliar often several heads are better than one.

There is a down side to traveling together also. The truth is that three rigs traveling together will have three times the mechanical problems. We have yet to see a caravan of RVs that wasn't being slowed by at least one rig with problems. If you do decide to travel with a group of other RV's make sure that they are in good mechanical condition before you start, otherwise there may be unexpected friction.

And that brings up another point. Only compatible people should travel together. We have met several groups who teamed up when they met at the border. Often these groups split within a week. Some people like to travel fast, others slow. Some like to get up early, others late. Some have rigs in great mechanical condition, some do not. If you must have a companion rig make sure you know them well, try traveling together north of the border first. Actually, a good place to meet compatible travel partners is on a commercial guided caravan trip.

As you travel around Mexico, even if you are a single rig, you will find that you are not really alone. Everyone trades tips about good camping spots and interesting places they have visited. Mexico is an adventure and people want to talk about it. You will get to know other people and you will find that you often run into them again, usually without planning it. After all, there are a limited number of campgrounds and even a dedicated free camper uses them occasionally.

Type of Rig

The truth is that you can travel Mexico in almost any type of vehicle, anything from a bicycle to the largest diesel pusher or fifth-wheel. Each kind of rig has its own advantages and disadvantages. The best rig depends upon where you want to go; how you travel, sightsee, and shop; and how much you want to spend. We've always felt that we want the largest possible rig when we're parked, and the smallest and most maneuverable when we're on the road.

Many people do visit Mexico on bicycles. We have never thought Mexico a great bicycle destination because many highways are narrow and heavily traveled. When you see a Mexican on a bicycle you will notice that he often climbs off his bike and steps off the road for all passing traffic, hardly the way to make much progress but sometimes necessary in the interests of safety. The obvious way to get around this problem is to travel back roads, something easier to say than to do. In many regions there are few minor roads and the ones that do exist don't go to the places you're likely to want to visit. There are some exceptions. Many people ride Mex 1 on the Baja Peninsula. They can do this because much of the road is not extremely busy. Other possible biking areas are the back roads in the Chiapas mountains, the Yucatán, and Oaxaca. Fortunately bike travelers in Mexico can easily use the extensive bus system to move from one area to another.

It is entirely possible to travel comfortably in Mexico with an automobile or light truck and tent. You'll want a good insect-proof tent to keep out both the flying insects you're probably familiar with at home and the stinging crawlers you may meet in Mexico. If you plan to do no backpacking there is no real reason to use a small tent, you'll be more comfortable in one that allows you to stand up. Folding cots of some kind will let you get a much better night's sleep.

If you are at all interested in exploring there are big advantages to using a smaller camping vehicle. On the Baja Peninsula there are many roads that are just not suitable for larger RVs. Four-wheel drive is nice to have on the Baja although just having good ground clearance is a big help. On the mainland a small rig is much cheaper to use on toll roads. Smaller rigs also are easier to shepherd along Mexico's narrow and often steep highways. The warm climate in this part of the world means that you can spend a lot of time outside the rig, many people bring along one of those screened tent-rooms where they can set up a card table or cots and effectively double the size of their rig.

We've traveled the highways of Mexico extensively in a 34-foot gas-powered motorhome pulling a pickup. We had no problems and feel that any reasonably cautious person can go almost anywhere where there are paved roads. The two Achilles heels of big rigs are ground clearance and poor maneuverability. Both of these are not nearly as limiting if you know what to expect. Hopefully this book will help in that area. While on the road the key is caution. Keep the speed down so that you have complete control and slow even more when large vehicles pass you in either direction. In spots with no shoulder a wheel off the pavement could mean disaster.

Units of Measurement

Mexico is on the metric system. Most of the world has already learned to deal with this. For the rest of us it takes just a short time of working with the metric system, and there is no way to avoid it, to start to feel at home. Conversion tables and factors are available in most guidebooks but you will probably remember a few critical conversion numbers as we have.

For distance runners like ourselves, kilometers were easy. A kilometer is about .62 miles (actually .6124). We can remember this because a 10 kilometer race is 6.2 miles long. For converting miles to kilometer, divide the number of miles by .62. For converting kilometers to miles, multiply the kilometers by .62. Since kilometers are shorter than miles the number of kilometers after the conversion will always be more than the number of miles, if they aren't you divided when you should have multiplied or vice versa.

For liquid measurement it is usually enough to know that a liter is about the same as a quart. When you need more accuracy, like when you are trying to make some sense out of your miles-per-gallon calculations, there are 3.79 liters in a U.S. gallon.

Here are a few useful conversion factors:

1 km = .62 mile	1 mile = 1.61 km
1 meter = 3.28 feet	1 foot = .30 meters
1 liter = .26 U.S. gallon	1 U.S. gallon = 3.79 liters
1 kilogram = 2.21 pounds	1 pound = .45 kilograms

convert from °F to °C by subtracting 32 and multiplying by 5/9
convert from °C to °F by multiplying by 1.8 and adding 32

Vehicle Preparation and Breakdowns

One of the favorite subjects whenever a group of Mexican campers gets together over cocktails is war stories about breakdowns and miraculous repairs performed by Mexican mechanics with almost no tools. Before visiting Mexico many people fear a breakdown above all else. Our experience and that of the people we talk to is that help is generally readily available and very reasonably priced. It is usually easy to find someone to work on the vehicle, it is often very hard to get parts.

Ford, General Motors, Chrysler, Volkswagen and Nissan all manufacture cars and trucks in Mexico and have large, good dealers throughout the country. Toyota does not. These dealers are good places to go if you need emergency or maintenance work done on your vehicle. However, many of the models sold in the north are not manufactured in Mexico and the dealers may not have parts for your particular vehicle. They can order them but often it takes several weeks for parts from the U.S. to arrive.

Often the quickest way to get a part is to go get it yourself. An acquaintances once broke an axle in Villahermosa. His vehicle is common in Mexico, but the type of axle he needed was not used in the Mexican models. Rather than wait an indeterminate length of time for a new axle he went and picked one up himself. He climbed on a bus, traveled to Matamoros, walked across the border, caught a cab to a dealer, picked up a new axle and threw it over his shoulder, walked back across the border, caught another bus, and was back in Villahermosa within 48 hours.

Avoid problems by making sure your vehicle is in good condition before entering Mexico. Get an oil change, a lube job, and a tune-up. Make sure that hoses, belts, filters, brake pads, shocks and tires are all good. Consider replacing them before you leave. Driving conditions in Mexico tend to be extreme. Your vehicle will be operating on rough roads, in very hot weather, with lots of climbs and descents.

Bring along a reasonable amount of spares. We like to carry replacement belts, hoses, and filters. Make sure you have a good spare tire even if you don't mount it on a rim. Tires can be mounted in Mexico but often the sizes used on RVs are not available. Don't bring much oil, good multi-weight oil is now available in Mexico.

RV drivers need to be prepared to make the required hookups in Mexican RV parks. RV supplies are difficult to find in Mexico so make sure that you have any RV supplies you need before crossing the border. Don't forget holding tank chemicals.

Electricity is often suspect at campgrounds in Mexico. It is a good idea to carry a tester that will tell you when voltages are incorrect, polarities reversed, and grounds lacking. Always carry adapters allowing you to use small 110V, two-pronged outlets. The best setup is one that lets you turn the plug over (to reverse polarity) and to connect a ground wire to a convenient pipe, conduit, or metal stake.

Sewer stations (*dranaje*) in many Mexican campgrounds are located at the rear of the site. Make sure you have a long sewer hose, one that will reach all the way to the rear of your RV and then another couple of feet. You'll be glad you have it.

Water purity considerations (see the *Drinking Water* title in this chapter), mean that you may need a few items that you may not already have in your rig. Consider adding a water filter if you do not already have one installed. You should also have a simple filter for filtering water before it even enters your rig, this avoids sediment build-up in your fresh water tank. Of course you'll also need a hose, we have found a 20-foot length to be adequate in most cases.

It is extremely hard to find parts or knowledgeable mechanics to do systems-related work on camping vehicles. Before crossing the border make sure your propane system, all appliances, toilet, holding tanks, and water system are working well because you'll want them to last until you get home. Marginal or jury-rigged systems should be repaired. Consider bringing a spare fresh water pump, or at least a diaphragm set if yours isn't quite new. Make sure your refrigerator is working well, you'll need it and replacement parts are impossible to find.

Make sure you have all the tools necessary to change a tire on your rig. Many large motorhomes no longer come with jacks and tire-changing tools. The theory must be that it is too dangerous for an individual to change a tire on one of these huge heavy rigs. This may be true but you need to have the proper tools available so that you can find help and get the job done if you have a flat in a remote location. Mexican roads are rough and flat tires common.

If you do have a breakdown along the road what should you do? It is not a good idea to abandon your rig. RVs are a tempting target, one abandoned along the road invites a break-in. This is one good reason not to travel at night. Daytime drivers can usually find a way to get their broken-down rig off the road before night falls. If you are traveling with another rig you can send someone for help. If you are traveling by yourself you will probably find it easy to flag down a car or truck. We find that Mexican drivers are much more helpful than those in the U.S. Ask the other driver to send a mechanic or *grúa* (tow truck) from the next town. Large tow trucks are common since there is heavy truck traffic on most highways in Mexico.

Weather

Most of Mexico really has two seasons: a wet season and a dry season. The wet season is the summer, from approximately June through some time in September or October. During this period in many parts of the country it rains each afternoon. Much of the country is also extremely hot during this period. If you can only visit in the summer plan on hot, muggy weather along the Gulf Coast, the Yucatán, Chiapas, and much of the west coast. On the Baja Peninsula and the deserts of northern Mexico expect extremely hot weather. Added excitement on the Yucatán and along the southern Pacific Coast may be provided by hurricane season from August through October.

The winter dry season is when most travelers visit Mexico. In a fortunate conjunction of events the extremely pleasant warm dry season in Mexico occurs exactly when most northerners are more than ready to leave snow and cold temperatures behind. Comfortable temperatures occur beginning in November and lasting through May. The shoulder months of November and May may be uncomfortably warm for some people.

For year-round comfort consider the higher elevations. Guadalajara and Cuernavaca are both famous for their year-round good weather and there are many other nearby cities with similarly decent weather during almost the entire year. Even in the highlands, however, expect afternoon showers.

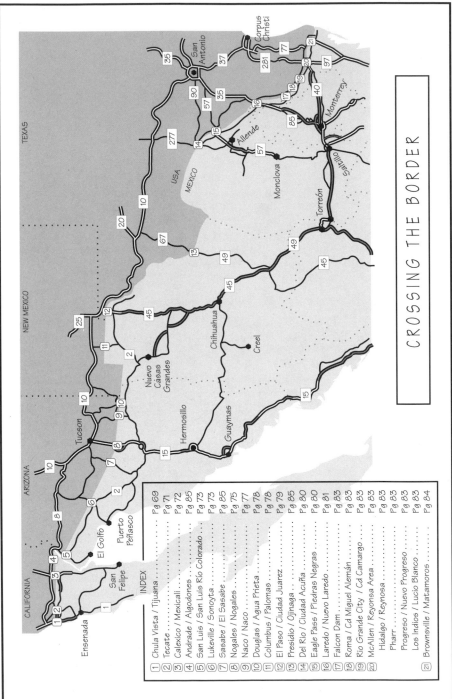

CROSSING THE BORDER

CHAPTER

. . . . 3

CROSSING THE BORDER

If you find that crossing the border into Mexico is a little intimidating you are not alone. The border crossing is probably the main thing that keeps most RVers from traveling south. This is understandable. Mexico is so different from the U.S. that you undergo something of a culture shock the first day. When we cross the border each time we immediately notice that there is more dust, more garbage along the roadside, more people on foot, and that the roads are much poorer. Part of this is due to the fact that the border region is probably the least attractive part of Mexico. Within a few days we become accustomed to these things and you probably will to. When you return to the U.S. you're likely to think that things seem sterile and uninteresting.

If you have your ducks in a row and know what to expect the border crossing will be a much less trying experience. In this chapter we'll try to tell you everything you need to know to make it easy. Below you'll find sections about documentation, insurance, and what you can take to Mexico without problems. Then we'll talk a little about coming back into the states. Finally, we'll give you some information about some of the more popular border crossings.

People Documentation

Any U.S. or Canadian citizen entering Mexico for more than 72 hours must have a *Tarjeta de Turista* or tourist card. These are also sometimes called an FMT (Forma Migratoria Turista). Don't leave home without proof or your citizenship because you will need it to get your tourist card (and are required to have it even for short visits to border areas). The best proof of citizenship is a passport but a certified copy of your birth certificate is also acceptable. If you use your birth certificate instead of a passport you will also need a picture ID like a driver's license. In parts of Mexico it is not unusual for roadblocks to be set up to check everyone who passes for identification. The army troops at these roadblocks often speak no English and prefer passports, this seems like reason enough to us for a person to go through the trouble of getting a passport if they don't have one already.

Tourist cards are required for any visit beyond border areas or if you are going to be inside Mexico more than 72 hours. You pick them up at the Migración office at the border crossing. Actually, you can pick them up before entering Mexico at Mexican government tourist offices and other travel agencies. If you pick up cards north of the border, however, they still must be validated when you cross the border. For that reason there seems to be no real advantage in picking up a card before you cross. These cards are issued for up to a 180-day stay and there is a charge, actually a tourist tax. You do not pay at the border, instead you take the card to any bank and they collect about $18 and stamp the form. Originally we were told that the fee had to be paid within three day but now it appears that it only must be paid before leaving the country. Also, now a few travel agencies north of the border are selling pre-paid forms so that you do not have to visit a bank in Mexico at all. You must have the stamped form to leave Mexico. At the time this is written the procedures seem a little loose, but just as has happened with the automobile permits described below we believe that procedures will be tightened up over time. Eventually it appears that the payment stamp will be required on the tourist card before a vehicle permit is issued but during the winter of 2000/2001 this was not the case. The tourist card is good for multiple entries, make sure you turn it in before its time limit is expired.

As a practical matter the tourist card tends to take second place in importance to the vehicle documentation discussed below but that doesn't mean it can be ignored. At the border you must get the tourist card at the Migración office before proceeding to the Banjercito for your vehicle permit.

The Baja Peninsula is a special case. Vehicle documentation is not required on the Baja but tourist cards are. If you are on the Baja south of the Ensenada area or are anywhere on the Baja for more than 72 hours you are required to have a tourist card. Many people don't get them, either because they don't know they're required or because they are not often checked. If you get caught you are at least subject to a fine. Spot checks are sometimes conducted in campgrounds and cards are being checked when vehicles cross the border between Baja and Baja Sur near Guerrero Negro.

Another special case is the Sonoran Free Trade Zone. This area encompasses north-western Sonora state and includes the area east to Sonoyta and Puerto Peñasco. The rules in this area are like those on the Baja. The zone includes both Puerto Peñasco and El Golfo de Santa Clara.

Many people do not worry about returning their tourist cards when they leave the country. The Mexican government has not kept track of tourist cards in the past. In fact, one time when we left Mexico the official we were dealing with waved us off when we tried to return our cards. However, now that fees are being collected we suspect that better record-keeping will follow.

Vehicle Documentation

In an effort to combat the illegal importation of vehicles from the U.S. and Canada the Mexican government has an elaborate procedure to make sure you bring yours back into the states. These procedures take some time and usually involve standing in a couple of lines, but it seems that things are better organized every year. The last time we crossed the border the entire process of vehicle and personal documentation took about forty-five minutes.

Each driver is allowed only one vehicle. This includes motorcycles and ATV's so the limit does cause problems. If you are pulling a tow car you and your wife or other companion must both have drivers licenses. Each one of you must sign up for one vehicle and the vehicle must be registered in the name of the driver. The limit on motorcycles and ATVs is one reason that the Baja and northwest Sonora are so popular, no vehicle import documents are required in these areas. Obviously these rules present a problem for folks traveling by themselves. We have met single travelers who get around the problem by making two visits to the border, perhaps to different border stations. We're not sure this is legal, but it seems to work. We have also talked with folks who have been able to get the Mexican official to put together two packages, one for each car but with the same driver, using different credit cards. Most officials, however, will not do this.

To get your temporary vehicle importation permit you must have proof of citizenship, a driver's license, and the vehicle's registration or title. Borrowed vehicles are not allowed. If your title or registration shows a lienholder (you have a loan secured by the vehicle) you must have a letter from the lienholder stating that you can take it into Mexico for a specified period of time. You should make sure these letters look very official. Make sure they are on letterhead and consider getting the signatures notarized. Rental cars require both a rental agreement and notarized permission letter for travel into Mexico.

You must also have a credit card (MasterCard, VISA, American Express or Diner's Club) issued in the registered owner's name and issued by a U.S. or Canadian bank. If you don't have such a credit card there is an alternate procedure. You can post a bond based upon the value of the vehicle. The bonding process is complicated and somewhat expensive so go the credit card route if at all possible.

When you cross the border you should have your documentation in hand as well as two Xerox copies of your proof of citizenship, driver's license, vehicle registration, and tourist card. For some reason we've never succeeded in having the right combinations of these copies even though we always give it our best shot. Never fear, there always seems to be a handy copy machine where the operator knows exactly what you need and can produce them for a reasonable fee. Last time we crossed the nearby pharmacy made the following copies: one sheet with the tourist card we had just received from Migración, a second sheet with the vehicle title, and a third sheet with our passports open to the first page, our driver's license, and our credit card.

Back at the Banjercito office you'll have your documents processed, go to a bank window where a fee of approximately $17 U.S. will be charged to your credit card, and then an official will accompany you to your vehicle where he/she will put a metallic sticker (*holograma*) on the upper left corner of your window. You will also be given a certificate, make sure the VIN (vehicle identification number) is correct and that the time limit is at least as long as the one on your tourist card.

This sticker must remain on the vehicle until you leave the country. It is good for multiple entries. When you leave the last time, but before your permit expires, you must stop and have the sticker removed at any border station with a Banjercito. The Mexican government does keep track of this and will fine you if you don't properly return the sticker. You may also have a lot of trouble trying to bring that vehicle back into Mexico in following years.

Vehicle Insurance

Your automobile insurance from home will not cover you in Mexico. Insurance is not required in Mexico, but you would be very foolish not to have it. Mexico follows the

Napoleonic code, you are guilty until proven innocent. If you have an accident and have no insurance to assure the authorities that you can pay for damages it is possible that you might be detained for a considerable time.

Don't believe the old saw that all Mexican insurance costs the same, this is not true. Get several quotes and compare coverages. People who go into Mexico for just a short time usually buy daily coverage. This is extremely expensive. Some people get this short-term coverage for the week or so it takes to get to their favorite campground. Once there they park the vehicle and don't use it until they buy more short-term coverage for the drive home.

Longer term coverage, for six months or a year, is much cheaper. It is comparable with the cost of insurance in the U.S. You can buy liability insurance only or a policy that also covers damage to your rig. Check with your U.S. insurance agency to see if damage to your vehicle might be covered by your U.S. policy. No U.S. policy will cover you for liability in Mexico, however. To keep costs down see if you can cancel your U.S. insurance while you are in Mexico and it is not providing any coverage. Here are names and addresses for a few of the brokers that offer Mexican insurance. Call them well before you travel and compare coverage and costs. They will charge the policy to a credit card and mail it to you so that you do not have to worry about insurance at the last moment.

Adventure Caravans, 124 Rainbow Dr. # 2434, Livingston, TX 77399-1024; (800) 872-7897 or (936) 327-3428.

Fantasy RV Tours, Inc., P.O. Box 97605, Las Vegas, NV 89193-5605; (800) 952-8496.

International Gateway Insurance Brokers, Inc., 3450 Bonita Road, Suite #103, Chula Vista, CA 91910; (800) 423-2646 and (619) 422-3022; Fax: (619) 422-2671; E-mail: igib@igib.com.

Miller Insurance Agency, Inc., 5805 SW Willow Lane, Lake Oswego, OR 97035; (800) 622-6347; Web Site: www.MillerRVInsurance.com.

Point South RV Tours; 11313 Edmonson Ave., Moreno Valley, CA 92555; (800) 421-1394 or (909) 247-1222; Web Site: www.rvtours.com.

Sanborn's Mexico Insurance, 2009 S. 10th (SH-336), P.O. Box 310, McAllen, TX 78505-0310; (800) 222-0158; Web Site: www.sanbornsinsurance.com; E-mail: mcallen@sanbornsinsurance.com.

San Xavier Mexico Insurance, 1777 N. Frank Reed Rd. #C, Nogales, AZ 85621; (888) 377-1570; E-mail: mexicobob@aol.com.

Tracks to Adventure, 2811 Jackson Ave., El Paso, TX 79930; (800) 351-6053.

Vagabundos del Mar Boat and Travel Club, Adventure Tours, 190 Main St., Rio Vista, CA 94571; (800) 474-2252.

Pets

You can take your dog or cat into Mexico. Birds and other pets are subject to additional restrictions, taking them to Mexico is not practical. We've not heard of anyone taking a pet into Mexico who has run into problems going south, whatever requirements are in effect do not seem to be observed, so the rules you want to watch for are the ones for bringing the animal back into the U.S. The U.S. Customs web site says that dogs coming back into the U.S. require a rabies vaccination certificate that is at least 30 days old with an expiration date that is not expired. Your vet will probably know the proper forms that are required, if not, check with customs. Your dog or cat may also be examined at the border to see if it seems to be sick, if there is a question you may be required to have it examined by a vet before it will be admitted to the U.S.

Trailer Boats

You will need a boat permit if you plan to use your boat for fishing (or even if you have fishing tackle on board). You can wait to get one until you get to Mexico, they are available from the Mexican Department of Fisheries (*Pesca*) offices in various port cities. In the U.S. they have an office at 2550 Fifth Avenue, Suite 101, San Diego, CA 92103. The Vagabundos del Mar Boat and Travel Club can also provide them, call (800) 474-2252.

ATVs and Motorcycles

Vehicle import documents are required for ATVs and motorcycles just as they are for cars and RVs. This means that the number of vehicles you bring can be limited (since each driver can bring only one vehicle). Since vehicle import permits are not required for the Baja Peninsula or for Sonora east to Puerto Peñasco these are both popular off-road destinations.

What Can You Take In To Mexico?

Campers tend to bring more things along with them when they visit Mexico than most people. When you cross the border you may be stopped and your things quickly checked. You are actually allowed to bring only certain specified items into Mexico duty free and most RVer probably have more things along with them than they should. Fortunately Mexican border authorities seldom are hard-nosed, in fact they usually don't do much looking around at all. Lately we have heard that people bringing large quantities of food sometimes have problems getting it across the border. Now that Mexico has such good supermarkets there is really little need to bring in food.

What Can't You Bring Along?

Guns and illegal drugs. Either of these things will certainly get you in big trouble. If you travel much on Mexican highways you'll eventually be stopped and searched. Guns and drugs are exactly what they will be looking for.

It is illegal for any non-Mexican to have a firearm of any type without a special Mexican permit. These are for hunters and must be obtained through licensed Mexican hunting guides.

Actual Procedures at the Border

The day before you plan to cross the border you should arrive fairly early in the day and find a campground on the U.S. side. The descriptions of the individual crossings below should help. You should have all the identification and papers discussed above in your possession and you should already have arranged your insurance. Spend the afternoon getting ready to go. Fill your tank with U.S. gasoline and hit the stores for last minute purchases. Have a nice dinner, pack things so you can get an easy start in the morning, and get to bed early.

In the morning there's no reason to get to the border much before the Banjercito office opens so time your arrival based upon the information we have included in the write-ups below.

When you cross the border you will not even stop at the U.S. customs. Once you enter Mexico, however, you will probably have to stop to talk with a Mexican official. Most crossings use a stoplight system. You pull up to a light and it will flash green or red. Green means you are not going to be searched or even talked to. Red means that the customs official will ask you a few questions and perhaps wave you to the side for a search. RV searches going south tend to be fairly cursory assuming that you are friendly and polite and do not seem to have a load of something you should not have. Usually they involve nothing more than a walk-through.

Regardless of whether you get a green or red light, once you are turned loose you must still take care of getting your tourist cards and vehicle papers. In many places this is done right at the border crossing station, other places have other stations to take care of this. See the individual crossing write-ups for this information. Parking at the border is sometimes a problem for big rigs, you may have to be creative. We discuss the stations with the best parking situations below.

You will need to visit two offices, Migración (mee-graw-see-OWN) and Banjercito (bahn-hair-SEE-toe), and in that order. If you don't see a sign just ask one of the

THE BANJERCITO AT THE NOGALES CROSSING

officials to point them out. While you're at it you might ask where they suggest that you park.

Migración is where you take care of the people paperwork. The official in the office will probably not speak much English but the form is simple. He'll help you fill it out. He'll ask where you are headed and perhaps how long you will be in Mexico. It probably makes sense to get the card for the maximum 180 days since you can never be entirely sure how long you will need one. For the last few years Migración officials have been issuing 180 day cards with few hassles, but like everything at the border this could change. There is a charge for the tourist card, but you don't pay it at the office. Instead you take the card into a bank and they collect the money from you. You should probably do this within a week or so of your entry although the rules seem to be loose.

Your next visit is to the Banjercito office for your vehicle paperwork, your vehicle import papers. Get in line armed with the documents outlined in the *Vehicle Documentation* section above. This process takes longer than the tourist card but is fairly simple. Once at the window your information is typed into a computer by the clerk. Usually you are sent to another nearby location to have copies produced of some or all of your documents. Then you will be issued a certificate and a window sticker which is known as a *holograma*. Check the certificate to make sure the information that has been input is correct, in particular check that your VIN number is correct and that the vehicle permit has the same time limit as your tourist card. The official will accompany you to your rig and check your VIN number, then he or she will affix the sticker to the inside upper left-hand corner of your windshield.

Once this procedure is complete you are ready to go. You're not quite finished with border officials yet, however. Some 15 miles south of the border you will come to another customs checkpoint. You'll go through the same red and green light procedure, perhaps be inspected again, and go on your way.

Coming Back Into the U.S.

There are a few things to consider when you come back into the U.S. First, you must turn in your window sticker, your *holograma,* to a Mexican Banjercito office. Second, U.S. customs is tougher to get through than Mexican customs, so choosing a crossing to avoid delays is important. Also, U.S. customs does not allow you to bring some things into the country. There are limits on dollar value of items purchased overseas that can be imported without tax. There are also prohibitions against bringing some Mexican food items into the country so you want to make sure you are prepared for this.

When you come back to the U.S. it is important to avoid rush hours. At many crossing points there are large cities on both sides of the border, many people commute to work both ways. Try to avoid the rush-hour crush.

In some ways turning in the *holograma* can be just as difficult as getting one. The sticker program is relatively new and most stations are not designed for the traffic flow required. Particularly for people driving huge rigs. This can be a problem since it is necessary to bring your rig right to the Banjercito office so that the official can remove the sticker in person. The worst case scenario is that you might have to actually cross the border into the U.S. and then come back again to get rid of it. Crossing the border three times instead of once is not fun, so take a look at the individual crossing write-ups below for information about crossings where this can be avoided. Actually, things are getting better each year as the Mexican government upgrades the border stations. While you're at the crossing don't forget to turn in your tourist cards too.

U.S. citizens are allowed to bring back a value of $400 each in goods purchased in Mexico. This includes one liter of spirits, 200 cigarettes, and 100 cigars. It is best to make up a detailed list before you reach the border and to have receipts, a helpful attitude will go a long way.

The U.S. government will not allow certain meats, fruits, and vegetables into the country because they may spread disease. Border agents are well aware that RVers have refrigerators, you can be pretty much assured that you will be questioned and probably searched. It's not worth fibbing, there are hefty fines. The list of prohibited items changes at times but here's the most current as we go to print.

All fruits are prohibited except bananas, blackberries, cactus fruits, dates, dewberries, grapes, lemons, limes (sour, the little ones), lychees, melons, papayas, pineapples, and strawberries. Avocados are prohibited but are allowed if you remove the seed, but not into California.

All vegetables are allowed except potatoes (Irish, sweet, and yams) and sometimes okra. Cooked potatoes, however, are allowed. Nuts are prohibited except acorns, almonds, cocoa beans, chestnuts, coconuts (without husks or milk), peanuts, pecans, piñon seeds (pine nuts), tamarind beans, walnuts, and waternuts.

Eggs are generally prohibited but are allowed if you cook them.

All pork; raw, cooked, or processed; is prohibited except some shelf-stable canned pork and hard cooked pork skins (cracklings).

Poultry is prohibited if it is raw, thoroughly cooked poultry is allowed.

Rules about these things are complicated and do change over time, see our web site at www.rollinghomes.com for links to government sites that have more complete and up-to-date information.

A Final Note About Border-Crossing Procedures and Regulations

The only sure thing about crossing the border is that rules change. The best plan is to stay calm and be polite and flexible. Thousands of people cross the border each year with few problems, you will too.

SELECTED BORDER CROSSINGS

You will find almost every border crossing between the U.S. and Mexico listed below. Here are some of the things you should consider in choosing a crossing.

Unless you will travel only on the Baja or in the Sonora free zone you will need to visit a Banjercito at the border. Vehicle permits are only issued by Banjercitos. Not all crossings have them and the ones that do have different hours than the crossings themselves. We've given the hours that the crossings are open and also the Banjercito hours.

Not all crossings have enough maneuvering and parking room for big rigs. We've included information about this also.

Where will you stay the night before crossing and where the evening of your first day in Mexico? You'll find some campground descriptions below as well as our recommendations for your first night's destination.

When you return from Mexico you will want to cross at a point where you can conveniently turn in your documentation. These might not necessarily be the same crossings that are the best for going into Mexico. Our favorites for returning are Tecate, Sonoyta, Nogales, Naco, Palomas, Ciudad Juarez, Piedras Negras, Nuevo Laredo (Columbia Port of Entry), Pharr, Lucio Blanco, and the new crossing east of Matamoros.

The crossings are described from west to east. Those we do not recommend have short descriptions at the end of the chapter.

CHULA VISTA, CALIFORNIA / TIJUANA, BAJA CALIFORNIA

There are two ports of entry in the Tijuana region. Both seem to be very busy almost all of the time. If we do cross here we like to drive south through the San Ysidro crossing but prefer the Otay Mesa crossing northbound. We would not use either of these crossings to get either tourist visas or vehicle papers, the crossing areas are just too crowded. Instead, get your tourist visa in the Migración office in Ensenada. If you are bound for the mainland get your vehicle papers at Tecate instead, or you can get them in La Paz if you are planning to take the ferry. If you are driving eastward on Mex 2 you could easily get your vehicle papers in Sonoyta or at the San Emeterio station 17 miles (27 km) east of Sonoyta along Mex 2.

The westernmost port is known as **San Ysidro** on the U.S. side, **Puerta Mexico** on the Mexican side. It is open 24 hours a day, seven days a week. This is said to be the busiest border crossing in the world. On the U.S. side access is from I-5, the main north-south highway through the western coastal states actually ends at this crossing. So does I-805. On the Mexico side the crossing is in downtown Tijuana, streets are crowded and there's lots of traffic. Still, if you follow signs for "Toll Road", "Cuota", "Rosarito-Ensenada Scenic Road" or "Mex 1D" you can easily travel west to the coast and follow Mex 1D south toward Ensenada without really dealing with much traffic. Almost immediately after crossing through the border station you loop around to the left, pass under the highway, and then travel westward along the border fence. You soon join another highway heading westward and it's easy sailing from there. We prefer this crossing southbound over the Otay Mesa crossing but going northbound the wait is usually at least an hour and driving through town is more difficult than it is headed south so we prefer Otay when headed north.

The easternmost crossing is known as **Otay Mesa** on the U.S. side, **Otay** on the Mexico side. This crossing is open 7 days a week from 6 a.m. until 10 p.m. It's located about 5 miles (8 km) east of the San Ysidro crossing and is accessed from the north by taking Hwy 905 eastward. From Mexico the crossing is on the eastern side of Tijuana near the point where Mex 2 enters the city. Easiest access is from Mex 2 to the east or

from Mex 1 Libre from Rosarito and then the Libramiento Oriente around Tijuana.
Expect at least a half-hour wait headed northbound at this crossing.

Campgrounds

Headed south the closest campgrounds are just north of Rosarito, see the *Rosarito*
section in Chapter 12 for information about them. It will take less than a half-hour to
reach them from the San Ysidro crossing.

On the U.S. side there are two excellent campgrounds in Chula Vista near San Ysidro.

⊟ CHULA VISTA RV RESORT

Address:	460 Sandpiper Way, Chula Vista, CA 91910
Telephone:	(619) 422-0111 or (800) 770-2878
Fax:	(619) 422-8872
E-mail:	chulavistarv@isat.com
Web Site:	www.gocampingamerica.com/chulavista

GPS Location: N 32° 37' 40.7", W 117° 06' 16.6"

This is a first class, very popular campground in an excellent location for preparing to
enter Mexico. Chula Vista is a convenient small town with all the stores and facilities
you'll need, and both San Diego and Tijuana are close by. Reservations are necessary.

This campground is located adjacent to and operated in conjunction with a marina.
There are 236 back-in and pull-through sites with 50-amp power and full hookups.
Parking is on paved drives with patios, sites are separated by shrubbery. Large rigs
and slide-outs fit fine. The bathroom facilities are excellent and there is a nice warm
pool as well as a hot tub, small store, and meeting rooms. The marina next door has
two restaurants and a shuttle bus provides access to central Chula Vista, stores, and
the local stop of the Tijuana Trolley. Paved walkways along the water are nice for that
evening stroll.

Take the J Street Exit from Highway 5 which is approximately 7 miles north of the
San Ysidro border crossing and about 8 miles south of central San Diego. Drive west
on J Street for 2 blocks, turn right on Marina Parkway, and drive north to the first
street from the left (about 1/4 mile) which is Sandpiper, turn left here and drive one
block, then follow the street as it makes a 90 degree right-angle turn, the entrance will
be on your left.

⊟ SAN DIEGO METRO KOA

Address:	111 North 2nd Ave, Chula Vista, CA 91910
Telephone:	(619) 427-3601
Res.:	(800) KOA-9877
E-mail:	reservations@sandiegokoa.com
Web Site:	www.koa.com/where/ca/05112.htm

GPS Location: N 32° 38' 57.1", W 117° 04' 39.3"

This large campground in Chula Vista also make a good base for exploring Tijuana
and San Diego. It has about 270 spaces. It's a well-equipped park with everything you
would normally expect at a KOA including a pool, hot tub, playground, and store.
There's a shuttle to the San Diego (Tijuana) Trolley. Reservations are necessary at this
campground, it is extremely popular.

To reach the campground take the E Street Exit from I-5 in Chula Vista. Travel east on
E Street until you reach 2nd Ave. Turn left here on 2nd and proceed about a mile.

TECATE, BAJA CALIFORNIA

Tecate, 25 miles east of Tijuana, offers a relaxed border crossing. We especially like to use the Tecate border crossing when headed north. Tecate is a small town without a lot of traffic. Mex 3 south from Tecate to Ensenada is a good alternative for folks heading north and south, it meets the coastal road just north of Ensenada. En route you pass across scenic mountains and through vineyards in the Valle de Guadelupe. There's even a campground near the wineries if you don't feel like driving on into Ensenada.

At the Tecate crossing there is no town on the U.S. side of the border. The crossing is open seven days a week from 6 a.m. to midnight. The Banjercito here is open from 8 a.m. until 8 p.m Monday through Friday, 10 a.m. until 2 p.m. on Saturday, and is closed on Sunday. If you are heading south you will immediately find yourself on city streets. Parking is limited but there is light traffic so you should have little problem stopping long enough to take care of paperwork. To find Mex 3 just jog left one block when you are able. You'll find yourself on the street that becomes Mex 3.

Campground

Heading south on Mex 3 the first campground you will encounter is the Rancho Sordo Mudo about 45 miles (73 km) from the border. You can also drive east on Mex 2 for 13 miles (21 km) to the Tecate KOA. See Chapter 12 for more information.

We have found the following campground to be a handy place to spend the night before crossing the border.

🚐 POTRERO REGIONAL PARK

Res.:	5201 Ruffin Road, Suite P, San Diego, CA 92123-1699
Telephone:	(Reservations) (858) 565-3600, (Info) (858) 694-3049
Web Site:	www.co.san-diego.ca.us/parks

GPS Location: N 32° 36' 45.6", W 116° 35' 41.2"

This is a good campground on the U.S. side of the border near Tecate. If you are headed south and want to get a good start in the morning consider spending the night here. It is only 5 miles (8 km) from Tecate, the small nearby town of Potrero offers a café. Another nearby town, Campo, has an interesting railroad museum.

There are 32 back-in sites with electrical and water hookups set under oak trees for shade. Large rigs will find plenty of room in most sites. Picnic tables and fire pits are provided. Areas are also set aside for tents and there are hot water showers. There is a dump station. Reservations are accepted but probably not necessary during the winter season.

Follow Hwy 94 from San Diego toward Tecate. Zero your odometer where Hwy 188 to Tecate cuts off to the right but continue straight. Drive 2.3 miles (3.7 km) to the outskirts of Potrero and turn left. Then after another .3 miles (.5 km) turn right on the entrance road to the campground.

CALEXICO, CALIFORNIA / MEXICALI, BAJA CALIFORNIA

Mexicali is the preferred border-crossing point for folks headed south to San Felipe on the Baja Peninsula's east coast. Most of these people do not worry about getting their paperwork done at the border. Tourist cards can be obtained in San Felipe and vehicle papers are not necessary unless you are headed for the mainland. If you are driving eastward on Mex 2 you could easily get your vehicle papers in Sonoyta or at the San Emeterio station 17 miles (27 km) east of Sonoyta along Mex 2.

CALEXICO / MEXICALI

Calexico on the U.S. side is a nice little town but most folks preparing to cross the border spend the night in El Centro a few miles to the north. El Centro has plenty of shopping facilities and several campgrounds. One of them is described below.

Mexicali is a big, sprawling city. There are two crossings. The downtown crossing is known as **Calexico Downtown** on the U.S. side and **Garita Mexicali I** on the Mexico side. This crossing is open 24 hours a day, seven days a week. From this crossing streets are crowded and traffic for San Felipe must pass directly through the middle of town. Fortunately the way is well-signed in both directions. The route follows Lopez Mateos boulevard until reaching both the east/west Mex 2 and Mex 5 to the south. Mex 2 passes south of the central area of Mexicali on city streets. Where it crosses Mex 5 things are somewhat confusing because the highway jogs through several intersections. As you pass through Mexicali on your way south you'll see several large supermarkets, good places to stop for groceries since San Felipe doesn't offer anything nearly as grand.

The second crossing is a few miles east. It is known as **Calexico East** on the U.S. side and **Mexicali II** on the Mexican side. It is open from 6 a.m. until 10 p.m. seven days a week. This crossing is much quieter and less crowded, the route south toward San Felipe goes south to Mex 2 and then follows that highway through the southern suburbs, it is well signed for San Felipe.

Campgrounds

Heading south the first decent campgrounds are just outside San Felipe, a distance of 120 miles (194 km). Plan on three hours to reach them.

North of the border El Centro makes a good place to get ready to cross. It's only 7 miles (11 km) north of Calexico.

DESERT TRAILS FIVE STAR RV PARK AND GOLF COURSE

Address: 225 Wake Ave., El Centro, CA 92243
Telephone: (760) 352-7275

This is a very large RV park, there are close to 400 spaces. There's also a nine-hole golf course. This campground often serves as the staging area for the El Dorado Ranch's guided tours to San Felipe.

The campground has almost 400 sites with full hookups. Many are pull-throughs and have 50-amp power. An overflow area is not quite as well equipped, parking is on gravel but hookups are provided. The resort has a wealth of amenities including excellent restrooms, a swimming pool and hot tub, a coffee shop, and a nine-hole golf course.

To reach the campground just go one block south from the junction of the I-8 freeway and 4th (Highway 86) street. Turn left on Wake Ave. and in a short distance you'll see the campground entrance on your right.

SAN LUIS, ARIZONA / SAN LUIS RÍO COLORADO, SONORA

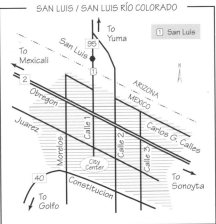

San Luis is the normal crossing for visitors headed south for Golfo de Santa Clara. It is open 24 hours a day, seven days a week. The Banjercito here is open from 8 a.m. to midnight, seven days a week. Parking for big rigs near the crossing is difficult.

In the U.S. the town is convenient to Yuma, Arizona 29 miles (47 km) to the north. On the Mexico side San Luis is a small town but east/west Mex 2 runs about a block south of the border through town. There's more traffic than you would expect in a town this size. Coming from the U.S. you'll see signs for Golfo de Santa Clara as soon as you cross the border. Headed north traffic lines up along the border fence east of the crossing, just as it does in most urban crossings on the border.

Campgrounds

On the north side of the border near Yuma there are dozens of large campgrounds. This is a very popular wintering area for snowbirds. In the middle of the winter most of these campgrounds are full so if you plan to stay in the area you should definitely make reservations.

South of the border the closest campgrounds are in Golfo de Santa Clara, a distance of 71 miles (115 km), plan on about two hours to get there from the border.

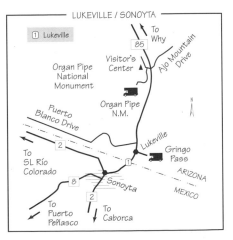

LUKEVILLE ARIZONA / SONOYTA, SONORA

Sonoyta is the crossing for traffic headed south to Rocky Point (Puerto Peñasco). Weekdays it is one of the quietest border crossings of all and seldom has a line. Weekends can be very crowded since much of the population of Arizona seems to go south to Puerto Peñasco to enjoy the beach. The port of entry is known as **Lukeville** north of the border and **Sonoyta** on the south. It is open from 6 a.m. until midnight seven days a week. The Banjercito here is open from 8 a.m. until midnight seven days a week. This is an excellent place to get both tourist cards and vehicle permits when the crossing is slow. The port of entry is outside the town of Sonoyta so parking is not difficult. The Banjercito office has a parking lot but access is tough and parking limited, you should probably park along the road south of the buildings and walk back to take care of your paperwork.

There's also a Banjercito office at San Emeterio which is 17 miles (27 km) east of Sonoyta on Mex 2. This station is there to check the papers of folks traveling in or out of the Sonora free zone. The Banjercito office at this checkpoint is open from 8 a.m. to midnight seven days a week. This crossing is not near a town, there is plenty of room to park near the offices, particularly on the north side of the road.

On the north side of the border at Sonoyta is Lukeville with a gas station, and a motel with an RV park out back. Organ Pipe National Monument also offers a large campground, it's just a few miles to the north. For shopping on your way to Puerto Peñasco we suggest Ajo, Arizona, some 40 miles (65 km) north of the border. The highway from the north is a good paved two-lane road.

Just south of the port-of-entry, in the small town of Sonoyta with 17,000 people, is east/west Mex 2. San Luis Río Colorado is 124 miles (203 km) west, Santa Ana and Mex 15 (the highway from Nogales south to the west coast) 159 miles (260 km) east. Puerto Peñasco is 62 miles (100 km) south of Sonoyta on good two-lane highway.

Campgrounds

North of the border there are two convenient campgrounds. They're described below.

Southward the closest campgrounds are just north of Puerto Peñasco, a distance of about 55 miles (89 km). It should take about an hour to reach the nearest. See Chapter 11 for more information.

ORGAN PIPE N.M.

GPS Location: N 31° 56' 28.3", W 112° 48' 39.8"

This national monument campground is an excellent place to stay on the U.S. side of the border before or after your crossing. It is only a few miles north of the border crossing at Sonoyta, the desert flora here is spectacular. This is the north end of the range for the organ pipe cactus, known as the pithahaya dulce on the Baja.

The campground has over 200 sites. They are all pull-throughs but due to their length are only suitable for rigs to 35 feet. There are no hookups. The restrooms have flush toilets but no showers. There is a dump station and water fill. The entrance road for the campground passes an information center, when we visited the fees were being collected there although there is also a fee station at the campground for busier seasons. There are excellent hiking trails from the campground and nearby, also some interesting drives.

The turn-off for this campground is at Mile 75 of Highway 85, not far north of the crossing at Lukeville/Sonoyta.

🚐 GRINGO PASS MOTEL AND RV PARK

Address: P.O. Box 266, Hwy 85, Lukeville, AZ 85341
Telephone: (602) 254-9284

GPS Location: N 31° 52' 54.2", W 112° 49' 04.4"

If you find that you have reached the border crossing at Lukeville/Sonoyta too late in the day to drive on to Puerto Peñasco before dark you can stay in this conveniently located RV park and go on in the morning.

The Gringo Pass Motel has a large number of sites out back. There are a variety of site types, some back-in and some pull-through. The sites have full hookups with 50 and 15-amp outlets. Sites have picnic tables and there is a swimming pool. Restrooms have hot showers and some sites have shade.

The motel is located just north of the border crossing on the east side of the road. There's a Chevron station, a grocery store, an insurance office, and a restaurant on the west side.

NOGALES, ARIZONA / NOGALES, SONORA

Nogales is the preferred crossing for folks headed down Mexico's west coast since it is serviced by U.S. Interstate Highway 17 from Tucson to the north and serves as the beginning of Mex 15, which is four-lane highway all the way to Mazatlán. The Nogales crossing is unique because you don't get your tourist card and vehicle import permit near the border crossing. Instead, there are modern facilities with quite a bit of parking room some 19 miles (31 km) south of the border on Mex 15 about 21 km south of Nogales. The place is known as the Km 21 Checkpoint. The Km 21 Checkpoint is also where you turn in your vehicle

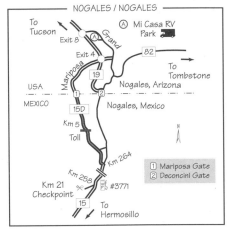

permit as you leave Mexico, there is a special north-bound lane with a person assigned to take the stickers. This is probably the easiest place along the entire border to give up your sticker when leaving the country. The Banjercito here is open 24 hours a day, seven days a week.

There is a new program for vehicle permits known as Sonora Only. You will see a separate line for this program when you approach the Km 21 Checkpoint. The program is designed to make it easier to get a vehicle permit if you only plan to visit Sonora. We have not done this ourselves but the only real difference in paperwork appears to be that no imprint is taken of your credit card so there is no charge. Think twice before taking advantage of this program. The southern Sonora border is just south of Navajoa. That means that Kino Bay, Guaymas/San Carlos, and Álamos are accessible to Sonoma Only participants, but not Los Mochis, El Fuerte, and points to the south. We met several RVers on the road last year who signed up for Sonoma Only and then later found they wanted to go farther south but could not do so.

There are actually two crossings in Nogales. The old crossing is downtown and is known as the **Deconcini Gate** on the U.S. side and **Garita #1** on the Mexican side. It is open 24 hours a day, seven days a week. This crossing is difficult for RVs because it is right in the middle of town. Barriers on the U.S. side make it very hard to get through with a big rig.

The second crossing is west of town. It is known as the **Mariposa Gate** on the U.S. side and **Garita #3** (Garita #2 is a third crossing for pedestrians only). This crossing is designed for heavy truck traffic and is one of the best crossings into Mexico for RVs. It is open from 6 a.m. until 10 p.m. seven days a week.

Here's a driving log for the route around Nogales through the Mariposa Gate from north to south to the Km 21 Checkpoint. Headed south on Highway 19 from Tucson you'll see the sign for the truck crossing at Exit 4 which is signed for Mariposa Road. Exit at this exit and zero your odometer. Drive west on Mariposa road. You'll reach the border at 2.9 miles (4.7 km), drive right across and at the junction just on the other side go straight following signs for Hermosillo Cuota 15D. A sign says Hermosillo 260 km, Santa Anna 92 km. You will find yourself on a fine four-lane highway with fences on each side that limit access to this short toll road. You'll reach a toll booth just after the Km 5 marker at 8.3 miles (13.4 km). The rates during the winter of 2000/2001 were approximately $3.25 for automobiles, and $11 for motorhomes pulling tow cars or pickups pulling fifth-wheels. Either dollars or pesos are accepted. Just beyond the toll booth there is a customs building, commercial trucks go to the right but automobiles and RVs go straight. You may or may not go through a customs search here, no checks were being conducted last time we went through. Traffic for Nogales Centro goes to the right at the Km 1 marker, you should continue straight following the signs for Hermosillo. At the end of the toll road it merges onto Mex 15 near the Km 264 marker, this is 11.3 miles (18.2 km) from where you zeroed your odometer as you turned off Highway 19. In 4.4 more miles (7.1 km) you'll be approaching the Km 21 Checkpoint, you'll see Pemex #3771 on the left and then you should take the cut-off to the right for parking for permits. This is 15.4 miles (24.8 km) from where you zeroed your odometer as you left Highway 19.

Campground

North of the border many people spend their last night before entering Mexico at the Mi Casa RV Park. It is described below.

South of the border the nearest campground is in Magdalena, a distance of about 44 miles (71 km) from the Km 21 Checkpoint. It is described in Chapter 5. Plan on about an hour to reach this campground.

⌷ MI CASA RV PARK

Address: 2901 N. Grand Avenue, Nogales, AZ 85621
Telephone: (520) 281-1150

GPS Location: N 31° 23' 07.2", W 110° 57' 05.2"

This little campground is a convenient place to stay the day before heading into Mexico. It is located a few miles north of central Nogales. South of the campground about 2 miles Mariposa crosses N. Grand. There are a Wal-Mart and a Safeway on the section of Mariposa that is just east of I-19 so last minute supply shopping is easy.

The campground has about 60 pull-through sites with 30-amp outlets and cable TV. The sites are closely packed and have little room for putting out an awning. Restrooms are older and basic but reasonably clean and have hot water showers. You need to get a key when you check in, there is a deposit. There's a coin-operated laundry and propane is available. A gas station with a Circle K is out front as is a Sanborn's agency where you can get Mexico insurance.

To find the campground as you travel south on Highway 19 take Exit 8 which will put you on N. Grand Ave. You will see the campground on the right in about .5 mile (.8 km). Watch for a Circle K quick-stop store and a Sanborn's Insurance agency, the campground is behind them.

NACO, ARIZONA / NACO, SONORA

This is a very small crossing, the towns on each side of the border are tiny and offer no problem when you pass through in an RV. The border crossing is open 24 hours a day, seven days a week. The Banjercito is open from 8 a.m. until midnight, seven days a week.

North of the border access to this crossing is via Highway 80 from Benson on I-10 through Tombstone and Bisbee. The road is mostly two-lane blacktop and is fine for big rigs.

South of the border the main east-west highway in Mexico, Mex 2, is 9 miles (15 km) south. On Mex 2 you can travel 80 miles (129 km) west to reach Mex 15 running south from Nogales or 164 miles (264 km) east through Agua Prieta to Nuevo Casas Grandes or 265 miles (427 km) to join Mex 45 south of El Paso. This is a two-lane blacktop road with some scenic mountainous sections, it is heavily traveled by trucks but should present no problems for well-driven RVs. Just cross early in the day so you have plenty of time to reach a campground in the evening.

Campgrounds

There are quite a few places to stay north of the border in the towns of Naco, Bisbee, Douglas and Tombstone. Our favorite is in Bisbee, it is described below. There's a Safeway along the road between Bisbee and Naco so you can quickly stop to pick up the few things you might have a tough time finding in Mexico.

South of the border the nearest campgrounds are quite a distance from the crossing. The nearest if you head west is in Magdalena, a distance of about 104 miles (167 km). See Chapter 5 for more information about this campground. Plan on about 2.75 hours to make this drive.

If you head east the nearest campgrounds are in Nuevo Casas Grandes, a distance of 173 miles (279 km). See Chapter 7 for information about these campgrounds. Plan on about 4.5 hours to make this drive.

🚐 QUEEN MINE RV PARK

Address: P.O. Box 488, Bisbee, AZ 85603
Telephone: (520) 432-5006

GPS Location: N 31° 26' 22.0", W 109° 54' 43.3"

This little campground sits on the brink of the Queen Mine copper mine. The mine is closed now, but the view is pretty spectacular over the cavernous mine pit to the south. Plus, the campground is within easy walking distance of interesting little downtown Bisbee.

There are 25 back-in sites arranged around the border of a large gravel parking area. Each has 30-amp power, water, sewer, and cable TV hookups. Restrooms are clean with hot showers and there's a coin-operated washer and dryer and modem hookup.

To find the campground just follow Highway 80, the campground entrance is just opposite the entrance to downtown Bisbee.

DOUGLAS, ARIZONA / AGUA PRIETA, SONORA

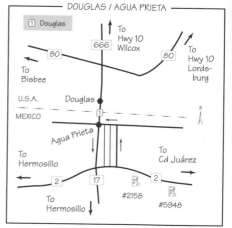

The Douglas - Agua Prieta crossing is just 30 miles or so east of the crossing at Naco. The crossing is a fairly busy one, it is open 24 hours a day, 7 days a week. The Banjercito here is also open 24 hours a day, seven days a week.

Douglas on the north side of the border is small and spread out, no challenge at all to an RVer. Agua Prieta, on the other hand, is a rapidly growing border town. Northbound traffic lines up along the border fence to the east of the port of entry, the wait is often over a half-hour. Because this crossing is in the center of a city parking is difficult for RVs but not impossible. We prefer the Naco crossing.

COLUMBUS, ARIZONA / PALOMAS, CHIHUAHUA

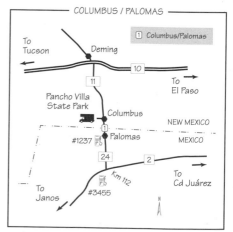

This crossing has become quite popular for RVers heading south into Chihuahua. It is open 24 hours a day, seven days a week. The Banjercito is open 8 a.m. to 10 p.m. seven days a week.

Columbus is a very small town famous only because Pancho Villa once raided it. Deming, a good-sized town along I-10 is about 40 miles north and is a good place to purchase last-minute supplies. The road north to Deming is two-lane blacktop.

South of the border the town of General Rodrigo M. Quevado, also known as Palomas, is a little larger, but not much. While the parking lot on the Mexico side of the port of entry is too small for RVs there should be no problem parking along the street while you are taking care of business.

A small two-lane blacktop road goes south 21 miles (34 km) to connect with the east-west Mex 2. From there you can go east 60 miles (96 km) to hook up with Mex 45 just south of El Paso and Ciudad Juárez or go southwest 95 miles (154 km) to Nuevo Casas Grandes.

Campgrounds

North of the border there is a large selection of campgrounds in Deming. There is also the Pancho Villa State Park in Columbus, a nice campground with electric and water hookups.

South of the border the closest campgrounds are in Nuevo Casas Grandes. This is a distance of 117 miles (188 km). See Chapter 7 for information about these camp-grounds. Plan on about 3 hours to reach Nuevo Casas Grandes from the border.

EL PASO, TEXAS / CIUDAD JUÁREZ, CHIHUAHUA

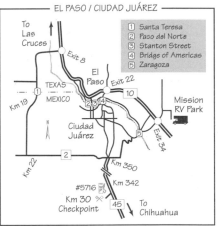

Both El Paso and Juárez are very large cities, they're not much fun to drive through with a big rig. Yet this is a good place to cross the border, largely because there are two outlying ports of entry that make crossing easy and let you avoid driving through these towns on city streets.

Like Nogales, Ciudad Juárez has a checkpoint south of town where you can take care of get-ting your tourist card and vehicle permit. It is at about the 30 Km marker, we'll call it the Km 30 Checkpoint. The Banjercito there is open 24 hours a day, 7 days a week. It has quite a bit of room for parking. Unlike the Nogales crossing there is no special kiosk to drop off your sticker when leaving Mexico, instead you must go back into the same park-ing area used by southbound traffic, not a major hardship.

Downtown El Paso has three major crossings. These are known as Bridge of the Americas - Cordova (also called the free bridge), Paso del Norte (the Santa Fe Bridge, northbound only), and Stanton Street - Reforma (southbound only). All are open 24 hours a day, seven days a week. We do not recommend any of them for RV crossings.

East of town is the **Ysleta - Zaragoza** crossing. It is open 24 hours a day, seven days a week. To reach it from I-10 take Exit 34, Avenida de las Americas. Drive south on the boulevard following signs for the crossings. There's a toll bridge across the Rio Grande, for cars it's $1.25, a motorcoach pulling a car or a pickup and fifth-wheel about $6. From the crossing there is good signage taking you around southeast Ciudad Juárez without going through any really congested areas. Generally you will follow signs for Chihuahua. The route eventually reaches Mex 45, and 3.7 miles (5.9 km) south you reach the Km 30 Checkpoint.

The other excellent crossing, this one with almost no traffic at all, is actually just across the border in New Mexico. It is our preferred crossing near El Paso. This one is called **Santa Teresa** on the U.S. side, **San Jeronimo** on the Mexico side. Santa Teresa is open from 6 a.m. until 10 p.m. 7 days a week. To reach Santa Teresa take Exit 8 from I-10 just north of the New Mexico - Texas border. Follow Aircraft Rd. west following signs for Santa Teresa Port of entry, the distance is about 12.5 miles (20.1 km). After crossing the border drive south on the two-lane paved highway for 7.4 miles (12 km) until you intersect with the east-west Mex 2. Turn left and follow Mex 2 some 8.7 miles (14 km) until it intersects Mex 45, then turn right and in another 3.7 miles (5.9 km) you'll be at the Km 30 Checkpoint.

Campgrounds

North of the border most folks preparing to cross into Mexico seem to spend the night at the Mission RV Park. It's convenient to the Zaragoza crossing and is described below.

South of the border the nearest campgrounds are in Chihuahua, a distance of 218 miles (352 km) on an excellent four-lane highway. See Chapter 7 for more information about these campgrounds. Plan on about 4 hours to make the drive.

🚐 MISSION RV PARK

Address: 1420 RV Drive, El Paso, TX 79927
Telephone: (915) 859-1133

GPS Location: N 31° 42' 02.7", W 106° 16' 50.3"

This large RV park is conveniently located just off I-10 to the east of central El Paso.

The campground has over 300 sites, many of them are pull-throughs. They have 50-amp power, water, sewer, and cable hookups. Restrooms are clean and have hot water. Other amenities include an enclosed swimming pool, a hot tub, a lounge room, a small store, a coin-operated laundry, an internet connection, basketball and tennis courts, and an RV parts and repair center. Right next door is the El Paso Museum of History.

From I-10 take Exit 34, it is marked Joe Battle and Americas Avenue. After the exit go around the block to the north by turning north on Joe Battle to Rojas, turning right and then right again onto RV drive, you'll soon see the RV park on your left. There are plenty of signs after you exit the freeway.

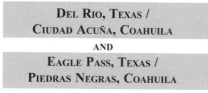

**DEL RIO, TEXAS /
CIUDAD ACUÑA, COAHUILA**

AND

**EAGLE PASS, TEXAS /
PIEDRAS NEGRAS, COAHUILA**

This double pair of towns both have crossings suitable for RVs. Ciudad Acuña has a Banjercito open 24 hours a day, seven days a week. There is also a checkpoint well south of the border near Ciudad Allende where there is a Banjercito that is open 24 hours a day, seven days a week. Many RVers like to drive south from these

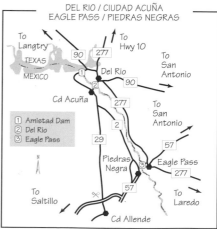

DEL RIO / CIUDAD ACUÑA
EAGLE PASS / PIEDRAS NEGRAS

To Langtry
To Hwy 10
TEXAS
90   277
To San Antonio
MEXICO
① Del Rio
90
Cd Acuña
277
To San Antonio
① Amistad Dam
② Del Rio
③ Eagle Pass
2
29
57
Piedras Negra
③ Eagle Pass
277
57
To Saltillo
To Laredo
Cd Allende

towns to reach Saltillo and then follow Mex 57 south into central Mexico. This route has the advantage of passing to the west of Monterrey so that you do not have to deal with the traffic and expensive toll bypasses around that busy city.

The Del Rio Port of Entry is open 24 hours, seven days a week. It is fine for RVs. North of town is another small crossing that goes across the Amistad Dam. This crossing is open from 10 a.m. to 6 p.m. seven days a week. From Ciudad Acuña you can follow either Mex 29 south to Ciudad Allende or Mex 2 along the border to Piedras Negras. These are two-lane paved highways.

Most RVers prefer the Eagle Pass - Piedras Negras crossing over the one in Del Rio. It too is open 24 hours a day but has the advantage of being connected to Ciudad Allende by Mex 57, a four-lane highway. The distance is shorter too.

Campgrounds

Del Rio is larger and has a better collection of campgrounds than Eagle Pass. It is something of a snowbird haven and is also home to the Amistad National Recreation Area northwest of town. The distance between Del Rio and Eagle Pass is 56 miles (90 km) so spending the night in Del Rio and then driving to Eagle Pass to cross into Mexico is easy to do.

Once you cross the border in Eagle Pass the closest campground is in Saltillo, a distance of 233 miles (376 km). Plan on about five hours to make this drive with additional time for the stop to get your paperwork done at the Ciudad Allende checkpoint.

LAREDO, TEXAS / NUEVO LAREDO, NUEVO LEÓN

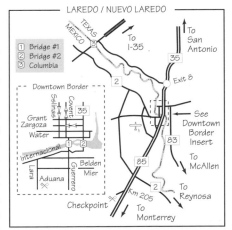

Nuevo Laredo is said to be the busiest of the border crossings in Texas. The town itself is often visited by day-trippers from north of the border which probably explains the statistic.

In town there are two bridges across the Río Grande, travelers headed south want to take the old International Bridge #1. Southbound Interstate 35 will lead you directly to International Bridge #2 (also called Lincoln-Juárez bridge), the easternmost bridge, if you aren't alert. Stay in the right-hand lanes. As you enter Laredo watch for signs leading to the western bridge which is also the truck crossing although it's a little tight. You want to get six blocks west of Highway 35 to a north-south parallel street called Salinas. This street will take you to International Bridge #1. There is a toll on the bridge, automobiles pay $1.50, a motorcoach with tow car or pickup pulling a fifth-wheel would pay $2.00. Northbound travelers want to use Bridge #2 because there is more room to get through the U.S. inspection station in that direction.

After crossing the bridge you want to find the customs and immigration offices to get your tourist card and vehicle import permits. Take the first street to the right and drive along the border fence until the road curves left and becomes Blvd. Lara. Now drive about .6 miles (1 km). You'll come to a statue of General Lara and see the Migración and Aduana building on the left. Turn into the big courtyard which has plenty of room for even big rigs. This is where you get your paperwork. When you are finished turn left after leaving the Migración and Banjercito offices. Follow signs for Monterrey which will lead you to Mex 85 south to Monterrey. Incidentally, the toll road to Monterrey is quite expensive and, in our opinion anyway, not worth the money. The Libre route is good enough although it will take longer.

Nuevo Laredo, like Ciudad Juárez and Nogales to the east, has a checkpoint along Mex 85 about 25 km south of the border. Here, however, no documents are issued and you cannot turn in your vehicle window stickers.

There is another crossing just west of Laredo known as the **Columbia** port of entry. This crossing is open from 8 a.m. to midnight, seven days a week. The Banjercito there is open from 8 a.m. until 11 p.m. seven days a week. This is a fairly new crossing. It is popular with trucks but also great for RVs because there is lots of room to park.

From the north you reach Columbia either by taking Exit 8 just north of Laredo on I-35 and following signs for the Columbia port of entry or by using a new toll road which is similarly signed and connects with I-35 farther from the city. There is a toll bridge at the Columbia crossing, it costs $1.50 for an automobile and $2 for larger RVs. The toll northbound is slightly higher.

From the south you reach Columbia by following Mex 2 westward from Mex 85. The junction is near Km 206 just north of the checkpoint. It is signed Puente Int. III. As you approach the border station at Columbia watch for the Y, trucks go right but you should go left (really straight) following signs for light and tourist traffic. Watch for a turn for busses that goes left quite a distance before the toll booths for the bridge across the river, this will take you over to the Mexican customs buildings on the left. There's lots of parking, this is an excellent place to turn in your sticker and tourist card. You'll then have to do a loop to get back into the U.S.-bound lanes.

Campgrounds

North of the border Laredo really has little to offer in the way of campgrounds. We do know several people, however, who have spent the night boondocking in Nuevo Laredo in the parking lot of the Migración building right in town. This seems a good idea, there are lots of people around and you can work on your paperwork all night if you want and get a good start in the morning.

Southbound the most convenient camping is in Saltillo because the only campground in Monterrey is on the far side of town. This is a distance of about 205 miles (330 km). See Chapter 7 for information about camping in Saltillo. Plan on 6 hours to make the drive using the free road.

RIO GRANDE VALLEY

The area stretching inland from the Gulf of Mexico to Falcon Lake for about 100 miles along the border is known as the Rio Grande Valley. There are a large number of crossings here. Two pairs of large cities are in the Valley: McAllen - Reynosa and Brownsville - Matamoros. The whole area is popular with snowbirds and makes a good place to prepare for crossing into Mexico. Here's a listing of the crossings from west to east. Our favorites are Pharr, Los Indios, and Zaragoza. All of the crossings except Falcon Dam have toll bridges with rates in the neighborhood of $1.50 for automobiles and $4.00 for RVs.

Falcon Dam - Also known as Puente San Juan. This small crossing is open from 7 a.m. to 9 p.m. There is no Banjercito so it's not used much by RVs.

Roma / Ciudad Miguel Alemán - A small crossing. Open from 8 a.m. to midnight, seven days a week. The Banjercito is open 24 hours a day, seven days a week. Poor for RVs due to lack of parking.

Rio Grand City, Texas / Ciudad Camargo, Tamaulipas - Also known as Puente Camargo. A small crossing. Open from 7 a.m. to 1 a.m.

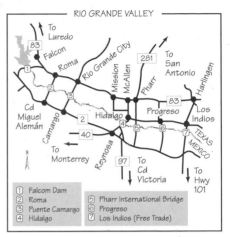

The Banjercito is open 8 a.m. to midnight. Poor for RVs due to lack of parking.

Hidalgo, Texas / Ciudad Reynosa, Tamaulipas - The large Mexican city of Reynosa is due south of McAllen. The crossing is open 24 hours a day, seven days a week. The Banjercito is also open 24 hours a day, seven days a week. Poor for RVs due to lack of parking and congestion.

Pharr International Bridge - This is a modern crossing built on empty land east of Reynosa. It is designed to provide an easy crossing for big rigs. The crossing is open from 6 a.m. to midnight, seven days a week. The Banjercito is open from 8 a.m. to midnight, seven days a week. There is plenty of room for big rigs to park to take care of paperwork southbound. Northbound you have to be careful not to get trapped into crossing the border before turning toward the Mexican border station to turn in your sticker and tourist cards.

From the north you will find the bridge just southeast of McAllen at the end of Hwy 281. After crossing the border the highway runs 1.5 miles (2.4 km) southward and meets Mex 2. You can go east for Brownsville to catch Mex 180 to the south or go west to the outskirts of Reynosa and catch Mex 97 southward. Westward is shorter but you must watch signs closely, the sign for the left turn onto Mex 97 is easy to miss and if you do you may end up in downtown Reynosa. The turn is 4.8 miles (7.7 km) from where you turned west onto Mex 2.

Progreso, Texas / Nuevo Progreso, Tamaulipas - Open 24 hours a day, seven days a week. The Banjercito is open from 8:30 a.m. to 6 p.m. Monday to Friday and from 9 a.m. to 5:30 Saturday and Sunday. This crossing is mostly used by local traffic.

Los Indios, Texas / Lucio Blanco, Tamaulipas - Also known as the Free Trade Bridge. This is another modern crossing built away from urban areas. It is open from 6 a.m. to midnight, seven days a week. The Banjercito is open 8 a.m. to 9 p.m. seven days a week. Like Pharr, there is room for southbound RVs to park and take care of paperwork but northbound traffic must be alert for a place to park to turn in their stickers and tourist cards.

Southbound the Los Indios bridge can be found just south of Harlingen. It is well-signed and easy to find. Once you cross the border follow signs for Ciudad Victoria, they will take you south on two-lane roads through the communities of Lucio Blanco, Empalme and Valle Hermosa to meet Mex 201 near the Km 255 marker. Northbound on Mex 101 watch for the Valle Hermosa cutoff near Km 255 and then follow signs to the crossing, the signage is good.

Brownsville, Texas / Matamoros, Tamaulipas - Brownsville and Matamoros are both large cities. There are two bridges: the **B&M Bridge** and the **Gateway Bridge**. The crossings here are open 24 hours a day, 7 days a week. The Banjercito in Brownsville has the same hours. This crossing is poor for RVs due to lack of parking and congestion.

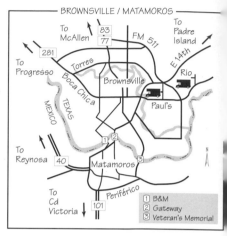

Veteran's Memorial Bridge / Puerto Nuevo Internacional - Also known as Ejido Los Tomates, and Puerto Fronterizo Matamoros III. Open from 8 a.m. until 11 p.m. Monday through Saturday, closed on Sunday. The Banjercito is open from 7 a.m. until 11 p.m. Monday through Saturday. This brand new crossing is just east of Brownsville and Matamoros but is similar to the Pharr and Los Indios crossings. There is plenty of room to park to get your paperwork done heading south. For northbound traffic a retorno has been provided just before the toll booths so that drivers needing to turn in their stickers and tourist cards can turn around and park, then use another retorno to head back north.

Heading south in Brownsville the crossing is easy to find because it is at the southern end of Hwy 77, a multi-lane expressway that cuts diagonally across the city. After crossing and taking care of paperwork zero your odometer and head south. Follow signs for Ciudad Victoria. You will pass a Soriana supermarket on your left and come to an intersection at 1 mile (1.6 km). Bear right, there is a sign for Ciudad Victoria. At about 2 miles (3.2 km) you will see that the road ahead rises to go over an overpass, instead exit onto the lateral to the right. Make sure you are in the second lane from the left and turn left onto Mex 180. This highway will take you out of town to the south toward Ciudad Victoria and La Pesca. Immediately after the turn there is a Gigante supermarket on the right and a Soriana and McDonalds on the left. Travelers north-bound should watch for the Gigante, Soriana, and McDonalds as landmarks showing where they should turn right to follow the bypass to the crossing.

Campgrounds

North of the border the whole valley is full of campgrounds. Many, however, are full of snowbirds and getting a place for just the night may put you in overflow parking. Our favorites are both in Brownsville and have the same ownership, they specialize in folks heading south and are described below.

South of the border the closest campgrounds described in this book are in Ciudad Victoria and La Pesca. Both are about 200 miles (325 km) distant. Plan on about 4.5 hours to Ciudad Victoria and 5 hours to La Pesca.

🚐 RIO RV PARK

Address: 8801 Boca Chica, Brownsville, TX 78521
Telephone: (956) 831-4653 and (800) 776-1895
Fax: (956) 831-0147
E-mail: RioRVpark@aol.com
Web Site: www.gocampingamerica.com/riorv/index.html

GPS Location: N 25° 55' 04.7", W 097° 23' 36.3"

This campground has over 100 sites, most are back-ins but there are also pull-through sites for people passing through. They have full hookups with 50-amp power and cable TV. Restrooms are excellent and there is a swimming pool, a hot tub, a laundry, and computer modem hookup.

From the point where Boca Chica Blvd. crosses Hwy 77 drive east for 7.5 miles (12.1 km), you'll see the campground on the left.

🚐 PAUL'S RV PARK

Address: 1129 N. Minnesota, Brownsville, TX 78521
Telephone: (956) 831-4852 and (800) 352-5010   **Fax:** (956) 831-7033
E-mail: paulRVpark@aol.com
Web Site: www.Texasusa.com/paulsrvpark

GPS Location: N 25° 55' 45.0", W 097° 25' 58.2"

This campground also has over 100 sites. Most are back-ins but there are pull-through sites available. The sites are full-hookup with 50-amp power and cable TV. Restrooms are excellent. There is a laundry and computer modem hookups are available. There is convenient bus service out front.

From the intersection of Boca Chica Blvd. and Hwy 77 drive east for 4 miles (6.4 km), turn north on Minnesota Ave. and in .9 miles (1.5 km) you'll see the campground on your left.

OTHER BORDER CROSSINGS

Crossings not mentioned above include the following:

Los Algodones, Baja California is just west of Yuma. This is a small crossing mostly used by people walking across to visit the doctors and pharmacies in the small town. There is no Banjercito office and the streets on the Mexican side are difficult to negotiate in large rigs, we do not recommend the crossing for RVs. The crossing is known as **Andrade** on the U.S. side, **Algodones** on the Mexican side. It is open from 6 a.m. until 10 p.m. seven days a week. There is no Banjercito.

El Sasabe, Sonora is located near Sasabe, Arizona, about 10 miles west of Nogales. The crossing is open from 8 a.m. to 8 p.m. Monday through Friday and 10 a.m. to 2 p.m. on weekends but there is no Banjercito office. The nearby crossing in Nogales is good and the roads on the Mexico side poor. We do not recommend this crossing.

Ojinaga, Chihuahua is across the border from Presidio, Texas and is open 24 hours a day, 7 days a week. The Banjercito here is also open 24 hours a day, seven days a week. This is a seldom-used remote crossing. Although there are paved two-lane roads to the border from both directions the one to the south toward Chihuahua, Mex 16, is slow and winding and poor for RVs. Rumors are circulating about a new toll road to be built over this route, probably a two-lane one. Until that happens this crossing is not recommended.

CHAPTER

. . . . 4

HOW TO USE THE DESTINATION CHAPTERS

The focus of this book is on campgrounds, of course. A question we often hear is "Which campground is the best in Mexico?" Usually the person asking the question has a personal favorite in mind. Our answer is always the same—we like them all. No one campground is the best in Mexico because everyone likes different things. Also, the personality of a campground depends upon the people staying there when you visit. People traveling on their own in an unfamiliar environment tend to be very friendly, this is one of the best things about Mexican camping. We can't tell you exactly who will be staying in each of the campgrounds in this book when you decide to visit, but we will try to give you a good feel for what to expect in the way of campground features and amenities.

Chapters 5 through 14 contain information about the many camping destinations you may visit in Mexico. The chapters are arranged somewhat arbitrarily into regions that fall naturally together for a discussion of their camping possibilities.

Introductory Material and Road Map

Each chapter starts with an introduction giving important information about the region covered in the chapter. Usually included is something about the lay of the land, the road system, and highlights of the area. Most of this information is important to a camping traveler and much of it is not necessarily included or easy to find in normal tourist guides. On the other hand, much information that is readily available in normal tourist guides will not be found in this book. Many other books do a good job of covering things like currency information, hotels, restaurants, language, and tour details. This book is designed to be a supplement to normal tourist guides, not to replace them. It provides a framework for camping travelers, other guides must be used to fill it the details.

The road map at the beginning of the chapter is included to give you a reference while reading about the road system and for planning purposes. There is not enough detail to use these as your primary map, see the section titled *Maps* in the *Details, Details, Details* chapter for information about available maps.

Campground Overview Maps

In each chapter, located just before the point where the *Selected Cities and Their Campgrounds* section begins, there is another regional map. This map shows only the cities that have campgrounds and for which there are city and campground descriptions on the pages that follow. You can use the campground overview maps as a table of contents to the cities and districts covered in the chapter.

Some of the maps also show the outline of an interesting district or region. These regions are arranged in their own individual write-up sections and are listed under the title given to the small outline maps.

Each chapter introduction also includes a distance table. Sometimes they are on the same page as the campground overview map but in chapters with many campgrounds they occupy their own page.

City Descriptions

Following the introductory material in each chapter is the *Selected Cities and Campgrounds* section. Cities are listed alphabetically in this segment. Each city has a few paragraphs describing the local attractions, then information about at least one campground. In some cases there is also information about interesting side trips that you may wish to take while continuing to use this particular town and campground as a base. Some of the destinations are famous and well known, others less familiar but still well worth a visit.

Our descriptions of the destinations in this book are intended to give you an idea of what the city or region has to offer. They are by no means complete, you will undoubtedly need additional guides during your visit. There is no way that complete information could be included in a conveniently-sized book, nor do we have the knowledge or time to write that kind of guide. Exploring travel guides is almost as much fun as exploring the destinations themselves, you will no doubt acquire a small library before you finish your travels.

We have also given population, altitude, and pronunciation information for some of the cities. The population and altitude information are our estimates. Population figures are difficult to obtain for Mexico since censuses are infrequent and the population is rapidly growing and also moving about. These are our best guesses based upon many sources. Altitude figures are also estimates. While we are not linguists we do think that it is nice to be able to pronounce the names of the cities we visit, hopefully the very amateurish pronunciation guides we have included will be of some help.

Campground Maps

Most of the campground descriptions include a small map to assist you in finding the campground. They show enough roads and other identifying features to allow you to tie them into the highway and city maps you will be using for primary navigation. You can use these maps to assist you in your search for campgrounds, they are meant to be used in conjunction with the written directions that we have included in the campground descriptions. A picture often *is* worth a thousand words, even if it only serves to give you a general idea of the campground location. We hope these maps will do more than that, we've spent a lot of time searching for campgrounds based upon little more than a rumor. May you never have to do the same.

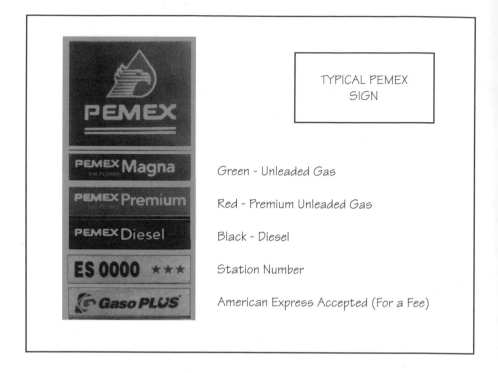

TYPICAL PEMEX SIGN

Green - Unleaded Gas

Red - Premium Unleaded Gas

Black - Diesel

Station Number

American Express Accepted (For a Fee)

In an effort to make our maps and descriptions more useful we have begun to include the Pemex numbers. Each Pemex has a unique identification number which is almost always boldly stated on the sign out front. This number seldom changes, it seems like Pemexes are the most reliable reference point on Mexican roads and they're often conveniently located near crucial intersections.

While the maps are for the most part self-explanatory here is a key.

MAP LEGEND

══════	Major Freeway	1D	Freeway or Road Number
▬▬▬▬▬	Toll Road	🚐	Campground with Text Write-up
───────	Other Paved Roads		Campground - no Text Write-up
▬·▬·▬	Unpaved Roads	P	Pemex Station
U.S.A. / MEXICO	Country or State Border	▲	Area of Interest
═▭═	Freeway Off-ramp	●	City, Town, or Village
San Antonio	Off-ramp - Name Indicated	✈	Airport

Campground Descriptions

Each campground section begins with address and telephone number. While it is not generally necessary or even possible to obtain campground reservations in Mexico you may want to do so for some very popular campgrounds. This is particularly true during the busy December to March season in popular areas. If reservations seem desirable or necessary we mention the fact in the campground description.

One thing you will not find in our campground descriptions is a rating with some kind of system of stars, checks, or tree icons. Hopefully we've included enough information in our campground description to let you make your own analysis.

Campground prices vary considerably. The price you pay depends upon the type of rig you drive, the number in your party, your use of hookups and sometimes even the time of year.

Generally you can expect that tents are least expensive, followed by vans and smaller RVs. The price range we give is for a van or small RV with two people using full hookups. In some places larger RVs may pay a little more but this is unusual.

A final price consideration is the value of the peso against U.S. or Canadian dollars. The prices in this book were determined during the 2000/2001 winter season when the peso was trading at 9.5 to the U.S. dollar. The peso was stable. Near the border, on the Baja, and on the northern west coast prices are often charged in U.S. dollars so the conversion rate makes little difference.

We've grouped campground fees into the following categories:

$	Up to $5 U.S.	$ $$$	Over $15 and up to $20 U.S.
$$	Over $ 5 and up to $10 U.S.	$$ $$$	Over $20 and up to $25 U.S.
$$$	Over $10 and up to $15 U.S.	$$$ $$$	Over $25

All of these prices are winter high season prices for a van conversion with two people using electricity and taking a shower. You should expect to pay slightly less for tents in many places and slightly more for very large rigs.

Campground icons can be useful for a quick overview of campground facilities or if you are quickly looking for a particular feature.

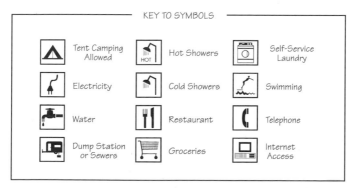

KEY TO SYMBOLS

Tent Camping Allowed — Hot Showers — Self-Service Laundry

Electricity — Cold Showers — Swimming

Water — Restaurant — Telephone

Dump Station or Sewers — Groceries — Internet Access

All of the campgrounds in this book accept RV's but not all accept tent campers. We've included the tent symbol for all campgrounds that do accept tents.

Hookups in Mexican campgrounds vary a great deal so we've included individual symbols for electricity, water, and sewer. For more information take a look at the written description section.

You'll note that we usually state that a campground has 15-amp or 30-amp outlets. This refers to the physical outlet type only. Sometimes it is impossible to determine the actual breaker size, sometimes there probably is no breaker at all. It seems that the 30-amp outlet type we are accustomed to north of the border must be expensive or difficult to come by in Mexico because often they are not used even when quite a bit of amperage is available. If you see a normal 30-amp outlet it's a sign that the electrical system might be more sophisticated than normal, or it might just mean that a previous occupant of your site brought his own outlet south one winter.

Showers in Mexican campgrounds often have no provision for hot water so we give separate shower symbols for hot and cold water. If there is provision for hot water but it was cold when we visited we list is as providing cold water only. You may be luckier when you visit.

If we've given the grocery cart icon then it has some groceries. This is usually just a few items in the reception area. Check the write-up for more information. The write-up will often mention a larger store located conveniently near the campground.

An on-site restaurant can provide a welcome change from home-cooked meals and a good way to meet people. In Mexico almost all restaurants also serve alcohol of some kind. Often campground restaurants are only open during certain periods during the year, sometimes only during the very busy Christmas and Semana Santa holidays. Even if there is no restaurant at the campground we have found that in Mexico there is usually one not far away.

Self-service laundries are uncommon in Mexican campgrounds outside the Baja and the west coast. Even if there is no laundry icon it is often possible to have laundry done for you, ask at the campground office. Ask the price before committing.

A swimming icon means that the campground has swimming either on-site or nearby. This may be a pool or the beach at an ocean or lake.

We've included a telephone icon if there is one on the premises or nearby.

The internet access symbol is included if access is available at the campground. Ask at the office for off-site internet access, it is often not far away.

You'll find that this book has a much larger campground description than most guidebooks. We've tried to include detailed information about the campground itself so you know what to expect when you arrive. While most campgrounds described in this book have a map we've also included a paragraph giving even more details about finding the campground.

GPS (Global Positioning System) Coordinates

You will note that for most of the campgrounds we have included a GPS Location. GPS is a new navigation tool that uses signals from satellites. For less than $150 you can now buy a hand-held receiver that will give you your latitude, longitude and altitude anywhere in the world. You can also enter the coordinates we have given for the campgrounds in this book into the receiver and it will tell you exactly where the campground lies in relation to your position. If our maps and descriptions just don't lead you to the campground you can fall back on the GPS information.

If you don't have a GPS receiver already you certainly don't need to go out and buy one to use this book. On the other hand, if you do have one bring it along. We expect that GPS will actually be installed in many vehicles during the next few years so we thought we'd get a jump on things. If you are finding that our readings are not entirely accurate you should check to see which Map Datum your machine is set to use. The coordinates in this book are based upon the World Geodetic System 1984 (WGS 84) datum.

Other Camping Possibilities

We've used the heading *Other Camping Possibilities* as a catchall for several kinds of information. If we have not had a chance to visit a campground but have heard that it exists we often put in this section. If a campground was listed in our previous book but is missing in the current edition we mention it in this section so you'll know we didn't just forget it. We also list some free camping possibilities under this heading. You should keep in mind that much of what is in the *Other Camping Possibilities* section is information we have gathered from others and have not confirmed so do not count on it being entirely accurate. Finally, if we've spent a lot of time looking for a campground that is listed in other guides but no longer exists we'll often mention it in this section to save you from having the same experience.

Side Trips

The *Side Trips* section included for some towns describes interesting places you may want to visit. If you have a tent or pull a trailer you can leave your camp set up at the base and avoid setting up camp each night. Even if you are in a van or motorhome and do take your camp along with you the base city always provides a place to return to if you can find no acceptable alternate campground during your side trip.

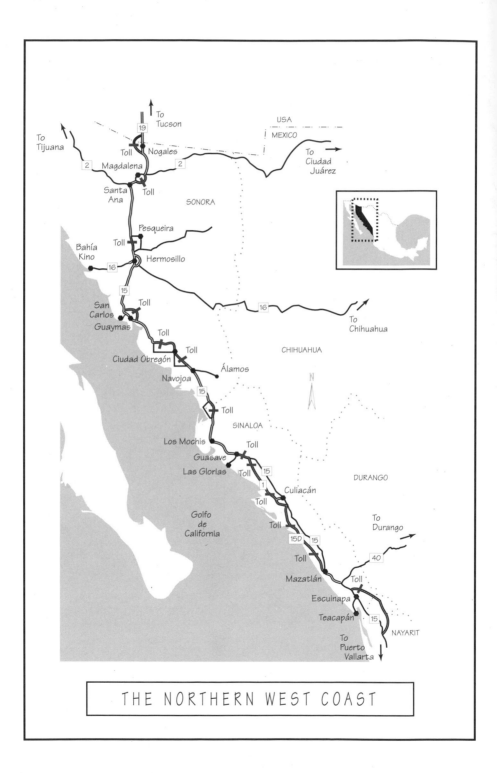

To Tucson

19

To Tijuana

USA
MEXICO

Toll   Nogales

2   Magdalena   2   To Ciudad Juárez

Santa   Toll
Ana

SONORA

Pesqueira

Toll

Bahía   16   Hermosillo
Kino

15

San   Toll
Carlos
Guaymas

Toll

16   To Chihuahua

Ciudad Obregón   Toll

CHIHUAHUA

Navojoa   Álamos

15

Toll

SINALOA

Los Mochis   Toll

Guasave   15
Las Glorias   Toll
1

Culiacán   DURANGO

Toll

Golfo
de
California   Toll

15D   15   To Durango

Toll   40

Mazatlán   Toll

Escuinapa

Teacapán   15

NAYARIT

To
Puerto
Vallarta

THE NORTHERN WEST COAST

CHAPTER

. . . . 5

THE NORTHERN WEST COAST: NOGALES TO TEACAPÁN

INTRODUCTION

The northern portion of the west coast is a premier destination for RVers in Mexico, it is second only to the northern Gulf of California in the number of camping visitors it receives each year. The popularity is no mystery. Access from north of the border is easy. There are four-lane highways from the border at Nogales all the way south to Mazatlán. Dozens of full-service campgrounds serve Kino Bay, Guaymas/San Carlos, Los Mochis, and Mazatlán. It takes only three easy days of driving to reach the farthest south of these major towns, Mazatlán.

For the RVer the west coast is probably the best choice for that first trip to Mexico. It offers an attractive combination of easy border crossing, excellent campgrounds, good roads, interesting ocean-side destinations, and lots of company in the form of other RVers.

Two states, Sonora to the north and Sinaloa in the south, define the region. These states have dry desert climates, but the big industries are fishing and agriculture. Guaymas and Mazatlán are fishing ports and there are huge areas of irrigated land, particularly around Los Mochis, Ciudad Obregón, and Culiacán. The landscape is generally flat so travel is easy. Only if you venture off the beaten path, say inland to Alamos or Durango, will you find mountains. The coast is often backed by lagoons and swampy areas so the road stays inland all the way to Mazatlán and then again until San Blas.

Strictly speaking the west coast probably should include the important RVing destinations of Puerto Peñasco and Golfo de Santa Clara. For several reasons we feel that these destinations fit better in their own chapter, we call it the Northern Gulf of California.

ROAD SYSTEM

Four-lane Mex 15 runs all the way from the border at Nogales to Mazatlán. It is the arterial of the region and provides quick and easy access. It is of particular benefit to RVers with big rigs. You will hardly know you've left the states.

When you first drive Mex 15 south you may think that the entire highway is a toll road. In actual fact there are many stretches that are free. The government of Mexico is committed to providing a free alternate to as much of the toll system as possible, so where there is not a free alternate the four-lane highway is usually toll free. Tolls on much of the road are reasonable for cars, but RVs can really get hit hard. As we have described in the *Details, Details, Details* chapter the toll rates for RVs can be as much as four times the automobile rates on Mexican toll roads. In early 2001 the car rate to travel all the way from Nogales to Culiacán was $35 U.S., the rate for a motorhome pulling a car or pickup with fifth-wheel trailer was about $90 U.S. These totals assume that you bypass the toll booths at Magdalena and Guaymas (see those sections later in this chapter).

Between Culiacán and Mazatlán there is a beautiful four-lane toll road. Unfortunately it is a very expensive one. Fortunately the two-lane free highway along almost the same route is pretty good although heavily traveled by trucks. If you take it easy the trip will take about an hour and a half longer than traveling the toll road and is almost the same distance. Headed south just drive right by the entrance to Mex 15D on the Culiacán western bypass, you'll soon intersect Mex 15 Libre south of town. If you are heading north in Mazatlán just follow signs for Mex 15 Libre instead of those for Mex 15D. When you approach Culiacán you want to take the left for Mex 15D at about Km 208, just .2 mile (.3 km) beyond Pemex #4365.

Travelers headed south generally make the trip to Mazatlán in three days. In the evening of the first day they stop in Guaymas having driven 257 miles (419 km), the second day they reach Los Mochis after 220 miles (359 km), and the third day of 259 miles (423 km) finds them in Mazatlán. Possible side trips on two-lane free roads to Kino Bay and Álamos can easily make this a longer trip, as can the temptation to make multiple-day stops en route.

HIGHLIGHTS

There are five good **ocean-side destinations** with good campgrounds in this section of the book. These are **Kino Bay**, **Guaymas/San Carlos**, **Guasave** (included here under Los Mochis), **Mazatlán**, and **Teacapán**. Each has its own unique personality and amenities so take a look at the individual listings to find the one (or ones) that will please you.

The lower end of the popular **Chihuahua al Pacífico Railroad along the Copper Canyon** is accessible from **Los Mochis** and **El Fuerte**. This is an excellent reason to visit the towns, as is the nearby ferry port for boats to and from the Baja Peninsula. Many people leave their vehicles in one of the RV parks and make a two-day train trip up along the Copper Canyon, spending the night in Divisadero, Creel or Chihuahua and then returning.

The old **colonial gold-mining town** of **Álamos** is an unusual and very entertaining destination. It may give you a taste for visits to similar cities in other parts of the country. The side road to Álamos from Navojoa is paved and only takes about an

THE CAMPGROUNDS

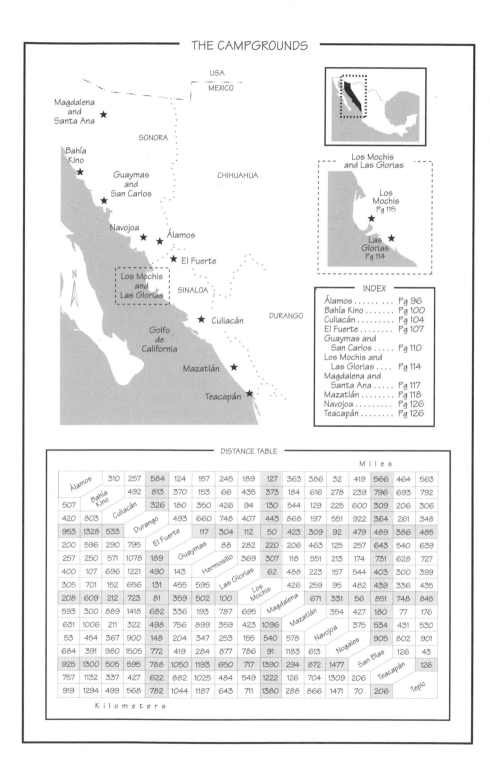

INDEX

DISTANCE TABLE

Miles (upper right) / Kilometers (lower left)

	Álamos	Bahía Kino	Culiacán	Durango	El Fuerte	Guaymas	Hermosillo	Las Glorias	Los Mochis	Magdalena	Mazatlán	Navojoa	Nogales	San Blas	Teacapán	Tepic
Álamos	Álamos	310	257	584	124	157	245	189	127	363	386	32	419	566	464	563
Bahía Kino	507	Bahía Kino	492	813	370	153	66	435	373	184	616	278	239	796	693	792
Culiacán	420	803	Culiacán	326	180	350	426	94	130	544	129	225	600	309	206	306
Durango	953	1328	533	Durango	493	660	748	407	443	868	197	551	922	364	261	348
El Fuerte	200	596	290	795	El Fuerte	117	304	112	50	423	309	92	479	489	386	485
Guaymas	257	250	571	1078	189	Guaymas	88	282	220	206	463	125	257	643	540	639
Hermosillo	400	107	696	1221	490	143	Hermosillo	369	307	118	551	213	174	731	628	727
Las Glorias	305	701	152	656	131	455	595	Las Glorias	62	488	223	157	544	403	300	399
Los Mochis	208	609	212	723	81	359	502	100	Los Mochis	426	259	95	482	439	336	435
Magdalena	593	300	889	1418	682	336	193	787	695	Magdalena	671	331	56	851	748	845
Mazatlán	631	1006	211	322	498	756	899	359	423	1096	Mazatlán	354	427	180	77	176
Navojoa	53	454	367	900	148	204	347	253	155	540	578	Navojoa	375	534	431	530
Nogales	684	391	980	1505	772	419	284	877	786	91	1183	613	Nogales	905	802	901
San Blas	925	1300	505	595	788	1050	1193	650	717	1390	294	872	1477	San Blas	126	43
Teacapán	757	1132	337	427	622	882	1025	484	549	1222	126	704	1309	206	Teacapán	126
Tepic	919	1294	499	568	782	1044	1187	643	711	1380	288	866	1471	70	206	Tepic

hour. El Fuerte is another town with some colonial features that is well worth a visit now that it has a few RV parks.

SELECTED CITIES AND THEIR CAMPGROUNDS

ÁLAMOS, SONORA (AH-LAH-MOHS)
Population 7,500, Elevation 1,350 ft (410 m)

Álamos had a population of 30,000 people in the late 1700's. The town was the supply and cultural center for the surrounding mining area. Much of this wealth went into impressive colonial casas (homes) and other buildings. Later the mines closed, the town declined, and the structures deteriorated. Fortunately, in the last fifty years Álamos has become popular with American and Canadian expats, many wealthy, and some of the former polish has returned. Many homes with traditional interior courtyard designs have been restored and can be toured. The town's colonial atmosphere is now protected by law.

You will want to explore Álamos on foot, the narrow streets and difficult parking make an automobile a real bother. You can easily walk from some of the campgrounds just outside town, from others you may want to take a taxi or catch a bus. One of the campgrounds, the Acosta, is located on the back side of town, staying there requires

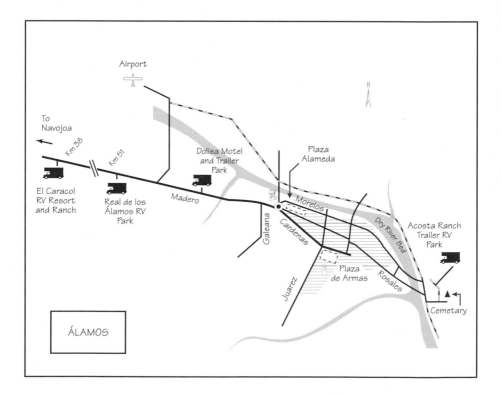

driving through Álamos, not something you should do in a rig of any size without scouting a route first but nothing to fear if you have a car, van, or pickup camper.

The town has a museum, the **Museo Costumbrista de Sonora**, which will give you some background on the area. There are two plazas in Álamos, the first you will see as you enter town is the **Plaza Alameda** which is not very impressive, it hosts a Pemex gas station and the municipal market. The nearby **Plaza de Armas** is much nicer but quieter with a central kiosk and a cathedral, **La Parroquia de la Purísima Concepción**. An overlook on a hill south of town, the **Cerro del Perico**, offers great views of the area. It is difficult to see much of the restoration work that has been done on the many casas in Álamos, they are typically Spanish with unimpressive exteriors. Tours are sometimes available. Check at your campground or the tourist office on the Plaza de Armas for information. Several hotels and restaurants have been built in these buildings, they are easier to visit.

The road to Álamos goes east into the mountains from Navojoa. The distance is 32 miles (53 km) on good two-lane paved road.

PLAZA DE ARMAS AT NIGHT

THE NORTHERN WEST COAST

Álamos Campgrounds

DOLISA MOTEL AND TRAILER PARK

Address: Calle Madero No. 72, Álamos, CP 85763 Sonora, México
Telephone: (6) 428-0131   **Fax:** (6) 428-0131

GPS Location: N 27° 01' 23.1", W 108° 55' 31.4"

The Dolisa is the closest RV park to town that you can reach with a full-size motorhome. For that reason (and because it has a laundry) you will often find it full when the other Álamos campgrounds have lots of room. Caravans often fill the facility.

The campground has 42 spaces, 35 have all hookups and the others only electricity and water. A few are pull-throughs and large rigs will fit. Electrical outlets are either 15-amp or 30-amp and air conditioners are allowed. The restrooms are clean and have hot water for showers. There is a self-service laundry with good machines, this is probably the best self-service laundry in town. The walk into town from the Dolisa is about a quarter of a mile, easily done on foot. The Dolisa has an operation that produces purified water, in fact, they sell water to much of Álamos.

To find the campground watch carefully as you near Álamos. Watch for the airport cutoff, the campground is .3 miles (.5 km) farther toward town on the left, it has a good sign located on the right side of the road opposite the entrance.

EL CARACOL RV RESORT AND RANCH

Address: Km 37 Carretera a Alamos (P.O. Box 124),
              Álamos, CP 85760 Sonora, México
Telephone: (6) 484-2079

GPS Location: N 27° 04' 43.3", W 109° 04' 26.9"

We think that El Caracol has the most pleasant setting of all the Álamos trailer parks. It is in the high desert on a 2,800 acre ranch and is very quiet and peaceful. Birding is great, you should inquire about hikes and the availability of rental horses. This is the Alamos eco-campground.

There are 65 pull-through spaces at the campground with plenty of room for big rigs. They have 15-amp outlets with 30-amp breakers, water, and sewer hookups. Most have patios and shade. The restrooms have hot showers. There is an unheated swimming pool open even in the winter. An hourly bus that stops at the front gate will whisk you in to Álamos to look around. The owner speaks excellent English.

Twenty-three miles (37 km) east of Navojoa watch for many signs at the entrance on the right side of the highway. The campground is 9 miles (14.5 km) from Alamos.

REAL DE LOS ÁLAMOS RV PARK

Address: Morelos 31, Álamos, CP 85760 Sonora, México
Telephone: (6) 428-0045 or (6) 428-0180

GPS Location: N 27° 01' 49.3", W 108° 57' 01.9"

This newest of Álamos' campgrounds is about a mile (1.6 km) from town on the right as you arrive. There's lots of maneuvering room for big rigs.

The campground's 60 back-in spaces all have 15-amp outlets with 30-amp breakers, water, and sewer hookups. They are arranged around the perimeter of a large field next to the highway. The restrooms have hot showers. This campground doubles as the local balneario (swimming resort), it has a pool. The pool is unheated and isn't kept up well during the winter.

As you approach Álamos watch for the Real de los Álamos on the right. You pass it before you reach the Dolisa. It's easy to spot because the campers parked there are easily visible from the road.

ACOSTA RANCH TRAILER RV PARK

Address: Apdo. 67, Álamos, CP 85760 Sonora, México
Telephone: (6) 428-0077, (6) 428-0246   **Fax:** (6) 428-0279

GPS Location: N 27° 01' 23.1", W 108° 55' 31.4"

The Acosta is a nice little campground in a quiet setting within walking distance of downtown Álamos, it is on the far side of town and unfortunately large rigs have a tough time negotiating Álamos' streets. If you are smaller than 25 feet and not towing you should have no problems. Large rigs can make it too, they just have a little more trouble.

The campground has 18 back-in RV slots, all have 30-amp outlets, water, sewer, a patio and most have some shade. The one restroom has a hot shower. This is also a local balneario (in the summer) and has a beautiful unheated pool near the motel units and also a couple of lap-type pools that are empty in the winter. Groups can arrange to have meals prepared and served in the very nice dining room and the manager specializes in guided bird-watching and hunting trips. You can easily walk into town from the campground, the distance is about a half-mile.

To reach the campground drive right into town. Zero your odometer as you pass the Pemex station. At the tiny glorieta in front of the Pemex you must choose your route carefully. You want to take the road to the right of the small square which you see ahead and slightly to your left. At .2 miles (.3 km) you will come to a stop sign. This is the only difficult-to-negotiate corner. Make the difficult right turn and then almost immediately turn left. Drive down this street which will eventually turn to cobblestones and make a dogleg left and cross the (hopefully) dry river bed. After the river bed you will see an Acosta TP sign pointing to the left at a Y, follow the indicated road until you get to a walled cemetery at .7 miles (1.1 km) from where you passed the Pemex. Follow the wall of the cemetery to the left and then right around the far end and you will see the entrance to the trailer park and motel ahead. Drive through the gate and past some houses into the trailer park. The managers are sometimes hard to find, they live in the house to the right at the far end of the trailer park. Large rigs will want to cut left to the dry arroyo just after reaching the Pemex station and then follow it to the right about .6 miles (1 km) until they see the second pedestrian bridge. On the far side of the pedestrian bridge turn left onto the main road and follow the signs to the Acosta.

Side Trips from Álamos

La Aduana is a nearby mining town. The mine has been abandoned but the church, **Iglesia de Nuestra Señora de la Balvanera**, remains. The church was built to celebrate a miracle which resulted in the discovery of silver in the town. A procession from Navojoa comes here on December 12 during the Festival Guadalupana. The town is located on a 2 mile (3 km) stub road off the main road into Álamos, watch for a sign in Minas Nuevas about 4.5 miles (7.3 km) outside Álamos along the main road from Navojoa. This is a drive for smaller vehicles only.

BAHÍA KINO, SONORA (BAH-HEE-AH KEY-NO)
Population 3,500, Elevation sea level

Bahía Kino or Kino Bay is really two villages. Both towns, of course, are named for the famed Jesuit missionary Padre Eusebio Francisco Kino. **Kino Viejo** (Old Kino) is a traditional fishing village with dusty streets arranged around a traditional square. Fishing is from skiffs or pangas, they pull up on the beach to unload. **Kino Nuevo** (New Kino) is a resort with small hotels and RV parks strung along several miles of beach to the northwest. Only one RV park is in Viejo Kino but the old town is where many of the services are located, including restaurants and the only gas station. Small grocery stores in both towns provide limited supplies, for bigger shopping trips the huge supermarkets in Hermosillo are only 66 miles (107 km) distant on a decent two-lane paved road. Closer, at 27 miles (44 km), along the road to Hermosillo is the farming town of Miguel Aleman with a population of 33,000. Miguel Aleman now has several medium-sized supermarkets. Kino Bay has streetside telephone booths but no banks.

Kino is Seri Indian country, some live in Bahía Kino but there are also villages located to the north along the coast. You can sometimes find stands selling ironwood carvings of dolphins and other animals. Most of the ironwood carvings, however, are not au-

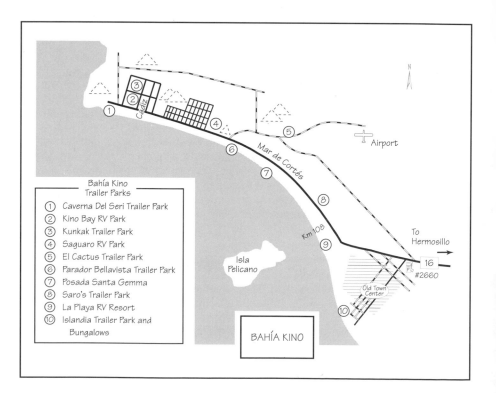

Bahía Kino Trailer Parks

① Caverna Del Seri Trailer Park
② Kino Bay RV Park
③ Kunkak Trailer Park
④ Saguaro RV Park
⑤ El Cactus Trailer Park
⑥ Parador Bellavista Trailer Park
⑦ Posada Santa Gemma
⑧ Saro's Trailer Park
⑨ La Playa RV Resort
⑩ Islandia Trailer Park and Bungalows

thentic Seri carvings, they are produced in small factories on the back streets of Kino Viejo. There is also a museum, **Museo de los Seris,** with displays of historical photographs and traditional articles of clothing and living utensils.

The fishing is excellent off Kino Bay and there are miles of coast to explore along rough sandy roads to the north toward El Desemboque.

Bahía Kino Campgrounds

🚐 CAVERNA DEL SERI TRAILER PARK

Address: Apdo. 72, Bahía Kino, CP 83340 Sonora, México

GPS Location: N 28° 51' 37.1", W 112° 01' 40.6"

The Caverna del Seri is at the end of the road through Nuevo Kino. It is the largest of the campgrounds that actually allow you to park next to the sand. When we last visited it was also in the poorest condition and virtually empty.

The campground has 28 spaces, half are right down on the beach and the others are on a terrace above. There is room for big rigs. The upper spaces have patios and some even have sun shades. All spaces have electricity with 15-amp outlets, sewer and water. The restrooms have hot-water showers. There is a boat ramp and fish-cleaning house.

To find the campground follow the main drag, Avenida Mar de Cortés, right to the end of the pavement. The white wall ahead is the campground, just drive around to the right and enter the gate.

🚐 KINO BAY RV PARK

Address: P.O. Box 57, Bahía Kino, CP 83340 Sonora, México
Telephone: (6) 242-0216, (6) 280-0000 (Hermosillo)
Fax: (6) 242-0083

GPS Location: N 28° 51' 34.2", W 112° 01' 29.2"

Bahía Kino's largest trailer park is organized and well run.

There are 200 full hookup spaces at the Kino Bay. These are rather barren pull-through spaces with 30-amp outlets (air conditioners are OK), sewer, water, and covered patios. They are large enough for big rigs. The restrooms are modern and clean, they have hot-water showers. The campground has a huge fenced storage area for boats and RV's and a fish-cleaning house that is well separated from the living areas. The beach is right across the street. The folks at the reception office speak English and are very helpful.

The campground is well-signed. If you zero your odometer as you pass Pemex #2660 at the entrance to Old Kino Bay and continue straight on the main highway you will find that the Kino Bay RV park is on your right at 5.7 miles (9.2 km).

🚐 KUNKAK TRAILER PARK

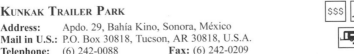

Address: Apdo. 29, Bahía Kino, Sonora, México
Mail in U.S.: P.O. Box 30818, Tucson, AR 30818, U.S.A.
Telephone: (6) 242-0088   **Fax:** (6) 242-0209

GPS Location: N 28° 51' 40.1", W 112° 01' 22.6"

The Trailer Park Kunkak is one of the few campgrounds in Bahía Kino that is not on

THE NORTHERN WEST COAST

Avenida Mar de Cortés along the water. It is not far away, however, it sits almost behind the Kino Bay RV Park.

The camp sites of the Kunkak are arranged around an attractive central building which houses the office, lounge, game room, restrooms and laundry room. There is no fence around this park, the spaces are attractively arranged and separated by rock walls and plants. The 60 spaces have 15-amp outlets with 30-amp breakers (air conditioners are OK), water, and sewer. Most are fine for big rigs. Restrooms are modern and clean, they have hot water showers. The well-liked manager speaks English and loves to talk politics.

To find the campground zero your odometer as you pass Pemex #2660 at the entrance to Old Kino Bay and continue straight on the main highway. At 5.6 miles (9 km) turn right on Cadiz and drive a block inland alongside the small pitch-and-putt golf course, the trailer park will be on your left.

🚐 SAGUARO RV PARK

Address: Apdo. 50, Bahía Kino, CP 83340 Sonora, México
Telephone: (6) 242 0165

GPS Location: N 28° 51' 17.7", W 112° 00' 12.1"

The Saguaro is one of the older trailer parks in Kino Bay, it is also one of the better maintained and managed places in town. It sits across the road from the beach, many people prefer to keep their rigs away from the salt water.

The campground has 25 spaces, they have 30-amp outlets, sewer, water, and satellite TV hookups. Eighteen of them have covered patios and many are pull-throughs. Parking is on gravel but the driveways are paved. The restrooms are older but extremely clean, they have hot water showers. There is a laundry with a self-operated washer, a recreation/meeting room, and an outdoor patio area. The Saguaro also has four rental rooms. English is spoken at this campground.

To find the campground zero your odometer as you pass Pemex #2660 at the entrance to Old Kino Bay and continue straight on the main highway. At 4.4 miles (7.1 km) you'll see the Saguaro on the right near the foot of the small hill.

🚐 EL CACTUS TRAILER PARK

Address: Camino a P. Chueca Km 2, Bahía Kino, Sonora, México
Telephone: (6) 216-1643 (Hermosillo), (6) 258-1200 (Kino Bay)

GPS Location: N 28° 51' 35.7", W 111° 59' 27.1"

The El Cactus is not located in Bahía Kino at all, it sits alone in the desert about a mile from the ocean. If you like your peace and quiet this is the place for you.

The El Cactus has 29 spaces. All are back-in sites with 15-amp outlets, sewer, water, satellite TV, and patios. Some have a little shade. The restrooms are clean and have hot water showers. There is a swimming pool. The campground is surrounded by a chain-link fence and lots of desert. Only limited English is spoken.

To reach the El Cactus zero your odometer as you pass Pemex #2660 at the entrance to Old Kino Bay and continue straight on the main highway. Turn right at 4.3 miles (6.9 km) just before the small hill, there is a sign for the El Cactus Trailer Park. Follow the gravel road for .9 miles (1.5 km), the trailer park is on the left.

🚐 **PARADOR BELLAVISTA TRAILER PARK**

Address: Mar de Cortés and Cochorit (P.O. Box 27),
               Bahía Kino, Sonora, México
Telephone: (6) 242-0868   **Fax:** (6) 242-0536

GPS Location: N 28° 51' 12.3", W 111° 59' 50.1"

The Parador Bellavista is a small beachside trailer park. The maneuvering room is limited but somehow the big rigs manage to get in here each year.

There are 16 spaces in the campground, nine along the front row overlooking the beach. All have electricity (15-amp or 30-amp outlets), sewer, and water hookups. Most of the spaces are back-in (or pull-in), two are parallel parking spaces. Most have patios, some with sun covers. The restrooms have hot showers and there is a laundry with a self-service machine.

To find the Bellavista zero your odometer as you pass Pemex #2660 at the entrance to Old Kino Bay and continue straight on the main highway. The campground is on the left at 4.1 miles (6.6 km).

🚐 **POSADA SANTA GEMMA**

Address: Alatorre No. 912, Colonia Pitic, Hermosillo,
               CP 83150 Sonora, México
Telephone: (6) 214-5579 (Hermosillo), (6) 242-0026 (Kino Bay)
Fax: (6) 214-5579

GPS Location: N 28° 51' 00.2", W 111° 59' 09.0"

This is another small campground next to the beach. The Posada Santa Gemma is also a motel.

There are 14 spaces, all are back-in or pull-in with 15-amp outlets, sewer, and water and covered patios. An additional seven spaces with no hookups are located across the road. Seven spaces overlooking the beach are usually full, the others are usually empty. The restroom are small but adequate and have hot-water showers.

To find the Santa Gemma zero your odometer as you pass Pemex #2660 at the entrance to Old Kino Bay and continue straight on the main highway. The campground is on the left at 3.3 miles (5.3 km).

🚐 **SARO'S TRAILER PARK**

Address: Avenida Mar de Cortés, Bahía Kino, Sonora, México
Telephone: (6) 242-0007

GPS Location: N 28° 50' 41.6", W 111° 58' 25.7"

Saro's is a simple RV park on the far side of the highway from the beach. There are seven back-in spaces along the north wall of an almost-empty dirt-covered lot, these spaces have patios and wood-framed palapas. Another eight spaces line the south fence. Each space has electricity (15-amp outlets), sewer, and water. There's lots of room for big rigs to maneuver. Restrooms are new, clean and have hot showers. There is also a laundry room with a washer and dryer. Across the street, on the ocean side of the road is the small Saro's Hotel which has rooms and a popular Italian restaurant which is only open from October to March. The owner, Saro, (he's Italian, of course) emphasizes that his is the least expensive trailer park in Kino Bay.

To reach Saro's Trailer Park zero your odometer as you pass Pemex #2660 at the entrance to Old Kino Bay and continue straight on the main highway. The campground is on the right at 3 miles (4.8 km).

LA PLAYA RV RESORT

Address: P.O. Box 15, Bahía Kino, CP 83340 Sonora, México
Telephone: (6) 242-0274   **Fax:** (6) 242-0273

GPS Location: N 28° 49' 48.5", W 111° 57' 18.1"

As you enter Nuevo Bahía Kino the first campground you'll see is the brand new La Playa. It's definitely the most upscale of Kino's campgrounds and plans are in the works to continue improving it.

There are 48 full-hookup sites with 30 and 50-amp outlets on two terraces overlooking the beach. These are big sites. Half have great view and half sit back away from the edge of the terraces and don't get much use. The restrooms are some of the nicest we've seen, of course they have hot showers. The owner of this campground is one of the towns top homebuilders, he is continuing work on the campground as time allows. A pool and hot tub will soon be added as well as rental rooms. Many RVers are contracting to have structures erected on the patios and plan to return every winter.

To reach La Playa zero your odometer as you pass Pemex #2660 at the entrance to Old Kino Bay and continue straight on the main highway. The campground is on the left at 1.1 miles (1.8 km).

ISLANDIA TRAILER PARK AND BUNGALOWS

Address: Puerto Peñasco s/n entre Guaymas y Mazatlán,
                Bahía Kino, CP 83340 Sonora, México
Telephone: (6) 242-0081

GPS Location: N 28° 49' 22.9", W 111° 56' 44.6"

The Islandia is the only one of the Kino Bay trailer parks located in Old Kino Bay. The location in the old town is the campground's biggest attraction and it also may be it's biggest problem, it just depends upon what you like.

The family-run water-front campground has 72 spaces with 30-amp outlets, sewer, and water. On our latest visit we found the condition of hookups and facilities to be much improved. Some spaces are along the water but most sit back away from the beach. There's lots of room for big rigs. Restrooms are in good condition and have hot showers. There's a self-service laundry with two washers and also a boat ramp. There are also several rental bungalows scattered around the property. You can easily walk to the center of town in a few minutes. The town has dusty streets, a square, several small stores and restaurants, and small fishing boats pulled up along the beach.

To get to the campground turn left just after Pemex #2660 as you enter Old Kino Bay on the main road from Hermosillo. Turn onto the paved road and follow it all the way through town until it rises to go onto the beach. Turn right just before the rise and drive three blocks until the road reaches the campground fence. Turn to the right and follow the fence around to the entrance.

CULIACÁN, SINALOA (KOO-LEE-AH-KAHN)
Population 950,000, Elevation 275 ft (84 m)

Few of the drivers who bypass Culiacán on the way south to Mazatlán know that the

THE NORTHERN WEST COAST

city is anything more than a large agricultural center. Culiacán was founded in the 16th century by the most-hated of the conquistadors, Beltrán Nuño de Guzmán, and today is the state capital of Sinaloa. It is a prosperous city intent upon building a more attractive environment for citizens and visitors.

You won't find a lot of tourist attractions in Culiacán. One worth a visit is the **Museo del Arte de Sinaloa** which has works by Diego Rivera, Pedro Coronel, Rufino Tamayo and López Sañez. Meteorites are in the news recently, one said to be the second largest ever recovered is in the **Parque Constitución**. There's also a nice riverfront malecón (walkway).

If you are traveling on Mex 15D you will bypass Culiacán and only see the town from a distance. About half way around the west side is the intersection where the Maxipista toll road south to Mazatlán takes off to the right, easy access to downtown Culiacán goes to the left at the same intersection, see the instructions for reaching the Tres Ríos Hotel given below. If you want to travel the free road south continue straight at this intersection, in 6.0 miles (9.8 km) you will intersect Mex 15 Libre.

Culiacán Campgrounds

🚐 HOTEL LOS TRES RÍOS

Address: Carretera México-Nogales Km 1423, Culiacán, CP80020 Sinaloa, México
Telephone: (6) 750-5280 and (800) 710-6177
Fax: (6) 750-5283

GPS Location: N 24° 48' 54.0", W 107° 24' 47.2"

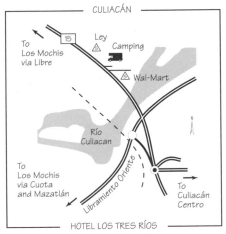

The Tres Ríos isn't a destination campground, but it makes a convenient place to stay if you find yourself near Culiacán when night falls. Unfortunately, you pay a lot here for poor camping facilities.

There are 16 RV parking slots with 30-amp outlets, water, and sewer hookups in a barren fenced field behind the hotel. All are back-in sites, a couple have paved patios and big rigs have lots of room once they've threaded their way through the hotel parking lot. The hookups are in poor repair. There isn't much shade or vegetation in the campground itself but the hotel has a pleasant pool area. The bathrooms at the pool double for the RV park, they have hot-water showers. The hotel also has a restaurant and a disco, fortunately the disco is on the far side of the grounds. Little or no English is spoken. There is a Ley supermarket next door on one side and a huge Wal-Mart and Sam's Club on the other.

The hotel is located on the east side of Mex 15 Libre so it is easy to find if you are following the free highway through town instead of using the bypass. Watch carefully if headed north and you will see the hotel .3 miles (.5 km) north of the river bridge, just past the Wal-Mart. Driving south it is just past the Ley supermarket but you can't enter from southbound lanes, you'll have to pull into the Wal-Mart parking lot to turn around.

The easiest access for most travelers, however, is from the west. At the intersection of the bypass and the Mazatlán toll road zero your odometer and follow signs toward Culiacán (also labeled Mex 15 Libre). At 2.1 miles (3.4 km) you will see a Ley super-market on your right and then an intersection. Go straight through, the intersection isn't square so make sure you pass to the left of the Pemex on the far side. You'll cross some railroad tracks at 2.6 miles (4.2 km) and see a big movie theater called the Cinepolis on the right at 5.1 miles (8.2 km). At 5.7 miles (9.2 km) slow to pass under some railroad tracks and turn sharply right immediately after them. The road will come to a big and sometimes crowded glorieta at 5.9 miles (9.5 km). You want to drive all the way around it so that you are heading back the way you came in but one street to the right. The proper road is signed as Mex 15 and Los Mochis. The river bridge is at 6.5 miles (10.5 km), you'll see the Wal-Mart on the right at 6.8 miles (11 km) and soon see the entrance to the Los Tres Ríos Hotel on the right. Pull into the driveway, bear left around the buildings, check in at the hotel office, and pull through the cobblestone parking lot to the RV park behind.

CENTRO RECREATIVO LAS CASCABELES

Address: Carretera Internacional Costa Rica
                 Km 6, Culiacán, Sinaloa, México
Telephone: (6) 717-2659 (Site) or
                 (6) 713-64-18 (Culiacán)

GPS Location: N 24° 35' 46.5", W 107° 18' 19.5"

CENTRO RECREATIVO LAS CASCABELES

The second camping area near Culiacán is a country location and has much easier access than the hotel in town. This is a balneario (swimming area) popular with folks from Culiacán. During the week during the winter you should have it pretty much to yourself, even weekends during the winter won't usually be too crowded. It is set on the shore of a shallow lake south of Culiacán. Swimming is in a pool, not the lake.

The recreation area has 29 pull-in parking areas. Most are suitable for rigs to about 30 feet, a few for rigs to about 35 feet. Larger rigs would have some trouble maneuvering here. The sites are called cabañas because each has a covered patio with a table, 15-amp electrical outlet, water faucet, light and sometimes a hammock. Normally these are rented for picnics but they make good camping sites. The area has restrooms with flush toilets and hot showers, be advised that their condition is a little grim. There is a swimming pool and a wading pool, a track for four-wheelers, and a sports field.

Access is from Mex 15 Libre south of Culiacán at about Km 193. Just north of two Pemex stations (#3675 and #3856) a paved road goes west signed for Costa Rica and Cascabeles Centro Recreativo. Follow this road for 4.2 miles (6.8 km) to the entrance on the right (signed Las Cascabeles Entrada #2). You will see another entrance before this one, but it is not the entrance to the RV parking area. The person minding the entrance will open a gate to allow you access. The gate should be manned from 8:30 a.m. to 6:30 p.m.

Side Trips from Culiacán

The Culiacán area is devoted to farming but people do need their time at the beach, you might want to take a look at the long beaches at **Altata**, **Playa el Tambor**, and **Playa Las Arenitas**. It can be fun to explore roads toward the ocean all along this coast. Most trips involve long drives across agricultural land and then through flats with shrimp farms. Often they end at small fish camps or villages on deserted beaches. There are definitely opportunities for boondocking with no amenities other than an occasional palapa restaurant.

The colonial mining town of **Cosalá** is an excellent side trip from either Culiacán or Mazatlán. To get there drive 34 miles (55 km) east from an intersection on Mex 15 Libre that is halfway between Culiacán and Mazatlán. This town could be another Álamos, except that no one has restored it. It has its own historical museum and is known for hand-crafted saddles.

EL FUERTE (EHL FWEHR-TAY)
Population 25,000, Elevation 350 ft (107 m)

A short 48 mile (78 km) drive inland from Los Mochis is the old **colonial town** of El Fuerte. Founded in 1564 this town was a way station on the Camino Real and has its share of colonial architecture. Some people say this is the way Álamos would be if it

THE DOWNTOWN SQUARE IN EL FUERTE

THE NORTHERN WEST COAST

had not been restored. In fact, El Fuerte is a bustling supply center for the surrounding agricultural area. We're told that plans are in the works to improve an old back road north to Álamos, a section of the old Camino Real. That will make a nice loop drive for RVers, if and when it happens.

The Chihuahua al Pacífico Railroad stops at a station near town and is a good place to catch the train to travel to Divisadero or Creel along the Copper Canyon. The train passes here about an hour and a half after leaving or before arriving in Los Mochis so you don't have to get up as early in the morning to catch it. It also arrives here earlier when you return. The section of the line between Los Mochis and El Fuerte is not very interesting so you don't really miss a thing. Use a taxi to reach the train station from the RV parks, the station is 3.5 miles (5.7 km) from town.

The distance from Los Mochis to El Fuerte on a paved two-lane highway is 48 miles (77 km). Alternately, you can take a short cut from Mex 15 about 33 miles (53 km) north of Los Mochis at Km 55 in the town of El Carrizo. This route is a paved two-lane road and lets you avoid a toll booth north of Los Mochis if you are southbound. From El Carrizo to El Fuerte the distance is 36 miles (58 km).

El Fuerte Campgrounds

🚐 RV PARK DE EL FUERTE

Address:	A.P. #93, El Fuerte, CP 81820
	Sinaloa, México
Telephone:	(6) 893-1138, Cell (6) 868-4052
E-mail:	bill@tsi.com.mx

GPS Location: N 26° 24' 41.4", W 108° 37' 46.1"

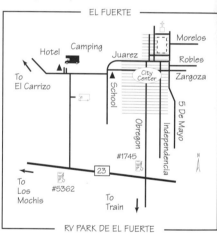

This campground is brand new, a welcome addition to west coast campgrounds and a great place to stay while taking the train up along the Copper Canyon.

The campground has 25 large pull-through RV sites, parking is on grass. Each site has electrical, water, and sewer hookups. Electricity is either 30-amp or 50-amp with the proper outlets. There are two bathrooms with hot showers and flush toilets in a building that has a cactus garden planted on the roof. There is also a thatch-roofed patio for social get-togethers. The laundry has two washers and two dryers.

The campground is located just southwest of El Fuerte. The distance from Los Mochis on a paved two-lane highway is 48 miles. As you approach El Fuerte you will see Pemex #5362 on the right, turn left immediately after the Pemex and drive .6 miles (1 km). The road turns to the left and the campground entrance is directly ahead. Alternately, you can take a short cut from Mex 15 about 33 miles (53 km) north of Los Mochis at Km 55 in the town of El Carrizo. This route is a paved two-lane road, you approach El Fuerte in 36 miles (58 km). As you do you should see the campground sign on your left.

THE NORTHERN WEST COAST

HOTEL BOUGAINVILLEA

Address: Apdo. 109, El Fuerte, Sinaloa,
             México.
Telephone: (6) 893-0985

GPS Location: N 26° 24' 36.8", W 108° 37' 35.5"

$$$ ▲ ⌂ ⌂ 🚿 ☎

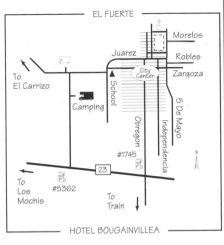

This motel primarily caters to fishermen and hunters visiting the El Fuerte area. It has installed six duplex 15-amp electrical outlets mounted on trees in the big parking area in front of the motel. The managers can show you where there is a water hose and also a place to dump your holding tanks. The place is best for self-contained rigs but you can arrange to use one of the hotel rooms for a shower. There is a wall surrounding the grounds.

Hotel Bougainvillea is located just southwest of El Fuerte. As you approach El Fuerte from Los Mochis you will see Pemex #5362 on the right, turn left immediately after the Pemex and drive .5 miles (.8 km). You'll see the hotel on your right. Alternately, you can take a short cut from Mex 15 about 33 miles (53 km) north of Los Mochis at Km 55 in the town of El Carrizo. This route is a paved two-lane road, you approach El Fuerte in 36 miles (58 km). As you do you should see the RV Park de El Fuerte sign on your left, turn the 90 degree corner to the right, and then see this campground on your left just .1 mile (.2 km) after the RV Park de El Fuerte. When we visited there was no sign.

RIO FUERTE CAMPGROUND

Address: Rodolfo G. Robles #105, El
             Fuerte, CP 81820 Sinaloa,
             México
Telephone: (6) 893-0308
E-mail: riofuertebb@yahoo.com

GPS Location: N 26° 27' 30.2", W 108° 36' 18.6"

$$ ▲ 🚿

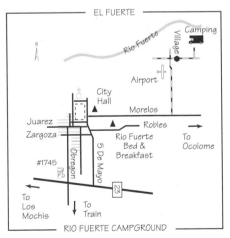

A new tenting campground is under construction about 3 miles outside El Fuerte on the banks of the El Fuerte River. It is being put together by the owners of the Rio Fuerte Bed and Breakfast. You should contact them before going out, they can give you detailed information.

The campground has room for plenty of tents but is not equipped for RVs. There is a platform next to the river with a table that makes an excellent place to relax. Restrooms, probably with cold showers, are planned for next year. Limited parking makes this campground inappropriate for RVs.

The campground is located 3 miles (5 km) out of town off the road to Ocolome that forms an extension of Morelos, the street just south of the city hall in El Fuerte. The route is complicated, however. To find the campground it is best to stop in at the Rio Fuerte Bad and Breakfast, the address above is the location of the bed and breakfast in town. This is on Robles which is the east-west street just south of Morelos.

Guaymas and San Carlos, Sonora (GWAY-mas and sawn-KAHR-loes)
Population 200,000, Elevation sea level

You can think of Guaymas and San Carlos as twin cities, fraternal twins, they are not at all alike. Guaymas itself is an old port, the first supply depot was set up here by the Jesuits in 1701 although they were driven out later by the tough and resistant local Indians. Today the major industry is fishing. Guaymas has a modern Ley supermarket which is the best place to lay in supplies in the area.

North of Guaymas is San Carlos, center of the tourist activity. The recent completion of a four-lane boulevard through San Carlos has really changed the ambiance. The dust is gone, now the town seems to be making real progress toward being an upscale resort. There are marinas, hotels, a golf course, and restaurants. There are also three good trailer parks.

Between Guaymas and San Carlos is the small town of **Miramar**. The main reason you will want to know this is that Miramar is home to a popular RV park for visitors passing through the area, the venerable Hotel Playa de Cortés.

The toll highway bypasses Guaymas entirely, if you want to visit you must take the Guaymas/San Carlos cutoff near Pemex #3531 and Km 139 when headed south. If you follow this cutoff through Guaymas it will eventually reconnect with the toll highway south of town at the Km 107 marker and you will have avoided one toll station.

Guaymas and San Carlos Campgrounds

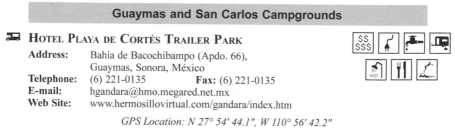

Hotel Playa de Cortés Trailer Park

Address:	Bahía de Bacochibampo (Apdo. 66), Guaymas, Sonora, México
Telephone:	(6) 221-0135 **Fax:** (6) 221-0135
E-mail:	hgandara@hmo.megared.net.mx
Web Site:	www.hermosillovirtual.com/gandara/index.htm

GPS Location: N 27° 54' 44.1", W 110° 56' 42.2"

This is a good place to pull into for a good night's sleep if you're headed for points farther north or south. The Hotel Playa de Cortés was built in 1936 as a railway resort hotel and is still a class joint. It is located in Miramar between the San Carlos cutoff from Mex 15 and the town of Guaymas.

Behind the hotel is a nice RV parking area with 52 very long full-hookup (30-amp outlets) back-in slots. Each has its own patio and long fifth-wheelers will find that they do not need to unhook. Twenty-seven additional full-hookup (15-amp outlets) back-in sites with no patios have recently been added as well as 6 more unmarked sites with only electrical and water hookups. The park advertises that it specializes in big rigs and there is even a sign out front asking smaller rigs not to ask to stay. This probably just means that everyone is expected to pay the full freight since vans seem to be welcome. Tents, on the other hand, are nowhere to be seen. This is a full-service hotel, it has a restaurant, bar, swimming pool, tennis courts, and small boat charters are available for fishing or sightseeing. There are no permanently-located rigs here.

The hotel is located at Playa Miramar, a beach community between Guaymas and Bahía San Carlos. Take the off ramp from Mex 15 just west of Guaymas and follow the wide road 1.9 miles (3.1 km) to its end. You'll be at the hotel. Just through the gate turn to the left to enter the campground.

EL MIRADOR RV PARK

Address:	Apdo. 439, San Carlos-Nuevo Guaymas, Sonora, México
Telephone:	(6) 227-0213 or (6) 227-0107 **Fax:** (6) 227-0108
E-mail:	mirador@tetakawi.net.mx
Web Site:	www.elmiradorrv.com

GPS Location: N 27° 56' 39.5", W 111° 05' 14.4"

This is the brand new RV park in San Carlos. The park is actually built to U.S. standards, many people think it is the best RV park in Mexico. If you judge strictly by the quality of the facilities it probably is. That's not to speak badly of the location either: the area is very scenic, the weather generally good, and it's an easy drive from the states.

The campground has about 90 large back-in sites, almost all are suitable for the larg-

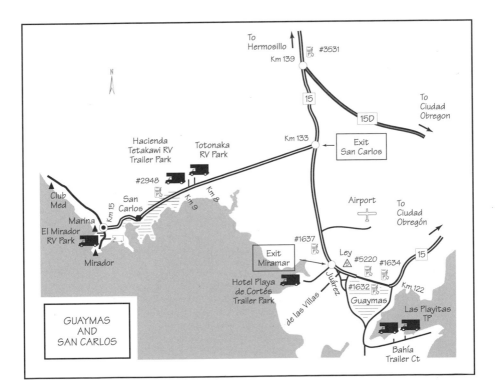

THE NORTHERN WEST COAST

est rigs. The parking pads are cobblestone and there are cement patios. Electrical outlets are 30-amp and each site also has water, sewer, and satellite TV connections. There is gravel between the sites and no shade. The amenities at this campground are excellent. Restrooms are first class with good hot showers. There is a swimming pool and hot tub, an excellent restaurant, a laundry room with coin-operated machines, a game room with pool and ping-pong tables, and two beautiful tennis courts. If you want to spend time here it is a good idea to make reservations ahead, during the winter it seems that every caravan coming through San Carlos stays here, and this campground honors their reservations, unlike some in Mexico. That means that individual travelers without reservations are often turned away or can only stay a night or two.

The campground is located west of central San Carlos. If you take the San Carlos exit from the highway north of Guaymas at the Km 133 marker and drive west you will reach San Carlos in about 4.4 miles (7.1 km), and reach a Y at 7.5 miles (12.1 km). Go right here following the sign to Algodones and climb up and over a low hill, then follow the road through a small area of holiday homes and then through a short valley between two hills. You will reach an intersection at 9.9 miles (16 km). Turn left here and the entrance to the campground is on the right at 10.4 miles (16.8 km).The route is well-signed for the entire distance.

▭ Totonaka RV Park

Address:	P.O. Box 211, San Carlos, Sonora, México
Telephone:	(6) 226-0323, (6) 226-0481
E-mail:	totonakarv@yahoo.com
Web Site:	www.totonaka.homepage.com

GPS Location: N 27° 57' 47.9", W 111° 01' 28.2"

The Totonaka Trailer Park is much like the Tetakawi next door, but in much better condition. Back in the trailer park itself you'd be hard pressed to tell one from the other if there weren't a fence between them. Instead of a hotel out front the Totonaka has a restaurant.

The campground has about 125 spaces, these are back-in sites with patios, electricity, water, sewer and cable TV. Electrical outlets are 15-amp but most spaces have 30-amp breakers. Many sites will handle big rigs. The park has a cobblestone central avenue with packed gravel side streets and parking areas. Restrooms are old but serviceable, they have hot water showers. A laundry room has many coin-operated washers and dryers. There is a swimming pool at the front of the campground and a restaurant on the street out front as well as several within easy walking distance. The beach is across the street. Internet access is available in the office and English is spoken there.

Zero your odometer as you take the cutoff from Mex 15 toward San Carlos. You will be driving on a nice four-lane highway that is virtually empty. At 5.6 miles (9.0 km) you will see the Totonaka Trailer Park on the right and a tenth of a mile later the Hacienda Tetakawi, also is on the right.

▭ Hacienda Tetakawi RV Trailer Park

Address:	P.O. Box 71, San Carlos/Guaymas,
	CP 85406 Sonora, México
Telephone:	(6) 226-0220 **Fax:** (6) 226-0248

GPS Location: N 27° 57' 48.2", W 111° 01' 32.9"

The Hacienda Tetakawi is a Best Western Hotel with a trailer park in the rear. You'll

THE NORTHERN WEST COAST

find a lot of people here who return every year and stay for the entire season. The campground is right across the new boulevard from the beach and there is now a sidewalk for taking a stroll.

There are about 40 spaces, they are back-ins with patios, 15-amp outlets with 15 or 30-amp breakers, sewer, water and cable TV hookups. Many sites have roofs on the patios. There are many more sites in the rear but they were not in use when we visited. The bathrooms are clean and well-maintained, they have hot-water showers. There is a swimming pool with a bar/restaurant up front next to the motel and a fish-cleaning room at the rear of the park. English is spoken at the hotel front desk and there is a bus that runs along the waterfront and into Guaymas every quarter hour.

To find the campground just follow the instructions given above for reaching the Totonaka RV Park. The Hacienda Tetakawi is just beyond and located right next door.

LAS PLAYITAS TRAILER PARK

Address: Apdo. 327, Guaymas, Sonora, México
Telephone: (6) 221-5196

One of two trailer parks located across Guaymas Bay from town, Las Playitas is quiet and friendly. According to the manager the place has been here for thirty-five years and in its heyday was very popular with fishermen. Today the fishing isn't as good and swimming in the bay just isn't done so the business has largely gone elsewhere. Unlike the similar campground listed below this one has no permanently-located rigs. Take a look, you may find the quiet and slow pace at Las Playitas to your liking. It also has low monthly rates.

The campground has about 30 back-in spaces with electricity (15-amp outlets), sewer, and water. The restrooms are old but clean and have hot water showers. The campground has a bar, it can be a little noisy some evenings. A bus goes in to Guaymas every half-hour from a stop nearby.

To reach the campground turn toward the south from Mex 15 through Guaymas at the stop light in front of the Ley supermarket. Zero your odometer here. Go .1 mile (.2 km) and turn left onto Blvd. Benito Juárez. Follow this boulevard through a right at a Y at .7 miles (1.1 km) and another right at 1.2 miles (1.9 km). There's a stop light at 2.2 miles (3.5 km), turn right toward Las Playitas. You'll pass a baseball stadium on your right and at the Y at 2.5 miles (4 km) turn left following signs toward Las Playitas. You'll pass the Bahía Trailer Court at 3.5 miles (5.6 km) and then come to the Las Playitas Hotel and Trailer Park at 4.3 miles (6.9 km) on the left.

BAHÍA TRAILER COURT

Address: Apdo. 75, Guaymas, Sonora, México
Telephone: (6) 222-3545

Like the Las Playitas this is a campground built to serve the fishermen who no longer come in very large numbers. It too has a quiet, pleasant ambiance and is well worth considering as a base for your stay in Guaymas.

The Bahía has about 65 spaces. Many have had permanent structures built on them. About half of the spaces remain available for travelers, each has a patio, electricity, sewer, and water. The restrooms are old but clean and maintained, the campground also has a meeting hall, boat ramp and dock. Buses pass every half-hour for Guaymas.

To get to the Bahía Trailer Court follow the instructions given above for reaching Las Playitas. The campground is on the left before you reach Las Playitas.

LOS MOCHIS, SINALOA (LOS MO-chees) AND LAS GLORIAS (LAS GLOW-REE-ahs)
Population 200,000, Elevation near sea level

Los Mochis is something of a transportation crossroads. If you are traveling south on Mex 15 this is probably where you'll spend your second night. Topolobampo, the city's port, is probably the best place to cross to/from the Baja Peninsula. The ferry runs daily. Also, Los Mochis is the western end of the famous Chihuahua al Pacífico Railroad with trains along the Copper Canyon to Chihuahua.

This is a farming town. The surrounding countryside is extensively irrigated using the waters of the Río Fuerte. Sugar-cane is the main crop although you will see many marigolds being grown too. These are used as chicken feed to yellow the yolks (much of the feed goes to the U.S.). This is also the reason often given for the yellow color of the plucked chickens seen in Mexican supermarkets.

While in town you may want to visit the huge sugar refinery (**Ingenio Azucarero**) to see how the process works. The **gardens** at the former home of the town's founder, an American named Benjamin Johnston, are now a park. There's also a local museum, the **Museo Regional del Valle del Fuerte**. The Los Mochis area is a popular hunting destination for ducks, geese, doves and deer. Fishing out of Topolobampo and inland behind the dams near El Fuerte is also excellent.

Los Mochis and Las Glorias Campgrounds

MR. MORO HOTEL AND RV RESORT

Address:	Apdo. 342 Playa Las Glorias, CP 81000 Guasave, Sinaloa, México
Telephone:	(6) 872-5511 **Fax:** (6) 871-1188
E-mail:	hotel@mrmoro.com.mx
Web Site:	www.mrmoro.com.mx

GPS Location: N 25° 17' 47.2", W 108° 31' 28.0"

$$$ (back) $$$ (front)

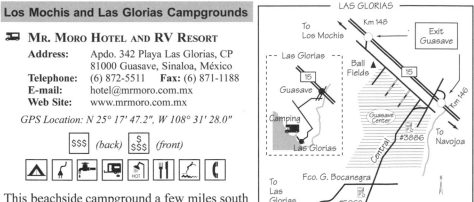

This beachside campground a few miles south of Los Mochis has acquired a loyal following in the past few years. To reach it you must drive some 26 miles (42 km) on back roads to coastal Las Glorias from Guasave which is 34 miles (54.8 km) south of Los Mochis on Mex 15. People in a hurry to get to southern destinations will find that it is too far off the highway for an overnight stop, the drive out takes about an hour each way. On the other hand, many folks stop here and never drive any farther south at all.

The trailer park is situated around a motel building: in the front, behind, and to the south. There are about 70 camping spaces, most are back-in but there are a few pull-throughs. Many can handle big rigs. The sites have 15-amp outlets, sewer, and water but no patios and little shade. This has rapidly become a very popular destination because there is a nice pool, a well-used bar with a pool table, a good palapa restaurant, and miles of sandy beach out front. The management is very friendly and English is spoken. Showers for RVers are in unused hotel rooms, separate rooms are set aside for the boys and girls. Supplies are very limited in Las Glorias, you will have to drive to Guasave for anything more than the basics.

To reach this trailer park leave Mex 15 at Guasave and follow the signs south from town toward Las Glorias. The route passes through farming country, it is full of tractors and old pickup trucks driving very slowly so be patient. The road is paved all the way to Las Glorias and well-signed.

From Mex 15 southbound take the Guasave exit just after the Km 148 marker. Follow the lateral road along the highway for .9 miles (1.5 km) and turn right on Blvd. Central. This is the **second** road to the right marked for Las Glorias, it is a divided boulevard. To get to Central from northbound Mex 15 take the Guasave exit just after the bridge over the Río Sinaloa at about Km 146. At the bottom of the ramp turn left, pass under the highway, and take the dogleg right on the far side. At the next set of stoplights turn left, this is Blvd. Central and you are heading for Las Glorias just a block beyond where the southbound traffic turned onto the boulevard as described above. You will know you are on the right boulevard when you see Pemex #3886 on the left. Follow central for about 1.2 miles (1.9 km) and turn right onto Calle Fco. Bocanegra. This turn is marked by a sign for Las Glorias. From here just follow the main road out of town. Twenty-six miles (42 km) after leaving Mex 15 you will enter tiny Las Glorias, in another .7 miles (1.1 km) you will see a sign for the trailer park pointing right down an unpaved but divided boulevard. The campground is .7 miles (1.1 km) down this road on the left, you can't miss the orange motel building.

COLINAS RESORT HOTEL AND TRAILER PARK

Address:	Carr. Internacional No. 15 y Blvd. Macario Gaxiola, Los Mochis, Sinaloa, México
Telephone:	(6) 811-8111 or 888 377-7876 (From U.S.)
Fax:	(6) 811-8181
E-mail:	hotelcolinas@coppercanyon hotels.com.mx
Web Site:	www.coppercanyon hotels.com.mx

GPS Location: N 25° 48' 49.4", W 108° 57' 33.6"

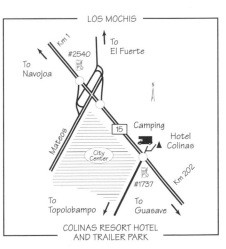

COLINAS RESORT HOTEL
AND TRAILER PARK

The Colinas Hotel is a favorite with caravans, you will often find it full. The draw may be the hotel facilities or it may just be that this is the easiest trailer park in Los Mochis to find. The hotel is perched on top of a hill to the right of Mex 15 as you enter Los Mochis from the south, you can't miss it.

The campground sits on level ground on the north side of the hill where the hotel perches. It is a level fenced gravel area with 53 large spaces. Each has a 30-amp outlet, water, sewer, and a patio. The use of air conditioners is allowed, you will need them because there is no shade here. Bathrooms are modern and clean, showers are hot. There is a palapa-style meeting room at the campground and a long stairway up to the hotel. Once up the hill you'll find a great view, a restaurant and coffee shop, swimming pools and tennis courts. Someone who speaks English is generally available and reservations are recommended.

The hotel is just south of Los Mochis near the Km 202 marker. It sits on a hill on the east side of the road, the entrance is just north of the hill, as is the campground. A big Pemex, #1737, is just across the highway next to the road that leads to the railroad terminal for trips to the Copper Canyon and also to Topolobampo for the ferry to La Paz.

LOS MOCHIS COPPER CANYON RV PARK

Address:	P.O. Box 50, Los Mochis, Sinaloa México
Telephone:	(6) 812-0021 (Reservations), (6) 812-6817 (Trailer Park)

GPS Location: N 25° 49' 13.2", W 108° 58' 25.8"

The Copper Canyon RV Park is showing its age and is quite noisy because it is located next to the main road between Mex 15 and downtown Los Mochis. There is usually room here if the other trailer parks in town are full. Caravans also use this park for Copper Canyon trips.

The trailer park has 100 pull-through and back-in spaces off gravel driveways. Each has electricity (15-amp outlets with 30-amp breakers), sewer, water and a small patio. There is limited shade. Restrooms are older ones with separate rooms each having stool, sink, and hot shower. There is a small restaurant and the campground specializes in tours of the Copper Canyon via the railroad. People leave their rigs here while making the two-day trip. Bus service downtown is available on the main road in front of the campground.

To find the Copper Canyon RV Park follow the signs off Mex 15 for Los Mochis. The exit is at Km 0, you can spot it because Pemex #2540 is on the east side of the highway just to the north. The exit is 1.4 miles (2.3 km) north of Pemex #1737 and the Colinas RV Park. After you exit you'll find yourself on Blvd. A. L. Mateos. From the interchange head west, you will see the campground on your right in about 1 mile (1.6 km).

Side Trips from Los Mochis

Los Mochis is a popular base for trips on the **Chihuahua al Pacífico Railroad**. People leave their vehicles in the various campgrounds (the Los Mochis Copper Canyon or the Colinas, or better yet, the El Fuerte RV Park in El Fuerte) and spend two days on the trip. They overnight in either Chihuahua or nearer to the Copper Canyon in Creel or Divisadero. You can arrange a tour through one of the campgrounds or do it yourself and save a bundle.

THE NORTHERN WEST COAST

MAGDALENA AND SANTA ANA, SONORA
(MAHG-DAH-LEH-nah AND SAHN-TAH ANN-AH)
Population 15,000, Elevation 2,275 ft (692 m)

Magdalena and Santa Ana are located within a few miles of each other some 54 miles (87 km) south of the border town of Nogales. Magdalena is an agricultural and mining town also known as the site of the grave of Father Kino. There is a **fiesta in honor of San Francisco Xavier** from September 22 to October 4 each year.

Santa Ana is little more than an important crossroads, Mex 2 which crosses northern Mexico meets Mex 15 here. Santa Ana is also the site of a Yaqui Indian gathering during the **Feast of St. Anne** from July 17 to 26. The Yaquis sometimes perform their famous deer dance during the feast.

These two towns are included here because they make a good stopping point if you cross the border late and want to spend the night or if you want to rest up before crossing into the U.S when headed north. They both have a campground, and Magdalena has a good-sized supermarket. A drive through Magdalena also saves you a few dollars on tolls, there is a toll station where Mex 15 passes town. The northern exit/entrance for Magdalena is near Km 194, the southern near Km 180.

Magdalena and Santa Ana Campgrounds

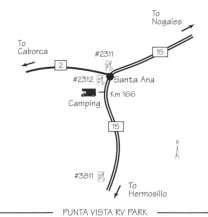

🚐 **PUNTA VISTA RV PARK**

Address:	Carretera Internacional #15 and Allende, Santa Ana, Sonora, México
Telephone:	(6) 324-0769

GPS Location: N 30° 32' 08.2", W 111° 06' 59.1"

This small trailer park near the intersection of Mex 15 and Mex 2 is a godsend for folks who just don't feel like driving all the way to Kino Bay or Guaymas after dealing with the border crossing in Nogales. It is also a good place to rest up before crossing if you are headed north. There's a wide shoulder out front so you can easily stop and take a look.

The Punta Vista has 12 spaces, 7 have 15-amp outlets, sewer and water, 5 have electricity only. The parking arrangement is flexible. There's plenty of room for a big rig or two to park without unhooking, the campground is seldom full. There's no official bathroom for the campground but if the rental casita isn't in use it has a bathroom with hot shower. The owners speak English.

The campground is right on Mex 15. It is .6 mile (1 km) south of the intersection where Mex 2 heads west, near the Km 166 marker, and is on the west side of the highway.

MOTEL KINO

Address: Dr. Ernesto Rivera M. #100,
Magdalena de Kino, Sonora,
México
Telephone: (6) 322-3684, (6) 322-3683

GPS Location: N 30° 37' 34.3", W 110° 58' 21.2"

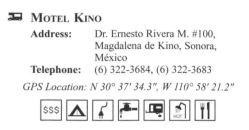

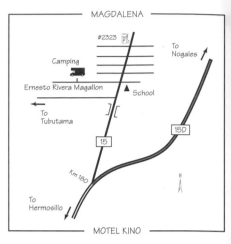

This is an alternative to the Punta Vista for folks seeking a campground between Nogales and Hermosillo. Knowledgeable travelers drive through Magdalena to avoid the toll gate on the four-lane highway bypass and save a few dollars so you're likely to be passing within a quarter-mile of the Motel Kino trailer park anyway.

The campground is located beside the motel in a fenced, gravel-covered lot. Fifteen back-in RV slots are arranged around the perimeter but there is no shade. Each RV slot has 15-amp electrical outlet, sewer, and water. There is lots of room for big rigs to maneuver. The one restroom is clean and modern and has hot water showers. You're likely to be one of only a few people who spend the night here so there's really going to be no reason to unhook or back into a space. The motel has a restaurant and a bar and some English is spoken at the desk.

If you are driving south on Mex 15 zero your odometer as you leave the toll road at the exit north of town at Km 194. You will find yourself entering town at about 3.5 miles (5.6 km) and see the VH supermarket on the right at 4.2 miles (6.8 km). You will pass through town and drive by two Pemexes, the first on the left and the second (#2323) on the right. At the second stop light after the second Pemex, a distance of .2 miles (.4 km), and at 4.9 miles (8 km) on your odometer turn right on Dr. Riviera M., it sometimes has a sign for the Motel Kino, and drive .1 mile (2 km) to the motel which is on the right.

Coming from the south take the Magdalena exit from the toll road near Km 180 and you will see the left turn for Dr. Riviera M. at 1.5 miles (2.4 km). The turnoff for Magdalena is 9 miles (14.5 km) north of the intersection of Mex 15 and Mex 2 from the west and is marked as the Libre route to Nogales.

MAZATLÁN, SINALOA (MAH-SAHT-LAHN)
Population 800,000, Elevation sea level

Mazatlán is the top RV destination on Mexico's west coast if you judge by the number of camping spaces available (we count nearly 700). It is also Mexico's top west-coast port. This is a bustling town that mixes everyday living with tourist activities. There is plenty to see and do and any service you require is available. Mazatlán is interesting also in that it has an acceptable climate year-round. Although temperatures do get warm in the summer July is the top tourist month, but not for campers from north of the border.

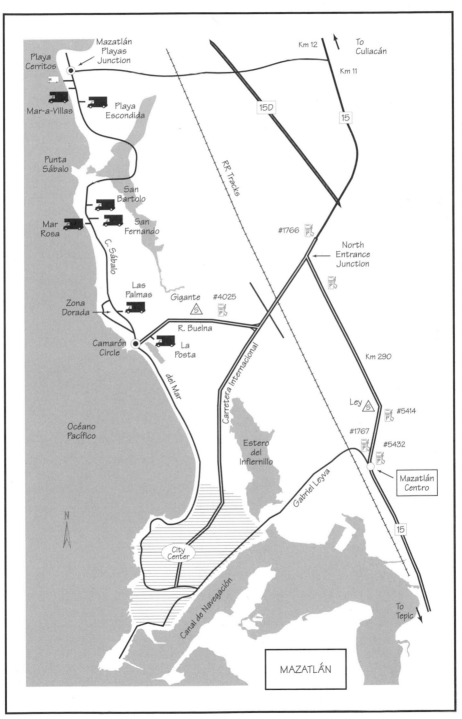

MAZATLÁN

All of the RV parks in town are strung out in northern Mazatlán in the Zona Dorada (Golden Zone) tourist area and even farther north. Only a few are actually on the beautiful beach that runs all along this stretch but all are within easy walking distance of it. There are also large supermarkets and shopping malls nearby. One road, Calz. Camarón Sábalo, runs along just inland from the coast and all of the RV parks are easily accessible from it. If you drive south on Calz. Camarón Sábalo the name changes and it will take you to old Mazatlán.

Visitors tired of the glitzy Zona Dorada can find relief in downtown old Mazatlán. You'll find the restored **Plazuela Machado**, the **Plaza Republicana**, and the **Plazuela Zaragoza** here, also the Mercado **José Pino Suárez**, a municipal market. If you haven't visited a municipal market yet don't miss this one. Virtually every Mexican town of any size has one and they are filled with wonderful colors and smells. They are a great place for an inexpensive meal. Mazatlán also has a museum, the **Museo Arqueológico** and an aquarium, the **Acuario Mazatlán**.

The city is known for its **Carnival**, the third largest in the world after Río de Janeiro and New Orleans. Like the others it is the week before Ash Wednesday when Lent starts. This, of course, means that it is variable but always in late February or March.

Since Mazatlán is often the first major city visited by campers new to Mexico a thorough description of the route to the beach-area campgrounds will probably be appre-

MAZATLÁN VIEW FROM MAR ROSA'S BEACH

THE NORTHERN WEST COAST

ciated. As you approach Mazatlán from the north on either the toll or free roads you will see a sign in the middle of nowhere for Mazatlán Playas. On the toll road it is 12 miles (19 km) south of the toll booth, on the free road it is between the Km 11 and 12 markers. You can take this road to reach the far north end of the boulevard along the coast which is called Cerritos in the north and which becomes Calz. Camarón Sábalo as you travel south. This is a low-traffic and easy way to drive to the campgrounds. On the toll road headed north you cannot access this road, there is no exit. Campground location directions given below show each campground's distance south of the point where the northern access road reaches Cerritos, in the instructions we call this the **Mazatlán Playas Junction.**

If you are coming into Mazatlán from the south or miss the northern playas access road have no fear, campground access is really not difficult. From the north 1.4 miles (2.2 km) after the Mex 15 Libre and toll roads meet you will see Pemex #1766 on the right. One tenth mile south of the Pemex the highway jogs left, you should go straight heading for Mazatlán centro. We'll call this the **North Entrance Junction**. If you approach Mazatlán from the south stay on the main highway past the first marked exit for Mazatlán centro. Eventually you'll see a big Ley store on your left, the **North Entrance Junction** is 2.2 miles (3.5 km) after the Ley store and goes to your left. If you pass Pemex #1766 on the left you've gone too far.

Zero your odometer at the North Entrance Junction. Drive south on a wide boulevard, in .7 mile (1.1 km) it will rise and cross some railroad tracks. Just at the bottom of the descent after the railroad tracks there is a confusing sign pointing right which appears to indicate that the first cross street goes to Zona Hotelera, don't take this right. Take the next major right, your odometer will read 1.1 miles (1.8 km). You are now on Calz. Rafael Buelna and will pass many businesses including a huge Pemex on the right, a bullring, and a Gigante supermarket, also on the right. The road T's at the beach at 3 miles (4.8 km) on your odometer . This T is really a glorieta and is called Camarón Circle. Directions to all Mazatlán campgrounds from Cameron Circle are given below in the individual campground descriptions.

Mazatlán Campgrounds

TRAILER PARK LA POSTA

Address: Rafael Buelna No. 7, Mazatlán, Sinaloa, México
Telephone: (6) 983-5310 **Fax:** (6) 985-1485
E-mail: topshoes@mzt.megared.net.mx

GPS Location: N 23° 14' 26.3", W 106° 26' 37.6"

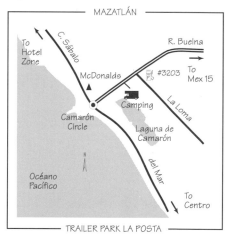

The La Posta is one of the largest trailer parks in Mazatlán and probably the easiest to find. It is also conveniently close to the Zona Dorada restaurants and shops.

This trailer park has 180 camping spaces, all have electricity with 15-amp outlets, sewer, and water. The use of air conditioners is prohibited. Most slots have patios, there is some shade. Restrooms are older but well-maintained and have hot water showers, there is a swimming pool. Grocery shopping is convenient with a Gigante, a Sam's Club and a Comercial Mexicana within walking distance.

This is the only campground in town that is not north of Camarón Circle. As you approach the circle from the east you will see La Posta on your left about a half block after Pemex #3203 but you cannot enter because you are on a divided street. Instead go on to Camarón Circle, pass all the way around, and then drive .1 miles (.2 km) back in the direction you came from and turn right into the campground. Some people with large rigs like to turn left on La Loma just after the Pemex and before the campground and go around the large block clockwise to enter the campground. This way they don't have to go around the fairly tight turn at Camarón Circle towing the car. For those using the northern playas entrance to town it is 6.7 miles (10.8 km) from the Mazatlán Playas Junction to Camarón Circle.

🚐 LAS PALMAS TRAILER PARK

Address: Ave. Camarón Sábalo 333 (Apdo.
                 1032), Mazatlán, CP 82110 Sinaloa,
                 México
Telephone: (6) 913-5311

GPS Location: N 23° 14' 40.1", W 106° 27' 07.0"

MAZATLÁN

LAS PALMAS TRAILER PARK

Las Palmas is a pretty well hidden Mazatlán campground. It is an older facility but still very popular because it is conveniently located right in the Zona Dorada. You may meet old timers here who have been coming here since before the Zona Dorada was even built.

The Las Palmas has about 70 spaces. They are in a palm grove behind a building just east of the main road through the Zona Dorada. Each slot has a15-amp outlet, sewer, water and a patio. Bathrooms are old but have hot water for showers and there is a swimming pool and meeting/banquet room

The entrance to the campground is easy to miss. It is marked only by a small circular yellow sign mounted high on a telephone pole. From Camarón Circle drive .6 miles (1 km) north, the entrance is on the right across from the Guadalajara Grill. Do not try to approach this campground from the north when you arrive, you can not turn in from southbound lanes and you'll have to go south to Camarón Circle to turn around.

🚐 MAR ROSA TRAILER PARK

Address: Av. Camarón Sábalo 702 (Apdo. 4
                 35 Playas del Sábalo), Mazatlán,
                 Sinaloa, México
Telephone: (6) 913-6187   **Fax:** (6) 913-6187
E-mail: www.mar-rosa@pacificpearl.com

$$$ *(back)* $$$ *(middle)* $$ *(front)*

GPS Location: N 23° 15' 24.6", W 106° 27' 36.9"

The Mar Rosa is the only trailer park in Mazatlán with sites right along the beach. It also has a convenient location within walking distance of the Zona Dorada. Site prices here are based upon your distance from the water, this is a very popular campground.

The campground has about 70 back-in spaces off sandy driveways. All sites have electricity (15 or 30-amp outlets), water, and sewer. Some sites have TV hookups. Bathrooms are modern and clean and have hot water. A central building houses a self-service laundry. The campground is fully fenced including a wire fence in the front along the beach. There are some additional sites located across the boulevard.

The Mar Rosa is 1.6 miles (2.6 km) north of Camarón Circle on the left, it is just past the Holiday Inn when you are traveling northward. You can easily turn into the campground from north or southbound lanes. For those using the northern playas entrance to town it is 5.1 miles (8.2 km) from the Mazatlán Playas Junction to the Mar Rosa.

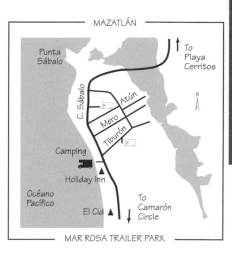

🚐 SAN FERNANDO RV PARK

Address: Av. Tiburón S/N, Fracc. Sábalo Country, Mazatlán, Sinaloa, México
Telephone: (6) 914-0173   **Fax:** (6) 914-0325

GPS Location: N 23° 15' 32.8", W 106° 27' 33.1"

$$$ *(small)* $ $$$ *(med)* $$ $$$ *(double)*

This is the newest of the Mazatlán campgrounds. It is conveniently located near the Zona Dorada and very popular. The beach is a short walk away and there is also a beautiful little swimming pool.

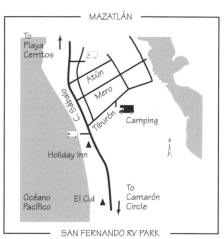

The campground has 65 back-in spaces. They all have electricity (15 and 30-amp outlets), water, and sewer hookups. The sites here are artfully packed into a pretty small area, individual gates to some of the outside spots are a unique way to do this. There is a swimming pool, a self-service laundry, a hot tub, cable TV, and internet access is promised for next year. Prices vary depending upon size of site.

The San Fernando is about a block inland from the Mar Rosa Trailer Park. Drive 1.6 miles (2.6 km) north of Camarón Circle, you will see the Mar Rosa on the left. Turn right at the next road, Av. Tiburón, and you will soon see the San Fernando on the right. For those using the northern playas entrance to town it is 5.1 miles (8.2 km) from the Mazatlán Playas Junction to the turn onto Av. Tiburón.

SAN BARTOLO TRAILER PARK

Address: Box 1388, Mazatlán, CP 82000
Sinaloa, México
Telephone: (6) 913-5755 **Fax:** (6) 913-5755

GPS Location: N 23° 15' 43.0", W 106° 27' 50.5"

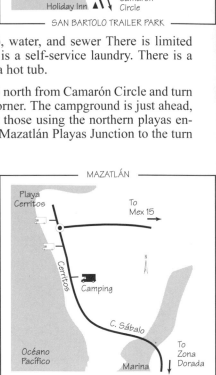

SAN BARTOLO TRAILER PARK

The San Bartolo is unusual in that it is located back away from the main north-south Camarón Sábalo in a quiet residential area. It is also south of the new El Cid marina development so access to the Zona Dorada is much better than the two campgrounds located farther north.

The campground has 47 spaces arranged in a long triangle-shaped fenced lot. All are back-in spaces and have electricity (30-amp outlets), water, and sewer There is limited shade. The restrooms are very clean and there is a self-service laundry. There is a small palapa-style meeting or lounge area with a hot tub.

To find the campground drive 2.1 miles (3.4 km) north from Camarón Circle and turn right on Calamar. There is a good sign on the corner. The campground is just ahead, one block from Camarón Sábalo on Pulpo. For those using the northern playas entrance to town it is 4.7 miles (7.6 km) from the Mazatlán Playas Junction to the turn onto Calamar.

TRAILER PARK HOLIDAY AND BUNGALOWS PLAYA ESCONDIDA

Address: Av. Sábalo-Cerritos No. 999 (Apdo. 682), Mazatlán, Sinaloa, México
Telephone: (6) 988-0077 **Fax:** (6) 982-2255

GPS Location: N 23° 17' 10.4", W 106° 28' 14.8"

The huge Playa Escondida trailer park is far north of the Zona Dorada and is very large. There is generally room here if the other Mazatlán campgrounds are full.

The campground has 236 spaces, all with electricity (15-amp style outlets), sewer, water, and patios. It is in a mature palm grove so there is quite a bit of shade. This large campground fronts on the beach and stretches far inland on the east side of Cerritos, the boulevard that is the northern extension of Camarón Sábalo. All camping is on the east side of the road, the water side is occupied by a few bungalows and many older but unused campsites. Bathrooms here are old but have hot water, there is a big pool, tennis courts, and a small meeting room. Campers here often complain that maintenance could be better. Some caravans stay at the back of the park in an area that seems to

THE NORTHERN WEST COAST

receive a little better maintenance.

Find the Playa Escondida by driving north from Camarón Circle. The road now circles far inland across two large bridges before coming back to the beach strip. The campground is 5.4 miles (8.7 km) north of Camarón Circle with the entrance on the right. For those using the northern playas entrance to town it is 1.2 miles (1.9 km) from the Mazatlán Playas Junction to Playa Escondida.

 **MAR-A-VILLAS RV PARK**

| Address: | Alfredo Tirado, Apdo. 1470 Playa de Sábalo-Cerritos, Mazatlán, Sinaloa, México |

GPS Location: N 23° 17' 50.1", W 106° 28' 49.1"

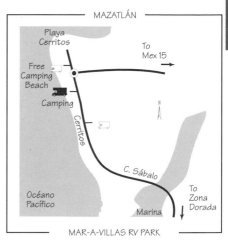

The Mar-a-Villas is a not-so-well-kept secret in Mazatlán. It is located far north next to the beach, you'll almost forget that you are in Mazatlán at all.

This is a small campground. There are about 30 back-in spaces near the beach with limited room for maneuvering (although 40 footers sometimes find room) and 9 new easier to enter back-in slots near the road. Each site has a 15-amp outlet, water, and sewer hookups. The lower area has more shade. The bathroom cubicles have a toilet and hot showers and each camper is given a key. There is a building between the beach and the campground with the owner's residence and a meeting room. Out front is a beautiful beach. Busses run frequently in to town so the isolated location is really no hardship. Only basic English is spoken by the owner but the campers here do a pretty good job of taking care of business. Reservations would be nice but are difficult to make unless you are actually at the trailer park and want to make them for the next season.

The Mar-a-Villas is located 6.4 miles (10.3 km) north of Camarón Circle. If you are coming from the south you will need to go on to a retorno and come back, no problem since there is virtually no traffic this far north. Park on the boulevard outside and walk in to make sure there is room if you have a big rig because turning around inside the campground will be tough, particularly if you are towing. For those using the northern playas entrance to town it is .3 miles (.5 km) from the Mazatlán Playas Junction to Mar-a-Villas.

Other Camping Possibilities

Free-camping RVers will find a popular location at the beach just north of the Mar-a-Villas RV park. Water vendors make this place a regular stop, there's a place to dump your holding tanks into the city sewer system, bus service to central Mazatlán runs nearby, and there is security in numbers. Many people use this place, and the local police usually do not seem to mind.

The Point South Mazatlán Trailer Park listed in the previous edition of this guide is now closed.

THE NORTHERN WEST COAST

NAVOJOA, SONORA (NAH-VO-HOH-AH)
Population 85,000, Elevation 125 ft (38 m)

Navojoa is the largest Mayo Indian center. It is located right on Mex 15, the road to Alamos runs east from the city. It is the hub of an agricultural region and is known for several Mayo celebration days including the **feast of St. John the Baptist** on June 24, **Day of the Dead** on Nov. 1 and 2, and the **Feast of Our Lady of Guadalupe**. These are celebrated in the barrio (neighborhood) of **Pueblo Viejo**. The surrounding region is popular for dove, deer and duck hunting and the town is a good place to buy Mayo crafts including baskets and masks. Navojoa has supermarkets, service stations, and banks.

Navojoa Campground

🚐 ALAMEDA TRAILER PARK

Address: Pesqueira Prolongacion Norte S/N,
            Colonia Los Naranjos, Navojoa,
            Sonora, México
Telephone: (6) 421-5202 and (6) 421-5203

GPS Location: N 27° 06' 02.2", W 109° 26' 54.4"

[$$] [⛺] [🦩] [🚰] [🚐] [🚿 HOT]

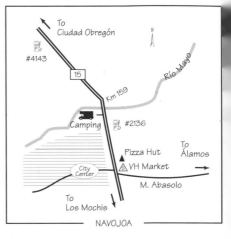

If you find yourself near Navojoa when darkness falls and turn into the Alameda TP you'll usually find a hard core of norteamericanos hidden beneath the trees in this campground. They've been coming here for years, primarily for the bird hunting.

The Alameda has about 80 spaces. Last time we visited only about 30 at the back of the campground were usable, the ones nearest the road were filled with the equipment of a construction company that works out of the campground. The pull-through spaces have electricity (15-amp outlets with various breakers), sewer and water hookups in poor repair. All of the slots have patios and there is lots of shade. The restrooms are old, dirty and poorly maintained but did have hot-water showers.

The campground is located just south of the Río Mayo Puente (bridge) on the west side of the road. As you approach Navojoa from the north you will cross the bridge as you enter town, turn right at the first road after the bridge and then almost immediately turn right into the campground entrance. There will probably be no sign at all. If there is no one at the entrance office building just drive on in and to the left, you'll probably find several rigs in the back and the watchman will find you to collect.

TEACAPÁN, SINALOA (TEE-ACK-AH-PAN)
Population 1,000, Elevation sea level

Teacapán is little more than a fishing village set at the end of a long peninsula that serves to enclose a virtually land-locked mangrove-lined **estuary**. The lagoon abounds in fish and bird life. You can rent a panga and guide in the village for birding, fishing, and crocodile watching. Kayaking is also excellent. On the outside of the peninsula is a long, empty **beach**. Dolphins are often seen near the estuary mouth. Teacapán has little in the way of services other than a restaurant or two and a few small grocery stores. There is a large supermarket in Escuinapa, about 23 miles (37 km) from Teacapán.

The old Pemex has been shut down and there was a new one under construction next door when we visited, we call this the new Pemex in our campground descriptions, it makes a good marker to use in telling how to find the campgrounds. However, big rigs will find it inconvenient to turn around in Teacapán after they reach the Pemex so we also use Rancho Los Angeles, 8.4 miles (13.5 km) outside of Teacapán and 15.1 miles (34.3 km) from Pemex #5274 just west of Escuinapa, as a marker.

Teacapán Campgrounds

RANCHO LOS ANGELES

Address:	Calle Gabriel Leyua No. 12, Escuinapa, CP 82400 Sinaloa, México
Telephone:	(6) 953-1609 (Escuinapa), (6) 956-6530 (Teacapán)
E-mail:	ernestotrivera@yahoo.com

GPS Location: N 22° 38' 45.4", W 105° 48' 52.5"

This is Teacapán's most popular campground. Rancho Los Angeles is about 8 miles (13 km) north of town, the first campground you reach, and has a large number of fully serviced sites overlooking the beach.

There are 40 full-hookup (15-amp outlets) sites installed along the beach fronting the sand. Another 20 pull-through sites are located on sometimes soft sand (beware) just inland. The restroom has flush toilets and hot showers, a self-service washing machine is available. The campground is about a mile from the road, you enter and drive through a cluster of ranch buildings and then follow a small road (the one on the far right) through a coconut palm plantation to the beach. A hacienda-style building with pool and restaurant is located just to the south, campers have full access to it.

The campground has a good sign on the main road from Teacapán. You will see it on the right 15.2 miles (24.5 km) after you cross the railroad tracks when leaving Escuinapa, it is 8.2 miles (13.2 km) from the Pemex on the outskirts of Teacapán.

LA TAMBORA

GPS Location: N 22° 33' 29.9", W 105° 45' 53.7"

There is an old RV park located at Playa La Tambora north of Teacapán. Surprisingly, in view of the hookups and price, there is seldom more than a rig or two parked here.

The camping area has 24 islands containing hookups for electricity (15-amp outlets), water, and sewer. If the place were full there would be two rigs parked alongside each of these islands for a total of 48 spaces, but usually the rig or two occupying the campground park haphazardly along the front. There should be plenty of room for the largest rigs. The restrooms are basic and not very clean, but they have flush toilets and hot showers. Next door is a palapa restaurant which is reported to be pretty good. The manager of the campground may not be around when you arrive but he will probably show up to collect the fee before you leave, perhaps in the morning.

The turnoff for La Tambora is signed and located 7.1 miles (11.5 km) on the far side of Rancho Los Angeles. It is 1.4 miles (2.3 km) north of the new Pemex at the entrance to Teacapán. Turn west toward the beach and follow the straight paved but badly potholed road for 1.3 miles (2.1 km). When you reach the beach turn sharply right and drive past the palapa restaurant to the campground.

☷ TRAILER PARK OREGON

Address: Domicilio Conocido, Colonia Centro,
Teacapán, CP 82560 Sinaloa, México
Telephone: (6) 954-5308

GPS Location: N 22° 32' 24.9", W 105° 44' 29.3"

The Trailer Park Oregon is located on a back street in the village of Teacapan. This is the place to stay if you want to walk to local restaurants or stroll around town in the evening.

The campground is a grassy lot with ten slots, all have patios and connections for electricity, water, and sewer. Electric outlets are 15-amp, there is room for the largest rigs. The park is fenced but gates are not closed at night, there isn't much concern in Teacapán about big city crime problems. The restrooms are basic but have flush toilets, showers are cold. The manager's house adjoins the campground and she speaks

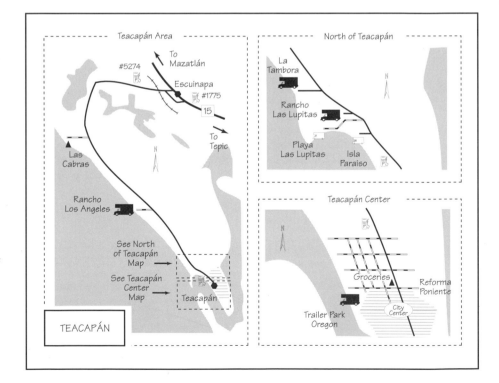

some English and is quite helpful.

From the Pemex at the entrance to town drive toward the center. In .3 mile (.5 km) at the fourth small dirt street (Calle Reforma Poniente) turn right and drive toward the water. In .2 mile (.3 km), just before you reach the water you will see the campground on your left. The roads in town are rough cobblestones and uneven dirt with puddles but passable for all rigs.

RANCHO LAS LUPITAS TRAILER PARK

Address: Teacapán, Sinaloa, México

GPS Location: N 22° 33' 23.0", W 105° 44' 40.8"

Just before you reach Teacapán you will see a small group of buildings on the right and perhaps a few RV's. This is Rancho Las Lupitas Trailer Park. There are 10 spaces with electricity (15-amp outlets), water, sewer, patios and some shade. Most of these are pull-through slots and not all had serviceable hookups last time we visited. The one restroom is clean and has a hot water shower. The owner speaks English and provides guided boat trips on the nearby estuaries for fishing and birding

From the new Pemex at the entrance to Teacapán drive north away from town for .9 mile (1.5 km). The campground is on the left. Coming from Escuinapa the entrance is 7.6 miles (12.3 km) after the entrance to Rancho Los Angeles.

Other Camping Possibilities

Playa Las Lupitas is a popular boondocking location (actually the nightly fee is $5) just north of Teacapan. A sandy road winds back to a cleared area along the north shore of the estuary mouth. There are few services although a dump station has been installed. Water is not available. From the new Pemex station at the entrance to Teacapán drive north away from town for .7 mile (1.1 km) and turn left down the dirt road toward the beach. You will drive through fields, turn inland to wind through trees, then come to a rope gate where a fee is collected. The road has ruts and dips but you'll usually find that large fifth-wheels have made it to the beach. The GPS location is N 22° 33' 07.5", W 105° 45' 06.6".

Isla Paraiso, a new housing development just outside Teacapán, was letting a few rigs park along the estuary mouth the last time we visited. This situation may or may not be permanent, it's hard to tell. Some electricity was available and there was a place to dump. The entrance is located .4 miles (.6 km) north of the new Pemex at the entrance to Teacapán. The GPS location is N 22° 32' 53.2", W 105° 44' 41.5".

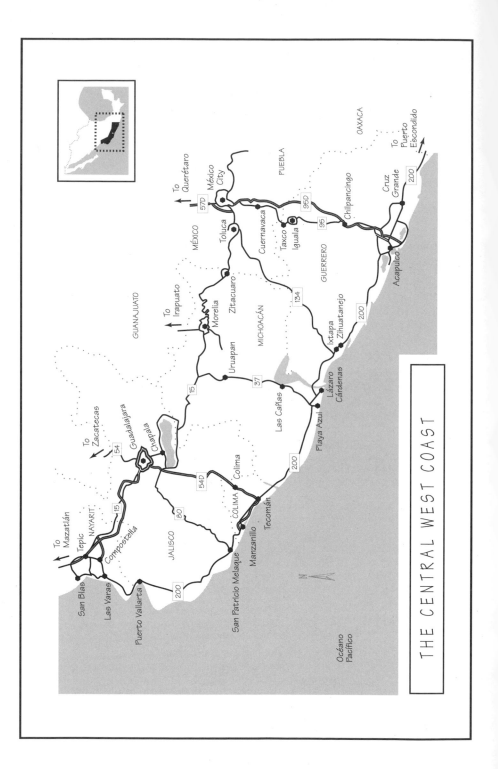

THE CENTRAL WEST COAST

THE CENTRAL WEST COAST: SAN BLAS TO ACAPULCO

INTRODUCTION

In this guide we've broken the very popular Mexican west coast into three parts. The section from the U.S. border to Mazatlán (actually just south of Mazatlán at Teacapán) is in Chapter 5. This chapter covers the section south of San Blas, the part of the coast south of the point where the four-lane Mex 15 heads inland to Guadalajara and the narrow two-lane Mex 200 takes over. Finally, Chapter 9, Chiapas and Oaxaca covers the far south.

The attractions of this part of Mexico are obvious: miles of empty beaches, months of terrific weather, some of Mexico's most famous resorts, great fishing, and dozens of excellent ocean-side RV parks filled with friendly people. The west coast isn't heavy on cultural attractions, don't expect much in the way of cathedrals or archeological sites.

The easiest access to this part of the coast is not necessarily down the west coast from Nogales. The distance down the coast from Nogales to Puerta Vallarta is about 1,000 miles (1,600 km), from Matamoros across central Mexico the distance is about 875 miles (1,400 km). Driving distance from the border to Acapulco is about 1,600 miles (2,580 km) along the coast, but across central Mexico from Matamoros and through Mexico City it is 975 miles (1,575 km). Even if you wisely opt to make a lengthy bypass of Mexico City this route is clearly quicker and easier than the coastal route.

Your sense of direction may play you false on this coast. From Puerto Vallarta to the south the coast bends eastwards and is actually running northwest - southeast. The Sierra Madre Occidental (Western Sierra Madre) back the coast at varying distances. Where they are near the ocean there are rocky headlands and smaller (but still long by most standards) beaches, where the mountains retreat there are marshes, lagoons, and long sandy beaches.

As you travel south you will find that by the time your reach San Blas you are definitely into the tropical region of Mexico. Although there are some dry areas there are also many sections that are jungle-like. Even during the winter the weather can be quite hot, especially farther south near Manzanillo. The ocean is definitely warm enough for swimming.

ROAD SYSTEM

It would be hard to get lost in this area of Mexico. There is really just one major highway, Mex 200. For the most part it is a two-lane road. The quality of the surface changes from year to year and section to section. Most of it is narrow and you shouldn't expect to average more than 35 miles an hour (55 km per hour) or so when traveling on it.

In the north, near Tepic, Mex 200 begins in the mountains. The grades are steep and there are many trucks. Fortunately it is now possible to bypass this section. There is a quiet little road out to the coast near San Blas, then south to an intersection in Las Varas. Most RVers now use this road as they travel north and south along the coast.

Toll roads are scarce. Along the coast there is only one, a 45 mile (73 km) stretch running from north of Manzanillo southeast to Tecomán. The road is nice but hardly necessary, the free road running just inland is not bad. Other toll roads connect the coast with inland destinations. The most famous is Mexico's first major toll road, the one running from Acapulco to Mexico City. This is a very impressive but expensive road, the tolls are outrageous. We've traveled the free road, which runs along almost the same route but passes through Taxco, in a large motorhome with tow car with no problems. Another toll road runs inland from Tecomán through Colima to the Guadalajara area, this road is recommended over the poor free road. A third connects Tepic with Guadalajara. This road also has a short section west of Tepic that makes the climb on Mex 15 from the San Blas cutoff into Tepic much easier than it was in the past. This Tepic to Guadalajara road is another expensive one, but the free road along here is poor, full of trucks, and slow. It is one toll road that we recommend. A short section of two-lane toll road connects the larger Tepic to Guadalajara road with Mex 200 at Compostela allowing traffic from Guadalajara to Puerto Vallarta to bypass Tepic. This is a less expensive toll road and is also recommended.

There are several smaller roads running north into the highlands from the coast. Two of these roads, Mex 80 and Mex 37, while narrow and full of curves, are used by travelers with large RVs. The trick is to take it slow and give yourself plenty of time. Many people bound for this southern coast travel through the interior of Mexico to get here and use these small roads to filter down to the ocean.

HIGHLIGHTS

The resort cities and beautiful waters and beaches of this coast are its highlights. In the far south is the queen of Mexican resorts, **Acapulco**. In recent years the popularity of Acapulco has dimmed and resorts farther north have taken over. First among these was and still is **Puerto Vallarta**. Newer and not nearly as popular among RVers is **Ixtapa/Zihuatanejo**. Manzanillo, despite the movie *10*, is more supply center and commercial port than resort, and little **Playa Azul** isn't known to airline tourists at all. All of these places, with the possible exception of Ixtapa/Zihuatanejo, make excellent destinations for campers and RVers. They have good campgrounds and lots of attractions to keep you just as busy as you want to be.

THE CENTRAL WEST COAST

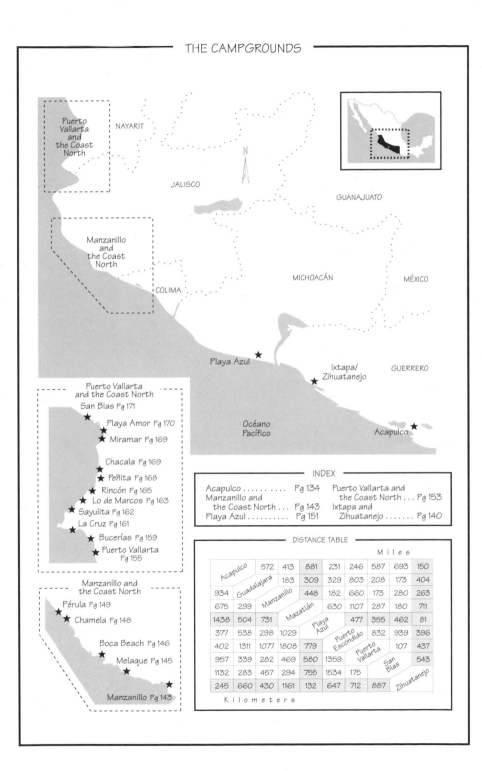

THE CAMPGROUNDS

Puerto Vallarta and the Coast North

NAYARIT

JALISCO

GUANAJUATO

Manzanillo and the Coast North

COLIMA

MICHOACÁN

MÉXICO

Playa Azul ★

Ixtapa/ Zihuatanejo ★   GUERRERO

Océano Pacífico

Acapulco ★

Puerto Vallarta and the Coast North

★ San Blas Pg 171
★ Playa Amor Pg 170
★ Miramar Pg 169
★ Chacala Pg 169
★ Peñita Pg 168
★ Rincón Pg 165
★ Lo de Marcos Pg 163
★ Sayulita Pg 162
★ La Cruz Pg 161
★ Bucerías Pg 159
★ Puerto Vallarta Pg 155

Manzanillo and the Coast North

★ Pérula Pg 149
★ Chamela Pg 148
★ Boca Beach Pg 146
★ Melaque Pg 145
★ Manzanillo Pg 143

INDEX

DISTANCE TABLE

Miles

Acapulco	572	413	881	231	246	587	693	150
	Guadalajara	183	309	329	803	208	173	404
934		Manzanillo	448	182	660	173	280	263
675	299		Mazatlán	630	1107	287	180	711
1438	504	731		Playa Azul	477	355	462	81
377	538	298	1029		Puerto Escondido	832	939	396
402	1311	1077	1808	779		Puerto Vallarta	107	437
957	339	282	469	580	1359		San Blas	543
1132	283	457	294	755	1534	175		Zihuatanejo
245	660	430	1161	132	647	712	887	

Kilometers

In addition to the well-known resorts there are many quiet little villages with great beaches and swaying palms. Some have RV campgrounds with reasonable facilities. Those along the coasts north of Manzanillo and Puerto Vallarta come to mind. Others offer a palapa restaurant or less, you can make camping arrangements with whomever seems to be in charge. Often the deal involves eating a few excellent meals in a nearby restaurant.

SELECTED CITIES AND THEIR CAMPGROUNDS

ACAPULCO, GUERRERO (AH-KAH-POOL-KO)
Population 1,000,000, Elevation sea level

Everyone wants to visit Acapulco. It is the largest, oldest, and most famous of Mexico's resorts. Acapulco wasn't built from virtual scratch in recent years like the FONATUR resorts of Cancún, Ixtapa, Cabo San Lucas, and Bahías de Huatulco. It has quite a bit of history and is even a bit seedy in places, but Acapulco is one of the world's great resort cities with beautiful beaches, lots of shops and restaurants, and lots to do. Essentials stops on your tourist agenda are few, you'll probably want to see the **La Quebrada cliff divers** and visit the beaches and restaurants. A short driving tour to Puerto Marqués gives a great view of the bay and city.

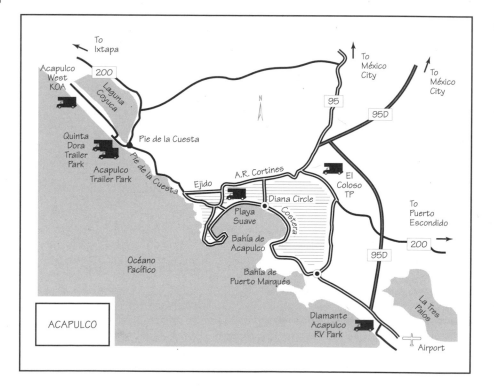

THE CENTRAL WEST COAST

Acapulco is also much more RV-friendly than many Mexican resorts. There are quite a few RV parks here, some in excellent locations. Shopping for essentials is easy, all the large Mexican supermarket chains are present, so are Wal-Mart and Costco.

Driving around Acapulco is not bad if you have a small vehicle. Roads aren't narrow, but traffic is heavy with lots of taxis so you have to be alert. Bringing an RV through town is possible but not advisable unless you are headed for the Playa Suave campground, you can pass around most of Acapulco pretty easily by using outer roads that serve as a bypass.

Acapulco Campgrounds

🚐 **ACAPULCO TRAILER PARK** | $$ | *(back)* | $$$ | *(middle)* | $ $$$ | *(front)*

Address: Playa Pie de la Cuesta (Apdo #1),
            Acapulco, CP 39300 Guerrero, México
Telephone: (7) 460-0010   **Fax**: (7) 460-2457
E-mail: acapulcotrailerpark@hotmail.com.mx

GPS Location: N 16° 54' 12.4", W 099° 58' 31.6"

Among traveling campers there is no question that Acapulco Trailer Park is the favorite campground for a short stay in Acapulco. The reason is that if you arrive in Acapulco from the northwest or north you never have to enter Acapulco at all with your own rig. This campground is located in Pie de la Cuesta which is on the beach about 5 miles (8 km) northwest of Acapulco.

The Acapulco has 48 spaces on the ocean side and 12 spaces on the lagoon side. They are arranged under coconut palms on packed sand. All have 15-amp outlets, water, and sewer service. Big rigs can maneuver in this campground with little problem. The park is fenced and the gate is kept closed, there is a small grocery store at the entrance that is also the camp office. Some of the sites can be used as pull-throughs if the park is not full. The restrooms have cold showers but are otherwise just fine. There is also a swimming pool. On the lagoon side there is boat ramp and a small beach for swimming. Some English is spoken.

The beach in front of Pie de la Cuesta is famous for its sunsets. It is really a beautiful place. Unfortunately it is not a good place to swim, the surf is so powerful here that swimming is dangerous. If you park at the front of the park along the beach the crash of the waves may actually shake your rig. This is not unpleasant, it just reminds you to stay out of the water. The lagoon side is a better place to swim, it is also popular for water skiing.

The somewhat remote location of the campground is not much of a problem. There are many restaurants in Pie de la Cuesta and access to Acapulco is easy by bus or taxi.

About 5 miles (8 km) outside Acapulco on Mex 200 you will see signs pointing toward the water for Pie de la Cuesta and Base Area Militar (there is a Mexican Air Force base past the campground). The road passes under an orange arch. The campground is on your left 1.0 mile (1.6 km) down this road.

🚐 **QUINTA DORA TRAILER PARK**

Address: Playa Pie de la Cuesta (Apdo. 1093),
            Acapulco, CP 39300 Guerrero, México
Telephone: (7) 460-1138 or (7) 460-0600

GPS Location: N 16° 54' 15.7", W 099° 58' 37.0"

When you find the Acapulco Trailer Park you've also found the Quinta Dora. It is located about 100 yards (or meters) past the Acapulco. It also is on both sides of the road with a big sign.

The main part of this campground is on the lagoon side of the road. It's cute as a bug and well-fenced. Only van-sized rigs will fit. There is room for 16 rigs, 8 sites have full hookups (15-amp outlets), 8 more lack sewer. There are restrooms with cold water showers. There is a small beach for swimming in the lagoon.

On the ocean side of the park the campground is very ragged. Storm damage is evident and there are about four large sites for camping, only a couple have working electrical outlets and sewer drains. There is no fence around this portion of the campground and no security.

ACAPULCO WEST KOA

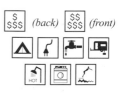

Address:	Carr. Pie de la Cuesta-Barra de Coyuca Km 4 (Apdo. 4-80), Acapulco, CP 39580 Guerrero, México
Telephone:	(7) 444-4062 **Fax:** (7) 483-2281
E-mail:	koaca@acabtu.com.mx

GPS Location: N 16° 55' 13.7", W 100° 00' 44.5"

The campground is located along the beach much farther west than the Pie de la Cuesta campgrounds. There are a variety of site types here. In front along the beach are 5 pull-in sites with palapas, patios, and palapa shades. Behind them are another 5

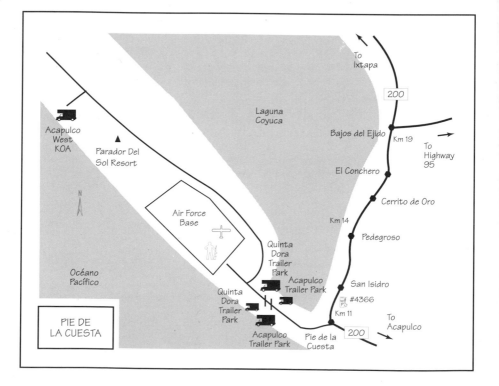

back-in spaces. At the rear of the park are 43 back-in full-hookup sites with shade. You'll find both 15 and 30-amp outlets at this campground, there is lots of room for large rigs to park. Between the front and rear sites are many small sites on sand with electricity and water. Some also have sewer. These sites have no shade and are probably only used during Mexican holiday periods when everyone in Mexico seems to come to the beach. The restrooms have hot water showers, there is a swimming pool and water slide, and a children's play area with wading pool. In addition there are miles of beach just out front. Limited English is spoken.

The campground is located on the same road as the Acapulco and Quinta Dora Trailer Parks, just much farther out. From the intersection where the Pie de la Cuesta road leaves Mex 200 drive 1.25 miles (2 km) and turn right (the Air Force base gates are straight), drive around the end of the airport and you will see the familiar KOA sign on the left at 3.9 miles (6.2 km). There is bus service into Acapulco from in front of the campground.

🚐 PLAYA SUAVE

Address: Av. Costera Miguel Alemán No. 276 (Apdo. 165), Acapulco, Guerrero, México

Telehone: (7) 485-1464 or (7) 485-0572 or (7) 485-1885

GPS Location: N 16° 51' 23.5", W 099° 53' 50.3"

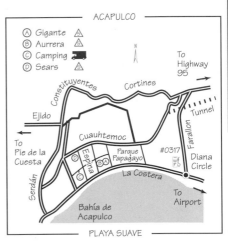

The Playa Suave is the only campground in Acapulco that is within convenient walking distance of the tourist strip on Costera Miguel Alemán and of the beach. Probably everyone would stay here if they could just find it.

The Playa Suave has 38 sites, all with 15-amp outlets, water, and sewer. Each site also has its own toilet and cold shower in a private little building. All sites are paved with patio areas, palm trees provide quite a bit of shade. This campground was built during the days of smaller rigs, now giant fifth-wheels with pull-outs fill the place, their maneuvers when entering and leaving can be quite entertaining for onlookers and frustrating for the owners. Big rigs will only find this worthwhile if they plan to stay for a long period. The area is fenced and the gate is kept closed. There is 24 hour security, if the gatekeeper isn't at the gate you can be sure he's close by. If you walk out the front door you are right on La Costera, cross the street and you are on the beach. One more benefit is that you can conveniently walk to a Comercial Mexicana, a Bodega A, a Sears, or a Gigante. All are just down the street. If you plan to make an extended stay here you should definitely make reservations. The manager is on-site during the day and speaks English.

Here's how find the campground. There are many ways to get down to the main coastal boulevard along the beach which is called La Costera. We like to approach from the east in the direction of the airport thereby avoiding driving complicated routes through heavy traffic. Zero your odometer at the Diana statue in Diana Circle at the corner of La Costera Miguel Alemán and Paseo del Farallon. This is a large glorieta so you can reach it from either the east or west and get turned so that you are facing west. You can identify Diana Circle by Pemex #0317 which is located next to it. Drive west along La Costera and the beach. At 1.3 miles (2.1 km) you will see a Gigante Bodega on the right, soon after that you will see a Bodega Aurrera. These will tell you that you are getting close, slow down. Although the trailer park address is on Miguel Alemán the park really fronts on the next street north, Vasco Nuñez de Balboa. You must turn right at the streetlight at 1.65 miles (2.6 km) on Capitán Mala Espina or one of the streets on either side. A restaurant on the beach side, the Tropicana, makes a good landmark. Drive one block up Mala Espina, turn left, and you will see the Playa Suave about halfway down the block on your left. Vasco Nuñez de Balboa is a wide, quiet street. Take your time looking and you will see the park even if you haven't taken exactly the right street off La Costera. The street address is Costera Miguel Alemán No. 276 (just in case you still have to hire a cab to lead you to it.)

⛟ TRAILER PARK EL COLOSO

Address:	Blvd. Lázaro Cárdenas Km 2.5, La Sabana, Acapulco, Guerrero, México
Telephone:	(7) 450-0067

GPS Location: N 16° 52' 38.6", W 099° 49' 05.2"

TRAILER PARK EL COLOSO

This is the most convenient place to stay if you are coming in to town from the east, up Mex 200 from the Puerto Escondido area. The huge suburban campground is well run and has good facilities, unfortunately it has no beach and is located somewhat out of the way. Nonetheless, it has some faithful long-termers who think it is an excellent place to spend the winter and there is a swimming pool. Monthly discount rates are available.

This trailer park is a large grassy area with trees for shade. It has about 75 large spaces with 15-amp outlets, water, and sewer. A wall surrounds the entire trailer park and there is a gate for security. There are two sets of clean restrooms with hot showers. There is also a swimming pool with a big water slide. The campground has a restaurant (with a dance floor) and there is a small grocery store out front. Limited English is spoken.

Busses pass right in front of the campground so transportation to downtown Acapulco or much nearer shopping is not a problem.

Coming from Cuernavaca or from Acapulco zero your odometer at the intersection where Mex 200 from the east meets Mex 95 going in to Acapulco from Cuernavaca. Drive east on Mex 200. The El Coloso will be on your left at 1.6 miles (2.6 km).

Coming from the Puerto Escondido direction on Mex 200 zero your odometer as you pass the cutoff for Bahía Puerto Marqués and Aeropuerto. The El Coloso is on your right at 1.3 miles (2.1 km).

DIAMANTE ACAPULCO RV PARK

Address: Avenida Copacabana 8, Colonia La
                Posa, Acapulco, Guerrero, México
Telephone: (7) 466-0200

GPS Location: N 16° 47' 01.2", W 099° 47' 45.1"

This is a nice park with the right price, unfortunately it is not near the beach or downtown. It is operated by the same folks who operate the Diamante in Cuernavaca. If you can reconcile yourself to the location you will probably like it here. It would be a comfortable and inexpensive place to spend some time. There are more long-term residents here than at the other trailer parks in town and the last time we visited the place was in excellent condition. Note that the campground is only open from November 15 to April 15.

The entrance road runs about .5 miles (.8 km) back into a large coconut palm grove where the park is located. It is a very large fenced area with room for lots of rigs of any

THE MOON RISING OVER DOWNTOWN ACAPULCO

THE CENTRAL WEST COAST

size. There are about 75 back-in spaces with electricity (both 15 and 30-amp outlets), water, and sewer. There are lots more with no services. The park has restrooms and showers with hot water. There is also a nice swimming pool and a wading pool.

To find the trailer park zero your odometer near Bahía Puerto Marqués where the short road between Mex 200 and the airport road (Carretera al Coloso) meet. Drive east toward the airport. At .5 miles (.8 km) you will see a big Costco on the left. The entrance road to the trailer park is on the right just past the entrance to the Mexico City toll road at 2.1 miles (3.4 km). You may not see the sign at first, it is very large and located on a tall column.

Other Camping Possibilities

The Trailer Park la Roca, listed in our last edition, is now closed.

IXTAPA/ZIHUATANEJO, GUERRERO (EES-TAH-PAH/SEE-WAH-TAH-NEH-HOH)
Population 40,000, Elevation sea level

Zihuatanejo was here long before Ixtapa resort was built. It was originally a fishing village, but now it is definitely a tourist resort. There are small hotels and people staying in Ixtapa come over for a visit to the beaches or the restaurants.

From Mex 200 which runs through a new section of Zihuatanejo it is about 2 miles (3.3 km) on a divided boulevard to the center of the old part of Zihuatanejo. This is a nice road, you can tell that a lot of money was spent to upgrade the streets when tourism hit town. Once you reach the old town the streets are much smaller and you won't want to bring a large RV down here. Zihuatanejo has lots of restaurants and shopping, you can spend several enjoyable hours strolling around. The new section of Zihuatanejo has a large supermarket so supplies are readily available.

East of town is the Playa la Ropa area. This is where Zihuatanejo's few campgrounds are located. The instructions for finding the campgrounds will show you how to get there. This is a popular beach and the streets behind it are even more restricted than those in town.

Nearby Ixtapa is another of those FONATUR instant resorts, just like Cancún and Bahías de Huatulco. If you've seen both of those you'll understand when we tell you that Ixtapa is behind Cancún and ahead of Bahías de Huatulco on the development timeline. There are no campgrounds in Ixtapa but there was a boondocking area when we recently visited. See *Other Camping Possibilites* below for more information.

You can make a quick tour of Ixtapa in your RV by driving through. You'll probably be able to find a spot to park for a few hours if you want to look around.

Ixtapa/Zihuatanejo Campgrounds

🚐 CAMPING LOS CABAÑAS

| **Address:** | Playa la Ropa, Zihuatanejo, Guerrero, México |
| **Telephone:** | (7) 554-4718 |

GPS Location: N 17° 37' 55.7", W 101° 32' 44.6"

This is a very small campground with room for maybe 5 vans. Larger vehicles won't fit. It is located in the Playa la Ropa area.

Los Cabañas is very small, and very cute. It is a shaded dirt pad in a back yard. There are 15-amp electrical outlets and water is available. Several restrooms with flush toilets and cold water showers are attached to the back and side of the house adjoining the camping area. It is a cozy place to camp within a couple of short blocks of Playa la Ropa.

From Mex 200, the main road through the newer section of Zihuatanejo, you want to follow the road out toward the beach to old Zihuatanejo. It is a little difficult to identify this road the first time you see it. It is marked Centro and joins Mex 200 at a glorieta with a large orange and yellow modernistic sculpture in the middle. Be advised that the sculpture is almost hidden by trees. This glorieta is handy since you can stay on the center lanes (not the laterals) of Mex 200 until you reach it from either direction and then turn directly onto the four-lane divided road into old Zihuatanejo. Zero your odometer as you leave the glorieta and follow signs to the Zona Hotelera (Hotel Area). At .2 miles (.3 km) the road curves right, at .4 miles (.6 km) it curves left, at .5 miles (.8 km) it curves right again. At .7 miles (1.1 km) take the left turn for the Zona Hotelera. This actually takes you around the block so you are heading back the way you came. Now take a right turn at a Y at .8 miles (1.3 km). You will come to a traffic circle at 1.0 miles (1.6 km), continue straight here. Follow the road up a hill, take the right at 1.3 miles (2.1 km). Now the signs change to say Zona Hotelera la Ropa. The road curves to the right and left around a bluff and then down towards the Playa la Ropa area. At 2.0 miles (3.2 km) at the statue of the dolphins turn right and

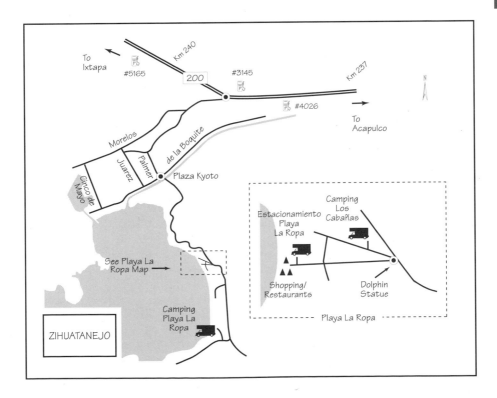

then take the far right fork of the streets ahead of you. Almost immediately you will see a sign for Los Cabañas and then see the campground on the right.

⛺ CAMPING PLAYA LA ROPA

Address: Playa la Ropa S/N, Zihuatanejo, Guerrero, México
Telephone: (7) 554-4967

GPS Location: N 17° 37' 33.6", W 101° 32' 40.9"

Campgrounds, particularly ones with hookups suitable to larger rigs, are scarce in this area. Recently some RVer who frequent the town convinced a local resident to put a few camping slots in his back yard. The result is Camping Playa la Ropa, Zihuataneho's best RV park for large rigs. The name given above is tentative, the owner hasn't really decided what to call this place.

The campground has eight back-in spaces with 15-amp outlets, sewer, and water hook-ups. There are presently no bathrooms so only self-contained rigs can stay here but restrooms are planned and under construction. Access for big rigs is excellent, there's a large gate at the back of the house. There are also some rental rooms under construction. The beach is a very short stroll away.

To reach the campground you follow the same route you would to Camping Los Cabañas. When you reach the dolphin fountain continue straight ahead and again zero your odometer. You'll come to a Y at .1 miles (.2 km), continue straight. At .6 miles (1 km) at another Y take the right and turn toward the beach. A third Y appears in another .1 mile (.2 km), go right here to reach the rear of the row of houses you see ahead. You will enter a large parking area, the campground entrance gate is ahead and to the left.

⛺ ESTACIONAMIENTO PLAYA LA ROPA

Address: Playa la Ropa S/N, Zihuatanejo, Guerrero, México

GPS Location: N 17° 37' 54.6", W 101° 32' 45.6"

This parking area, also known as "Temo's Place" has been here for a while. In former years it was the only place with hookups that was near the beach and could take larger rigs. The facilities are very basic and there is a lot of activity in this area but one or two RVers come back here year after year.

There is room for about 4 larger rigs to park in this lot, electricity is available from cords strung from a few outlets. Water is available and there is also a place to dump. A small restaurant run by the same people is nearby and the beach is a short walk away although it is not within sight of the campground. There are rustic flush toilets and cold showers available.

To reach the campground follow the directions for reaching Las Cabañas. When you reach the dolphin statue you want to turn right, but not into the road that you would take to Camping Los Cabañas. Instead you want the next one to the left. You might want to park and walk the short distance down this road to the campground to check it out before driving a big rig in, it is on the right just as you reach the end of the road.

Other Camping Possibilities

At Playa Linda at the west end of Ixtapa there is a walk-on ferry landing and a small tourist market. Between the two, next to a sidewalk that runs from the market area out to the ferry terminal is an undeveloped parking lot. Boondockers are sometimes allowed to camp here. Security is said to be good since there is a police office right next to the market. Cold showers and toilets are available at the market. To get there follow signs to Playa Linda, and when you reach the market follow the small road around to the left, access is actually fine for big rigs. The GPS location is N 17° 40' 54.3", W 101° 38' 45.6".

MANZANILLO, COLIMA AND THE COAST TO THE NORTH (MAHN-SAH-NEE-YOH)
Manzanillo population 110,000, Elevation sea level

RVers who have formed their expectations of Manzanillo from the movie 10, which was set here, may be disappointed by the town. There are beautiful hotels and beaches, just like in the movie, but you'll probably never see them since they are in the resort area where access is limited. This isn't really a problem since some of the best camping in Mexico is located along the coast for 50 miles to the north along what is known as the **Costa Alegre**.

The town of Manzanillo has an industrial side and a tourist side. This is one of the largest west coast cargo ports in Mexico, the port area spawns lots of trucks heading inland. Unfortunately the one campground in Manzanillo is itself near the port area and shares the atmosphere. The main reason for spending the night is that the drive to the next campground south, Playa Azul, is a long one.

If you do decide to stop in Manzanillo you can have a good time. South of the port is the real town of **Manzanillo**. There is a pretty little square here, an evening visit is enjoyable. North of the port area there are many beaches, hotels, and restaurants. The nicest hotels are actually off the main road on the **Peninsula de Santiago**. There is also an excellent modern Comercial Mexicana mall north of town, it provides supplies for campers all along this coast.

Don't give up on Manzanillo just because there is limited camping in town. There are some very popular places along the 50 miles (80 km) of road to the north. Many norteamericanos look forward all summer to their annual migration to places like Boca de Iguanas and San Patricio Melaque.

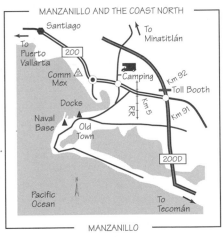

Manzanillo and the Coast to the North Campgrounds

🚐 **LA MARMOTA TRAILER PARK**

Address: Crucero Pez Vela, Carretera a
                 Minatitlán Km 0, Manzanillo,
                 Colima, México
Telephone: (3) 336-6248

GPS Location: N 19° 04' 44.3", W 104° 17' 09.6"

Manzanillo's campground situation is quite limited these days. The La Marmota is it.

There are 24 back-in spaces with 30-amp electricity, water, and sewer. Each site has a paved pad and patio and some shade. The campground

THE CENTRAL WEST COAST

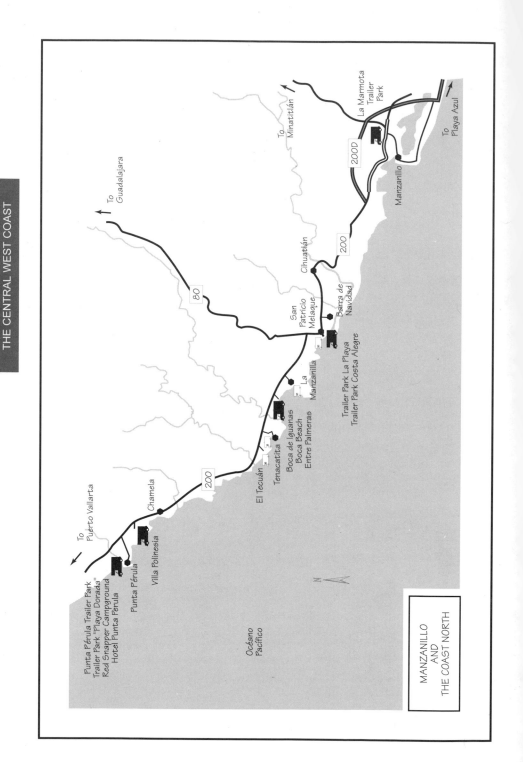

MANZANILLO
AND
THE COAST NORTH

is a fenced compound with room for more rigs to free camp if all of the spaces with services are filled. There are also many motel-style rooms. Restrooms are no longer usable. Dust from traffic is a big problem here.

La Marmota is located about 100 yards toward Minatitlán from the Crucero Pez Vela (Sailfish Intersection), so named because it formerly had a large sailfish statue marking it. This crossing is just northeast of central Manzanillo and near the port where Mex 98, the road to Minatitlán, goes inland. A large intersection including a highway overpass was under construction when we last visited making access difficult. The statue of the sailfish was nowhere in sight and we are unable to give better access instructions since it is unclear exactly what the final configuration of the roads will be.

⊞ TRAILER PARK LA PLAYA

Address: Gomez Farias #250 (Apdo. 59), Melaque,
                CP 48980 Jalisco, México
Telephone: (3) 355-5065

GPS Location: N 19° 13' 25.2", W 104° 42' 21.2"

The La Playa is deservedly popular. It has a beach-side location, easy access, full hookups and is located in the small town of San Patricio Melaque so you can shop, visit restaurants, and stroll around the small friendly town in the evening.

There are 45 spaces with 15-amp outlets, water and sewer sized large enough for big rigs. All of the sites have paved patios. Some of the sites are right above the beach.

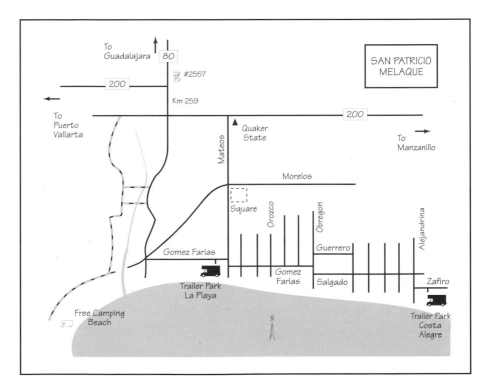

Restrooms have flush toilets and cold showers. There is a fence and a gate that is kept closed at night, but there is no fence on the beach side so the fence really serves no purpose except to keep people from using the campground as a thoroughfare. There are enough people around that security isn't really a problem as long as you keep smaller items locked up so they don't grow legs. Little English is spoken. People aiming to spend a while here should make reservations.

The La Playa is located in the town of San Patricio Melaque. Turn toward the beach from Mex 200 on the town's main cobblestone street. Unfortunately the street is not well marked at the highway end, it has a ferretería (hardware store) on one corner and the Refraccionaría Wynter (an auto parts store) on the other. The cutoff is .2 miles (.3 km) east of the point where Mex 200 makes a right angle turn to head away from the ocean. You'll know you are on the right street when you see the town's square on your left at .2 miles (.3 km). The campground is on the right at .4 miles (.7 km), on the beach. If you've taken the wrong street you can always drive along the street running parallel to the beach, but one block back.

TRAILER PARK COSTA ALEGRE

Address: Zafiro No. 41, Villa Obregón, Jalisco, México
Telephone: (3) 355-5276

GPS Location: N 19° 13' 08.1", W 104° 41' 44.8"

This is a small campground that is an alternative to the La Playa if you like the San Patricio Melaque area. It is actually in the small town of Villa Obregón which adjoins San Patricio Melaque to the east.

The campground has about 10 back-in spaces with 15-amp electricity, water, and sewer. Parking is on sand and the beach is directly out front although it is on the far side of a wire fence. Restrooms are basic with flush toilets and cold showers. Rental rooms are also available. Security here seems pretty good due to the fence and an on-site manager.

To find the campground make your way to the road paralleling the beach, perhaps at the La Playa, and work your way southeast. The road jogs in and out a bit, but .9 mile (1.5 km) south of the La Playa you will find the Costa Alegre.

BOCA DE IGUANAS

Address: Playa Boca de Iguanas, Km 16.5 Carr. Melaque-Pto.
                Vallarta, Jalisco, México

GPS Location: N 19° 18' 25.8", W 104° 49' 07.9"

This is a medium-size camping area in a grove of palm trees right on the beach. The 1.7 mile access road from the highway is now paved. This same road provides access to the Boca Beach Trailer Park and the Entre Palmeras. These three campgrounds sit at the western end of a beautiful wide three-mile-long beach.

Boca de Iguanas is a large sandy area shaded by palms. There are scattered electrical outlets and water taps, if you have a long cord and lots of hose you'll be able to find a way to hook up. Restrooms with flush toilets and cold water showers are provided. There is a dump station. Old timers warn that it is best to keep a sharp eye on small dogs here since crocodiles inhabit the swamp behind the camping area.

The three campgrounds in this location (see Boca Beach and Entre Palmeras also) make up a very comfortable winter community of campers from north of the border.

They sit on a beautiful isolated beach and even have a restaurant located between them. Things start to get crowded soon after Christmas as the snowbirds arrive and stake out their spots. Reservations are not taken at Boca de Iguanas.

The entrance road to Boca de Iguanas is near the 17 Km mark of Mex 200 some 10.3 miles (16.6 km) north of the point where Mex 80 from Guadalajara meets Mex 200 near Melaque. The entrance road is paved so access is much improved over the former dirt road. Unfortunately, Boca de Iguanas sits in front of a swamp area with an outlet that drains across the campground entrance. There is no bridge, and if the tides, winds, and rain conspire the entrance can be very difficult to negotiate. Take a close look before committing yourself or you may find yourself calling for a grúa (tow truck).

BOCA BEACH

Address: Apdo. 18, San Patricio Melaque, Jalisco, México
Telephone: (3) 381-0393   **Fax:** (3) 381-0342

GPS Location: N 19° 18' 27.8", W 104° 49' 03.9"

This is the campground formerly known as Tenacatita Trailer Park. It is located right next to Boca de Iguana. Of the two campgrounds this is now the most popular, Boca de Iguana's problem entrance and refusal to take reservations have led to a decline in its fortunes.

There are about 40 spaces with 15-amp outlets, water and sewer under lots of palm

THE CENTRAL WEST COAST

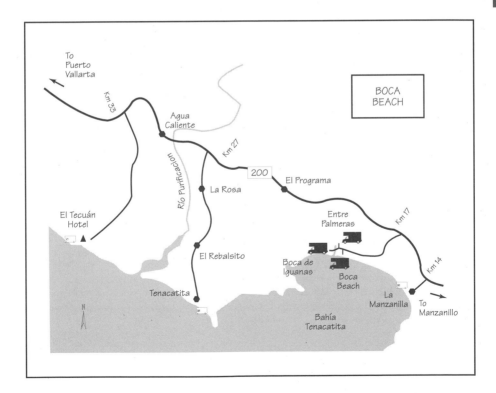

THE CENTRAL WEST COAST

trees. Another 80 sites offer electricity and water. Big rigs can use this campground. There is also a separate dump station. Many of the sites border the beach. The restrooms have flush toilets and hot water showers. Many campers keep small boats on the beach out front for fishing in the bay. Limited English is spoken and reservations are accepted.

To find Boca Beach just follow the directions given above for Boca de Iguanas. You'll come to the Boca Beach entrance just before you reach that of Boca de Iguanas.

🚐 HOTEL, BUNGALOWS Y CAMPAMENTO ENTRE PALMERAS

Address:	Playa Boca de Iguanas, Km 16.5 Carr.
	Melaque-Pto. Vallarta, Jalisco, México
Res.:	Donato Guerra No. 321, Guadalajara, México
Telephone:	(3) 613-6735 (Guadalajara)
E-mail:	letnika@hotmail.com

GPS Location: N 19° 18' 27.3", W 104° 49' 06.8"

The Entre Palmeras is a small hotel located behind the Boca de Iguanas and Boca Beach campgrounds. It does not sit directly on the beach but is very near.

Plans are afoot to add formal electricity, water, and sewer hookups to the ten spaces behind the hotel. Currently they do not have hookups although some electricity and water are available. Hot showers and flush toilets are available and the hotel has a small restaurant out front. When we visited a group of the local RVers were taking Spanish lessons there.

To find Entre Palmeras just follow the directions given above for Boca de Iguanas. You'll come to the Boca Beach entrance on the left and just beyond the entrance to Entre Palmeras on the right.

🚐 PARAISO COSTALEGRE EN VILLA POLINESIA

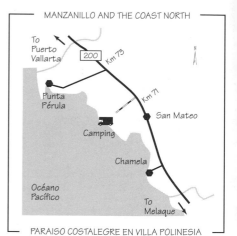

PARAISO COSTALEGRE EN VILLA POLINESIA

Address:	Carretera No. 200 Km 72,
	Chamela, Jalisco, México
Telephone:	(3) 333-9778 (Chamela) or
	(3) 122-3940 (Guadalajara for
	reservations)
Fax:	(3) 121-2534 (Guadalajara)
E-mail:	paraiso@paraisocostalegre.com.mx
Web Site:	www.paraisocostalegre.com.mx

GPS Location: N 19° 34' 51.3", W 105° 06' 18.2"

Villa Polinesia is an unusual campground. It is a resort fronting a beautiful beach with a few nice palapa-style bungalows and meeting areas in front, strange little concrete tents behind, and then a trailer park behind all this. Usually the place is almost empty which makes it a really nice place to stay.

There are 16 usable camping spaces arranged in a long row. Only eight have electricity (15-amp outlets), water, and sewer hookups. Some of the sites have palapas that you can use to lounge out of the sun. Big rigs can use the campground. There are very basic restrooms with flush toilets and cold-water showers.

To reach Villa Polinesia take the road toward the beach near the 71 Km marker. These kilometers markers start at the Melaque Junction near San Patricio Melaque so the turnoff is 44 miles (71 km) north of the Melaque junction. Drive .9 miles (1.5 km) along this unpaved but otherwise fine road following signs left into the campground.

PUNTA PÉRULA TRAILER PARK

Address:	C/O Jose Ventura Preciado, Mojarra 2,
	Ejido La Fortuna, Pérula, Jalisco, México
Telephone:	(3) 638-3593

GPS Location: N 19° 35' 19.1", W 105° 07' 46.4"

This trailer park has a devoted following. They arrive soon after Christmas (or even before) and don't leave until the end of March. After that, they report, it just gets too hot. It is one of four trailer parks in the small town of Pérula.

There are 19 spaces, all have electricity (mostly 15-amp, three 30-amp), sewer, and water. Good clean restrooms with cold showers are provided. The spaces are all back-ins and have patios. The ground is sandy and there is little shade. There was a big TV with satellite hookup in the central lounge area which is open to the breezes and looks out over the ocean. The campground is right next to a beautiful big open beach and fishing is said to be excellent. Limited supplies are available in the village and there are a few small restaurants.

Take the Pérula cutoff just south of the Km 73 marker on Mex 200. Follow the paved road for 1.2 miles (1.9 km) until you enter the village. Continue straight ahead, you'll soon see the square on your right, the trailer park is on the left on the fifth cross-street after the square.

HOTEL, BUNGALOWS, Y TRAILER PARK "PLAYA DORADA"

Address:	Pérula, Jalisco, México
Telephone:	(3) 333-9710 (Pérula), (3) 122-6853 (Guadalajara)
Fax:	(3) 285-51-32 (Pérula)
E-mail:	pdorada@cybercable.net.mx
Web Site:	www.geocities.com/pdorada

GPS Location: N 19° 35' 19.3", W 105° 07' 35.9"

This is a trailer park associated with the hotel just across the street. It fronts the ocean at one end.

There are 10 spaces, all back-in and all with lots of room for big rigs. There isn't much shade, the owner explains that customers prefer maneuvering room to shade. All sites have 15-amp outlets, water, and sewer and room for big rigs to maneuver and park. The restrooms are spotless and have hot water showers. If you are looking for some shade you have access to the swimming pool at the hotel next door which has plenty and is quite nice. Laundry service is available and there is a restaurant next door. The owner speaks excellent English and will probably correct yours if you aren't careful.

To reach the campground turn off Mex 200 near the 73 Km marker. Follow the paved road 1.2 miles (1.9 km) until you reach the village. Continue straight ahead past the square, the campground is to the left at the second cross street after the square. It is well signed.

THE CENTRAL WEST COAST

RED SNAPPER CAMPGROUND

Address:	Pérula, Jalisco, México
Telephone:	(3) 333-9784
E-mail:	redsnapper@hotmail.com

GPS Location: N 19° 35' 19.1", W 105° 07' 25.2"

The Red Snapper is one of the newer campgrounds in Pérula. It is run by an expat American and his wife and has a very popular restaurant.

The campground has about 13 spaces, all are pull or back-in with six overlooking the beach. Electricity is 30-amps with the appropriate outlets, there are also sewer and water hookups. The restaurant also overlooks the beach and is a popular meeting area. Restrooms are excellent with flush toilets and hot showers. A washing machine is available. Internet access is promised but not yet available.

To reach the campground turn off Mex 200 near the 73 Km marker. Follow the paved road 1.5 miles (2.4 km) to a cross street marked with a sign telling you to turn left to the Red Snapper. It is on the street a block before the square.

HOTEL PUNTA PÉRULA

Address:	Juarez y Tiburon S/N, Punta Pérula, Jalisco, México
Telephone:	(3) 333-9782

GPS Location: N 19° 35' 25.6", W 105° 07' 39.2"

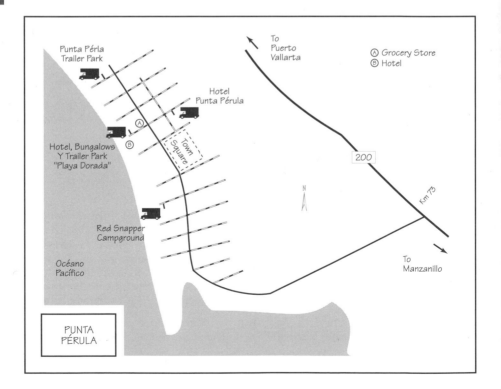

THE CENTRAL WEST COAST

This is **another** new campground in Pérula. It is located in a field of palms behind the hotel. There are four full-hookup sites with 15-amp outlets, water, and sewer. They have brick patios. There are plans for another six sites to go in sometime in the next few years. Restrooms have flush toilets and cold showers.

Take the Pérula cutoff just south of the Km 73 marker on Mex 200. Follow the paved road for 1.2 miles (1.9 km) until you enter the village. Continue straight ahead, you'll soon see the square on your right. Turn right on the second cross-street after the square and drive inland. The campground is on the right in about a block and a half.

Other Camping Possibilities

At the north end of San Patricio Melaque is a large gravel parking lot next to the water filled with free campers. Don't be surprised to find 50 rigs in here. Some people spend all season at this one location. Unfortunately the sanitation standard here is questionable, there are no adequate sewer facilities. It is no longer possible to access this camping area by driving along the street that follows the beach. Instead it is best to start at the intersection where Mex 80 enters San Patricio Melaque from the north and makes a 90-degree left. Turn right instead, go .2 miles (.3 km) and take the small dirt road to the left. The camping area is .6 miles (1 km) down this road. It might be best to drive this in your tow car before committing yourself with your big rig, the road is definitely not very good. Watch for low-hanging wires.

A few years ago the Tenacatita campground next to Boca de Iguanas campground changed its name to Boca Beach. They did this because people were confusing it with Tenicatita beach, a popular free camping beach a few miles to the north. Tenicatita beach is reached from near the Km 28 marker off Mex 200 about 7.8 miles (12.5 km) north of the road to Boca de Iguanas and Boca Beach. It is 5.3 miles (8.5 km) in to the ocean.

The El Tecuán Hotel turnoff is just south of the 33 Km marker on Mex 200 north of the Melaque Junction. There is a long twisting but paved road to the hotel. This place used to have a very popular campground, then it closed. There were various rumors involving drugs, movies, and airplanes. Now there are no camping facilities and the place is now clearly signed that camping is not allowed. The hotel was abandoned when we last visited.

PLAYA AZUL, MICHOACÁN (PLI-YAH AH-SOOL)
Population 5,000, Elevation sea level

What can you say about Playa Azul? It isn't even in most guide books. Still, this is the state of Michoacán's claim to fame in the beach resort category. There aren't any other beach resorts in the state. AAA and most authorities claim that this is the only safe place to camp on the coast between Ixtapa and Manzanillo.

Playa Azul is a sleepy but pleasant little town with a good beach. Relaxing in the sun will be the main thing on your daily agenda here. There are a few restaurants, the best one is probably in the Playa Azul Hotel but there are others along the beach and in town. This is a resort frequented primarily by Mexican families, a pleasant change and one that will help your budget although the campground itself is no deal.

You may want to visit the much larger nearby industrial town of Lázaro Cárdenas

THE CENTRAL WEST COAST

THE QUIET BEACH AT PLAYA AZUL

because it has supermarkets and larger stores. Busses and collectivos run between Playa Azul and the city.

Playa Azul Campground

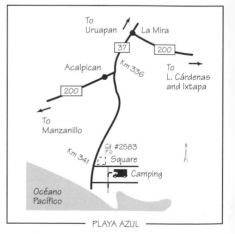

PLAYA AZUL

🚐 **PLAYA AZUL HOTEL**

Address: Av. Venustiano Carranza s/n, Playa Azul, CP 60982 Michoacán, México
Telephone: (7) 536-0024

GPS Location: N 18° 25' 51.1", W 095° 05' 28.5"

The Playa Azul Hotel and its trailer park are an oasis in a long stretch of road with few RV Parks suitable for larger rigs. Located near the beach this is a worthwhile rest stop or even a decent semi-long-term destination.

The campground sits behind the hotel. There is room for about 12 larger rigs. Electricity (15-amp outlets), water, and sewer are all available, although not necessarily at all sites. Several restrooms with hot showers are provided for the campground. The hotel has a two nice pools and a restaurant. Little English is spoken by the staff but there may be a long-term camper or two to help you out with translation or logistics questions. You're only a half block from the beach. Have fun!

From Mex 200 you must drive a short stub road to reach Playa Azul. At 2.7 miles (4.4 km) from Mex 200 you will enter the town, there is a small Pemex with decent access on the left, directly ahead you will see that the road ends at the beach. The grid of streets branches off to the right and left. Turn left one block before reaching the beach. Drive one block, turn right on a rough dirt street, the campground entrance is halfway down the block on the left. There is a gate that is usually closed, ring the bell or walk around to the hotel to register.

PUERTO VALLARTA, JALISCO AND THE COAST TO THE NORTH
(PWERT-TOE VAH-YAHR-TAH)
Population 250,000, Elevation sea level

Puerto Vallarta (also known as PV) is a full-scale, extremely popular tourist destination with all that that entails. Hundreds of thousands of people each year visit for a week at a time, they come by jet and cruise ship. Every tourist service you can imagine is offered: great restaurants, booze cruises, tours, para-sailing, time-share sales, you name it. The whole thing can be hard to take for more than a few days at a time, but never fear, a slower-paced paradise of small towns and quiet beaches stretches to the north.

In Puerto Vallarta the crowded **downtown** area is the center of activities. There's a **malecón** along the waterfront for strolling, across the street and up the hill are restaurants and shops along small cobblestone streets. The selection of Mexican crafts in Puerto Vallarta is one of the best in Mexico and prices aren't really too bad. South of downtown and the Río Cuale a hotel and restaurant area backs **Playa de los Muertos** while to the north toward the airport are big hotels, more beaches, and a marina and **golf course**. Big rigs are a real problem in the old town, use a tow car or bus to get there, you'll be glad you did because streets are narrow and parking very limited. If you approach PV from the south you can avoid most of the traffic by following a bypass that runs around the back side of the old town. Just watch carefully for the sign pointing right as you enter town.

A few miles north of Puerto Vallarta but still along the shore of Banderas Bay is **Bucerías**. Between the highway and the beach are wide cobblestones streets lined with many expensive homes, most have high walls so you really can't get a good look. There are small restaurants and stores so if you stay in Bucerías you probably won't visit PV very often.

The small town of **Sayulita**, some 27 miles (43 km) north of Puerto Vallarta, is one of the quietest places you're likely to find in this area. The beach is a popular surfing destination (swimming is dangerous), there are a couple of good restaurants, some tiny grocery stores, and that's about it.

A short distance to the north is the slightly larger ocean-side town of **Lo De Marcos**. It is neatly arranged along cobblestone streets and has an excellent swimming beach. Here you'll also find small restaurants, hotels, and shops.

THE CENTRAL WEST COAST

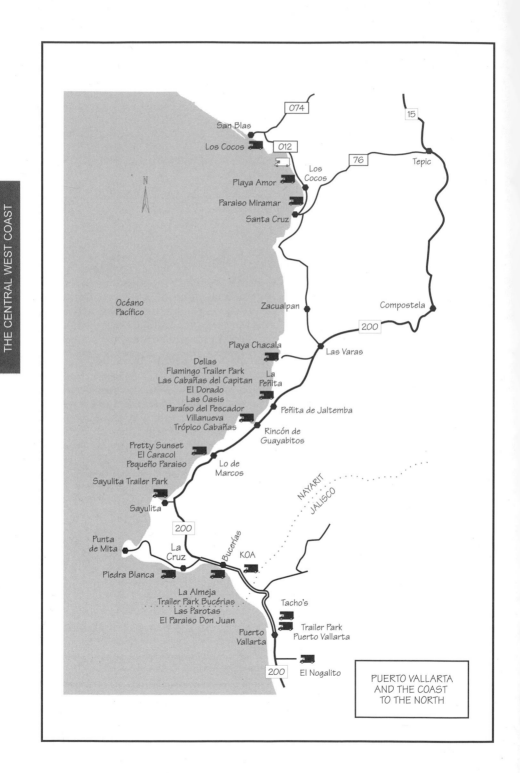

San Blas

074

15

Los Cocos

012

Los Cocos

76

Tepic

Playa Amor

Paraiso Miramar

Santa Cruz

Océano Pacífico

Zacualpan

Compostela

200

Playa Chacala

Las Varas

Delias
Flamingo Trailer Park
Las Cabañas del Capitan
El Dorado
Las Oasis
Paraíso del Pescador
Villanueva
Trópico Cabañas

La Peñita

Peñita de Jaltemba

Rincón de Guayabitos

Pretty Sunset
El Caracol
Pequeño Paraiso

Lo de Marcos

Sayulita Trailer Park

NAYARIT

JALISCO

Sayulita

200

Punta de Mita

La Cruz

Bucerías

KOA

Piedra Blanca

La Almeja
Trailer Park Bucérias
Las Parotas
El Paraiso Don Juan

Tacho's

Puerto Vallarta

Trailer Park Puerto Vallarta

200

El Nogalito

PUERTO VALLARTA
AND THE COAST
TO THE NORTH

North again is **Rincón de Guayabitos**. This town seems to cater more to Mexicans than norteamericanos, you'll see many family groups on the beach. Prices tend to be lower than in PV. There are many restaurants and hotels, as well as a variety of small stores. This is also a popular fishing destination for campers, with nine campgrounds in town RVers are obviously an important part of this community. These campgrounds are all older and sites can be cramped for big rigs but RVers always seem to find a way to fit.

Farther north a paved road runs out to the coast at **Chacala**. RVers have recently discovered this easily-reached piece of paradise with its beautiful beach and many are beginning to boondock near the palapa restaurants there.

Moving north again, we leave Mex 200 in the town of **Las Varas** and drive through tobacco farms and then rolling hills until we reach the water again near the tiny towns of **Aticama, Los Cocos, Miramar** and **Santa Cruz**. There are a couple of campgrounds along here and the mosquitoes aren't quite as bad as in nearby **San Blas**.

San Blas today is a small fishing village but one with a surprising amount of history. The town was an important port even in the 1500s. The Manila galleons visited and expeditions north to California departed from here. You can still visit the ruins of an old **Spanish fort** just inland. San Blas also has beaches, they start south of town near the campground. Behind San Blas is an area of **swamps and lagoons**, small boats are available to take you exploring, birding, and crocodile watching. The swamps are also responsible for another memorable San Blas attraction, the **mosquitoes**. Be sure you bring bug dope and have good screens on your rig if you stay in the San Blas campground.

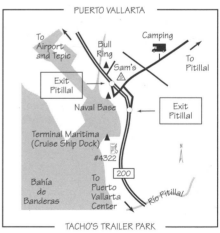

PUERTO VALLARTA

TACHO'S TRAILER PARK

Puerto Vallarta and the Coast to the North Campgrounds

🚐 TACHO'S TRAILER PARK

Address:	Prisciliano Sánchez s/n Frente Aramara, Puerto Vallarta, Jalisco, México
Telephone:	(3) 224-22163 **Fax:** (3) 222-1818
E-mail:	siesta20@prodigy.net.mx

GPS Location: N 20° 39' 19.4", W 105° 13' 57.1"

Tacho's is a popular big-rig campground. The wide cobblestone streets make access easy and the widely spaced sites with patios and clipped grass are very pleasant. The location north of town and outside the busy traffic area is also a plus.

The campground has about 150 spaces, each with 15-amp outlet, water, and sewer. All are back-in sites. The clean restrooms have hot showers. There is a nice big pool here to make up for the distance from the beach. You'll have to use your own car or public transportation to reach beaches, shopping, or downtown.

The key to finding this trailer park is locating the correct intersection north of Puerto Vallarta. From the north watch for the airport. The left turn to El Pitillal and the trailer

THE CENTRAL WEST COAST

THE CENTRAL WEST COAST

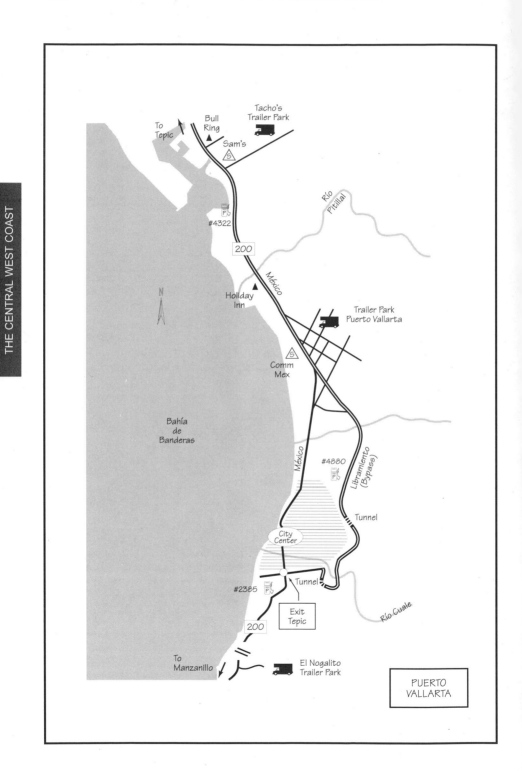

PUERTO
VALLARTA

The Gift that Comes 12 Times a Year . . .

PLEASE PRINT

Your Name _____

Address _____

City _____

State _____ Zip _____

☐ Renewal   ☐ New Subscription

$ _____ Payment enclosed ☐ Bill me later

Give 12 issues of the Wellness Letter for Christmas. Order the 1st subscription (your own or a gift) at the regular price of $28.00. Each additional subscription (ordered at the same time) is only $24.00. Offer expires January 31, 2003.

Gift to _____

Address _____

City _____

State _____ Zip _____

☐ Renewal   ☐ New Subscription

Gift to _____

Address _____

City _____

State _____ Zip _____

☐ Renewal   ☐ New Subscription

72KXMA

Limited to Continental U.S. only.

WNL XP002

BUSINESS REPLY MAIL

FIRST-CLASS MAIL   PERMIT NO 114   FLAGER BEACH FL

POSTAGE WILL BE PAID BY ADDRESSEE

UNIVERSITY OF CALIFORNIA, BERKELEY
WELLNESS LETTER
PO BOX 420149
PALM COAST FL 32142-9822

park is 1.6 miles (2.6 km) south of the airport. There is a stop light but you must make your turn from the lateral lane on the right so watch carefully ahead for the overhead sign for El Pitillal (a Puerto Vallarta suburb). The new Sam's Club on the corner just before the turn makes it easier to spot. From the south the intersection for the right turn to El Pitillal and the trailer park is 1.8 miles (2.9 km) north of the point where the ring road around old PV joins the four-lane (plus laterals) road north out of town and .2 miles (.3 km) north of Pemex #4322 on the left. From the south you must also make the right turn from a lateral but access is easy and the turn easier to see as you approach. Once you make the turn toward El Pitillal the trailer park is .5 miles (.8 km) ahead on the left. The park has its own turn lane so the entry is easy, however if you have a low ground clearance rig you should exercise caution crossing the entrance threshold.

⛟ TRAILER PARK PUERTO VALLARTA

Address: Calle Francia #143, Colonia
              Versailles, Puerto Vallarta, Jalisco,
              México
Telephone: (3) 224-2828

GPS Location: N 20° 38' 06.8", W 105° 13' 42.1"

For the most convenient place to stay to enjoy PV's delights you should give the Trailer Park Puerto Vallarta a try. It is located almost within walking distance of downtown (really a pretty good hike of about 2 miles (3.3 km)) and with great access to busses and supermarkets.

The trailer park has 49 spaces, several are pull-throughs for big rigs while most are back-in sites. This is a walled campground in a close-in PV suburb. There is no gate and poor security but this is apparently not much of a problem here. All sites have 15-amp outlets, water, sewer, and patios. They are close together. Shade is abundant, in fact the campground is much like a *vivero* (gardening nursery). The bathroom building is only adequate but the showers are hot. To reach the beach you'll have to walk for about 10 minutes.

The campground is not on a main road and there are no signs so it is not easy to locate. It sits east of Mex 200 on a side street named Francia not far from the point where the ring road meets four-lane Mex 200 leading north out of town. The best landmark marking the turn onto Francia is the four-story white Plaza del Sol Hotel (with a Bital bank on the ground floor) on the east side of the highway. The road just north of the hotel is Francia. Coming from the north the turn for the campground is 1.6 miles (2.6 km) from the stop light at the Sam's Club, make sure you get into the lateral in plenty of time since you must turn left from it. Coming from the south the turn into Francia is the second (after a very short block) after the bypass meets the main highway. Once on Francia drive 2.5 blocks east, you'll see the unsigned entrance to the campground on the left.

EL NOGALITO TRAILER PARK

Address: Naranjo 123, Colonia El Nogalito,
                 Puerto Vallarta, Jalisco, México
Telephone: (3) 221-5419

GPS Location: N 20° 33' 41.4", W 105° 14' 32.4"

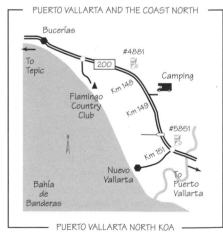

This is a new campground suitable for tents, vans and small trailers. It is located in the tiny village of El Nogalito which is hidden in the mountains less than a mile off Mex 200 south of Puerto Vallarta. The interesting small-village location away from the coast makes this campground very different from others in the area.

The El Nogalito has 12 back-in spaces. Most are long enough only for 20-foot rigs although two or three will accept rigs to 24 feet. The larger rigs that sometimes camp here are really too large, they tend to block access to the remaining sites. Each slot has a 15-amp outlet and a water hookup, there is also a dump site. Restrooms are excellent and have hot showers. There's a small wading pool and sunning area. The campground sits next to the little Punta Negra River and is surrounded by a fence for security. Rental bungalows are also available.

Driving south from Puerto Vallarta the left turn onto the gravel road into El Nogalito is at about Km 5. Watch for the Blue Bay Club, the turn is .5 miles (.8 km) south of the club. The turn was marked with a sign to the campground when we visited, be careful since it is on a fairly blind curve. After the turn you'll reach the village of El Nogalito in .6 miles (1 km). Continue on through the village and in another .3 miles (.5 km) you'll see the gate of the campground on the right.

PUERTO VALLARTA NORTH KOA

Location: Km 149 on Mex 200 North of
                 Puerto Vallarta
Address: Apdo. 2-107, Col 5 de Diciembre,
                 Puerto Vallarta, CP 48350 Jalisco,
                 México
Telephone: (3) 296-5053   **Fax:** (3) 296-5053
E-mail: pvkoan@pvnet.com.mx
Web Site: http://www.koakampgrounds.com/
                 where/MEXICO/77101.htm

GPS Location: N 20° 43' 28.2", W 105° 16' 41.7"

The new KOA north of Puerto Vallarta has some of the best facilities in Mexico. Many campers we meet have stopped for an overnight stay and remained for months. Even in the states this would rate as one of the nicest KOAs around.

There are 70 large full-hookup sites (50-amp outlets), many are pull-throughs. There are also tent sites and camping cabins. Camping is on grass, many trees are beginning to provide quite a bit of shade. Restrooms are excellent with hot showers. There is a self-service coin-operated laundry, a small general store, a restaurant and bar, and a very nice swimming pool. There is also internet access and English is spoken.

The campground is located east of Mex 200 near the Km 149 marker. This is about 8 miles (13 km) north of Puerto Vallarta. The access road is directly off the highway and is only accessable from the north-bound lanes. South-bound traffic must travel on south and turn around to enter the campground.

▭ TRAILER PARK BUCERÍAS

Address: Apdo. 148, Bucerías, CP 63732 Nayarit, México
Telephone: (3) 298-0265   **Fax:** (3) 298-0300

GPS Location: N 20° 45' 02.5", W 105° 19' 55.2"

A camper we met at Boca de Iguanas once warned us that Bucerías was the most expensive campground on the coast. "They know what they've got" he told us.

Bucerías has about 45 spaces with full hookups and a few more with electricity only. There is plenty of room for big rigs and all of the full-service sites have patios. The restrooms have hot showers, the women's is particularly cute. There is a brick fence completely around the park, great for security but blocking any beach view. The beach is the park's best feature, this is the closest ocean-side park to Puerto Vallarta, but not by much. English is spoken and reservations are a must during the high season.

The trailer park is located next to the beach on the south side of Bucerías. The easiest access from Mex 200 is on a road toward the coast near the Km 143 marker. The stoplight at this corner is the third in Bucerías if you are driving from north to south, the first if you are driving from south to north. The cobblestone road passes under a golden arch which is visible from the highway and then leads .5 mile (.8 km) to an intersection in front of the Decameron Hotel. Turn right here on Lazaro Cardenas. The trailer park is on the left in the third block after this turn.

▭ LAS PAROTAS COUNTRY PARADISE GARDENS
VILLAS AND RV PARK

Address: #119 Calle Canal, Bucerías, Nayarit, México
Telephone: (3) 298-1788   **Fax:** (3) 298-1787
E-mail: tedpenner@lasparotas.com   **Web Site:** www.lasparotas.com

GPS Location: N 20° 45' 37.5", W 105° 19' 16.8"

This is a new campground located inland on the mountain side of Bucerías. The lots here are for sale and many are available on a rental basis.

When we visited in the spring of 2001 there were 21 back-in sites with full-hookups (50-amp electrical outlets). A total of 80 are planned. The sites are on 2000 square-foot lots so there is plenty of room. Other amenities include excellent restrooms with hot showers, a swimming pool, a self-serviced laundry, and a lounge area which may become a restaurant and bar. English is spoken.

To reach the campground you follow Av. Estaciones north toward the mountains from an intersection with Mex 200 in the middle of Bucerias. The proper road is marked by two businesses located on the corner, to the east is the Fumar Restaurant (excellent), to the west is Mini Super La Fuente. The easiest way to find the right street is to approach from the east. Zero your odometer at Pemex #4266 as you travel west on

THE CENTRAL WEST COAST

Mex 200. Enter the lateral as soon as possible which is almost immediately. You'll come to a stop light in .3 mile (.5 km). From there you'll pass 3 streets in this order: Rio Colorado, Jacarandas, and then Primavera which is at a 45-degree angle. The next street is Estaciones, turn right here. Follow Estaciones, which is a dirt road, for .3 miles (.5 km) and it will curve to the right. In another .5 miles (.8 km) you'll see the Las Parotas on your right.

⬛ El Paraiso de Don Juan

Address:	Primavera #119, Col. Buenos Aires, Bucerías, Nayarit, México
Telephone:	(3) 298-0581

GPS Location: N 20° 45' 14.1", W 105° 19' 41.0"

This is another new campground in Bucerías, this is a small one located in the built-up area on the mountain side of Mex 200. The facilities are brand new and excellent, and the location is good if you are attracted to the goings-on in a small Mexican neighborhood.

The campground has 10 back-in spaces suitable for large rigs but with maneuvering room a little tight, they all have full hookups (30-amp outlets) and patios. The excellent restrooms have hot showers and there is an attractive swimming pool. The campground is fenced for security. Across the street is a private camping area of about the same size. French is the language of choice at this campground but you can certainly get by with English.

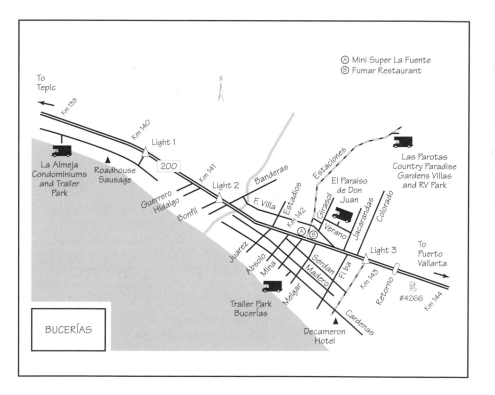

Easiest access for large rigs is from the westbound Mex 200 because you must turn into a side street from a lateral. Zero your odometer at Pemex #4266 as you travel north on Mex 200. Enter the lateral as soon as possible which is almost immediately. You'll come to a stop light in .3 mile (.5 km). The next street is Rio Colorado and the following is Jacarandas. Turn right on Jacarandas, there may not be a sign marking the street. Drive one block and turn left on Verano, the campground is just ahead and on your right.

▭ LA ALMEJA CONDOMINIUMS AND TRAILER PARK

Address: Km 139 Carr Compostela a Pto. Vallarta (Apdo. 163),
                Playas de Huanacastle, Bucerías, CP 63732 Nayarit, México
Telephone: (3) 298-0137

GPS Location: N 20° 45' 47.1", W 105° 21' 27.2"

The La Almeja is small and usually fully reserved during the January to March high season (reportedly for several years in advance), but since it is near the highway and such a nice place you should always stop on your way by to see if there is a free space. We think the atmosphere here is more like a Mediterranean villa than a trailer park.

There are 28 sites, 11 on one end of the buildings and 17 newer ones on the other. The campground sits on a low bluff above a beach that extends far to the north and south. Sites have 15-amp outlets, water, sewer and patios, they are all back-in slots and are fine for big rigs. The bathrooms are clean and modern with lots of hot water. Two beautiful swimming pools sit in front of the condominiums and above the ocean, you'll probably be spending quite a bit of time there. The only drawback to the campground is the presence of the nearby highway, road noise is quite noticeable. Campers here often hike into nearby Bucerías for groceries and busses on the highway go into Puerto Vallarta. English is spoken and reservations are definitely recommended.

You drive into this campground from a stoplight on Mex 200 near the Km 140 marker west of Bucerías. Turn toward the ocean at the light, then immediately turn right again on a frontage access road. You'll reach the La Almeja in .8 miles (1.3 km), it will be on your left.

▭ HOTEL PIEDRA BLANCA Y TRAILER PARK

Address: Calz. Independencia Nte. 914,
                Guadalajara, CP 44340 Jalisco,
                México (Reservations)
Telephone: (3) 617-6051   **Fax:** (3) 617-6047

GPS Location: N 20° 44' 47.5", W 105° 23' 10.7"

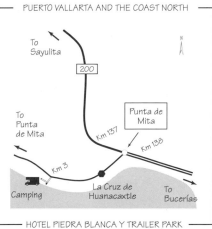

The Trailer Park Piedra Blanca is located next to the beach near the small town of La Cruz de Huanacaxtle, when someone recommends that you stay at La Cruz this is the place they're talking about.

The campground is situated next to the beach. There are 26 sites, all with patios and 15-amp outlets, water and sewer. The sites are fine for big rigs. The bathrooms are barely adequate and have hot water. The associated hotel has a swimming pool. You may find this campground slightly easier to get into than Bucerías and La Almeja during the high season, particularly if you are willing to park in the row back from the beach. Before committing to a long stay make sure to ask residents how the drainage system is working. Some English is spoken and reservations are accepted.

To reach the trailer park take the Punta de Mita road just north of the Km 138 marker on Mex 200 north of Bucerías. After 1.5 miles (2.4 km) you will reach La Cruz de Huanacaxtle and at 1.9 miles (3.1 km) you should very carefully turn 90 degrees left and drive about 200 yards on a dirt road to the entrance gate on your right. Exercise caution leaving the paved highway, the drop can cause problems for those with poor ground clearance. Open the gate and drive down the long entrance (make sure someone isn't coming in the opposite direction, this is a one-lane road). Check in at the hotel office on the far side of the pool and parking lot.

🚐 SAYULITA TRAILER PARK

Address:	Apdo. 11, La Peñita de Jaltemba, CP 63726 Nayarit, México
Telephone:	(3) 275-0202　**Fax:** (3) 275-0202
E-mail:	sayupark@prodigy.net.mx

GPS Location: N 20° 52' 16.8", W 105° 26' 12.5"

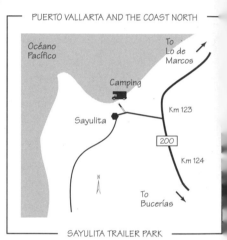

SAYULITA TRAILER PARK

This campground is a real find. It is located next to a beautiful beach in the so-far almost undiscovered village of Sayulita. The owner makes his guests promise only to recommend it to nice people, we assured him that our readers would qualify.

There are 38 sites in this campground, all with 15-amp outlets, water, and sewer hookups. The sites have patios and shade. Some are small sites but several can take the largest rigs. Amenities are shared with 7 bungalow units and are generous. The bathrooms are tiled and very clean with lots of hot water. A TV room and patio provide a place for people to get together and two more terraces provide places for ping-pong and watching the surfers. Someday there may be a pool but right now no one seems to miss it. The beach is one of the prettiest around and increasingly popular for surfing. When the surf is down it makes a great place to swim. Sayulita village has several places to buy groceries and also a couple of excellent restaurants.

During the off season you can arrange reservations with Thies and Cristina Rohlfs, Revolucion 349, CP 54030 Tlalnepantla, México. The telephone number is (5) 572-1335 and the fax number (5) 390-2750. Call the campground itself to reach them from November to March. English is spoken.

The road to Sayulita is near the Km 123 marker of Mex 200 north of Puerto Vallarta. A paved road leads .9 miles (1.5 km) to the village. Turn right down an unsigned dirt street just after entering the village, the campground is at the end of the street.

🚐 PRETTY SUNSET TRAILER PARK

Address: Camino a las Minitas s-n, Lo de Marcos, Nayarit, México
Telephone: (3) 275-0055   **Fax:** (3) 275-0024

GPS Location: N 20° 57' 20.9", W 105° 21' 24.0"

This is the newest of the trailer parks in the village of Lo de Marcos. There are 8 sites stretching from the road to the beach. Each site has its own patio, shade, 30-amp power, water, and sewer. There's plenty of room to park long rigs but maneuvering room is cramped. The bathrooms are new and clean and have hot showers. All of the campers we talked to loved the place. The beach out front may have something to do with that.

When we visited during the spring of 2001 another section of camping sites was under construction just to the east along the road. There are going to be 10 larger sites with full hookups in this area.

This is the first of three campgrounds you will find as you drive south along the beach out of the little village of Lo de Marcos. From Mex 200 the turnoff for Lo de Marcos is near the Km 108 marker. If you zero your odometer as you turn off the highway you will reach the village square at .5 miles (.8 km) and the road doglegs left just beyond it. Drive until you see the ocean ahead, you want to turn left two blocks from the beach at .7 miles (1.1 km). The road soon becomes paved (it was cobblestone before) and at .8 miles (1.3 km) you will see the campground on the right.

THE CENTRAL WEST COAST

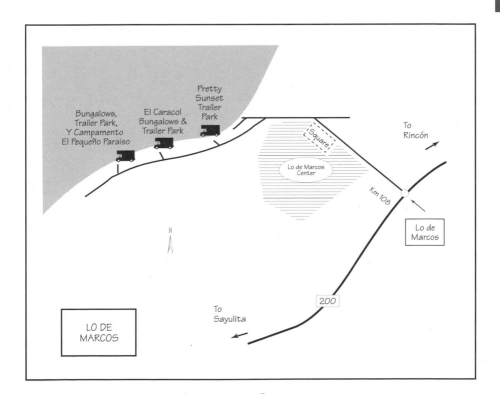

EL CARACOL BUNGALOWS & TRAILER PARK

Address: Apdo. 89, La Peñita de Jaltemba, CP 63726 Nayarit, México
Telephone: (3) 275-0050
E-mail: elcaracol_mx@hotmail.com

GPS Location: N 20° 57' 15.3", W 105° 21' 29.7"

El Caracol is the luxury trailer park in Lo de Marcos. This campground is usually full during the high season so if you want to stay here you had better make reservations.

There are 17 parking slots but a few are taken by permanently installed rigs. They all have 15-amp outlets, water, and sewer, patios, and plenty of shade. This is a very tidy facility with cobblestones for paving. Bathrooms are very clean and showers are hot. There are even special areas for hanging your wash to dry that are screened from the view of passersby. There is a patio area separating the campground from the beach, it has tables and a small wading pool.

El Caracol is on the same road as the Pretty Sunset Trailer Park described above. Just drive .2 miles (.3 km) farther and you will see the trailer park on the right.

BUNGALOWS, TRAILER PARK, Y
CAMPAMENTO EL PEQUEÑO PARAISO

Address: Carrt. Las Minitas No. 1938, Lo de Marcos, Nayarit, México
Telephone: (3) 275-0089

GPS Location: N 20° 57' 12.4", W 105° 21' 35.6"

BEACH VENDOR IN RINCÓN DE GUAYABITOS

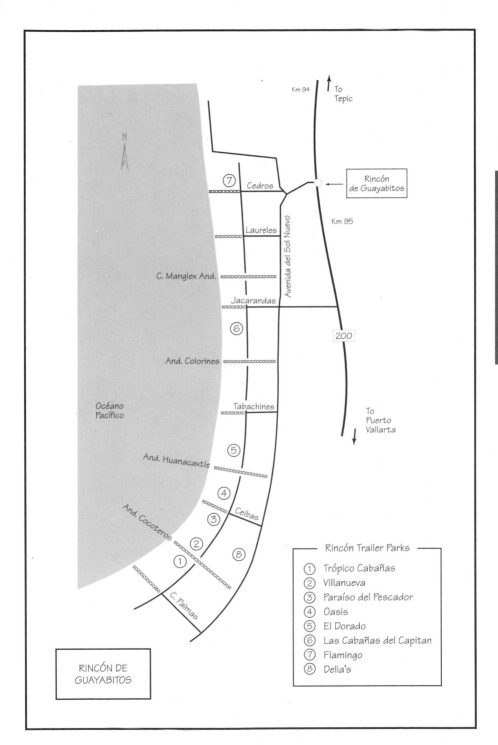

The El Pequeño Paraiso is the farthest east of the Lo de Marcos campgrounds. There are about 15 developed back-in sites, all with 15-amp outlets, water, sewer, patios, and shade. Large rigs use the campground. The bathrooms are very basic, they have hot water showers. The campground also has some rental motel-style bungalows.

To reach the campground follow the directions given above for the Pretty Sunset Trailer Park. Once there continue on for another .3 miles (.5 km) and you will see El Pequeño Paraiso on the right.

⊞ TRAILER PARK TRÓPICO CABAÑAS

Address: Retorno Palmas No. 22, Junto al Cocos,
                 Rincón de Guayabitos, Nayarit, México
Telephone: (3) 274-0662

GPS Location: N 21° 01' 21.2", W 105° 16' 31.5"

The Trópico Cabañas is the farthest east ocean-side trailer park in Rincón de Guayabitos. This campground is very much fishing oriented, it is also a favorite of big rigs since the parking slots are especially long. Maneuvering room, however, can be tight.

There are 30 spaces in this campground, all with 15-amp outlets, water, and sewer. The entire campground is paved and there is a boat ramp onto the beach. The bathrooms are very clean and there are hot water showers. This is a popular campground and reservations are recommended.

The campground is the only one on the Palmas Retorno.

⊞ TRAILER PARK VILLANUEVA

Address: Retorno Ceibas S-N, Rincón de Guayabitos,
                 Nayarit, México
Telephone: (3) 274-0658

GPS Location: N 21° 01' 20.5", W 105° 16' 29.8"

A new hotel and swimming pool have been built on the grounds of this campground. The personality has changed, it's half the size it was, but it's still popular.

There are about 19 spaces with all utilities (15-amp outlets) and patios. Big rigs fit, maneuvering room can be tight. Bathrooms are nice and there is hot water. Palm trees provide shade and the new swimming pool is great. There is a boat ramp onto the beach. There's also a small restaurant in the new hotel building.

The campground is located off the Ceibas Retorno. This is a popular location, two other campgrounds are also located on this one.

⊞ PARAÍSO DEL PESCADOR TRAILER PARK AND BUNGALOWS

Address: Retorno Ceibas No 1 & 2, Rincón de Guayabitos
                 CP 63727 Nayarit, México
Telephone: (3) 274-0014   **Fax:** (3) 274-0525

GPS Location: N 21° 01' 21.0", W 105° 16' 26.4"

Complete with boat ramp onto the beach, Paraíso del Pescador is another fisherman's favorite. There are about 30 spaces in a fully paved, carefully-gated beach-side campground. All sites have 15-amp outlets, sewer, and water. Most have patios. Big rigs fit but maneuvering room is tight. The bathrooms are beautifully clean, have lots of tile and hot water showers. There is an additional charge for the use of air conditioners. The manager speaks some English.

Paraíso del Pescador is located on the Ceibas Retorno.

⛟ TRAILER PARK LAS OASIS

Address: Retorno Ceibas s-n, Rincón de Guayabitos, Nayarit, México
Telephone: (3) 274-0361

GPS Location: N 21° 01' 20.7", W 105° 16' 22.3"

The Oasis is the newest of the Rincón campgrounds. The parking area is completely paved and has hookups for 19 rigs with full hookups (some 15-amp and some 30-amp outlets). Palms provide limited shade. There is plenty of room for big units. Between the camping area and the beach are two buildings, but in front of them is a sunning area and a small hourglass-shaped pool. The bathrooms are fairly modern and there is hot water. This campground has it's own boat ramp onto the beach.

The Oasis is located on the Ceibas Retorno.

⛟ EL DORADO TRAILER PARK

Address: Retorno Tabachines s-n, Rincón de Guayabitos,
                 Nayarit, México
Telephone: (3) 274-0152   **Fax:** (3) 274-0747

GPS Location: N 21° 01' 21.4", W 105° 16' 19.3"

This is the last campground with its own boat ramp as you go north along the beach in Rincón. Fishing is important here but so is lying in the sun.

The El Dorado has 21 spaces arranged around a central parking area. All sites have patios and full hookups with 15-amp outlets. Large rigs fit in some sites but maneuvering room can be tight. There is a sunning platform above the beach at the front. The bathrooms are tucked away behind the owner's house but are clean and showers have hot water.

The El Dorado is located on the Tabachines Retorno.

⛟ LAS CABAÑAS DEL CAPITAN

Address: Retorno Jacarandas s-n, Rincón de Guayabitos,
                 Nayarit, México
Telephone: (3) 274-0304   **Fax:** (3) 274-0301

GPS Location: N 21° 01' 27.6", W 105° 16' 07.9"

This campground was formerly known as the Trailer Park Number 1. Improvements have appeared on a regular basis here over the past few years. There are back-in parking slots for 14 units with full hookups but plans are in the works to widen them so there will be fewer in the future. Large rigs do use this campground. The bathrooms are nice and have hot water showers. There's a new swimming pool out next to the beach, a gift shop near the entrance, and many new rental rooms along one side of the property. The owner here speaks English.

Las Cabañas del Capitan is located on the Retorno Jacarandas.

⛟ FLAMINGO TRAILER PARK

Address: Apdo. 58, Rincón de Guayabitos, Nayarit, México

GPS Location: N 21° 01' 37.9", W 105° 15' 55.3"

At the far north end of the Rincón strip is the Flamingo Trailer Park. This trailer park is showing its age but has its own attractions. There are about 20 spaces with hookups in varying stages of repair and additional spaces for vans and tents. The Flamingo probably has the nicest beach of all of the trailer parks in town, Rincón's beach gets wider as you go north. Bathrooms are adequate and the showers are hot. We've seen caravans using this campground, probably because it is the only one in Rincón with any room during the busy season. There's also more room to maneuver and park here than in many of the Rincón campgrounds.

The Flamingo is on the Retorno Cedros, this is the first one you come to after entering the main entrance to Rincón and turning left on Avenida del Sol Nuevo.

⛟ DELIA'S TRAILER PARK

Address:	Retorno Ciebas No. 4, Rincón de Guayabitos, CP 63727 Nayarit, México
Telephone:	(3) 274-0226 **Fax:** (3) 274-0399
E-mail:	deliabond@hotmail.com

GPS Location: N 21° 01' 18.4", W 105° 16' 28.5"

Delia's is the least expensive of the Rincón trailer parks and the only one not on the beach. There is room for about 10 rigs under trees behind a building that contains the owner's house and restrooms. Most sites have 15-amp outlets, water, and sewer. While space can be tight there's usually a large bus conversion camping here, he found a way to fit. There's a good bathroom with a hot shower as well as several toilets and showers in individual stalls.

The entrance to Delia's is off Avenida del Sol Nuevo, not one of the retornos. There is poor signage, watch closely as you drive between the entrances to the Ceibas and Palmas Retornos. To reach the beach just go out the campground's back gate and walk the block to the sand.

⛟ LA PEÑITA TRAILER PARK

Address:	Apdo 22., Peñita de Jaltemba, CP 63726 Nayarit, México
Fax:	(3) 274-0996

GPS Location: N 21° 02' 46.8", W 105° 14' 30.8"

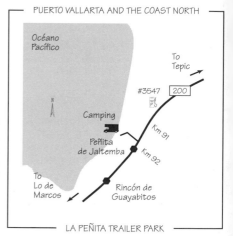

This campground is a little different than the others in the area. It is located on a small hill above, but close to, a nice beach. The facilities have a rustic feel to them and the folks are friendly. Unfortunately, during the winter of 2000/2001 word was circulating that this campground would close after the season, e-mails that we have received before printing indicates that it will not be open for the 2001/2002 season. However, since we customarily take word of new campgrounds and facilities with a grain of salt until we actually see them we'll do the same here and continue to list the campground until it actually closes.

Campsites are spread all along the hillside on terraces. There are about 130 spaces, most have full utilities (15-amp outlets) and some have patios. There is plenty of room for big rigs. There is lots of shade and some sites have great views of the coast and beach below. Restrooms have hot showers and there is even a swimming pool. The many fishermen at this campground must either go down the road to launch their boats or manhandle them across a wide beach below the campground. The town of Peñita, about a mile south, provides adequate shopping.

The entrance to this campground is well-signed and is right on Mex 200 between the 91 and 92 Km markers. This is just north of the town of Peñita de Jaltemba.

PLAYA CHACALA

GPS Location: N 21° 09' 43.3", W 105° 13' 23.5"

Now that there is a paved highway out to Playa Chacala the place has become an increasingly popular destination for those looking for a palm grove paradise next to a beautiful beach. Playa Chacala has a few palapa restaurants and little else in the way of facilities. You'll find no hookups here, that's one of the attractions to the folks who love it. Actually, a few campers have been able to run extension cords from one of the few palapas along the beach, but the power is low amp and not available to most campers. There is room for a few rigs to park overlooking the beach and lots more room under the trees behind.

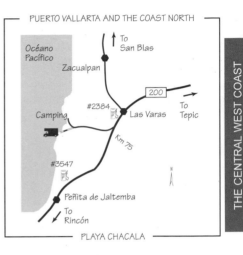

The road out to Playa Chacala leaves Mex 200 between Las Varas and La Peñita near the Km 75 point. There is a good sign, you will reach the turnoff to the camping area 4.7 miles (7.6 km) after leaving the highway. Turn left on the gravel road and you'll spot the campers in just a short distance.

PARAISO MIRAMAR RV-TRAILER PARK

Address: Calle Cerrada en Playa La
                 Manzanila s-n, Miramar, Nayarit,
                 México
Telephone: (3) 212-0411 (Tepic)

GPS Location: N 21° 26' 24.7", W 105° 11' 28.6"

The long cobblestone driveway into Paraiso Miramar may give you pause but press on, this almost unknown trailer park is well worth the trouble.

Paraiso Miramar is a small motel-style resort set above a small rocky beach. Behind and alongside the bungalows is a small RV park with about eight usable sites. Each has 15-amp

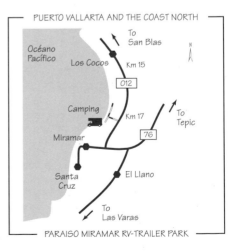

outlets, water and sewer. Some have cement parking pads and all are back-in spaces. The bathrooms are clean and modern and have hot water showers. There are an additional 15 or so spaces on grass nearby but it is difficult to imagine them being used except perhaps during the Christmas or Easter holidays. This is a very pleasant camping area with well-clipped green grass and a park-like setting. In front above the ocean are small swimming/wading pools and sunning areas. The Paraiso Miramar has a cute little restaurant overlooking the ocean and the tiny towns of Miramar and Santa Cruz are just a short stroll away along the beach.

The turnoff for Paraiso Miramar is just 2.5 miles (4.0 km) south of the well-known Playa Amor RV Park (see below). The entrance road has a small sign, follow the good dirt road toward the ocean for .2 miles (.3 km), turn left at the T and drive .3 miles (.5 km) on cobblestones to the campground entrance at the end of the road. Big rigs should have no problems with reasonable caution.

⛺ PLAYA AMOR RV PARK

Address: Playa Los Cocos, Aticama, Nayarit, México

GPS Location: N 21° 28' 29.6", W 105° 11' 45.6"

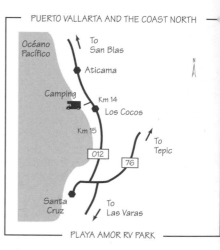

PUERTO VALLARTA AND THE COAST NORTH

PLAYA AMOR RV PARK

We were pleased on our last visit to find that the Playa Amor has been getting some much-needed improvements. New toilet and shower buildings help a lot. Now that most folks headed south use the small road that bypasses Tepic along the coast many people spend the night at Playa Amor. It is a good place to break the drive from Mazatlán to Puerto Vallarta. A lot of other people like Playa Amor for itself, this is one of the few places where you are almost guaranteed to find an unoccupied site on a low bluff overlooking the ocean, even during the high season.

Playa Amor really has two different camping areas. One has 38 spaces with 15-amp outlets, water, and sewer. Another area next door has 35 spaces with only electricity and water. This second area is usually reserved for caravans, they often spend a day or two here on the way up and down the coast. Some sites in both areas have patios and some are pull-throughs. The bluff sites seem to be eroding away, take a look before you park too near the edge! The restrooms in the large building are barely adequate, but recently added small bathrooms and showers are much better. English is spoken.

Playa Amor is located on the highway between San Blas and Santa Cruz to the south. This road heads south at a junction some 1.3 miles (2.1 km) east of the bridge at the edge of San Blas. The campground is 8.5 miles (13.7 km) south of the junction, you will drive through the small town of Aticama about a mile before you reach it.

⛐ TRAILER PARK LOS COCOS

Address: Av. Temiente Azueta(Apdo 8),
San Blas, CP 60340 Nayarit,
México
Telephone: (3) 215-0055

GPS Location: N 21° 31' 57.7", W 105° 17' 00.3"

$$$	⛺	🚰	🚽	🛻	🚿 HOT	📞

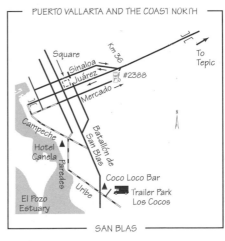

Given the fact that San Blas has an unfortunate (but true) reputation for harboring hordes of biting insects it is probably not too surprising that Los Cocos always has lots of room. The campground itself, set in a grove of coco palms, is pleasant enough. It sits within walking distance of both the historical town of San Blas and the beach.

The sign out front says there are 100 spaces in the campground. There must be at least that many, the campground is a large flat well-clipped grass field under coco palms with services islands widely spaced in rows throughout the campground. Each has a 15-amp outlet, water, and sewer. There are no patios or roadways so every site can be a pull-through. The bathrooms are poor, they have hot water showers but unfortunately harbor even more mosquitoes than you will find outside. When you arrive check in with the bartender in the Coco Loco Bar out front, that's the office. There is a low fence around the campground and a gate that is closed at night.

As you enter San Blas on Mex 74 you will pass over a bridge and in .6 mile (1.0 km) be confronted with a three-way fork. Take the right fork. Drive straight ahead until you come to the square, turn left on the road on the far side of the square. In .7 miles (1.2 km) you will see the Los Cocos straight ahead behind a fairly respectable-looking bar, the Coco Loco. A side road on the right gives you access to the campground gate.

Other Camping Possibilities

There's a new campground under construction between San Blas and Los Cocos. If you are coming from the north and following the coastal bypass route you will turn south just outside San Blas. From that point it is 4.3 miles (6.9 km) to the campground on the beach. When we stopped to look there appeared to be about 30 full-hookup sites being laid out as well as a hotel to the south. A worker told us it would be called the "Motel Y Trailer Park". We expect the owner will come up with something more elaborate. The beach here is very wide with very nice sand. The GPS location is N 21° 30' 35.7", W 105° 12' 41.5". We're guessing the place will be in operation for the 2001/2002 season.

THE CENTRAL WEST COAST

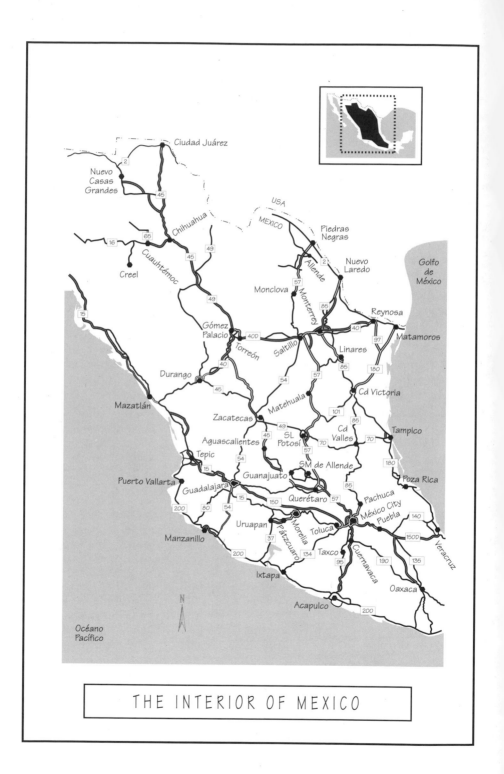

THE INTERIOR OF MEXICO

CHAPTER

. . . . 7

THE INTERIOR OF MEXICO

INTRODUCTION

This chapter covers a huge area, much larger than any of the other chapters in this book. The interior, as organized here, has 27 cities with good camping accommodations. For anyone new to the interior of Mexico it is no easy task to arrange it into an understandable whole in their mind.

Most of the interior is comprised of high plateau or mountains. Two mountain ranges define the borders of the northern interior. The Sierra Madre Occidental are in the west and the Sierra Madre Oriental in the east. Between them is a highland plateau, far from flat, that slopes gradually upward toward the south. This area is called the Altiplano. At the U.S. border the altitude is about 4,000 feet, but in the south near Mexico City it is 8,000 feet.

At the south end of the plateau is a unique east-west volcanic fault area called the Cordillera Neo-Volcánica. It runs from the Cape Corrientes, near Puerto Vallarta on the west coast, to the Tuxtla Mountains near Veracruz on the east coast. Following the fault from west to east you will find some of the highest and most active volcanic mountains in the world including Ceboruco, Nevado de Colima, Pico de Tancitaro, Paricutín, Nevado de Toluca, Popocatépetl (second highest in Mexico, fifth highest in North America), Iztaccíhuatl (third highest in Mexico), La Malinche, and Pico de Orizaba (highest in Mexico, third highest in North America). Within the folds of the Cordillera are the cities of Tepic, Guadalajara, Morelia, Pátzcuaro, Uruapan, Toluca, Mexico City, Cuernavaca, and Puebla.

Almost all of the towns covered in this chapter are above 4,000 feet in altitude, many are over a mile high. This means that the weather, especially in the winter, can be brisk. Daytime temperatures are quite comfortable. During the summer the northern desert cities can be very hot while farther south and higher up temperatures are milder. Both the Guadalajara area and the Cuernavaca area are known for their year-round springtime climates.

ROAD SYSTEM

Most of the cities with camping facilities in the northern interior sit astride one of three major routes south to Mexico City.

The farthest-west of the three routes is Mex 45/49. This highway crosses the border at El Paso/Ciudad Juárez and runs south through Chihuahua, Torreón, Durango, Zacatecas, and Aquascalientes to the Guadalajara and Bajío (Guanajuato, San Miguel de Allende, Querétaro) regions. Much of this route is fast toll roads but often there are alternate free roads.

The next road corridor to the east is Mex 57. This highway crosses the border at Eagle Pass, Texas/Piedras Negras but it is also easily accessed through Monterrey from Laredo/Nuevo Laredo and McAllen/Reynosa. Along this route are the cities of Monterrey, Saltillo, Matehuala, San Luis Potosí, San Miguel de Allende, and Querétaro. This is the quickest route from the border to Mexico City. Much of it is toll road, there are often alternate free routes.

The farthest east of the interior road corridors is the old Pan American Highway, Mex 85. This was once an important route but is sinuous and slow, most people only drive selected sections of the route now. It crosses the border at Laredo/ Nuevo Laredo and runs through Monterrey, Ciudad Victoria, and Ciudad Valles to Pachuca and then Mexico City.

There are many east-west highways connecting these three corridors. One of the most popular is Mex 40 which runs from McAllen/Reynosa to Mazatlán through Monterrey, Saltillo, Torreón, and Durango. Between Durango and Mazatlán this highway descends the famously scenic "Devil's Backbone" which is quite steep in places, use your engine for braking and take it slowly. Trucks use this route so most RVs should be OK.

Once you reach the Bajío, an east-west breadbasket region with some of the most famous and attractive cities in Mexico, you have a choice of several east-west routes. These routes actually run between Guadalajara, Mexico's second largest city, and Mexico City itself. The northernmost is a combination of Mex 80, Mex 45, and Mex 57 and begins in Guadalajara, passes south of Guanajuato and San Miguel de Allende, to Querétaro and on to Mexico City. Much of this highway is toll road. The second is the new Guadalajara to Mexico City toll road, Mex 15D, which starts in Guadalajara, passes just north of Morelia, then through Toluca to Mexico City. The third is the old free Mex 15. This slow but extremely scenic two-lane road runs from Guadalajara, through Morelia, across the mountains past Los Azufres and north of Valle de Bravo, to Toluca and then Mexico City.

You can see that all of these routes funnel in to Mexico City (you've no doubt heard the phrase "all roads lead to Mexico City"). This is great if Mexico City is your destination, but for many people the capital city is a huge roadblock. How do you go on to Puebla and the Yucatán or Cuernavaca and Acapulco? With the proper directions in hand this is no real problem, we've included a bypass section which follows the Mexico City campground section below to show you several bypass routes.

From the interior there are of course many good highways to the coast. Here are a few of them. Starting in the northwest and traveling south along the Sierra Madre Occidental Mex 2 is the traditional east - west route at the top of Mexico just south of the

U.S. border. Farther south there is a scenic but slow and long paved road, Mex 16, connecting Chihuahua with Hermosillo. Mex 40, mentioned above, runs down the "Devil's Backbone" to Mazatlán from Durango. Mex 15 is a major four-lane route (toll with alternate free roads) connecting Guadalajara with Tepic and then running north along the west coast all the way to the border. From Guadalajara you can also follow winding little Mex 80 to the ocean at Barra de Navidad/San Patricio Melaque or the better toll route, Mex 54D through Colima to Tecomán and Manzanillo. Farther south Mex 37 runs from the Bajío through Uruapan to the coast at Playa Azul.

Eastward now, Mex 134 runs from Toluca past Valle de Bravo to the coast near Ixtapa/ Zihuatanejo. This is a long isolated road and is not recommended for travel, there have been attempted holdups and other problems along this highway. From Mexico City a major toll road, Mex 95D, passes through Cuernavaca and down to the coast at Acapulco. This is the first and most famous of Mexico's toll roads but there is also a free route. The free route is quite steep near Taxco but we've done it in a big motorhome towing a car so most rigs should have no problem if they take it easy and use their engines for braking. From near Cuernavaca 160 leads southeast, meets Mex 190 from Puebla, and goes on south to Oaxaca. This is a long and lonely two-lane road, expect to spend two days en route unless you are in a small vehicle. A much quicker route to Oaxaca is from Puebla on Mex 135D, a fairly new two-lane toll road through Tehuacan. You can easily make the trip in one day on this road, it is possible to drive from Puebla to Oaxaca in about 5 hours

On the east side of the country the four-lane toll highway Mex 150D descends to Veracruz from Mexico City and Puebla but there is also a free route, Mex 140, that circles toward the north around Pico de Orizaba and through the interesting and little-visited city of Jalapa. Moving toward the north through the Sierra Madre Oriental we find a new toll highway from Mexico City to Tuxpan under construction. There are several smaller routes through the Sierra Madre on this eastern side of Mexico. A popular one is Mex 70 from San Luis Potosí through Ciudad Valles to Tampico. Finally, Mex 85 from Monterrey to Ciudad Victoria actually passes through the Sierra Madre before heading south to climb toward Mexico City, the Monterrey to Ciudad Victoria section is not a bad road at all.

HIGHLIGHTS

The interior is chock full of interesting destinations. First, of course, have to be the cities. But there are also several regions with lots of interesting sights outside the cities. If you are a lover of hiking and the outdoors the interior has some of the best hiking areas in the country.

Mexico City (Ciudad de México) is the number one interior city. This huge metropolis, the area has somewhere in the neighborhood of 20,000,000 inhabitants, is not difficult for a camper to visit. The number two city is **Guadalajara**, it is even easier to visit than Mexico City and has almost as much to offer. The entire area around Guadalajara and **Lake Chapala** is extremely popular with North Americans, many make it their home. **San Miguel de Allende**, another popular norteamericano hangout, has three good RV parks. The **Cuernavaca area** is full of campgrounds used mostly by Mexico City residents, some are balneario (spa) campgrounds in the countryside outside Cuernavaca. Other attractive colonial cities include **Guanajuato,** **Puebla, Tlaxcala, Morelia, Zacatecas, Querétaro**, and **San Luis Potosí**. A smaller town loved by many tourists, it can't properly be called a city, is **Pátzcuaro**. This is a

DISTANCE TABLE

Miles

	Aguas-calientes	Chihuahua	Ciudad Valles	Creel	Cuernavaca	Durango	Guadalajara	Guanajuato	Los Azufres	Matehuala	México City	Monterrey	Morelia	Nuevo Casas Grandes	Pachuca	Pátzcuaro	Puebla	Querétaro	Saltillo	San Luis Potosi	S.M de Allende	Tepic	Tequisquia-pan	Tlaxcala	Toluca	Torreón	Uruapan	Valle de Bravo	Zacatecas
Aguascalientes	600	263	754	367	265	153	113	273	220	313	360	197	802	323	233	388	181	308	103	165	285	225	382	301	316	273	343	80
Chihuahua	979	800	154	954	480	721	712	872	585	899	480	797	202	908	832	974	764	428	640	765	756	807	968	883	286	873	942	520
Ciudad Valles	429	1306	954	1108	345	465	366	288	429	277	291	318	403	1002	237	438	348	284	371	160	297	498	327	328	330	512	479	380	280
Creel	1231	252	1558		563	875	867	1026	739	1053	634	951	356	1062	987	1129	918	582	794	919	911	961	1123	1037	440	1027	1097	674
Cuernavaca	600	1557	564	1809	618	389	278	192	431	55	621	239	1156	108	275	109	186	562	314	224	521	167	124	94	664	315	144	432
Durango	433	667	760	919	1009	386	378	538	423	563	345	462	610	571	498	639	429	293	306	431	348	473	633	549	151	538	599	186
Guadalajara	250	1177	597	1429	635	631	181	239	323	334	481	164	923	363	200	410	220	429	206	234	132	264	404	295	437	167	310	201
Guanajuato	184	1163	471	1415	454	617	296	189	246	224	434	114	914	234	149	299	92	405	129	53	314	135	293	211	429	190	260	192
Los Azufres	445	1424	700	1676	314	878	391	309	436	138	628	75	1074	192	111	213	195	601	318	233	372	238	207	99	589	151	87	352
Matehuala	360	955	453	1207	704	691	528	402	712	377	209	361	787	386	396	452	241	157	118	255	456	285	446	367	299	437	418	238
México City	511	1468	475	1720	89	920	546	365	225	615	566	185	1101	54	220	75	132	507	259	170	467	113	69	39	610	261	89	378
Monterrey	588	783	520	1035	1014	563	786	708	1026	342	925	553	682	551	589	642	434	52	317	454	614	477	636	553	194	629	603	280
Morelia	322	1301	658	1553	391	755	268	186	123	589	302	903	989	239	36	260	119	526	243	157	296	163	254	146	513	76	146	277
Nuevo Casas Grandes	1293	327	1615	574	1863	983	1488	1473	1731	1269	1775	1099	1594	1110	1034	1176	966	630	842	967	958	1009	1170	1085	488	1075	1144	722
Pachuca	528	1482	387	1734	177	933	592	382	313	630	88	900	390	1789	274	111	142	516	268	180	495	129	91	93	625	315	143	386
Pátzcuaro	380	1359	716	1611	449	813	326	244	181	647	360	961	58	1667	448	296	155	562	279	193	332	198	290	181	549	40	181	312
Puebla	634	1591	569	1843	178	1043	669	488	348	738	123	1048	425	1896	182	483	207	582	334	245	542	188	20	115	685	336	165	453
Querétaro	296	1247	463	1499	304	701	360	150	318	394	215	708	195	1557	232	253	338	407	124	38	353	43	201	119	475	195	170	244
Saltillo	503	698	605	950	917	478	701	662	982	257	828	85	859	1016	843	917	951	664	275	412	562	450	576	526	141	602	576	228
San Luis Potosi	168	1045	261	1297	512	499	336	210	520	192	423	517	397	1357	438	455	546	202	449	137	338	167	328	250	356	319	300	120
S.M de Allende	270	1249	485	1501	366	703	382	86	380	416	277	741	257	1559	294	315	400	62	673	224	366	81	239	157	481	233	208	245
Tepic	466	1235	813	1487	851	568	216	512	607	744	762	1002	484	1544	808	542	885	576	597	552	598	396	536	427	499	299	442	333
Tequisquia-pan	367	1318	534	1570	273	772	431	221	389	465	184	779	266	1627	211	324	307	71	735	273	133	647	182	152	518	239	202	287
Tlaxcala	624	1581	536	1833	202	1033	659	478	338	728	113	1038	415	1886	149	473	33	328	941	536	390	875	297	108	679	330	159	447
Toluca	491	1442	539	1694	153	896	482	345	161	600	64	903	238	1749	152	296	187	195	859	408	257	698	248	177	594	222	50	363
Torreón	516	467	836	719	1085	247	714	700	961	488	996	316	838	787	1020	896	1119	775	231	582	786	815	846	1109	970	589	644	236
Uruapan	446	1425	782	1677	515	879	272	310	247	713	426	1027	124	1733	514	66	549	319	983	521	381	488	390	539	362	962	222	353
Valle de Bravo	560	1539	621	1791	235	978	506	424	142	682	146	985	238	1844	234	296	269	277	941	490	339	722	330	259	82	1052	362	413
Zacatecas	130	849	457	1101	706	303	328	317	575	388	617	458	452	1164	630	510	740	398	373	196	400	544	469	730	593	386	576	675

Kilometers

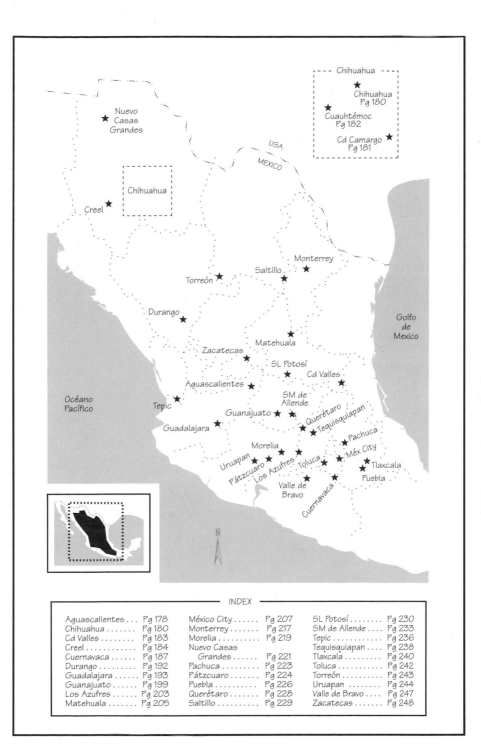

Chihuahua

Chihuahua
Pg 180

Cuauhtémoc
Pg 182

Cd Camargo
Pg 181

Nuevo
Casas
Grandes

USA

MEXICO

Chihuahua

Creel

Monterrey

Saltillo

Torreón

Durango

Golfo
de
Mexico

Matehuala

Zacatecas

SL Potosí

Cd Valles

Océano
Pacífico

Tepic

Aguascalientes

SM de
Allende

Guanajuato

Querétaro

Tequisquiapan

Guadalajara

Morelia

Pachuca

Uruapan

Méx City

Pátzcuaro

Los Azufres

Toluca

Tlaxcala

Valle de
Bravo

Cuernavaca

Puebla

N

THE INTERIOR OF MEXICO

long list but it is difficult to leave out any of these destinations, they all have a lot to offer.

If you are more interested in the countryside your first destination should probably be the **Copper Canyon**. The best access point is Creel, just east of Chihuahua. Other areas of outdoors interest are Los Azufres and the **monarch butterfly reserves** and **La Malinche** volcano near Tlaxcala.

SELECTED CITIES AND THEIR CAMPGROUNDS

AGUASCALIENTES, AGUASCALIENTES (AH-GWAHS-KA-LEE-EHN-TAYS)
Population 750,000, Elevation 6,250 ft (1900 m)

The city of Aguascalientes, capital of a state of the same name, is known for its orderliness and well-being. The attractive central area of the city holds most of the sights interesting to visitors, it has colonial buildings interspersed with more modern structures, including many stores and shopping centers. The city is not known as a tourist destination, many of the visitors it does get come for the **Feria de San Marcos** in late April and early May. The surrounding region is known for producing the best **fighting bulls** in Mexico, also for its **vineyards**. Aguascalientes is named for its **hot springs**, the **Centro Deportivo Aguascalientes** described below is one of them.

Aguascalientes Campgrounds

HOTEL MEDRANO

Address:	Blvd. José Ma. Chávez 904, Aguascalientes, CP 20270 Aguascalientes, México
Telephone:	(4) 915-5500 **Fax:** (4) 916-8076
E-mail:	medranoh@prodigy.net.mx

GPS Location: N 21° 52' 11.8", W 102° 17' 35.9"

The Hotel Medrano is located just a mile or so south of central Aguascalientes. It is a place where the camping facilities aren't considered very important in the scheme of things, but with this convenient location it is difficult to complain and Aguascalientes offers few alternatives.

RV parking is limited to five pull-through spots arranged around a square garden area and surrounded by hotel rooms. The sites have electricity (15-amp outlets) and sewer. There is also a water hookup in the area. Larger rigs can maneuver into this campground with caution. There are no restrooms set aside for campers, a room is available with showers and toilets. The hotel has a restaurant and a swimming pool. You can walk to the central area of town in 15 minutes or catch a bus. Limited English is spoken at the front desk.

The easiest access to the hotel is from Mex 45 entering town from the south. From other directions take one of the two outer ring roads around town until you meet Mex 45 (José Má. Chávez). The hotel is on the east side of the road .8 miles (1.3 km) north of Aguascalientes Ave. Watch for the sign (it is a Best Western Hotel) and swing wide to enter beneath a high arch. If you miss the turn or when you leave the campground you can drive clockwise around the neighborhood to get back to José Má. Chávez and either head out of town or back to the hotel.

CENTRO DEPORTIVO EJIDAL OJOCALIENTE

Address: Km 1 Carr. a San Luis Potosí, Aguascalientes,
               Aguascalientes., México
Telephone: (4) 970-0698

GPS Location: N 21° 52' 45.4", W 102° 15' 43.2"

The Centro is a balneario and sports center east of central Aguascalientes. They allow overnight dry camping. This can be a pleasant place to stay, especially if you like to swim.

There is a grassy area behind the squash courts for tent camping, RVs park in a paved and fenced lot with space for large rigs. Water is available but there are no hookups. The squash courts have restrooms with hot showers. The balneario also has swimming pools, saunas, steam baths, a restaurant, squash and tennis courts and sports fields.

This campground is most easily found if you enter town on Mex 70 from San Luis Potosí to the east. From other directions follow the outer ring road around the east side of town (3er Anillo) until you reach Mex 70. Once headed toward the city center you will cross the second ring road at .9 miles (1.4 km) and see the balneario on the right in 1.4 miles (2.2 km). The ramp down to the gate might cause problems for some rigs with low ground clearance so exercise caution. There is a low arch over the entrance road but RVs can use an alternate gate.

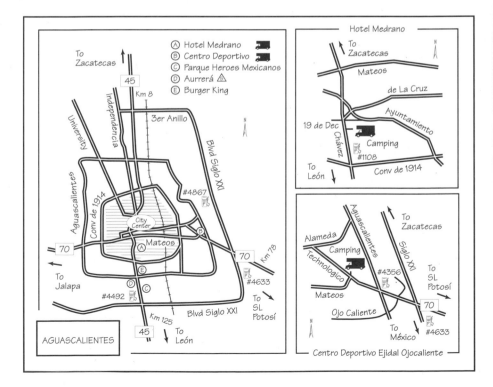

THE INTERIOR OF MEXICO

CHIHUAHUA, CHIHUAHUA (CHEE-WAH-wah)
Population 625,000, Elevation 4,700 ft (1429 m)

Chihuahua is the trade center for a huge area of northern Mexico and the capital city of the state of the same name. For such a large city there is surprisingly little to interest the traveler. One attraction is the **Museo de la Revolución** which is probably the best Pancho Villa museum in Mexico. Chihuahua is also often used as a departure point for rides on the **Chihuahua al Pacífico Railway** to Los Mochis along the Copper Canyon. Travelers with their own vehicles will probably find that Creel makes a better departure point for this trip since it has better places to leave your vehicle and allows you to bypass the least interesting portion of the trip. Chihuahua boasts a fine selection of large supermarkets so it makes a good place to stock up.

Chihuahua Campgrounds

⌦ CHIHUAHUA CITY KOA

Address:	1 de Mayo #3600, Colonia Pacifico, Chihuahua, CP 31030 Chihuahua, México
Location:	Km 14.5 Carr. Chihuahua- Cd. Cuauhtémoc, Chihuahua, Chihuahua, México
Telephone:	(1) 421-7088

GPS Location: N 28° 32' 30.3", W 106° 10' 06.6"

$$ 🏕 👤 🚰 🚐 🚿 🍴 ⚓

Chihuahua has a new and much-needed campground. It is located just east of the city and is handy for travelers needing a place to spend the night and also for visits to the city. While this place does have a KOA sign out front, or did when we visited in 2000/2001, it is not listed in the KOA guide and may not be one for long.

There are 35 large spaces, mostly pull-throughs, on a large lot with no shade. Trees have been planted but they'll need time to grow. There are modern full hookups with 15-amp and either 30-amp or 50-amp outlets although when we visited all had 10-amp breakers. Well-tended grass separates the sites and all sites have picnic tables and barbecues. The campground is located behind a large Pemex. A swimming pool has been completed but bathroom facilities for the campground are still under construction. The Pemex is set up as a truck stop which has good bathroom facilities including hot showers and also a restaurant. There is room for the largest rigs in this campground and access is excellent, no English is spoken. Pay at the office of the Pemex out front.

To find the campground drive westward on Mex 16 toward Cuauhtémoc from the western Chihuahua periférico or bypass road. The campground is 4.9 miles (7.9 km) from the intersection where the southern bypass connects with the western portion of the bypass. The campground is near the Km 14 marker. If you are traveling south it is 8.5 miles (13.7 km) past the Wal-Mart. The big Pemex out front and a large KOA sign make it hard to miss.

CENTRO DEPORTIVO

Address: Av. Division del Norte and Av.
Tecnologico, Chihuahua,
Chihuahua, México

GPS Location: N 28° 39' 20.4", W 106° 04' 53.8"

$$ | 🚰

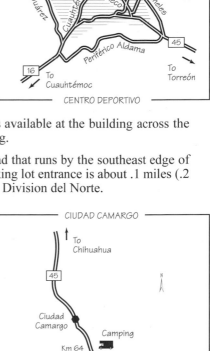

For a visit to central Chihuahua this sports cen-
ter is the best alternative. The camping area is
the parking lot of the stadium in the large
Ciudad Deportivo park on Avenida
Tecnologico. Camping vehicles are allowed to
spend the night there, for a fee. There are no
hookups but there are overhead lights. The
restrooms in the stadium are available but there
are no showers available to RVers. Security
personnel are on duty all night. Potable water is available at the building across the
street, watch for the line that forms each morning.

From Av. Tecnologico turn southwest on the road that runs by the southeast edge of
the park, this is Av. Division del Norte. The parking lot entrance is about .1 miles (.2
km) from the corner of Av. Tecnologico and Av. Division del Norte.

 MOTEL Y TRAILER PARK VILLA DEL CHARRO

Location: Mex 47 (Toll) Jiménez-Chihuahua,
Km 63

GPS Location: N 27° 39' 00.0", W 105° 08' 44.7"

$$ | ⛺ | 🍴 | 🅿

This campground is really a full 95 miles (155
km) south of Chihuahua and just south of the
town of Ciudad Camargo, but it is a good place
to overnight for travelers driving through the
area along the north-south Mex 45 highway.
Access is easy and there are some hookups.

At first glance this campground appears to be
pretty much abandoned. However, there is gen-
erally someone manning the reception desk for the motel units on a hill behind the
camping area and camping is permitted. The campground has 45 pull-through slots
with very poorly maintained full hookups. You will want to do a check before parking
to find one of the slots that has electricity. Water is sometimes available but you might
have to ask to have the pumps turned on. The dedicated restroom building is not in
service so campers must be self-contained. There are eight motel rooms behind the
camping area, campers may be able to negotiate use of the bathroom facilities in one
of the rooms if it is not full. You might even want to just rent a motel room, they are
quite reasonable and there is room to park your rig. However, make sure that hot
water is available first if that is important to you.

THE INTERIOR OF MEXICO

The Villa del Charro sits on the east side of Mex 45D (the toll road) near the Km 64 marker about 1 mile (1.6 km) south of Ciudad Camargo.

LOEWEN'S RV PARK

Address: Km 14 Carr. a Col. A. Obregón, Cd. Cuauhtémoc, Chihuahua, México

Telephone and Fax: (1) 582-6523

GPS Location: N 28° 31' 21.2", W 106° 54' 36.6"

In past years full-service campgrounds have been scarce in this region and Loewen's has always been a popular stop for caravans bound for La Junta for loading onto rail cars for the Copper Canyon transit. If there is no caravan in the campground you're likely to be alone. Cuauhtémoc is a large agricultural center with a population of some 150,000 people sitting in the middle of a rich farming region famous for its apples. Mennonites farm much of the surrounding land.

THE INTERIOR OF MEXICO

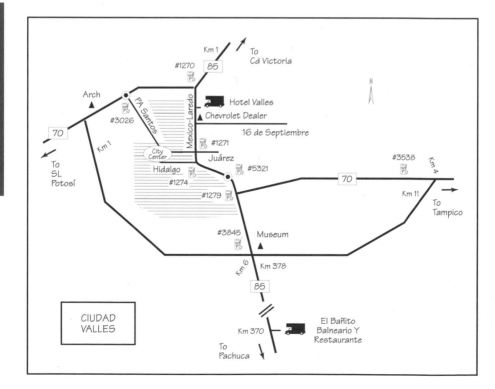

There are 23 pull-through spaces in a large flat grassy field with electricity (15-amp outlets), sewer, and water hookups. Back-in sites along the perimeter also have some utilities. There's lots of room for big rigs. A nearby building has restrooms with hot showers, coin-operated laundry, and a meeting room. There are a few supplies for sale.

Mex 16 runs west from Chihuahua 61 miles (98 km) to Ciudad Cuauhtémoc. Mex 65 cuts off to the north from Mex 16 both east and west of Ciudad Cuauhtémoc, they meet north of town and continue north. If you take the more direct western cut-off and drive north you will see Loewen's on the right after 8.4 miles (13.7 km).

CIUDAD VALLES, SAN LUIS POTOSÍ (SEE-OOH-DAWD VAH-YES)
Population 105,000, Elevation 300 ft (91 m)

Once an important overnight stop on Mex 85 to Mexico City, Ciudad Valles receives fewer visitors now that there are alternatives to the slow and winding highway that makes its way south through rugged mountains. Today the city serves as a hub for exploring the surrounding Huasteca region, there is a **Huastec Regional Museum of Anthropology and Archeology** in Valles which makes a good introduction to the Indian culture and surrounding attractions. Travelers descending from the higher areas to the west and south may be surprised by the climate here, the area is known as part of the **northernmost tropical rain forest** in North America.

Ciudad Valles Campgrounds

HOTEL VALLES

Address:	Boulevard México-Laredo 36 Norte,
	Ciudad Valles, CP 79050 S.L.P., México
Telephone:	(1) 382-0050

GPS Location: N 21° 59' 32.5", W 099° 00' 42.4"

Hotel Valles is by far the most conveniently located of the two Ciudad Valles campgrounds. It also is a very nice hotel, almost resort-class (not the campground, however).

The campground area is very near the front entrance. Parking is under trees on an area paved with rockwork. There are about 25 spaces in three rows, vehicles park parallel so with today's large rigs there probably is really room for about 12 rigs. Hookups are old, some are in poor repair. Most sites have some combination of 15-amp power, water, and sewer. There is also a grassy area for tent campers and those not needing hookups. Several private bathrooms near the pool offer toilets and hot showers and are in good condition. There are two good restaurants and a nice swimming pool. English is spoken at the front desk.

Ciudad Valles has a ring road with highways approaching from the north (Ciudad Victoria), south (Pachuca), east (Tampico) and west (San Luis Potosí). From east or west just follow the ring road around until you get to either the intersection with Mex 85 from the south or Mex 85 from the north. The campground is located on Blvd. Mexico-Laredo which is also Mex 85 as it passes through town on the north-south axis. From the north at the intersection of Mex 85 from Cd. Victoria and the ring road head south, the Hotel Valles will be on the left in .4 miles (.6 km). From the south on Mex 85 from the intersection with the ring road zero your odometer and drive north.

In .9 miles (1.5 km) you'll see Pemex # 1279 on the left. Continue straight through the intersection at the Pemex and at 1.2 miles (1.9 km) you will come to a traffic circle with another Pemex, this one #5321. Continue straight and at 2.2 miles (3.5 km) you will see the hotel on the right.

EL Bañito Balneario y Restaurante

> **Address:**   Km 370 Carr. 85 (Apdo. 66), Cd. Valles, S.L.P., México
>
> *GPS Location: N 21° 54' 53.7", W 098° 57' 04.7"*

The El Bañito is a good place to let down your hair and relax. There's nothing fancy about this balneario, in fact we've had people tell us that they drove by and it looked closed to them, and this while we were actually staying there.

The campground has about 20 usable back-in spaces with 15-amp outlets, sewer, water and patios. The lower spaces nearer the front are suitable for big rigs. There is quite a bit of shade and the orange blossoms next to the campground smell great in the spring. The grass sometimes isn't clipped as closely as it could be and the facilities are old and a little run down. There are several restrooms near the pools and lots of changing rooms, but, amazingly for a balneario, no showers to be seen. If you ask the manager he'll give you a key to the one cold shower, it is in an outbuilding and not available to the balneario customers, don't expect much of a shower. The two swimming pools smell of sulfur, one strongly and the other only slightly. This second pool is actually very pleasant, a morning swim before the first customers arrive about 10:30 a.m. is one of the best parts of this stop. The other is the little restaurant, we know people who come here just for the French fries.

El Bañito is south of Ciudad Valles on Mex 85. It is on the east side of the highway very near the Km 370 marker. This is 5.4 miles (8.7 km) south of the outer Ciudad Valles ring road.

Side Trips from Ciudad Valles

The **Tamasopo waterfall** area is located about 35 miles (57 km) west on Mex 70 and then north about 5 miles (8 km). There are swimming areas and primitive tent camping sites.

The **Zona Arqueológica El Consuelo** is located in the other direction, 19 miles (31 km) east on Mex 70 and then 3 miles (5 km) south from Tamuín village. These are excavations of a large Huastec ceremonial center.

Winding Mex 85 south to Pachuca crosses remote mountains and is quite narrow in places. During certain times of the year fog is common, this isn't a route for folks in a hurry. The highway passes through the heart of the Huastec region, some interesting Huastec towns center around **Pedro Antonio de los Santos** some 31 miles (50 km) south of Ciudad Valles.

CREEL, CHIHUAHUA (CREH-EHL)
Population 3,500, Elevation 7,659 ft (2,328 m)

Creel is the gateway to the **Copper Canyon** area. Activity centers on the railway station and nearby plaza, almost everything in town is within walking distance and there are restaurants and grocery stores. The real attraction is the nearby Copper Can-

THE INTERIOR OF MEXICO

yon. This is the approximate midpoint of the Chihuahua - Pacífico Railway and an excellent place to catch the train to Los Mochis or El Fuerte. If you are interested in some of the best hiking and tent camping in North America this is the place. Hotels in town run tour vans to various sights in the area and also offer hiking tours.

Creel Campground

🚐 HOTEL VILLA MEXICANA & KOA RV PARK

Location:	Calle Adolpo Lopez Mateos S/N, Creel, Chihuahua, México
Address:	Ave. Tecnologico #4904, Col. Granjas Industriales, Chihuahua, CP 31160 Chihuahua, México
Telephone:	(1) 421-7088 or (888) 610-2095 (Toll Free)
Fax:	(1) 421-7089
E-mail:	koacreel@infosel.net.mx
Web Site:	www.koacoppercanyon.com

GPS Location: N 27° 44' 45.5", W 107° 38' 11.9"

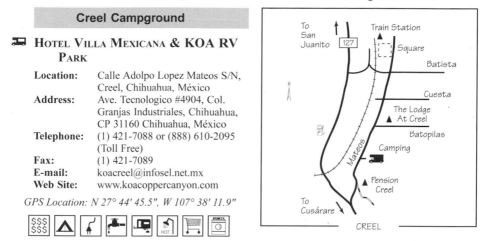

This new KOA campground fills a desperate need in Creel, gateway to the Copper Canyon. You now have a base for exploring the area, as well as a place to leave your RV if you wish to take the train along the edge of the canyon to El Fuerte or Los Mochis.

The campground offers full hookups in sites large enough for modern big rigs, some sites even have 50-amp outlets. There are about 80 spaces. Restrooms are modern with hot showers and there is a convenience store and an enclosed food preparation and eating area for the tenters. The campground even has a self-service laundry. For folks wanting to ride the train the campground is within easy walking distance of the central square and the train station. You can leave your rig here and take the two-day rail trip with little fear for your rig's safety since the campground has 24 hour security.

As you approach Creel from the north pass through town on the paved road until you reach the southern entrance road at the far end of town. Turn left onto this cobblestone street, you will see the campground entrance on your right in a short distance.

Other Camping Possibilities

It is possible to camp at a primitive area near Lago de Arareco known as Valle de los Hongos. This campground has little in the way of facilities. It is a few miles down the road toward Batopilas from Creel on the left side of the road. The GPS location is N 27° 42' 04.5", W 107° 35' 42.4". No security is provided.

Side Trips from Creel

Access into the **Copper Canyon** for hiking and camping is not really difficult. Don't attempt a serious hike, however, without proper maps and supplies. You should use a guide or at the very least obtain a good guidebook. This can be complicated camping country because you must contend with both the country and its inhabitants, the Tarahumara Indians. The canyons are their home and proper etiquette is essential.

THE INTERIOR OF MEXICO

Many people use the train as an access route. There are trails or roads into the canyon from several stops including **Divisadero** where there is an extremely strenuous hiking trail down to the river and Bahuichivo where you can catch a bus down to the town of **Urique** in the canyon on the river. The best way to get into the canyon country is probably the bus from Creel to **Batopilas**. Remote Batopilas has some interesting hiking routes that are not nearly as difficult as an on-foot descent into (and ascent out of) one of the canyons. It is also possible to drive to Divisadero in almost any vehicle (the entire route is being paved) and high-clearance smaller vehicles can drive farther along the rail line or make the long and dusty drive on a different road all the way to Batopilas. Creel itself has some good hiking routes including ones to the **Cristo Rey** statue overlooking town and to the **San Ignacio de Arareco** mission village.

A good side trip to make in your vehicle is **Basaseachic Falls National Park**. The falls themselves have a drop of almost 1,000 feet and there are marked hiking trails. There are **several** different tent-camping **and boondocking** areas with pit toilets in the park, they are near the entrances off Mex 16 and Chih 330. To reach the park from Creel backtrack 19 miles (30 km) on Chih. 127 to San Juanito, then follow Chih 330 north for about 59 miles (95 km) to the park entrance. This road also goes on to meet Mex 16 a few miles past the park entrance so you can continue either east to Chihuahua or west to Hermosillo.

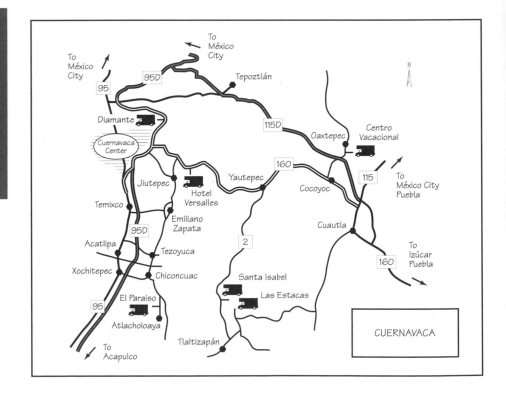

CUERNAVACA, MORELOS (KWER-NAH-VAH-KAH)
Population 1,000,000, Elevation 5,100 ft (1,550 m)

The Cuernavaca area is the weekend playground for people from Mexico City. The weather is usually warmer and far more pleasant than that of the capital since the altitude is far lower. We've certainly always had good weather when we've visited Cuernavaca. By Cuernavaca we mean the entire region around the city because the whole area is full of interesting sights and destinations, as well as many campgrounds.

Like many Mexican cities Cuernavaca's interesting sights tend to be clustered near the central square, in this case a double one called the **Plaza de Armas** and the **Jardin Juárez**. Next to the squares on the southeast side is a large **home built for Cortés**, he lived in Cuernavaca for several years. The building is now a museum with colonial and Indian artifacts from the area. Also near the square are the **Palacio Municipal** and the **Catedral de la Asunción**. A few blocks to the west is the Jardín Borda, a large park with lakes and gardens. The city is well supplied with excellent restaurants.

In the surrounding area you will find many other attractions. There are several balnearios (bathing resorts) including three with campgrounds which are listed below. The ex-hacienda at **Temixco** is also worth a visit. The mountain-side town of **Tepoztlán** makes a good day-trip. It has an old Dominican convent, an archeological museum, and the **Tepozteco Pyramid** perched on the mountain above Tepoztlán and offering great views to those willing to hike the 2 miles (3 km) up from town. The **Xochicalco** archeological site is probably the most impressive in the area. It is located about 25 miles (41 km) from Cuernavaca to the south and is best known for it's **Pyramid of the Plumed Serpent**.

THE INTERIOR OF MEXICO

Cuernavaca Campgrounds

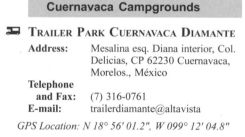

🚐 **TRAILER PARK CUERNAVACA DIAMANTE**

Address:	Mesalina esq. Diana interior, Col. Delicias, CP 62230 Cuernavaca, Morelos., México
Telephone and Fax:	(7) 316-0761
E-mail:	trailerdiamante@altavista

GPS Location: N 18° 56' 01.2", W 099° 12' 04.8"

TRAILER PARK CUERNAVACA DIAMANTE

This trailer park is the most popular in the Cuernavaca region for caravans and RVers passing through. Its popularity stems from its location near the toll highway and also inside the city. Cuernavaca is a popular vacation and weekend retreat for people from Mexico City, the Diamante is really designed to service those people. Up to now you probably have believed that Mexican people really don't own RVs, but a few do. This park is home to a large part of them. Mexico City residents rent spots here on an annual basis and come up for the weekend. The nicer spaces in the upper park are generally occupied by these permanently-parked rigs. There is a separate area for those of us who are passing through.

The temporary area is located below the main park and just above Mex 95. Freeway noise is noticeable but not a major problem. The area is much-improved over the last few years. Parking is now on grass. Spaces are back-in and have full hookups with 15-amp outlets. They're large enough for big rigs however you must exercise caution descending the ramp to the parking area if you have a rig with low ground clearance. New restrooms are provided for this lower area with hot showers, others are also available above.

The key to enjoying this park is knowing that it is a beehive of activity on weekends but almost deserted during the week. The facilities are quite nice and include three swimming pools, a tennis court, and a billiard room. You'll have a great time during the quiet of the week. Weekends are busier, you will probably have a chance to meet some Mexican RVers.

The campground is outside walking distance of central Cuernavaca. Taxis are the most convenient way to get around this crowded town. You can generally flag one down if you walk the short distance up to Diana Street.

To reach the campground take the Diana Street off ramp from Mex 95D. Diana is just south of the Km 87 marker and has a huge supermarket right at the exit. Take the Diana exit and head up the hill on Diana. If you are traveling north on Mex 95 you should know that there are two exits for Diana, right next to each other. If you take the first one you will not be able to turn left at the bottom of the ramp. Make sure to take the second exit lane and then turn left at the bottom and drive under the toll road and up the hill. At .6 miles (1 km), just as you are cresting the hill, you want to take a left on Mesalina. It is marked with a trailer park sign on the left side of Diana but facing you as you come up the hill, watch carefully. Follow the entrance road as it zigzags right, then left, then right again and then left to the gate. You may have some problems raising the gate guard but there's a buzzer, eventually he'll open the gate and check you in.

We hear that the owners are looking for a new location for this park, watch our web site (www.rollinghomes.com) for news of this change.

🚐 EL PARAISO DE LOS ACAMPADORES TRAILER PARK

Address: Atlacholoaya, Morelos, México
Telephone: (7) 361-3454   **Fax:** (7) 361-3456

GPS Location: N 18° 45' 52.9", W 099° 13' 19.7"

 $$$ *(small)* $$$ *(large)*

EL PARAISO DE LOS
ACAMPADORES TRAILER PARK

This large, well-run campground in a country setting caters primarily to Mexico City weekenders. Unlike the Diamonte there are not a lot of permanent rigs here. It would no doubt be more popular with RVers if it were easier to find. If you are a Taxco fan this is the closest campground to that city. It is also a fine campground for larger rigs, but you'll want to have a smaller vehicle to do your sightseeing, public transportation is not very accessible from here.

The El Paraiso has about 100 spaces, all have 15-amp outlets (some 30-amp breakers) and water, 40 also have sewer. The spaces are grass under shade trees and are large enough for big rigs. There are big tiled restrooms with hot water showers. There is also a swimming pool, playground equipment and a small store. Reservations are unnecessary except during holidays, use the phone if you want to make them because the mail is slow and erratic. English is spoken.

Access to this campground has been greatly improved with the construction of an off-ramp from Mex 85 to service Cuernavaca's airport. From north or south take the exit near Km 105 marked Aeropuerto and Tepetzingo. Zero your odometer and drive eastward, signs say Tepetzingo is this way. You want to go in the opposite direction from the airport. At 1.3 miles (2.1 km) you will reach an intersection, turn right, a sign pointing this way says Chiconcuac. At 2.2 miles (3.5 km) you will pass through a small town and at 2.8 miles (4.5 km) you will see a small airstrip on the right. You will reach an intersection at 3.6 miles (5.8 km), turn right here and then at 4 miles (6.5 km) reach the entrance road for the campground. Turn right on a small road through fields and you will find the entrance to the campground in another .4 mile (.6 km). When we last visited it was possible to travel from Cuernavaca to this campground without paying a toll if you drove past the airport off-ramp for another 3.1 miles (5 km), reversed course using a handy retorno, and then exited at the Airport exit northbound. No telling how long this will last.

LAS ESTACAS

Address:	Km 6 Carretera Tlaltizapán-Cuautla, Tlaltizapán, Morelos, México
Telephone:	(7) 345-0077 or (7) 312-4412 (Cuernavaca)
Fax:	(7) 345-0159
Web Site:	www.lasestacas.com

GPS Location: N 18° 43' 40.9", W 099° 06' 40.3"

Las Estacas is a balneario in a class by itself. It has a half-mile crystal-clear jungle river running through the grounds. Another great feature is the beautiful RV park. However, this is one of the most expensive RV parks in Mexico, in effect you get charged for camping and also an entrance fee. If you think of it that way, that you are also getting entrance to one of Mexico's premier balnearios, the price doesn't seem quite so steep. Here it is, as of the winter of 2000/2001: $47 for two people in an RV for one night (and two days), $37 per night if you stay two nights (and three days)!

The RV park has 13 back-in spaces with 15-amp outlets, sewer, and water hookups. The pads are gravel arranged off a paved driveway, well-clipped grass separates them, tall palms and other trees provide shade, and flowers complete the picture. The slots are a little short for big rigs but by now you probably are accustomed to making your rig fit into a short space, since the park is usually practically empty a long rig should cause no problems. There is also an extremely large area set aside for tent camping. Restrooms are basic and have cold showers but are well maintained.

Las Estacas has many swimming pools, an open-air restaurant/bar, a mini-mart, miniature golf, and horse rentals. Best of all is the river. The water is cool but not cold, you can easily drift through the grounds for a half-hour using a snorkel to watch the many fish as you float along. A few deeper pools provide areas for diving and you can wave at the folks at the bar as you drift by. When you reach the edge of the property you can climb out and go back for more.

To reach Las Estacas turn south near Km 26 of the Cuernavaca-Cuautla road (Mex 160). Road signs point to Jojutla and Zacatepec. Note the large sign advertising Las Estacas here, you will see several of these as you approach the park. Zero your odometer here. Follow the road south, it goes through several small built-up areas until at 6.7 miles (10.9 km) there is a Y, go left following the sign for Balneario Estacas. The new section of road is one of the best that you've seen in Mexico. At 11.3 miles (18.5 km) you pass the Balneario Santa Isabel on the left. There is also an entrance to Las Estacas here, but it is for cars and pedestrians, not RVs. At 11.9 miles (19.4 km) the road T's, go left. Watch closely now, at 14.1 miles (23.0 km) there is a concrete road on the left that goes down a short hill and meets another small road, where you turn left. This is a short cut that allows you to bypass a sharp difficult turn ahead. If you miss the concrete road at 14.1 miles (23.0 km) just continue on for .5 mile (.8 km), make the difficult turn just past the Pemex station #3650, and come back to this point. You will soon pass over a single lane bridge and then go straight at a Y at 14.8 miles (24.2 km). Finally at 16.0 miles (26.1 km) turn left, Las Estacas will be on the left at 17.0 miles (27.8 km).

🚐 CENTRO ECOTURISTICO EJIDAL SANTA ISABEL "LAS POCITAS"

Address: Col. Alejandra, Tlaltizapán, Morelos, México

GPS Location: N 18° 43' 58.4", W 099° 06' 53.8"

CENTRO ECOTURISTICO EJIDAL SANTA ISABEL "LAS POCITAS"

If Las Estacas is a little rich for your blood try the balneario next door, the Santa Isabel. The amenities are much more basic but the price is better (although still pretty steep).

The Balneario Santa Isabel has lots of room for camping on two large grassy fields, some have palapas. There are no hookups other than two electrical outlets on one light pole in the middle of one of the fields. Restrooms are very basic with flush toilets and cold showers. Swimming is in two nice dammed pools, this is the same river used by Las Estacas. There is also a palapa bar on the property.

To reach the Santa Isabel turn south near Km 26 of the Cuernavaca-Cuautla road (Mex 160). Road signs point to Jojutla and Zacatepec. Note the large sign advertising Las Estacas here, you will see several of these as you approach the parks. Zero your odometer here. Follow the road south, it goes through several small built-up areas until at odometer 6.7 there is a Y, go left following the sign for Balneario Estacas. At odometer 11.3 you will see the Balneario Santa Isabel on the left just before the Las Estacas parking and pedestrian entrance.

⊟ HOTEL VERSALLES

Address: Carretera Cuernavaca-Cuautla Km
                  15.5, Cuernavaca, Morelos, México
Telephone: (7) 323-0099

GPS Location: N 18° 53' 29.9", W 099° 07' 42.9"

The Hotel Versalles has just five RV slots in a fenced yard next to the small motel and restaurant. They are short back-in slots, 15-amp outlets and water are available and three have a sewer drain. There are no dedicated restrooms but a room is available for showers and the restaurant has restrooms. There is also a decent swimming pool. There is frequent bus service along the road in front of the hotel and

even a small bus station just a short distance to the east so bus transportation into Cuernavaca should be easy.

Watch for the Hotel Versalles on the south side of the Cuernavaca-Cuautla free road (Mex 160) near the Km 15.5 marker.

⊟ IMSS CENTRO VACACIONAL OAXTEPEC

Address: Oaxtepec, Morelos., México
Telephone: (7) 356-0101

GPS Location: N 18° 54' 05.2", W 098° 58' 47.4"

The IMSS (Mexican government social security) runs this huge balneario but anyone is welcome. There are over twenty swimming pools here, you'll want to visit just to see the place. It was originally constructed for the 1968 Olympic Games in Mexico City.

The RV camping area is a small grassy field with room for about 18 large rigs to hook up to electricity (15-amp style outlets) and water, there is no sewer hookup or dump station. There is also room for another 10 or so rigs to boondock. The sites have a moderate slope, leveling may be difficult. A tent camping area next door has grassy fields with room for hundreds of tents. There are restroom available to the campgrounds with toilets (and cold showers for the tenters), hot showers are available in the large dressing room buildings near the pools. In addition to the swimming pools there are several restaurants, a small supermarket, hotels and rental cabañas (each with a small wading pool), a geodesic dome covering a garden, play areas, rental boats on a small lake, and even an overhead tram. Virtually no English is spoken here.

The campground is located right next to Mex 115D near Cuautla. Take the exit marked Oaxtepec near the Km 27 marker and then turn north, you'll see the entrance almost immediately. Alternately, from Mex 160, the Cuernavaca to Cuautla highway, turn north at the sign to Oaxtepec near Km 36, the balneario is 1.2 miles (1.9 km) ahead after you pass under Mex 115D.

Other Camping Possibilities

If you find that you like camping at balnearios you have some other choices. Here are a couple that advertise camping areas but that we have not had the time to check out: Balneario Los Limones in the center of Cuautla and Centro Turístico Ejidal El Bosque in Oaxtepec. We suspect that they are more suitable for tents than RVs.

Side Trips from Cuernavaca

Mexico's colonial silver town, **Taxco**, doesn't currently have a campground but it is an easy day trip from the Cuernavaca region, the distance is about 60 miles (96 km). There's easy toll road access and also a decent free road. Parking in Taxco is difficult for big rigs so if you don't have a tow car consider taking a bus from Cuernavaca.

Once you get familiar with the long-distance bus stations you might consider another excellent bus destination from Cuernavaca, **Mexico City**. The ride takes about an hour and a half on a luxury bus and you can leave your vehicle safe in a Cuernavaca campground.

DURANGO, DURANGO (DOO-RAIN-GO)
Population 400,000, Elevation 6,200 ft (1,885 m)

Durango is often visited by travelers crossing Mexico from Texas to the Mazatlán area. The city and the surrounding area was a filming location for many westerns, there are several **movie set locations** just to the north of town that you can visit. Durango has been declared a national monument because of the colonial architecture, especially a number of churches in the central area. Durango's plaza and surrounding neighborhood are good places to explore on foot.

Durango Campground

🚐 **CAMPO MEXICO HOTEL**

Address:	Av. 20 de Noviembre y Heroico
	Colegio Militar, Durango, Dgo. México
Telephone:	(1) 8-18-79-84 **Fax:** (1) 818-3015

GPS Location: N 24° 01' 49.8", W 104° 38' 33.3"

Like many campgrounds in central Mexico this one is located on the grounds of a motel. In this place the grounds have a very large open grassy field and the RV sites are nicely placed away from the hustle and bustle of the entrance and rooms. It's a nice relaxing location although there is heavy traffic on the far side of the fence directly behind the sites.

There are 7 large parking spaces with full hookups, or perhaps 14 with partial hookups. Electricity is from seven 15-amp outlets with space to plug in two cords. In the past some of these have been wired for 220 volts, but we tested them all and they are now all 110. Actually, the voltage was about 135 volts and some had open grounds, others had reversed polarity, and some tested fine. About normal for Mexico. There are also 14 water faucets and 7 dump drains. The sites are located in a large area so there is lots of room for tent campers and those not needing hookups. The motel has no restrooms for the camping area but has let us use one of the rooms for a toilet and shower. The motel has a restaurant, a pool, and a children's play area. Several supermarkets are within a mile or so. Some English is usually spoken at the desk.

DURANGO

To find the motel start at the big intersection where Mex 45 from Zacatecas and Mex 40 from Torreón meet. This is the corner of Boulevard Fco. Villa and Ave. Filipe Pescador. As Blvd. Fco Villa crosses Pescador toward town it becomes Blvd. Heroico Colegio Militar. You can identify the corner by the big statue of Pancho Villa on a horse that is located next to it (recently moved from the center of the intersection). Head southwest toward central Durango on Colegio Militar for .4 miles (.6 km), you'll see the motel's large fenced field on your right, it has a water tank looking like a golf ball on a tee in the middle. Take the right turn on Ave. 20 de Noviembre just beyond and then turn immediately right into the motel entrance. Really big rigs may find this a difficult turn so swing well out as you make the turn, often there are cars parked under the portico at the entrance blocking it so you may have to park outside and make another swing around the block once you check in.

GUADALAJARA, JALISCO (GWAH-DAH-LAH-HAH-RAH)
Population 4,000,000, Elevation 5,100 ft (1,550 m)

Guadalajara is the second largest city in Mexico, much easier to visit than Mexico City and very rewarding. This and a climate with year-round decent weather have made Guadalajara a favorite retirement city for Americans and Canadians. The large norteamericano population also means that it is easy to find information, activities, and friends.

There are many attractions in Guadalajara, here are just a few. The center of town is the **cathedral**. It is surrounded by four elegant squares and many walking streets, this is probably the most attractive central area in all of Mexico. Nearby is the **Mercado Libertad**, a huge municipal market that is without a doubt also the cleanest and most attractive in the country. It takes massive self-control to walk through the food section without sitting down to at least a small snack. Probably the most important museum in Guadalajara is the **Regional Museum of Guadalajara** with archeological, crafts, and painting exhibits. It is located in the block northeast of the cathedral. You should also visit the **Cabañas Cultural Institute** at the east end of the Plaza Tapatía to see some of local artist José Clemente Orozco's murals.

In the suburbs of Guadalajara you will want to visit famous **Tlaquepaque**. The town is a favorite with home decorators, it is a source of pottery, glassware, silver, copper ware, furniture, leather goods and even sculpture. **Tonalá**, a little farther from the center of Guadalajara, is the source of some of the things you'll see in Tlaquepaque, especially pottery. Tonalá has open-air markets on Thursday and Sunday where you may find some excellent pottery bargains as well as many other items.

The month of October is an excellent time to visit the city. The city holds it's **Fiestas de Octubre** with continuing cultural events. During the same month the suburb of Zapopan celebrates the end of the 4-month **pilgrimage of the Virgin of Zapopan** with a huge bash on October 12.

Driving in Guadalajara can be confusing. The city is criss-crossed by wide boulevards, but they run at odd angles. You must keep a close eye on the map. Many of the main boulevards have lateral streets running along both sides. You are usually not allowed to turn from the center lanes, either left or right. This is confusing at first, watch to see what other drivers are doing.

The region around Guadalajara is full of interesting destinations. Two are especially popular with RVers since there are convenient campgrounds nearby. **Lake Chapala** is south of Guadalajara about 24 miles (38 km). You can reach it by driving south on

THE INTERIOR OF MEXICO

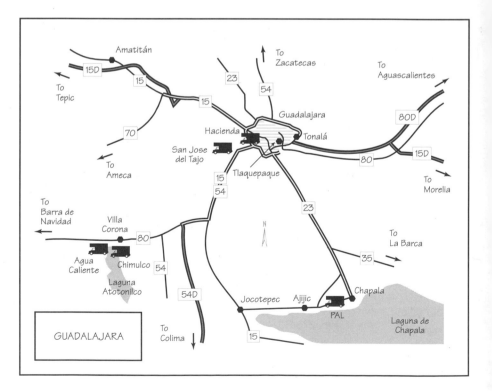

Mex 23 or Mex 54 past the San Jose del Tajo campground. The PAL campground is in Ajijic near the north shore of the lake. About 15 miles (24 km) west of the lake there are two campgrounds in the hot-water-springs town of **Villa Corona**. All of these campgrounds are listed below in this section.

Guadalajara Campgrounds

🚐 HACIENDA TRAILER PARK

Address:	Circunvalación Pte. 66, Ciudad Granja (Apdo. 5-494), Guadalajara, CP 45000 Jalisco, México
Telephone:	(3) 627-1724, (3) 627-1843
Fax:	(3) 627-2832

GPS Location: N 20° 40' 52.0", W 103° 26' 53.3"

The large city of Guadalajara has only one campground within the ring road. This is the charming Hacienda Trailer Park. It is easy to reach without driving on crowded roads and easy to find, especially if you are approaching the city on Mex 15 from the west.

The Hacienda has 98 spaces with patios arranged along cobblestone paths under spreading shade trees. All spaces have 15-amp outlets, water, and sewer and some have TV hookups. These are all back-in spaces. Very large rigs find the Hacienda crowded but usually manage to enter, if you are longer than 35 feet you might find the other Guadalajara parks a better match. The central building houses the bathrooms with hot showers, a lounge, billiard room, and staffed laundry room. The adjoining swimming pool is especially well maintained and surrounded by comfortable lounge chairs. English is spoken at the check-in desk and the people are helpful.

Access to downtown Guadalajara by bus is convenient and inexpensive. Ask for directions at the desk. Shopping is equally easy. There are huge Wal-Mart and Costco stores a 25-minute walk from the campground, you can also use the bus to reach them.

There are rumors that this campground will close in the next few years, keep an eye on www.rollinghomes.com for updates.

To find the campground start at the point where the ring road (Anillo Periférico) and Mex 15 from Tepic meet (actually Mex 15 passes over the ring road). Zero your odometer at this point and head southeast into town on Av. Vallarta which is the continuation of Mex 15. Av. Vallarta is a boulevard with lateral roads along the side, you should get on the lateral as soon as possible. In 1 mile (1.6 km) you will see a Nissan Dealer on the right, you want to turn right on the street immediately after the dealer. The turn is a difficult one for big rigs. You may need to go to the next stoplight, turn left and cross to the lateral on the far side, come back and turn left to cross the boulevard again and drive up the street next to the Nissan dealer. After the turn proceed .4 mile (.6 km) to a traffic circle, as you go to the right around it take the second exit (there is a sign here for the campground) onto Poniente and you will find the campground on the right in about .2 mile (.3 km).

SAN JOSE DEL TAJO TRAILER PARK RESORT

Address:	P.O. Box 31-242, Guadalajara, Jalisco, México
Location:	Highway 15, Km 15
Telephone:	(3) 686-1738

GPS Location: N 20° 35' 02.3", W 103° 27' 14.5"

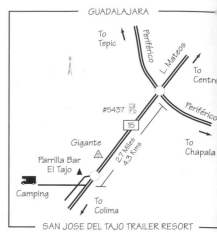

SAN JOSE DEL TAJO TRAILER RESORT

Located just a few miles outside the Guadalajara periférico in a pleasant country setting, San Jose del Tajo is the campground of choice for many visitors to the area. The largest rigs will fit here.

The campground has about 175 spaces, all back-in with patio and paved parking strips. Most sites will take large rigs. All sites have 15-amp outlets (some also have 30 amp outlets, probably installed by RVers), water, and sewer. There is also quite a bit of shade. The restrooms are older but are kept clean and have hot showers. There is a swimming pool but it does not seem to get much use, it needed cleaning when we visited. There are TV hookups, a large meeting room/lounge/library, some groceries in the reception office, a Telmex phone, and a popular nearby restaurant. English is spoken at the desk and tent camping is only available from May to September. Busses to downtown Guadalajara stop near the entrance to the campground.

To find the campground take the exit for Mex 54 (Morelia, Colima) from the Guadalajara periférico. This is a four-lane highway. At 2 miles (3.2 km) you will see a Gigante supermarket on the right. Slow down as you reach 2.5 miles and make sure you are in the right lane and do not drive over the overpass. The entrance to the campground is on the right next to the overpass at 2.7 miles (4.4 km). Turn in and follow the cobblestone road for .6 miles (1 km) to the campground. Coming from the south you will have to bypass the campground and make a 180, probably at the retorno opposite the Gigante supermarket, and then return to enter.

PAL LAKE CHAPALA RV PARK

Address:	P.O. Box 84, Chapala, CP 45900 Jalisco, México
Telephone:	(3) 766-0440, (3) 766-0040 or (3) 766-1447

GPS Location: N 20° 17' 54.1", W 103° 14' 31.3"

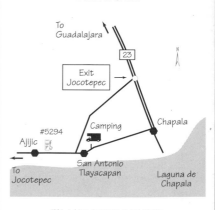

PAL LAKE CHAPALA RV PARK

The north shore of Lake Chapala has been a resort area since the mid-nineteenth century. The top trailer park in the area is the PAL RV Park.

The park originally had about 100 back-in

spaces, but this number is down to about 89 because many people have built permanent casas around their units. All spaces have patios and there is plenty of room for big rigs. All sites have 30-amp outlets, sewer, and water. Most also have TV hookups. Air conditioners are OK in this park, but you probably won't need them with Chapala's near-perfect weather. This campground is known for its spic-and-span tiled bathrooms, they have hot showers. There is a beautiful clean swimming pool that is well used, a self-service laundry, a club house with terrace, a playground, and a computer set up to allow internet access. The people at the front desk speak English, they'll answer all your questions.

There is a small supermarket across the road with many norteamericano items not found in most supermarkets in Mexico, and both Ajijic and Chapala are not far away.

To most easily reach the campground follow Mex 23 south from the Guadalajara periférico (ring road). Just before reaching Chapala watch for the Chapala bypass as the road descends toward the lake, it is marked as going to Ajijic and Jocotepec. Follow the bypass for 3.6 miles (5.8 km), it terminates at the Chapala-Ajijic road. Turn left, the campground is on your left in .2 miles (.3 km).

🚐 PARQUE ACUÁTICO CHIMULCO

Address:	(Res) Cir. Agustin Yañez No. 2640, Guadalajara, CP 44140 Jalisco, México
Location:	Km y Medio Car. a Estipac, Villa Corona, CP 45730 Jalisco, México
Telephone:	(3) 778-0209 (Villa Corona), (3) 616-9393 (Guadalajara)
Fax:	(3) 778-0161
E-mail:	chimulco@hotmail.com

GPS Location: N 20° 24' 37.8", W 103° 40' 12.4"

If you've been missing your evening soak in the tub while you travel around Mexico you'll enjoy this place. Chimulco has many hot swimming pools, they empty them each night and refill them each morning with hot water from natural springs. The use of the pools is included in the price, a special pool is filled each evening except Sunday for the use of the RV park guests. Since almost everyone meets in the pool this is a very friendly place to stay.

This combination water park and RV park has about 50 camping sites. About half are pull-through and half back-in. Even the largest rigs seem to find room to park although the overall length of the largest spaces is really only about 30 feet. All have patios, 15-amp outlets, water, and sewer. Trees provide shade. The bathrooms are clean and have hot water showers. You'll have to wait a bit for the hot water to arrive in the showers, but eventually it does. There is a meeting room reserved just for the campground, a computer residents can use to send e-mail, and also a tennis court. Limited English is spoken at the office but resident campers will fill you in on anything you need to know about the park or surrounding region. Shopping in Villa Corona is limited but residents find they can get by with the help of visits to the Tuesday village market and the nearby small tiendas. Note that this campground is only open during the winter season, from October through March, although the water park is open all year long.

To reach Villa Corona and Chimulco head south from the Guadalajara periférico on Mex 54 and 15 toward Colima. Zero your odometer as you leave the periférico. At 2.6 miles (4.2 km) you will pass the entrance to the San Jose del Tajo Trailer Park. Continue along the four-lane highway until you come to a Y at 16 miles (25.8 km), take the left fork following signs for Colima and Barra de Navidad. Soon after, at 16.2 miles (26.1 km) at another Y go right following signs for Barra de Navidad (Mex 80). You are now on a two-lane road. Another Y soon appears at 18.5 miles (29.8 km), go right to Barra de Navidad and Villa Corona. There is a railroad crossing at 21.5 miles (34.7 km). You enter Villa Corona (population 12,000) at 24.5 miles (39.5 km). Watch carefully for Chimulco signs, you turn left at 24.7 miles (39.8 km) onto an unlikely-looking cobblestone road (Morelos) in the center of the village, turn right at the T, and then reach the entrance to the park at 25.4 miles (40.1 km). Tell the person at the entrance booth that you want to go to the trailer park, they'll let you drive in and go to the office to check in. Then you can pull in to the trailer park.

🚐 Agua Caliente Parque Aquático

Address: Km 56 Carr. Guadalajara-Barra de Navidad, Villa Corona, Jal., México
Telephone: (3) 778-0022   **Fax:** (3) 778-07-84

GPS Location: N 20° 25' 29.1", W 103° 40' 41.0"

Just a few miles down the road from Chimulco is another water park, Agua Caliente. Agua Caliente also offers camping.

There are 62 sites, all with patios and all with 15-amp outlets, water and sewer. Some are pretty small and the largest sites would accommodate only a 32-foot rig. The camping area is in a fairly thick pine grove. The restrooms have hot showers. Use of the huge water park and tennis court is included in the camping fee and there is a pool set aside for RV park use although it was not filled when we visited. The management of this park wants to attract more RVers from north of the border. To accomplish this they are thinning the trees in the park so large RVs will fit better, and removing all permanents. We'll have to see how things go, if more RVers do start using the park that will make it more attractive to others. Very little English is spoken here but this may change also.

To find this campground follow the directions given for the Chimulco trailer park. When you reach Villa Corona remain on Mex 80, drive directly through town, and 1.0 mile (1.6 km) west of the turnoff for Chimulco you will see Agua Caliente on the left. Do not enter at the main entrance, the campground entrance is on the far end of the big parking lot.

Other Camping Possibilities

There are apparently two new campgrounds under construction near Lake Chapala. People we have met along the road talk of a small new one near the Pal park but we have been able to dig up no further information and we did not spot it when we visited the area. We do know for sure that there is a new place called **Sunset Bay RV Park** located in the village of Puruagua somewhere south of Lake Chapala but do not have any further information about this place either. Watch our web site, rollinghomes.com, for updates.

For several years we've been hearing about a RV park on a ranch owned by the same family as Delia's in Rincón de Guayabitos. We still haven't visited but if you are feeling adventurous Delia says it is located in the town of Etzatlán, Jalisco which is south of Magdalena (on Mex 15 Libre between Guadalajara and Tepic). Once you reach Etzatlán you'll have to ask around for the place, she gave us the address Mina 345, Etzatlán, Jalisco. If you visit please send us an e-mail with the details so we can post them on rollinghomes.com.

GUANAJUATO, GUANAJUATO (GWAH-NAH-HWAH-TOH)
Population 100,000, Elevation 6,700 ft (2037 m)

Of all the colonial cities in Mexico, Guanajuato is probably the most interesting and fun to visit. Its small size and cramped bottom-of-a-ravine location combine to make it a walker's paradise. The town is a maze of crooked little streets, alleys, and even tunnels. Guanajuato was a colonial silver mining town, one of the more important cities of that era and on a par in importance with cities like Querétaro, San Miguel de

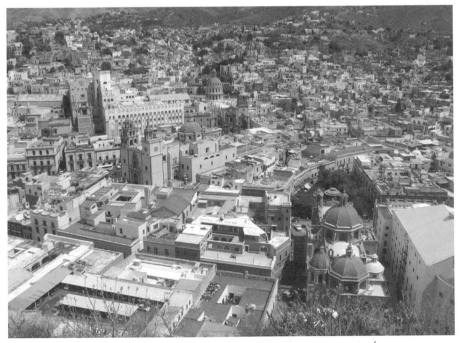

DOWNTOWN GUANAJUATO VIEW FROM NEAR THE STATUE OF PÍPILA

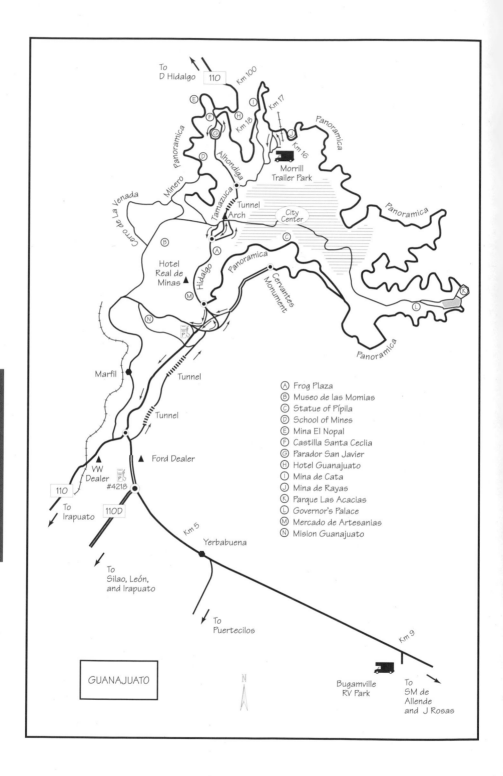

To D Hidalgo
110 Km 100
Panoramica
Km 17
Panoramica
Km 18
Km 16
Morrill Trailer Park
Panoramica
Minero
Alhondiga
Panoramica
Cerro La Venada
Tamazuca
Tunnel Arch
City Center
Panoramica
Hotel Real de Minas
Hidalgo
Panoramica
Cervantes Monument
Panoramica
Marfil
Tunnel
Tunnel
Ford Dealer
VW Dealer
#4218
110
To Irapuato
110D
Km 5
Yerbabuena
To Silao, León, and Irapuato
To Puertecilos
Km 9
Bugamville RV Park
To SM de Allende and J Rosas

Ⓐ Frog Plaza
Ⓑ Museo de las Momias
Ⓒ Statue of Pípila
Ⓓ School of Mines
Ⓔ Mina El Nopal
Ⓕ Castilla Santa Ceclia
Ⓖ Parador San Javier
Ⓗ Hotel Guanajuato
Ⓘ Mina de Cata
Ⓙ Mina de Rayas
Ⓚ Parque Las Acacias
Ⓛ Governor's Palace
Ⓜ Mercado de Artesanias
Ⓝ Mision Guanajuato

GUANAJUATO

N

Allende, Zacatecas, and San Luis Potosí. Most of these cities have grown and lost their colonial atmosphere. Guanajuato hasn't had room to grow so it has retained a great deal of charm. Guanajuato has been declared a **national monument** and is a popular destination for Mexican and international tourists so there are many restaurants, interesting shops, and things to see.

Guanajuato doesn't have much in the way of large flat areas for a central plaza so instead it has several smaller ones, **El Jardín de La Unión** and **Plaza de la Paz** are the largest. Sights of interest in town include the historically important **Alhóndiga de Graniditas**, the **statue of Pípila** overlooking town, the **Mercado Hidalgo**, and any number of churches, museums, and shops. Slightly farther from town are the **La Valenciana** mine and church and the ghoulish **Museo de las Momias** (Mummy Museum). Both of these destinations can be reached by bus from central Guanajuato.

The small streets that are so attractive to walkers are a nightmare for drivers. Do not take a large RV anywhere near central Guanajuato. Unfortunately, travelers headed for Dolores Hidalgo or to the Morrill Trailer Park must find their way around town. The periférico on the east side of town (allowing you to circle counter-clockwise) is accessible from the south, which is the direction of approach for most visitors, but it is definitely the long, scenic route. The periférico on the west is more direct but is only accessible by driving through a section of town. This route is OK for rigs up to small RV size, follow signs for Dolores Hidalgo. Young men standing along the road just outside town will undoubtedly try to flag you down and offer to guide you to local hotels, you should probably ignore them since they are unlikely to know the location of a campground.

Travelers with only RVs for transportation should use a bus to get into the central area of town or, if their rig is small enough, stay at the Morrill RV Park which is close enough to the central area to make walking practical.

Guanajuato Campgrounds

🚐 **BUGAMVILLE RV PARK**

Location:	Km 9.5 Carretera Guanajuato-J Rosas, Guanajuato, Guanajuato, México
Address:	Apdo. 340, Guanajuato, CP 36000 Guanajuato, México
Telephone:	(4) 733-0521 **E-mail:** bugamvillervpark@prodigy.net.mx

GPS Location: N 20° 56' 44.2", W 101° 15' 30.7"

This place is also known as the Cactus or Buganvilia, but the sign out front says Bugamville. It is Guanajuato's main campground and is suitable for large rigs.

There is room for at least a hundred rigs on a flat open graded area with no shade. There are 18 sites with electric hookups (15-amp outlets) and another 24 being installed. Water is available at some sites and there is a primitive dump area, ask the manager about this. There are no restrooms except in the restaurant and hotel rooms, if you need access to a shower make arrangements to use the hot ones in the hotel rooms. The restaurant, called the Cactus, is only open when caravans or large numbers of rigs are visiting the campground. Access to Guanajuato is easy using frequent busses that pass the gate.

The campground is located off the road from Guanajuato to Juventino Rosas and San Miguel de Allende. The entrance road has a sign, it is on the south side of the highway very near the 9 Km marker. The campground is about .2 miles (.3 km) back from the highway, don't be surprised when you find that the road passes through a junk yard.

⛴ MORRILL TRAILER PARK

Address:	Carretera Escenica y Subida de Mellado,
	Guanajuato, Guanajuato., México
Telephone:	(4) 732-1909

GPS Location: N 21° 01' 29.3", W 101° 15' 08.9"

Perhaps you've heard rumors of this place but never been able to track it down. Here are the directions you need to find the only Guanajuato campground within walking distance of town. We think this campground is only suitable for rigs up to 24 feet, if yours is larger please check it out on foot or with a tow car before committing yourself.

There are about 6 parking spaces, four with electricity (very poor 15-amp outlets), some sewer and water hookups are also available. The sites are arranged on a terrace on the hillside above Guanajuato. There is a second terrace below for tents. The restrooms are old but tiled and clean and have hot water showers. There is a gate and the steep terraces provide pretty good security, the managers live on the property. You can walk downtown in 15 minutes via a tunnel at the bottom of the hill, ask someone in the trailer park for detailed directions. Guanajuato has a Comercial Mexicana store in the central area so supplies are easy to find. You may want to take a taxi back up to the campground, however, since the climb is challenging. The campground also rents out parking spaces to area residents so you may awake in the morning to the sound of warming engines as drivers prepare to drive up the hill out of the campground.

The campground is located just off (below) the Panoramica near the Mina de Cata and the Km 17 marker. The easiest access is from the highway to Dolores Hidalgo. If you are approaching on the other highway from San Miguel de Allende and Silao you can either follow the Panoramica counterclockwise for almost 17 kilometers or drive through town following signs for Dolores Hidalgo and Mina de Cata. The Panoramica leaves the highway to Dolores Hidalgo just outside town near the Parador San Javier and is marked Panoramica and M. de Cata. Zero your odometer at the Parador San Javier. As you drive clockwise around town you'll reach the Mina de Cata at 1.2 miles (2 km) and reach the road going downhill to the right to the trailer park at 1.7 miles (2.7 km). If you pass over some railroad tracks you've gone too far. Drive down the hill a short distance to a Y and stop. The trailer park is just to the left, unfortunately this is a one-way road coming up the hill. Easiest access to the trailer park is along this route so send someone down the hill to stop traffic and then head down the left fork. You might also want to walk down to take a look before committing yourself. The trailer park is the second gate on the left. If you are coming around the Panoramica in a counter-clockwise direction watch for the railroad tracks after the Km 16 marker, the road to the campground is the first one on the left after passing over the tracks.

Other Camping Possibilities

Travelers with large rigs which can not fit into the Morrill RV Park in Guanajuato often stay in one of the San Miguel de Allende RV parks. The bus trip to Guanajuato takes less than two hours and is inexpensive, this is a great way to avoid Guanajuato parking hassles.

LOS AZUFRES, MICHOACÁN (LOES AH-SOOF-RAZE)

Los Azufres (the Sulfurs) is an area of sulfur hot springs located some 75 miles (123 km) east of Morelia along Mex 15. While Los Azufres itself probably isn't of more than passing interest to the traveler it is included here because campgrounds in this area are few and far between. Mex 15 between Morelia and Toluca is extremely scenic and not to be missed. Attractions along the way include the **Mirador de Mil Cumbres** (thousand peaks viewpoint), the **Monarch Butterfly winter sanctuaries at El Rosario and Sierra Cincua**, and the **Los Alzati** archeological site.

From the campground at Balneario Erendira (see below) you can continue up the hill toward **Los Azufres National Park**. If you have zeroed your odometer at the point where the Balneario Erendira entrance road meets the highway you will come to the road to the Motel Tejamaniles at 3 miles (4.9 km), take a right at the Y at 3.6 miles (5.9 km), and come to the Campamento Turístico at 4 miles (6.5 km). This is the park, don't expect much and you won't be disappointed. Next door is the Balneario Doña Celia which looks nice, we didn't visit because it was closed when we were in the area. Farther along the road are many geothermal wells that have been drilled to produce power.

Los Azufres Campground

🚐 **CABAÑAS Y BALNEARIO ERENDIRA**

Address: Morelos Pte. 43, Cd. Hidalgo,
               Michoacan, México (Res.)
Telephone: (7) 154-0169

GPS Location: N 19° 45' 28.0", W 100° 41' 32.5"

| $$$ | ▲ | ⚡ | 🚿 HOT | 🍴 | 〰 |

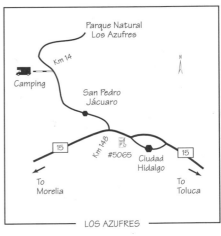

Like most other popular balnearios this one is loud and crowded on weekends and holidays, but during the week you're likely to have it mostly to yourself. The minerals in the pools give them a disturbing green color, but they're warm and there's no smell.

The balneario has no formal RV spaces but has several flat grassy areas suitable for RV parking. Some have good shade. Larger rigs may end up in a less secluded area near the restaurant where busses park because the access road to the normal camping area is a little steep, you'll have to decide if you can handle it. In the various areas there is room for at least 10 RV's during the week, but you probably won't have any other campers for company. It is possible to run an electric cord to one of the many lamp posts but don't count on much juice, a hair dryer will trip the remote breaker. The restrooms are balneario-style with group shower rooms but have fairly warm water and are clean when they're not getting heavy use. There are two small groups of pools, they're open at all times so you can take an early or late dip. There are a few rental cabañas but most visitors are day-trippers. There is also a restaurant. Little English is spoken.

From Mex 15 some 2 miles (3.3 km) west of Cd. Hidalgo near the 148 Km marker the road to Los Azufres goes north. Turn left onto the gravel Erendira driveway at 8.6 miles (13.9 km). You'll reach the gate in .3 miles (.5 km). They'll check you in there.

Other Camping Possibilities

The Campamento Turístico at Los Azufres National Park has tent camping, you would probably be allowed to camp overnight in the parking lot if you have an RV but access is poor for rigs over about 22 feet long. There is a cafeteria, a playground, some pools and a bathroom with hot shower. There is also a private balneario next door which may allow tent camping. Follow the road past Balneario Erendira to find these places.

Many visitors to this area are here to see the Monarch butterflies, unfortunately camping possibilities near the butterfly reserves are limited. See the *Side Trips* section below for information about the two reserves that are accessible.

Caravans that stop to see the butterflies stay at the **Villa Monarch Hotel** which is about a mile east of San Felipe (the location of the cutoff up to Angangueo from Mex 15). It has room for 15 to 20 rigs to boondock in a field behind the hotel. Use the eastern-most entrance to the hotel when you arrive. From there it is very easy to drive up to Ocampo and Angangueo in a tow car. This is probably the very best way to see the butterflies in an RV.

Here are a few more possibilities. We have talked with folks who have parked their RV overnight in the square in front of the auditorium in central Angangueo. No one gave them a bit of trouble. We ourselves have stayed in the parking lot of the Don Bruno Hotel in Angangueo but it would only be suitable for camping vans due to height and space restrictions.

We know folks who have camped in a small RV at the Sierra Cincua reserve itself, but there are no facilities and the road in from the highway is pretty bad. In fact, they got stuck and had to be pulled out with a tractor. The Campamento Turístico which is on the highway across from the entrance road to Cincua Reserve is said to accept tent campers and RV boondockers but was closed up tight when we visited in December.

Finally, with the new improved road up to El Rosario from Ocampo it will probably not be long until people are camping there. Until then we have talked to folks who have spent the night at the sports field just outside Ocampo (toward San Felipe) but there is no formal security and it is a somewhat isolated location.

Side Trips from Los Azufres

The two Monarch butterfly reserves at **El Rosario** and **Sierra Cincua** are both in the same general area, they have become a top tourist destination during the past few years, and for good reason. During the months of December through March millions of Monarchs cling to the drooping branches of trees in these reserves waiting for warmer weather. On sunny days, especially during February and March, they warm up and begin to fly, actually filling the air with the sound of their wings. You will need to hike when you reach the reserves, probably at least 2 miles on steep terrain although this depends upon the locations of the butterfly concentrations.

The best road to the two main towns near the reserves, Ocampo and Angangueo, leaves Mex 15 toward the north at San Felipe which is about 4.4 miles (6.8 km) west of Zitácuaro. The paved road climbs (but not too steeply for RVs) for 7.9 miles (12.9

km) to Ocampo. Just before reaching Ocampo you will see a soccer field on the right, if you have a big rig this is probably the best place to park, trucks will take you up to the El Rosario reserve for a fee from Ocampo. We recommend making sure that someone watches your rig while you are gone if you do this, it is never safe to leave a rig alone outside a campground, particularly for an extended period.

From Ocampo it is now also possible to drive directly to the El Rosario reserve in a passenger car or rig up to van size, the distance from town is 8.5 miles (14 km) on a rough but passable road. This road is an extension of Melchor Ocampo leading right from central Ocampo and there is a 20 pesos toll collected en route. It may also be possible to boondock at the reserve if you are willing to pay for the privilege. There is a huge new parking lot but we have not talked with anyone who has yet spent the night there.

Alternately, you can drive on from Ocampo following the paved road another 6.5 miles (10.5 km) to the mining town of Angangueo where there is limited parking but also a rougher and much steeper dirt road suitable for hiking or driving in high clearance (and preferably four-wheel drive) vehicles to El Rosario. This route can be hiked if you are in absolutely great shape, the walk up takes at least two hours and has a lot of altitude gain. Then there's the hike back! The road out of town is not marked as being the route to the reserve, it is called Matamoros as it climbs out of central Angangueo, then you ask for directions from villagers you'll meet along the way to reach the "mariposas". Small trucks and guides are also available in Angangueo to take you into El Rosario along this route or to the Sierra Cincua reserve for a fee.

Sierra Cincua is located farther up the main road from Angangueo. Pick your way through the town of Angangueo and continue for another 5 miles (8 km). Be advised that the route through Angangueo is very tight for even small rigs, we wouldn't try it in anything longer than 24 feet. Following the paved highway upward you will reach the turnoff for the reserve. The road in to the reserve parking area is dirt and is only suitable for small vehicles. Once you do reach the parking area you must hike with a guide or ride a horse on in to the butterfly reserve, a considerable distance.

New Mexican travelers coming from the west won't have had many opportunities to visit archeological sites. The road to Los Alzati leaves Mex 15 about 1.3 miles (2 km) east of San Felipe (the turnoff for the Monarch reserve). **Los Alzati** is a Matlatzinca Indian city which was at the height of its power about 900 A.D. and has a pyramid.

MATEHUALA, SAN LUÍS POTOSÍ (MAH-TEH-WAH-LAW)
Population 80,000, Elevation 5,300 ft (1,611 m)

There are two good reasons to stop in Matehuala. The first is that this is a very convenient stop if you are traveling north or south on Mex 57. The other is that this is the best place to overnight if you are planning a trip to Real de Catorce. See the *Side Trip* section below.

Many people have stopped at Matehuala for years and never visited the town because a bypass road makes this unnecessary. The town is much more attractive than it appears from the bypass road, it is definitely worth your time to take a stroll in to town in the evening.

Matehuala Campgrounds

🚐 LAS PALMAS MIDWAY INN

Address:	Carretera Central Km 617 (Apdo. 73), Matehuala, CP 78700 S.L.P., México
Telephone:	(4) 882-0001
Fax:	(4) 882-1396 or (4) 882-3620

GPS Location: N 23° 39' 38.9", W 100° 38' 08.5"

The Las Palmas has long been a popular over-night stop for RVs traveling Mex 54. Unfortu-nately, today's large RVs often must park out front since to enter the RV park you must pass under a roof that is marked as being 11' 8". Readers tell us it actually measures 12'4" but exercise extreme caution if you have a tall rig and decide to attempt the entrance, have someone outside the rig watching carefully because the cement driveway is not flat.

The Las Palmas has 24 back-in spaces with electricity (15-amp outlets), water and sewer hookups and about 6 more with electricity and water. Since the campground will probably not be full there is a good chance that big rigs can park sideways and avoid unhooking or backing. The campground is actually a large oiled gravel lot be-hind the hotel and has its own restroom building with hot showers. The hotel has a restaurant, nice swimming pool, 2 lane boliche (bowling) alley, mini-golf, children's play area, and a 1.7 km paved bike trail. English is spoken at the front desk.

The hotel is located on the east side of Mex 57 north of town. It is .2 miles (.3 km) north of the north entrance intersection and difficult to miss because there is a huge sign. Note that the kilometer markers along this section do not reflect the address advertised by the hotel, the hotel is actually located .5 miles (.8 km) south of the Km 5 marker so it is actually very near Km 4.

🚐 OASIS MOTEL

Address:	Carretera Central Km 617, Matehuala, S.L.P., México
Telephone:	(4) 882-3362

GPS Location: N 23° 40' 18.2", W 100° 37' 51.9"

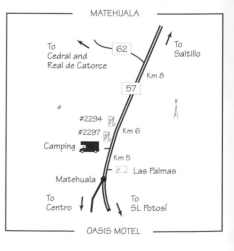

The Oasis Motel, just up the road from the Las Palmas Midway Inn, offers much less in the way of facilities, but the price is better too.

The motel has 4 spaces with room for rigs to about 30 feet. Electricity (15-amp outlets) is available to these sites. There is also a large area toward the rear of the motel suitable for any size rig, this is a boondock area. No restrooms are available to campers so this campground is only suitable for self-contained rigs, but there is a restaurant and a swimming pool. The entrance here, like at the Midway Inn, is height-restricted at about 12' 9". However, you may be able to bypass the arch on the right or use the alternate gate at the left side of the property.

The Oasis is located .7 mile (1.1 km) north of the Las Palmas Midway Inn but on the west side of the road. Like the Las Palmas Midway the Km markers along the road do not agree with the advertised address, the hotel is .2 mile (.3 km) north of the Km 5 marker.

Side Trips from Matehuala

During the 1800's **Real de Catorce** was a thriving silver-mining town with a population of 40,000. Then came the lower silver prices in the first part of the 20th century and the town was virtually abandoned. Today there are about 900 inhabitants and Real de Catorce is virtually a ghost town except at the end of September and beginning of October when over 100,000 people visit the town for the festival of San Francisco pilgrimage.

Driving to Real de Catorce can be something of a trial. You might want to just take a bus or tour from Matehuala. To drive yourself go west 17 miles (27 km) past the town of Cedral on a paved highway, then 15 miles (25 km) south on a rough cobblestone road. Just before reaching Real you must drive through a 1.4 mile (2.3 km) tunnel. This is a one-way passage, tolls are taken and traffic is regulated so that you won't meet someone coming the other way inside the tunnel. That means that you can wait up to 20 minutes before being allowed to continue. The tunnel is said to provide clearance to about 3 meters.

MEXICO CITY (CIUDAD DE MÉXICO), DISTRITO FEDERAL
(SEE-OOH-DAWD day MAY-HEE-KOH)
Population 20,000,000, Elevation 8,000 ft (2,432 m)

For most travelers the idea of visiting Mexico in their own vehicle is more than a little intimidating. The city is famous for terrible traffic jams, pollution, predator cops, confusing traffic laws and street crime. The truth is that Mexico City does indeed have all of these things, but a visit, perhaps even an extended visit, is well worth the trouble.

This is perhaps the largest city in the would. No one really knows how many people live there. The sights and activities in Mexico City place it on a level with other world capitals including London, Paris, New York and Tokyo as far as tourist interest is concerned. Sure there are problems, but remember, 20,000,000 people deal with them on a daily basis. The fact is that once you actually arrive you will be amazed that you were ever concerned. Most visitors never have a problem.

When you visit Mexico City it is important to do it right. First, and most importantly, don't drive into Mexico City for your visit. Base yourself either north of the city in the campgrounds at Tepotzotlán or Teotihuacán, or in one of the Cuernavaca campgrounds. Use the excellent bus service from these locations to get downtown. Consider spending several days in a reasonably priced hotel. Get a good guidebook and pack light. When you get to the city exercise normal precautions like you would in any major city. Only visit well-traveled places. Don't stay out late at night. Don't drink too

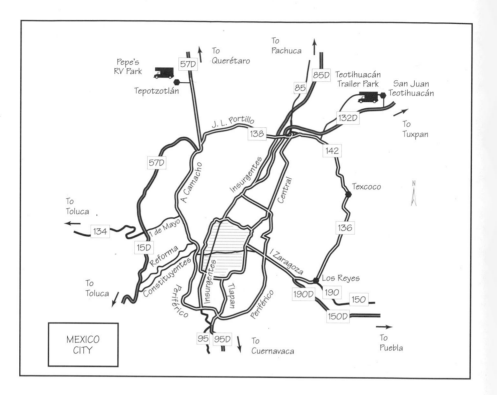

much. Don't carry any more valuables than you can afford to loose and keep credit cards, passports, and most of your cash in a belt safe. Don't carry anything of value in a purse, in fact, avoid carrying one at all if possible. And finally, a special Mexico City precaution, don't take a taxi that you have hailed on the street, only use one that you have ordered by phone.

There are really too many attractions in Mexico City for even inadequate coverage in this book. The most popular ones include the **Ballet Folklórico de México**, the **National Museum of Anthropology**, the **Shrine to the Virgin of Guadalupe**, the **Zona Rosa**, the **Zócalo** and surrounding area, **Chapultepec Park,** the **University,** the **Xochimilco Floating Gardens**, and the **San Angel** and **Coyoacán** districts. This only scratches the surface. Transportation is easy, there is an extensive subway and bus system which can be supplemented by cautious use of taxis.

Mexico City Campgrounds

⊟ PEPE'S RV PARK

| Address: | Eva Sámano de López Mateos No.
62, Tepotzlán, Edo. de México, México |
| Telephone: | (5) 876-0515, (5) 705-2424 (Res.) |

GPS Location: N 19° 43' 24.3", W 099° 13' 16.2"

Pepe's is situated in the small town of Tepotzotlán, about 25 miles (40.8 km) north of the center of the city. The campground makes a convenient base for your visit to this amazing city, and you don't have to take your own vehicle anywhere near the terrible traffic. It is suitable for any size rig.

There are about 60 full service back-in spaces with 30-amp outlets, sewer, and water hookups. Virtually the entire spacious park is paved with attractive red bricks, there are some grassy areas for tent or van campers. A large and a small restroom area are both clean and modern and have hot water showers. The park is fenced and gated and has continuous 24-hour security. English is usually but not always spoken. Caravans use this campground quite a bit but there are enough spaces that reservations are not usually necessary.

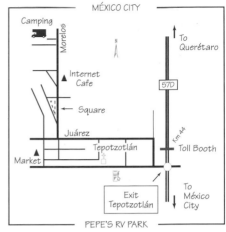

The trip into town is quite easy. A city bus stops at a nearby stop, an hour-long bus ride takes you to the nearest subway station, and then you can travel easily and very cheaply to any area of the huge city. The owner of the RV park also owns a travel agency, you can make arrangements at the campground for tours of the city and surrounding areas or book a room for an overnight stay downtown. You can also use the agency to make reservations at the RV park:

SAN FRANCISCO JAVIER IN TEPOTZOTLÁN

THE INTERIOR OF MEXICO

Mallorca Travel Service, Paseo de la Reforma No. 105, México, D.F., telephone (5) 705-2424 or fax (5) 705-2673. Don't forget to explore Tepotzotlán. This is an interesting little town with it's own important tourist attraction, the **Museo Nacional de Virreinato**, which includes the beautiful church of San Francisco Javier. This is an excellent museum of the colonial period. Don't miss the museum or the gilded church interior.

Finding the campground is not difficult with decent directions. As you drive south on Mex 57D toward Mexico City you will pass through the last toll booth at Km 44. Take the first exit after the toll booth, it is just .1 mile (.2 km) south and is labeled Tepotzotlán. At the end of the off ramp zero your odometer and drive right (west) toward town. Drive to odometer .1 mile (.2 km) and turn right onto an avenue under high-tension electrical cables (look up). Turn left at odometer .3 miles (.5 km). You will find yourself on an uneven brick road with lots of topes. Follow it up the hill and past a long rock wall on the left. Turn right at 1 mile (1.6 km), there is usually a sign for the trailer park visible here if you look carefully. There is lots of room to make the turn although you may have to wait for other traffic, semis and big busses make the turn all day long so even if people stare they really are accustomed to big rigs coming through here. At odometer 1.1 miles (1.8 km) there is a Y, take the right fork. You will see the campground entrance on your left at 1.7 miles (2.7 km). The gate will probably be closed, you can ring the bell to get someone's attention.

⛟ TEOTIHUACÁN TRAILER PARK

Address:	López Mateos #17, San Juan Teotihuacán, CP 55800 Edo. de Mex, México
Telephone:	(5) 956-0313
E-mail:	teotipark@correoweb.com

GPS Location: N 19° 40' 58.0", W 098° 52' 12.4"

$$ \boxed{\$\$} \quad \boxed{\triangle} \quad \boxed{\text{⛟}} \quad \boxed{\text{⊓}} \quad \boxed{\text{⬚}} \quad \boxed{\text{⬚}}_{HOT} $$

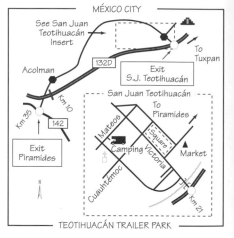

This is a rare find, a second campground in the Mexico City area. This one is in the town of San Juan Teotihuacan which is just a few kilometers from the Teotihuacán archeological site. It is a little harder to find than Pepe's, but is convenient to the pyramids and also allows use of busses to reach downtown Mexico City.

The campground is a grassy lot with 15-amp outlets, water, and sewer hookups. There are 42 sites, but with today's larger rigs that translates into parking for perhaps 25 rigs. A restroom building was being upgraded when we visited, when finished it will provide hot showers. The campground is within a block or so of the central square of this little town, you can easily stroll to the central square and the town's small shops. Collectivos run frequently to the ruins from near the campground. Some English is spoken.

The campground is located in San Juan Teotihuacán which is just two kilometers southwest of the archeological site. Easiest access is from the road that enters town from the east off Mex 132D. There is an exit marked San Juan Teotihuacán off that highway, take the exit and follow signs for the town. You will be entering from the east. The campground is near the church you can see rising above the town's buildings ahead and to the left. You will cross a bridge as you enter town. Take the first left in just .1 mile and follow the road for .3 miles (.5 km). You will enter a large parking plaza in front of the church. Collectivos often park right where you enter the plaza. Drive straight ahead across the parking plaza and near the opposite side you will see the campground on your right. Turn right on Lopez Mateos and then take the right turn into the campground.

Other Camping Possibilities

Don't forget that Mexico has lots of excellent reasonably-priced bus service, especially to Mexico City. You can easily visit the city for several days by taking a bus and staying in an inexpensive but conveniently located hotel. Here are the approximate travel times by bus from several cities with good campgrounds: Cuernavaca - 1.5 hours, Puebla - 2 hours, Querétaro - 3 hours, San Miguel de Allende - 4 hours, Acapulco - 5 hours, Guadalajara - 7 hours.

Side Trips from Mexico City

Teotihuacán is probably the most impressive archeological site in Mexico, especially if size is what impresses you. The huge **Pyramid of the Sun** and smaller **Pyramid of the Moon** rival those in Egypt. You can drive to Teotihuacán easily, follow the first portion of our driving log around northeastern Mexico City in the section below. Even better, stay in the nearby campground. You can also catch a tour bus from Mexico City, check with a travel agency about this.

Tula is another archeological site, this one much smaller but known for its Atlanteans, carved fifteen-foot-high stone warriors. To get there from Pepe's follow Mex 57 north for 8.3 miles (13.4 km) and then a secondary highway north another 21.5 miles (34.7 km) to Tula. As you approach the town of Tula watch for signs for Las Ruinas or Parque Nacionál Tula. A smaller and sometimes rough road will take you another 7.9 miles (12.7 km) to the ruins.

Driving Through or Around Mexico City

Mexico City is a wonderful destination, but when you decide to continue south you have a problem. How do you get through the city? This is probably one of the big reasons many people don't visit Mexico City on their way to other destinations in the south like Chiapas or the Yucatán. They hate the idea of driving through the largest city in the world.

It is really quite amazing, but true, that there is no toll ring road allowing motorists coming south on Mex 57 to easily bypass the city and continue south on Mex 150 to Puebla and beyond or to Mex 95 to Cuernavaca. Most other cities in Mexico now have bypasses, why not the capital?

We don't know the answer to that question, but we do know several useful routes around and through the city.

Hoy No Circula Driving Restrictions

You should be aware that in an effort to fight pollution Mexico City has extended rules making it illegal to drive your vehicle in the city on certain days. These driving restrictions, known as **Hoy No Circula** (Today Don't Drive) are based upon the last digit of your license plate and apply to all vehicles. The digits and days are as follows: 5 or 6 - Monday, 7 or 8 - Tuesday, 3 or 4 - Wednesday, 1 or 2 - Thursday, 9 or 0 - Friday. If pollution is particularly bad there may be additional restrictions. Do not drive your vehicle in Mexico City on these days. If you are pulling a trailer or tow car use the towing vehicle's license number. The rules do not apply as far out as Tepotzotlán so you can arrive at Pepe's RV park on any day. The covered zone also does not extend far enough from Mexico city to apply to the Pachuca bypass route or the Toluca bypass route described below. However, they do apply to the northeastern Mexico City bypass route, the routes directly through Mexico City, and the western toll bypass to Toluca.

EASTERN BYPASS ROUTE THROUGH PACHUCA

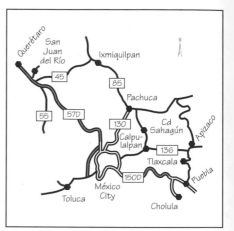

To bypass Mexico City to the east follow Mex 45 from an intersection with Mex 57 just a few miles south of the San Juan del Río exits. This is known as the Palmillas intersection but probably not marked as such. Mex 45 meets Mex 85 after 56 miles (92 km). Turn south on Mex 85 and drive to Pachuca, a distance of 51 miles (84 km). Now follow two-lane highways southeast through Ciudad Sahagún to meet Mex 136 at Calpulalpan and then east to Tlaxcala, altogether a distance of 92 miles (150 km). Puebla and Mex 150D are then only about 18 miles (30 km) farther south, you can then easily travel east to the coastal route on Mex 150D. This entire bypass route is relatively quiet and easy to drive, only the city bypass south around Pachuca is at all challenging. The entire drive should take about 5 hours. The entire route is outside the Hoy No Circula zone.

WESTERN BYPASS ROUTE THROUGH TOLUCA

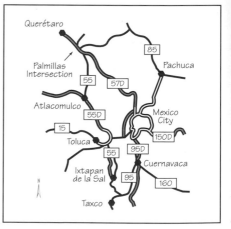

The western bypass of Mexico City starts on Mex 57 very near the Palmillas intersection, just south of the exit for the eastern bypass. Follow Mex 55 south to Atlacomulco, then join Mex 55D south to Toluca. From Toluca Mex 55 continues south to a point near Taxco where you can join Mex 95 and travel back north to Cuernavaca or south to Acapulco. This bypass, from Mex 57 to Mex 95, is about 150 miles (250 km) long and takes about 5 hours. This route is busier than the eastern route and has several sections of toll roads. You must also follow the bypass around Toluca which can be busy, and pass through Ixtapan de la Sal, which is easy. Still, this route avoids Mexico City, a worthwhile achievement. The entire route is outside the Hoy No Circula zone.

NORTHEASTERN MEXICO CITY BYPASS HEADING SOUTH

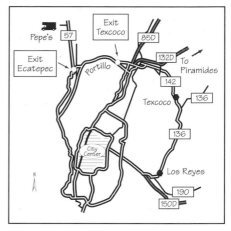

There is a bypass route that runs around northeast of Mexico city from south of Tepotzotlán to the toll highway running east to Puebla. The route is 40 miles (65 km) long and will take you about an hour and thirty minutes if you avoid rush hours. The ultimate time to do it would be Sunday morning. It is all on four-lane or better streets, much of it on secondary highway without stop lights. You will be passing through the Hoy No Circula zone so see the rules above. You'll get an expensive ticket for sure if you try to ignore them. Also be advised that many folks taking this route are stopped by police, be sure that your equipment and driving are impeccable if you drive this route.

Zero your odometer at the overpass on Mex 57 that is just south of the toll plaza near Tepotzotlán. This is a good place to start because it is the exit associated with Pepe's RV Park, the place most people will stay while visiting Mexico City. Head south.

At 7.7 miles (12.6 km) take the exit for Ecatepec. This exit road is just past an overpass, you loop around and take the overpass over Mex 57 so that you are headed east. You can identify the overpass because there is a big McDonald's sign nearby on the west side of Mex 57.

For the next few miles you will be following the signs towards Ecatepec. For the first mile stay to the left as several roads, detailed below, split off from this route.

Roads split off to the right at 8.4 miles (13.7 km) (Perenorte) and again at 8.8 miles (14.4 km) (Cd. Labor). At 9.0 miles (14.7 km) you will merge left into a boulevard that you will be following for the next few miles, the street's name is J.L. Portillo but you may never see a sign identifying it.

You will follow J.L. Portillo for 8.9 miles (14.5 km), until your odometer reading is 17.9 miles (29.2 km). This street is six lanes wide with many stop lights. If you stay in the second lane from the left you should have easy sailing. Checkpoints along this road are a big Bodega Comercial Mexicana on the right at 10.3 miles (16.8 km), a big Bodega A store on the left at 12 miles (19.6 km), a McDonalds, Burger King, and Kentucky Fried Chicken (did we leave anyone out?) near 14.4 miles (23.5 km), and both a Bodega Gigante store and a Comercial Mexicana at 15.9 miles (26.0 km).

As you approach 17.5 miles (28.6 km) on your odometer move to the right lane to be ready to take the exit to the right at 17.9 miles (29.2 km). This exit is marked with an overhead sign for Texcoco and Los Reyes. The route will curve to the left and run over J.L. Portillo. From here you will be following the signs for Los Reyes, although you really will have few route choices to make. This is Hwy 142, it is four lanes wide and divided in most places. You will want to keep your speed down because the there are many unexpected dips and heaves. There are occasional unmarked speed bumps, so watch out.

Here are some checkpoints for this portion of the route. You will pass over freeways at 19.9 miles (32.5 km) and again at 20.9 miles (34.1 km), there is an off ramp to the right for the Teotihuacán Pyramids (see the pyramid discussion in the Side Trips section of this chapter, you may want to take this exit to see Teotihuacán or stay at the campground near the archeological site) at 25.7 miles (42.0 km), there is a Comercial Mexicana at 34.1 miles (55.7 km) and a Cuota road to Mexico City cutting off to the right. There is a stop light at 34.7 miles (56.7 km) and you cross railroad tracks at 36.7 miles (60.0 km).

Just past the railroad tracks the highway merges left into another road, Mex 136. Stay in the second lane from the left to avoid being forced to turn off this road. There is a Pemex on the right at 40.9 miles (66.8 km)and another small railroad crossing at 46.1 miles (75.3 km). Near here you may see signs pointing off this highway labeled Los Reyes, do not follow them, continue on straight.

At 46.9 miles (76.6 km) you will see the cutoff for the Mex 190 free road to Puebla, do not take this exit, continue straight. You now pass through a fairly congested area but don't worry. Stay in the middle lanes and take it easy, the end is near. At 48.0 miles (78.4 km) you will see another big Comercial Mexicana store on the right.

At 48.3 miles (78.9 km) you should move to the left to follow the sign to Mex 150D, the Cuota to Puebla. Finally at 48.5 miles (79.2 km) you exit to the right to enter Mex 150D towards Puebla.

See how easy that was?

NORTHEASTERN MEXICO CITY BYPASS HEADING NORTH

This is the same route detailed above, just going the other way. Remember, you will be passing through the Hoy No Circula zone so see the rules above. As we said above, you'll get an expensive ticket for sure if you try to ignore them. Also be advised that many folks taking this route are stopped by police, be sure that your equipment and driving are impeccable if you drive this route.

From the Cuota road from Puebla, called both Mex 150D and Mex 190D, take the exit for Mex 136, signed as Texcoco Libre. This exit is about 9.5 miles (15.5 km) from the last toll booth as you approach Mexico City from the east. Zero your odometer as you leave the freeway so you can stay in step with these directions.

You will be following signs towards Texcoco during this first section of the route. Follow these signs through a fairly congested area with three lanes in each direction, stay in the middle lane because the far left one will force you to turn and the far right one is extremely slow and crowded. The road will shrink to two lanes and then go back to three. At 1.4 miles (3.3 km) you will pass under the free road to Puebla, continue straight following the Texcoco signs.

At 11.0 miles (18.0 km) make sure you are in the left lane. From here you will be following the signs to Lecheria. At 12 miles (19.6 km) follow the Lecheria signs to the left. You will immediately have a stop sign, a railroad crossing, and speed bumps, not necessarily in that order.

You will be following this highway for about 19 miles (31 km). It is two lanes in each direction and is divided most of the way. Keep your speed down, however, because there will be unexpected swoops and bumps. Checkpoints along here are a Comercial Mexicana store on the right at 14.2 miles (23.2 km) with the entrance to a cuota road to downtown Mexico City (don't take it), an exit for Highway 132 to the pyramids at 22.7 miles (37.1 km), and a V in the road at 25.5 miles (41.6 km), go left towards Lecheria.

As you approach odometer 30 get into the right lane and take the exit to Lecheria that goes to the right. There will be a couple of good sized speed bumps and you will merge left onto J.L. Portillo.

J.L. Portillo has three lanes in each direction along much of its course, you will be following it for about 9 miles (14.7 km). This road will be slower than the one you have been traveling on, it has quite a few stop lights and more traffic, if you stay in the middle lane whenever possible you should have no problems.

Some checkpoints along this route are a Comercial Mexicana on the left at 32.0 miles (52.3 km) and many U.S. fast food places around 33.0 miles (53.9 km).

Near 37.0 miles (60.4 km) you will begin to see Querétaro signs, follow them from now on instead of Lecheria signs. You will see a Lecheria sign at 38.8 miles (63.4 km), do not follow it, continue straight ahead.

Finally, at 39.9 miles (65.2 km) you will see a sign pointing to Querétaro, Mexico, and probably also Lecheria, follow these signs over an overpass above many railroad tracks until you see the Querétaro sign at 39.8 miles (65.0 km), exit here and you will find yourself heading north away from Mexico City on Mex 57.

If you are planning to stay in Mexico City you will want to exit at Tepotzotlán. This exit is to the right at 47.4 miles (77.4 km), you will know you are getting close when you see the marker for kilometer 42 and a Pemex station on the right at 47.2 miles (77.1 km).

Once off the freeway take the always crowded left turn so that you cross the freeway and are heading west. From here follow the directions to the campground given in the campground section.

THROUGH MEXICO CITY HEADING SOUTH

It is also not difficult to drive right through Mexico City on multi-lane highways. If you try to do this in the morning when traffic is light, say between 9 a.m. and 11 a.m., there is a good chance that you will not even run into much in the way of slow traffic. The best time is Sunday morning. This route goes through the Hoy No Circula zone so see the rules above. Also, big rigs are almost always hassled on this route, they are supposed to follow the laterals but this is just not possible without lots of local knowledge. We know people who go to Acapulco every year who expect to be

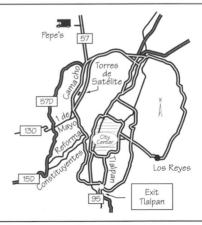

stopped and pay a fee to the police of at least $50 U.S. as a matter of course, often the transaction includes an escort through town. Our advice is to only use this route in small rigs like vans and pickup campers without duals.

This route involves little other than staying on a major limited-access highway until it is time to get off and catch the Cuernavaca highway. We'll give a few checkpoints to give you something to watch for.

As you approach Mexico City on Mex 57 from the north zero your odometer as you pass the Tepotzotlán off ramps just south of the last toll booth. At 7.6 miles (12.4 km) you will pass the overpass and exit for Ecatepec, this is where the route around the northeast side of the city exits as detailed above. Just past this point is an exit for an expensive new toll bypass that leads to the Toluca toll road, do not take it but see *The Western Toll Bypass to Toluca* below if it sounds interesting. The hard-to-miss Torres de Satélite monument is on the left at 16.0 miles (26.1 km). The exit for Mex 130 to Toluca is at 18.3 miles (29.9 km). The exit for Palmas and Mex 15D to Toluca, Morelia, and Guadalajara is at 21.1 miles (34.5 km). There is a Y at 23.8 miles (38.9 km), stay left. You'll see a Costco on the right at 24.1 miles (39.4 km). At 32.9 miles (53.7 km) you'll see an exit for Cuernavaca and Mex 95, do not take it. Instead take the exit for the Viaducto Tlalpan at 35.5 mile (58.0 km). Follow signs for Cuernavaca that take you to the right, merge you to the left with a lateral and then merge you left again onto the main street. At 37.2 miles (60.7 km) you'll see signs for Cuernavaca Libre and Cuernavaca Cuota, and if you merge left to Mex 95D you'll come to the first toll booth at 40.1 miles (65.5 km).

THROUGH MEXICO CITY
HEADING NORTH

This is the same route as described above, just the opposite direction. See the preface to that section for cautions and advice.

If you are heading north the route is also easy. Zero your odometer at the last toll booth of Mex 95D from Cuernavaca. At 2.7 miles (4.4 km) follow signs right for Viaducto Tlalpan and Periférico. Go right again at 3.9 miles (6.4 km) following the signs for Periférico. At 4.3 miles (7.0 km) go right again following signs for Reino Av., Insurgentes, and Querétaro. At 4.7 miles (7.7 km) you merge left onto the Periférico and should have smooth sailing the rest of the way through the city.

Here are a few checkpoints. The Costco is on your left at 15.4 miles (25.1 km). An exit for Mex 15D to Toluca, Morelia, and Guadalajara is at 17.1 miles (27.9 km), there is another at 19.0 miles (31.0 km). Mex 130 to Toluca exit is at 21.5 miles (35.1 km). The Torres de Satélite monument is on the right at 24.2 miles (39.5 km). The new Toluca toll bypass route is at 31.4 miles (51.3 km) and the exit for Tepotzotlán and Pepe's RV Park is at 40.2 miles (65.6 km). Immediately after this exit is the first toll booth of Mex 57 to the north.

THE WESTERN TOLL BYPASS
TO TOLUCA

There is an easy to drive but expensive toll bypass leading from Mex 57 south of Tepotzotlán but north of Mexico City around the west side of town through the hills to meet Mex 15D to Toluca. It passes through the Hoy No Circula zone so see those rules above. To travel it from north to south just take the right fork following signs for Toluca Cuota when the freeway splits 8.9 miles (14.4 km) south of the Tepotzotlán off ramp. Follow signs for Toluca. Northbound, coming from Toluca, follow signs for Mexico Cuota and then Querétaro Cuota. Either way you'll pay at 2 toll booths, a car in the winter of 2000/2001 paid $11.50 U.S. for the route, a motorhome/toad or pickup/fifth wheel combination paid $46 U.S. The distance from Mex 57 to Mex 15D is about 26 miles (42 km).

MONTERREY, NUEVO LEÓN (MOHN-TEH-RAY)
Population 3,000,000, Elevation 1,750 ft (532 m)

Busy, prosperous Monterey is the third largest city in Mexico and the capital of the state of Nuevo León. Travelers who have already had a chance to see some of the rest of the country will not be surprised to hear that Monterrey has the highest standard of living in all of Mexico. The city lies in a valley surrounded by mountains with the Río Santa Caterina bisecting the town in a east-west direction.

The huge central **Gran Plaza,** just north of the river, with its modern orange obelisk topped with a laser and called the **Faro de Comercio** sets the tone for the city. It is very different from the central plazas in other Mexican cities. Running for many blocks in a north-south orientation many of the interesting attractions of Monterrey surround it or are not far away. These include the **Zona Rosa** pedestrian mall which makes a good place to stroll and introduce yourself to Mexican shopping and also the **Catedral de Monterrey**.

El Obispado, at the western end of the downtown area near the river, was built as a bishop's residence in 1797 and has also served as a fort during the Mexican-American war of 1846, as Pancho Villa's headquarters during the Revolution, and today as a regional museum. It sits on a hill and offers good views of the city.

Lead crystal glassware fans will want to tour the **Cristalería Kristaluxus** factory and showrooms. Visitors with other interests may want to visit the giant **Cervecería Cuauhtémoc** which brews Bohemia and Carta Blanca beer. The brewery also houses a **Sports Hall of Fame** and the **Monterrey Museum**.

Monterrey fiestas include the **Feria de Primavera** which begins on Palm Sunday and lasts two weeks and the **Fiestas de Septiembre**, in September, of course. In December Monterrey hosts the **Feria del Norte de México** and also the **Fiesta of the Virgin of Guadalupe**.

Monterrey Campground

BAHÍA ESCONDIDA HOTEL AND RESORT

Address:	Av. Eugenio Garza Sada 2116, Col. Roma, CP 64710 Monterrey, Nuevo León, México (Reservations)
Location:	El Cercado, Santiago, Nuevo León, México
Telephone:	(8) 285-2323 (Resort), (8) 359-7400 (Monterrey)
Fax:	(8) 285-1518 (Resort), (8) 359-8773 (Monterrey)

$$ / $$$ (Winter) $$$ / $$$ (Summer)

GPS Location: N 25° 24' 50.6", W 100° 07' 28.9"

The Bahía Escondida is a first-class operation that has been around a while, it has recently become a KOA. Unfortunately it is somewhat inconveniently located some

15 miles (24 km) south of Monterrey on the road to Ciudad Victoria and is not a good place to overnight if you are heading west to Saltillo and then south to the central area of Mexico via Mex 54. It is good however, if you are by-passing Monterrey on the east and south on secondary roads. With the closure of the Nueva Castilla this has become Monterrey's only campground.

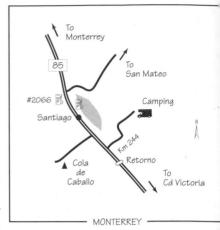

This very large resort has lots of amenities, the campground is very nice but hardly the center of attention. There are 26 back-in spaces with electricity (30-amp outlets), sewer (small 2 ¾" tubes for some reason), water, picnic tables, barbecues and plenty of shade. Access to 13 of the sites is restricted for high vehicles because an aqueduct crosses the driveway, work seems to be underway to correct this problem. The access drive in the campground is gravel with curbs, there is well-clipped grass everywhere else. The restroom building is large, modern, clean and tiled, it has hot water showers. There is a children's play area in the camping area and also a self-service laundry. Really long rigs won't fit in this campground, we estimate 32 feet to be about the maximum although you could park a tow vehicle away from your space but nearby.

As mentioned above, the campground is only a minor part of this huge resort. Here's a short list of some of the other offerings: swimming pools (including one with waves), boat launch, restaurant, hotel, and a huge water slide.

The entrance to the resort is on the east side of Mex 85 south of Monterrey near the Km 244 marker. If you are traveling away from Monterrey you must go beyond the Km marker, use a retorno to turn around and head back toward the city. Just beyond the Km 244 marker take the right marked Bahía Escondida. Follow this small paved road for 1.4 miles (2.3 km) until your reach the entrance gate and office. After checking in you head down the hill to the left, take a left fork as you climb again, and follow the driveway up and over the small hill to the campground which sits down next to the lake.

Other Camping Possibilities

The northern Monterrey camping area at Hotel Nueva Castilla has been closed effective spring 2001 and will not reopen.

If you have a tow car or don't mind a bus ride and wish to visit Monterrey you might consider basing yourself in Saltillo. That city has a decent camping area and is much smaller and much easier to navigate than Monterrey.

Side Trips from Monterrey

Sights outside the city but in the immediately surrounding area include **Horsetail Falls**, **Huasteca Canyon**, and the **Grutas de García**.

The distance between Saltillo and Monterrey is only 51 miles (82 km) on a good multi-lane free highway. This means that if you would like to base yourself in one of these cities and visit the other on a day trip you can easily do it.

Bypass Routes

Maps of the Monterrey area are likely to confuse you because many of them show a bypass road from north to south on the east side of town that does not yet exist. A beautiful toll bypass road does scribe a semicircle around from Mex 40 to the west, north to meet Mex 85 from Nuevo Laredo, and then east to meet Mex 40 from Reynosa. Unfortunately it does not extend south to meet Mex 85. This is a very expensive toll road, but there is a free bypass road just south (toward the city) that virtually parallels the toll bypass, you will probably want to use it instead if you are traveling around the north side of town.

Travelers bound south for the campground there or wanting to bypass Monterrey on the south can do it pretty easily. There is a small but paved and uncrowded two-lane highway from Cadereyta de Jiminez on the east side of the city that goes south to Allende on Mex 85. Then there is Mex 31 which connects Mex 85 at Linares to Mex 57. Both of these roads are suitable for RVs driven carefully.

MORELIA, MICHOACÁN (MOH-RAY-lee-ah)
Population 750,000, Elevation 6,400 ft (1,946 m)

Morelia is the capital of the state of Michoacán, one of the most handsome state capitals in Mexico. Originally the city was called Valladolid but in 1828 it was named after the Mexican War of Independence hero General José María Morelos. The city is extremely well endowed with colonial-style buildings, building ordinances preserve what is there and restrict the construction of clashing designs in the central area.

The state of Michoacán is known for its handicrafts and Morelia has a good selection. Try both the **Casa de las Artesanías** at the **convent of the Church of San Francisco** and the **Mercado de Dulces** (Candy Market). You'll also find many smaller shops scattered around town.

The **central square** and **cathedral** are rewarding, just as they are in most Mexican colonial cities. Morelia is special, however, the cathedral is considered one of the most impressive in Mexico. Morelia also has an **aqueduct**. It is no longer in use but you'll probably see at least some of its remaining 253 arches. There are two museums to the city's namesake, **Museo Casa Natal de Morelos** (where he was born) and **Museo Casa de Morelos** (where he lived later in life). Morelia also has a good zoo and, at the modern convention center, a **planetarium** and an **orchid house**.

Morelia is also well-endowed with shopping centers, supermarkets, and discount stores so it is a good place to stock up. Several are located off the ring road in the southeastern section of town. There's a Wal-Mart just inside the ring road where the highway from Pátzcuaro joins it.

Morelia has few campgrounds, none actually are at the city but there are several in the surrounding area. Most visitors use Pátzcuaro as a base but that's not the only possibility. A balneario near Zinapécuaro is one alternative, there's also a small balneario in the town of Quiroga along Mex 15 to the east.

THE INTERIOR OF MEXICO

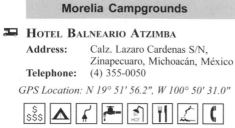

Morelia Campgrounds

🚐 **HOTEL BALNEARIO ATZIMBA**

Address: Calz. Lazaro Cardenas S/N,
                Zinapecuaro, Michoacán, México
Telephone: (4) 355-0050

GPS Location: N 19° 51' 56.2", W 100° 50' 31.0"

HOTEL BALNEARIO ATZIMBA

Morelia has few campgrounds, none actually are in the city but there are a few in the surrounding area. The Balneario Atzimba is about 30 miles (48 km) northeast of the city beyond the airport.

The camping area at Atzimba is really designed for car campers using tents. Camping spaces are not delineated, you just pick a place to park. Electricity is available from a large number of outlets (15-amp) nailed to the trees and water is also available, there is no provision for dumping. Restrooms at the campground area are in poor condition but there are better ones a short distance away near the pools with warm showers. The campground has several nice warm swimming pools, tennis courts, and a restaurant. Expect this place to be crowded on weekends, but it is quiet during the week, particularly during the winter. Maneuvering room is limited, this campground is suitable only for rigs to about 30 feet. No English is spoken.

From Morelia follow Mex 43 north from the ring road at the northern edge of town. Near Km 8 take the exit for the airport and Zinapecuaro. Follow the two-lane highway east for about 23 miles (38 km), you'll see the Atzimba on the left as you near Zinapecuaro. There is a large lot for parking cars near the front entrance, this makes a good place to park while you walk in and make arrangements to have the rear gate to the camping area opened. This rear gate is about one hundred yards down the highway in the direction from which you have come but there is not sufficient room to park at that entrance while waiting for a attendant. Approaching from the east in big RVs is not advisable, the town of Zinapecuaro is difficult to negotiate in a large rig.

🚐 **BALNEARIO SAN JOSÉ DE AGUA TIBIA**

Address: Lopez Mateos Y Juárez, Quiroga,
                Michoacán , México
Telephone: (4) 354-0295

GPS Location: N 19° 40' 05.1", W 101° 31' 30.4"

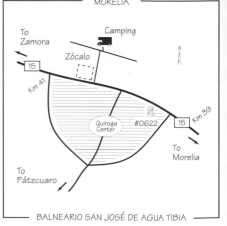

BALNEARIO SAN JOSÉ DE AGUA TIBIA

This is the town balneario in Quiroga, one of the main arts and crafts market centers around Lake Pátzcuaro in Michoacán. Quiroga is also only 30 miles (48 km) from Morelia so it is also a fairly convenient place to stay while visiting the city. There is frequent bus service into Morelia.

The balneario has two large grass fields behind its pool area. RV's can park along the edge of one field near the changing room building and run a cord for electricity. Tenters have a large area to themselves. Rigs over about 25 feet long will probably not be able to enter the gate as turning space is limited. The restrooms are old and nothing special but have hot showers. The pool here is heated using a boiler so it is popular all year long. Weekends at the balneario can be crowded but the camping area is slightly removed so there is some privacy. Security is pretty good since a decent fence is the only way to make sure the local teens pay for their pool use. The central plaza is only a block away so you are in a very convenient location when you stay here. Some readers have reported the balneario closed during the week during the winter. If you do find it closed the campgrounds at Pátzcuaro are within easy driving distance along the east shore of Lake Pátzcuaro.

Passing through Quiroga on Mex 15 turn north at the east side of the central plaza. The balneario is two blocks straight ahead. Large RV's may have some trouble entering the camping area because swing room is limited. We estimate that a 30 foot motorhome is about the maximum size for this campground.

Other Camping Possibilities

A small motel on the eastern outskirts of Morelia has a few camping slots in the rear courtyard. The **Hotel Meson Tarasco** is 2.3 miles (3.7 km) west of the ring road near the Km 7 marker. There are no longer any hookups or restrooms. The GPS location is N 19° 41' 31.4", W 101° 16' 39.4". Parking for vehicles longer than 30 feet is difficult and involves backing your rig around several corners.

We've met several groups who have spent the night in the **Wal-Mart** parking lot just inside the Morelia ring road where the highway from Pátzcuaro meets it.

Don't forget **Pátzcuaro** as a base for exploring Morelia. It's only 36 miles (58 km) away on an excellent highway.

NUEVO CASAS GRANDES (NEW-AY-voe CAWS-aws GRAHN-days)
Population 50,000, Elevation 4,760 ft (1,450 m)

This modern town in northern Mexico, an easy day's drive from the New Mexico border, has become a good option for a first night in Mexico. You can easily get there from the crossings at Palomas or Naco/Agua Prieta if you get a reasonably early start. The town has banks with cash machines, supermarkets, and a couple of small RV parks that have appeared in the last few years. It's a farming town and home to a sizable Mormon population.

The most important reason for visiting Casas Grandes is the nearby **Paquimé** or Casas Grandes archeological site. Paquimé was the largest pre-Hispanic trading settlement in northern Mexico and was populated until about 1300 A.D. The ruins are of adobe and that means that they have eroded to fairly low walls, but today the former and current inhabitants of the area are probably best known for their beautiful Paquimé-style pottery. The archeological site has an outstanding museum which highlights this pottery.

Nuevo Casas Grandes Campground

HOTEL LOS ARCOS

Address: Casas Grandes-Chihuahua
Highway Km#2, Nuevo Casas
Grandes, Chihuahua, México
Telephone: (1) 694-4260

GPS Location: N 30° 24' 02.0", W 107° 53' 52.1"

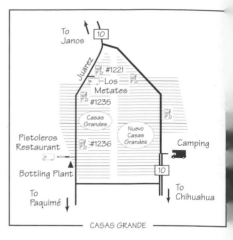

CASAS GRANDE

The Hotel Los Arcos, located at the southern edge of Nuevo Casas Grandes, is about 7 km from the archeological site. It makes a convenient place to stay when you visit. The RV sites are slowly being developed as you will see in the description below.

The RV parking area is inside the walled hotel. There are 10 electrical outlets (actually five boxes) with 15-amp outlets and room to back in probably 7 large rigs next to them). Unfortunately there is not enough power available to run even one air conditioner on the one circuit so it is doubtful that seven rigs would be happy with the available power. Water hookups are available and there is a dump station. A restroom

PAQUIMÉ ARCHEOLOGICAL SITE NEAR CASAS GRANDE

THE INTERIOR OF MEXICO

with shower has been constructed but when we visited (twice over a five-month period during the winter of 2000-2001) water had not been connected, this does not seem to be a priority. There is a great deal of room to park in the lot where the sites are located, truckers using the motel often park there but there is usually room for at least five large rigs in addition to the RV sites.

The campground is located on the east side of Mex 10 as it enters town from the south. This is very near the cutoff to the town of Casas Grandes and the Paquimé site. Exercise caution as you turn into the motel entrance, the drop has caused large bus-type rigs with little ground clearance to drag.

Other Camping Possibilities

Nuevo Casas Grandes will soon have a second campground, unfortunately when we visited in the spring of 2001 there was no one around and we were unable to get complete information. The place is called **Los Metates**. There appear to be about 30 sites although they are too small for large rigs. If the campground were not full large rigs could, of course, find room to park. Sites have full hookups with 30-amp outlets. We have talked with folks who have visited this campground and the owner is planning to be open for business soon. It is located at the northern edge of Nuevo Casas Grandes. As you enter town from the north do not turn left on the signed bypass, Instead continue straight. You will spot Pemex #1221 on the left and just .1 mile (.2 km) later see the campground, also on the left. The GPS location is N 30° 26' 20.0", W 107° 54' 52.3".

We have talked with a group who recently spent several very enjoyable days camped on the grounds of **Pistoleros Restaurant** in Nuevo Casas Grandes. There is plenty of room for at least 10 large rigs to boondock on the grounds and the restaurant seems happy to have them if they are good restaurant customers. If enough people visit this could easily become a formal RV park. To find the restaurant drive west from the intersection on Mex 10 near the Los Arcos Hotel toward the Casas Grandes site. You will come to an intersection where you would turn left to go to Casas Grandes. Instead turn right and watch for a small Carta Blanca bottling plant on your left, you will see Pemex #1236 ahead on the right. After the bottling plant there is a large empty lot on the left side of the highway before you reach the Pemex, turn left either immediately after the bottling plant or on the far side of the field, you should be able to see Pistoleros off to the left on the far side. There are several routes across the field. The GPS location is N 30° 23' 55.9", W 107° 55' 00.1".

PACHUCA, HIDALGO (PAH-CHOO-KAH)
Population 300,000, Elevation 8,000 ft (2,432 m)

Pachuca is one of the closest capitals to Mexico City, it is only 55 miles (88 km) away on a good toll road. It is the capital of the state of Hidalgo. Historically this is a mining area, and it continues to produce a great deal of silver, but today the town is becoming more and more industrial.

Few people visit Pachuca and it really has little to attract tourists. Many Cornish miners came to Pachuca in the 19th century so it has a personality slightly different than other Mexican cities. While the central area is on flat land much of the suburban area rises onto the mountains behind, the roads in this area are narrow and difficult to

negotiate, don't get trapped on them if you are in a larger rig. A ring road around the
east side of town makes it relatively easy to get to Mex 105 northeast to El Chico.

Pachuca Campground

🚐 **EL CHICO NATIONAL PARK**

$$ ▲

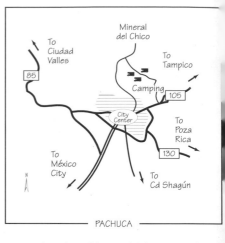

El Chico National Park just north and far above
Pachuca has many flat grassy areas for dry
camping. Most are provided with pit toilets by
locals and a small fee is charged for camping.
There is also a more formal area called El
Oyamel just inside the entrance gate to the park.
It is run by a local ejido and has (GPS Loca-
tion: N 20° 10' 40.9", W 098° 41' 43.8") 10 full
hookup sites with electricity, sewer, and water.
Also a large building with restrooms and meet-
ing rooms. Unfortunately when we visited there
was no power or water and it was only open on weekends. This could be a good
campground but apparently there is not enough demand to make its operation worth-
while.

To find El Chico National Park follow Mex 105 northeast from Pachuca. After a 2.8
miles (4.5 km) climb from the ring road you'll see a sign for Mineral del Chico to the
left. Take this road and after another 3.5 miles (5.6 km) you'll pass through the park
entrance and find campsites at various locations for the next several miles.

PÁTZCUARO, MICHOACÁN (PAHTZ-kwah-row)
Population 65,000, Elevation 7,150 ft (2,174 m)

Pátzcuaro is a treasure. It is a town from another time and place and seems to be a
favorite with everyone who visits. It is a friendly-sized town, there are adequate fa-
cilities for camping, many good restaurants, lots of shopping for crafts, and interest-
ing side trips around the surrounding countryside.

Life in town centers around the two plazas. The **Plaza Grande** is slow-moving and
shaded. Restaurants and shops occupy porticos around the perimeter. The **Plaza Chica**
is much different. It is full of activity and vendors, especially during the Friday mar-
ket, and the town mercado (market) is adjacent. The third location of interest is the
lake front, it is about 2 miles (3 km) from the central area and quite near the camp-
grounds. There are several seafood restaurants there and two dock areas where you
can catch boats to Janitzio Island.

Crafts are readily available in Pátzcuaro. The **Friday market** is an excellent place to
find them, you should also check out the **Casa de los Once Patios** (house of eleven
patios) where you can watch craftsmen work and buy their handiwork.

One thing not to be missed in the Pátzcuaro area is the **dance of "Los Viejitos"** (old
men). Young dancers dress in masks of old men and carry canes, their dance is hilari-
ous. The easiest place to see it is at a show at the Hotel Don Vasco, these shows were

on Thursday night when we last visited.

If you decide to stay in Pátzcuaro for an extended period you shouldn't forget that Morelia is just 36 miles (58 km) away on good roads. You can easily run in for a day of shopping for supplies in the big stores. Do not drive a large RV into Pátzcuaro since the streets are confusing and some would be hard to negotiate. The campgrounds are well outside the central area but small combi busses provide easy access to town.

Pátzcuaro Campgrounds

🚐 VILLA PÁTZCUARO

Address:	Avenida Lázaro Cárdenas 506
	(Apdo 206), Pátzcuaro, CP 61600
	Michoacán, México
Telephone:	(4) 342-0767 **Fax:** (4) 342-2984
E-mail:	vpatzcuaro@yahoo.com
Web Site:	www.geocities.com/vpatzcuaro

GPS Location: N 19° 32' 02.6", W 101° 36' 36.2"

This is a cute little place conveniently located and with good facilities. It is best for smaller rigs, anything over about 30 feet will have some maneuvering problems although we've seen some huge rigs here.

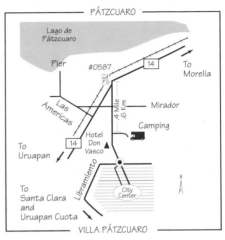

There are 12 short back-in spaces with 15-amp outlets, sewer, and water. A much larger grassy area is available for dry and tent camping. The restrooms are well-maintained and have hot water. There is a small swimming pool and also a small cottage that serves as a shared kitchen area, very useful for tenters. The docks for boats to Janitzio are a 10 minute walk in one direction and the center of town is 30 minutes in the other. Small busses along the highway provide convenient motorized transport.

As you arrive in Pátzcuaro from the direction of Morelia on Mex 14 you will see Pemex #589 on the left. Zero your odometer. In .3 miles (.5 km) you will see the El Pozo Trailer Park on the right and then at 1.1 miles (1.8 km) come to an intersection. Go left here toward central Patzcuaro, the small road to the Villa Pátzcuaro is on the left at 1.5 miles (2.4 km).

🚐 EL POZO TRAILER PARK

Address:	Route 120 At Kilometer 20 (Apdo.
	142), Pátzcuaro, CP 61600
	Michoacán, México
Telephone:	(4) 342-0937

GPS Location: N 19° 32' 02.6", W 101° 36' 36.2"

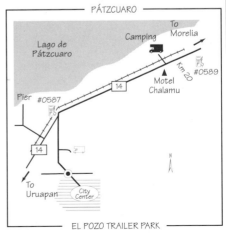

This is the first campground you'll see when you come into Pátzcuaro from Morelia. It is the best of the campgrounds in town for big rigs, there's plenty of room. It is popular with caravans.

There are 20 back-in spaces arranged on both sides of a very large grassy field. Each has 15-amp outlets, sewer, and water. Restrooms are clean and well-maintained, they have hot water showers. There is a playground for the kids and busses pass in front of the campground for transportation into town or to the dock area. There is room for any size RV and English is spoken.

As you come into Pátzcuaro from Morelia watch for the Pemex on the left. Just after the Pemex you'll see the 20-Km marker and then the El Pozo on the right. Watch for the campground's large sign on the far side of the railroad tracks running alongside the highway.

Side Trips from Pátzcuaro

When you visit Pátzcuaro don't miss the boat trip to **Isla Janitzio**. These waterborne busses are used by both tourists and residents. The trip takes about a half-hour each way. On weekends you are likely to be treated to a mariachi band en route, be sure to kick in a few coins when they pass the hat. Once on the island you climb to the statue of Morelos on the summit of the island. The view from the base of the statue is good but you'll probably want to climb up into the torch, if only for the thrill. All the way up the hill you'll be tempted by vendors with handicrafts and wonderful smelling restaurants. You can catch any boat back to the mainland, the return is included in the price you paid on the way out.

Santa Clara del Cobre (also called Villa Escalante) is 12 miles (20 km) south of Pátzcuaro. This town is famous for its copper metalwork. You'll find most of the stores concentrated near the plaza, they're filled with plates, pots, and almost anything you can think of made of copper. Take a tour of one of the *fábricas* (factories) to see the work in progress.

Nine miles (15 km) north of Pátzcuaro near the shore of the lake is the pre-colonial village of **Tzintzuntzan**. **Las Yácatas** archeological site has five round tombs built by ancient Tarascan Indians. The village produces a green-colored pottery.

PUEBLA, PUEBLA (PWEH-BLAH)
Population 1,100,000, Elevation 7,100 ft (2,158 m)

Like many Mexican cities Puebla sits surrounded by mountains, they include the volcanoes of Popocatépetl, Iztaccíhuatl, La Malinche, and Pico de Orizaba. This is a sophisticated city with an elegant colonial central area. It is also Mexico's fourth largest city. There is a lot of history in Puebla and the **food** is famous throughout the country. Puebla's mole poblano is the country's national dish. The city is synonymous with **Talavera**, both tiles and pottery.

On May 5, 1862 Mexican military forces won a huge and unexpected victory here over invading French forces. The victory was a temporary one, a year later the French were back with reinforcements from home and this time they were victorious. The May 5 victory is celebrated by a well-known holiday known as Cinco de Mayo. You can visit the fort where all of this happened, it is located just northeast of the center of the city and has a museum.

Another very attractive town, **Cholula**, is almost a suburb of Puebla. Cholula is known for its churches, there are sometimes said to be 365 of them in this small town of approximately 50,000 people. The most unique is built atop a huge Indian pyramid. Today the pyramid looks like a pyramid-shaped hill but if you take the tour through the interior you will see that it definitely is a pyramid to rival those at Teotihuacán, in fact this one is even larger.

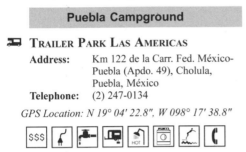

Puebla Campground

🚐 **TRAILER PARK LAS AMERICAS**

Address: Km 122 de la Carr. Fed. México-
                  Puebla (Apdo. 49), Cholula,
                  Puebla, México
Telephone: (2) 247-0134

GPS Location: N 19° 04' 22.8", W 098° 17' 38.8"

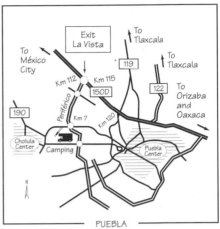

PUEBLA

Las Americas is located in Cholula, a pleasant Puebla suburb with lots to see. The famous Cholula pyramid, largest in the western hemisphere, is only a 20 minute walk from the campground. It's the tall hill to the south with the church on the summit.

The campground has 17 back-in spaces with 15-amp outlets, sewer, water and patios arranged around the outside wall of a cobblestone courtyard with grass surfaces for parking. There is plenty of room for big rigs to maneuver. An additional 11 full-service back-in spaces occupy the entrance courtyard, they are seldom used for camping, usually this area is used by the adjoining motel for parking. The campground has three tiled restroom cubicles with toilet, sink and shower. There is also a pool, a wading pool, playground equipment, and a dormitory room that can be rented by groups. The gate is closed at night. Access to both Puebla and Cholula by public transportation is easy, dozens of small collectivos (VW vans) ply the road two blocks away. The central Cholula square can be reached in a half-hour stroll.

To reach the campground it is best to use the new ring road around Puebla known as the Periférico Ecological, it runs very near the campground and makes getting there a snap. From Mex 150D the exit for the ring road is near Km 115, the exit is marked as La Vista and Periférico Ecological. Follow the Periférico southward for 4.3 miles (7 km) and take the exit marked Cholula and Puebla Libre. You will merge onto a two lane westbound highway and must make a left turn almost immediately onto a gravel road to the left, Calle 6 Norte. It is marked with a faded billboard for Las Americas. If you follow the highway around a gradual 90 degree left bend you've gone too far. After making the turn at the Las Americas sign you will follow a rough dirt road for two blocks and turn left. The campground is on the left about half way down the block.

Other Camping Possibilities

In the past the **Hotel Cuatro Caminos** was one of Puebla's campgrounds, but when hotel units were added they took the space needed for campers. It is still possible to spend the night boondocking in the parking lot of this hotel but not nearly as comfort-

THE INTERIOR OF MEXICO

able as camping at the Las Americas. The ownership of the two facilities is the same. The hotel is located at Av. Hermanos Serdan No. 406 at the northern edge of Puebla near the toll road, the GPS location is N 19° 05' 35.5", W 098° 13' 43.9"

QUERÉTARO, QUERÉTARO (KEH-RAY-TAH-ROW)
Population 500,000, Elevation 6,100 ft (1,855 m)

The city of Querétaro has played an important part in Mexican history. Querétaro was the headquarters for the Franciscan monks as they founded missions throughout the country, the revolution against Spain was planned here, Maximilian made his last stand and faced the firing squad in Querétaro, the constitution was drafted here, and here the PRI was founded.

The colonial center is the prime attraction for visitors. It has a very Spanish flavor, some of the center is closed to automobile traffic. You'll want to visit the central square which is called the **Jardín Obregón**, the **Ex-Convent and Church of San Francisco** which also houses a museum, the **Casa de Corregidora**, and the **Temple and Ex-Convent of Santa Cruz**. About a half-hour walk from the central area is the **Cerro de las Campañas**, the hill where Maximilian was executed. Querétaro has a still-working **aqueduct** on the east side of town which was finished in 1738.

Querétaro Campgrounds

🚐 **FLAMINGO HOTEL**

Address:	Av. Constituyentes Pte. 138 Centro, Querétaro, CP 76000 Querétaro, México
Telephone:	(4) 216-2093

GPS Location: N 20° 34' 51.8", W 100° 23' 56.7"

$$$ 🏕️ 🎣 🚰 🚿 HOT 🍴 🏊

If a little heavy traffic doesn't bother you this is the place to stay for your Querétaro visit. The center of town is a twenty-minute stroll away. This camping area is only suitable for rigs to about 30 feet because maneuvering room into and inside the grounds is limited.

The Flamingo has 7 camping spaces. They are parallel parking spots next to a lawn area, in effect they are pull-throughs. All have electricity (15-amp outlets) and water is available. There are no sewer drains. The lawn is good for tent camping. The small restroom is adequate, it has a hot water shower and is relatively clean. The hotel has a swimming pool and a restaurant.

Access to the hotel is from near the intersection of Mex 45 and Mex 57 on the southwest side of Querétaro. The road that the hotel sits next to (Av. Constituyentes Pte.) is the continuation of Mex 45 Libre as it enters town after passing under Mex 57. Unfortunately the hotel is on the north side of the boulevard and the necessary U-turn is difficult for big rigs. The best access is by taking Av. Ignacio Zaragoza east from Mex 57 (Zaragoza is marked from the highway, it is near what would be Km 213 from the south, Km 1 from the north), turning right on Ezequiel Montes (the 5th streetlight east of Mex 57) or any other convenient street, to head south to Constituyentes. Once established westbound on Constituyentes you can easily make the right turn into the hotel. The entrance is tight and maneuvering room inside is limited.

AZTECA PARADOR HOTEL

Address:	Km 15.5 Carr. Querétaro-S.L.P., Querétaro, Querétaro, México
Telephone:	(4) 294-0592, (4) 294-0593

GPS Location: N 20° 41' 56.5", W 100° 26' 09.1"

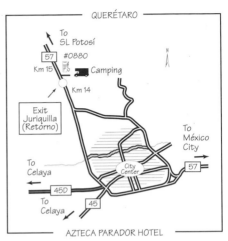

QUERÉTARO

AZTECA PARADOR HOTEL

If you don't want to drive your big rig into town or if you are just looking for an easily accessible place to spend the night when passing through this is the place. Some hard-chargers use this campground as their only stop between the U.S. border and Acapulco.

The hotel has about 70 camping spaces on grass or gravel. Some 50 have electricity (15-amp outlets), sewer, and water. There is lots of room to maneuver large rigs. The hotel and campground are located next to a modern Pemex with the same ownership, the bathrooms are located at the back of the Pemex but only used by campers. There is a good restaurant at the Pemex and a swimming pool and children's play area at the hotel for use by camping guests. It is possible but not really convenient to catch a bus into town from along the highway out front. A tow car would work better. This is also a good place to gas up, it seems to have excellent and honest service.

The hotel and campground are located on the east side of Mex 57 near the Km 15 mark. Mex 57 is a four-lane divided highway at this point. Headed north just take the exit at the Pemex. Headed south you must continue for .6 miles (1 km) to the Juriquilla Exit to reverse direction and access the hotel. A convenient retorno to the north will allow you to head south the next morning.

SALTILLO, COAHUILA (SAHL-TEE-YOH)
Population 600,000, Elevation 5,250 ft (1,596 m)

Saltillo is close to Monterrey and shares the booming industrial economy of that city. On the other hand, Saltillo is much smaller and much easier to deal with. Traffic is less of a problem and the colonial central area quite walkable. Saltillo has the best **colonial center** of any city near the U.S. border.

The streets in the city center are crowded and narrow, they are not suitable for big rigs. Park outside the central area and either walk or catch a bus. The town centers on a plaza, of course, in this case called the Plaza de Armas. The churrigueresque **Cathedral de Santiago Saltillo** faces out onto the plaza. A few blocks away is the city market building, the **Mercado Juárez**.

Saltillo Campground

🚐 HOTEL IMPERIAL DEL NORTE

Address: Blvd. Venustiano Carranza No.
             3800, Saltillo, Coahuila, México
Telephone: (8) 415-0011   **Fax:** (8) 416-7543
E-mail: imperial@mcsa.net.mx

GPS Location: N 25° 27' 24.5", W 100° 59' 08.4"

There's nothing too fancy about the camping facilities at the Imperial, but they're in a quiet location back from the road and the central area of Saltillo is just a short bus ride away. There are many restaurants in the immediate area.

There are about 16 back-in sites on a flat paved area behind the hotel. Each has a 15-amp outlet, sewer, and water hookups although they are in poor repair and some may not be serviceable. There is plenty of maneuvering room for large rigs. Since there are seldom many people staying here you will undoubtedly be able to find a spot with utilities that work. There are two restrooms, one for caballeros and one for dames, they are rooms containing a toilet, sink and hot shower. Last time we visited they were poorly maintained and dirty. The hotel also has a restaurant and a swimming pool, although it is not in operation during the winter.

The Imperial del Norte is located on Blvd. Carranza to the northeast of central Saltillo. If you are approaching on Mex 40 from Monterrey you will already be on Blvd. Carranza when you arrive. If you are arriving from the south follow the Periférico Luis Echeverria around to the northeast side of town and then take Blvd. Nazario S. Ortiz Garza north to intersect with Blvd. Carranza. From either direction watch for the Soriana supermarket on the northeast corner of Blvd. Carranza and Blvd. Nazario S. Ortiz Garza. The hotel is on the right .7 miles (1.1 km) south of this intersection, watch for a Kentucky Fried Chicken just before the hotel. Turn right into the road between the KFC and the hotel, the campground entrance is directly ahead. If you are approaching from the south on Blvd. Carranza it is more difficult, there is no break in the median so you must go north to a retorno which has little swing room, big rigs will probably have to pull through a Pemex station there to turn around or go on to the Soriana parking lot. When leaving, if you are bound for Monterrey or want to turn left on Carranza you can not do so because of the median strip. Instead turn left immediately after exiting the gate of the campground to drive behind the KFC, left again at the next block, right at the next block, and right again at the next block. This should put you on the road that reaches Carranza at the Pemex where there is a break in the median allowing you to turn left. You might want to walk this first to make sure you can make it.

SAN LUIS POTOSÍ, SAN LUIS POTOSÍ (SAHN LOO-EES POH-TOE-SEE)
Population 750,000, Elevation 6,175 ft (1,877 m)

Few tourists seem to make it to San Luis Potosí, this really isn't a popular tourist city.

For a long period of Mexican history San Luis Potosí was the largest and most important city of northern México, today that spot is taken by Monterrey. San Luis Potosí remains an economic powerhouse however, it is a transportation center sitting astride railroads and highways.

Because it was historically prominent and powerful the center of San Luis Potosí has impressive buildings and parks. The streets tend to be narrow but quite a few are closed to traffic to make a pedestrian shopping area. There are many squares, often in the form of well-tended gardens. Centrally located ones include the **Alameda**, the **Jardín Hidalgo**, the **Plaza de los Fundadores**, and the **Jardín San Juan de Dios**. Many of these are flanked by neoclassical or republican-style buildings and connecting walking streets. The historical importance also means that San Luis Potosí is also full of churches. These include the centrally located **Santa Iglesia Catedral** and the churrigueresque-style **Templo del Carmen**, but there are many others. Important museums include a **bull-fighting museum** at the bull ring and the centrally located **Museo Regional Potosino** and **Mexican mask museum**.

San Luis Potosí Campgrounds

🚐 **EL MESQUITE MOTEL**

Address: Carretera 57 a Matehuala - San Louis Potosí Km 13, San Louis Potosí, S.L.P., México

GPS Location: N 22° 14' 45.7", W 100° 53' 02.6"

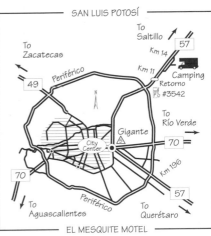

The El Mesquite was for many years the only place to stay in San Luis Potosí. A few years ago the place was closed and construction of a hotel begun. Then construction stalled for several years. The campsites behind the hotel remained available to campers although there were no services, it was essentially boondocking for a fee.

When we visited during the winter of 2000/2001 the situation was unchanged, work was not progressing and it was possible to boondock for a pretty substantial price. However, the caretaker said that the hotel has changed hands and work will soon resume. He assured us that the new hotel would have camping facilities. We'll have to wait and see what develops.

At the present time there is space for 30 or so rigs to park behind the hotel. Big rigs will find that there is room to maneuver. There is really no security although the caretaker is sometimes on the grounds. Children from the village often visit. Busses to central San Luis Potosí pass on the highway in front of the motel. English is not spoken.

The motel is located in the village of Enrique Estrada on Mex 57 north of San Luis Potosí. It is on the east side of the road near the Km 13 marker. Lateral streets in the village make access to the motel only possible if you are northbound and are on the lateral. Be sure to enter the lateral when you enter the village if you are approaching from the south. From the north you must now go all the way to the south end of the village and use a retorno to turn around and enter the northbound lateral lane.

▣ HOTEL QUINTA SAN JORGE

Address: Carretera a Matehuala Km 11.6,
              San Louis Potosí, S.L.P., México
Telephone: (4) 814-6794

GPS Location: N 22° 13' 55.3", W 100° 53' 48.7"

Just a short distance south of the El Mesquite is another small hotel which offers boondocking for a fee. The Hotel Quinta is fairly new, there is room for about 5 rigs to park in the field behind the motel near the swimming pool. The entire motel is fenced so security seems pretty good here. There are no hookups but there are restrooms with hot showers available to campers. Big rigs will find that there is room to maneuver and smaller rigs may find it possible to park near the rooms and string an electrical cord from the utility room. English is not spoken.

The hotel is just south of the village of Enrique Estrada on Mex 57 north of San Louis Potosí. It is on the east side of the road near the Km 11 marker. This is just before the laterals in the village start.

▣ CENTRO VACACIONAL GOGORRÓN

Location: Km 9 Carretera Villa de Reyes - San
              Felipe Gto., Villa de Reyes, S.L.P.,
              México
Res.:   Alvaro Obregón 660, S.L.P., S.L.P.,
              México
**Telephone
and fax:**   (4) 822-0806 or (reservations)
              (4) 812-3636 and (4) 812-1550

GPS Location: N 21° 44' 04.3", W 100° 57' 15.8"

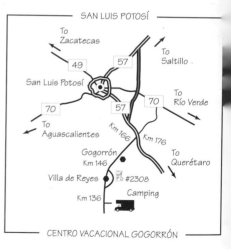

This balneario has been around for quite a while but the management seems to be interested in becoming an RVing destination. Keep in mind that the $27 fee for two includes full use of the facilities. The location is 19 miles off Mex 57 from an intersection some 13.5 miles (21.7 km) to the south of San Luis Potosí.

Management has set aside an area for RVs and plans to install electric and water hookups. The sites are essentially parallel parking on pavement adjacent to one of the pools, there should be room for about five large rigs. Plans are also afoot for a larger area with hookups if there seems to be enough RV visitors as the place becomes known. This balneario has four pools as well as hot tubs and a restaurant. There are also hotel rooms. English is spoken and large rigs will fit although maneuvering room is somewhat limited in the area set aside for camping.

THE INTERIOR OF MEXICO

To drive to the campground take the Villa de Reyes exit from Mex 57 near Km 176. Zero your odometer and drive southwest on the two-lane paved highway. You will pass through several villages, the largest is Villa de Reyes at 13 miles (21 km). Soon after entering Villa de Reyes watch for a bypass (Libramiento) to the left at 13.2 miles (21.3 km). Turn onto the Libramiento and follow it for 1 mile (1.6 km) until it rejoins the main road at a T and turn left to continue on the highway toward the southwest. At 18.9 miles (30.5 km) you'll see the balneario on the left. It is probably best to park on the pull-off across the highway and walk in to register and see how things are laid out.

SAN MIGUEL DE ALLENDE, GUANAJUATO
(SAHN MEE-GEHL DAY AL-YEHN-DAY)
Population 50,000, Elevation 6,100 ft (1,854 m)

This small colonial town is justifiable popular with North American visitors. Many have made it their home so there are lots of the kinds of amenities demanded by visitors from north of the border. San Miguel is second only to the Guadalajara area in popularity with expats. The Allende Institute which offers art and language classes is one of the major reasons for San Miguel's popularity. It and other schools draw many art and language students to the town. Like Guanajuato, San Miguel has been named a national monument, and changes to the town's buildings are carefully controlled.

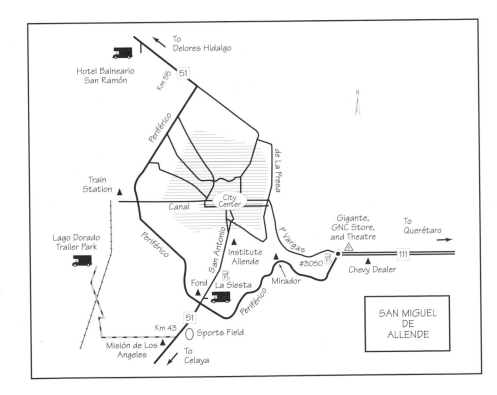

THE INTERIOR OF MEXICO

Here, as elsewhere in central México, a plaza marks the city center. This one is the **Plaza Allende**. Next to it is the unusual **La Parroquia** church which has French gothic features. The central streets are narrow, hilly, and cobblestone-covered. Park outside the central area, there are few places where there is room to park inside it. Near the plaza are many shops and restaurants.

San Miguel de Allende Campgrounds

La Siesta Hotel

Address:	Salida a Celaya No. 82 (Apdo. 72), San Miguel de Allende, CP 37700 Guanajuato., México
Telephone:	(4) 152-0207 **Fax:** (4) 152-3722
E-mail:	lasiesta@unisono.net.mx
Web Site:	www.naftaconnect.com/hotellasiesta

GPS Location: N 20° 53' 59.9", W 100° 45' 07.0"

Many people use the La Siesta during their San Miguel stay because it is conveniently located. It is easy to walk into town from the La Siesta in twenty minutes.

The Hotel has about 45 usable back-in spaces located in a lot behind the motel-style hotel units. Many of the 15-amp outlets, sewer, and water connections for these back-in spaces are in poor repair. There is quite a bit of shade. A small restroom building has been redone recently and has hot showers. The hotel has a restaurant and a swimming pool, but only for summer use. Little English is spoken.

The La Siesta is located next to the bypass road on the south side of San Miguel. From the intersection of the bypass and the road to Celaya go north toward town. You'll see a Ford agency on the left, the La Siesta has a much smaller sign and is on the right.

Lago Dorado Trailer Park

Address:	Jacob van Dijk, Apdo. 523, San Miguel de Allende, CP 37700 Guanajuato, México
Telephone:	(4) 152-2301 **Fax:** (4) 152-3686

GPS Location: N 20° 54' 00.5", W 100° 46' 33.2"

The Lago Dorado is a nice little campground. It is less convenient than the La Siesta, but also much quieter. At one time it was a KOA, the signs have been changed but still look a lot like KOA signs. While named for the nearby lake it is seldom near the water, the reservoir's dam apparently can no longer withstand the pressure of a full lake.

There are 65 camping spaces at the campground. All have electricity (15-amp outlets) and water, twenty have sewer hookups and are pull-throughs. They are arranged on grass under pines that provide lots of shade, the trees are spaced just right for hanging a hammock. Some have picnic tables. The bathrooms are modern, clean, and nice, they have hot water showers. There is also a swimming pool for spring and summer use and a children's play area. English is spoken if the owner is around.

The entrance road to the campground is off the highway leading south from San Miguel toward Celaya and Guanajuato. From the intersection at the south side of San Miguel (near the La Siesta Hotel) drive south .8 miles (1.3 km). The entrance road goes right at the Hotel Misión de Los Angeles. There is a good sign. Zero your odometer here and drive down the cobblestone road for .8 miles (1.3 km) to the end, turn right and follow the turns of a smaller road that crosses railroad tracks at 1.3 miles (2.2 km) and reaches the campground at 1.7 miles (2.7 km).

⛟ HOTEL BALNEARIO SAN RAMÓN

Address:	Km 3 Carretera a Dolores Hidalgo,
	San Miguel de Allende, Guanajuato, México
Telephone:	(4) 152-3669

GPS Location N 20° 56' 52.2", W 100° 45' 35.3"

This small hotel and balneario is located a few miles outside San Miguel. Few RVers seem to stay here, perhaps because they don't know about it.

The balneario has 7 back in spots, all have electric (15-amp outlets) and water hook-ups, a few also have sewer drains. There is maneuvering room for large rigs. Restrooms are clean and modern and have hot showers. There are several pools, we have found them empty during the week but in use on weekends, even in the winter. This is one of several balnearios using the natural hot springs in this area.

From the intersection of the San Miguel ring road and the highway from San Miguel to Delores Hidalgo drive 1 mile (1.6 km), the balneario will be on your left.

San Miguel Bypass Route

San Miguel does have a ring road bypass. It is absolutely essential that you use the bypass if you have a rig that is larger than a van because the town is a maze of very narrow cobblestone streets with few direction signs. Unfortunately the bypass is not marked well so many people, particularly when approaching San Miguel from the east, blunder into town. It is an experience they long remember.

When approaching from the east watch for the Gigante store on the right. The paved road to the left, marked Celaya, is the one you want to take to bypass town. It also takes you on an easy route to the RV parks. A Pemex station stands on the corner next to the turn, it is #3050.

Approaching from the south, from the direction of Celeya, watch the Km markers, the bypass is .7 mile (1.1 km) past the Km 43 marker.

Side Trips From San Miguel

An easy day trip from San Miguel is the drive up to **Delores Hidalgo**. Historically famous as the site of the Grito de Hidalgo, Mexico's declaration of independence from Spain, the town is also known for its Talavera pottery. The distance from San Miguel to Delores Hidalgo is about 23 miles (37 km).

En route to Delores Hidalgo be sure to stop and see the **Santuario de Atotonilco**. The church here is impressively decorated inside, it is a pilgrimage destination from all over Mexico. A banner from here was used as the flag of the rebels during the first stages of the Mexican War of Independence. Atotonilco is about a mile off the San Miguel-Delores Hidalgo road about 8 miles (13 km) from San Miguel.

The drive over to **Guanajuato** also makes a good day trip. You could do a loop drive through Delores Hildago and then Guanajuato although there is so much to see that you would be rushed if you stopped for long in either city.

TEPIC, NAYARIT (TEH-PEEK)
Population 240,000, Elevation 3,000 ft (915 m)

Most guidebooks don't devote many words to Tepic, but it is an important stopover point for RVers. If you are traveling to Guadalajara from either Mazatlán or Puerto Vallarta you will find that Tepic is a great place to break up the long drive. The altitude cools the evening air and the atmosphere is pollution free, there is a big cigarette factory here however.

Tepic has few tourist attractions. The **State Museum** has displays of Indian crafts and also pre-Columbian ceramics. Tepic is the place to buy **Huichol and Cora Indian crafts**.

The city has several large supermarkets, including a Comercial Mexicana. To reach it follow Mex 200 in to town from the intersection with the southern Mex 15 bypass. Turn right at Av. Insurgentes, the store is .7 miles (1.1 km) from the turn.

There is one campground in Tepic and one about 27 miles (44 km) southeast toward Guadalajara at Laguna Santa Maria, a lake inside an old volcanic crater.

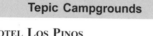

Tepic Campgrounds

🚐 **HOTEL LOS PINOS**

Address: Boulevard Tepic Xalisco #150
                 (Apdo. 329), Tepic, Nayarit, México
Telephone: (3) 213-1232

GPS Location: N 21° 28' 54.1", W 104° 53' 33.2"

Los Pinos is one of those places that might make you think of abandoning your rig. Their rate for camping is quite reasonable but it is almost exactly the same as the rate they charge for their motel-style rooms.

The campground is a large grassy field behind the home/office of the owners. There are 21 long back-in sites with plenty of maneuvering room. All have full utilities (15-amp outlets). Each also has level parking pads and a patio. The entire area has a high wall for security and there are 18 rental bungalows. The central driveway is cobbled so wet weather is no problem here. The small baño buildings have two private bathrooms each with each bathroom having it's own toilet, shower, and sink. Each is tiled in a different color. They are quite clean and have hot water. The owners speak a little English. Some people are bothered that the rooms here cost about the same as the camping. Take a look, you might want to spend a night in a motel room.

To reach central Tepic from the campground you can either walk 2.2 miles (3.5 km) north to the central square or catch a convenient bus on the road in front of the campground.

Los Pinos is not hard to find. Start from the intersection of the Libramiento (ring road) which circles Tepic to the south with Mex 200. From the Libramiento this exit is marked Puerto Vallarta and is at approximately Km 5. Drive north into town on Blvd. Tepic Xalisco, which is the street that becomes Mex 200 as it heads south. Los Pinos is on the left exactly .85 miles (1.4 km) north of the junction. There is a gap in the barrier between lanes to allow you to turn left into the campground.

 **KOALA BUNGALOWS AND RV PARK**

Address:	Apdo 14, Santa María del Oro, CP 63830 Nayarit, México
Telephone:	(3) 244-0237
E-mail:	koala45@latinmail.com
Web Site:	www.geocities.com/TheTropics/Reef/2688

GPS Location: N 21° 21' 42.7", W 104° 34' 26.9"

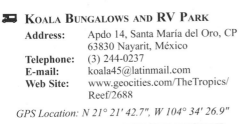

Some 15 miles (24.2 km) east of Tepic off Mex 15 is Laguna de Santa Maria, a pleasant lake located down inside the crater of an extinct volcano. Best of all, there is a trailer park there. Limited maneuvering room and the steep de-

LAGUNA DE SANTA MARIA NEAR TEPIC

THE INTERIOR OF MEXICO

scent to the lake mean that rigs over 30 feet probably shouldn't try to visit this camp-ground.

Koala Bungalow and RV Park has about 12 back-in spaces placed behind the motel-style bungalow building. Most spaces have electricity (15-amp outlets) and water, some also have sewer. Restrooms have hot showers and are clean and in good repair. Visitors relax on the front lawn next to the lake surrounded by citrus trees. There is a children's swimming pool, a kiosk-style refreshment stand, and a boat launching ramp. Swimming in the lake, fishing, hiking and birding are all excellent. English is spoken.

From Mex 15 Libre some 14.6 miles (23.5 km) east of the junction of the toll and free roads near Tepic follow signs north for Sta. Maria del Oro. You'll pass over the toll Mex 15D (from Mex 15D take the Santa Maria del Oro exit to reach this point) in .5 mile (.8 km) and in 6.1 miles (9.8 km) reach the town of Sta. Maria del Oro with 3,000 residents. Pass straight through town on the main road and at 7.8 miles (12.6 km) reach the crater rim which has a viewing pull-off. There is a steep descent to the lake which you reach at 12.0 miles (19.4 km). Turn left and you will find the Koala at the end of this short access road along the lake.

Other Camping Possibilities

The Kampamento KOA, long a fixture in Tepic but seldom visited, has closed and the property is being developed for other purposes.

TEQUISQUIAPAN, QUERÉTARO (TEH-KISS-KEY-AH-PAN)
Population 20,000, Elevation 5,600 ft (1,701 m)

Tequisquiapan is a spa town that is very popular with weekenders from México City. Access for them is easy, the town is just 75 miles (120 km) north on Mex 57D and then another 12 miles (20 km) east on Mex 120 which is a good two-lane road. It is a small town with lots of hotels, restaurants and cobblestone streets. Incidentally, this town occupies the official geographic center of México.

Don't drive a rig of any size into central Tequisquiapan, while good at first the roads narrow and become a trap for the adventurous. The three campgrounds below are well outside town.

Tequisquiapan Campgrounds

TERMAS DEL REY

Address:	Carretera Tequisquiapan a Ezequiel Montes Km 10, Tequisquiapan, Querétaro, México
Telephone:	(5) 554-6587 **Fax:** (5) 658-1926

GPS Location: N 20° 37' 08.2", W 099° 54' 50.2"

Here's another example of a balneario with sites for RVs. This one is off the beaten path for norteamericanos. On weekends and holidays this balneario will probably be crowded, but during the week you'll have it almost to yourself. It isn't a world-class place but the pools are well maintained and clean and the people friendly.

The RV camping area has electrical (15-amp outlets) and water hookups for at least twenty rigs. Tent campers can use the grass. The RV area doubles as parking for the other balneario visitors but you will probably be able to set up out of the way. The area is suitable for any size rig. The balneario changing room doubles as the restrooms, they are cavernous but clean and have warm water showers. There's a small refreshment stand open during the day and a restaurant for busy weekends and holidays. No English is spoken.

From Tequisquiapan head northeast on Mex 120. The balneario is on the right near the 31 Km marker, which is about 6 miles (10 km) out of town.

EL OASIS

Address: Carretera Tequisquiapan a Ezequiel Montes Km 10, Tequisquiapan, Querétaro, México
Telephone: (4) 273-0412

GPS Location: N 20° 36' 31.8", W 099° 54' 48.1"

This is the largest of the three balnearios in this area offering camping. The El Oasis has three swimming pools, one with waves, a water slide and a "dino-slide" (you'll have to see it yourself).

Camping is in a large grass-covered field. There are 45 15-amp outlets but no other hookups. There is room for big rigs to maneuver. Restrooms have hot showers and there is a snack bar. English is spoken.

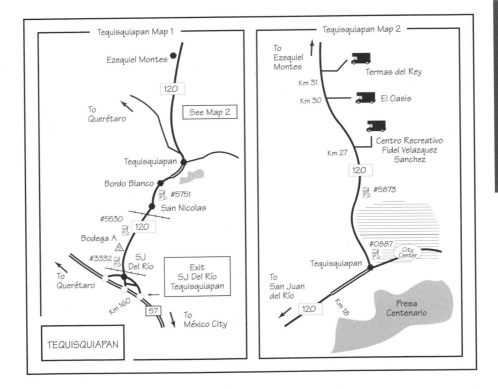

This campground is east of the highway near the Km 30 marker. Despite their advertised addresses the Oasis and Termas del Rey are a couple of kilometers apart.

⛟ CENTRO RECREATIVO FIDEL VELAZQUEZ SANCHEZ

Address: Carretera Tequisquiapan a Ezequiel Montes Km 7, Tequisquiapan, Queretaro, México

GPS Location: N 20° 35' 32.6", W 099° 54' 08.8"

This campground near Tequisquiapan is also a balneario. During the winter the two pools are open only during the weekends, but the campsite are open all week long.

There are 45 back-in spaces with electricity (15-amp outlets), water, and sewer hookups. All are on cobblestones with a line of trees providing some shade. You can probably pretend these spaces are pull-throughs, there isn't likely to be a crowd except on holidays. Big rigs are no problem. There are new modern changing rooms with hot showers. There are two swimming pools and a snack bar for weekends. No English is spoken.

To reach the campground drive northeast on Mex 120 from Tequisquiapan. Just after the Km 27 marker turn right into the entrance driveway. The road surface is cobblestone. At .3 miles (.5 km) you reach a Y, go right, then at .5 miles(.8 km) take a ninety-degree turn to the left. You'll pass alongside a vineyard and at 1 mile (1.6 km) arrive at the balneario. The camping spaces are through the gate and to the left. If it isn't a weekend you'll probably have to look around for someone to accept your registration.

TLAXCALA, TLAXCALA (TLAS-KAH-LAW)
Population 53,000, Elevation 9,800 ft (2,979 m)

Although Tlaxcala is located just a half-hour or so north of Puebla it seems like most people never take the time to visit. This is a mistake. Tlaxcala is a small, easy to visit Indian town with colonial features. The area around the central plaza offers good shopping and several restaurants. This is an easy town in which to spend some time strolling around.

If you have a larger rig you will probably find yourself parking some distance from the center, arrive in a smaller rig if possible. The campgrounds listed below are quite a distance from town and not really good places to use as a base for exploring the city. A visit to Tlaxcala is a good day trip from Puebla.

Tlaxcala Campgrounds

⛟ IMSS CENTRO VACACIONAL LA TRINIDAD

Address: Santa Cruz Tlaxcala, Tlaxcala, México
Telephone: (2) 461-0700 or (800) 711-0614
Fax: (2) 461-0692

GPS Location: N 19° 21' 34.2", W 098° 09' 08.6"

The Mexican social security department (IMSS) maintains several resorts near México City to give residents a chance to get out into the country. Several have camping facilities and non-Mexican visitors are more than welcome. RV campers are something of an afterthought at this facility but don't let that stop you.

The RV camping area is actually two large brick covered parking lots above and behind the hotel building. You'll be boondocking here, there are no hookups. A reasonably good restroom with no showers is provided for the RV area. There are lots of showers with hot water in the changing rooms for the pools. Tenters have a separate grass-covered area, this area is more heavily used than the RV area at this resort. The resort itself is very large, it is set in a reconstructed textile factory but is really quite elegant. It has hotel facilities, two very large pools (one inside), two restaurants, a museum, a small store, and lots of other attractions. You'll enjoy just seeing this place. Access is tight, only rigs to about 30 feet should attempt this campground.

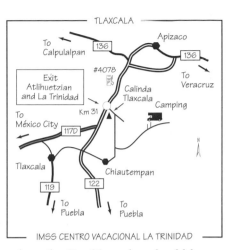

IMSS CENTRO VACACIONAL LA TRINIDAD

From Tlaxcala follow Mex 136 toward Apizaco. After about 5.5 miles (8.9 km) near where the Km 31 marker should be you'll see a small exit for Atlihuetzian and Centro Vacacional Trinidad. Take the exit and head south, zero your odometer at the exit. At .2 miles (.3 km) there is a Y, go right. Only after the turn will you see a sign for La Trinidad saying it is 4 km ahead. At 1.4 miles (2.3 km) turn left, there should be a sign at this corner. The first La Trinidad gate appears at 2.6 miles (4.2 km), go on to the second just a short distance ahead. Tell the gate person you want to camp and he'll direct you to the proper area.

IMSS CENTRO VACACIONAL LA MALINTZI

Address: Huamantla, Tlaxcala, México
Telephone: (2) 461-0222

GPS Location: N 19° 16' 51.0", W 098° 02' 37.1"

This is another IMSS resort near Tlaxcala. This one has even less provision for RVs but they are welcome, as are tent campers. The campground is a fenced and gated compound set in a pine forest, it is a 6 mile (10 km) hike to the top of La Malinche volcano from this campground. The campground itself is at 10,115 feet (3,083 meters).

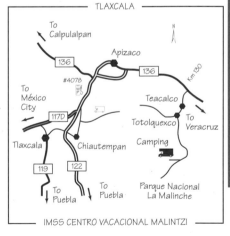

IMSS CENTRO VACACIONAL MALINTZI

There is a large parking lot here where RV's are allowed to park, it has no hookups. Tent campers have their own grass-covered area. There is a restroom near the tent area, it has flush toilets and hot showers. This campground also offers rental cabañas, a small grocery store, a restaurant, play fields and a children's play area. There is plenty of room for big rigs once you reach the campground but the climb through the park probably limits really big rigs from visiting, we wouldn't bring anything over about 30 feet up here.

To reach La Malintzi head south on the road up to the volcano which cuts off Mex 136 at about the 130 Km marker between Apizaco and Huamantla, it is signed for Teacalco.

After 2.6 miles (4.2 km) you will reach the small village of Totolquexco. Turn left at the intersection and drive another 3.4 miles (5.5 km) to the gated park entrance. A ranger will let you in and then it is another 1.8 miles (2.9 km) to the gated campground entrance on the right.

TOLUCA, MÉXICO (TOW-LOO-KAH)
Population 500,000, Elevation 8,800 ft (2,675 m)

Toluca has the highest altitude of any major city in México. It is definitely an industrial city. The city's location means that you will probably pass through some day, either on the east-west routes between Mexico City and Guadalajara or when bypassing Mexico City on the north-south route. Tourists visit Toluca primarily for its famously huge Friday Indian market which offers a great selection of handicrafts. It is located near the bus station and is really open all week, Friday is just the best day. Toluca may seem like a good base for visiting Mexico City since it is so close but we recommend instead either Pepe's RV Park which is listed in this book under Mexico City or one of the Cuernavaca campgrounds.

Toluca Campgrounds

 PARQUE SIERRA MORELOS

GPS Location: N 19° 18' 42.7", W 099° 41' 09.8"

$$ ⛺

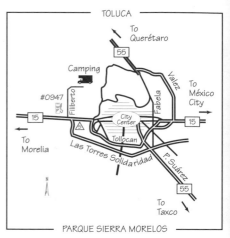
PARQUE SIERRA MORELOS

The Sierra Morelos is a public park located outside of Toluca to the east. It has picnic facilities, lots of play fields, and paths through pine forests. Camping facilities are minimal but this is a place you can park for the night although we would hesitate to do so in a single rig.

There is an unmarked flat open field near a large picnic area that is used for parking by RVs. There are no hookups and the restrooms are in poor condition and usually dirty but do have flush toilets. There are no showers. The park is very large and has full-time watchmen but the fences are not secure and people wander through at will. The neighborhood isn't great. Busses stop at the gate of the park which is about a mile from the RV parking area.

The park is well signed off Mex 15 to the east of Toluca. The road to the park goes north about 1.1 mile (1.7 km) west of the Toluca ring road. If you are driving toward the east watch for Pemex #947 on your left and then watch for the sign for the left turn soon afterwards. If you pass a Comercial Mexicana on your right you've gone too far.

 PARQUE EL OCOTAL

Address: Parque El Ocotal S/N, Timilpan, Edo. de México, México
Telephone: (7) 261-1681

GPS Location: N 19° 48' 21.6", W 099° 45' 36.6"

It is a bit of a stretch to consider this a Toluca campground but since campgrounds in the region are scarce it is entirely possible that a visitor to Toluca will spend the night here. Toluca is the nearest large city.

The Parque El Ocotal is a state campground. There are several hundred acres filled with pine trees and walking trails. This is a government-owned wilderness campground in the tradition of those we're accustomed to in the states and Canada, except this one has a nice little hotel tucked away in one corner with a convenient and very nice restaurant.

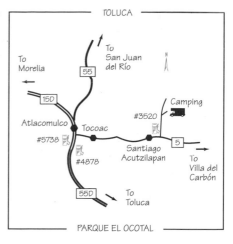

The camping areas are open pine-needle covered areas with scattered picnic tables and grills. There are also some flat parking areas for RVs. There are no hookups. Large rigs will have to be cautious on the interior dirt roads, this campground is really best for those under 30 feet. The restrooms have flush toilets and cold showers. There are several children's playgrounds. This is a quiet and isolated spot so you'll really feel like you are in the woods, but just over a rise is the hotel with restaurant, tennis courts, horse rentals, sauna, steam bath and Jacuzzi. There is 24-hour security at the gate to the park. No English is spoken.

From the eastern side of the Atlacomulco ring road, 44 miles (71.8 km) north of Toluca, drive east toward Villa del Carbón on Mex 5. After 7.2 miles (11.6 km) you will reach the small village of Santiago Acutzilapan. On the far edge just past the Pemex a paved road goes north 1.1 miles (1.8 km) to El Ocotal. The attendant at the gate will let you in and take your money (but not very much).

Other Camping Possibilities

The volcanic Nevada de Toluca looms over Toluca. This 15,390 foot (4,690 meter) peak actually has a road that runs almost to the top. Along this road is a camping area, we've talked with campers who have spent the night there. The altitude at the campground is very high, our friends report that it was so difficult to breath that sleeping was very difficult. To get to the road to the top follow Mex 134 about 13 miles (21 km) southwest from Metepec (a southern suburb of Toluca) and then turn left on Mex 10. The volcano road goes left in another 5 miles (8 km). It is 12 miles (19 km) from there to the top on a gravel road. This trip is only suitable for small rigs like autos, vans and pickups.

TORREÓN, COAHUILA (TOE-RAY-OHN)
Population 450,000, Elevation 3,700 ft (1,125 m)

This is really a triple city: Torreón, Gómez Palacio, and Lerdo. Torreón is in the state of Coahuila while nearby Gómez Palacio and Lerdo are in Durango. The three cities form a railroad, farming and industrial center. Torreón is a relatively new city, founded in 1897, and has more to offer than the other two cities including parks, museums and stores.

THE INTERIOR OF MEXICO

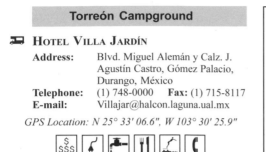

Torreón Campground

🚐 HOTEL VILLA JARDÍN

Address: Blvd. Miguel Alemán y Calz. J.
Agustín Castro, Gómez Palacio,
Durango, México
Telephone: (1) 748-0000   **Fax:** (1) 715-8117
E-mail: Villajar@halcon.laguna.ual.mx

GPS Location: N 25° 33' 06.6", W 103° 30' 25.9"

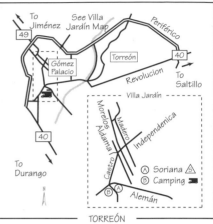

The Hotel Villa Jardín offers campers little more than four parking slots behind the motel, but there is not much else available in this area. The hotel itself is quite nice, the management seems to like RVers.

Parking is parallel parking for about eight rigs of any size along a paved driveway. There are five electrical sockets, really nothing more than outlets tapped into light pole circuits, a water faucet, and the area is lighted. It is behind the hotel and seems secure. Every time we've checked in a maintenance man had to come out and set up the very low-amp electrical hookup, then in the morning it was accidentally switched off when the lights were extinguished. The swimming pool is nearby and there are restrooms available with toilets and sinks but no showers. There are also a tennis court and a children's play area behind the hotel. The hotel has a restaurant and some English is spoken. A huge new Soriana supermarket is across the street. The laundry service here is reported by a reader to be very expensive.

Easiest access is from the north where Mex 49 meets the Periférico. Cross under the Periférico and continue straight ahead passing a Soriana supermarket on your left. Continue south for .7 miles (1.1 km) until the street makes a right turn and you come to a stop at a T, you have reached Morelos. Turn left on Morelos and drive 1.3 miles (2.1 km) to a cross street named Independencia. Turn right and follow Independencia. After .3 miles (.5 km) it will dog-leg left and become A. Castro. Follow A. Castro for .9 miles (1.5 km) to a major intersection with a stop light. The hotel is directly ahead and to the right, the Soriana supermarket ahead and to the left.

Side Trips from Torreón

At the point where the three states of Chihuahua, Durango and Coahuila meet is the **Zone of Silence**. This is an area of remote desert. There are reports of mysterious happenings in the zone: radio signals are blocked, meteorites fall, and UFO's land. To get here drive north on free Mex 49 about 67 miles (110 km) to a road going east. The Zone of Silence is about 55 miles (90 km) away on poor gravel roads requiring a high-clearance vehicle. You should also have a good map and supplies for the desert.

URUAPAN, MICHOACÁN (OOH-ROO-AH-PAN)
Population 250,000, Elevation 5,500 ft (1,672 m)

With a semi-tropical climate Uruapan is one of Mexico's top agricultural centers.

Coffee, avocados, bananas, and oranges are grown in the region. Travelers often find this a convenient place to stop on the trip down Mex 37 to the coast at Playa Azul. Sights worth a look in Uruapan include the **Parque Nacionál Eduardo Ruiz** and the headwaters of the **Río Cupatitzio**, and the **Plaza Principal** with the **Museo Regional Huatapera** alongside. Interesting side trips from the city include the **Paricutín Volcano** and **Tzaráracua Waterfall**.

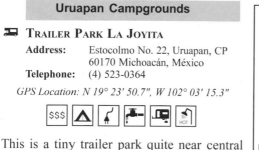

TRAILER PARK LA JOYITA

Address:	Estocolmo No. 22, Uruapan, CP 60170 Michoacán, México
Telephone:	(4) 523-0364

GPS Location: N 19° 23' 50.7", W 102° 03' 15.3"

This is a tiny trailer park quite near central Uruapan. The facilities are old and simple but fine for a quick stopover. We think that the best feature of the campground is that it is only a few blocks from a newish Comercial Mexicana and a good multi-screen movie house. Since many U.S. movies shown in Mexico are in their original English with Spanish subtitles you can catch up on a first-run movie while staying here and walk home afterwards.

The campground has three back-in slots with electricity (15-amp style outlets), sewer, and water. There are about seven more slots with electricity and water only. All are located in a courtyard with a few motel rooms and quite a few parked cars. The restrooms are old and reasonably clean and have hot water for showers. We think of this as a small-RV campground but we are aware of at least one group of three large rigs that has spent the night here. By the time you reach Uruapan you will no doubt have become adept at maneuvering your big rig into tight places.

The campground is in the southeastern section of Uruapan just off Paseo Gral Lazaro Cardenas. Headed south on Paseo Gral. Lázaro Cárdenas (the turn from B. Juárez is marked Ave Chiapas, Ave. Chiapas becomes Cárdenas as it goes south) from B Juárez for 1.8 miles (2.9 km) you will see the Comercial Mexicana on your left. You want to turn left on the second road after the Commercial Mexicana but it is probably easiest to continue south for .3 miles (.5 km) until you come to a glorieta. Make a U-turn using the traffic circle and drive north two blocks to Estocolmco. Drive east one and a half blocks, you'll see the campground entrance on your right. The street out front can be a little loud at night, several street-side stall-type restaurants are located there and it is a busy place on weekend nights.

MOTEL PIE DE LA SIERRA

Address:	Km 4 Carretera Uruapan-Carapán (Apdo. 153), Uruapan, Mich., México
Telephone:	(4) 524-2510, (4) 524-9712 **Fax:** (4) 522-2510
E-mail:	piesierra@vel.com.mx

GPS Location: N 19° 26' 36.1", W 102° 04' 33.0"

The Motel Pie De La Sierra is located high above Uruapan to the north. It has very nice facilities except that the RV park serves as over-flow parking for the popular party facilities offered by the hotel. During the week this is the place to stay in Uruapan, on weekends you might wish that you had a quieter location.

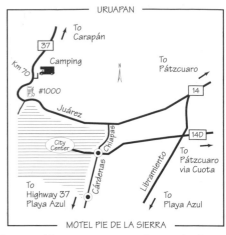

MOTEL PIE DE LA SIERRA

There are 20 back-in parking spaces with elec-tricity (15-amp outlets) and water. There is sewer too, unfortunately the drains are smaller than normal, suitable only for a small hose. Campers use the pool restrooms which are tiled and clean, they have hot water showers. This very nice hotel has a beautiful pool area over-looking town and also a restaurant/bar and game room. Access for big rigs is tight, you will want to park outside the gate and take a look to see if you can get past the two bad spots. These are at the gate itself, you have to make a quick left just inside it, and up the hill in front of the reception office where you have to make a tight 180 degree turn. This may be no problem, it just depends upon how cars are parked in the driveway. Bus and taxi service to downtown Uruapan are available.

From Uruapan drive north out of town toward Carapán on Mex 37. You'll see the motel on the right just past the Km 71 marker. This is 3 miles north (4.8 km) of the intersection in town of Mex 37 and Mex 14 (Av. Chiapas) from Pátzcuaro.

🚐 CENTRO TURÍSTICO DE ANGAHUAN

Address:	Domicilio Conocido, Camino al Volcán Paricutín, Angahuan, Michoacán, México
Telephone:	(4) 520-8786 (Angahuan), (4) 523-3934 (Uruapan)

GPS Location: N 19° 32' 31.3", W 102° 14' 03.3"

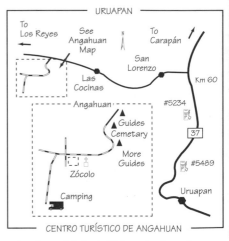

CENTRO TURÍSTICO DE ANGAHUAN

At the edge of the village of Angahuan, right where you leave town on the way to the vol-cano, there is a tourist center. It has a museum devoted to the volcano, a small restaurant, park-ing, rooms for rent, and even overnight park-ing for RVs. The difficult entrance route through the village makes this campground only suitable for pickups, vans, and motorhomes to about 24 feet. Take a look at the *Side Trips from Uruapan* section below for more information about Paricutín.

The tourist center has a tent-camping area with a covered picnic shelter as well as lots of room for overnight parking for RVs. Hookups are not provided, this is boondocking except that you may be able to convince the manager to let you run an extension cord to one of the rental rooms. The center is on a bluff, you can sight the church that has been buried by the lava from a mirador in front of the restaurant. The trail to the church runs right by the front of the campground and is easy to follow without a guide, the one-way walk takes about a half-hour. Guides can provide horses to make the trip even easier.

North of Uruapan about 8 miles (13 km) on Mex 37 near the Km 59 marker a good paved road goes east to Angahuan. Zero your odometer at the intersection and head east. After 11.9 miles (19.2 km) you will enter the outskirts of Angahuan and see a paved road to the left, probably signed Volcán. Turn left here and again zero your odometer. The road will curve to the right and pass a group of men with horses. These are guides, they will flag you down and you should stop and talk, otherwise at least one will probably chase you all the way through town on his horse in hopes of talking you into a guided trip to the buried church. Once you have talked and either made arrangements or not continue straight. The road passes into the village and is surfaced with rough cobblestones. There are very few signs telling you where to go. You want to turn left on a street that is .8 miles (1.3 km) from where you turned off the main road just before meeting the guides. This is about a tenth of a mile past the square, the left may be signed for Centro Turistico, and one of the houses at the intersection can be identified by it's satellite dish, an unusual sight in Angahuan. After turning the cobblestones soon come to an end and you are on dirt, then there is a very large tope that seems to be designed to keep large rigs with long wheelbases from passing. You will see several restaurants with parking for travelers to the church, and then .6 mile (1 km) from the turn you will see the gate for the Centro Turistico on your left just before the road descends steeply.

Side Trips from Uruapan

Most people have probably heard the story of **Paracutín**. In 1943 a farmer was plowing his field when the ground began shaking and a brand-new volcano began building where there had been nothing before. For 9 years the volcano erupted, in the process burying two nearby villages and rising to approximately 1,700 feet above the corn field. Today you can drive to the village of Angahuan and then make the half-hour hike or ride a horse with a guide to view the mountain or even visit a church that is partially buried in lava. Angahuan itself is of interest, it is a Purépecha Indian village. You can reach Angahuan by driving north on Mex 37 from Uruapan for 10 miles (16 km) and then following a small paved road to the left for 13 miles (21 km) to the village. See the campground description above for Centro Turístico de Angahuan for a place to stay during your visit.

The 60-meter high **Tzararacua Falls** are located about 6 miles (10 km) south of Uruapan on Mex 37. The river here, the Cupatitzio, is the same one that arises in Uruapan at the National Park. There is a car park and many stairs leading down to the viewpoint.

VALLE DE BRAVO, MÉXICO (VAH-yay day BRAH-voe)
Population 16,000, Elevation 5,950 ft (1,808 m)

The town of Valle de Bravo is another favorite weekend destination for crowds from Mexico City which is only 87 miles (140 km) distant. This upscale resort village overlooks a large *presa* or reservoir called Lake Avandaro. The high surrounding mountains are covered with pines, the town sometimes feels like it is located in Switzerland or the mountains above the French Riviera instead of Mexico. There are lots of good tourist facilities here, especially restaurants. Good campgrounds are scarce in this neighborhood but there is one place as we detail below.

RVers bound for Valle de Bravo should be aware that it sits in a valley far below Mex 15, the usual highway used for access. If you have a heavy rig and would not enjoy a relatively steep 10-mile (16 km) grade you should stay away from Valle de Bravo.

Valle de Bravo Campground

▥ EMBARCADERO LAUMASE

> **Address:**   San Gaspar del Lago, Carr. Valle de
> Bravo-Colorines, Valle de
> Bravo, México, México
> **Telephone:**   (7) 262-3935, (7) 262-2642
>
> *GPS Location: N 19° 13' 28.2", W 100° 08' 38.7"*

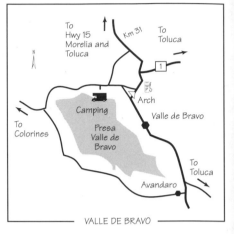

VALLE DE BRAVO

The Embarcadero Laumase is a boat launching and storage facility conveniently located for a visit to Valle de Bravo. You'll also see some Mexican RVs stored here. It is particularly good if you are driving a big rig and have a smaller vehicle for driving on into town.

There is a lot of room on a large sandy and grassy field extending to the water. There are no hookups although the owner may stretch an electrical cord for you. Water is also available. There are nice new tiled bathrooms with hot showers. This is a popular boating facility with storage and launching, weekends and holidays are likely to be very crowded and busy. At other times things are peaceful. The restaurants and shops of Valle de Bravo are about 3 miles (4.8 km) away, busses run past the gate of the campground, and there is a very small store across the street. One problem, at least one reader has reported not being allowed to spend the night when the owner was absent but this appears to be an unusual occurrence.

As you descend into Valle de Bravo from the north you will come to a Pemex on the left and see an arch across the road ahead. A road going right here goes toward Colorines although it was not marked last time we visited. Turn right toward Colorines, you will see the Embarcadero Laumase on your left on the lakeshore in 1.1 miles (1.8 km).

ZACATECAS, ZACATECAS (SAH-KAH-TAY-KAHS)
Population 150,000, Elevation 8,200 ft (2,493 m)

Zacatecas is a well-kept secret. It gets few visitors from outside Mexico. This colonial mining city has a spectacular site in a valley below two peaks. There is a **aerial tramway** between the two for great views of the city. The **cathedral** here is generally considered the best example of a churrigueresque church in Mexico and the downtown area, built of rose-colored sandstone, would seem straight out of an earlier century if it weren't for the cars. Two museums in this town shouldn't be missed: the **Museo Pedro Coronel** with a large and varied art collection and the **Museo Rafael Coronel Mexican mask collection**.

Heavy vehicles, those with duals on the rear or trailers, are not allowed to drive through Zacatecas on Mex 45/49. They are likely to be ticketed. Instead there is a long truck bypass that circles the town on the south. The western entrance is right next to the Hotel del Bosque, one of the town's campgrounds. The eastern entrance is east of the suburb of Guadalupe. The junction is just west of the Bonito Pueblo Convention Center, another of the Zacatecas campgrounds, see the write-up below. From the east follow signs for *Trafico Pesado* (heavy traffic) Ciudad Cuauhtémoc, and Libramiento.

Zacatecas Campgrounds

🚐 **HACIENDA DEL BOSQUE HOTEL & RV PARK**

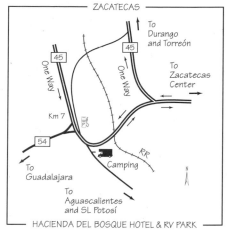

HACIENDA DEL BOSQUE HOTEL & RV PARK

Address:	Heroes de Chapultepec 801, Zacatecas, CP 98057 Zacatecas, México	
Telephone:	(4) 924-6666	**Fax:** (4) 924-6565
E-mail:	hhbosque@prodigy.net.mx	

GPS Location: N 22° 46' 26.6", W 102° 37' 11.6"

Zacatecas has an excellent first-class campground. Owned by the same people who run the Motel del Bosque, the Hotel Hacienda del Bosque is a popular caravan stop.

There are 34 back-in spaces in a fenced, rock-paved courtyard with additional partial-hookup overflow parking available for a few more rigs. There are 30-amp electricity (some 50-amp), sewer, and water hookups. The restrooms are very good, they are modern, tiled, clean, and have hot showers. The hotel has a good restaurant and a bus into town stops nearby. English is spoken and reservations are recommended since caravans often fill the whole campground. There is, unfortunately, a fly in the ointment. Trains on the nearby line run through the night, and this seems to be one of their favorite spots to blow the whistle.

The campground is near the intersection of Mex 45 from Durango and the Mex 54 cutoff south to Guadalajara. This is not the same intersection discussed in the driving directions to the Servicio Morelos Trailer Park below, it is about 6 miles (9.7 km) south toward Zacatecas from that one. To reach the hotel continue east from the intersection for .3 miles (.5km) to an intersection with a stop light. The main highway curves left to go around the left side of the hotel, the heavy vehicle bypass route around Zacatecas goes straight. Go straight yourself and then park along the shoulder. Walk across to the hotel, ask them to open the large RV gate and let you in. Large vehicles often sustain significant damage trying to use other entrances to this campground so don't even try.

🚐 **MOTEL DEL BOSQUE**

    Address: Periférico Diaz Ordaz S/N, Zacatecas, Zacatecas, México
    Telephone: (4) 922-0745

GPS Location: N 22° 46' 43.9", W 102° 34' 27.4"

It would be tough to beat the location of this campground for campers interested in visiting central Zacatecas. The motel overlooks the downtown area, the walk to the central area is less than a mile. The teleférico (overhead tram) terminal to La Bufa is right below the campground.

There is room for about 8 rigs to back in on a large rock-paved area near the entrance to the motel. The spaces have four duplex 15-amp outlets and a few water hookups, they have no view. There is a place to dump, ask about it at the desk. The parking area slopes quite a bit so you'll have to level your rig. There are older restrooms with hot showers. The motel has a reasonably-priced restaurant that overlooks the town. Access to the campground is down a short winding road from the Periférico, rigs to 28 feet should have no problems although they may

MOTEL DEL BOSQUE

have to do a little careful maneuvering to make one turn. You can walk a short distance down the hill to catch a bus to the central area or walk there in less than 15 minutes.

The motel is located on a hill overlooking Zacatecas. It is accessed from a Periférico which branches off Mex 45 and 54, the main highway through the city. However, as detailed above, heavy rigs are not allowed to drive through Zacatecas. Heavy rigs should approach this campground from the north. From the north zero your odometer as you pass the Hotel del Bosque, described above. In 2.2 miles (3.5 km) you will see the exit to the Periférico. Take this exit, it is marked Quebradilla, Centro, and Teleférico from both directions. The exits from both directions enter a traffic circle above the highways, follow the sign for La Bufa, there is also a sign for the Motel del Bosque painted on a wall next to this road. After .8 miles (1.3 km) you'll see the motel entrance on the right.

 Servicio Morelos Trailer Park

> **Address:**　　Panamericana Guadalajara - Saltillo Km 678, Zacatecas, Zacatecas, México
> **Telephone:**　(4) 921-0367

GPS Location: N 22° 51' 43.1", W 102° 37' 23.9"

SERVICIO MORELOS TRAILER PARK

The Servicio Morelos Trailer Park has long been a popular stopover for folks heading south to Guadalajara or the coast through the interior. It is well away from any urban traffic and is an excellent place for a late arrival and early start.

The campground has 16 back-in spaces with electricity (15-amp outlets), sewer and water hookups. There's lots of room for big rigs and access is easy. Since the campground is rarely crowded many people don't bother to unhook. The service station out front is a big modern one with toilets but no showers. It also has a modern Telmex phone, a small store, and a restaurant. The campground is fenced and gated. Someone will be by to collect, ask for a receipt for proof of payment to insure that you don't have to pay twice. Lots of trucks stop and park at this intersection so there are also many taco and other food stands in the area.

The campground is located at the junction of Mex 45 from Durango and Mex 54 from Saltillo about 8 miles (13 km) northwest of Zacatecas near the 15 Km marker of Mex 45. Mex 45 is four-lane with the opposing lanes about 1.4 miles (2.3 km) apart at this point, you won't be able to see the Pemex and campground if you are traveling toward Zacatecas on Mex 45 but it is obvious from both Mex 45 northwest-bound and Mex 54.

⛺ BONITO PUEBLO CONVENTION CENTER

Address:	Km 117.5 Carretera Panamericana Aguascalientes - Zacatecas, Guadalupe, Zacatecas, México
Telephone:	(4) 923-8001
Fax:	(4) 923-8002

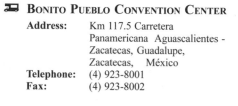

Bonito Pueblo is a new convention center in Guadalupe, a suburb just east of Zacatecas. The location is convenient for people heading south on Mex 45 or 49 or arriving from that direction. The huge parking lot will hold 200 rigs or more. Limited electricity is available for a few rigs. Water and dump stations are also available. Very limited English is spoken.

The city bus into Zacatecas will stop in front of Bonito Pueblo. The bus is marked as Trancoso-Zacatecas on the front headed into town, the return bus is marked Zacatecas-Trancoso.

The campground is located just east of the junction of the south Libramiento around Zacatecas and Highway 45. It is located north of the highway and has a large "Bonito Pueblo" painted on the front. If the gate is closed, park in front of it and walk to the building to request someone to open the gate.

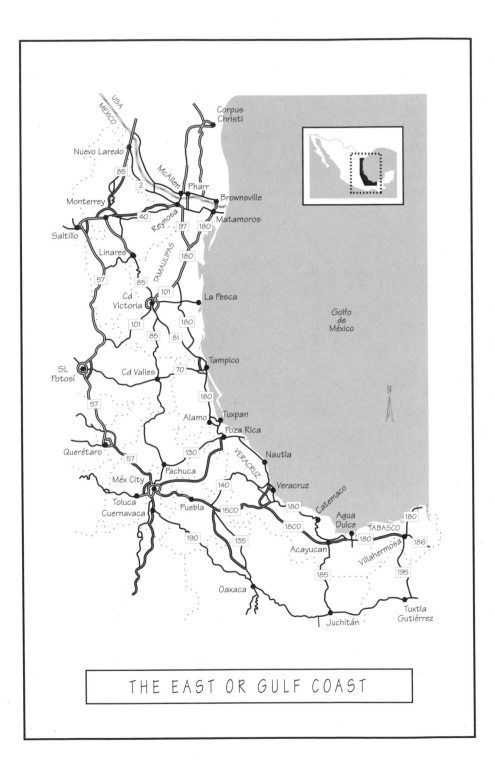

THE EAST OR GULF COAST

THE EAST OR GULF COAST

INTRODUCTION

Mexico's Gulf Coast is a long semicircle of mostly deserted beaches backed by often swampy flatlands. Because of vast wetlands behind the coast access is sometimes difficult or not possible. Fortunately, if you can get to the beach, it is likely to be uncrowded and very good for fishing, birding, and beachcombing. For our purposes in this book the Gulf Coast stretches from the border at Reynosa to the town of Villahermosa in the State of Tabasco, a driving distance of about 900 miles (1,470 km). The coast east of Villahermosa is covered in our Yucatán chapter.

Much of the Mexican Gulf Coast is oil country. This means that you will pass through areas that are industrial, full of trucks, and generally not very pleasant. Don't let the bad places bother you. The Yucatán, Belize and Chiapas at the end of your journey are outstanding, and even the Gulf Coast has its rewarding destinations.

Winter is the time to visit the Gulf Coast. Summer, from May to October, is extremely hot and humid. Temperatures from October to April can be hot also, but bearable. Summer is also hurricane season, but the risk of a hurricane drops to nearly zero by the beginning of November.

ROAD SYSTEM

The Gulf Coast serves as the shortest route south to both the Yucatán Peninsula and Chiapas. Unfortunately the roads are not great. Most are two lanes, and many stretches are heavily used by trucks and do not get nearly enough maintenance. In general the condition of roads tends to be bad at the end of the summer rainy season and gets better as they are gradually repaired during the winter dry season.

Mex 180 serves as the main arterial. It snakes down the coast from Matamoros and eventually ends at Puerto Juárez, now a Cancún suburb. For the most part traffic along the Gulf Coast stays on 180 although there are a few shortcuts and bypasses around larger towns.

A new addition to the coastal route is a toll road which runs from just north of Veracruz to a point near La Venta, about 80 miles (130 km) west of Villahermosa. This is a very expensive route. It does effectively cut a day from the drive south, you can now easily drive from the campgrounds on the Emerald Coast to Rancho Hermanos Graham near Villahermosa in a single day. Unfortunately to do this you must bypass both Veracruz and Lake Catemaco, a difficult decision.

If you are not bound for the Yucatán there are several places along the coast where you might choose to turn inland. Mex 85 (the Pan American Highway) is a good road leading from the border at Nuevo Laredo through Monterrey and then into the Gulf Coast area at Ciudad Victoria before winding its way south through mountains to Mexico City. Mex 101 from Ciudad Victoria to the southwest is small and uncrowded as it crosses rugged mountains and desert until connecting with Mex 80 and then Mex 57 into San Luis Potosí. Mex 70 provides a direct route from Tampico to San Luis Potosí while Mex 130 does the same from Poza Rica to Pachuca where you can catch a good toll road south to Mexico City. There's a well-traveled toll road from Veracruz to Mexico City, Mex 150D. In the south, near Minatitlán, the two lane Mex 185 cuts south across the Isthmus of Tehuantepec to the Pacific, a relatively low-altitude route to the Pacific.

At Villahermosa travelers bound for the Yucatán face a choice of routes. Mex 180 goes north to the coast and crosses a string of sandy islands until reaching the Yucatán. This route now has bridges across all of the inlets and is very popular. The alternative is Mex 186 which runs inland and passes near Palenque before heading to the north-east through Escárcega to the Yucatán. Both routes take about the same time. Many folks follow one route while bound for the Yucatán and the other on their return.

HIGHLIGHTS

The Gulf Coast is often considered little but a corridor to the south, but there are many places along the way that are destinations in themselves or well worth a short visit.

The far north near the Texas border is very popular with sportsmen. It has good fishing and hunting. **Lake Vincent Guerrero** to the northeast of Ciudad Victoria is known for its bass fishing as are several other lakes in the region. The coast through here also offers great fishing where it is accessible. There are campgrounds at **La Pesca** to the east of Ciudad Victoria which offers both fishing and a beach.

The **Emerald Coast** between Poza Rica and Nautla offers several good campgrounds with an excellent beach and some good side trips. The **El Tajín** archeological site nearby is a well-known site off the beaten track that does not get many visitors be-cause there are no big tourist destinations nearby. The small city of Papantla is home to the flying *Voladores* you'll see performing far from home in many other parts of Mexico.

Veracruz is the historic port for Mexico City. It has great historical importance, its own ambiance, and plenty to see and do. Fortunately there is a campground here so you can easily make an extended visit.

The **Sierra de los Tuxtlas** to the south of Veracruz offer a mountainous break from the sometimes monotonous lowlands. You can stay at Lake Catemaco, make day trips to the nearby towns, and take a boat tour of the lake while enjoying cool evenings.

Finally, the modern town of **Villahermosa** is known for its **La Venta Park Museum**

THE CAMPGROUNDS

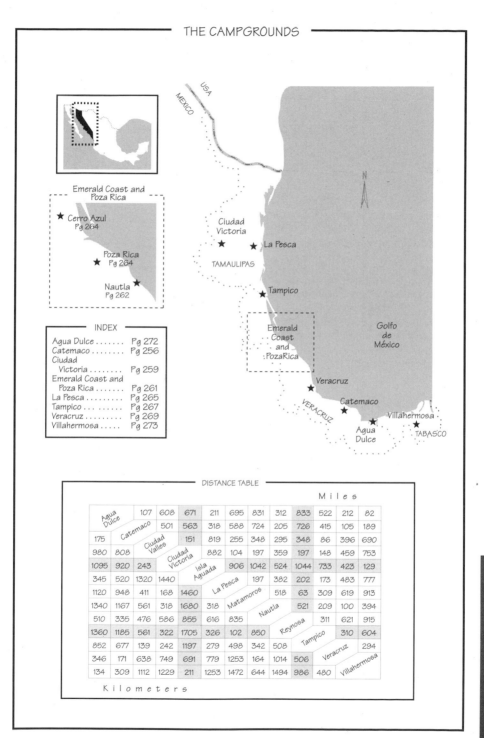

Emerald Coast and Poza Rica

★ Cerro Azul
Pg 264

Poza Rica ★
Pg 264

Nautla ★
Pg 262

Ciudad Victoria ★

★ La Pesca

TAMAULIPAS

■ Tampico

Emerald Coast and PozaRica

Golfo de México

★ Veracruz

Catemaco ★

★ Agua Dulce

★ Villahermosa

VERACRUZ

TABASCO

MÉXICO   USA

INDEX

DISTANCE TABLE

Miles

	Agua Dulce	Catemaco	Ciudad Valles	Ciudad Victoria	Isla Aguada	La Pesca	Matamoros	Nautla	Reynosa	Tampico	Veracruz	Villahermosa
Agua Dulce		107	608	671	211	695	831	312	833	522	212	82
Catemaco	175		501	563	318	588	724	205	726	415	105	189
Ciudad Valles	980	808		151	819	255	348	295	348	86	396	690
Ciudad Victoria	1095	920	243		882	104	197	359	197	148	459	753
Isla Aguada	345	520	1320	1440		906	1042	524	1044	733	423	129
La Pesca	1120	948	411	168	1460		197	382	202	173	483	777
Matamoros	1340	1167	561	318	1680	318		518	63	309	619	913
Nautla	510	335	476	586	855	616	835		521	209	100	394
Reynosa	1360	1185	561	322	1705	326	102	850		311	621	915
Tampico	852	677	139	242	1197	279	498	342	508		310	604
Veracruz	346	171	638	749	691	779	1253	164	1014	506		294
Villahermosa	134	309	1112	1229	211	1253	1472	644	1494	986	480	

Kilometers

containing giant Olmec heads in an outdoor setting. If this park helps you develop a deeper interest you might also want to visit the Museo Regional de Antropologiía at CICOM.

SELECTED CITIES AND THEIR CAMPGROUNDS

CATEMACO, VERACRUZ (KAH-TEH-MAH-KO)
Population 41,000, Elevation 1,200 ft (354 m)

The Sierra de los Tuxtlas are a small isolated range of mountains sitting near to the coast south of Veracruz. These are volcanic mountains with lush vegetation, a pleasant change from the hot surrounding flatlands. You'll appreciate the altitude in the evenings, they are cooler than down on the flats. Mex 180 runs right through the mountains, you can now bypass them on a toll road from Veracruz to La Venta but the tolls are high and you will probably enjoy spending at least one night at Lake Catemaco.

There are really three interesting towns in these mountains: **Santiago Tuxtla**, **San Andrés Tuxtla**, and **Catemaco**. You'll pass through all of them as you follow Mex 180 but only the last has campgrounds, and it sits beside very scenic **Lake Catemaco**. The town has become something of a ecotourism destination lately. **Boat tours** on the lake are very popular, you can see a great variety of bird life and even some Asian monkeys on one of the islands in the lake. Catemaco is famous in Mexico for its brujos, or witches. You can consult with one or buy charms and herbs at the markets here to fix what ails you.

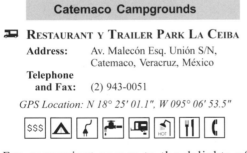

Catemaco Campgrounds

🚐 **RESTAURANT Y TRAILER PARK LA CEIBA**

Address: Av. Malecón Esq. Unión S/N, Catemaco, Veracruz, México

Telephone and Fax: (2) 943-0051

GPS Location: N 18° 25' 01.1", W 095° 06' 53.5"

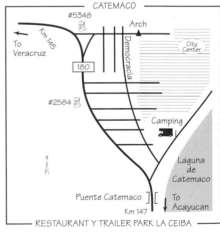

For convenient access to the delights of Catemaco this campground can't be beat. It is located on the waterfront malecón, or sea wall road, across the street from the lake. Boat tours and the central area of town are a short stroll away. The camping area here is a grassy yard next to and behind a small restaurant.

This campground does not have a lot of formal facilities. There are 10 duplex 15-amp outlets with low amperage if many folks try to hook up, water is available, there is also a dump station. The bathroom has a flushing toilet and showers, nothing fancy but the water in the showers is hot. The restaurant can provide good meals and they are more than happy to arrange boat tours of the lake. In the past we've thought of this as a small campground but we recently saw 18 rigs here at one time, and many were over 35 feet. Parking is on grass and since 18 rigs at one time is unusual tent campers should also be comfortable here.

At first glance the easiest access appears to be from the southern-most town entrance right next to the lake, just before you cross the Puente Catemaco if you're heading south. However, we have received many reports of rig damage due to the steep slope and abrupt concave angle of the road surface after the descent from the highway. A better access route is to take the main Catemaco exit some six-tenths of a mile north which is marked by Pemex #5348. You'll see an arch ahead, turn right on the road just before it. You will find yourself on a quiet city street named Democracia. Follow it down a gradual hill for .5 mile (.8 km) until it comes to a T at the malecón along the water. Turn left here and you'll see the La Ceiba on your left in just .1 mile (.2 km). We should alert you that boys on bicycles will intercept you near the Pemex. They will want to lead you to a campground for a fee. Even if you ignore them they are likely to follow you all the way to the campground hoping you'll get lost. Don't make a wrong turn, they'll be watching.

PLAYA AZUL

Address:	Km 2 Carretera a Sontecompan, Catemaco, CP 95870 Veracruz, México
Telephone:	(2) 943-0001 **Fax:** (2) 943-0042
E-mail:	hotelplayaazul@prodigy.net.mx

GPS Location: N 18° 25' 51.1", W 095° 05' 28.5"

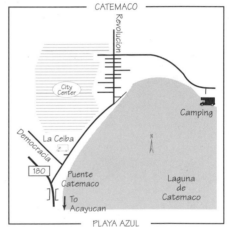

Playa Azul is a hotel with some room set aside for RV parking. It sits on the lakeshore about 1.5 miles (2.4 km) from Catemaco and will work quite well for RV's of all sizes, and also for tenters.

The hotel has set aside the small lawns in front of several bungalows as its campground for tents. One room is reserved so that campers can use it for their washroom and for showers, there are no furnishings. Small RVs are allowed to park in front and can run an extension cord. Larger rigs park in a paved lot at the back of the property with no hookups. This campground is fine for large rigs except for the problem at the entrance mentioned below.

The Play Azul has a nice swimming pool and terrace area next to the pool and a dock where launches for lake tours can embark. There's a restaurant but this often is not open.

To find the Playa Azul follow the instructions to get to the La Ceiba campground above. Drive on along the Malecón until you reach its end about .6 miles (1 km) from the La Ceiba. Watch carefully because you might get stuck in a short road extension at the end of the Malecón and be forced to back out. Turn 90 degrees left just before the extension and drive about .2 mile (.3 km), until you see a road to your right marked with a sign with an arrow for Playa Azul, which is 1.2 miles (2.0 km) away. You will see a big sign painted on the wall marking the entrance to the hotel on the right. Exercise caution entering the driveway, the turnoff is off the side of a banked roadway

LAKE CATEMACO

which forms a hump, vehicles with long wheelbases sometimes hang up. It is probably better to drive another mile or so farther and turn around at the y-shaped intersection to enter from that direction. You should take a look and make your own decision.

Side Trips from Catemaco

The town of **Santiago Tuxtla**, 16 miles (26 km) toward Veracruz on Mex 180 has an Olmec head in the central square and a small museum with Olmec sculptures. If the museum piques your interest you may want to continue on to the important Olmec ceremonial site of **Tres Zapotes**. Take the paved Mex 25 south from town toward Isla for 13 miles (21 km) to Tibernal. From there a small road takes you west and north about 19 miles (31 km) to the town of Tres Zapotes with its own museum and the site. There's not much to see at the site but many of the finds are in the museum. The road is only suitable for small vehicles.

San Andrés Tuxtla is the largest town in the Tuxtlas, it has a population of about 50,000. It is 7 miles (12 km) from Catemaco. You might want to visit one of the cigar-manufacturing factories nearby and take an informal tour. This city is the transportation hub for the Tuxtlas, if you don't feel like touring in your car you can use the local busses to go almost anywhere.

Salto de Exipantla is a 150-foot waterfall near Catemaco. The road to the waterfall cuts off Mex 180 about 2.5 miles (4 km) on the Catemaco side of San Andrés Tuxtla. About 4 miles (6 km) down the small road you'll see some small restaurants and the beginning of the steps to the falls. This trip is only suitable for small vehicles.

CIUDAD VICTORIA, TAMAULIPAS (SEE-OOH-DAWD VEEK-TOH-REE-AH)
Population 300,000, Elevation 900 ft (274 m)

Ciudad Victoria is a small city without much in the way of tourist attractions. Still, it is a pleasant place to kick back and get accustomed to being in a foreign country, the perfect stop for your first night in Mexico. Banking, groceries, and supplies are easy to find. You can drive around town without worrying much about traffic or finding a place to park.

The city is the capital of the state of Tamaulipas. People here work for the government, for suppliers for the agriculture in the area, or in light manufacturing. All of this activity makes Ciudad Victoria relatively prosperous by Mexican standards.

If you do feel like taking in a sight or two you might take a look at the **Anthropology and History Museum** which has a variety of artifacts from the area or take a short 25 km drive to **El Chorrito** waterfall where the Virgin of Guadalupe is said to have once appeared.

There is a huge new Soriana supermarket only a half-mile from the Victoria Trailer Park. It's an easy walk if you don't feel like moving your vehicle. Just turn to the left when you leave the park. You'll enjoy exploring the store and seeing the relative prices of things here compared to back home. Since this is likely to be your first stop

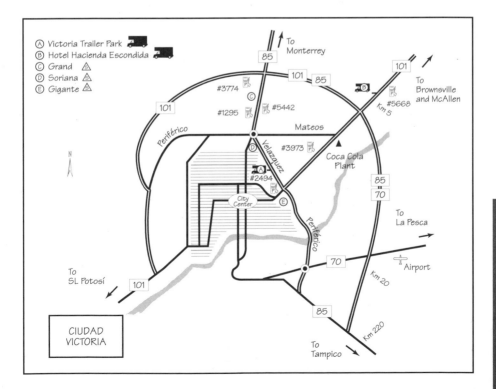

in Mexico you will probably need money, there's a cash machine at the store. There's also an internet café in the shopping center.

Ciudad Victoria Campgrounds

⛟ VICTORIA TRAILER PARK

Address:	Blvd. F. Velazquez 1940 (Apdo. 475),
	Cd. Victoria, Tampaulipas, México
Telephone	
and Fax:	(1) 312-4824

GPS Location: N 23° 44' 37.1", W 099° 08' 09.2"

This is a very large park with about 90 spaces with electricity (15-amp outlets), water and sewer. Many of these spaces are pull-throughs unless the park is full. There are also a few 30-amp sites along the back wall. The Victoria is a very large grassy field sitting behind the owner's house. It is enclosed by a wall, there are a few small rental rooms along one side. It is fine for any size rig.

Amenities include older restrooms with hot showers, a covered patio area used by caravans for get-togethers and a small gift shop. The owners have put together quite a bit of information about places to see, camping locations to the south, and border crossings. Much of it is posted on boards or available as hand-outs.

The park's location is quite convenient, bus service from just in front of the park will take you downtown. Ciudad Victoria is small enough that driving into the central downtown area is no problem.

The owner/managers speak English and have done quite a bit of RVing in the U.S. themselves so they are simpatico. It seems like every RVer who ever stayed in their park is on a first name basis with either Russ or Rosie. RV caravans love this place because it is such a good introduction to Mexico. If you're here during their season you're likely to share the campground with at least one of them. This is no problem since this is a big campground.

The best way to get to the campground, especially with a big rig, is from the point where Mex 85 from Monterrey meets the outer bypass ring. Arriving from other directions you can use the ring road to get to this point. Drive toward the center of town for 1.9 miles (3.1 km) until you reach a glorieta or traffic circle. Go around it and take the exit that is about 300 degrees from where you entered. The street is Blvd. F. Velazquez, you can recognize it because it is a divided road with trees growing in the middle. A large Soriana shopping center will be on your right after the turn. Drive east on Blvd. F. Velazquez for .6 mile (1 km), the entrance to the park is on the right. Watch carefully for a cement fence with the trailer park sign painted on it, the entrance is just past the fence and is a little bit obscure. Don't miss it or you'll have to go on down the road and use a retorno.

⛟ HOTEL HACIENDA ESCONDIDA

Address:	Km 5 Carretera a Matamoros, Col. Residencial	
	Granjas Campestre, Cd. Victoria, Tamaulipas, México	
Telephone:	(1) 314-0542	**Fax:** (1) 314-0543

GPS Location: N 23° 46' 17.0", W 099° 06' 37.0"

This is a motel with a few RV slots in a barren dirt field. There are 12 back-in sites with electricity, water, and sewer (30-amp outlets), and 16 pull-through sites with only electricity and water. No restrooms are available so this is a campground for self-contained rigs only. There is a restaurant out front and a swimming pool which was empty when we visited.

The campground is located on Mex 101, the highway that connects Cd. Victoria with Matamoros and Reynosa. It is north of the Km 5 marker, about .5 miles (.8 km) north of the outer Ciudad Victoria ring road.

Other Camping Possibilities

The **El Jardin Motel and Trailer Park**, mentioned in our last edition, has closed.

There are several places dedicated to sportsmen north of Ciudad Victoria near **Lake Guerrero**. These might be viable for those coming directly south from McAllen or Brownsville, Texas, especially bass fishermen.

EMERALD COAST (NEAR MONTE GORDO) AND POZA RICA, VERACRUZ
Poza Rica Population 160,000, Elevation near sea level

The Emerald Coast (Costa Esmeralda) and its continuous beach stretch for about 25 miles (40.8 km) north of the small town of Nautla. It is a popular holiday destination for residents of Poza Rica to the north and Veracruz to the south. There is an unsophisticated cluster of campgrounds, hotels and condos some 9 miles (14 km) north of

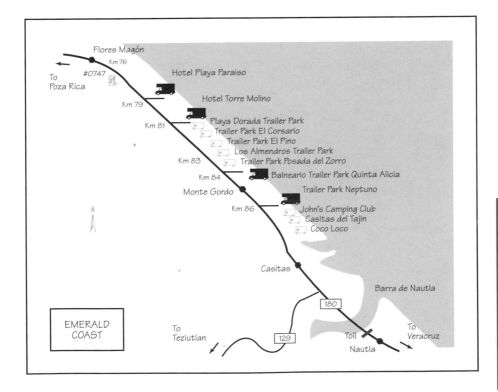

THE EAST OR GULF COAST

Nautla clustered around the small town of Monte Gordo. As you drive down the Gulf Coast from Texas this may be the first place you'll be tempted to stay for another day, then another, and another. The beach can be walked for miles, swimming is fine if you watch for undertow. Coconut palms run continuously for miles between the highway and the water. There are no large stores nearby but small local ones supply the basics.

There are attractions in the area other than the beach. The **El Tajín** archeological site and the city of **Papantla** are discussed in the *Side Trip* section below.

We've listed the campgrounds below from south to north. Also included in this section are two campground not actually on the Emerald Coast, one is in Poza Rica, 44 miles (71 km) north, and one near Cerro Azul, 97 miles (156 km) north. The Poza Rica campground is actually a more convenient base for visits to El Tajín than the campgrounds on the coast, the other campground far to the north is solely for those drivers who find themselves in need of a place to stop as darkness approaches.

Emerald Coast and Poza Rica Campgrounds

⛟ Trailer Park Neptuno

Address:	Carretera Federal Poza Rica, Monte Gordo, Veracruz, México
Telephone:	(2) 321-0102 **Fax:** (2) 321-0442

GPS Location: N 20° 16' 55.6", W 096° 49' 36.0"

Last time we drove through Monte Gordo the Neptuno seemed to be the most popular campground. It offers excellent access, good clean facilities that are being upgraded, and English is spoken.

The campground has 45 sites with 15-amp outlets, water, and sewer. Eighteen of them are back-in sites arranged around an oblong drive, another 12 are on grass nearer the ocean. Most are suitable for large rigs. The restroom building is older but clean, hot water is available in the morning. A palapa bar/restaurant is being built overlooking the beach and a self-service clothes- washing machine is being installed.

The Neptuno is located on Mex 180 some 6 miles (9.7 km) north of the Puente Nautla near Km 86 on the ocean side of the road.

⛟ Balneario Trailer Park Quinta Alicia

Address:	Carretera Nautla-Poza Rica Km 84, Monte Gordo, Veracruz, México
Telephone:	(2) 321-0042

GPS Location: N 20° 17' 38.1", W 096° 50' 21.5"

The Quinta Alicia is a small campground with a very attractive location right on the beach. For such a small campground it has good facilities and the management is first rate, this is a favorite for all kinds of campers. Even if you're in a hurry to get south you'll be tempted to stay for a few days. Space is a little tight for big rigs so caravans usually choose to stay in one of the other campgrounds nearby.

The campground has about thirty spaces. They are located in a coconut grove between the highway and the ocean. At the entrance there is a small restaurant and store with a few necessities, including beer. Eighteen level sites with 15-amp outlets and water are arranged off the entrance drive, half of them also have sewer. A grassy area beyond has parking for 12 more rigs and has electricity and water hookups, sewer for these sites may be installed soon. There's a well-maintained swimming pool and beyond is the beach. Swimming on the beach is fine, ask the managers about the safest places. The bathroom and shower building is clean and has hot showers. The manager does not speak English.

The Quinta Alicia is located on Mex 180 some 7.1 miles (11.5 km) north of the Puente Nautla near Km 84 on the ocean side of the road.

HOTEL TORRE MOLINO

| Address: | Km 80.5 Carretera Fed. 180, Monte Gordo, Veracruz, México |
| Telephone and Fax: | (2) 321-0045 |

GPS Location: N 20° 18' 53.0", W 096° 51' 36.8"

We've never seen anyone camped at the Torre Molino, perhaps that's because there are so many nearby alternates. The camping sites are on the highway side of the hotel, most other campgrounds in this area have sites much closer to the ocean.

The Torre Molino is a nice hotel with 29 back-in RV spaces with 15-amp outlets, water, and sewer. There's plenty of room for large rigs. Their restrooms have hot showers and there's a swimming pool and restaurant.

The Torre Molino is located on Mex 180 some 9.1 miles (14.7 km) north of the Puente Nautla near Km 81 on the ocean side of the road.

HOTEL PLAYA PARAISO

| Address: | Km 86 Carretera Poza Rica-Nautla, Costa Esmeralda, Veracruz, México |
| Telephone: | (2) 321-0044 |

GPS Location: N 20° 19' 30.0", W 096° 52' 13.3"

As you turn in the gate of the Playa Paraiso there's a big two-story white motel building on the right. The entrance road runs around the left of the motel building, down almost to the beach, and then left about 100 yards to a very large lot filled with palms. There are at least 40 usable spaces here in varying stages of repair. Most have 15-amp outlets, water and sewer. While not quite as popular as the Neptuno or the Quinta Alicia the Playa Paraiso has its own charm. Large rigs are fine here.

Facilities at Playa Paraiso include two swimming pools at least one of which is well-maintained. One is located in the trailer park area, the other in front of the motel. Both can be used by people staying at the trailer park. The trailer park bathroom facilities are somewhat marginal but include working toilets and showers. The motel also has a restaurant.

The Playa Paraiso is located on Mex 180 some 10.1 miles (16.3 km) north of the Puente Nautla near kilometer marker 79 on the ocean side of the road. We've never been able to figure out the address here, they used to say it was at Km 83, now they say it's at Km 86, but we think it's really nearer Km 79. We could probably ask but it's more fun to wonder.

⊞ HOTEL POZA RICA INN RESORT

Address: Blvd. Poza Rica Km 4.5, Col. Anahuac, CP 93270, Poza Rica, Veracruz, México
Telephone: (7) 826-0300 **Fax:** (7) 823-1922
E-mail: ohp@prodigy.net.mx

GPS Location: N 20° 31' 01.9", W 097° 26' 30.6"

This is an upscale hotel on the outskirts of Poza Rica, it is some 44 miles (71 km) north of the campgrounds listed above. It is convenient for visiting both the booming oil town of Poza Rica and the ruins of El Tajín. It has become a popular caravan stop, probably because there is lots of room for larger rigs.

Camping is in two areas. Both are paved parking lot areas provided with electrical outlets and water hookups. The upper lot has eight 15-amp duplex outlet boxes and the lower lot beyond the lobby entrance has two more. There is a place to dump, ask at the front desk. Restrooms are near the pool, they offer hot showers, and there is a nice restaurant.

The hotel is off Mex 180 as it enters Poza Rica from the south. If you are approaching from the south watch for Pemex #2600 on the right, the hotel driveway is .9 mile (1.5 km) beyond on the right. If you are approaching from the north you will see a large shopping center with a Chedraui supermarket and a Pizza Hut on your right. Zero your odometer here. The road right in .8 mile (1.3 km) is the one to El Tajin, don't take it, continue straight. At 1 mile (1.6 km) you'll see a small Pemex, #0762 on the left. Continue straight and you'll see the hotel on the left at 3 miles (4.8 km).

⊞ CONDADO WESTERN

Address: Carretera Tampico-Tuxpan Km 55, Cerro Azul, Veracruz, México

GPS Location: N 21° 08' 14.9", W 097° 45' 04.7"

We've included this campground here just because it doesn't really fit anywhere else. It is 53 miles (85 km) north of Poza Rica and 90 miles (145 km) south of Tampico.

The Condado Western is a small motel with just a few camping sites in the back yard. It's kind of an unusual place, all of the clientele seems to be male and they only stay for a short time. There's a yellow beacon mounted next to the entrance that is usually flashing as dusk approaches. Not to be too cute about it, even with all the activity out front the camping area in back is reasonably quiet, this makes a possible place to stop that is in about the middle of the long 140-mile drive on poor roads between Tampico and Poza Rica.

The camping area has room for quite a few rigs but only a few hookups. Parking is on grass. There are 3 duplex 15-amp outlets, 1 water hookup, and four sewer drains. Big rigs are fine. Bathrooms are located next to the sites and have flush toilets and hot showers.

Heading south watch for Pemex #2353 on the left just south of the small town of Cerro Azul. The campground is on the right 5.8 miles (9.4 km) south of the Pemex. Heading north the motel is 3.5 miles (5.6 km) north of the intersection near El Alazán of Mex 127 and Mex 180.

Other Camping Possibilities

There are several additional campgrounds along the Costa Esmeralda near the first four described above. These include the **El Pino Trailer Park**, **Trailer Park RV Center El Corsario**, and the **Playa Dorada**. All of these are between the Playa Paraiso and the Quinta Alicia.

We have talked with several people who have spent the night boondocking in the parking lot of the **El Tajín archeological site**. They were in groups of several rigs.

Side Trips from the Emerald Coast and Poza Rica

The important **El Tajín** archeological site and the city of **Papantla** make a good day trip from the Costa Esmeralda. Papantla is a Totonac Indian town and with its own unique atmosphere. You may see a few Totonac men dressed in their traditional costume of loose shirts, tapered white pants, and high-heeled black ankle boots. A lot of vanilla is grown here, you'll have many opportunities to buy the pods, the liquid extract, and *figuras* created by weaving the pods. Papantla is the home of the *Voladores*. You'll see these men perform their unique spectacle which involves descending on whirling ropes from the top of a tall pole in many places in Mexico, but this is their home. On Sunday evening they perform near the cathedral. There's also a volador monument. The big celebration here is the **Corpus Christi festival** at the end of May.

The El Tajín site can be reached from both Poza Rica and Papantla. Follow the signs from Papantla for about 7.5 miles (12 km) on back roads to reach this large grouping of pyramids and ball courts, best known for its unique Pyramid of the Niches. The Voladores often perform here using a pole mounted in front of the site entrance buildings, it's easier to catch them here than in Papantla, they perform a couple times during the afternoon.

LA PESCA, TAMAULIPAS (LAH PES-KAH)
Elevation near sea level

La Pesca is a small village on the coast directly east of Ciudad Victoria. The Río Soto La Marina empties into the ocean here and there are miles and miles of wetlands. The road follows the north side of the river as it nears the coast and then crosses a sand spit that connects to a sandy barrier island. Fishing is excellent in the area and the long outside beach can be very popular during Mexican holidays. It is known as one of the few decent surfing spots on the Gulf Coast.

Most travelers headed south toward the Yucatán from McAllen and Brownsville travel through Ciudad Victoria but it is also possible to use Mex 180 and overnight in La Pesca. The drive out to the coast from Mex 180 is about 30 miles (48 km) and you will have to retrace your steps to continue south.

La Pesca Campgrounds

🚐 LA GAVIOTA RESTAURANTE Y HOTEL

Address:	Pino Suares 602 Sur, Monterrey, Nuevo León, México (reservations)
Telephone:	(1) 327-0738, (8) 344-5210 (Res.)

GPS Location: N 23° 47' 23.3", W 097° 47' 57.0"

This is a beautiful new facility set on the north bank of the Río Soto La Marina. There's a large perfectly mowed lawn with a small number of hotel buildings near the river. The RV spaces here don't really seem too important in the scheme of things but caravan companies have discovered it and some are now bypassing Ciudad Victoria and staying in La Pesca.

There are about 20 back-in spaces with 15-amp electric, water and sewer hookups set along the fence next to the gate. Parking is on grass and there is lots of maneuvering room. The restroom building is adjacent and is in excellent condition with hot showers. Other facilities include a new swimming pool next to the river, tennis and basketball courts, a boat ramp, and a restaurant (it was not open when we visited).

As you approach La Pesca you will see a large naval base on your right and cross a series of topes, the campground is on the right 2.6 miles (4.2 km) beyond near Km 45.

🚐 HOTEL LA QUINTA

Address:	Km 42 Colonia B. Juarez, La Pesca, Tamaulipas, México
Telephone:	(1) 327-0642 **Fax:** (1) 327-0691
Web Site:	www.lapesca-fishing.com

GPS Location: N 23° 47' 03.4", W 097° 49' 47.1"

The La Quinta is a small group of bungalows used primarily by people on guided fishing trips. However, there is room for 3 to 4 large rigs to park in the yard between the buildings. Two duplex 15-amp outlets are available for power as are water hookups and a dump station. Restroom are in good condition and have hot water showers.

As you approach La Pesca you will see a large naval base on your right and cross a series of topes, the campground is on the right .5 mile (.8 km) beyond near Km 42.

TAMPICO, TAMAULIPAS (TAHM-PEE-ko)
Population 650,000, Elevation sea level

The large and active port city of Tampico is often bypassed by traveler's on their way south. The city is a large port and oil and fishing are also important. If you do venture into town you'll find that it has an active street scene, a sort of run-down Veracruz flavor. Cruise ships actually stop here occasionally so it is difficult to say that the city holds no attraction for the tourist. The city's **Huastec Museum** is worth a look if you are interested in this pre-Hispanic culture. **Playa Miramar** is the city beach, it is located about 3 miles (5 km) west of town.

Tampico has a bad reputation among RVers, they are often ticketed as they pass through town. That may be because there is a prohibition on driving heavy rigs through town. Problems are easily avoided, however, there's a good bypass route. See the *Driving Route to Bypass Tampico* section below for detailed driving instructions.

Tampico Campgrounds

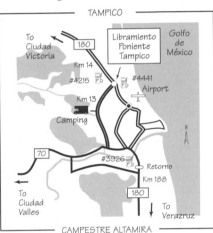

▭ **CAMPESTRE ALTAMIRA**

    Address: 2 Km Maxilibramiento, Tampico, Tampaulipas, México
    Telephone: (1) 226-7255   **Fax:** (1) 226-7040

    GPS Location: N 22° 19' 41.5", W 097° 53' 21.7"

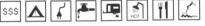

Campestre Altamira is a welcome alternative to the Tampico airport parking lot, the traditional stop-over point in Tampico for RVers heading south along the coast. It's easy to find on the Libramiento Poniente bypass.

This is really a holiday resort. It has 10 individual cottages, extensive grounds with two swimming pools, a bar and restaurant, and tennis courts. There's also a boat ramp for access to the huge wetland area surrounding Tampico and known for bass fishing. It is a dry camp for most RVs. There are several grass fields for parking, big rigs have lots of room. The management may be able to arrange to have an extension cord strung to give you limited electricity and there is a dump site. The restrooms near the pool have toilets and cold showers, you may be able to use one of the cottages for a hot shower if they're not all full.

From the north follow signs for the Libramiento Poniente Tampico, a toll road which completely bypasses the crowded town of Tampico to the west. Campestre Altamira is at 2 miles (3.2 km), on the right. You reach it before the toll booth so if you do want to drive through town you can return after a night in the campground and not pay a toll.

▭ **TAMPICO AIRPORT** $$$ ☎

    GPS Location: N 22° 17' 23.4", W 097° 52' 15.3"

Many people spend the night in the Tampico Airport parking lot. This is a traditional camping location, the entry station even has a sign with the rate for RV parking. There's lots of room for large rigs and the airport restrooms are close by as are easy bus connections into town.

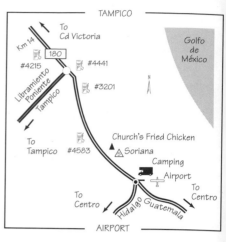

The airport is not hard to find. As you come into Tampico from the north on Mex 180 continue straight at the Libramiento Poniente bypass. If you zero your odometer as you pass the bypass entrance with its mounted fishing boat and continue to follow the main road, which is a divided boulevard, you'll come to a sort of glorieta intersection at 3.8 miles (6.2 km). Turn left here and follow the signs into the airport.

Other Camping Possibilities

We've talked to many folks who have spent the night at **Playa Miramar** east of town.

If you are traveling south the **Condado Western** in Cerro Azul is about half way to the Emerald Coast. See the *Emerald Coast* section for information about this campground.

Driving Route to Bypass Tampico

HEADING SOUTH

As you approach Tampico from the north on Mex 180 be aware of the kilometer posts. As you pass Km 15 watch for Pemex #4215 on the right. Just beyond the Pemex is the entrance to the bypass route, it is signed as the Libramiento Poniente Tampico (Tampico Western Bypass). It is also marked by a large fishing boat mounted next to the highway.

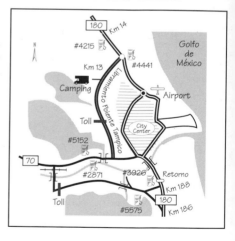

Zero your odometer here and turn right onto the Libramiento. In just 2 miles (3.2 km) you will see Tampico's camping area, Campestre Altamira, on your right. You will reach a toll booth in 6 miles (9.7 km) and then come to an intersections at 9.4 miles (15.2 km).

You have reached Mex 70, the highway between Tampico and Ciudad Valles. Turn right here and you will soon pass Pemex #2871 on the left and Pemex #5152 on the right.

At 13 miles (21 km) you will see a road joining Mex 70 from the left. It is marked as Tuxpan via Corta. Turn left here and immediately cross some railroad tracks. You will cross a bridge and at 14.7 miles (23.7 km) come to a toll booth.

The road after the toll booth is relatively rough, hopefully it will get some attention soon. At 20.8 miles (33.5 km) you will cross a bridge and at 21.8 miles (35.2 km) see Pemex #5575 on the right. Soon after, at 22.1 miles (35.6 km) there is a Y, take the left fork and drive up the hill. At 22.7 miles (36.6 km) you will come to a T. You have reached Mex 180 coming into Tampico from the south. Turn right for points south.

HEADING NORTH

As you approach Tampico from the south watch for Km 186. At this point a road goes to the left marked for Ciudad Valles. This is the beginning of the bypass road around the southern edge of Tampico, however, when we last visited heavy vehicles were not being allowed to make this turn. Signage at that time was very poor along this entire route, we suspect that the turn, the bypass road, and the signage will be upgraded soon.

If the situation has not changed, instead of turning continue north for another 1.5 miles (2.4 km), you will see Pemex # 3926 on the left. Make the left turn into the Pemex and use the driveway to complete a U-turn so that you can go back the way you came. Zero your odometer here.

In just .1 mile (.2 km) turn right at the first road to the right. This is the entrance to the bypass route for heavy vehicles. It is unmarked. Follow the fairly rough two-lane road down the hill and when you arrive at a Y at .7 miles (1.1 km) turn right. At 1 mile (1.6 km) you will see Pemex #5575 on the left.

When you reach another Y at 1.8 miles (2.9 km) take the left fork and cross the bridge. At 8.1 miles (13.1 km) you will reach a small toll booth. A mile beyond you will cross a bridge, then at 9.8 miles (15.8 km) reach a level crossing of some railroad tracks and come to a T intersection.

You have reached Mex 70, the main road between Ciudad Valles (to the left) and Tampico (to the right). To reach the Tampico campground or continue toward the north make a right turn at this T.

You will pass Pemex #5152 on the left and Pemex #2871 on the right and at 13.4 miles (12.8 km) come to another intersection.

Turn left at the intersection and you will be on a nice new toll road known as the Libramiento Poniente Tampico. At 16.8 miles (27.1 km) is a toll booth and at 20.8 miles (33.5 km) you will see Tampico's campground (Campestre Altamira) to the left. Finally at 22.8 miles (36.8 km) the road comes to a T as it meets Mex 180. To the right is downtown Tampico, to the left Ciudad Victoria and points north.

VERACRUZ, VERACRUZ (VEH-RAH-CROOZ)
Population 550,000, Elevation sea level

Veracruz is one of Mexico's main east-coast seaports, and has a long history as the gateway for entry into Mexico. The Spanish, French, and Americans have all used this port for invited and uninvited visits to Mexico.

As in most Mexican cities the central focus of life in the city for visitors is the main square, in this case the **Plaza de Armas**. Cafes are located in arcades around this small friendly square. The atmosphere is much more Caribbean than in the cities farther north. Veracruz, like other seaports such as New Orleans, Mazatlán, and Buenos Aires, has an excellent pre-Lentan *Carnaval* (Mardi Gras).

Another attraction here is **Fuerte San Jose,** the old fort built to protect the harbor. It is located on the island of San Juan de Ulúa which is connected to the mainland.The waterfront **malecón** makes a good place to walk and has good views of the harbor.

We find driving aroung Veracruz in a small vehicle to be pretty easy. Alternately, you can easily catch busses into town from near the campground.

Like Tampico, many RVers driving big rigs have trouble with the police in Veracruz. You can easily avoid trouble by driving the ring road around the city to bypass it or to access the campground from the south. The route can be confusing so we've written detailed driving instructions. See the *Driving Route to Bypass Veracruz* section below.

Veracruz Campground

BALNEARIO MOCAMBO

Address: Playas de Mocambo s/n, Boca del Río, Veracruz, México
Telephone: (2) 921-0288   **Fax:** (2) 921-2727
E-mail: b_mocambo@artedigital.com

GPS Location: N 19° 07' 52.5", W 096° 06' 18.6"

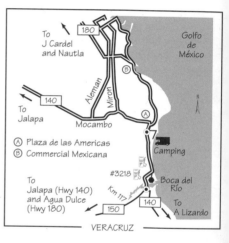

Ⓐ Plaza de las Americas
Ⓑ Commercial Mexicana

Since this is the only RV park in Veracruz it is used by most visitors. The other side of the coin is that few campers actually stop in Veracruz so the campground is usually not crowded. Caravans do visit, they usually park in the balneario's parking lot. Many campground guides list it as having up to 100 sites. There probably are if you include boondocking in the parking lots but the number of spaces with utilities is much smaller. There is plenty of room for big rigs both in the parking lots and the camping area.

The campground has 14 sites with 15-amp outlets and water hookups. They are much improved in the last few years but are still in poor repair. There is a place to dump your holding tanks, ask for the location at the office, it's not marked.

Hookups, however, are not where this campground shines. The location is the attraction. Balneario Mocambo is located right on one of the nicest and most interesting beaches around Veracruz, Playa Mocambo. The grassy campground area is situated with only a small grove of palm trees between it and the beach. You will probably have no trouble securing a parking spot with a beautiful view of the water and beach activities.

The RV park is really part of a balneario, or swimming pool and beach facility, but the pools have always been empty in the winter when we have visited. Toilet facilities are basic, they're the same ones used by balneario visitors. There is no hot water for showers, lots of cold though. Access to the campground is not well controlled, we've had several reports of stolen property at this campground, including bicycles stolen from the back of a rig during the night, and they were chained and locked!

This beach is good for sunning and walking, but the most interesting activity on it is the fishing. Small skiffs pull a long net out to sea and then bring them back in a loop, then a crowd of people pull on both ends of the net from the beach to bring in the school of fish caught in the trap. As the fish are pulled ashore an even larger crowd assembles to see the results, many people buy their evening meal right there.

Access to downtown Veracruz by bus is not difficult. The busy Adolfo Ruiz Cortines runs very close to the park, and there are many busses running along it towards town and the other way towards Boca del Río and its restaurants.

To drive to the campground it is best to approach town from the south. If you happen to be coming from the north use the bypass instructions below to get to the intersection of Mex 180 and Mex 150 south of the city. Zero your odometer at the intersection and drive north into town. In .9 mile (1.5 km) you will cross some railroad tracks and come to a Y at 5.8 miles (9.4 km). Take the left toward Veracruz. You'll cross a river at 6 miles (9.7 km) and enter Boca del Río. Here the road becomes a four-lane divided boulevard and you'll soon find yourself driving along the coast. At 8.6 miles (13.9 km) you should see the Hotel Mocambo on the right. Drive on by and take the right turn just beyond the hotel to circle down toward the water to the entrance of the campground.

Driving Route to Bypass Veracruz

NORTH TO SOUTH

Driving south toward Veracruz watch for the Puente Antigua where the bridge crosses a river just after a toll booth. Six miles (9.7 km) beyond the bridge, just beyond Km 232, is an exit marked for Cordoba, Veracruz, and Coatzacoalcos. Take this exit. Immediately after the exit is a toll booth, zero your odometer here. In 3.8 miles (6.1 km) you will come to a stop sign at an intersection. The crossing road is Mex 140 from Xalapa. Continue straight.

At 12.9 miles (20.8 km) the highway you are following crosses toll Mex 150D from Mexico City. This is also the road that you would take

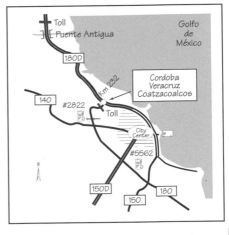

to get to toll Mex 145D running east to Coatzacoalcos, Villahermosa, and the Yucatán. There are on-ramps to the toll highway from our road going both east and west. Continue straight if you wish to stay in the Veracruz campground or if you wish to follow free roads south.

At 15.8 miles (25.5 km) you will see Pemex #5562 on the left and at 18.7 miles (30.2 km) you will reach the intersection of Mex 180 and Mex 150. Turn left here to drive the 8.6 miles (13.9 km) into Veracruz to the campground or continue straight for Mex 180 to Catemaco and points south.

SOUTH TO NORTH

This route begins at the intersection of Mex 180 and Mex 150 about nine miles (15 km) south of Veracruz. Zero your odometer and follow the two-lane paved highway northward following signs for Xalapa. At 1.2 miles (1.9 km) you will see a Km 4 marker. At 2.9 miles (4.7 km) you will see Pemex #5562 on the right.

At 5.8 miles (9.4 km) the road passes over the toll road Mex 150D from Mexico City. This is also the road that you would take to get to toll Mex 145D running east to Coatzacoalcos, Villahermosa, and the Yucatán. There are on-ramps to the toll highway from our road going both east and west. Continue straight.

At 14.9 miles (24 km) we come to a stop sign at an intersection. This is where Mex 140 from Xalapa to Veracruz crosses our Veracruz bypass highway. Left will take you to Xalapa, right in to Veracruz. Off to the left, on the road to Xalapa, you will see Pemex #2822, a good way to identify this intersection if you happen to be coming from Xalapa.

Continue straight across Mex 140. At 15.5 miles (25.0 km) you will see a Km 1 marker and at 16 miles (25.8 km) cross some railroad tracks on a level crossing. At 18.7 miles (30.2 km) you will reach a toll booth. No toll was being collected last time we passed this way. You have reached Mex 180D, the main toll road that enters Veracruz from the north. A right would take you to Veracruz, enter the toll road heading north by following signs for Poza Rica. It is a four-lane expressway, almost new.

VILLAHERMOSA, TABASCO (VEE-YAH-EHRR-MOH-SAH)
Population 390,000, Elevation near sea level

Villahermosa has money, you can see it in the wide boulevards, the parks, and the heavy traffic. The main reason most RVers stop here is to visit the **La Venta** outdoor museum. This is the best place to learn about the early pre-Hispanic Olmec culture. The museum is justifiably famous, it contains the oversized heads originally unearthed at La Venta, near the Hermanos Graham RV Park. They are set in a well-tended garden. Visitors follow a walking path around the grounds, many of the trees are identified and there is even a zoo containing Mexican animals.

La Venta is easy to find. You can often actually park near the museum with a big rig if you drive past the parking area and then park along the street. Even on a Sunday we had no problem finding plenty of room, we just had to walk back about 200 yards.

Unfortunately, there are no formal campgrounds in Villahermosa. There is one quite a distance north of town and also a secure boondocking location just outside town at La Choca fairgrounds. You can also take a look at the *Other Camping Possibilities* section below for other ideas.

Villahermosa Campgrounds

RANCHO HERMANOS GRAHAM

Location:	Km 83, Carr Villahermosa-Veracruz, Agua Dulce, Veracruz, México
Address:	Paseo Tabasco 426 Planta Alta, Villahermosa, Tabasco, México (Res.)
Telephone:	(9) 212-3137

GPS Location: N 18° 03' 17.1", W 094° 06' 06.9"

Rancho Hermanos Graham is a tradition with RVers journeying to the Yucatán, it makes a great place to stop between Veracruz and Palenque or the Yucatán. Villahermosa is just another hour and a half down the road, but there are no campgrounds there. The distance from Rancho Hermanos Graham to Villahermosa is about 80 miles (131 km). For the past several years this campground has been closed which left visitors to the area in something of a bind, but during the 2000/2001 winter season it was open again and pretty much unchanged.

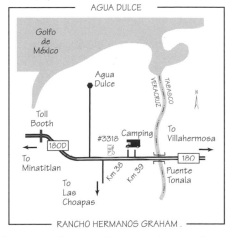

Hermanos Graham can seem isolated and run-down, almost abandoned, or it can seem like a busy crossroads with lots of activity. It just depends upon the luck of the draw. If a caravan is scheduled things will be in pretty good shape. Otherwise you may find long grass and no water because the pump is turned off. This is a good place to meet caravanners and find out how the other half lives. On the other hand, a caravan taxes the electrical system here, if you have a lot of company you probably won't get your air conditioner to work.

The camping area sits well back from the highway so traffic noise is not a problem. The sites are shaded and grassy, very pleasant if it doesn't rain. Unfortunately, if it does rain the ground gets soft and big rigs often get stuck. There are 24 pull-through sites with 15-amp outlets, water, and sewer. An additional 20 sites at the top of the campground have no electricity and are seldom used. The restrooms are in very poor shape and are generally dirty, few people use them. The toilets do work, however. There is a swimming pool but we have not seen it clean and in use for years. English is sometimes spoken, depending upon who is managing the campground when you arrive.

If you are interested in birds you should keep an eye open for parrots. At dusk you can often see them flying in pairs across the big open field behind the campground. You can recognize them because they are heavy fliers, almost like ducks, they seem to be working pretty hard to stay aloft.

Hermanos Graham is well-signed and located right on Mex 180 near Km 38. There are two entrance roads separated by about .1 mile, the south one is often blocked by a locked gate so take the north one through the rancho's yard and between the houses. Be careful when you try to turn here because it is very likely that as soon as you start to slow down the trucks behind you will grab the opportunity to pass, don't accidentally turn in front of them and don't rely on a left blinker to keep them from passing.

From the entrance the campground is about .6 miles (1 km), take the obvious right and then a left away from the road and past a pond and then a balneario or swimming pool area. You'll start to climb a small hill and see the camping sites ahead.

NEW LA CHOCA FAIRGROUNDS

In the last edition of this book we suggested boondocking in the lot of the La Choca Fairgrounds. The fairgrounds are still the best placed in town to camp, but they have moved. They're now a little farther out of town on the far side of the river. This is a secure parking area, there are guards at the gate. And it's free!

To find the fairgrounds when you arrive from the west on Mex 180 you should be alert as you cross the river into town. Take the first possible off-ramp after crossing the river, the exit is marked Teapa 195, and turn left to pass under the highway. From the east on Mex 180 through town the Carrefour store makes a good marker for the turn. Zero your odometer at the bottom of the ramp. After the turn you'll drive between a Sam's Club on the left and a Carrefour on the right, and then follow the riverbank to circle around Villahermosa. After 1.5 miles (2.4 km) turn left to cross the river. In another .7 mile (1.1 km) you'll see the La Choca gate on the right.

VILLAHERMOSA

Ⓐ La Venta
Ⓑ Tabasco 2000
Ⓒ Restaurants

Camping

LA CHOCA FAIRGROUNDS

Other Camping Possibilities

The big fenced parking lot at the old La Choca fairgrounds is gone, now there's a park called Parque Tabasco and a very small parking area at that location, it's not large enough for RVs. However, behind the park are a couple of **restaurants with fairly large parking lots** that are occasionally used by RVers. Be sure to ask permission and have dinner in the restaurants so other RVers will be welcome. To find these restaurants when you arrive from the west on Mex 180 you should be alert as you cross the river into town. Take the first possible off-ramp after crossing the river, the exit is marked Teapa 195, and turn left to pass under the highway. From the east on Mex 180 through town the Carrefour store makes a good marker for the turn. Zero your odometer at the bottom of the ramp. After the turn you'll drive between a Sam's Club on the left and a Carrefour on the right, and then follow the riverbank to circle around Villahermosa. After 1.5 miles (2.4 km) turn right on a good-sized road just before the park, follow it a short distance to the restaurants.

We've also received reports that it is possible to spend the night in the lot of the **Carrefour store**. To find this store when you arrive from the west on Mex 180 you should be alert as you cross the river into town. Take the first possible off-ramp after crossing the river, the exit is marked Teapa 195, and turn left to pass under the highway. From the east on Mex 180 through town the Carrefour store should be visable on the right as you approach the western outskirts of the city.

Some campers have been able to stay at the **La Venta Museum** itself. The parking area is not particularly spacious but once it has emptied for the night you should have no problem with maneuvering even a big rig. You should ask at the museum itself about the possibility of doing this and expect to pay a fee.

It is entirely possible to **visit Villahermosa from Palenque**, the distance is only 87 miles (141 km) each way. Perhaps a day trip from Palenque is the best way to visit Villahermosa and Palenque.

Driving Through Villahermosa

Although Villahermosa isn't a really big town the traffic can be heavy and the signs a little confusing. If you don't take a wrong turn this is an easy town to pass through, take a wrong one though and you'll have problems. Construction related to a bypass and work on the bridge that connects to Mex 180 as it enters Villahermosa from Isla Aguada and Frontera further complicated the situation in 2000/2001, we can not determine how long the construction will continue. When it is finished it may make passing around Villahermosa very easy.

Ⓐ La Venta
Ⓑ Tabasco 2000
Ⓒ Fairgrounds

To Frontera and Jalpa

To Frontera

Periférico Under Const 2001

Bridge Under Const 2001

Universidad

Mina

Lergo

Tabasco

186

To Palenque

Km 165

Sam's

180

Cortines

Usumacinta

To Agua Dulce

Carrefour

Periférico Cámara

N

Approaching the city on Mex 180 from the west you'll cross a bridge, the Puente Carrizal, near Km 164. If you plan to overnight at La Choca Fairgrounds you would take the first exit on the Villahermosa side of the bridge. Eventually we believe this will be a bypass route following the river to the left around town, but in 2000/2001 when we visited the route was under construction so until the bypass is finished only take this exit for camping.

If you want to pass straight through Villahermosa bound for Escárcega and Palenque you want to stay in the middle lanes and just follow the highway. Although the name of the highway changes from Mex 180 to Mex 186 in Villahermosa you do not want to leave the main boulevard through town, it is called Av. Adolfo Ruiz Cortines.

If, on the other hand, you want to visit the La Venta Museum or follow Mex 180 to the coast and Isla Aguada you will need to exit the main boulevard and get onto the laterals. Zero your odometer as you leave the Puente Carrizal. In 3.3 miles (5.3 km) you will reach the cross street Paseo Tabasco. You will want to be on the lateral by this time because the La Venta Museum is on the right just beyond. To continue on toward Isla Aguada remain in the laterals. You will pass another cross street, called both Av. Universidad and José Pages Lergo, at 4.5 miles (7.3 km). At this point get into the left lane of the lateral. At 5.1 miles (8.2 km) you want to turn left through an underpass onto Paseo Fco. Javier Mina following signs for Frontera. From this point continue to follow signs for Frontera to pass out of town on Mex 180. Mex 180 out of town crosses a bridge that was under construction in 2000/2001 but signage on the route described above should let you bypass it if it continues to be under construction or use it if it is finished.

Driving westward up the coast the situation is less confusing. Signage through Villahermosa tends to be better in this direction. Follow signs for Veracruz and Cardenas. Coming in to town on Mex 186 from Escárcega and Palenque you'll want to stay on the main boulevard through town. Coming in from Isla Aguada and Frontera on Mex 180 you are on a smaller road and should have no problem recognizing Mex 180/Mex 186, called Av. Adolfo Ruiz Cortines as it passes through Villahermosa. Watch for signs for Veracruz and Cardenas to mark the right turn onto Cortines. Once on Cortines just follow it westward out of town. It is not possible to give more specific directions at this time due to the bridge construction mentioned above so be alert and watch for those signs.

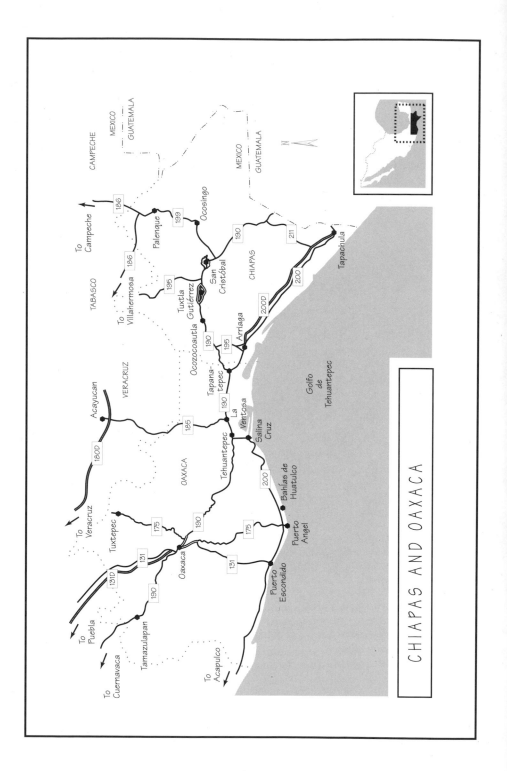

CHIAPAS AND OAXACA

INTRODUCTION

More than anything else it is the Indian cultures that attract visitors to the southern states of Chiapas and Oaxaca. The Chiapas Indians, dressed in bright colors and descended from the Mayas, are ubiquitous throughout the region. Even if you don't visit their remote villages you will see them along the roads and in the towns, especially in San Cristóbal de las Casas. The Oaxacan Indians have a different lineage, they are descendants of the Zapotec and Mixtec cultures and are known for their handicrafts.

Geographically the southern states are composed primarily of highland areas with the low Isthmus of Tehuantepec crossing between them. In northern Chiapas the town of Palenque is at 200 feet (61 m) elevation while only 70 miles (114 km) away (as the crow flies) the town of San Cristóbal de las Casas is at 6,900 feet (2,098 m). Moving west from San Cristóbal de las Casas the country becomes lower and hotter. When they reach Tehuantepec the Oaxacan Pacific coast lures travelers with empty golden beaches while the highland valleys at over 5,000 feet near the state capital city of Oaxaca are filled with ancient archeological sites and small villages famous for their crafts.

ROAD SYSTEM

The road system in this part of Mexico is not really extensive but the area is something of a crossroads. At the Isthmus of Tehuantepec, the narrowest part of Mexico, the distance from the Caribbean to the Pacific coast is only about 125 miles (200 km). Mex 185 runs north and south across the Isthmus from near Coatzacoalcos in the north to La Ventosa Junction near Tehuantepec. This is the easiest route for large rigs from coast to coast since the road does not gain much altitude or have steep grades.

From La Ventosa near the Pacific Coast roads lead east and west. Each soon splits with a leg heading inland and a leg following the coast. East of La Ventosa Mex 190 soon forks into Mex 200 (at times a toll road) along the coast through Arriaga and Tapachula to Guatemala and Mex 190 running inland through Tuxtla Gutiérrez and

San Cristóbal de las Casas. This road also eventually enters Guatemala, but branches lead north directly to Villahermosa (Mex 195) and to Palenque and then Villahermosa or the Yucatán (Mex 199) .

West from La Ventosa junction the highway soon reaches Tehuantepec where it splits, one branch following the coast (Mex 200) and the other (Mex 190) climbing to the inland city of Oaxaca. These forks are joined farther west by a small steep road (Mex 175) which descends precipitously from Oaxaca to the coast near several excellent resorts. From Oaxaca several good roads lead north into central Mexico. One is a toll road leading north to Tehuacán and Puebla. The others are Mex 190, a slower route leading eventually to Cuernavaca and Puebla and scenic Mex 135 north to Tehuacán and Puebla.

HIGHLIGHTS

The states of Chiapas and Oaxaca are blessed with some of Mexico's most interesting archeological sites. **Palenque**, a Mayan site set in the jungle, is easy to reach and probably most people's favorite of all of the ruins they will see in Mexico. A visit to two more remote sites south of Palenque, **Bonampak** and **Yaxchilán**, is much easier than it used to be. A paved road has recently been completed from Palenque to Bonampak. Also easy to reach is **Toniná** near Ocosingo on Mex 199 between Palenque and San Cristóbal.

PALENQUE

THE CAMPGROUNDS

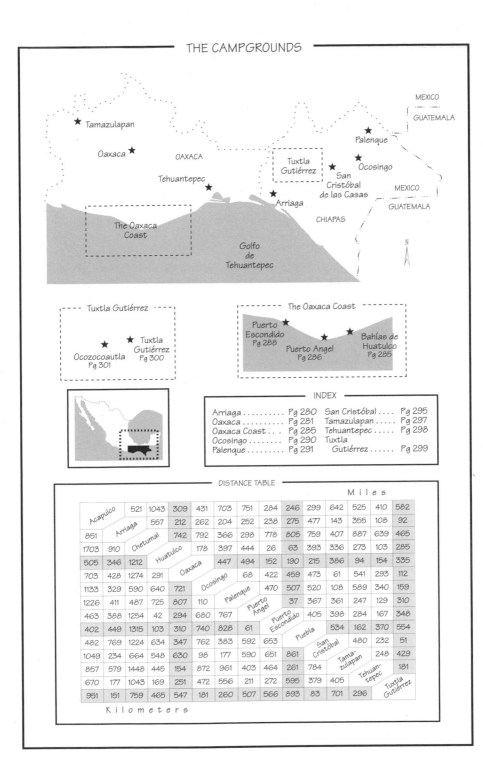

Tamazulapan

Oaxaca

OAXACA

Tehuantepec

The Oaxaca Coast

Golfo de Tehuantepec

Palenque

Tuxtla Gutiérrez

Ocosingo

San Cristóbal de las Casas

Arriaga

CHIAPAS

MEXICO

GUATEMALA

MEXICO

GUATEMALA

N

Tuxtla Gutiérrez

Tuxtla Gutiérrez Pg 300

Ocozocoautla Pg 301

The Oaxaca Coast

Puerto Escondido Pg 288

Puerto Angel Pg 286

Bahías de Huatulco Pg 285

INDEX

DISTANCE TABLE

Miles

Acapulco	521	1043	309	431	703	751	284	246	299	642	525	410	582
	Arriaga	557	212	262	204	252	238	275	477	143	355	108	92
851		**Chetumal**	742	792	366	298	778	805	759	407	887	639	465
1703	910		**Huatulco**	178	397	444	26	63	393	336	273	103	285
505	346	1212		**Oaxaca**	447	494	152	190	215	386	94	154	335
703	428	1274	291		**Ocosingo**	68	422	459	473	61	541	293	112
1133	329	590	640	721		**Palenque**	470	507	520	108	589	340	159
1226	411	487	725	807	110		**Puerto Angel**	37	367	361	247	129	310
463	388	1254	42	294	680	767		**Puerto Escondido**	405	398	284	167	348
402	449	1315	103	310	740	828	61		**Puebla**	534	162	370	554
482	769	1224	634	347	762	383	592	653		**San Cristóbal**	480	232	51
1049	234	664	548	630	98	177	590	651	861		**Tamazulapan**	248	429
857	579	1448	445	154	872	961	403	464	261	784		**Tehuantepec**	181
670	177	1043	169	251	472	556	211	272	595	379	405		**Tuxtla Gutiérrez**
951	151	759	465	547	181	260	507	566	893	83	701	296	

Kilometers

CHIAPAS AND OAXACA

The Oaxaca Valley was home to the pre-Columbian Zapotec and Mixtec Indian cultures. **Monte Albán**, located just outside Oaxaca is huge, and unusually impressive because it sits on top of a mountain. Another very popular site near Oaxaca is **Mitla**, known for its geometric mosaic facades.

The mountains surrounding San Cristóbal in Chiapas are filled with Tzotzil and Tzeltal Indian villages. Two near the city, **San Juan Chamula** and **Zinacantán**, are easy to visit with local guides. You will pass through others on Mex 199 between San Cristóbal and Palenque or on Mex 195 leading to Villahermosa. Further exploration off the main highways is not difficult, it just requires a vehicle with high clearance.

The **villages around Oaxaca** are known for their crafts and markets. The towns include **Atzompa** (green pottery), **Arrazola** (brightly painted wooden animals), **San Bartolo Coyotepec** (black pottery), **Teotitlan del Valle** (wool rugs), and **Ocotlán** (green pottery, reed crafts). Some of these towns have market days, mini-bus tours to the villages are available from Oaxaca and are really the easiest way to visit.

The Oaxaca Coast offers some of the best beaches in Mexico. Three very different destinations; **Huatulco**, **Puerto Angel**, and **Puerto Escondido**; all have campgrounds of some kind and many tourist amenities.

SELECTED CITIES AND THEIR CAMPGROUNDS

ARRIAGA, CHIAPAS (AHR-EE-AH-GAW)
Population 25,000, Elevation 184 ft (56 m)

Arriaga is little more than a place to stop for the evening if you are bound east along the Chiapas coast toward Guatemala or wish to explore the beaches around Puerto Arista. It does have a hotel with adequate maneuvering room to accommodate campers and RVs. Arriaga is only 27 miles (44 km) from Mex 190 between Tuxtla Gutiérrez and Tehuantepec (via either of two different highways) and makes a decent place to spend the night if you find yourself on this stretch of road as darkness approaches.

Arriaga Campground

🚐 **EL PARADOR AUTO HOTEL**

    Address: Carr. Arriaga-Tapachula Km 46.7,
                       Arriaga, Chiapas, México
    Telephone: (9) 662-0199, (9) 662-0164

    GPS Location: N 16° 14' 14.7", W 093° 52' 59.6"

$SSS | ⛺ | 👤 | 🚰 | 🚿 | 🍴 | 🏪 | 🏊

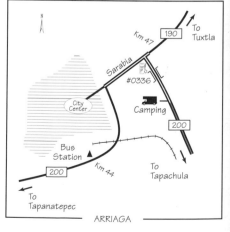

No one would mistake the El Parador Auto Hotel for a destination resort, but it does make a good secure place to pull in for the night. The hotel has room for three to four rigs to park on dirt at the left end of the buildings as you go in the gate. Large rigs will fit. Park away from the wall of the hotel because people staying in the back units drive through here. You can string a long extension cord from your rig into the laundry room for electricity. There is a cold shower and toilet for camper use, also in the laundry room. The hotel has a decent restaurant, one of the best in town, and there is a pool.

Coming into Arriaga from the east on Mex 200 you can't miss the hotel. It will be on your left just before you enter town. From other directions follow signs for Tonalá, Tapachula, and Mex 200. You will see the motel on your right just after you enter Mex 200. This is a divided four-lane highway but there is a turn-around just past the motel so you can easily head back west in the morning.

OAXACA, OAXACA (WA-HAH-KA)
Population 300,000, Elevation 5,100 ft (1,540 m)

Oaxaca state has more different Indian groups than any other in Mexico, and the city of Oaxaca **shows** more Indian influence than any other large Mexican city. This is the home of many of those handicrafts that you have been seeing in other areas of Mexico, and this is the place to buy them.

The main square (**Plaza de Armas**) area is a good place to start your visit. It has a personality of its own and also a lot of nearby locations to shop, including the **Old Market**, a block south of the square. Many crafts are offered from collections spread

THE ABASTOS MARKET IN OAXACA

right on the square itself. Later you will probably visit other market locations like the **Abastos Market** (it's huge) a few blocks farther southwest and other weekly markets in surrounding villages.

Oaxaca is a great walking town. It is filled with churches and colonial houses. There are also several streets set aside just for pedestrians. Be sure to visit the **Regional Museum of Oaxaca**. It is located in the very interesting Convent of Santo Domingo and contains the treasure found in a tomb at Monte Albán. The Santo Domingo Church is right next door.

Oaxaca is also known for fiestas. The **Guelaguetza**, in July, is a time for regional dances. The **Night of the Radish**, on December 23, with carvings made from radishes, is one of several pre-Christmas celebrations. The **Day of the Dead** on November first and second is also an important celebration in Oaxaca.

Your daily necessities are easy to find in this large city. There are several supermarkets but the most convenient for campers is an older Gigante within easy walking distance (two blocks) of the Oaxaca Trailer Park.

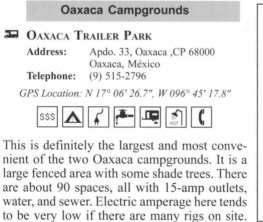

Oaxaca Campgrounds

OAXACA TRAILER PARK

Address:　　Apdo. 33, Oaxaca ,CP 68000
　　　　　　　Oaxaca, México
Telephone:　(9) 515-2796

GPS Location: N 17° 06' 26.7", W 096° 45' 17.8"

This is definitely the largest and most convenient of the two Oaxaca campgrounds. It is a large fenced area with some shade trees. There are about 90 spaces, all with 15-amp outlets, water, and sewer. Electric amperage here tends to be very low if there are many rigs on site. Water pressure is also very low at times. None of the spaces are pull-throughs, but some are quite large. Many have patios. Those of you with big rigs will find that there is adequate maneuvering room. The campground has older restrooms with hot showers.

Although located in town the campground is still about 2.5 miles (4 km) from the center, perhaps too far to walk. Busses do run close to the park so even if you don't have a small vehicle you will be able to get around.

The campground is located a few blocks north of Mex 190, called Heroes de Chapultepec at this point, where it passes north of central Oaxaca. Turn north on Manuel Ruiz, one block east of the Volkswagen dealer. The road is marked as going to Colonia Reforma. As you drive north the name of the road changes to Violeta After .5 mile (.8 km) you will see the Oaxaca Trailer Park on the left.

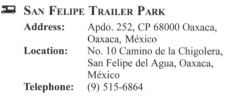 **SAN FELIPE TRAILER PARK**

Address:	Apdo. 252, CP 68000 Oaxaca, Oaxaca, México
Location:	No. 10 Camino de la Chigolera, San Felipe del Agua, Oaxaca, México
Telephone:	(9) 515-6864

GPS Location: N 17° 06' 31.9", W 096° 42' 48.5"

This new campground in Oaxaca is small and suitable only for smaller rigs due to the tight access route. It has a rural location high above Oaxaca to the north. Birders we met at the campground loved it, they say that a park farther up the hill offers excellent hiking and bird-watching opportunities.

The campground offers 4 or 5 back-in spaces with 15-amp outlets, water, and sewer hookups. The parking slots are widely spaced at the border of a small cactus field. A restroom for the campers has a flush toilet and hot shower. The owner is an American, he produces and sells mescal (a very respectable occupation here) and, of course, speaks English.

The driving route to the campground is a little bit complicated. From Heroes de Chapultepec (Mex 190 north of central Oaxaca) drive north on Nezahualcoyotl. This road goes north just east of Pemex #0638. The first part of the route has many signs for the Hotel San Felipe, you will find that following them makes route-finding much easier. If you zero your odometer when you leave Heroes de Chapultepec the road jogs a block left at .8 miles (1.3 km) to a fountain, then right toward San Felipe. From the fountain the road trends pretty much north up the hill for another .6 miles (1 km) to a church in the center of San Felipe. Watch carefully for the church, which is on your right, because you want to turn left just before it on Iturbide. Now heading west, you will make a jog to the right after a block and then continue west. The road dips steeply into a valley and then climbs the opposite side. Four-tenths mile (.7 km) from where you turned onto Iturbide you will see the campground entrance on your left. We think that if you are pulling a trailer or over about 24 feet long you should drive this route in something smaller before attempting it.

Side Trips from Oaxaca

The very large and famous Zapotec and Mixtec archeological site **Monte Albán** is located on a hilltop about six miles (10 km) from town. Believe it or not it is different from all of the ruins you have seen so far, you won't want to miss it. There is room to park your RV at the site although you will have to drive up the mountain to get there. A tow car or taxi might be a better option.

The **Árbol de Tule** is a 2,000 year old Mexican Cyprus that is 164 feet high and 161 feet in circumference at the base. This is said to make it the largest tree in the world, it is about 2,000 years old. It sits in a church yard and you are asked for 1 peso if you want to get really close, seems like a reasonable fee to us for protecting the tree. It is located only 7 miles (12 km) from Oaxaca on Mex 190 toward Mitla and Tehuantepec in the town of El Tule.

Mitla, much smaller than Monte Albán, is another well-known Zapotec/Mixtec archeological site near Oaxaca. The ruins are unusual because they are covered with geometric stone carvings known as mosaics. Mitla has a church built in the middle of the ruins and there is a crafts market nearby to serve the many tours that visit the ruins. Mitla is located about 27 miles (43 km) from Oaxaca, also southeast on Mex 190 but off the main road about 2.5 miles (4 km). Also impressive is **Yagul**. It is reached by a .9 mile (1.5 km) paved road leading off Mex 190 about 22 miles (35 km) from Oaxaca. You might also look for **Dainzú**, off the road near the 23.5 km marker and **Lambityeco**, also located near the road about 29 km from Oaxaca.

The villages surrounding Oaxaca are known for their crafts and folk art. They can be visited in your own vehicle or by reasonably-priced bus tours available through Oaxaca travel agencies. Some of these villages have their own market days and some do not. If you don't want to visit the individual villages you can find their products in the Abastos Market in Oaxaca on Saturday.

Atzompa is the nearest village to Oaxaca off Mex 170 about 5 miles (8 km) from town and at the foot of Monte Albán. It is known for green-glazed pottery.

Arrazola is south of Oaxaca on the short road to the village of Zaachila, about 7.5 miles (12 km) from town. Arrazola is known for its *alebrijes*. These weirdly-playful carved and brightly painted figures are probably the most popular craft produced in the Oaxaca valley. The first ones were done here by Manuel Jiménez about 15 years ago, they are now widely copied in the Oaxaca area and elsewhere in Mexico. The best are still produced in this village, most of these go directly into galleries.

Ocotlán is a large town located about 20 miles (32 km) southwest of Oaxaca on Mex 175. It is known for green-glazed pottery, rugs, and also for products made of reeds by inmates of the prison here. Ocotlán has an excellent market on Friday.

San Bartolo Coyotepec is known for its black pottery. The village is located south of Oaxaca about 7.5 miles(12 km) on Mex 175 toward Puerto Angel. This style of pottery was invented by Doña Rosa Nieto in 1934. She is no longer alive but her shop is still open. You can watch a a demonstration of the process that is used to produce the black color and shine.

Santo Tomás Jalieza is known for cotton textiles. This village is off Mex 175 just before you reach Ocotlán.

Teotitlán del Valle produces hand-woven wool products, especially rugs and serapes. It is located about 17 miles (28 km) southeast of Oaxaca off Mex 190.

Tlacolulu, 19 miles (30 km) southeast of Oaxaca on Mex 190, also has a market, this one on Sunday. It is a close rival to the one in Oaxaca on Saturday. The town is known for its Mescal and castor oil but at the market you'll find many other products from the surrounding Indian communities.

Zaachila, south of Oaxaca and past Arrazola has an Indian market on Thursday. You will find a wide range of crafts here. There are also a few Mixtec ruins.

THE OAXACA COAST

BAHÍAS DE HUATULCO, OAXACA (WA-TOOL-KO)
Elevation sea level

If the Mexican government and FONATUR have their way the Bahías will some day become a mega-resort to rival Cancún and Ixtapa. The natural beauty is certainly here, there are nine bays along 22 miles (32 km) of coastline with wide protected beaches and pristine water. Rocky headlands separate the bays. There are already miles of four-lane boulevard running behind the largely undeveloped coastline. Some of the first road that was installed is already starting to look like it could use a refurbishment but several large hotel chains have taken the plunge, including Club Med and Sheraton.

It appears that the remote location of the resort is slowing development. Right now the big hotels are mostly clustered around Bahía Tangolunda to the east. Santa Cruz de Huatulco on Bahía Santa Cruz seems more a Mexican-oriented resort, and as such is really much more interesting and fun. Tour busses from all over Mexico arrive, especially during the Christmas holidays, and visitors throng the beach, restaurants, and shops.

RVers do not currently appear to be part of the government's plan. The only real

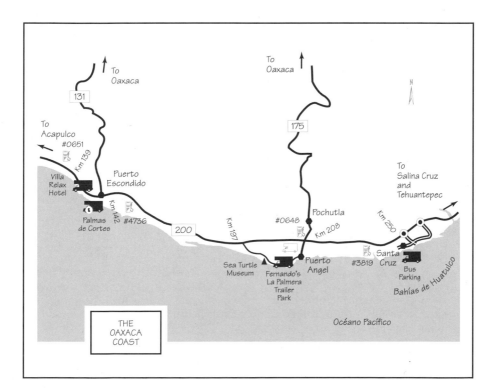

camping area has now disappeared. We visited the tourist office and were told that RVers should park in the bus parking area described below.

Bahía de Huatulco Campground

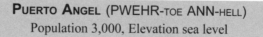

🚌 **Bus Parking on the Street in Santa Cruz**

GPS Location: N 15° 45' 12.3", W 096° 07' 58.0"

THE OAXACA COAST
#3867
To La Crucecita
To La Crucecita and Hwy 200
Juárez
To Playa Entrega and Bahía Maguey
To Tangolunda
Blvd Santa Cruz
Mitla
Ⓐ Plaza
Ⓑ Pedestrian Streets
Bus Parking   Camping
Bahía de Santa Cruz
N
BAHÍA DE HUATULCO

Santa Cruz is the small marina, restaurant, and shopping area located on the shore of Bahía Santa Cruz. When Bahías de Huatulco is mobbed by Mexican tourists during the Christmas holidays and during Semana Santa at Easter many arrive in busses. These busses park along Mitla, a street near the marina. Mitla actually makes a loop through the area, the parking is on a part of the street that is a very wide with parking on both sides that is reserved for busses and other large rigs. There are no hookups although there is a place for the busses to dump their holding tanks, you can do the same. Restrooms are located nearby with flush toilets and cold showers. There are also restaurants and shops in the immediate area and police patrol it regularly. There is no charge.

If you zero your odometer at the point where Mex 175 meets Mex 200 near Puerto Angel and drive east, at 25 miles (40.8 km) you will see a divided six-lane road leading toward the water on your right near Km 250. This is the first of two Huatulco cutoffs. Follow the road to a T at 2.5 miles (4 km) from the highway, turn right, and in another .7 miles (1.1 km) you'll see Mitla on your left. Turn on Mitla and follow it as it curves left, after the turn you are in the bus parking area.

Puerto Angel (PWEHR-toe ANN-hell)
Population 3,000, Elevation sea level

Puerto Angel really is the small, sleepy fishing village that everyone says it is. Now you see a few tourists, mostly young Europeans and North Americans, wandering around town, but this is no resort town.

Most of the camping and tourist action is west of town on **Zipolite Beach**. The visitors here tend to be tenters and van campers although the Palmera Trailer Park does have enough room for a few large rigs. There is a paved road out to Zipolite from Puerto Angel and also a paved road that leads from Zipolite past Playa Mazunte to the west and connects with the main road some 7.6 miles (12.3 km) west of the old Puerto Angel cutoff. This back way in has been a good route for larger rigs because it avoids the steep winding descent into Puerto Angel on the main access road. Unfortunately, last time we visited a storm had taken out a bridge on this back route and larger rigs could not negotiate the detour.

You can buy some groceries in Puerto Angel. There is a small supermarket on the west end of the town.

CHIAPAS AND OAXACA

Puerto Angel Campground

FERNANDO'S LA PALMERA TRAILER PARK

Address: Apdo 12, Puerto Angel, CP 70902, Oaxaca, México

GPS Location: N 15° 39' 42.4", W 096° 30' 28.9"

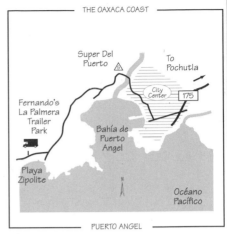

The Palmera is suitable for small to medium rigs. Larger rigs also sometimes squeeze in here, there are few alternatives along the Oaxaca coast. The Palmera is not on the water, but it is very near beautiful Playa Zipolite. You can stroll over to the beach any time you wish.

The spaces here are not really marked out, but there are 15-amp outlets for 10 rigs (actually 20 since they are duplex outlets) fastened to trees around the campground. There are also several water faucets. Parking is on grass under the palms. Before parking check to make sure you are not under a hanging coconut, they can do considerable damage to your rig when they drop. Restrooms are very basic palapa-style huts, there are flush toilets and cold water showers. The entrance to this campground is narrow and difficult for very large rigs, although we know of several that have visited. If you come in from the east (from Puerto Angel) you will probably enter directly and find a way to turn once you are in the campground. From the west you probably will not be able to turn sharply enough to enter directly but will need to back into the campground. An alternative would be to continue on toward Puerto Angel to one of the Ys and turn around there. Some English is spoken by the manager of this campground.

Zero your odometer at the point where Mex 200 and Mex 175 meet, follow the road leading south from the intersection toward Puerto Angel. At 6.0 miles (9.7 km) you will reach the village of Puerto Angel, turn right when you get to the street along the water at 6.1 miles (9.8 km). Follow the road along the coast, you will see occasional signs for your destination, Zipolite beach. This is a decent paved road with some steep sections but large rigs can negotiate it.

At 6.4 miles (10.3 km) you will see the Super Del Puerto on the right, this is your source for groceries in Puerto Angel. At 6.5 miles (10.5 km) and again at 7.3 miles (11.8 km) you will come to Y's in the road, go right at both of them staying on the main track and following the signs to Zipolite. At 7.8 miles (12.6 km) you will see the La Palmera Trailer Park on the right in a grove of palm trees.

You can also reach this campground without driving through Puerto Angel from a cutoff 7.6 miles (12.3 km) west of the main Puerto Angel access road. This entrance road is less steep. Be advised, however, that when we visited during the spring of 2001 larger rigs could not negotiate a detour on this road that passed around a washed-out bridge. There's no telling how long this situation will last.

Other Camping Possibilities

There is a small campground located on Mex 175 where it descends into Puerto Angel from Mex 200. The place is called **Los Tamarindos Hotel and Trailer Park** and is 3.2 miles (5.2 km) from the highway. It has about 10 very small camping spaces, some with electrical outlets. It has an unfortunate location on a hot hillside and is not near the water. Bathroom arrangements are marginal. The GPS location is N 15° 41' 40.8", W 096° 28' 56.5"

Zipolite Beach is lined with places offering rental palapas and refreshments. Many of these have room to park a smaller rig. No doubt some of these places would be happy to accommodate overnight campers. A few even have camping signs out.

Side Trips from Puerto Angel

A few years ago **Playa Mazunte** was notorious as a place where turtles were slaughtered. Now the harvest of turtles is illegal in Mexico and instead you'll find the **Museum of the Sea Turtle** here. Drive west 3.7 miles (6 km) from La Palmera Trailer Park at Zipolite beach on the new road, you can't miss it.

PUERTO ESCONDIDO, OAXACA (PWEHR-TOE ES-CON-DEE-DOH)
Population 38,200, Elevation sea level

The most mature of the Oaxaca Coast resort towns, Puerto Escondido may be a pleasant surprise to you. Once known primarily as a surfer hangout it has developed into an attractive but relaxed beach resort with all the services you could desire. There is a barricaded pedestrian street along the bay, Pérez Gasga, lined with reasonably priced restaurants, some quite good. There are also lots of places to shop for the usual tourist items. Puerto Escondido has a supermarket, it is located in town on the upper side of the highway.

Puerto Escondido Campgrounds

VILLA RELAX HOTEL

    Address: Colonia Granjas del Pescador,
                    Puerto Escondido, Oaxaca,
                    México
    Telephone: (9) 582-2977

GPS Location: N 15° 52' 00.4", W 097° 04' 38.4"

THE OAXACA COAST

To Sola de Vega and Oaxaca

#0651

Villa Relax Hotel

To Oaxaca

131

To Acapulco

Guelatao

#4496

200

131

Km 140

Puente Regadillo

Km 142

Océano Pacífico

To Puerto Angel

PUERTO ESCONDIDO

If you have a large rig your choices in Puerto Escondido are very limited. This new campground is probably your best choice in town.

This is a motel with a large dirt parking lot in front shaded by mango trees. The parking area is fenced and secure. Ten full-hookup large back-in sites (15-amp outlets) have been installed in the lot. There is a restroom with hot shower available, also a nice swimming pool and an inexpensive but very good open-air restaurant. The downside is that this is also used as a parking area for a half-dozen or so large busses. They're nice busses, but they arrive until about 9 p.m. and then leave about 7 a.m. The woman who manages this campground is extremely accommodating and speaks some English.

The Villa Relax is easy to find since it is located right on Mex 200. If you are coming from the direction of Acapulco watch for the campground on your left as you approach town, it is located .2 miles (.3 km) after the intersection with Mex 131 from Sola de Vega and Oaxaca. Coming from the direction of Puerto Angel the campground is 1.2 miles (1.9 km) from Puente Ragadillo and .7 miles (1.1 km) from the stoplight.

PALMAS DE CORTES

Location: Puerto Escondido, Oaxaca, México

GPS Location: N 15° 51' 41.0", W 097° 03' 44.7"

The Palmas de Cortes is located right on the beach in downtown Puerto Escondido. There are fifteen spaces for tents, vans and small RV's set under palm trees next to the beach. The park is fenced but limiting unauthorized access in this area is almost impossible, if you camp here you should watch your belongings carefully. Most of the spaces have 15-amp outlets and there are a few water spigots. The surface is packed sand with no patios. Clean restrooms and cold showers are provided.

To reach the trailer park take the first left (toward the beach) west of the Puente Regadillo. When you reach the barriers marking the pedestrian area turn left. You will see the campground sign ahead down the alley and to the right. This campground is only suitable for smaller rigs. Maneuvering space inside the campground is very tight.

Other Camping Possibilities

The very popular **Puerto Escondido Trailer Park**, also known as Bahía de Carrizalillo, is gone. It was severely damaged in a hurricane several years ago. For two years after the storm RVers were allowed to camp without services at the site, but during the winter of 2000/2001 this was not allowed. A difficult-to-negotiate dirt berm was placed at the entrance to discourage RVers from even trying to enter.

Inland from the old Puerto Escondido Trailer Park about a block a **homeowner has opened a lot** next to his house for camping. There is only room for one rig here, or perhaps two or three vans. He will string an electrical cord and water hose but there are no bathroom facilities available. The site is well-clipped grass, has shade, and is surrounded by a locked fence. He puts out a sign when there is room for a rig. To find the place drive westward from the Hotel Relax (see above) for .2 mile (.3 km), turn left on Av. Guelatao or one of the other small roads, and work your way down toward the ocean as far as you can go. The camping area is on one of the streets a block or two inland from the bluff.

The **Neptuno Trailer Park** is located on the beach near downtown Puerto Escondido. To reach the park you also take the first turn west of the Puente Regadillo just as you do when headed for the Palmas de Cortes. The Neptuno will be on your left almost immediately after the turn. This trailer park has a lot more room than the Palma de Cortes, but even less security. It is also in a palm grove. There is probably room for 30 RVs, some spaces have electricity. Restrooms have cold showers and are usually extremely dirty. There seems to be absolutely no security here.

We have occasionally seen campers along the beach east of town (**Zicatela Beach**) along the road that runs past the Hotel Santa Fe, which has a very good restaurant. One little café along this stretch, Carmen's Cafacito, has a few very small and funky camping spaces in the rear. The camping place is called **Cabañas El Eden**. Some have electricity and water hookups. Only tents or small vans will fit. Access is extremely difficult, they actually have to move the restaurant tables for you to pass, most of the little rigs here appear to be long-term.

OCOSINGO (OH-KOH-SIHN-GO)
Population 25,000, Elevation 2,950 feet (900 m)

The Chiapas highland market town of Ocosingo is located along the driving route, Mex 199, from San Cristóbal to Palenque—56 miles (90 km) from San Cristóbal and 72 miles (116 km) from Palenque. It is truly an Indian town, much more than San Cristóbal. Some of the worst fighting of the Zapatista rebellion was in this town. There is a Pemex station here and also a bank with a cash machine.

While the Indian market area here is interesting the big attraction is the **Toniná** archeological site. Smaller than Palenque but also an impressive jungle site, Toniná was only excavated recently, in 1979. There is a new museum at the site.

Ocosingo Campground

⊟ RANCHO ESMERALDA

Address:	Apdo. 68, Ocosingo, CP
	29950 Chiapas, México
Fax:	(9) 673-0711
E-mail:	ranchoes@mundomaya.com.mx

GPS Location: N 16° 54' 12.0", W 092° 01' 10.7"

$$$ ▲ 🔌 🚰 HOT 🍴

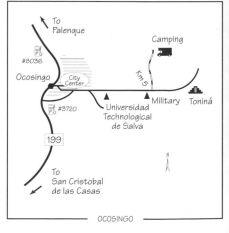

The Rancho Esmeralda is a macadamia nut and coffee plantation located very near the ruins at Toniná. It is no ordinary plantation, however. The well clipped fields and beautiful vistas make it one of the most pleasant places to stay in Chiapas. Long a popular guest ranch with small cabins the rancho began during the 2000/2001 season to accept RVs. The owners, an American couple, have been RVers themselves, so they are in tune with the lifestyle. RV visitors here should be aware that the Rancho Esmeralda's owners place great importance upon courteous and respectful relations with their Indian neighbors, they rely upon you as guests to do the same.

The rancho has set aside a flat grassy area for RVs. This is a boondocking area, there are no hookups available. Very small rigs could park in an area near the maintenance buildings and obtain electrical power, however, this area is not nearly as attractive as the normal RV area and we doubt that many will feel that electricity is that important. Toilets are outhouses (but nice ones) hot showers are available, and there is a bar/restaurant building on a knoll with great views of the countryside, family-style meals are served here. The rancho has horses and offers horseback tours of the surrounding area including trips to the nearby (about a mile) Tonina archeological site. Or you can hike to the site on a trail from the rancho. The rancho produces its own coffee, some is usually available for purchase by visitors.

To drive to Rancho Esmeralda follow the road to the ruins that leaves Mex 199 just east of the Pemex station (#3720) west of Ocosingo. The road is signed, however, when we visited the sign had been damaged and was difficult to make out, the location of the Pemex station makes it easy to determine the proper road. Follow the road for 1.2 miles (1.9 km) to a Y. Take the right fork and drive another 3.2 miles (5.2 km). You will see a large army base (which could be decommisioned by the time you visit) on the right and just past it a sign for Rancho Esmeralda pointing left. The road you have been driving on is marked with kilometer signs, the turn is just past Km 5. Up to now you have been on paved roads. The entrance road to the Rancho is not paved and is just a rural farm access road, but the rancho has laid a considerable amount of gravel and improved the road so that large rigs should have no problems. Not far down the entrance road there is gate with side posts that are a little narrow, this may have been removed by the time you arrive. Even if it has not with care you should be able to negotiate it and you will see the rancho on the right 1 mile (1.6 km) from the paved road.

PALENQUE, CHIAPAS (PAH-LEHN-KEH)
Population 25,000, Elevation 195 ft (60 m)

The town near the archeological site is really named Santo Domingo de Palenque, but everyone, including the signs, now calls it Palenque or Palenque Village. It is about five miles (8 km) from the ruins and the campgrounds are near the ruins, not the town. Many visitors never see the town. You won't want to drive a large rig into Santo Domingo, the roads aren't laid out for anything larger than a small bus, but you should be able to catch a bus, collectivo, or taxi in from the camping areas if you want to visit and don't have a smaller vehicle available.

There are several small grocery stores in town for essential supplies. There are also some nice restaurants. Palenque is visited by a lot of tourists so it has developed more services than you would normally expect in such a small remote town. The square can be pleasant, especially in the evening and if you are not planning to drive farther into Chiapas you may wish to do some shopping for handicrafts here.

The **Palenque Archeological Site** is not to be missed. If you have been on the Yucatán Peninsula you may feel that you have maxed out on ruins. Palenque is different enough to renew your interest. It is in a moist, jungle environment. Plants that we are accustomed to seeing indoors in pots grow everywhere. The crowds of Chichén Itzá and

Tulúm are not in evidence. Most importantly, the ruins themselves are extensive and very interesting. Many frescos and inscriptions are at least partially intact and can be viewed. This is also the site known for the crypt found in the largest pyramid, the Temple of Inscriptions. You can climb down a long steep set of stairs inside the pyramid and take a look.

One big recent improvement in the Palenque area is a brick walking path that follows the road all the way from Santo Domingo to the Museum just below the archeological site. This means that you can walk (or bike) in to town from either campground without fear of being run down by a taxi or bus.

Palenque Campgrounds

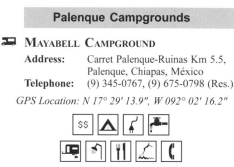

MAYABELL CAMPGROUND

    Address: Carret Palenque-Ruinas Km 5.5,
                   Palenque, Chiapas, México
    Telephone: (9) 345-0767, (9) 675-0798 (Res.)

GPS Location: N 17° 29' 13.9", W 092° 02' 16.2"

The Mayabell is the place to stay at Palenque, not because the facilities are great but because of the location. The campground is near the archeological site, right on the edge of the un-developed forest. At night campers are almost always serenaded by howler monkeys, their call is an exotic sound you will long remember. The Mayabell tends to be a little funky, you'll see more Volkswagen campers here than you've seen in years. Larger rigs can get in and find room to park but there is a lot more room at Los Leones.

There are up to 35 full-service spaces with 15-amp outlets, water, and sewer. The spaces are small but if you have a big rig you will just take up a bit more than one space. The hookups have recently been refurbished and there is now a new restroom building. Some of the spaces are pull-throughs if the campground isn't crowded. There are cold water showers, some rental rooms, a small restaurant and a pool formed by damming a jungle stream. There's a Telmex pay phone at the campground.

The Mayabell also has a large area for tent campers on a small hill above the RV parking area that is complete with a number of palapas.

The Palenque site lower entrance is only a kilometer or so up the road. The walk to the upper entrance is about a mile and a half, you might take a bus up and then walk back to the Mayabell using the lower entrance when you come home. There are some nice pools in a stream near the bottom entrance, swimming is theoretically forbidden but the pools are extremely popular after a hot day climbing around the ruins above.

It is easy to find the Mayabell. The road to the ruins is well-marked, just follow the signs toward the archeological site from Mex 199 near town. The Mayabell is on the left at 3.5 miles (5.6 km) from the cutoff from Mex 199.

CHIAPAS AND OAXACA

☎ LOS LEONES HOTEL, RESTAURANT, AND TRAILER PARK

Address:	Carret. Palenque-Ruinas Km 2.6, Palenque, Chiapas, México
Telephone:	(9) 345-1110 **Fax:** (9) 345-1140

GPS Location: N 17° 30' 06.7", W 092° 00' 45.0"

Los Leones is a newer campground located behind a restaurant and motel on the road to the ruins. There are 50 sites, all with 15-amp outlets, water, and sewer hookups. All are back-in sites and there are no patios. This campground has been designed to give big rigs lots of room and will probably be much better drained and dryer than the Mayabell during wet weather. Unfortunately, there is absolutely no shrubbery and little grass. The restrooms are very clean and nice, cold water showers however. There are two covered picnic shelters with lights. Out front there is a good restaurant.

To find the campground follow the signs toward the ruins. Los Leones is on the right 1.4 miles (2.3 km) from the cutoff from Mex 199.

Other Camping Possibilities

Without a doubt you will visit **Agua Azul**, you may also wish to camp here. The *Side Trips* section describes the site. The entrance fee allows you to stay overnight. There are designated camping areas which sometimes require an extra fee but camping outside them in RVs seems to be OK. There are no hookups but there are dirty restrooms requiring a fee. Theft is a problem at Agua Azul, under no circumstances leave your things unwatched. Camp where there are other people if possible. We do not recommend camping at Agua Azul, particularly tent camping. We are personally aware of two separate armed robbery incidents here during the 2000/2001 season.

Camping is also allowed at **Misol Ha**. We've heard of no problems from campers here. There is not a lot of room for large rigs and most of the parking area has a sloping surface although there is a flat dirt area just outside the gate.

On the road toward San Cristóbal 2 miles (3 km) from Palenque is the **Nututun Hotel**. It has camping for tents on grass next to a river and a great swimming hole out front. RVs are sometimes allowed to park in the parking area (for a fee) when the hotel is not busy. The GPS location is N 17° 29' 02.8", W 091° 58' 27.9".

If you drive to Bonampak there is a small camping area called **Camping Margarito** about 6 miles (9 km) away from the site at the cutoff for Lacanjá Chansayab. It is suitable only for small rigs like vans and pickup campers.

Side Trips from Palenque

Thirty-five miles (57 km) up the road towards San Cristóbal de las Casas is one of the most well-known cascades in Mexico. It is known as **Agua Azul**. The pale blue water flowing across the light colored rocks in a green jungle setting is just part of the story.

This is also a great place to swim. The water is a comfortable temperature and there are lots of pools with a slower current. The falls are located three miles (5 km) from the highway on a nice paved road that descends into the river valley. The area is formally known as the Parque Natural Turístico Cascadas de Agua Azul. It is run by local people, the entry fee is low. There is plenty of room for larger rigs to park. This is a regular stop for tour busses so there are vendor stalls and small restaurants. There's also an airstrip. Unfortunately there is a downside. The facilities here are not adequate for the large number of visitors, it's often muddy and restrooms are terrible. Restaurants often charge more than menus state (if called on this some have a second menu with different prices), children want coins to watch rigs and minor damage can occur if you don't hire them, and it is no longer considered safe to wander far from the parking area. Swimming can also be dangerous, crosses placed next to the river mark the spots where you probably shouldn't swim. We still like to visit, but it is important to be armed with the facts.

THE CHURCH AT SAN JUAN CHAMULA

The waterfall known as **Misol-Ha**. is a popular destination. The falls drop about 100 feet (30 meters) into a pool. The spray keeps the area cool and the falls are surrounded by lush vegetation. There's a viewpoint, a short trail leading under the falls, and a restaurant and souvenir store as well as clean restrooms. This place is much better managed than Agua Azul. A small entrance fee is charged.

There is now a paved road from Palenque leading 93 miles (150 km) to the famous ruins at **Bonampak**. This site is known for it's murals and in the past a visit required an airplane ride. Visitor facilities are still fairly undeveloped here since large numbers of visitors have begun arriving only recently. You can also visit the site at **Yaxchilán** by boat on the Río Usamacinta from nearby Frontera Corozal. If you don't feel like driving yourself consider a guided tour from Palenque.

SAN CRISTÓBAL DE LAS CASAS, CHIAPAS
(SAHN KREES-TOE-BALL DAY LAHS KAH-SAHS)
Population 120,000, Elevation 6,900 ft (2,150 m)

San Cristóbal de las Casas is another of those Mexican cities that has been designated a national historic monument. It is different, however, because it is far enough out of the way so that it is not overrun by holiday tourists. It does receive many visitors, many are from Europe. San Cristóbal is isolated and surrounded by Indian villages so the atmosphere here is unlike that in other small colonial towns like Guanajuato and San Miguel de Allende. This is a good place to shop for Indian crafts. It is also a good base for exploring the surrounding villages and countryside.

Most shopping, including groceries, will probably be done in the central area of the city. There are several small supermarkets located there.

San Cristóbal Campgrounds

🚐 **HOTEL BONAMPAK TRAILER PARK**

Address: Calzada México No. 5, Barrio de
                Fátima, San Cristóbal de las Casas,
                Chiapas
Telephone: (9) 678-1621   **Fax:** (9) 678-4310
E-mail: bonampak@mundomaya.com.mx

GPS Location: N 16° 43' 52.9", W 092° 39' 12.8"

SAN CRISTÓBAL DE LAS CASAS

HOTEL BONAMPAK TRAILER PARK

This motel has a very tidy park with 22 spaces, all with full utilities (15-amp outlets). The sites sit along the sides of a large grassy field surrounded by a wall, there is not much shade but at this altitude this isn't as much of a problem as it would be in the hot lowlands. All sites are back-in sites with no patios but the campground is usually empty if a caravan is not visiting and you can pretend they are pull-through sites. The campground has clean restrooms with hot water showers. The hotel out front has a good restaurant. It also has a tennis court.

This campground is not hard to find. Approaching from Tuxtla do not take the Periférico

CHIAPAS AND OAXACA

Sur. Continue straight in to town. When you see Pemex #0349 on the right the hotel entrance is just beyond on the right. Unfortunately the entrance is narrower than it looks and an overhanging roof is positioned so that it can easily catch the top of your rig. If yours is a big rig you might want to drive on by and turn around at one of the parking lots for the athletic fields you'll soon see on your right or even at Pemex #0347 on the far side of town. The entrance is easier from that direction.

Coming into town from the south (from the direction of Palenque) you want to follow the highway right through town, do not take either of the periféricos. As you enter town you'll see Pemex #0347 on your right. Zero your odometer. You'll come to the sign pointing right for Centro at .6 miles (1 km). Do not follow it, continue on the main highway. You will see the Bonampak on the left in another 1 mile (1.6 km).

⛺ RANCHO SAN NICHOLÁS

    Telephone: (9) 678-0057
    E-mail: snnicholas@hotmail.com

    GPS Location: N 16° 44' 02.6", W 092° 37' 18.2"

The San Nicholás is in a pleasant area outside town. It is suitable for only smaller rigs because access is through the center of town. You don't want to try getting to the San Nicolás if you are longer than about 24 feet. There are 10 grassy spaces separated by trees with electric (15-amp outlets), water, and sewer hookups. There are also tent spaces on the hillside above. The campground has good clean restrooms and hot showers and is fenced and gated. There is a Telmex phone on the street outside the campground.

From Mex 190 which runs south of the central part of town take the "Centro" cutoff onto Insurgentes. After turning towards Centro watch for a street called Francisco Leon (it is about the 7th intersecting street) at .4 mile (.6 km). Turn right on this street and follow it all the way to the end, about 1 mile (1.6 km). When you see the arch ahead the campground is on your right.

Side Trips from San Cristóbal de las Casas

Seeing the Indians along the highways and in the town of San Cristóbal may inspire you to visit their villages. There are two major groups of Indians near San Cristóbal, the Tzotzil and the Tzeltal, but each village has it's own dress and customs. The two easiest villages to visit are **San Juan Chamula** and **Zinacantán**. Both of these villages are near San Cristobál. The people speak Tzotzil. The unusual practices of worship in the San Juan Chamula church make it a popular visitor destination, you must ask for permission to enter at the village tourist office. Under no circumstances enter the church without permission and never take pictures inside. The most fun and popular way to visit is with a local woman named Mercedes. You'll find her twirling her trademark, a striped umbrella, in the main square in San Cristóbal at 9 a.m. If enough people show up, and they usually do, she'll lead a very reasonably-priced all-day mini-bus and walking tour to San Juan Chamula and Zinacantán. Be advised, you'll have to walk several miles between the villages on dirt roads and steep trails. Other folks lead tours to these towns too, many other tours do not require the hike between towns.

If you feel like going farther afield but don't have a high-clearance vehicle there are villages along the major highways that are easy to visit, these include Huixtán (Tzotzil), Oxchuc (Tzeltal) and Abasolo (Tzeltal) on Mex 199 to Palenque and Ixtapa (Tzotzil), Soyaló (Tzotzil), and Bochil (Tzotzil) on Mex 195 to Villahermosa.

The **Lagunas de Montebello** are an easy day's drive from San Cristóbal. They are located about 90 miles (145 km) south near the Guatemala border. They get mixed reviews. Some people say they are the prettiest part of Mexico, other consider them overrated and not nearly as attractive as some unimportant lakes in the Pacific Northwest. It probably depends upon what you are accustomed to.

TAMAZULAPAN, OAXACA (TAHM-AH-ZOO-LAH-PAHN)

This small town located along Mex 190 between Oaxaca and Cuernavaca (and Puebla) makes a great place to spend the night. There is also a Pemex station. It is difficult to make the approximately 275 miles (450 km) trip along this free road from Oaxaca to Cuernavaca in one day. Tamazulapan is 94 miles (154 km) north of Oaxaca. If you elect not to take the toll route to Puebla you'll probably enjoy spending the night at this town's balneario. You may have to be persuasive with the young man in the entrance booth, but regardless of what he thinks, people do occasionally camp here. Hopefully you will prevail.

Tamazulapan Campground

BALNEAREO ATONALTZIN

| $$$ | ⛺ | 🚶 | 🚿 | 🏊 |

The Balneario Atonaltzin is not a formal campground, in fact few campers ever stop here. We heard about it from someone who had traveled the route with the Point South caravan company and found it an excellent place to overnight.

This small balneario has only two small electrical outlets for hookups but there is a fairly large parking area inside the fence near the pools that is accessible with large rigs. The large pool is beautiful with a large rock face along one side. The water at this balneario is cool, very refreshing after a long day on the road. Bathroom facilities are about normal for a rural balneario, not great, and showers are cold. In the evening the gates are locked and you are left alone with only the night watchman for company.

The balneario is located about 1.2 miles (2 km) north of Mex 190 on a road that soon becomes gravel. The road heads north from the center of Tamazulapan, it leaves Mex 190 between the red-domed church and the central square.

Tehuantepec (teh-wan-teh-PECK)
Population 45,000 Elevation 330 ft.(100 m)

For RVers Tehuantepec is usually just a good place to spend the night. It is conveniently located near La Ventosa, the crossroads where four important routes meet: Mex 200 coming down the west coast, Mex 190 from Oaxaca, Mex 189 coming across the Isthmus of Tehuantepec from the Gulf Coast, and Mex 190 from Chiapas.

The town's attractions are limited, you will enjoy a stroll around the square and market area. Tehuantepec is known for its women, they have always played a much more important part in business and social life than women in other parts of the country. Their traditional costumes are elaborate with headdresses, huipiles, and lots of jewelry.

Travelers heading east on Mex 185 toward Tuxtla Gutiérrez or planning to cross the Isthmus should be aware that the section of road near La Ventosa is known for its very strong winds. Even if the wind is not blowing in Tehuantepec it may be blowing at over 50 mph across the road just a few miles to the east. The most common problem RVer have is damaged awnings, both the main one and window awnings. The wind will deploy them and once they get loose you'll have a very tough time saving them. Always secure all awnings as securely as possible before trying to cross this stretch of road.

Tehuantepec Campgrounds

🚐 **Santa Teresa Trailer Park**

Address:	Km 6.5 Carr. a Mixtequilla (Ferrocarril #34 (Res.), Tehuantepec, Oaxaca, México
Telephone:	(9) 715-0500, (9) 715-0353
Fax:	(9) 715-0212

GPS Location: N 16° 22' 05.8", W 095° 14' 59.8"

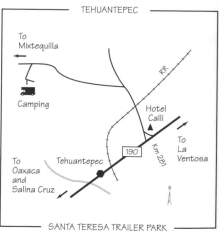

The Santa Teresa has a pleasant country location, it was once a sugar hacienda. The surrounding fields are actively farmed. Ox carts frequently trundle through the campground, that's atmosphere! The campground is much-frequented by caravans. The friendly owners put on a fiesta for them with traditional costumes, music, and food.

There are 25 or so spaces scattered under big shade trees. Fluorescent fixtures are hung for light but there are no hookups other than a water faucet. The campground has restroom facilities and cold showers. Watch for bugs here, biting flies are the most common complaint and if you ignore them they can cause serious damage. Sometimes they're here, sometimes not.

The Santa Teresa is located down the road marked by the Hotel Calli which is some 1.3 miles (2.1 km) toward the La Ventosa Junction from Tehuantepec. This is the

CHIAPAS AND OAXACA

Carretera a Mixtequilla. Zero your odometer as you pass the hotel. You will cross some railroad tracks at 1 mile (1.6 km). There is sometimes a campground sign at 1.5 miles (2.4 km) as the road comes to a Y, take the left fork. The road curves left after 3.6 miles (5.8 km). Stay on the main road until you have gone 4.0 miles (6.5 km), you will cross a tope and then hopefully see a faded sign for the campground pointing left down a small paved lane between typical rural Mexican houses. Turn here. There will be one of the ubiquitous basketball courts on the right just .1 mile (1.6 km) from the turn and the dirt entrance road for the campground (unsigned when we last visited) goes right .2 miles (.3 km) from the turn. Watch carefully and don't pass this entrance by mistake because turning around farther down the lane is difficult.

HOTEL CALLI

Address: Carretera Cristóbal Colón Km 790, Tehuantepec, Oaxaca, México

Telephone: (9) 715-0085

GPS Location: N 16° 20' 43.2", W 095° 13' 03.2"

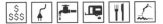

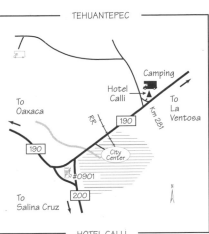

The Calli is easy to find, and if you are arriving late and planning to leave early in the morning this is a good place to stay. It's also the only place in the area with hookups.

This is a nice hotel, perhaps the best in town, but the campground facilities consist of a paved area behind the hotel that you share with the tour busses. There is room for at least four large rigs to park. There are 15-amp electrical outlets and water faucets and also a place where the busses dump their holding tanks, ask someone if you can't spot it. There's a nice swimming pool and also a fairly expensive restaurant. Restrooms for the pool area can be used by campers but there are no showers and management was unwilling to let us use the shower in a room last time we visited. Security is provided by a night watchman. It is entirely possible to walk the mile or so into town from here.

The hotel is located right on Mex 190 some 2.1 miles (3.4 km) east of the intersection where the road out to the coast at Salina Cruz meets Mex 190 in Tehuantepec.

TUXTLA GUTIÉRREZ (TOOKS-tlah goo-TYEH-rehs)
Population 475,000, Elevation 1,722 ft (525 m)

Tuxtla is a modern commercial city. It has at least two attractions that make it an attractive stopping point.

The **Sumidero Canyon** with very tall steep cliffs falling to a narrow river can be seen two ways. You can catch a boat in Chiapa de Corzo to see the canyon from the bottom. This is not a whitewater trip, in the canyon the river is really a lake formed by the Chicoasén Dam. You can also see the cliffs from the top by driving up into the Sumidero National Park which overlooks Tuxtla and the Canyon. The road is good but steep, the end about 15 miles (25 km) from the Tuxtla northern bypass (Libramiento Norte). There are several miradors (overlooks) before you reach the main one at the end of the road.

Tuxtla also has a fine **zoo** filled with local animals in natural settings. It is well signed off the Libramiento Sur.

Tuxtla Campgrounds

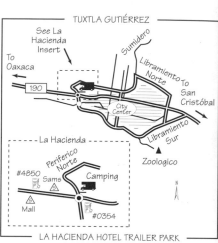

🚐 LA HACIENDA HOTEL TRAILER PARK

Address: Blvd. Dr. B. Dominguez 1197,
                 Tuxtla Gutiérrez, Chiapas, México
Telephone: (9) 611-3844   **Fax:** (9) 612-7832

GPS Location: N 16° 45' 23.2", W 093° 08' 30.9"

Tuxtla is difficult for larger rigs. The one good trailer park in town, La Hacienda, is a little tight. Take a look at the following campground and at the *Other Camping Possibilities* section for ideas if you are in a big rig.

La Hacienda is a motel-style hotel with a central well-shaded parking area that doubles for an RV park. There are 7 RV spaces. Four of these are normal car-size parking spaces only suitable for vans or pickup campers. The other three are longer, a couple of them large enough for a 35-footer. All parking slots have water and 15-amp electrical outlets. Three of them have sewer drains. La Hacienda sits on a busy intersection, the slots near the road (the big ones) will be noisy. There is a very small swimming pool in the middle of the parking area with lots of greenery, the hotel also has a restaurant. There are bathrooms for the trailer park, they are clean and have barely-warm showers. There is a large shopping center with a supermarket a ten-minute walk down the road in the opposite direction than the center of town. It is modern and flashy. There's also a Sam's Club.

To find the campground when you are coming from the west on Mex 190 just stay on the main highway until you come to the glorieta a short distance past the McDonalds and Sam's Club (they'll be on your left). The hotel is located right next to the glorieta, go around 270 degrees to the third road, get in the center lane because you have to turn sharply right almost immediately into the entrance road which descends into the motel parking lot. The entrance is narrow so swing wide, the descent is gradual enough that it should cause no problems if you're not longer than about 35 feet.

If you are coming into town from the east on Mex 190 follow the southern bypass (Libramento Sur) past the zoo, which you will pass at 2.1 miles (3.4 km). Watch carefully once you pass the zoo signs, in 3.0 miles (4.9 km) from the zoo cutoff at a tall monument the bypass turns right but another four-lane road which appears to be the main road continues straight. Turn right here, you will see a Pemex on your right in .6 miles (1 km) and immediately after that a glorieta. Go straight through, get as far left as possible, and almost immediately turn right into the La Hacienda.

CHIAPAS AND OAXACA

🚐 HOGAR INFANTIL

Location: Ocozocoautla, Chiapas, México
E-mail: hogar2@aol.com
Web Site: www.hogarinfantil.org

GPS Location: N 16° 46' 37.0", W 093° 23' 01.5"

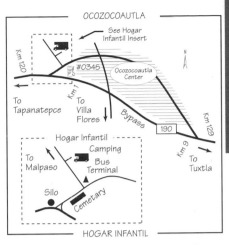

The Hogar Infantil is a children's home located just outside the town of Ocozocoautla. This is some 21 miles (34 km) from Tuxtla Gutiérrez but really the best place in the area for larger RVs. It also makes an interesting place to spend the night.

There are four back-in slots, they're suitable for large rigs. They have electric (15-amp) and water hookups. Larger groups are allowed to park on the soccer pitch. There is provision for dumping gray water here, ask for instructions. A restroom is available with hot showers. You may find yourself giving impromptu English lessons, most visitors remember a visit to the Hogar as a highlight of their trip to Mexico.

Stays here are limited to five days unless you have permission from the director. Payment for staying at this campground is neither expected nor allowed. If, however, after spending some time at the facility, you decide that you would like to help with its support you can do so through the funding agency in the U.S. This is Hogar Infantil, Inc. (a U.S. Non-Profit Corporation with no paid employees), PO Box 7049, Salem, OR 97303-0031. Their e-mail address is hogar2@aol.com. The person in the U.S. in charge of the RV operation is Bob Herlocker, you can reach him at bobnpeg@pocketmail.com, he'd love to hear from you.

If you are approaching Tuxtle from the west, the direction of Tehuantepec, you'll drive right through Ocozocoautla. The campground is located near the west end of the bypass that passes south of Ocozocoautla. Take the road into town from here, you'll see grain storage silos nearby. You will pass a cemetery on the right and at .5 miles (.8 km), just before the bus terminal on the left, turn left. Drive .4 miles (.7 km) down the road, you'll see the Hogar Infantil entrance on the right.

Other Camping Possibilities

Many individual campers and caravans boondock in the parking lot at the **zoo**. There is lots of room, there are watchmen on duty during the day and you can probably get one to watch at night for a tip. We've also had people report that the police kept a watch over them. Check with the zoo office before parking here, there is generally no problem if you leave the lot in the morning before they need it for visitors.

We have heard that caravans arrange to stay at the **convention center** which is located near the intersection east of town where the highway from San Cristobol meets the ring road that circles town on the south side. That's all we know, you can give it a try if you like.

We've also talked with RVers who have boondocked in the parking lot at the **boat docks near Chiapa de Corzo**.

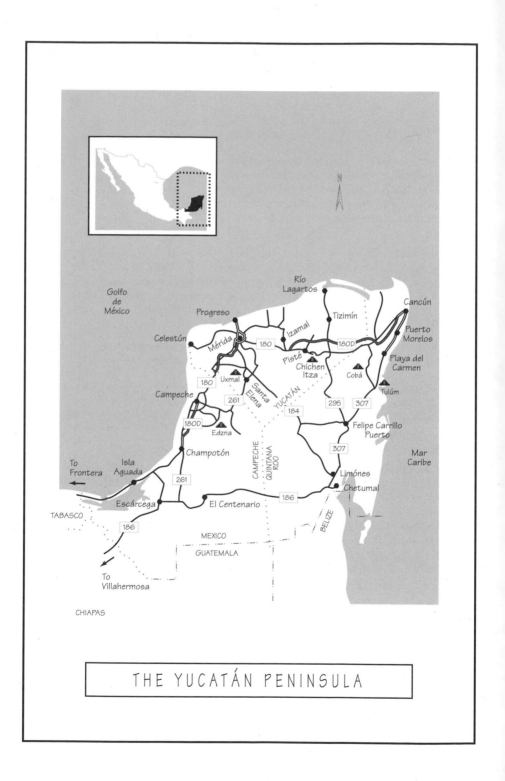

THE YUCATÁN PENINSULA

CHAPTER

. . . . **10**

THE YUCATÁN PENINSULA

INTRODUCTION

The Yucatán Peninsula is one of the most-visited region of Mexico. Most visitors are bound for the east coast mega-resort, Cancún. It is no surprise that this relatively young destination, developed from nothing since 1974, is a big success. The Yucatán has lots to offer visitors: sun, sand, crystal clear waters, archeological ruins, the unique Mayan culture, crafts, wildlife (especially birds) and even several colonial cities.

When you visit the Yucatán today it is difficult to believe that forty-five years ago there was no road to the Yucatán, travelers had to take a train from Coatzacoalcos to Campeche. There was also no road to the Quintana Roo coast. Once the traveler reached Quintana Roo, not yet a state, the only population centers were Isla Mujeres, Cozumel, and Chetumal.

The Yucatán is a huge limestone plateau. Much of it is very dry, and what rain does fall quickly percolates into the ground. Cenotes, natural wells where the limestone has collapsed when the underground water undercut the surface, are one of the few sources of water. There are a few small ranges of hills near the west coast of the peninsula, but the remainder is very flat. Miles and miles of dry scrub cover everything including hundreds, if not thousands, of Mayan structures. Surrounding it all is warm tropical water, and particularly on the east coast, beaches and coral reefs for diving.

Politically the peninsula is divided into three states. In the west along the Gulf is Campeche with its colonial capital, also called Campeche. In the north is Yucatán, Mérida is the capital. Finally, along the east coast is the state of Quintana Roo. Most people think of Cancún as the major city in this state but in fact the capital is in the far south, the city of Chetumal.

Campgrounds are not plentiful in the Yucatán, but they are well-located. You can visit all the more interesting attractions and spend the night in full-service campgrounds. There are also some prospects for boondocking along the coasts.

Probably the best time to visit the Yucatán is in the late fall or early winter beginning toward the first half of November. The rains have stopped and things are a little cooler. Later in the winter the weather is usually nice but occasionally there are spells of cool weather. These spells, which often last several days, make a good time to leave the beach and explore the usually hot interior of the peninsula. The rains start again in April. With rain, extreme heat, and the occasional hurricane, most campers give the Yucatán a wide berth in the summer.

ROAD SYSTEM

The majority of the visitors traveling to the Yucatán come by air. For automobile and RV visitors the region is remote. The driving distance from McAllen, Texas to Campeche is 1,240 miles (2,000 km). Today there are two routes into the peninsula from the west. Mex 180 follows the coast from Villahermosa into the Campeche area, Mex 186 runs inland and, although there are also good roads connecting it to the eastern and northern peninsula, it is generally thought of as the most direct route for those in a hurry to reach the eastern Quintana Roo coast and Cancún.

The nature of the peninsula, a flat limestone plateau, makes roads easy to build and there are many of them. The major ones are Mex 180 running all the way across the peninsula through Campeche and Mérida to Cancún, Mex 186 running across the southern Peninsula to Chetumal, and north-south Mex 307 which connects the two along the east coast. Smaller highways connect these major roads making it easy to get from almost any location to any other location in a day of driving. The only thing to slow you down are the topes. They are very popular, most villages have a complete collection. Since the roads run through the villages you will see many of them.

There are few divided highways yet but they are coming. There is an expensive toll road, Mex 180D from east of Mérida to Cancún and another, also labeled Mex 180D that runs for a few miles south of Campeche. The coastal highway Mex 307 has been four-laned from Cancún to a few miles south of Playa del Carmen but is not a toll road.

HIGHLIGHTS

For many visitors the first priority is sun and sand. For this you will probably be attracted to the Cancún area. Campers are not particularly well served here, however. The **hotel zone beaches** are nice but difficult to enjoy if you aren't staying in one of the hotels. After at least a week in the real Mexico on your drive south you will probably quickly tire of the Cancún tourist scene. Before you leave Cancún however, you should make a visit to laid-back **Isla Mujeres** and perhaps even a tour to **Isla Contoy** bird reserve.

From Cancún it is not far to beach destinations that are much more attractive to campers. All along the Cancún-Tulúm corridor running for 85 miles (139 km) south there are many campgrounds and quiet beaches.

The most popular archeological sites on the Yucatán are **Chichén Itzá**, **Tulúm**, **Cobá** and **Uxmal**. There are dozens more. An interesting and easy-to-reach lesser-known group is the **Puuc Sites** near Uxmal. Between Chetumal and Escárcega off Mex 186 are many more sites, popular with hikers and more eco-oriented travelers. **Dzibilchaltún**, north of Mérida has a famous cenote.

THE CAMPGROUNDS

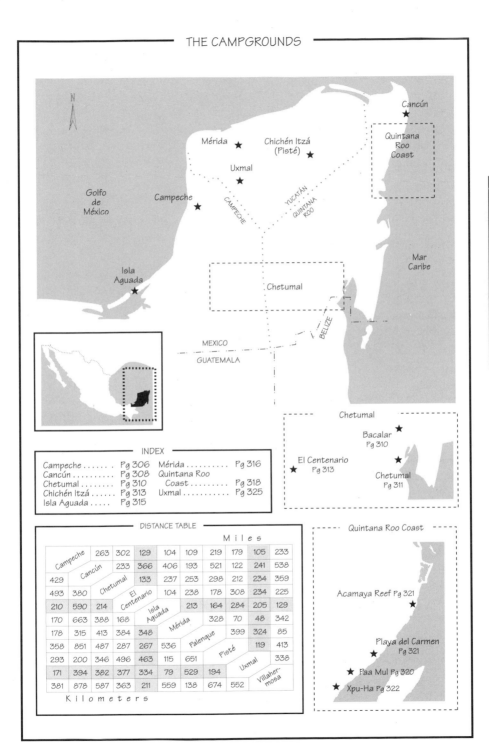

Chetumal

Bacalar ★ Pg 310

El Centenario ★ Pg 313

Chetumal ★ Pg 311

DISTANCE TABLE

Miles

Campeche	263	302	129	104	109	219	179	105	233
	Cancún	233	366	406	193	521	122	241	538
429		Chetumal	133	237	253	298	212	234	359
493	380		El Centenario	104	238	178	308	234	225
210	590	214		Isla Aguada	213	164	284	205	129
170	663	388	168		Mérida	328	70	48	342
178	315	413	384	348		Palenque	399	324	85
358	851	487	287	267	536		Pisté	119	413
293	200	346	496	463	115	651		Uxmal	338
171	394	382	377	334	79	529	194		Villahermosa
381	878	587	363	211	559	138	674	552	

Kilometers

Quintana Roo Coast

Acamaya Reef Pg 321 ★

Playa del Carmen Pg 321 ★

Paa Mul Pg 320 ★

Xpu-Ha Pg 322 ★

THE YUCATÁN PENINSULA

If you are interested in the Spanish culture in Mexico there are two cities you'll want to visit: **Mérida** and **Campeche**. You might also find the churches and monasteries in places like **Izamal**, **Valladolid**, **Muna**, and **Ticul** of interest. They're all located within easy driving distance of campgrounds in Mérida, Uxmal or Chichén Itzá.

Bird watchers will love the Yucatán. For flamingos the destinations are **Celestún** near Mérida and the **Parque Natural Río Lagartos** on the Yucatán north coast. **Isla Contoy**, north of Isla Mujeres, is uninhabited and home to 70 species. The **Sian Ka´an Biosphere Reserve** south of Tulúm also has possibilities. You can see both ruins and birds if you visit the **Cobá** archeological site which is mostly unexcavated and covered by jungle.

If you are a diver you'll be attracted by the **Belize Barrier Reef**, the fifth longest reef in the world that runs from just south of Cancún all the way to the Gulf of Honduras. The **Isla Cozumel** is the real center for divers on the coast but there are plenty of dive shops on the mainland too. Experienced divers may want to try a unique Yucatán specialty, the cenote dive.

SELECTED CITIES AND THEIR CAMPGROUNDS

CAMPECHE, CAMPECHE (KAHM-PEH-CHEH)
Population 170,000, Elevation sea level

Few people stop at Campeche the first time they visit the Yucatán. Some are in a hurry to reach the ruins farther east, some just don't know about Campeche's attractions.

Campeche is an old city, it was founded in 1542. To protect it from pirates (who hid out near Isla Aguada) it was encircled by a wall in 1686. Much of the wall still remains with the guard towers or *baluartes* often housing small museums or government offices. The old city is a national historical monument and has a very Spanish atmosphere. It has a pleasant central plaza with a cathedral. The town's museum, the **Regional Museum of Campeche**, has both colonial and Mayan exhibits.

Campeche Campgrounds

🚐 **SAMULA TRAILER PARK**

Address: Calle 19, Campeche, Campeche, México

GPS Location: N 19° 49' 04.3", W 090° 33' 09.5"

$$ | ▲ | 🚻 | 🚰 | 🔌 | 🚿HOT

The Samula Trailer Park is a favorite of veteran Yucatán campers. It sits in the Campeche suburb of Samula. The grounds are planted with orange trees, there's lots of greenery and shade. The owner speaks English and will make you feel right at home.

Campeche Campground has 15 level sites on

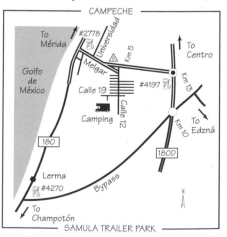

grass, they have full hookups with 15-amp outlets but are in poor repair. There are two toilets and two showers with hot water. Last time we visited the water was being heated with a wood fire that was fired up only for morning showers. We've seen some pretty big rigs here but watch for the branches on the orange trees when maneuvering. They've been pruned and the soft-looking leaves hide some sharp branches. Access through the neighborhood streets can also be difficult, see the instructions for reaching the campground below.

The campground is a great base for exploring the city of Campeche. Like almost everywhere in Mexico bus service is available nearby, just walk out to Calle 12. Taxis are also inexpensive and easy to use. Don't be surprised if a student from the nearby university drops by in the afternoon. They like to practice their English with the campers. Some of them are quite knowledgeable about the nearby Mayan archeological sites.

There is a nice small supermarket less than a mile away from the campground. Head out again on the same route you used to get to the campground and you will see it on the right in about .9 mile as you reach Avenue Agustin Melgar.

Finding this campground can be interesting. The easiest approach is from the waterfront 1.5 miles (2.4 km) south of the Centro area. Watch for Pemex #2778. This gas station marks the point where Avenue Agustin Melgar cuts inland from the waterfront. Turn inland on Melgar and you'll soon pass the university on the right. In .5 mile (.8 km) the boulevard will bend to the left but you want to stay on the street that branches off and continues straight ahead. Go straight ahead for another .2 miles (.3 km) to a T, and turn right. You are now on Calle 12. Drive eight blocks (.6 miles or 1 km) and turn right on Calle 19. There is a small grocery store on the corner called Abarotes Noemy that should help you identify the right street. The turn is tight and can be difficult. We've done it in a 34-footer towing a pickup and have seen some huge fifth-wheels in the campground so most people will be able to make it. Proceed 2.5 blocks and the campground will be on your left.

 **CLUB NAUTICO**

Address:	Calle 10, No. 293, Campeche, CP 24010 Campeche, México (Res)
Telephone:	(9) 816-7545 (Res)

GPS Location: N 19° 46' 39.7", W 090° 38' 11.8"

This is a brand-new campground, a welcome addition to the Campeche area. The sites and hook-ups actually seem to be built to U.S. standards, big rigs will appreciate that. The camping area was so new that it was not yet planted with trees and grass when we visited.

Club Nautico has 35 back-in full-hookup spaces arranged around a paved circular drive. Nineteen of the sites have 50-amp outlets, the remainder have the 30-amp style. The RV campground is located behind a large nautical club which has a bar, restaurant, sauna, swimming pool, game room, tennis courts, and lots more. During the week in the winter, however, you can count on pretty much everything except the camping area being shut down. The restrooms are really the locker rooms for the entire facility and have lots of hot showers but may not be accessible if only a rig or two are camping here.

The facility is located on the coast some 7 miles from central Campeche. It is off the free Mex 180 near Km 192 which is south of Lerma. The gatehouse was empty when we visited, we just drove right in.

Other Camping Possibilities

Caravans now often spend the night boondocking in the parking lot of the **information center** in downtown Campeche. It's OK for individuals to stay here too. It may be possible to have the center's night watchman keep an eye on you if you talk with him and offer a reasonable tip. The advantage of this location is that you can easily stroll the city streets in the evening.

Side Trips from Campeche

Edzná is a nice ruin to visit before you get spoiled by Uxmal. The parking lot is large enough for large rigs to turn around in, although people pulling cars may have to unhook to do so if there are many cars in the lot. There is no parking charge. Edzná's location well to the south of the majority of the Puuc area sites means that you probably won't visit if you don't stop when en route to Uxmal.

CANCÚN, QUINTANA ROO (KAHN-KOON)
Population 200,000 (and rapidly growing), Elevation sea level

There are really two Cancúns. One is the **Hotel Zone**, a strip of hotels, restaurants, beaches, and expensive shopping malls located on a spit of land running for miles off the Quintana Roo coast. The other is the town of **Ciudad Cancún** located on the mainland nearby which is home to many of the area residents and an excellent place to shop for supplies.

If you spend much time on the Quintana Roo coast you will probably visit Ciudad Cancún a few times to shop for the necessities of life. There's even a Costco now.

The tourist Cancún is also worth a visit, especially if you haven't seen it before. This is Mexico's premier fly-in international resort, truly world class. The hotels are fantastic and the shopping malls are first rate. If you don't watch yourself you could drop a wad here. You will also probably feel out of place. By now you're a true Mexico travel veteran with several weeks and 1,500 miles (2,500 km) under your belt, the tourists here hardly seem to know that they are in Mexico.

Cancún Campground

TRAILER PARK MECOLOCO

Address: Km 3 Carretera Puerto Juárez a Punta Sam,
              Cancún, Quintana Roo, México
Telephone: (9) 843-0324 or (9) 843-0325

GPS Location: N 21° 12' 42.3", W 086° 48' 11.4"

THE YUCATÁN PENINSULA

This is really the best choice for a campground near Cancún. It is located north of town between Punta Sam and Puerto Juárez. These are the mainland terminals for the ferries to Isla Mujeres, the park is ideal for those wishing to visit the island. It also has convenient bus service to Ciudad Cancún.

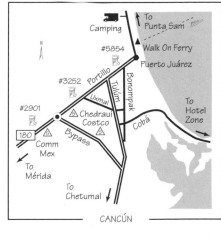

CANCÚN

There are about 100 spaces, almost all of them have full hookups with 15-amp outlets. There is lots of room for large RVs, parking is on packed dirt. Unfortunately this park has little shade and even less charm. There is a thatched-roof restroom building with hot showers. There is also a laundry and a small store associated with the campground which serves as an office and offers a computer with internet connection. Some English is spoken.

Although the campground is close to the water beach access is limited. The beach across the street is not at all attractive, a city beach about a mile toward Cancún is probably a better choice for sunning and swimming. Better yet, take the half-hour ferry ride to Isla Mujeres which has some of the nicest beaches in Mexico. The campground sometimes has a mosquito problem but frequent breezes help a bit and there are usually not many bugs until dusk.

To find the campground follow signs for Punta Sam which is the automobile ferry terminal for trips to Isla Mujeres. You will follow Lopez Portillo toward the ocean until it bends to the left. From this point the distance to the campground is 2.1miles (3.4 km). It is on the left.

Other Camping Possibilities

Some people take smaller RVs and vans to Isla Mujeres on the Punta Sam car ferry. They find a quiet spot and inconspicuously dry camp for the night. You might also try one of the balnearios on the west side of the island. Possibilities are very limited, however.

Side Trips from Cancún

Isla Mujeres is largely known as a day trip destination for people spending the week at nearby Cancún. There are also small hotels and restaurants for folks with a slightly different idea of the perfect Cancún-area vacation.

The island is located a few miles offshore just north of Cancún. You can reach it by taking a half-hour ferry from either Puerto Juárez or Punta Sam. The Punta Sam ferry is the automobile ferry. If you don't like small boats you might prefer this ferry. It runs six times daily each way. The smaller Puerto Juárez boats run at least hourly, they serve as marine busses for the island residents and visitors.

Day-trippers usually head for either the snorkeling at El Garrafón park or the beaches on the west and north edges of the town on the north end of the island. If you've already maxed out on diving and beaches you can wander around Isla Mujeres Town and have lunch at one of the restaurants. You can rent a bike, mo-ped or golf cart to tour the island. There are also lots of taxis.

Isla Contoy is a small uninhabited island that is a national park. It is located north of Isla Mujeres and day trips can be arranged from Isla Mujeres. It is a birders paradise but also a good place to snorkel and lie in the sun.

CHETUMAL, QUINTANA ROO (CHEH-TO-MAHL)
Population 95,000, Elevation sea level

This isolated Mexican town seems like it could easily be part of Belize rather than Mexico. You will be impressed by the wide boulevards running all over town, probably the result of the frequent rebuilding that this town gets after destruction by hurricanes. A lot of the economic activity here is related to trade with Belize, this is also a shallow water port requiring that lighters be used to load freighters.

The downtown area here is really not too inspired. A few blocks south is the waterfront with a nice boulevard and walkway along the ocean. There is a new museum in Chetumal that is well worth a visit. It is the **Museo de la Cultura Maya (Museum of Mayan Culture)** located two blocks east and four blocks north of the main square on Efraín Aguilar and Av. Héroes. The other attractions for visitors are the **Laguna Bacalar** area to the north, **Belize** to the south, and the **ruins** lining Mex 186 to the east. See *Side Trips* below for more about these destinations.

Chetumal Campgrounds

🚐 **CENOTE AZUL TRAILER PARK**

  Location: Kilometer 15 Mex 307, Bacalar, Quintana Roo, México

  GPS Location: N 18° 38' 46.7", W 088° 24' 49.4"

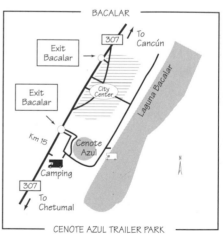

Located just south of Bacalar near the Cenote Azul, about 18 miles (29 km) north of Chetumal, this campground is a handy place to spend the night if you are traveling between Palenque and the coast of the Cancún-Tulúm corridor to the north. It is also a good destination in its own right. The nearby Laguna Bacalar and Cenote Azul are interesting attractions.

There is room for about 30 rigs or tent set-ups at Cenote Azul, depending upon their size, the campground is a grassy field with trees. Hookups are limited to a very few small electrical outlets on the light poles and in the shelter palapas (four that we could find). There is a dump station and water faucet. The restrooms are clean and have hot showers. The campground has lots of shade. No English is spoken and it is a good idea to have the correct change when you arrive, the owners never seem to have any.

The really important amenity at Cenote Azul Trailer Park is the cenote, located across the street and down the hill. It is quite large and very deep. Swimming is great, the water is warm. The best place to swim is next to the restaurant, they may let you jump off the roof. The restaurant is handy if you don't feel like cooking.

The entrance road to the campground is at the 15-kilometer post, about 1.7 miles (2.7 km) south of the south entrance to the town of Bacalar. There is a pictogram sign pointing to the east or left side of the road if you are driving south. Follow the second of two roads at the sign, drive about 100 yards and the campground is on the right. After passing the campground this road curves down to the Laguna Bacalar and then back along the shore to the town of Bacalar. If you miss the road off Mex 307 there is a second entrance about 50 yards farther south leading directly into the campground from the main road.

⛺ BALNEARIO LOS COQUITOS

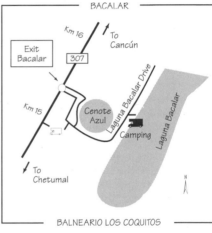

Location: Laguna Bacalar Road, Bacalar, Quintana Roo, México

GPS Location: N 18° 39' 06.8", W 088° 24' 33.2"

If you have tried the campground at Cenote Azul and would like to try a campground down on the Laguna you are in luck.

Balneario Los Coquitos is little more than a grassy field next to the lake. A Mexican family lives in a palapa on the property and parking is on a well-trimmed lawn. Facilities are limited to two open-topped bathrooms with bucket-flush toilets. Tents and RVers are welcome to spend the night.

Follow the entrance road to the Laguna Bacalar Drive. It is on Mex 307 at the 15-kilometer post, about 1.7 miles (2.7 km) south of the south entrance to the town of Bacalar. There is a pictogram sign pointing to the east or left side of the road if you are driving south. Follow the second of two roads at the sign, drive about .9 mile (1.5 km) and the campground is on the right.

⛺ RV PARK AND BUNGALOWS CALDERITAS (also known as Sunrise on the Caribbean)

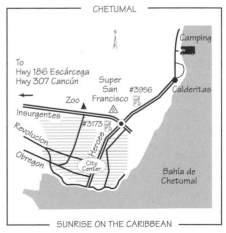

Address: Km 8 Carr. Chetumal-Calderitas (Apdo. 1), Chetumal, CP 77000 Quintana Roo, México

GPS Location: N 18° 33' 39.3", W 088° 14' 56.5"

This campground is located on Calderitas Bay north of Chetumal. It sits right next to the ocean. There is no beach, the campground has a low rock wall boundary for defense from the

waves. The ocean is very shallow here but popular for swimming.

Sunrise on the Caribbean has spaces for about 20 rigs. The campground was badly damaged in a storm a few years ago and is being slowly restored under new ownership. Right now it is little more than a place to boondock (for a fee) on a beautiful site. There is a faucet to get water, a place to dump that the attendant will show you, and no restrooms. We've seen two caravans in here at one time, big rigs will fit.

People have a terrible time finding this campground. There has been no entrance sign for years, if you don't know exactly where it is you will drive right on by and find yourself on a narrow road with no good places to turn if your vehicle is larger than a van. Zero your odometer at the intersection of Mex 307 and Mex 186 west of Chetumal. Head east towards Chetumal. The road to Belize goes right at a glorieta at 6.6 miles (10.8 km), continue straight toward Chetumal. There is a Pemex on the left at 6.8 miles (11.2 km). Follow Ave. Insurgentes to the left at a Y at 7.7 miles (12.6 km). You'll see a zoo on the left at 11.3 miles (18.5 km), then a Pemex on the right at 12.2 miles (19.9 km). Directly across the street from the Pemex, on your left, is a handy supermarket that you might want to remember. You'll come to a glorieta at 12.3 miles (20.1 km). Go three-quarters of the way around it (about 270 degrees) and take the third exit, you may see a sign for Calderitas marking this road. At 15.1 miles (24.7 km) the road dog-legs right at a small traffic circle. At 15.6 miles (25.1 km) take the road to the left which is immediately after the center divider ends, you'll pass a few small seafood restaurants and then come to the campground entrance at 16.3 miles (26.3 km). Do not pass any entrances without checking them carefully. The campground has a wall on the road side, cement pedestals on both sides of the entrance gate, water is on two sides of the property, there is a boat ramp, and there are 4 houses along the inside of the roadside wall. We give you these details so you can recognize the place since there was no sign when we were there. It you drive in the attendant usually appears immediately.

Other Camping Possibilities

There are several balnearios north of Chetumal near Laguna Bacalar that allow camping but have little in the way of hookups. Some are quite primitive, others are well-developed. Some, unfortunately, even have discos.

As you drive along Mex 307 north of Laguna Bacalar you may see a sign for a trailer park called **Fredericos Laguna Azul**. It is near Km 58 just south of the village of Pedro A. Santos. This is a new place on the north shore of Laguna Bacalar. It has a small stretch of lakefront and is suitable for boondocking for vans, pickup campers, and other small rigs. The 2-mile (3 km) entrance road is narrow and rough. It is not suitable for larger rigs and spots to turn around are not easy to find.

Adventure-camping aficionados will want to explore the beaches along the long deserted coast north of Chetumal and south of the Sian Ka´an Biosphere Reserve, especially the **Xcalak Peninsula**. Access is from Mex 307 just south of the town of Limónes 28 miles (46 km) north of Bacalar. There's a paved road to the coast, a distance of 35 miles (56 km) and then more paved roads running both north and south. Small sand roads run out to the coast from the paved roads. You can arrange a camping spot with one of the small resorts that are being built along the water. Everyone expects this to be the next area where campgrounds will develop because access highways are good, electricity is arriving, and big money development is still some distance off.

The drive from Chetumal to Palenque, or the other way, is a long one, a distance of 300 miles (485 km) that takes all day. There is a restaurant near El Centenario called the **Restaurante Familiar Campestre La Laguna**, that sometimes allows RVers to camp in their large well-kept grassy yard if they have dinner at the restaurant. The La Laguna is 133 miles (215 km) from Chetumal and 167 miles (270 km) from Palenque. The GPS location is N 18° 38' 36.3", W 090° 17' 43.3".

Side Trips from Chetumal

The town of **Bacalar** is located about 17 miles (38 km) north of Chetumal on the west shore of the **Laguna Bacalar** (Bacalar Lagoon). The town is old, it was the Spanish settlement here before Chetumal, and now is a small local resort with many nice homes along the lagoon. There is an old fort with a museum covering the history of the area. The Bacalar Lagoon, also known as Las Lagunas de Siete Colores (The Lagoons of Seven Colors) is now a landlocked lagoon, very shallow with a light-reflecting bottom, that changes colors depending upon the time of day and lighting conditions. Several balnearios along the shore provide a places to swim and perhaps to camp.

Just south of the town of Bacalar is **Cenote Azul**. It is separated from Lake Bacalar by only a narrow strip of land but is entirely different. Reported to be over 175 feet deep, this large circular cenote is very familiar to Yucatán campers, the popular Cenote Azul Trailer Park is just across the road. There is a decent restaurant on the shore with swimming in the deep water just in front and the opportunity to jump into the water off the roof, hard to pass up a combination like that!

East of Chetumal off roads on either side of Mex 186 are many Mayan archeological sites. The easiest-to-visit and most well-known is **Kohunlich**, located 42 miles (67 km) west of Chetumal and 5 miles (8 km) south on a side road. Another cluster of sites; **Becán**, **Xpujil**, and **Chicana**; is two hours farther west, about 124 miles (200 km) from Chetumal and clustered around the village of Xpujil. Finally, even farther west is the huge but largely undiscovered site of **Calakmul**. These places are difficult to visit in one day, perhaps the more eastern sites could be explored using the La Laguna restaurant near El Centenario as a base, see *Other Camping Possibilities* above.

CHICHÉN ITZÁ, YUCATÁN (CHEE-CHEN EET-SAH)

Chichén Itzá is one of the top archeological sites in Mexico, a must-see attraction. The site covers many acres, has eighteen excavated structures including a huge pyramid, and two cenotes. Chichén Itzá has been largely restored.

Pisté is a small town next to the site which seems totally devoted to supporting the tourist attraction next door. The archeological site is located about a mile to the east. There are several hotels with restaurants in Pisté if you feel like giving them a try. The grocery shopping possibilities are limited, but there are a few small places where you can pick up basic things.

Chichén Itzá Campgrounds

STARDUST INN

Address: Carretera Mérida-Puerto Juárez Km 118, Pisté, Yucatán, México

Telephone: (9) 851-0122

GPS Location: N 20° 41' 37.6", W 088° 34' 58.7"

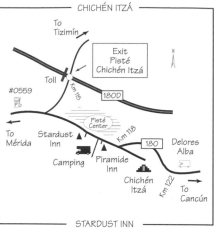

This campground is run by the Stardust Inn but the entrance is 50 yards or so east of the hotel next to the Pyramid Inn. The caretaker lives at the rear of the campground and will probably greet you and collect the fee when you arrive.

There are 20 spaces in the small campground, all with 15-amp electric and water hookups, and many with sewer, arranged along two sides of a grassy lot enclosed with a rock wall. Unfortunately, last time we visited the electric outlets were dead and most water faucets were inoperable. Very low amp electricity was only available using extension cords from the restrooms. Flowering plants and banana trees grow along the wall, they don't create much shade but they are attractive. There are restrooms with hot showers at the campground, and you can follow a trail to a back entrance to the Stardust Inn and use their pool for free, it is a nice pool. There's room for large rigs in this campground.

The RV park is located at the edge of Pisté near the archeological site, the distance is about a mile and there is a sidewalk the entire distance. If you wish to drive there is plenty of parking at the site, although you will have to pay. You'll easily spot the campground since it is on the main road through town.

PIRAMIDE INN

Address: Calle 15-A, No.28x20, Pisté, CP 97751 Yucatán, México

Telephone: (9) 851-0115 **Fax:** (9) 851-0114

E-mail: piramide@yahoo.com

Web Site: www.piramideinn.com

GPS Location: N 20° 41' 36.5", W 088° 34' 57.4"

Located right next to the Stardust Inn's camping area, and often preferred because it is cheaper, the Piramide Inn has room for two large RVs to park out front and run electrical cords to a low-amp outlet. There's also a water faucet available. Tent campers are allowed to set up in the nice garden area near the attractive swimming pool. There are restrooms back by the pool with cold water showers. This small hotel also has a restaurant.

Other Camping Possibilities

Caravans traveling through Pisté often camp in the **ball field** across from the Piramide Inn. Apparently the Inn owns the field and there is a fee to camp there. The Piramide is the place to check on this, if there is no ballgame scheduled this might be the best place in town to spend the night although you will undoubtedly be approached by youngsters selling various trinkets.

East of Pisté 3 miles (4.8 km) is the **Hotel Delores Alba**. The hotel has room for small rigs to park on grass near but off the highway. There is shade and the fee is reasonable although there are no hookups. The GPS location is N 20° 39' 51.8", W 088° 33' 00.1"

Side Trips from Chichén Itzá

The **Balankanche Caves** are only 4 miles (6 km) east of Chichén Itzá. They were discovered in 1959 and were a Maya ceremonial site. There's a restaurant, a museum, and each night a sound and light show.

Valladolid is just 27 miles (44 km) east of Chichén Itzá. It is a colonial town with many churches and an active central square. Largely ignored by visitors until recently it is being spruced up but still isn't full of tourists.

Izamal is located about 10 miles (16 km) north of the place where Mex 180D begins on the road between Mérida and Chichén Itzá. It is, therefore, about 41 miles (70 km) from Pisté. The downtown area is almost all painted yellow, the Pope visited a few years ago and the town was spiffed up for the visit. The Convent of St. Anthony de Padua, built on top of a Mayan temple, is located here as are unrestored Mayan ruins. History buffs will be interested to know that John L. Stephens visited these ruins during his trip described in the book *Incidents of Travel in Yucatán* and also that the fanatic friar Diego de Landa, responsible for much of the destruction of Mayan culture, was originally posted to this convent. Just to the west of town is a reconstruction of a Mayan sacbe or "white road". A small sign points it out, otherwise you would drive right past and never see it, although it is less than 100 feet from the road.

Río Lagartos (Lizard River or Alligator River) National Park is another place to see flamingoes and water birds on the Yucatán. The flamingos are not at Celestún and Río Lagartos at the same time of the year. Here's the cycle. The birds come to Río Lagartos in April, lay eggs in June, and hatch and raise the chicks until November. Then they fly to outlying lagoons, including Celestún, to feed. They return again to Río Lagartos then in April. The Río Lagartos birds should only be visited during the pre-nesting period in April and May. To reach the Río Lagartos National Park drive east to Valladolid and then north on Mex 295. The distance from Chichén Itzá is about 90 miles (150 km). You must rent a boat and guide to see the birds.

ISLA AGUADA, CAMPECHE (EES-LA AH-GWAH-DAH)
Population 2,900, Elevation sea level

Fishing is the main preoccupation in Isla Aguada. Each morning you'll hear the outboards as the fishermen head out to sea in skiffs. We walked out onto the toll bridge and watched some men fishing with hand lines and nets for fish to sell to the passing cars. Each time a net was thrown it came up with several fish, they must be thick down there. Shelling is pretty good on the outer coast almost everywhere in the vicinity of Isla Aguada.

You can walk to the center of town by following the streets east from the campground. The distance is about a mile. There are a few small grocery stores, a phone office, and you can watch the fish unloaded from the skiffs each day. Other than that not a lot happens in Isla Aguada.

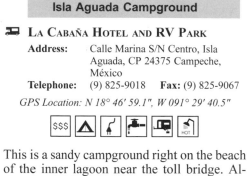

Isla Aguada Campground

🚐 **LA CABAÑA HOTEL AND RV PARK**

Address: Calle Marina S/N Centro, Isla
            Aguada, CP 24375 Campeche,
            México

Telephone: (9) 825-9018   **Fax:** (9) 825-9067

GPS Location: N 18° 46' 59.1", W 091° 29' 40.5"

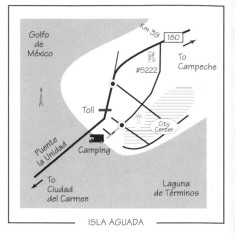

ISLA AGUADA

This is a sandy campground right on the beach of the inner lagoon near the toll bridge. Although called a hotel it is actually much more of an RV park, there are some rooms in the middle of the RV parking area. If you follow the beach around to the right and under the bridge you can walk for miles along the water and find tons of shells. The bridge is actually about a quarter-mile away and there is little traffic so road noise is no problem at all.

The campground has at least 60 spaces with 15-amp electrical outlets and water, and some sites also have sewer drains. There is a dump station and plenty of room for big rigs. Pines and other trees of various sizes shade many of the sites, there are several very large ones near the water. Our favorite sites were under the big trees with the nose of the RV about 50 feet from the lagoon. The campground is fully fenced. Five clean shower rooms, each with it's own toilet, have hot water. English is spoken.

You can drive right to the campground by taking the first possible right after leaving the bridge toll booth. Drive toward the lagoon, you'll see signs for the campground.

Other Camping Possibilities

There is an old ferry dock next to the campground (to the southeast) where we often see boondockers parked.

MÉRIDA, YUCATÁN (MEH-ree-dah)
Population 610,000, Elevation 30 ft (9 m)

Mérida is the largest city on the Yucatán Peninsula and capital of the state of Yucatán. It is also one of Mexico's oldest cities and a designated national historic monument.

Mérida is very much a tourist city. When you tour the downtown area you'll see lots of Americans and Europeans. Many visitors to the Cancún area make side trips here for the nearby ruins and for the shopping. The real bargains are local products like hammocks, Panama hats, guayabera shirts and huipile dresses. Other items from all over Mexico are available, but unlike the other visitors here you will probably have an opportunity to buy these other things much nearer their point of creation, and you can get better prices. Be forewarned that Mérida's vendors can be some of the pushiest around.

The central downtown area is well worth a visit for the shopping in the market and to tour the **plaza**, **cathedral**, and streets of the city. You can rent a horse-drawn buggy called a *calesa* if you wish. Do not take a large rig into town, the streets are narrow and crowded.

The best way to drive in to town is to drive around the ring road so that you enter the city on the road from Progreso. This is the road where the Rainbow RV Campground is located so you can follow the directions given below to find it. As you continue in towards the centro area the road becomes the **Paseo Montejo** which is one of the city's tourist attractions. During the late 19th and early 20th century Mérida was a very rich town because of it's sisal fiber exports, the Paseo is lined with mansions, Mérida's version of a fashionable Paris-style boulevard.

The Paseo ends before it reaches the centro area. You should jog a block or so to the right and then turn left. The central area is bounded by Calle 57 on the north, Calle 69 on the south, Calle 66 on the west and Calle 54 on the east. You should be able to find street parking on the borders of this area for cars and smaller vehicles or take a bus into town from the campground.

Mérida Campground

🚐 **RAINBOW RV CAMPGROUND**

Address:	Calle 61, No. 468 Bajos, Mérida, CP 97000-3 Yucatán, México (Reservations)
Location:	Carretera Mérida - Progresso, Mérida, Yucatán, México
Telephone:	(9) 926-1026 or (9) 926-1029
Fax:	(9) 924-7784

GPS Location: N 21° 02' 29.3", W 089° 37' 49.2"

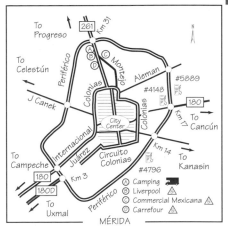

The Rainbow is now the only Mérida campground, and if you look at the recent development in the neighborhood you will probably conclude, as we have, that its days are numbered. A very upscale department store, the Liverpool, has just gone in next door and property values are obviously increasing.

The campground has about 50 sites, most with 15-amp outlets and water and sewer hookups. Some sites have patios and some are pull-throughs. The entire campground is grassy with lots of room for big rigs and a few sites have some shade. The restroom building is usually clean and has hot showers.

Grocery shopping is convenient to this campground with several large supermarkets and other stores along the boulevards toward the central area. These include a

Carrefours, a Comercial Mexicana, Liverpool, Sears, Costco, and a Sam's Club.

The Rainbow is easy to find and has very good access that does not require driving through town. Just follow the ring road to the north side of Mérida. At the Progreso interchange drive toward town, almost immediately you'll see the Rainbow on the right or west side of the road.

Other Camping Possibilities

We've spoken with people who have boondocked in the parking lot at the boat dock in Celustún. There is room for a few large rigs and a night watchman is on duty.

Side Trips from Mérida

Located north of Mérida on the road to Progreso the **Dzibilchaltún Ruins** are unusual because they were in use for such a long time, from 2000 BC until the arrival of the Spanish. They are largely unexcavated. There's a good museum. The Temple of the Seven Dolls has been restored and there is a Cenote where divers have recovered artifacts. The cenote is now used as a public swimming hole.

Celestún is located west of Mérida on the Gulf Coast in the Parque Natural del Flamingo. This is one of the places on the Yucatán to see flamingos, you must rent a boat and guide to do this. There's a nice building with restrooms, a store, and information displays at the landing. The flamingo-watching season is from November to March.

Progreso is a beach resort on the coast north of Mérida. The distance from Mérida is about 19 miles (30 km). The town has a malecón (beachside walkway) and good beaches. The water is so shallow here that there is a four-mile-long pier stretching out toward the north to allow ships to unload. It is a good side trip from town if you can't wait until you reach Cancún for a beach, and there are few fly-in tourists.

QUINTANA ROO COAST SOUTH OF CANCÚN, QUINTANA ROO
(KEEN-TAH-NUH ROW)

For purposes of this guide we define this area as starting near Puerto Morelos about 19 miles (31 km) south of Ciudad Cancún and running all the way south to Tulúm, which is about 75 miles (123 km) south of Ciudad Cancún. This coastal area is becoming increasingly popular as people discover that it offers a less crowded, less expensive, and much less developed alternative to Cancún.

The main town along the coast is **Playa del Carmen**. It is full of small hotels, good restaurants, small shops, and is the departure point for foot-passenger ferries to the Island of Cozumel. Playa del Carmen also has a Pemex station and a small supermarket so it is the supply center for campers not willing to trek north to Ciudad Cancún.

Smaller **Puerto Morelos**, much nearer to Ciudad Cancún, is another ferry departure point for Cozumel, this one for automobiles. Puerto Morelos has a couple of good restaurants but shopping is limited.

Along the coast from Puerto Morelos to Tulúm there are many resort communities, all with beaches and many open to the public with restaurants and limited shopping. They range from luxurious to almost undeveloped. Some of the larger ones are **Punta**

Bete, **Puerto Aventuras**, and **Akumal**. If you spend much time on the coast you'll probably explore them all.

Tulúm marks the south end of the developed section of coast. There's a Pemex and limited supplies here. If you head coastwards just south of the archeological site you'll find the Boca Paila Road which quickly becomes a gravel and sand track leading 35 miles (57 km) south to Punta Allen. You'll find many simple cabaña resorts for the first few miles.

There are so many campgrounds, beaches, towns and sights on the Quintana Roo coast that it can be difficult to organize them all in your mind. This listing of campgrounds will start with Paa Mul, probably the most popular campground along the coast. Then it will list the others, from north to south, along with their odometer readings from the intersection of the southern branch of Mex 180D and Mex 307 near Cancún. Addresses along the north-south highway use a kilometer marking system that runs from north to south, unfortunately the markings now on the highway start far south and get larger as you go north. To make things even more difficult the road has just been widened to four lanes to a point just south of Playa del Carmen. To avoid confusion we use the current kilometers markers and also give the distance south of the Mex 180D and Mex 307 interesection.

THE YUCATÁN PENINSULA

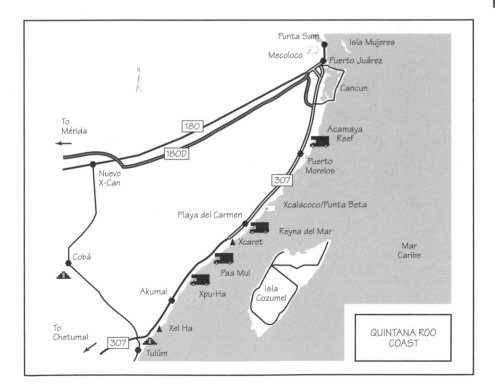

Quintana Roo Coast Campgrounds

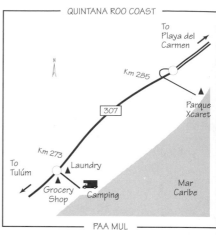

PAA MUL

Location:	Km 85 Carretera Cancún-Tulúm, Ciudad de Carmen, Q. Roo, México
Address:	705 Martens Ct. PMB 8-481, Laredo, TX 78041 (Reservations)
Telephone and Fax:	(9) 875-1051

GPS Location: N 20° 31' 22.5", W 087° 11' 36.2"

This campground is located right on the water. The bay in front is beautiful, it is well known for good snorkeling and has a nice beach. With full hookups and room for large rigs this is a popular place.

There are now about 120 spaces at Paa Mul, most with 15-amp outlets, water and sewer. The best spaces, 30 of them along the water, are occupied by people who rent them on an annual basis. This phenomenon, common on the Baja Peninsula and the west coast, is unusual here on the Yucatán. The North American RVers build semi-permanent roofs, patios, and sometimes walls enclosing their RV's. With most of the conveniences of a permanent building, some are so elaborate that you would be hard pressed to tell that there is really an RV inside. There are also nice motel-style rental rooms and cottages along the beach. Unfortunately, the RV sites available for rent are all back from the beach and have no views.

The resort has two clean restroom buildings, each with several hot water showers. There is also an open-air restaurant and bar overlooking the beach and an active dive shop with charter boats. English is spoken, you just have to find the right people. Out on the main road there are two small stores and a self-service laundromat.

Paa Mul is so self-contained that you may never need to leave it. It is popular with caravans because it has a combination of features not found at other parks on this coast. If you want to insure a spot you should make an advance reservation. Many people stay for several months.

You can walk north along a small road behind the beach for about two miles (3 km) from the campground. If you are seeking a quiet beach this is the place to find it. It's also a great place for a daily constitutional.

Paa Mul is located 41.3 miles (67.4 km) south of our reference point, the intersection of the southern branch of Mex 180D and Mex 307 near Cancún. It has hard-to-miss signage on the main road, turn toward the coast on a good paved road near the Km 273 marker and drive for .4 miles (.7 km).

The downside of this park is that the RVs are crowded together in what is essentially a sandy parking lot with little shade (the trees are getting bigger, however). The nicer spaces are reserved for the permanent residents and transients are relegated to the space between the permanent resident's palapas and the jungle. If you must have all of the conveniences, though, this is the place for you. Otherwise, read on.

ACAMAYA REEF MOTEL-CABAÑAS-CAMPING

Location: Km 29 Carretera Cancún-Chetumal, Quintana Roo, México
Address: Apdo 1510, Cancún, CP 77501, Quintana Roo, México
Telephone: (9) 871-0131   **Fax:** (9) 871-0132
E-mail: daisy@acamayareef.com
Web Site: www.acamayareef.com

GPS Location: N 20° 52' 22.4", W 086° 52' 01.3"

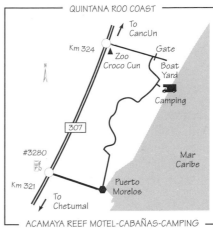

ACAMAYA REEF MOTEL-CABAÑAS-CAMPING

The Acamaya Reef is a small place sitting right next to a long, mostly deserted, open beach. It is relatively close to Cancún and within hiking distance (2 miles) of Puerto Morelos and its restaurants. An added benefit, especially for those with family joining them for the holidays, is that the Acamaya has a few clean, simple cabaña style rooms where the extra guests can comfortably be put up.

There are ten spaces, all with electricity and water. The outlets are 15-amp style but the breakers are 30 amp. There is an extra charge for the use of air conditioners. These are small spaces, to get 10 rigs in here they would all have to be van-size. All of the parking spots slope slightly so you'll have to work out an arrangement to level your vehicle.

There is a very clean restroom building with hot showers. A thatched shelter near the beach provides shade and there are scattered tables and chairs. A small restaurant is sometimes open.

The turn from Mex 307 is next to the well-signed Croco Cun crocodile farm near the Km 324 marker. It is 9.6 miles (15.7 km) south of the Mex 180D and Mex 307 intersection. You must make a U-turn if you are traveling south-bound. From the highway drive 1.3 miles (2.1 km) toward the beach on a paved but potholed road. Then turn right at the sign and follow an even poorer but passable road for another .3 miles (.5 km) to the campground. A road also runs behind condos and hotels north along the beach from the little town of Puerto Morelos, located a couple miles to the south. This road is pretty bad, vehicles should use the road from the highway.

REYNA DEL MAR ESTACIONAMIENTO

Address: Av. 6, Zona Federal Maritima y Av. 5, Playa del Carmen, Quintana Roo, México

This place has a bit of a split personality, it is labeled as a parking lot and charges a 24-hour

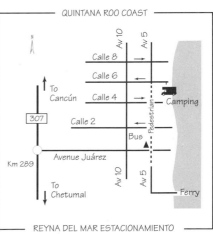

REYNA DEL MAR ESTACIONAMIENTO

THE YUCATÁN PENINSULA

parking fee, yet it is a camping area in one of the most desirable locations in Mexico: right on the beach in Playa del Carmen. It's hard to see how this will last very long, but it was in operation during the 2000/2001 winter season.

This is a fenced parking area, with electric hookups (15-amp). It is located right next to the beach in central Playa del Carmen. About 12 medium-size rigs can park with electricity, there are another eight or so sites without electricity. There's also a restroom with one toilet and a cold-water shower with no door. One faucet provides water and a dump station is promised but not yet available. Tent campers are welcome. Twenty-four hour security is advertised.

The campground is located where Avenida 6 reaches the beach. Since this is on the ocean side of the pedestrian walkway in town, and since Playa del Carmen has lots of one-way streets, it takes a roundabout route to get to the campground. Drive in to town on the main road, Av. Juárez from about Km 289 on the highway. Turn left on Av. 10 norte, that's the second road inland from the beach, it should be about the eighth crossroad from the highway. Drive four blocks and turn right on Av. 8. Now drive one block and turn right on Av. 5 Norte, this is the pedestrian walkway street but the walkway ends one block south. Drive one block, to the beginning of the pedestrian walkway, and turn left toward the ocean. You'll see the campground/parking area entrance on your right. If we were driving a big rig we'd scout the route and check the campground for a site before driving the big rig into the beach area.

XPU-HA CAMPGROUNDS (The X Beaches)

Location: Carretera Playa del Carmen-Tulum, Quintana Roo, México

GPS Location: N 20° 28' 15.2", W 087° 15' 32.3"

Some 46.6 miles (76.1 km) south of the intersection of Mex 307 and the southern branch of Mex 180D near Km 264 you will come upon several small roads running toward the beach. They are between the gates for the Copacabana and Robinson Club resorts. These roads provide access to a beautiful beach. Land along the beach is owned by various members of a Mayan family and is relatively undeveloped.

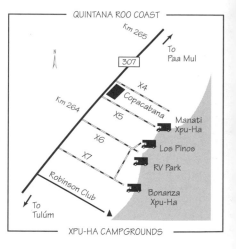

Rumors of buyers with suitcases of money are flying and there's no telling exactly what will be happening here when you arrive. When we last visited one area had been leased to a cruise company and they were building a restaurant that will attract busloads of visitors to this beautiful beach.

There are at least four different camping areas with facilities ranging from full hookups (always occupied by regulars) to boondocking sites on the sand. Low amperage electrical hookups are sometimes available and arrangements can be made for dumping using trolley tanks or buckets. Restrooms vary but most have flush toilets and cold showers.

The access road situation changes from year to year, as does signage. Roads may be marked for Bonanza Xpu-Ha, Los Pinos, Manati Xpu-Ha, X-4, X-5, X-6 or X-7. The best road in the near future will probably be the one for accessing the new restaurant (X-6), it should be suitable for any rig but maneuvering room will undoubtedly be tight, you should probably investigate in a smaller vehicle before driving a big rig in here.

Other Camping Possibilities

Playa Chemuyil and Playa Xcacel listed in our previous book are now closed.

At **Punta Beta** or Xcalcoco there are several small resorts with cabañas, restaurants, and a beautiful beach. Some of them have room for a few small RVs or for tent campers. The road to the beach where these campgrounds are located is 27.2 miles (44.4 km) south of the intersection of Mex 307 and the southern branch of Mex 180D near Km 295. The 1.3 mile long road is small and sometimes sandy with several Y's, each one with many signs pointing towards various establishments. You should find cold showers, no hookups, and a very relaxed ambiance.

Just south of the Tulúm archeological site there is a beachside cabaña city. It is known as **Camping Santa Fe**. There are dozens of thatched-roof huts and room for some van and tent camping with no hookups, cold showers and a few restaurants. Access is from the side road that runs toward the beach just south of the Tulúm archeological site (the Boca Paila Road). From Mex 307 drive east, at the T turn left and watch for the Don Armando Cabañas and Restaurant. Turn in here, bear left at the restaurant, the campground is just ahead. We've had reports of theft here so exercise caution.

THE XPU-HA BEACH

South along the Boca Paila Road there are a number of small resorts, some have room for vans and small RVs. Follow the side road that runs toward the beach just south of the Tulúm archeological site (the Boca Paila Road), and turn right. You'll immediately start seeing possibilities, you should stop and inquire if you see a place that looks interesting. Few have much in the way of facilities.

Side Trips from the Quintana Roo Coast

If you are a scuba diver you are probably well aware of the island of **Cozumel**. There are two Cozumels just as there are two Cancúns. One is a world-famous scuba diving destination making its living by catering to divers. The other is a port for cruise ships and everything that that implies. If you've never had the experience of traveling on a Caribbean cruise, you should know that the ports visited are generally tacky and expensive because they cater to the boatloads of passengers who come ashore for a few hours looking for souvenirs before moving on to another port. Cozumel is no exception. Don't plan on shopping here. Prices are actually quoted in U.S. dollars. If you want to dive, that's another story.

The easiest way to get to Cozumel is by ferry from Playa del Carmen. There are fast ferries running both ways every couple of hours, the trip takes about 45 minutes. The boat trip is a highlight for us, we've seen flying fish from the hydrofoil. To see them you should ride on deck, the fish launch themselves from the bow wave and fly for distances of over 50 yards before they splash in.

There are a number of what are known as eco-parks along the road south of Cancún. These include (from north to south) **Tres Rios**, **Xcaret**, **Kantun-Che**, **Actun-Chen Caves**, **Bahía Principe**, **Xel-Ha**, and **Hidden Worlds Cenotes**.

You'll want to visit **Xel-Ha**, it's not like anything you've seen elsewhere. It is a beautiful saltwater lagoon where you can actually watch tropical fish from the shore. It became so popular with snorkelers that it was declared a national park so that it wouldn't be destroyed. Extensive paved pathways have been built around the lagoon so you can easily walk around and watch the fish. Swimming is also allowed, in fact most people come here to snorkel. The inner lagoon is closed to swimming but a large part of the outer lagoon is open. If you are uneasy swimming in open water you may find that Xel-Ha is your favorite snorkeling site ever. Xel-Ha is located off Mex 307 near Km 245.

If you decide to visit **Xcaret** you had better set aside a whole day for it. Not only is there lots to keep you busy, it is so expensive that you will want to make them earn every cent. Here's what you can do. Float an underground river. Visit a wild bird breeding area. View a Mayan archeological site. Lie on the beach. Swim with a dolphin. Ride a horse. Tour a botanical garden. View tropical fish in an aquarium. Snorkel or scuba dive. Open from 8 a.m. to 5 p.m. Xcaret is located off Mex 307 between Playa del Carmen and Paa Mul.

Tulúm archeological site is famous not for the quantity or quality of its buildings (no pyramids) but for its setting. The site sits on a rocky bluff above the sea, it was one of the first Mayan cities discovered by the Spanish since they could actually see it from their ships when they sailed past. Probably the most common and beautiful photograph of Mexico is a shot of El Castillo (the watchtower) backed by dark blue Caribbean water.

Cobá is a very large site, actually covering more than 50 square miles, it is largely

TULÚM

unrestored. There are miles of hiking trails through the brush so if you like to hike, this is the place. Two large pyramids have been partially restored, stairs lead to the top. If you've come to like climbing pyramids you can visit both of them and not walk more than about 5 kilometers. After the crowds at Tulúm these ruins will seem empty, kind of nice. We know people who have boondocked in the parking lot here.

A huge area just south of the Cancún-Tulúm corridor has been set aside as a wildlife refuge called the **Sian Ka´an Biosphere Reserve**. Access is a little difficult but rewarding, especially for nature lovers. The rough unsurfaced Boca Paila Rd. running south from Tulúm to Punta Allen, a distance of 35 miles (57 km) is the best access. There's no gas so be sure to fill up before heading out, this road is slow going. This is a terrain of sand dunes, scrub jungle, and swampy lagoons. It is home to lots of birds and lots of mosquitoes. Also visit **Chunyaxché** archeological site on the main road (Mex 307) 27 miles (43 km) south of Tulúm. It sits at the edge of a lagoon and is surrounded by jungle.

UXMAL, YUCATÁN (OOSH-MAHL)

Uxmal is one of what we call the "big 4" archeological destinations in this part of Mexico. The others would be Chichén Itzá, Tulúm, and Palenque. They are included in the big 4 because they are important and interesting. They are also well-promoted and are visited by lots of tourists. This doesn't make them places to be avoided, just expect to see a lot more tourists than you have so far on this trip.

Almost everyone who visits Uxmal wants to see the "sound and light" show which is given every night at 8 p.m. For this reason many people think that they should camp at the ruins so they don't have to drive at night. See the camping section about this. We prefer to camp nearby and drive a small vehicle. We don't often break our no-night-driving rule, but this is one time we think it's OK.

Uxmal is in the center of a number of archeological sites, you will be missing a lot if you limit yourself to Uxmal only. Many people spend several days here and don't see all that they wish to. This is also a good area to do some bicycle touring. Services at Uxmal are limited but several hotels in the area do have decent restaurants.

Uxmal Campgrounds

🚐 CAMPING SACBE

Address:	Fam. Portillo, Apdo. 5, Ticul, CP 97860 Yucatán, México
Telephone:	(9) 955-9795
E-mail:	sacbehostel@hotmail.com

GPS Location: N 20° 19' 05.3", W 089° 38' 37.7"

This small family-run campground has a lot going for it. It is located 9 miles (14.5 km) south of Uxmal on Mex 261. This places it conveniently close to many of the other archeological sites that you will probably wish to visit while you are in the area.

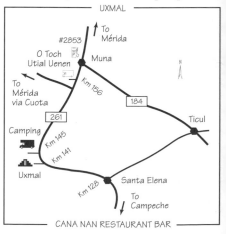

Sacbe has ten RV sites, six of them with 15-amp outlets (30-amp fuses) and sewer. Water is not available. The sites are large enough for big rigs and there is adequate maneuvering room. The bathroom facilities are in excellent condition and there are hot showers. The facilities are exceptionally clean and well maintained, as are the grounds.

The campground also has a very nice tent area with concrete picnic tables and palapas. There is a bulletin board with information about the bus service to the various sites. There are also maps and even a listing of birds that can be seen in the area. The owner will prepare meals if they are ordered ahead. English is spoken here.

🚐 CANA NAH RESTAURANT BAR

Location:	4 Kms Antes de Uxmal, Carretera a Muna, Yucatán, México
Telephone:	(9) 991-3889

GPS Location: N 20° 23' 53.3", W 089° 46' 04.9"

Four kilometers north of Uxmal on Mex 261 there is a restaurant with sites for four medium-sized rigs. Parking is on grass and is not quite level. There are two 15-amp duplex outlets and a water faucet. Restrooms were in good shape last time we visited with cold showers. The restaurant has a gift shop and a swimming pool.

Other Camping Possibilities

Many people dry camp in the parking lot at the **Uxmal archeological site**. The advantage of this is that you can walk to the sound and light show in the evening. There's a special area set aside for RV overnight parking, as you enter the archeological site you will see the gate to the right. It is chained at night. A nominal fee is charged.

North of Uxmal on Mex 261 on the southern outskirts of Muna there was a campground under construction when we drove through in January 2001. It was identified by a sign out front as **O Toan utial Uenen** The caretaker told us it will be "natural", which we interpret to mean there will be no hookups. Bathrooms were finished and looked good, they had cold showers. There was a swimming pool beginning to take shape. Parking slots had not been laid out and this may turn out to be a cabaña and tent place. The GPS location is N 20° 28' 32.9", W 089° 42' 55.9".

Side Trips from Uxmal

There are several smaller archeological sites located near Uxmal, a tour of them is known as the **Puuc Route**. They include **Kabah**, **Sayil**, **Xlapak**, and **Labná**. The roads to these sites are good and parking is uncrowded and fine for RVs so if you don't have a tow car you can easily use your RV for transportation.

Ticul, 18 miles (29 km) from Uxmal and 9 miles (14.7 km) from Camping Sacbe in Santa Elena is the place to go to buy shoes and replicas of Mayan artwork.

The **Loltún Caves**, 37 miles (60 km) from Uxmal and 27 miles (44 km) from Camping Sacbe in Santa Elena are the most impressive caves on the Yucatán. They have huge limestone chambers complete with stalagmites and stalactites and a Mayan wall carving. You are required to tour with one of the guides you will find there.

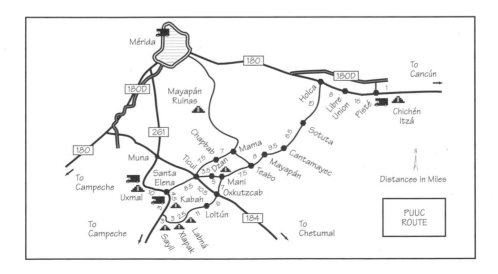

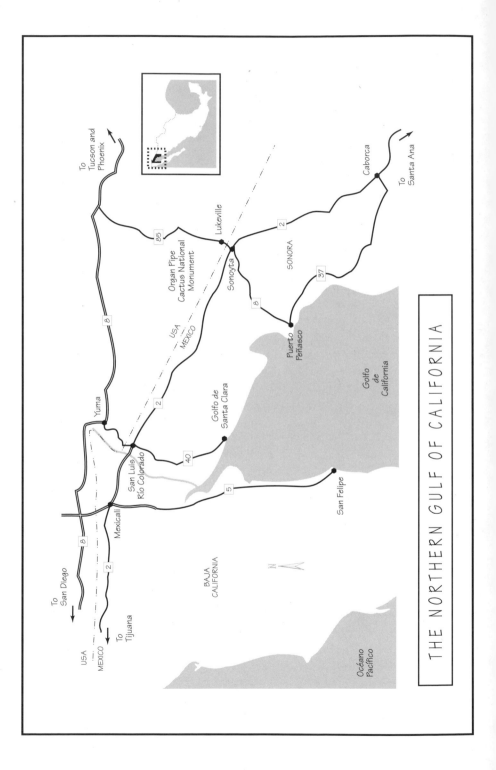

THE NORTHERN GULF OF CALIFORNIA

THE NORTHERN GULF OF CALIFORNIA

INTRODUCTION

The northern Gulf of California destinations: Puerto Peñasco, San Felipe, and Golfo de Santa Clara; are so close to the border, so easy to reach, and so full of Americans that you can almost consider them to be part of the U.S. Each of them can be reached by driving only a few hours south of the border on decent and mostly uncrowded two-lane roads.

Another great feature of these destinations is that they all fall within special zones in Mexico. Paperwork formalities are minimized, particularly regulations limiting the number of vehicles that you can bring south of the border. Off-roaders particularly appreciate these special rules. For details see the *Vehicle Documentation* heading in our *Crossing the Border* chapter.

The Sea of Cortez or Gulf of California is a long narrow body of water extending 700 miles (1,125 km) northward from the Tropic of Cancer which almost exactly traces a line between Cabo San Lucas and Mazatlán. The waters of the Sea or Gulf teem with fish and have some of the highest tides in the world. The northern reaches including the three towns featured in this chapter have a tidal range exceeding 20 feet between high and low water. This can be an interesting place to operate a boat.

Winter is probably the most pleasant time to visit this area because it is a desert area with extremely high temperatures during the summer, even along the water. Many people do visit in the summer, however, because that's when the fishing is best.

ROAD SYSTEM

All of these towns are within 110 miles (175 km) of each other as the crow flies, driving between them is another matter.

Puerto Peñasco is arguably the easiest of the three to reach. There is an excellent 61-mile (100 km) two-lane paved road running south from the Lukeville/Sonoyta border crossing. The crossing itself is excellent. It is uncrowded, has lots of room for RVs, and generally takes only a few minutes to negotiate. On the U.S. side of the border the roads are also pretty good, Hwy. 85 south from Interstate 8 is 80 miles (129 km) long and there are conveniently located campgrounds in the town of Lukeville and in the Organ Pipe Cactus National Monument. Mexican insurance is available in Lukeville. Vehicle-import permits are not necessary for a visit to Puerto Peñasco, tourist cards are available at the crossing.

Golfo de Santa Clara access is also easy. The closest crossing is at San Luis Río Colorado just south of Yuma, Arizona. Follow signs south and then southwest for Golfo de Santa Clara. The distance between the two towns is 70 miles (114 km). Like Puerto Peñasco, a visit to Golfo de Santa Clara requires no tourist cards or vehicle-import permits.

The closest crossing point for San Felipe is Calexico/Mexicali. This is a large town, the population approaches a million people, but it is not difficult to drive through. It has wide boulevards that make driving southeast from the central border crossing quite easy. You can get a vehicle-import permit here but you don't need it if you are heading south for San Felipe and the Baja. A tourist card, however, is necessary and should be picked up at the border crossing or in San Felipe. Many people do not do this and occasionally fines are levied during surprise inspections of San Felipe RV parks. The road south from Mexicali to San Felipe is 122 miles (200 km) long and takes about 3 hours to drive. Most if it is decent two-lane paved highway, some of the northern portion has four lanes. Many folks from southern California whip over to Mexicali on Interstate 8 for a quick weekend visit to San Felipe.

There are few additional roads in this region. Mex 2 runs just south of the U.S. border across the entire area, and is fine for local access, but it is generally two-lane and the heavy Mexican truck use that it receives is hard on the surface and makes driving some sections of it less than fun.

There is a newly-paved road that runs from Puerto Peñasco to Caborca, if you are approaching the area from the east you may want to give it a try rather than following Mex 2 all the way up to Sonoyta and then back down to Puerto Peñasco. Heading west you might want to have your tourist card and vehicle permit in hand since they are required.

HIGHLIGHTS

For folks accustomed to spending their winters in arid Arizona and New Mexico the highlights of this area are obvious, this is the closest salt water with its accompanying beaches and watersports. Californians find warmer winter weather and much better access to beaches and many watersports than they have back home. Fishing, sailing, and sailboarding are extremely popular. Added to that are huge areas to explore in off-road vehicles.

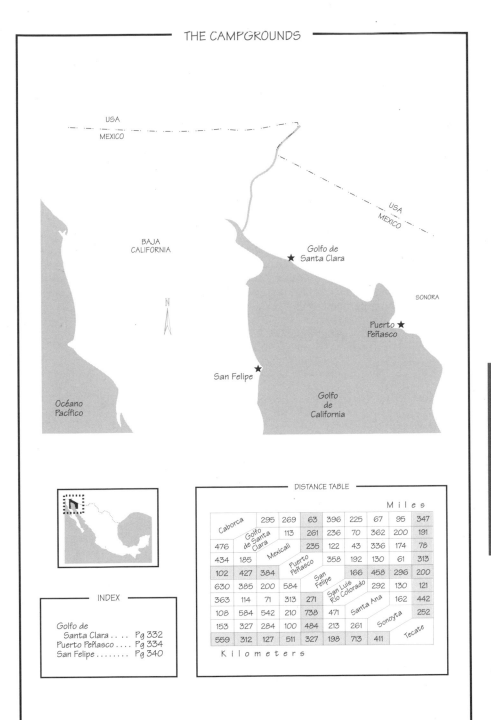

SELECTED CITIES AND THEIR CAMPGROUNDS

GOLFO DE SANTA CLARA (GOLF-OH DAY SAHN-TAW CLAW-RAH)
Population 1,500, Elevation sea level

If you are looking for a piece of the real outback Mexico with no tourist glitz Golfo de Santa Clara is the place for you. This is a small fishing village surrounded by miles and miles of sand. Most tourist guides don't even mention the town but it is becoming something of a popular camping destination. Recently a camping club took over the best campground in town, however, so your choices of campgrounds are limited if you are not a member. The beach south of town stretches for miles and ATVs are welcome.

Golfo de Santa Clara is built entirely on sand. This means that driving can be challenging. The streets in town aren't much of a problem, they are packed and if you are careful you aren't likely to get stuck, even with a big rig. The road out of town toward the cluster of campgrounds located a mile south on the beach is another story. This road is usually passable and big rigs, even fifth-wheels and 40-foot motorhomes can make it to the campgrounds if they do not slow and stop in the loose sand. Momentum is everything so stay to the part of the road that seems best and forge ahead! You might be smart to stop before starting down this road and see if other traffic is having problems, you can see almost the entire mile of soft sandy road straight ahead.

Golfo de Santa Clara Campgrounds

NUEVO EL GOLFO MOTEL

    Address: Av. Almejas y 1ra., Golfo de Santa Clara, Sonora, México
    Telephone: (6) 538-0221

GPS Location: N 31° 41' 20.0", W 114° 29' 58.6"

There are two campgrounds in town. These campgrounds have a big advantage, they can be reached without driving the sand road a mile south to where the other Santa Clara campgrounds are located. This can be important if the sand happens to be soft or if you are driving a big heavy rig.

There are three back-in slots behind the motel. They have full hookups with 30-amp outlets and are suitable for large rigs. The motel has toilets built for the camping area but no showers. They may let you use one of the showers at the motel. There's a laundry next door.

The motel is well signed so it is easy to find. Zero your odometer at the Pemex as you enter town. The left turn for the motel is at .1 mile (.2 km) on Almejas.

GOLFO RV PARK

    Telephone: (6) 538-0221

GPS Location: N 31° 41' 08.3", W 114° 29' 52.8"

This second campground in town is some distance from the motel but has the same owners.

There are 26 back-in slots with 30-amp outlets, sewer, and water on a gravel lot with

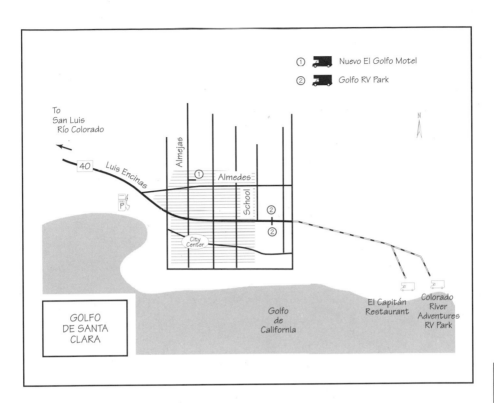

room for large rigs. There are no restroom facilities. When we visited a manager was living on site.

To find the RV park zero your odometer as you come to the Pemex at the entrance to town. Continue straight on the pavement for .2 miles (.3 km), the park is on both sides of the road and you reach it just before you reach the end of the pavement.

Other Camping Possibilities

There is an RV park about a mile south of town on the beach. We stayed there several years ago, it had a great location but terrible facilities. The new operator has improved the facilities so this is probably the best place in Golfo. It is operated by **Colorado River Adventures**, a camping club with 5 campgrounds along the lower Colorado River. You must be a member to stay there. They are affiliated with Coast to Coast so members of that organization may also find a spot. Call (760) 663-4941 to check.

Also out the road to the south **is El Capitán Restaurant**. This place has a restaurant and places to park with no hookups except perhaps some very low amperage electricity. On weekends and holidays it can be very popular with folks from San Luis Río Colorado and Mexicali. During the week, however, it is usually very quiet and a decent place to stay.

PUERTO PEÑASCO (PWEHR-TOE PEN-YAHS-KOE)
Population 13,000, Elevation sea level

Many Mexico travel guides ignore Puerto Peñasco as if it weren't even part of Mexico. This attitude is understandable, the town really does have a great deal of American influence. To ignore Puerto Peñasco in a camping guide to Mexico would be something of a crime, however. RVers virtually own this town, hordes of them fill RV parks and boondock in the vicinity. On weekends and holidays Puerto Peñasco is even more popular. After all, it is only a little over an hour's driving time south of the Arizona border, it is located in a free zone requiring little governmental paperwork, and there are beaches, desert, fishing, and Mexican crafts and food. Don't forget to pick up Mexican auto insurance, however.

Americans often call the town Rocky Point, you'll see why when you see the location of the old town. The road to Rocky Point was built by the American government during World War II when it was thought that it might be necessary to bring in supplies this way if the west coast was blockaded by Japanese submarines. That never happened, but the road, now paved and in good shape, makes the town easy to reach. Puerto Peñasco is also a fishing port, not everything here is tourist oriented.

Campgrounds are located in three areas: most are along the beach to the east of the old town, two others are along the beach to the northwest. Some campgrounds are also starting to appear along the main highway north of town. Boondockers congregate farther west toward La Choya on Sandy Beach and north of La Choya. There is lots of talk of major tourist developments in Rocky Point in the next few years, perhaps even with a golf course. Supplies of all kinds are available, but no large supermarkets have appeared yet.

Puerto Peñasco Campgrounds

PLAYA BONITA RV PARK

| Address: | 147 Balboa Blvd. (Apdo. 34), Puerto Peñasco, Sonora, México |
| Telephone: | (6) 383-2596 or 800 569-2586 (U.S. Res) |

GPS Location: N 31° 19' 06.4", W 113° 33' 15.9"

This is the larger of two trailer parks located northwest of town on Playa Bonita. The Playa Bonita RV Park is affiliated with a nice hotel next door.

There are 300 spaces in this huge campground. All are back-in slots with 30-amp outlets, sewer, water, and satellite TV connections. Restrooms are modern and clean and have hot water. The campground has a small recreation room with a TV, a self-service laundry, and the affiliated hotel next door has a restaurant. The beach out front is beautiful.

As you enter town you will pass two Pemexes, the first on the left and then one on the right. A half-mile (.8 km) after the second Pemex is a crossroad marked with many large green signs over the road. Turn right here on Calle 13. Proceed across the railroad tracks and drive for .3 mile (.5 km), turn right on sandy Armada Nacional. The turn is marked with a sign for the campground. Drive up this road for .9 miles (1.5 km) to the gate of the trailer park.

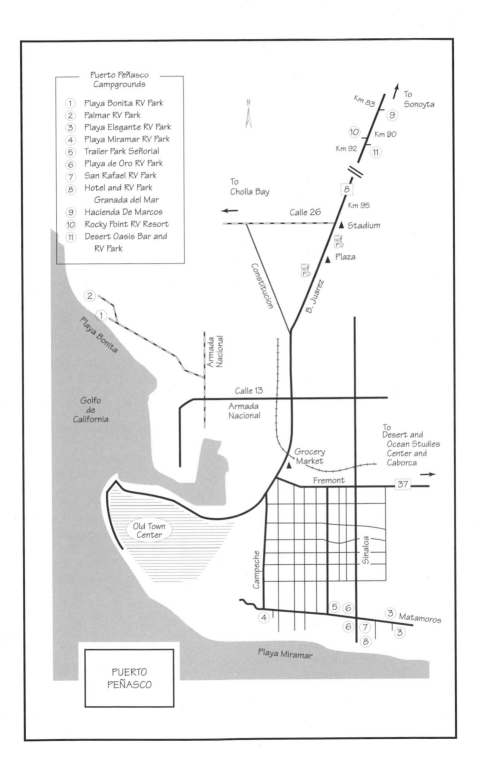

Puerto Peñasco
Campgrounds

1 Playa Bonita RV Park
2 Palmar RV Park
3 Playa Elegante RV Park
4 Playa Miramar RV Park
5 Trailer Park Señorial
6 Playa de Oro RV Park
7 San Rafael RV Park
8 Hotel and RV Park
    Granada del Mar
9 Hacienda De Marcos
10 Rocky Point RV Resort
11 Desert Oasis Bar and
    RV Park

N

To
Sonoyta

Km 83

9

10   Km 90

Km 92   11

8

To
Cholla Bay

Calle 26

Km 95

Stadium

Plaza

Constitucion

B. Juarez

2

1

Playa Bonita

Armada
Nacional

Golfo
de
California

Calle 13

Armada
Nacional

To
Desert and
Ocean Studies
Center and
Caborca

Grocery
Market

Fremont

37

Old Town
Center

Campeche

Sinaloa

5 6

3 Matamoros

6 7

4

8   3

Playa Miramar

PUERTO
PEÑASCO

NORTHERN GULF OF CALIFORNIA

PALMAR RV PARK

Address:	348 Balboa Blvd (Apdo. 24), Puerto Peñasco, CP 83550 Sonora, México
Telephone:	(6) 383-6633

GPS Location: N 31° 19' 12.7", W 113° 33' 49.1"

This is the second trailer park on Playa Bonita. It's a large, well-run park with only one disadvantage, no electricity.

The campground has about 150 generously-sized spaces, 100 of these have sewer and water hookups. The restrooms are modern and clean, they have hot water showers that cost a dollar. There is also a meeting room. The beach in front is very nice.

To reach the campground follow the instructions for finding the Playa Bonita given above. Just before you reach the Playa Bonita gate you will see a sign pointing right to a road running around the Playa Bonita. Follow this another .5 mile (.8 km) to the Palmar.

PLAYA ELEGANTE RV PARK

Address:	91 Matamoros Ave., Puerto Peñasco, Sonora, México
Res.:	P.O. Box 56, Lukeville, AZ 85341
Telephone:	(6) 383-3712　　　　**Fax:** (6) 383-6071
E-mail:	elegante@infotech.net.mx

GPS Location: N 31° 17' 45.5", W 113° 31' 54.2"

The Playa Elegante is the farthest-east trailer park in the look-alike group clustered along Calle Matamoros on the oceanfront east of the old town. It is a large beach-fronting campground with easy access. There is another section of the campground located a short distance away, not along the water.

The campground has 350 spaces. They are all back-in slots with 30-amp outlets, sewer, water, and satellite TV hookups. None of the spaces has a patio or shade, they all have a gravel parking surface. The bathrooms are in the main building which also houses a self-service laundry and meeting room. The bathrooms are modern and clean and have metered hot showers, they cost a quarter. There is a sun deck on the top of the main building, the beach is better for sun but the deck offers a good view. This campground also has a boat ramp. English is spoken.

To reach the campground when approaching Puerto Peñasco from the north on Mex 8 zero your odometer as you pass the airport. At 1.3 miles (2.1 km) you'll enter Puerto Peñasco, at 2 miles (3.2 km) you'll see the town square on the left, at 3.1 miles (5 km) you'll cross Armada Nacional Avenue/Hidalgo which is marked with cluster of green overhead signs. At a stoplight at 3.5 miles (5.6 km) Fremont Boulevard cuts off to the left, this is Son 37 to Caborca. Continuing straight and bear left at the Y at 3.6 miles (5.8 km) and at 4.1 miles (6.6 km) you'll reach Matamoros Ave. which runs east and west along the beach. Turn left here and pass a series of campgrounds and finally reach the right turn for the Playa Elegante at 4.7 miles (7.6 km). The campground is just down the road toward the water and to the left, the entrance is obvious.

If you are approaching from Caborca on Son 37 watch carefully as you enter town. You'll see a paved road with wide shoulders on the left that is well marked with campground signs. This is Sinaloa, if you turn here you'll soon reach the beach and can make a left and then a right to reach the Playa Elegante. The other Calle Matamoros campgrounds are to the right stretching westward along the beach.

CAMPING ON THE BEACH AT PLAYA BONITA

NORTHERN GULF OF CALIFORNIA

🚐 PLAYA MIRAMAR RV PARK

Address:	27 Matamoros Ave. (Apdo. 2), Puerto Peñasco, CP 83550 Sonora, México
Res.:	P.O. Box 456, Lukeville, AZ 85341
Telephone:	(6) 383-2587 **Fax:** (6) 383-2351

GPS Location: N 31° 17' 52.4", W 113° 32' 25.2"

This is the last (or first) of the three big RV parks between Ave. Matamoros (Calle 1) and the beach. The Playa Miramar has 146 spaces, all are back-in with 30-amp electricity, sewer, water and satellite TV. The restrooms are very clean and have hot water for showers that are metered and cost a quarter. There is a recreation room and a laundry. This campground is close to the base of the big rock that gives Rocky Point it's name, as a result there is no sandy beach, instead the shoreline is made up of bowling ball-sized black rocks. English is spoken.

If you follow the instructions given above for reaching the Playa Elegante Trailer Park the Playa Miramar is the first trailer park you'll see after turning onto Matamoros. It is on the right.

🚐 TRAILER PARK SEÑORIAL

Address:	Apdo. 76, Puerto Peñasco, CP 83550 Sonora, México
Telephone:	(6) 383-3530

GPS Location: N 31° 17' 50.6", W 113° 32' 10.7"

The Trailer Park Señorial is located just across the street and slightly west of the Playa de Oro and has the same owners. It is a smaller park and has a swimming pool to make up for the fact that it is not on the beach. Many of the spaces are filled with rigs that appear to be permanently located.

The campground has 65 spaces. All are back-in slots with 30-amp outlets, water, and sewer. The parking pads are cement but there are no patios or shade. The bathrooms are clean and in good repair, the showers are hot and require a $.25 payment. The swimming pool sits at the upper end of the campground and is quite nice. There's also a laundry.

To find the campground follow the instructions given for the Playa Elegante above. After turning left onto Matamoros proceed .3 miles (.5 km), you'll see the Playa de Oro entrance on the left.

PLAYA DE ORO RV PARK

Address: 60 Matamoros Ave (Apdo. 76), Puerto Peñasco, CP 83550 Sonora, México
Telephone: (6) 383-2668

GPS Location: N 31° 17' 51.6", W 113° 32' 06.7"

This huge campground is one of the oldest ones in Puerto Peñasco. It bills itself as the only full service RV park in Rocky Point. This is somewhat true, the campground does have many amenities, but is also is showing it's age in some ways.

There are now 350 spaces at the Playa de Oro. They are located south of Matamoros Ave. along and back from the beach and also extending well inland to the north of Matamoros. The sites have 30-amp electricity, sewer, and water. They have gravel surfaces, no shade, and no patios. The bathrooms are older but clean, the showers require a quarter for 4 to 5 minutes and the hot water was intermittent when we visited. The campground has a small, simple restaurant, a mini-mart, a self-service laundry, and a boat ramp. There is also a large long-term storage yard for those wishing to leave a trailer or boat when they go back north.

To find the campground follow the instructions given for the Playa Elegante above. After turning left onto Matamoros proceed .4 miles (.6 km), you'll see the Playa de Oro entrance on the right.

SAN RAFAEL RV PARK

Address: Apdo. 58, Puerto Peñasco, CP 83550 Sonora, México
Telephone: (6) 383-5044, (6) 383-2681

GPS Location: N 31° 17' 48.7", W 113° 31' 58.0"

This is a smaller campground with no beachfront sites even though it is south of Calle Matamoros.

The campground has 53 slots, all have 30-amp outlets, sewer, and water. These are gravel-surfaced back-in spaces without patios or shade. The campground has clean modern restrooms with hot showers, a TV room, a self-service laundry, and English is spoken.

To find the campground follow the instructions given for the Playa Elegante above. After turning left onto Matamoros proceed .5 miles (.8 km), you'll see the San Rafael entrance on the right.

⛺ HOTEL AND RV PARK GRANADA DEL MAR

Address: 41 Durango Ave., Puerto Peñasco, Sonora, México
Res.:   PO Box 30806, Tucson, AZ 85751
Telephone: (6) 383-2742

GPS Location: N 31° 17' 46.8", W 113° 32' 01.5"

The Granada del Mar is a new trailer park in Puerto Peñasco, it occupies the beach in front of the San Rafael and also some of the beach in front of the Playa de Oro. The trailer park is an addition to a hotel that has occupied the site for some time.

The campground has 40 back-in spaces, they all have 30-amp electricity, sewer, and water. These spaces have the customary Puerto Peñasco gravel surface with no patio or shade. About a third are beachfront sites. The small bathroom cubicles are new and clean and have hot water. There is a bar/disco on the water to the west of the hotel building that serves some food and is popular with the younger folks from this park and also the Playa de Oro next door.

To find the campground follow the instructions given for the Playa Elegante above. After turning left onto Matamoros proceed .5 miles (.8 km), you'll see the San Rafael entrance on the right. Turn right down the street just before the San Rafael, the Granada is at the end of the street next to the water.

⛺ HACIENDA DE MARCOS

Res.:   PO Box 379, Lukeville, AZ 85341
Telephone: (6) 385-1030

GPS Location: N 31° 25' 36.2", W 113° 28' 09.1"

This new campground is located north of town on the road to Sonoyta. If you are looking for a small friendly place you should stop in here.

The campground has 9 back-in spaces with full hookups (50 and 30-amp outlets) and another 32 or so with water and sewer only. There's a laundry and restrooms are modern and clean with flush toilets and hot water showers. The owner/managers are from north of the border.

The Hacienda De Marcos is located on the east side of Mex 8 some 7.5 miles (12 km) north of Puerto Peñasco.

⛺ ROCKY POINT RV RESORT

Address: Carr. Sonoyta-Peñasco Km 91.5,
                Puerto Peñasco, Sonora, México

GPS Location: N 31° 22' 05.4", W113° 30' 28.8"

The campground is located right in the middle of barren desert north of Puerto Peñasco. There are 28 large pull-through spaces, each with 15-amp outlets, sewer, water and satellite TV hookups. The restrooms are clean with hot showers. There is a recreation room and a self-service laundry. The campground is fenced and there is 24-hour security.

You'll find the campground on the west side of Mex 8 some 2.7 miles (4.4 km) north of Puerto Peñasco.

NORTHERN GULF OF CALIFORNIA

▭ DESERT OASIS BAR AND RV PARK

Address: Carr. Sonoyta-Peñasco Km 91, Puerto Peñasco, Sonora, México
Telephone: (6) 385-2961

GPS Location: N 31° 21' 51.8", W 113° 30' 27.6"

This is a modern campground that was in use but still under construction when we visited. There's a nice bar/restaurant here and the facility was in use as a checkpoint for an off-road race. The facilities are nice and this might be a good place to stay if you don't mind being a bit removed from the water and town.

The campground has 50 back-in spaces with full hookups. Power outlets are 30-amp and parking is on gravel. The restrooms have hot showers and flush toilets. There is no shade in the RV park.

The park is located at Km 91 which is 2.5 miles (4 km) north of Puerto Peñasco.

Other Camping Possibilities

About 4 miles (6 km) east of town on the road to Cholla Bay is **Sandy Beach**, a popular free camping area, especially for ATV owners.

SAN FELIPE (SAHN FAY-LEE-PAY)
Population 15,000, Elevation sea level

Although San Felipe is a Baja town its location in the far northeast portion of the peninsula means that it is not normally part of a visit to the peninsula's destinations farther south. That doesn't mean that this isn't a popular place, like Puerto Peñasco this town is full of Americans looking for easily accessible sun and sand. The majority of them seem to be RVers.

In many ways San Felipe and Puerto Peñasco are very similar. Both are small towns at the north end of the Gulf of California pretty much devoted to RV tourism. Both are probably on the cusp of a development boom, both need a golf course or two to really become big-time tourist resort areas. It is beginning to look like the folks in Puerto Peñasco will get their golf course first and that's fine, San Felipe can retain its dusty, small-town, no-big-money charm for a while longer.

Most of the action in San Felipe is found along its **malecón** (waterfront promenade) and the street one block inland - Mar de Cortez. Overlooking the malecón and the strip of sandy beach that fronts it is Cerro El Machorro, a tall rock with a shrine to the Virgin de Guadalupe at its top. This is a great place for photo. The bay in front of town goes dry at low tide, the panga fishermen who use the beach launch and retrieve their boats by driving out on the solid sand. Several of the campgrounds are located along the southern extension of Mar de Cortez so strolling in to central San Felipe is very easy. The town has a selection of decent restaurants and small shops as well as two Pemex stations.

Most of the important streets in town are paved and the rest present no driving problems. Watch for stop signs, however. They are in unexpected places. Sometimes the smallest dusty side street has priority over a main arterial.

It seems like San Felipe always has some kind of celebration in the works. The **San**

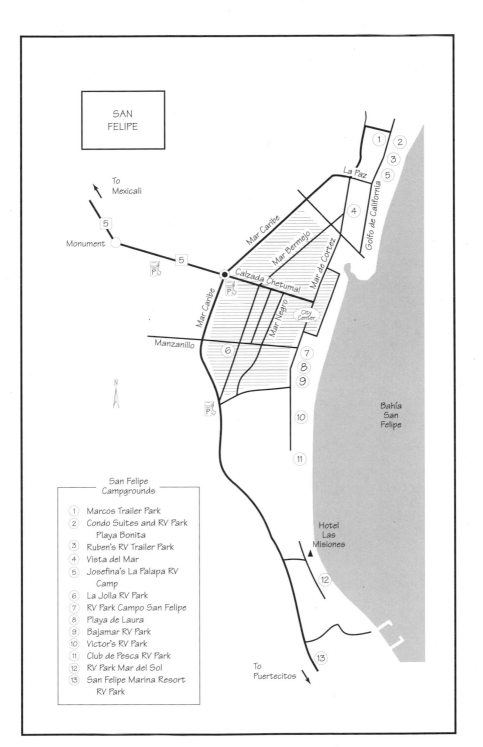

SAN FELIPE

To Mexicali

5

Monument

5

Calzada Chetumal

Mar Caribe

Mar Caribe

Mar Bermejo

Mar Negro

Mar de Cortez

La Paz

Golfo de California

City Center

Manzanillo

Bahía San Felipe

Hotel Las Misiones

To Puertecitos

N

1
2
3
5
4
6
7
8
9
10
11
12
13

San Felipe Campgrounds

1 Marcos Trailer Park
2 Condo Suites and RV Park Playa Bonita
3 Ruben's RV Trailer Park
4 Vista del Mar
5 Josefina's La Palapa RV Camp
6 La Jolla RV Park
7 RV Park Campo San Felipe
8 Playa de Laura
9 Bajamar RV Park
10 Victor's RV Park
11 Club de Pesca RV Park
12 RV Park Mar del Sol
13 San Felipe Marina Resort RV Park

THE WATERFRONT IN DOWNTOWN SAN FELIPE

Felipe 250 is a big off-road race at the end of March. Just before the off-road race is the **Mid-Winter West Hobie Cat Regatta**. Like many Mexican ports San Felipe celebrates **Carnival** (Mardi Gras) at the appropriate time in late February or early March. **Spring Break** is big here, just as on the rest of the peninsula, it happens during the third and fourth weeks of March. **Semana Santa**, the week up to and including Easter, is a big Mexican beach holiday and San Felipe is very popular as it hosts a number of sporting events. During the summer the town celebrates **Día de la Marina** on June 1. And in November there's the **Shrimp Festival**, one of the biggest celebrations of the year in San Felipe.

San Felipe Campgrounds

▣ **Marcos Trailer Park**

Address:	Av. Golfo de California 788, San Felipe, B.C., México
Telephone:	(6) 577-1875

GPS Location: N 31° 02' 08.6", W 114° 49' 42.5"

Marcos isn't on the water and all San Felipe campers seem to want to be in a campground next to the beach, even if they're parked so far back that they never see the water. Nonetheless Marcos succeeds in staying relatively full, perhaps because it is *almost* next to the beach.

There are 20 back-in spaces arranged around the perimeter of the campground. There is lots of room in the middle of the campground but large rigs have some difficulty parking because the lot slopes and the leveled parking pads aren't very long. Each space has 15-amp outlets, sewer, water, and a nice little covered patio. There is even a little shrubbery to separate the sites, unusual in San Felipe. The restrooms are old but clean and in good repair, they have hot water showers. There is a small meeting room with a library and a sun deck on top.

From the glorieta (traffic circle) at the entrance to town take the road that leads northeast. This is Mar Caribe Norte and is the road to the left as you come from Mexicali. It will curve to the right at .8 miles (1.3 km) and come to a T at 1 mile (1.6 km). Turn left and you'll see the entrance to the campground on the left in one block.

⛺ CONDO SUITES AND RV PARK PLAYA BONITA

Address: 475 E. Badillo Street, Covina, Cal. 91723 (Reservations)
Telephone: (6) 577-1215 (Mex), (818) 967-8977 (U.S.)

GPS Location: N 31° 02' 08.6", W 114° 49' 42.5"

This is another beachfront campground at the north end of town. Some day the campground may be replaced by condo suites, but so far only one building has been completed and it cohabits peacefully with the RVs and trailers.

There are 36 camping spaces in this campground. Ten are large back-in spaces with 30-amp outlets, sewer and water. Another 26 spaces are suitable only for vans, tents or small trailers. Most of these smaller spaces have electricity, sewer, and water. All spaces have paved patios with palapa-style roofs and picnic tables. The restrooms are older and rustic, the showers were barely warm when we visited. There's a nice beach out front.

From the glorieta (traffic circle) at the entrance to town take the road that leads northeast. This is Mar Caribe Norte and is the road to the left as you come from Mexicali. It will curve to the right at .8 miles (1.3 km) and come to a T at 1 mile (1.6 km). Turn left and you'll see the entrance to the campground on the right across from Marco's.

⛺ RUBEN'S RV TRAILER PARK

Address: Apdo. 59, San Felipe, CP 21850 B.C., México
Telephone: (6) 577-1442

GPS Location: N 31° 02' 03.6", W 114° 49' 43.0"

Ruben's is well known in San Felipe for its two-story patios. These are very popular with tenters during the Mexican holidays, it is easy to enclose the patio below and use the roof for added room. Some people think the two-story patios give the crowded campground the atmosphere of a parking garage but Ruben's remains a popular beachfront campground. There's always a lot of activity at this place, maybe too much.

There are 45 camping spaces, all with 15-amp outlets, sewer and water. Most spaces are small and maneuvering room is scarce. The restrooms are adequate and have hot water showers. There is also a well-liked bar/restaurant. The campground has a boat ramp and also a special rig for launching boats at low tide.

From the glorieta (traffic circle) at the entrance to town take the road that leads northeast. This is Mar Caribe Norte and is the road to the left as you come from Mexicali. It will curve to the right at .8 miles (1.3 km) and come to a T at 1 mile (1.6 km). Turn left and you'll almost immediately see the two entrances to Ruben's on the right.

VISTA DEL MAR

Address: 601 Ave. de Cortez, San Felipe, B.C., México

GPS Location: N 31° 01' 49.7", W 114° 49' 51.2"

The Vista del Mar is another campground suffering from a location far from the water. The facility is really very good, but often virtually empty.

There are 21 back-in spaces arranged on both sides of a sloping lot with a view of the ocean and hills to the north of town. Each space has 15 and 30-amp outlets, sewer, and water. Large rigs will have trouble parking because the level parking pad is not very long. The entire campground is paved, much of it with attractive reddish bricks. Each campsite has a tile-roofed patio with a table and barbecue. The restrooms are spic-and-span and have hot water showers. At the upper end of the campground is a group barbecue area.

From the glorieta (traffic circle) at the entrance to town take the road that leads northeast. This is Mar Caribe Norte and is the road to the left as you come from Mexicali. It will curve to the right at .8 miles (1.3 km). You must take the turn to the right at .9 miles (1.4 km) just before the fenced sports field, the campground is a short way up the hill on the left.

JOSEFINA'S LA PALAPA RV CAMP

GPS Location: N 31° 01' 52.5", W 114° 49' 41.6"

This little trailer park is located right next to the much better known Ruben's. At first glance it even looks like Rubens, it has some of the same two-story palapas. It's much quieter, however.

There are 22 spaces in this park. Six are along the front next to the beach. Most spaces are really van-size or short-trailer-size but a few will take large rigs. The camping slots have 15 or 30-amp outlets, sewer, water, and paved patios with a roof serviced by a ladder. You can use them for the view or pitch a tent up there. The bathrooms are old and need maintenance, they have hot water showers.

From the glorieta (traffic circle) at the entrance to town take the road that leads northeast. This is Mar Caribe Norte and is the road to the left as you come from Mexicali. It will curve to the right at .8 miles (1.3 km) and come to a T at 1 mile (1.6 km). Turn left and the campground will be on the right almost immediately, the sign is very small.

LA JOLLA RV PARK

Address: 300 Mar Bermejo, San Felipe, B.C., México
Res.:   P.O. Box 9019, Calexico, CA 92232
Telephone: (6) 577-1222

GPS Location: N 31° 01' 11.0", W 114° 50' 28.6"

The La Jolla isn't on the beach and suffers as a result. It is a friendly, well-run place and has spaces available when the campgrounds on the beach are full. If you want a quieter atmosphere you might give this place a try.

There are 55 camp sites, each with 15-amp outlets, sewer, water, and covered patios. These are pull-through spaces. Unfortunately they are closely spaced and do not have

(sidebar, left margin): NORTHERN GULF OF CALIFORNIA

room for modern slide-outs. Only the end spaces are suitable for wider rigs. The restrooms are in a simple cement block building with an unfinished interior but are in good condition and have hot water showers that are metered and cost a quarter. The La Jolla has a nice new swimming pool and hot tub. English is spoken.

As you enter town zero your odometer at the glorieta (traffic circle). Turn right toward the airport and drive .4 miles (6 km) to a stop sign at Manzanillo. Turn left and drive about .2 miles (.3 km) and you'll see the La Jolla on the right.

RV PARK CAMPO SAN FELIPE

Address:	Ave. Mar de Cortez #301, San Felipe, B.C., México
Mail:	P.O. Box 952, Calexico, CA 92232
Telephone:	(6) 577-1012

GPS Location: N 31° 01' 04.7", W 114° 50' 08.6"

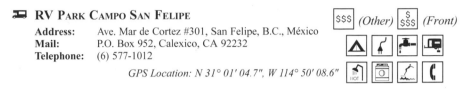

You'll find the San Felipe to be very much like the Playa de Laura next door but in much better condition. It has the distinction of being the closest campground to central San Felipe.

The campsites are arranged in several rows parallel to the beach, the closer to the beach you are the more you pay. Thirty-four sites have 30-amp outlets, sewer, water, and covered patios with tables. Most are pull-throughs. Another 5 are small and have sewer and water only. The restrooms are clean and in good repair, they have hot water showers. There is a handy telephone next to the office. English is spoken.

As you enter town zero your odometer at the glorieta (traffic circle). Turn right toward the airport and drive .8 miles (1.3 km) to the Pemex. Turn left here and drive down the hill toward the beach. You'll come to a T at 1.2 miles (1.9 km). Turn left and almost immediately you'll see the Campo San Felipe on the right in .2 miles (.4 km).

PLAYA DE LAURA

Address:	P.O. Box 549, Calexico, CA 92232 (U.S.)
Telephone:	6) 577-1128

GPS Location: N 31° 01' 03.4", W 114° 50' 06.3"

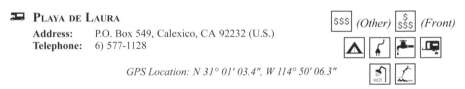

This older RV park doesn't seem to have been kept up to quite the same standards as the ones on either side. Still, it has a good location and is quite popular.

Forty-three campsites are arranged in rows running parallel to the beach. The front row is really packed and limits beach access by campers in the rows farther from the beach. Pricing varies with beach slots much more expensive than those farther back. Each camping spaces have 15-amp outlets, water and covered patios with tables and barbecues. Many have sewer hookups. Most of the spaces are pull-throughs. Restrooms are older and need maintenance, they have hot water showers.

As you enter town zero your odometer at the glorieta (traffic circle). Turn right toward the airport and drive .8 miles (1.3 km) to the Pemex. Turn left here and drive down the hill toward the beach. You'll come to a T at 1.2 miles (1.9 km). Turn left and almost immediately you'll see the Playa de Laura on the right in .2 miles (.3 km).

NORTHERN GULF OF CALIFORNIA

☵ BAJAMAR RV PARK

Address:	Av. Mar de Cortez s/n, San Felipe, B.C., México
Telephone:	(6) 553-2363 (Res.)
Fax:	(6) 563-1360 (Res.)

$$$ *(Other)* $$$ *(Front)*

GPS Location: N 31° 01' 05.8", W 114° 50' 10.5"

The Bajamar is the newest of the downtown San Felipe campgrounds. Rather than having rows of sites on sand, this campground has large back-in spaces off paved access roads. It's on a nice beach and you have convenient strolling access to central San Felipe.

There are 60 full-service spaces with 30-amp breakers (15-amp outlets however), sewer, and water. The central access roads are paved with curbs and the parking pads are gravel with patios, some have sun shades. This campground has left the waterfront open so that it can be enjoyed by all of the residents, there is a large patio with a palapa there and some small tables with umbrellas on the sand. The Bajamar has a much less crowded feel than the other campgrounds in this area. The campground has no apparent permanents yet. Restrooms are new and clean and have hot water showers. There is a self-service laundry and a playground.

As you enter town zero your odometer at the glorieta (traffic circle). Turn right toward the airport and drive .8 miles (1.3 km) to the Pemex. Turn left here and drive down the hill toward the beach. You'll come to a T at 1.2 miles (1.9 km). Turn left and almost immediately you'll see the Bajamar on the right.

☵ VICTOR'S RV PARK

Address:	PO Box 1227, Calexico, CA (Res.)
Telephone:	(6) 577-1056

$$$

GPS Location: N 31° 00' 48.6", W 114° 50' 11.7"

This 50-space campground is older with a lot of permanently located or long-term rigs. A few slots are available for daily rent. It is jointly run with the El Cortez Motel located just next door so the facilities are really pretty good for such a small park.

Victor's parking slots have 30-amp outlets, sewer, and water. Each space has a covered patio. The restrooms are clean and showers have hot water. The campground has a meeting room near the front next to the beach and the motel next door has a swimming pool and restaurant for the use of campground residents. There is also a laundry. This campground is fully fenced, even along the beach, and has an attendant.

As you enter town zero your odometer at the glorieta (traffic circle). Turn right toward the airport and drive .8 miles (1.3 km) to the Pemex. Turn left here and drive down the hill toward the beach. You'll come to a T at 1.2 miles (1.9 km). Turn right and almost immediately you'll see Victor's on your left.

☵ CLUB DE PESCA RV PARK

Address:	P.O. Box 3090, Calexico, CA 92232
Telephone:	(6) 577-1180
Fax:	(6) 577-1888
E-mail:	clubdepesca@canela.sanfelipe.com.mx

$$$ *(Other)* $$$ *(Front)*

GPS Location: N 31° 00' 47.7", W 114° 50' 08.4"

This is an old San Felipe favorite. The campground has many permanents, but also some choice slots for smaller rigs along the ocean and others toward the rear of the park.

There are 32 slots along the beach with 30-amp outlets and water but no sewer hookups. These spaces are paved and have palapas. We've seen rigs to 34 feet in them but usually only shorter rigs park here. At the rear of the park are 22 slots with 15-amp outlets, sewer, and water. Larger rigs fit here better. Restrooms are neat and clean and have hot water showers. There is a small grocery store and a room with a ping-pong table next to the beach dividing the beachside sites.

As you enter town zero your odometer at the glorieta (traffic circle). Turn right toward the airport and drive .8 miles (1.3 km) to the Pemex. Turn left here and drive down the hill toward the beach. You'll come to a T at 1.2 miles (1.9 km). Turn right and you'll find the Club de Pesca at the end of the road.

RV PARK MAR DEL SOL

Address:	Av. Misión de Loreto No. 130, San Felipe, B.C., México
Res.:	Baja California Tours, Inc., 7734 Hersihel Ave., Suite "O", La Jolla, Ca 92037
Telephone:	(6) 577-1088 (Mex), (619) 454-7166 or (800) 336-5454 (U.S. Res.)

GPS Location: N 30° 59' 52.3", W 114° 49' 59.2"

The Mar del Sol is another very nice but rather expensive trailer park located a short distance south of San Felipe. It is affiliated with the very nice Hotel Las Misiones next door. There's a beautiful beach out front.

The campground has 85 spaces with 30-amp outlets, sewer and water. These are back-in sites but are large with lots of room for bigger rigs. There are another 30 spaces with no utility hookups, these cost a lot less. The restrooms are individual cubicles for toilets and showers, they are tiled, clean, and in good repair. The showers have hot water. The campground has a swimming pool overlooking the beach, a palapa and meeting room for get-togethers, and a laundry. The nearest restaurant is in the Hotel Las Misiones next door and there's a handy public telephone by the office.

To find the Mar del Sol zero your odometer as you reach the glorieta (traffic circle) at the entrance to town. Turn 90 degrees right toward the airport and head south. At 2 miles (3.2 km) turn left on the well-marked road to the Hotel Las Misiones and the RV Park Mar del Sol. The road winds down a short hill to a T, turn right and you will find the campground at the end of the street.

SAN FELIPE MARINA RESORT RV PARK

Address:	Km 4.5 Carr. San Felipe-Aeropuerto, San Felipe, CP 21850 B.C., México
Telephone:	(5) 677-1455, (800) 291-5397 (U.S. Reservations)
Fax:	(6) 577-1566
E-mail:	snmarina@telnor.net
Web Site:	www.sanfelipe.com.mx/sfmarina/index.htm

GPS Location: N 30° 59' 18.3", W 114° 49' 40.4"

This campground may have the nicest facilities you will find in Mexico. It is only a few years old and is affiliated with a resort hotel below the campground on the beach. The campground itself is not next to the beach, it is set on a hillside above and has a great view.

NORTHERN GULF OF CALIFORNIA

There are 143 large back-in spaces with lots of room for bigger rigs. They have 50-amp and 30-amp outlets, sewer, water, and satellite TV. The campsites are all paved and have patios but no shade. The central facilities building has clean modern restrooms (an understatement) with hot showers, a beautiful pool and a lounge area. There is also a laundry in the building. The affiliated hotel has two more pools, tennis courts, and a restaurant. The campground and hotel are gated and have tight 24-hour security.

To find the San Felipe zero your odometer as you reach the glorieta (traffic circle) at the entrance to town. Turn 90 degrees right toward the airport and head south. At 2.9 miles (4.7 km) you'll see the campground on the left.

EL DORADO RANCH

Res.:	P.O. Box 3088, Englewood, CO 80155
Telephone:	(303) 790-1749 or (800) 404-2599 (U.S.), (6) 577-0010
Fax:	(6) 577-0009
E-mail:	email@eldoradoranch.com
Web Site:	www.eldoradoranch.com

GPS Location: N 31° 08' 09.4", W 114° 54' 37.1"

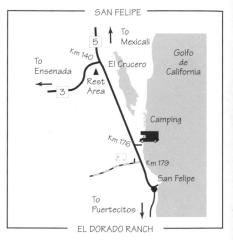

The El Dorado Ranch is a land development a few miles north of San Felipe along the coast. The area to be developed is huge, the project complex, and the promotion very active. Most importantly, to us anyway, there is a nice new RV park incorporated into the project.

There are 100 sites with 15 and 30-amp outlets, sewer, and water. All are on packed sand and separated by rows of painted white rocks. There are no patios and no shade but lots of room for large rigs. There is a very nice swimming pool pavilion with bar, a pool that is kept at bath temperature, and hot tubs that are even hotter. The campground has modern restrooms with flush toilets and hot showers. There's also a restaurant, a store, beautiful tennis courts, horse-back riding, desert tours, and lifestyle (sales) presentations.

The El Dorado Ranch is located about 8 miles (13 km) north of San Felipe. Take the well-marked road toward the beach between the 176 and 177 km markers. There's also a second campground that has been developed as part of this project, El Cachanilla, we talk about it below.

You should be warned that while this is a great RV park it is also a membership-type real estate development. They have a friendly but active sales force. The park often offers promotional escorted RV tours south to the campground from the border, this is an excellent way to make your first RV trip into Mexico. Call the reservation number for details.

NORTHERN GULF OF CALIFORNIA

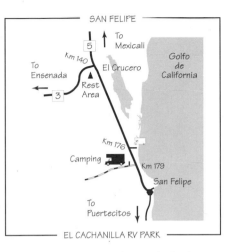

SAN FELIPE — EL CACHANILLA RV PARK

EL CACHANILLA RV PARK

Res.:	P.O. Box 3088, Englewood, CO 80155
Telephone:	(303) 790-1749 or (800) 404-2599 (U.S.), (6) 577-0010
Fax:	(6) 577-0009
E-mail:	email@eldoradoranch.com
Web Site:	www.eldoradoranch.com

GPS Location: N 31° 06' 54.0", W 114° 54' 21.6"

This campground is also part of the El Dorado Ranch. It is located in the desert away from the ocean, but is a good facility.

The latest word is that there are 130 sites here, 50 have full hookups and 80 are dry, hookups have been increased since our last visit. Some sites have covered patios and picnic tables. There are modern restrooms with flush toilets and hot showers, also a clubhouse and a self-service laundry.

To reach the campground turn toward the mountains near the Km 179 marker, this is about a mile closer to town than the El Dorado Ranch cutoff and is well signed. The campground is on the right a short distance up the side road.

Other Camping Possibilities

The campgrounds listed above only scratch the surface in San Felipe. Starting about 10 miles (16 km) north of town you will see many roads heading for the beach. Most of these roads end at small campgrounds with few services or facilities. If you don't need hookups you can explore some of them and find a place that suits you.

Side Trips from San Felipe

South of San Felipe the road is paved another 56 miles (91 km) to **Puertecitos**. There are many campgrounds along the beach north of Puertecitos and one in town. The one in town has electricity for a few hours each day. Puertecitos also has a restaurant, a small store and a Pemex. The road continues for 87 more miles (123 km) to connect with Mex 1 near the Laguna Chapala dry lake bed at the 223 Km mark. There have been rumors for several years that this stretch of road is about to be paved, until it is the road is said to be suitable for all sturdy rigs but has many miles of washboard bumps and lots of dust. Check road conditions before heading down it yourself and be prepared for many miles of road with no services.

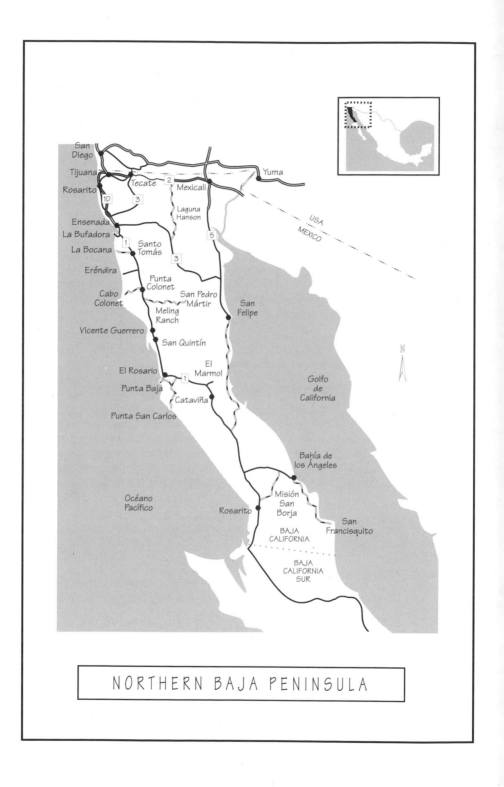

NORTHERN BAJA PENINSULA

CHAPTER

. . . . 12

NORTHERN BAJA PENINSULA

INTRODUCTION

The Baja Peninsula is an extremely popular camping destination. There are so many people living so close by in California that the peninsula, especially the northern part, seems almost an extension of that state. There are many campgrounds on the peninsula, fully a third of all formal Mexican campgrounds are located there. Additionally, this is without a doubt the most popular area of Mexico for boondocking outside formal campgrounds. There is much more information available about the Baja than about the remainder of the country.

One good reason for the Baja's popularity is the lack of bureaucratic nonsense required for a visit. Only if you plan to stay for more than three days or continue south of Maneadero (on Mex 1 about 10 miles (16 km) south of Ensenada) do you need a tourist card. Vehicle permits are not necessary at all.

The Baja Peninsula extends for approximately 1,000 miles (1,600 km) from the California border of the U.S. to its tip near Cabo San Lucas. For most of its length the peninsula's eastern portion is make up of rugged mountains. Bordering the Baja on the west is an often harsh Pacific Ocean coastline. On the east is the Gulf of California, also called the Sea of Cortez (Golfo de California or Mar de Cortés in Spanish). The fascinating gulf coast is by far the more accessible to visitors, particularly if they hesitate to use the many rough unpaved roads that are often the only way to reach long stretches of the west coast.

The Baja has an arid climate. Much of the peninsula is desert. Throughout most of the region the only relief from the dry climate is the occasional oasis, irrigated farm area, or seashore. There is a lot of seashore, about 2,000 miles (3,250 km) of it, no location on the peninsula is really far from the ocean.

A lot of people visit the Baja Peninsula during the winter because they are traveling to avoid the harsh weather in the north. This is not the best time for weather on the peninsula either, many northern sections are cool, especially on the Pacific coast. The southern Baja is more comfortable, but still not overly hot. The spring after Easter brings much better weather. It is not extremely hot yet but most of the tourists have gone home. During the summer both the air and water are very warm. It is still possible to stay comfortable along the coast however, and this is the best time of the year for fishing and watersports.

For the sake of convenience we have broken the Baja Peninsula into three areas in this book. The eastern portion of the northern peninsula is included in Chapter 11 covering the Northern Gulf of California. The easiest access to this part of the peninsula is by Mex 5 south from the Mexicali area and it has much in common with Puerto Peñasco and Gulfo de Santa Clara in the state of Sonora. This chapter will cover the remainder of the northern state of Baja California which stretches from the U.S. border south to the 28th parallel, a distance of about 350 miles (570 km) as the bird flies. Chapter 13 covers the southern portion of the peninsula, that part that comprises the state of Baja California Sur. From the 28th parallel to the tip if the peninsula the distance is about 425 air miles (690 km).

ROAD SYSTEM

The most important road on the Baja is Mex 1. This mostly two-lane paved road runs from the border crossing at Tijuana for 1,061 miles (1,711 km) south to the very tip of the Baja Peninsula at Cabo San Lucas. This highway was finished in 1973 and completely changed the character of the peninsula because it provided easy access for tourists and for commercial haulers.

Mex 1 is well supplied with kilometer markers and they make a convenient way to keep track of both your progress and the location of campgrounds. They do not progress in a uniform manner, however. In the state of Baja California there are four different segments of signed road. Kilometer markers in each section count from north to south: Tijuana to Ensenada, 109 kilometers; Ensenada to San Quintín, 196 kilometers; San Quintín to the junction of the road to Bahía de los Ángeles, 280 kilometers; and Bahía de los Ángeles junction to the Baja Sur border, 128 kilometers. This is a total distance of 713 kilometers or 436 miles.

Mex 1 begins in Tijuana. From Tijuana to Ensenada there are actually two different segments, one is the free road, Mex 1 Libre, the other is a toll road Mex 1D. The toll road is by far the best road, it is four lanes wide and for most of its length a limited access highway. There are three toll booths along the 65-mile road, an automobile or van was being charged about $ 7 U.S. during the late winter of 1999/2000 to cover the entire distance. A four-axle rig would pay about $14 for the same section of road. For more information about Mexican toll roads see our section titled *Toll Roads* in the *Details, Details, Details* chapter of this book. This is the only section of toll road on all of Mex 1.

From Ensenada south Mex 1 is a two-lane road except for short sections of boulevard through some towns and a section of four-lane highway near San Jose del Cabo. All of the highway is paved but much of it is relatively narrow and the surface in some places is potholed or rough. The key to a successful trip down this highway is to keep your speed down and, especially if you are in a big rig, slow down and exercise extreme caution when meeting larger vehicles coming from the opposite direction. There is always enough room to pass but often not much more than that. Inexperienced drivers sometimes tend to crowd the center line because they fear the often shoulderless outside pavement edge. We have met a surprising number of people who have had unnecessary problems because they weren't careful enough while passing traffic traveling the opposite direction.

Mex 1 follows a route that crosses back and forth across the peninsula. In the northern state of Baja California the highway never does reach the Gulf of California after leaving Ensenada. It heads south slightly inland until reaching El Rosario just south of San Quintín, then turns inland to pass through the mountainous interior before coming back toward the Pacific near Guerrero Negro and the border with Baja California Sur. It is important to gas up at El Rosario because gas stations are unreliable from there almost to Guerrero Negro, about 216 miles (353 km) south. This section is known to many as the "gas gap".

In the north there is a good alternate to Mex 1 as far south as Ensenada. This is Mex 3 which runs from Tecate on the border to Ensenada. Actually this is a very useful highway if you are headed north since the Tecate border crossing has much shorter waits while traveling north than the Tijuana crossings. See Chapter 3 for more information about crossing the border.

Most Baja visitors probably never have a chance to drive Mex 2, an east/west route that actually crosses all the way across Mexico from Tijuana to Matamoros on the east coast. The northern Baja section of this trans-continental highway is a decent route, often with four lanes. The section crossing the mountains east of Tecate and then

MUCH OF HIGHWAY 1 IN THE NORTH WAS RECENTLY REPAVED

dropping into the Central Valley near Mexicali is called the Cantu Grade. It is especially spectacular although if you are traveling from east to west it can be a long hot climb up the grade.

Mex 3 also continues from Ensenada to meet with Mex 5 about 31 miles (51 km) north of San Felipe on the Gulf of California. This 123 mile (201 km) two-lane paved highway offers an alternative to Mex 5 south from Mexicali for San Felipe-bound travelers and is one of only two paved routes across the peninsula in Baja Norte other than the Mex 2 border route. The other is a potholed two-lane paved road that goes east from Mex 1 to Bahía de los Angles from a point 364 miles (594 km) south of Tijuana. This road is 42 miles (68 km) long and is the only paved access to the Gulf of California south of San Felipe.

Most RVers will probably want to stay pretty close to paved roads but there are several routes that will accommodate smaller carefully driven RVs if drivers are willing to put up with lots of dust and the occasional washboard surface. From Mex 3 there is a road north to Laguna Hanson, see *Side Trips from Ensenada* for this trip. The road to La Bufadora just south of Ensenada is paved and easy to negotiate, see the *Punta Banda* description section. Roads lead to the Pacific coast at La Bocana and Ejido Eréndira from Mex 1, see *Side Trips from Santo Tomás*. There is a road east from north of San Quintín to the Meling Ranch, see *Side Trips from San Quintín*. El Marmól quarry is accessible from Mex 1 north of Cataviña, see *Side Trips from Cataviña* for this road. Finally, there is a road south from San Felipe that eventually connects with Mex 1 some 34 miles (56 km) south of Cataviña near Km 229, see the *Side Trips from San Felipe* section in Chapter 11 for a description of this road.

Smaller rigs with good clearance will find it possible to do some exploring. The following roads are reported to be fine for pickups and small sturdy vans, you need decent clearance but not necessarily four-wheel drive. You should make sure that your rig is in good mechanical condition and that you are well supplied before attempting these roads because help is scarce. You should also avoid these tracks in wet weather since many of them become virtually impassable when wet. Check with the locals before attempting them to make sure they are passable. It is always better to travel with several rigs so that help is available if a rig has a problem. The road connecting Laguna Hanson with Mex 2 to the north is covered in *Side Trips from Tecate*. For the road from Meling Ranch to the Astronomical Observatory in the Parque Nacionál Sierra San Pedro Martír see *Side Trips from San Quintín*. There is a road south from Bahía de los Ángeles to San Francisquito, see *Side Trips from Bahía de los Ángeles*. Misión San Borja is accessible from near Rosarito, see *Side Trips from Cataviña*. *Side Trips from El Rosario* covers roads to Punta Baja and Punta San Carlos.

HIGHLIGHTS

The Northern Baja Peninsula covered in this chapter, like the Southern Baja, has few large towns. In fact, other than those along the border and Ensenada there are really only small settlements. Popular San Felipe is covered in Chapter 10 in this book.

The Baja Peninsula is a paradise for outdoors enthusiasts. It offers unequaled opportunities for off-road exploration, hiking, fishing, kayaking, whale-watching, sailing, surfing, windsurfing, clam-digging, and even bicycling.

The area surrounding Ensenada and north to Tijuana is full of campgrounds and very easy to visit. It is virtually an extension of the U.S. and is very popular with California residents for short visits. Visitors staying for less than 72 hours are not even required to get a tourist card. People come down for the shopping, the restaurants, and the ocean-side campgrounds. During the summer this coastal area has pleasant California-like weather but in the winter it is cool. Tijuana is probably best visited on day trips from north of the border but Ensenada is a good camping destination. Probably the only other interesting city of any size in the area covered by this chapter is Tecate, one of the nicest border towns in Mexico.

As you head south down the peninsula there are two major regions offering fishing and water sports, on the Pacific side is San Quintín and on the Gulf side is Bahía de los Ángeles. Both of these regions are easily accessible and provide lots of opportunities for anglers and boaters of all kinds.

There are two mountain regions in the northern Baja that make good destinations for hikers and campers. One of these is the Laguna Hanson area between Mex 2 and Mex 3. The formal name for this area is Parque Nacional Constitución de 1857, see the *Side Trips from Ensenada* section below. The other is the Parque Nacional Sierra San Pedro Martír which is located east of San Quintín, see the *Side Trips from San Quintín* section.

Many of the communities on the Baja Peninsula grew up around missions founded by Jesuit, Franciscan, and Dominican missionaries. About 30 were built beginning in 1696 in Loreto. These missions were an important part of the peninsula's history and many can be visited today. Some are ruins, some are restored, some are in use, some are remote, and a few are lost. Some of those you might want to visit in North Baja are the Misión Santo Tomás ruins (*Santo Tomás* section), the Misión Rosario ruins (*El Rosario* section), and Misión San Borja ruins (*Side Trip from Cataviña* section).

Fishing along both coasts of the peninsula is excellent. In the Northern Baja favorite destinations accessible on good roads include Bahía de los Ángeles and San Quintín. Fishing is generally considered to be better in the late summer and early fall but there is what would be considered decent fishing by most standards available almost everywhere all year long.

Kayaking is extremely popular along the Sea of Cortez. The Bahía de los Ángeles is often used as a departure point for coastwise trips to the south all the way to La Paz.

Surfing is a west coast activity since the Gulf of California offers little in the way surf except at the far south end. Remote beaches all along the coast are popular. Easily accessible surfing opportunities include the coast between Tijuana and Ensenada, south from Ensenada to El Rosario, in some spots north of Guerrero Negro.

NORTHERN BAJA PENINSULA

THE CAMPGROUNDS

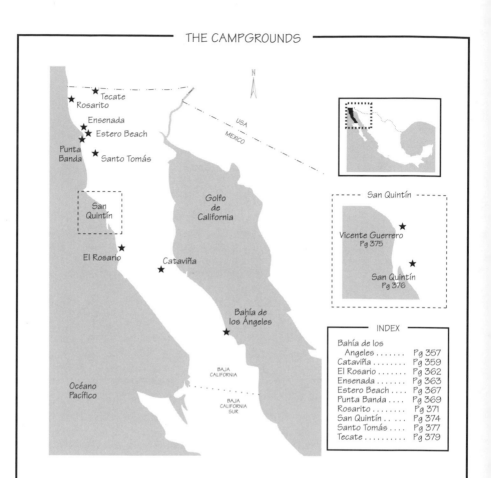

DISTANCE TABLE

Miles

Bahía de los Ángeles	109	182	333	121	486	384	489	219	307	408	400
	Cataviña	73	227	145	379	277	383	110	198	301	293
178		El Rosario	154	216	306	205	310	37	125	228	220
297	119		Ensenada	371	152	51	156	116	29	75	67
544	370	251		Guerrero Negro	524	422	527	255	342	446	438
198	236	353	606		Mexicali	116	122	269	181	78	104
793	619	500	249	855		Rosarito	207	167	80	46	16
627	453	334	83	689	190		San Felipe	273	185	200	223
799	625	506	255	861	200	338		San Quintín	88	191	183
358	180	61	190	416	439	273	445		Santo Tomás	103	96
501	323	204	47	559	296	130	302	143		Tecate	30
666	492	373	122	728	127	75	327	312	169		Tijuana
653	479	360	109	715	170	26	364	299	156	49	

Kilometers

SELECTED CITIES AND THEIR CAMPGROUNDS

BAHÍA DE LOS ÁNGELES, BAJA CALIFORNIA (BAH-HEE-AH DAY LOES AHN-HAIL-ACE)
Population 500, Elevation sea level

The Bahía de los Ángeles (Bay of the Angels) is one of the most scenic spots in Baja California with blue waters and barren desert shoreline backed by rocky mountains. The huge bay is protected by a chain of small islands, and also by Isla Angel de la Guarda, which is 45 miles (75 km) long. Even with this protection boating is often dangerous because of strong winds from the north and evening "gravity" winds that whistle downhill from the west. Fishing, boating, diving, and kayaking are good in the bay, among the islands, and offshore and there are several launch ramps in town. Exercise caution, these are considered dangerous waters due to the frequent strong winds.

There is a **turtle hatchery** in Bahía de los Ángeles near the Brisas Marina RV Park where you can see some of these endangered animals. The village itself doesn't offer much except a couple of motels, several RV parks and a few small stores. Electricity in town is produced by a generator that only runs part time.

Bahía de los Ángeles Campgrounds

This area offers many places to camp. You may find, as we do, that the campgrounds in town with hookups are much less attractive than the much more informal places outside town to the north and south.

GUILLERMO'S HOTEL AND RV PARK

Address:	Expendio #11, Boulevard Bahía de los Ángeles, CP 22950 B.C., México
Telephone:	(6) 650-3209, (6) 176-4946 (Ensenada)

GPS Location: N 28° 56' 52.3", W 113° 33' 32.5"

This campground has about 40 camping spaces, some have working full hookups with 15-amp outlets, others are in poor repair. Sites have patios and some palapas. This is a dirt and gravel lot next to the road with a few small trees to provide a little shade, permanents here block any view of the water. The restrooms around front have hot showers. There is a restaurant, bar, store and also a launch ramp. Bear in mind that electricity in Bahía de los Ángeles gets turned off during the middle of the day and at night.

To find Guillermo's drive into town, pass the Villa Vitta, and you'll soon see the campground on the left.

VILLA VITTA HOTEL RESORT

Res.:	509 Ross Drive, Escondido, CA 92029 (Res. in U.S.)
Telephone:	(760) 741-9583 (Res. in U.S.)

GPS Location: N 28° 57' 03.9", W 113° 33' 29.7"

The Villa Vitta RV Park is located across the street from the hotel of the same name. This is a flat dirt lot with no landscaping, however, it is right next to the beach. There are 46 pull-through slots with electricity, all have patios. The campground also has a dump station, water is not available. Bathrooms and hot showers are available at the hotel, so is a restaurant and bar. Campers are not given use of the swimming pool. This motel/campground has a good launch ramp, available for an extra fee.

You'll find the that the Villa Vitta is hard to miss, you'll see the hotel on the right and the RV park on the left soon after entering town.

🚐 CAMP GECKO

Telephone: (5) 151-9454

GPS Location: N 28° 54' 50.2", W 113° 32' 24.8"

This waterside campground has an idyllic location on a long sandy beach with a few rocks. Unfortunately you must drive almost four miles of washboard gravel road to reach it.

Camp Gecko has about 10 camping spaces with palapas, a few are suitable for RVs. There are no hookups but the camping area does have flush toilets and hot water showers. There are also cabins and cabanas for rent and a small paved boat ramp.

As you head south through Bahía de los Ángeles village you will come to a rock wall and the entrance to Diaz RV park. Go to the right around it and follow a washboard gravel road south. At 4.0 miles (6.5 km) take the sandy road left toward the beach and Camp Gecko.

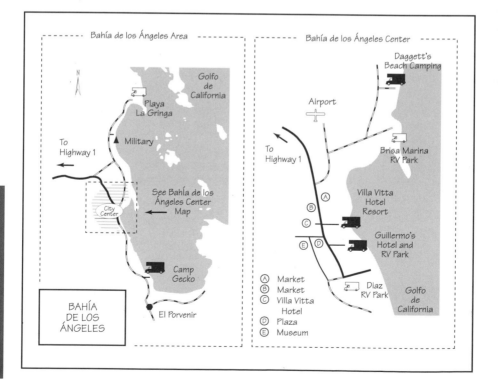

DAGGETT'S BEACH CAMPING

GPS Location: N 28° 58' 30.8", W 113° 32' 48.2"

This is one or our favorite places to stay in Bahía de los Ángeles. There are 18 beachside palapas with room to park an RV alongside. There are no hookups but there is a dump station, flush toilets, and hot showers. There's a restaurant next door, kayak rentals, and fishing and snorkeling charters.

To drive to the campground follow the north beaches road from Bahía L.A. After .8 mile (1.3 km) the road jogs right, than in .5 miles (.8 km) it jogs left to continue north. Three tenths of a mile (.5 km) after this last turn you'll see the sign for Daggett's Beach to the right. Follow the road to the beach and campground.

Other Camping Possibilities

There is an old government-built campground like the others you've seen on the peninsula which is located just north of town, follow signs for Brisa Marina RV Park. There are about 50 spaces but none of the hookups work. Most people camp nearby at turtle ponds. There is a small fee and no facilities.

At the south end of the village is the old Diaz RV Park which is associated with the Casa Diaz Motel with the same management. There are 6 poorly-maintained sites with electricity, water, sewer and cement palapas. The bathrooms were basic and none too clean when we visited. The location across the street from the beach offers no views. There are also a restaurant, store and boat launching ramp.

North of town along the beach there are several places with beachside camping, no facilities, and small fees. The one at the end of the road (about 7 miles (11 km)) is known as Playa La Gringa. The lack of facilities is more than compensated for by the isolated beachfront location.

Side Trips from Bahía de los Ángeles

You can drive to **Bahía (bay) or Cala (inlet) San Francisquito**, about 85 road miles south of Bahía de los Ángeles. The road south from town is obvious, it is usually suitable for small RVs and trucks with boat trailers. This is a long drive through empty country so make sure you have supplies and a vehicle in good condition, ask about the road in Bahía de los Ángeles before leaving because it occasionally gets washed out. Primitive campsites are available in San Francisquito for a small fee. Nearby Punta San Francisquito Resort also has some facilities including cabins and a restaurant. Bahía San Francisquito can also be accessed from El Arco by a road suitable only for rugged vehicles, see *Side Trips from Guerrero Negro* in the next chapter.

CATAVIÑA, BAJA CALIFORNIA (KAT-AH-VEEN-YAH)
Population 200, Elevation 1,900 ft. (580 m)

You can't really call Cataviña a town. There is little more here than a Hotel La Pinta, a closed-down Pemex, an old government-built campground, and a few shacks and restaurants. The area, however, is one of the most interesting on the Baja. The Cataviña boulder fields (formal name is Las Virgines - the Virgins) are striking. The road threads its way for several miles through a jumble of huge granite boulders sprinkled liberally

with attractive cacti and desert plants. It is a photographer's paradise. Gas is sometimes still available at the La Pinta Motel, they have a Pemex gas pump with limited
and irregular supplies.

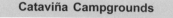

Cataviña Campgrounds

 PARQUE NATURAL DESIERTO CENTRAL
TRAILER PARK

GPS Location: N 29° 43' 51.6", W 114° 43' 19.6"

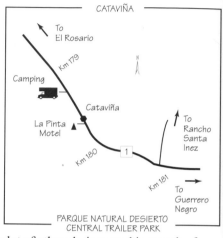

PARQUE NATURAL DESIERTO
CENTRAL TRAILER PARK

This is one of the fenced compounds that were
built by the government soon after the road
south was finished. None of the hookups other
than sewer work any more, but this is still an
attractive campground. The landscaping has
boulders and cactus, just like the surrounding
area. There are bathrooms with toilets that are
flushed with a bucket of water but no showers.
Many people use this campground, there aren't a lot of other choices on this stretch of
road.

The campground is located in Cataviña off Mex 1 just west of the La Pinta motel and
the abandoned Pemex on the south side of the road.

 RANCHO SANTA INEZ

GPS Location: N 29° 43' 47.9", W 114° 41' 53.0"

Many folks drive right by the entrance road to
this camping spot, and that's a mistake. We
think it is the best place to stay in this area.

The camping area is a large flat dirt lot with
only one tree for shade. There's room for lots
of rigs, that's why many of the caravans stay
here. Other facilities include a water faucet and
a small building with a flush toilet. Best of all
is the small restaurant.

To reach the campground turn north on the well-
marked road near Km 181, less than a mile east of the La Pinta Motel. Follow the
paved side road for about .8 miles (1.3 km), the camping area is on the left.

Other Camping Possibilities

It is tempting to just follow one of the many roads into the boulder field north of
Cataviña and set up camp. This might be fine for a group of several rigs but there have
been reports of robberies in the area so think twice before doing this.

NORTHERN BAJA PENINSULA

BOOJUM TREES IN THE CATAVIÑA DESERT

Side Trips from Cataviña

The virtually abandoned onyx mining area called **El Marmól** makes an interesting day trip. The access road is near the Km 143 marker about 19 miles (31 km) north of Cataviña. This is a graded road that is about 10 miles long. Take a look at the old school house built entirely of onyx. This mine was very active in the early part of the century, the quarried onyx slabs were shipped by water from Puerto Santa Catarina about 50 miles west on the Pacific coast. You might also want to make the 3-mile hike (6 miles round trip) to El Volcán where you can see a small seep forming new onyx.

A mission, **Misión San Borja** is accessible if you have four-wheel drive with good ground clearance. From Rosarito, located about 97 miles (158 km) south of Cataviña on Mex 1 drive east, roads leave the highway both north and south of the bridge over the arroyo. At about 15 miles (24 km) the road reaches Rancho San Ignacio, the mission is beyond at about 22 miles (36 km). Misión San Francisco de Borja was built in 1759 and has been restored by the government.

EL ROSARIO, BAJA CALIFORNIA (EL ROE-SAR-EEH-OH)
Population 4,000

For many years El Rosario was as far south as you could drive unless you were an off-roader. Today's road turns inland here and heads for the center of the peninsula, it won't return to the west coast until it cuts back to Guerrero Negro, and even there it won't stay for long. **Espinosa's Place**, a local restaurant, has been famous for years for its seafood burritos (lobster and crab meat). The town of El Rosario is actually in two places, El Rosario de Arriba is on the main highway, El Rosario de Abajo is 1.5 miles (2.4 km) away down and across the arroyo (river bed). Each has the ruins of an old mission, the first is in El Rosario de Arriba, it was abandoned when the mission moved to El Rosario de Abajo. Little remains of the first except the foundations, there are still standing walls at the second, which was abandoned in 1832.

El Rosario Campground

🚐 **MOTEL SINAI RV PARK**

Address: Carret. Transp. Km 56 #1056, El Rosario, B.C., México
Telephone: (6) 165-8818

GPS Location: N 30° 04' 00.6", W 115° 42' 55.0"

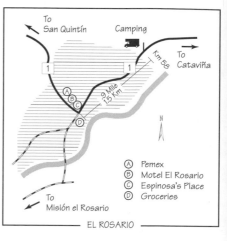

In the last few years this little hotel has installed RV spaces on the hillside behind. This is a welcome addition to the peninsula campgrounds because it reduces the longest gap between campgrounds with utilities by about 30 miles (49 km). It is 219 miles (358 km) between El Rosario and the next ones to the south in Guerrero Negro (unless you make a side trip to Bahía de los Ángeles).

There are 12 paved pads for RVs, but they are so close together that there will probably be room for fewer campers most of the time. All sites have electricity (15-amp outlets), water and sewer drains are available to most of them. There is a very nice toilet cubicle and two nice little shower rooms with hot water. The campground is up a small slope behind the motel. There is plenty of room for big rigs to maneuver and sites are flat. The motel also has a little restaurant. Limited English is spoken.

The Motel Sinai is near the eastern outskirts of El Rosario on the north side of the highway. It is exactly .9 miles (1.5 km) east of the 90-degree turn in the middle of town.

Side Trips from El Rosario

You can drive 10.5 miles (17 km) west on a decent road to **Punta Baja**, a fish camp and beach hangout where free camping is possible. Surfing here is said to be excellent. This road is usually suitable for pickups and sturdy vans, but probably not RVs.

It is also possible for similar vehicles to drive about 48 miles (74 km) southwest to

Punta San Carlos for primitive camping and wind surfing. Roads are dirt but generally not too bad by Baja standards.

ENSENADA, BAJA CALIFORNIA (EHN-SEH-NAH-DAH)
Population 400,000, Elevation sea level

Ensenada is the Baja's third most populous town and one of the most pleasant to visit. It is an important port and is more than ready for the tourist hordes that make the short-and-easy 68 mile (109 km) drive south from the border crossing at Tijuana or disembark from the cruise ships that anchor in Todos Santos Bay. There are many, many restaurants and handicrafts stores in the central area of town, English is often spoken so this is not a bad place to get your feet wet if you have not visited a Mexican city before. Try walking along **Calle Primera**, also called Avenida López Mateos, it is lined with restaurants and shops and is located just one block inland from the coastal Blvd. Costero (also known as Blvd. Gral. Lázaro Cárdenas). There are also many supermarkets and Pemex stations so Ensenada is the place to stock up on supplies before heading down the peninsula. Many banks have ATM machines so you can easily acquire some pesos.

When you tire of shopping and eating Ensenada has a few other attractions. The best beach is at **Estero Beach** which also has several campgrounds, they are discussed below. The **fishing** in Ensenada is good, charters for yellowtail, albacore, sea bass,

ENSENADA'S WATERFRONT WALKWAY

halibut and bonito can be arranged at the fishing piers. Ensenada has the largest fish market on the Baja, it is called the **Mercado Negro** (black market) and is located near the sport fishing piers. Nearby is a nice **Malecón** or waterfront walkway where you can take a good look at the fishing fleet. The waterspout at **La Bufadora**, located 10 miles beyond Punta Banda (see below) is a popular day trip. **Whale watching trips** are a possibility from December to March.

Important fiestas and busy times here are **Carnival** in February, spring break for colleges in the U.S. during late March, the Rosarito to Ensenada Bicycle Race and Newport to Ensenada Yacht Race in April, a wine festival in August, another Rosarito to Ensenada bicycle race in October, and the Baja 1000 off-road race in November.

If you did not get a tourist card when you crossed the border in Tijuana you can obtain one and get it validated at the immigration (Migración) office in Ensenada. It is located on the north side of the road soon after you cross the speed bumps next to the port when entering town from the north on Mex 1.

We have listed only four campgrounds in the Ensenada area. There are really many more. Some are very poor and really not very good choices. Others are located in outlying locations that are really destinations in their own right, see the Estero Beach and Punta Banda listings below for some of these. Finally, we've not listed others because we just don't have room in this book for them all. We hope, however, that we have included the best of them here.

Ensenada Campgrounds

🚐 CAMPO PLAYA RV PARK

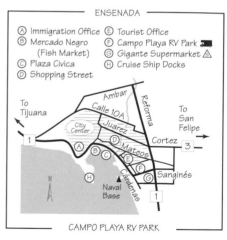

Address:	Blvd. Las Dunas & Calle Agustin S anginés (Apdo. 789), Ensenada, B.C., México
Telephone:	(6) 176-2918

GPS Location: N 31° 51' 01.4", W 116° 36' 50.1"

The Campo Playa is the only RV park actually in urban Ensenada and is the best place to stay if you want to explore the town. The downtown area is about 2 miles distant, the campground is right on the preferred route that you will probably be following through town, and there is a large Gigante supermarket just up the street.

There are about 50 spaces in the park set under palm trees. Most are pull-throughs that will accept big rigs with slideouts. The spaces have 15-amp outlets, sewer, water and patios. There are also some smaller spaces, some with only partial utilities availability. The restrooms are showing their age but are clean and have hot showers. The campground is fenced but the urban location suggests that belongings not be left unattended. Reservations are accepted.

The campground lies right on the most popular route through Ensenada. Entering town from the north on Mex 1 zero your odometer as you cross the obnoxious topes (speed bumps) next to the harbor. You'll pass a shipyard on your right with huge fishing boats almost overhanging the highway. Take the first major right in .5 miles (.8 km) following signs for La Bufadora, this is Blvd. Lázaro Cárdenas. You'll pass a Sanborn's coffee shop on the right and also a plaza with statues of three heads. At 1.8 miles (2.9 km) turn left onto Calle Agustin Sanginés, drive one block and turn left. The trailer park will be on your right after the turn.

BAJA SEASONS BEACH RESORT, VILLAS, RVS, AND MOTEL

Res.:   1177 Broadway Ave., Suite 2, Chula Vista, CA 91911

Telephone: (800) 754-4190 or (619) 422-2777 (U.S. Res.) or (6) 155-4015 (Mex)

GPS Location: N 32° 03' 55.0", W 116° 52' 42.3"

BAJA SEASONS BEACH RESORT, VILLAS, RVS, AND MOTEL

The Baja Seasons is a large and very nice beachside RV park within reasonable driving distance of Ensenada. The drive into town is about 30 miles (50 km) on good four-lane highway, complicated only by a fascinating area where there seems to be an unending construction project to stabilize the road and keep it from sliding into the ocean. The only problem is that you'll pay more to stay here than you would north of the border, about $40 in the winter and $50 in the summer.

The campground has about 140 very nice camping spaces with electricity (some 50 amp, the rest 30 amp), sewer, water, TV, paved parking pad, patios and landscaping. The streets are paved, they even have curbs. There's a huge central complex with a restaurant and bar, swimming pool, hot tub, small store, tennis courts, sauna and steam baths, mini golf, game room, library and coin-op laundry. There are also restrooms with hot showers. The entire setup is on a wide, beautiful beach. English is spoken and reservations are accepted.

The campground is right next to Mex 1D just south of the Km 72 marker. Going south watch the kilometer markers and turn directly off the highway. Going north you will see the campground on your left but cannot turn because of the central divider. Continue north 4.1 miles (6.6 km) to the Alisitos exit to return.

RANCHO SORDO MUDO

Address: P.O. Box 1376, Chula Vista, CA 91912 or Apdo. 1468, Ensenada, B.C., México

GPS Location: N 32° 06' 41.3", W 116° 32' 47.7"

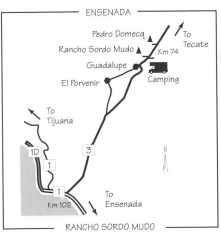

RANCHO SORDO MUDO

If you decide to follow the inland route on Mex 3 south from Tecate to Ensenada you might decide to spend the night at Rancho Sordo

NORTHERN BAJA PENINSULA

Mudo, about 24 miles (39 km) north of Ensenada. The ranch is actually a school for deaf-mute children, the campground is really maintained for the use of visitors helping at the school. The income from the RV park goes to a good cause and the surroundings are very pleasant. Donations are accepted in lieu of a fee.

There are 9 back-in spaces in a grassy field with full hookups including 50-amp outlets. Eighteen more pull-through spaces offer electricity and water only. The bathrooms are modern and clean and have hot water. The campground is likely to be deserted when you stop, just pull in and park and someone will eventually come across from the school to welcome you. The campground is located in a beautiful valley, the Domecq winery is just a mile up the road and offers tours.

The campground is well-signed on Mex 3. Driving south start watching as you pass the Domecq winery, it will be on your left right next to the highway just after the Km 74 marker. Heading north it is even easier to spot just north of the village of Guadalupe.

▭ HOTEL JOKER

Address: Carretera Transpeninsular Km 12.5,
Ensenada, B.C., México
Telephone: (6) 177-4460   **Fax:** (6) 177-4460

GPS Location: N 31° 48' 12.3", W 116° 35' 42.6"

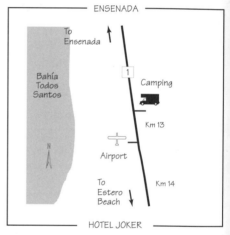

Just south of Ensenada, right on Mex 1, is a quirky little motel with a few RV slots. Once you enter the gates you'll probably find you like the place. The hotel specializes in special-event parties, there are play areas with castle-like crenellations, a piñata party plaza, a barbecue area and a general atmosphere of good clean family fun.

The Joker has about 6 spaces, although most are pull-throughs they are small, rigs larger than 24 feet or so will have difficulty maneuvering and parking. The slots have 15-amp outlets, sewer, water, and patios with shade, flowers, and barbecues. There's also a large grass area that is perfect for tents. The restrooms are older but clean and in good repair and have hot water. The hotel also has a restaurant and a tiny swimming pool.

The Joker is south of Ensenada on the east side of Mex 1 just north of the Km 13 marker. Heading north watch for it after you pass the airport, about 1.4 miles (2.2 km) north of the Estero Beach road. Heading south there are really no good markers, just watch for the hotel on your left.

Side Trips from Ensenada

A Mexican national park, **Parque Nacional Constitución**, is accessible from Mex 3 east of Ensenada. Near the Km 55 marker a road goes north to the shallow Laguna Hanson, the distance to the lake is 22 miles (36 km). There are primitive campsites at the lake. This lake is also accessible from Mex 2 to the north but the road is much worse and not suitable for small RVs like this one from the south.

ESTERO BEACH

The Estero Beach area is really a suburb of Ensenada. The road to Estero beach leads west from near the Km 15 marker of Mex 1 about 7 miles (11 km) south of Ensenada. There's not much here other than beaches, the resorts, and vacation homes.

Estero Beach Campgrounds

ESTERO BEACH HOTEL/RESORT $\frac{\$}{\$\$\$}$ *(Winter)* $\frac{\$\$}{\$\$\$}$ *(Summer)*

Address:	Apdo. 862, Ensenada, B.C., México
U.S. Res.:	PMB 1186, 482 W. San Ysidro Blvd., San Ysidro, CA 92173
Telephone:	(6) 176-6225 **Fax**: (6) 176-6925
E-mail:	estero@tlenor.net
Web Site:	www.hotelesterobeach.com

GPS Location: N 31° 46' 40.8", W 116° 36' 15.0"

The Estero Beach Hotel has one of Mexico's finest RV parks, comparable in many ways with the very expensive places on the road between Tijuana and Ensenada. For some reason, perhaps because it is slightly off the main road, it doesn't cost as much as those places. This is really a huge complex with a hotel as the centerpiece and many permanent RVs in separate area from the RV park. Reservations are recommended because caravans often fill this place unexpectedly. English is spoken.

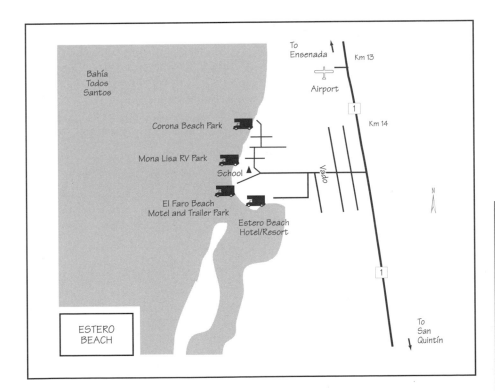

Bahía Todos Santos

To Ensenada   Km 13

Airport

Km 14

Corona Beach Park

Mona Lisa RV Park

School

El Faro Beach Motel and Trailer Park

Estero Beach Hotel/Resort

Vado

N

To San Quintín

ESTERO BEACH

The modern RV park has 38 big back-in spaces with 30-amp outlets, sewer, and water. There is also a very large area for parking if you don't want utilities. There is grass under trees for tenters. The parked RVs look across an estuary (excellent birding) toward the hotel about a quarter-mile away. There's a paved walkway along the border of the estuary to the hotel. The restrooms were showing some age last time we visited and there was no hot water, but we're assured that normally there is. The hotel also has another area with full hookups for about 20 smaller units, they call it their trailer park. Check to see if there is room there for you if the RV park happens to be full.

The resort also has a restaurant, bar, museum, several upscale shops, boat launching ramp, tennis courts, and playground. There's also a brand-new beautiful swimming pool with hot tubs.

To reach the Estero Beach Hotel take the Estero Beach road west from Mex 1 some 5.2 miles (8.4 km) south of the Gigante supermarket on the corner of Ave. Reforma (Mex 1) and Calle General Agustin Sanginés. Drive 1 mile (1.6 km) west and turn left at the sign for the Estero Beach Hotel. You'll soon come to a gate. There is a very long entrance drive and then a reception office where they'll sign you up and direct you to a campsite.

⏚ EL FARO BEACH MOTEL AND TRAILER PARK

Address: Apdo. 1008, Ensenada, CP 22800 B.C., México
Telephone: (6) 177-4620

GPS Location: N 31° 46' 48.1", W 116° 37' 04.0"

The El Faro is a popular destination for beach-goers from Ensenada. Busses bring loads of them to the small beach that is located between the El Faro and the Estero Beach Hotel. That means that on sunny days there are probably too many people wandering through the camping area for a really enjoyable experience. The mascot here is Leonardo, a huge male lion kept in a cage near the entrance. At one time it was a cute little cub, but, they say, "it just kept getting bigger!"

This is a simple place, parking is right next to the beach on a sandy lot surrounded by a low concrete curb. There is room for about 3 rigs to back in for spaces with low-amp electricity. Much more space, enough for some 20 more rigs is available without hookups. Showers are old, in poor repair, and cold. You'll be happier if you bring your own bathroom facilities along with you. However, hot showers are available for a fee at a place about a quarter-mile up the road.

To reach the El Faro take the Estero Beach road west from Mex 1 about 5.2 miles (8.4 km) south of the Gigante supermarket on the corner of Ave. Reforma (Mex 1) and Calle Agustin Sanginés. Drive 1.9 mile (3.1 km) west, taking the left fork of the Y at 1.6 miles (2.6 km). The El Faro is at the end of the road.

⏚ MONA LISA RV PARK

Address: Apdo. 200, Chapultepec, B.C., México
Telephone: (6) 177-4920

GPS Location: N 31° 47' 07.5", W 116° 36' 55.2"

This is a interesting family-run campground, a fun place to visit. The name apparently comes from the murals painted on every available wall. They depict scenes from Mexico's history and are themselves worth a special trip to the Mona Lisa.

The campground has 13 fairly large back-in spaces. All are paved and some have palapa-shaded tables. All also have 50-amp outlets, sewer, and water. The restrooms are old and last time we visited they were so dirty that they were unusable although this may not always be the case. There is also a restaurant, bar, and motel on the property. The Mona Lisa is near beaches but rock rip-rap fronts the actual RV park property, the current RV sites don't overlook the water. There's also a playground. English is spoken and reservations are accepted.

To reach the Mona Lisa take the Estero Beach road west from Mex 1 about 5.2 miles (8.4 km) south of the Gigante on the corner of Ave. Reforma (Mex 1) and Calle General Agustin Sanginés. Drive west and then north, taking the right fork of the Y at 1.6 miles (2.6 km). At 1.8 miles (2.9 km) turn left and you'll see the Mona Lisa ahead.

⊒ **CORONA BEACH PARK**

Address: P.O. Box 1149, Ensenada, México

GPS Location: N 31° 47' 21.9", W 116° 36' 53.3"

This is a simple campground with parking in a large flat area with no view of the beautiful sandy beach to the north of the campground. There is parking for 28 rigs with 15-amp outlets and water. There is also a dump station. The restrooms are clean and have cold water showers. A small grocery store sits next to the camping area. English is spoken.

To reach the Corona Beach take the Estero Beach road west from Mex 1 about 5.2 miles (8.4 km) south of the Gigante on the corner of Ave. Reforma (Mex 1) and Calle General Agustin Sanginés. Drive west and then north, taking the right fork of the Y at 1.6 miles (2.6 km). At 1.9 miles (3.1 km) the road makes a quick right and then a left to continue straight. You'll reach the campground at 2.1 miles (3.4 km).

PUNTA BANDA

Punta Banda is another small area that is virtually a suburb of Ensenada. To get there follow the road west from near the center of Maneadero near the 21 Km marker, about 11 miles (18 km) south of Ensenada on Mex 1. It is then another 8 miles (13 km) out to Punta Banda. Punta Banda has grown up around the large RV parks here. The beach is known for its hot springs, you can dig a hole and make your own bath tub. A few miles beyond Punta Banda is the **La Bufadora** blow hole. There are several small campgrounds without hookups or much in the way of services near La Bufadora.

Punta Banda Campgrounds

⊒ **VILLARINO CAMPAMENTO TURISTICO**

Address: Km 13 Carr. a la Bufadora, Apdo. 842, Ensenada, B.C., México

Telephone: (6) 154-2045   **Fax:** (6) 154-2044

GPS Location: N 31° 43' 03.5", W 116° 40' 00.9"

This campground with lots of permanents also has a good-size transient area. It's close to Ensenada, on the beach, and a little off the beaten path.

Behind a glass-fronted terrace overlooking the beach is a large packed dirt area with some trees and about 20 larger sites. Some sites have 15-amp outlets, sewer, and

water and some have only electricity and water. Most sites have picnic tables, some
have fire rings. The restrooms are very clean and well maintained, they have hot
showers. In front of the campground is a restaurant, a small store, a post office, and a
public phone.

Take the road toward La Bufadora from Mex 1 about 9.1 miles (14.7 km) south from
the Gigante on the corner of Ave. Reforma (Mex 1) and Calle General Agustin Sanginés
in Ensenada. You will see the Villarino on the right 7.9 miles (12.6 km) from the
cutoff.

LA JOLLA BEACH CAMP

    Address: Apdo. 102, Punta Banda, Ensenada, CP 22791 B.C., México
    Telephone: (6) 154-2005   **Fax**: (6) 154-2004

GPS Location: N 31° 43' 00.1", W 116° 39' 52.2"

The La Jolla Beach Camp is a huge place. There are a lot of permanently-located
trailers here but most of the transient trade is summer and holiday visitors using tents
or RVs. Several big empty dirt lots, both on the waterfront and on the south side of the
highway, have room for about 400 groups. During the winter these areas are practically empty. You can park on the waterfront and run a long cord for electricity from a
few outlets near the restroom buildings. Water is available and there's a dump station.
Restrooms are very basic, like what you'd expect next to a public beach, there are a
few hot showers available. There is a small grocery store and basic English is spoken.

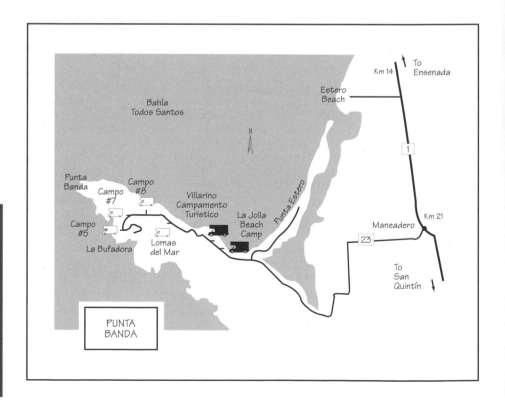

Take the road toward La Bufadora from Mex 1 about 9.1 miles (14.7 km) south from the Gigante on the corner of Ave. Reforma (Mex 1) and Calle General Agustin Sanginés in Ensenada. You will see the Villarino on the right 7.8 miles (12.6 km) from the cutoff.

ROSARITO, BAJA CALIFORNIA (ROE-SAH-REE-TOE)
Population 60,000, Elevation sea level

The main attraction in Rosarito is a nice beach close to the U.S. and Tijuana. On school breaks and weekends, particularly during the summer, Rosarito is a busy place. At other times, particularly during the winter, the town is much more quiet. Virtually everything in town except the beach is right on Avenida Benito Juárez, the main road, so a drive through will give you a good introduction. Watch for the stop signs!

Rosarito has a large Commercial Mexicana supermarket so if you are not planning to go as far as Ensenada you may want to stop and do some shopping there. The town also has curio and Mexican crafts stores, just like Tijuana and Ensenada so you will have a chance to do some shopping if you haven't yet had a chance.

The beach here is probably the main attraction. Unfortunately it is often polluted so swimming is not recommended.

For many years the top hotel in town has been the **Rosarito Beach Hotel**. It's been around since the 20s, and has grown over the years. Today a tour of the place is on most folk's itineraries.

Rosarito Campgrounds

ROSARITO CORA RV PARK
Res.: Box 430513, San Ysidro, CA 92143
Telephone: (6) 613-3305

GPS Location: N 32° 25' 33.1", W 117° 05' 32.2"

Rosarito Cora RV Park (formerly called the Rosarito KOA) is the closest campground to the border crossing in Tijuana. It could be a good overnight stop if you don't want to face the line in the evening.

The campground has about 200 grass-covered level campsites on a sloping hillside. Most are pull-throughs and have 15-amp electrical outlets and water. They also have great views of the coast far below. Unfortunately almost all of the spaces are filled with trailers that have been there for years. Travelers will have a choice of perhaps 10 spaces. While the campground is virtually full there aren't usually many people around, the facilities won't be crowded. The bathrooms are old but reasonably clean and have hot water showers. There is a laundry and a small store, a playground, and a dump station at the top of the campground. You can find groceries in Rosarito, a short drive away.

The campground is just off the toll highway Mex 1D. If you are headed south follow the signs from the border for Rosarito, Ensenada and *cuota* (toll) highway Mex 1D. Take the San Antonio exit 7.6 miles (12.2 km) south of the toll station. Use the overpass to cross the road and then follow the cobblestone driveway up the hill for .2 miles (.3 km). If you are coming from the south or if you have taken the free road to Rosarito you should take the toll road north and exit at the San Antonio exit at the 22 Km marker. There is no toll booth between the intersection of the free road and toll road in Rosarito and the KOA so free-road users won't have to pay to get to the campground if they use this route.

OASIS RESORT

Address:	Km 25 Carretera Escénica No. 1
	Tijuana-Ensenada, B.C., México
Res.:	P.O. Box 158, Imperial Beach, CA 91933
Telephone:	(6) 613-3255 (Mex), (800) 462-7472 (Reservations)
E-mail:	Oasis@telnor.net
Web Site:	www.oasisbaja.com

GPS Location: N 32° 23' 47.8", W 117° 05' 18.6"

This is one of the two most expensive campgrounds we've found in Mexico, reason enough to spend a night here just for the novelty. The other is the Baja Seasons farther south on this same coast. You won't spend much more than you would for a motel in the states and the facilities are great! In the winter the rates are $39 per day and summer rates about $10 higher during the week, $20 higher on weekends. Popular destinations in this part of the Baja have higher summer rates because that's when most people visit.

There are 57 back-in campsites available for visitors. Several others have big fifth-wheels permanently installed that the hotel rents as rooms. Each slot has a paved

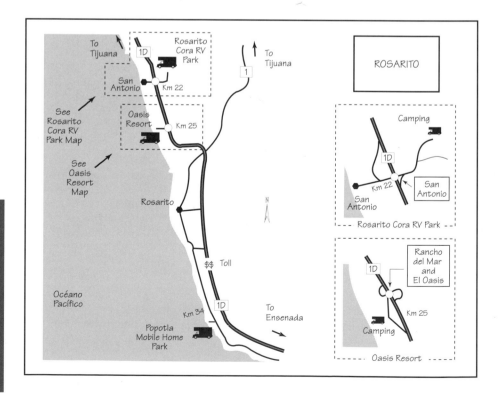

parking area, a patio, 50-amp outlets, sewer, water, TV hookup, patio, and barbecue. The whole place is beautifully landscaped, this is a posh place. Before accepting a campsite check it to make sure that you can level your rig, many have an excessive slope. Make sure too that you can extend your slideouts, some sites have trees that could interfere. There are very nice restrooms with hot showers, several swimming pools including one with a geyser-like fountain in the middle, a hot Jacuzzi next to the pool, a weight room and sauna with ocean view, a tennis court, a pool room, ping-pong, a putting course, a laundry, and a very nice restaurant. There is also a convention center for groups of up to 1,200, if you need one of those. The campground is next to the beach and has beach access. Security is tight and English is spoken. Pets are not allowed. Don't be run off by this description, the place really isn't as big or threatening as it sounds.

Heading south on the toll road Mex 1D the exit for the Oasis is labeled El Oasis, it is at Km 25 and is 9.4 miles (15.1 km) south of the northernmost toll booth. Heading north there is also an exit, it is labeled Rancho del Mar.

POPOTLA MOBILE HOME PARK

Address:	Km 33 Carr. Tijuana-Ensenada Libre, Rosarito, B.C., México
Res.:	P.O. Box 431135, San Ysidro, CA 92143
Telephone:	(6) 612-1501

GPS Location: N 32° 16' 48.5", W 117° 01' 48.0"

This is a large gated RV park mostly filled with permanent residents, but is has a very nice area set aside for short-term campers. We usually find these sites mostly empty, perhaps surprising considering the location next to the ocean, but probably reflecting the fact that we visit mostly during the winter.

There are 40 spaces here for overnighters, all with ocean views. They are large back-in spaces suitable for large rigs with full hook-ups. Electrical outlets are 30-amp and all sites have parking pads. Some sites are set near the water near a small cove, others are above along the bluff. There are bathrooms with hot showers and a swimming pool. The campground is fenced and secure and there is a bar and restaurant on the grounds. No dogs are allowed.

The campground is located near Km 34 on the free road about 7 km (4 miles) south of Rosarito.

Other Camping Possibilities

There are quite a few campgrounds along the beach south of Rosarito. If you want to check them out just follow the free road south from Rosarito, most are full of permanents or are very basic and aimed at the surfing trade.

Side Trips from Rosarito

Mex 1 (Libre) meets the toll highway Mex 1D at the north end of Rosarito. The free highway runs through town while the toll road bypasses it, then they meet and run side by side for about 25 miles (41 km) south. There are lots of developments of various types along this double road, one of the most interesting is **Puerto Nuevo**, about 13 miles (21 km) south of Rosarito. This has become the place to go to get a lobster dinner, there are about 30 restaurants in the small town, they cover the spectrum in price and quality.

NORTHERN BAJA PENINSULA

SAN QUINTÍN, BAJA CALIFORNIA (SAHN KWEEN-TEEN)
Population 25,000 in the area, Elevation near sea level

San Quintín is an interesting place, both geological and historically. The area is a large salt water lagoon system which fronts a fertile plain. Long sandy beaches stretch north and south. The lagoon and plain probably would have eroded away long ago except that there are eight small volcanoes (seven onshore and one an island offshore) that shelter the area from the sea. For the last few decades the plain has been heavily farmed, unfortunately there is not enough fresh water in the aquifer and salt water has started to displace the fresh water. Farming has gradually retreated to the east side of Mex 1.

Farming is also responsible for the interesting history of the area. During the late 19th century the region was the focus of a settlement scheme by an American company and then later an English company under a grant from Mexican President Porfirio Díaz. The plan was to grow wheat but it turned out that there wasn't enough rainfall. Today there are several ruined structures to remind visitors of the colony, they include the Molino Viejo (old mill), the Muelle Viejo (old pier), and the English cemetery.

Outdoorsmen love the area. Goose and duck hunting is good in the winter, fishing offshore is excellent. The protected waters are a good place to launch a trailer boat if you've pulled one south, but the shallow waters of the bay are difficult to navigate and

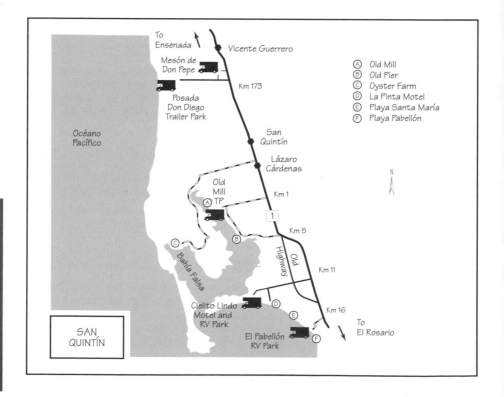

the offshore waters can be dangerous.

In the interests of simplicity we've included several campgrounds in this section that are not properly in the San Quintín area. The two farthest north are 8 miles (13 km) north in the town of Vicente Guerrero, the farthest south are 10 miles (16 km) away from San Quintín. None of the campgrounds in this section, in fact, are actually in the town of San Quintín.

San Quintín Campgrounds

MESÓN DE DON PEPE

Address: Callejon del Turista No. 102, Apdo. No. 7,
Col. Vicente Guerrero, CP 22920 B.C., México
Telephone: (6) 166-2216   **Fax:** (6) 166-2268

GPS Location: N 30° 42' 44.7", W 115° 59' 50.1"

This campground and the one following are in the town of Vicente Guerrero, about 8 miles (13 km) north of San Quintín. Both of these parks have been popular for a long time with traveler's heading south or north, they are a comfortable day's drive from the border. Both are located on the same entrance road, they're within a half-mile of each other. The Don Pepe is the one on the highway and the first one the visitor reaches, it is also the smaller of the two.

There are really two transient camping areas at this park. Just below the restaurant is a grassy area with electrical outlets and water that is set aside for about 10 tent and van campers. Farther from the restaurant on the far side of a few permanents is the RV camping with about 20 pull-through spaces with electricity (15-amp outlets), sewer, and water. Both camping areas have restrooms, they are older but clean and have hot water showers. The restaurant at the Don Pepe is well-known and considered to be very good.

The entrance to the trailer park is on the west side of Mex 1 just south of Col. Vicente Guerrero where the road starts to climb a small hill at the Km 173 marker. There are actually two entrances, the farthest north is well signed and will lead you into the RV camping area. The second is near the top of the hill, just north of the gas plant, this will take you to the restaurant/office. After checking in you'll see a road curving around the back of the trailer park to lead you back down the camping areas.

POSADA DON DIEGO TRAILER PARK

Address: Apdo. 126, Col. Vicente Guerrero, CP 22920, B.C., México
Telephone: (6) 166-2181

GPS Location: N 30° 42' 58.9", W 115° 59' 21.7"

This second Col. Vicente Guerrero trailer park is very popular with caravans, it is roomy and has lots of spaces, in fact it is the only large campground with full hookups in this area.

The campground has 100 spaces, almost 50 of these are usually occupied by permanents. Most of the available slots are large enough for big rigs with pull-outs, they have 15-amp outlets, water, and patios. About half have sewer, there is also a dump station available. The restrooms are in good repair and clean, they have hot water showers. The campground also has a restaurant/bar, a store, a meeting room and a playground.

To reach the Posada Don Diego follow the road going west from just north of the propane plant at Km 173. This is just south of Col. Vicente Guerrero. The same road runs right past the restaurant at the Don Pepe, described above. The campground is about .5 miles (.8 km) down this sometimes rough but passable gravel road.

OLD MILL TRAILER PARK

Address:	Apdo. 90, Valle de San Quintín, B.C., México
Telephone:	(800) 479-7962 (U.S. Reservations) or
	(619) 428-2779 (U.S. Reservations)

GPS Location: 30° 29' 09.8", W115° 58' 32.5"

The Old Mill Trailer Park is becoming more and more popular both as an overnight stop and a fishing destination. It is located some 3 miles (5 km) off Mex 1 on a washboard but otherwise fine dirt road. Big rigs don't hesitate to come here.

The campground has 20 spaces. They all have paved parking pads, patios, electricity with 15-amp outlets, sewer, and water. Fifteen are in the front row with a good view of the estuary and its birds. There is also an area set aside for dry or tent campers. The bathrooms are only a few years old, they have hot water showers. Check in at the bait shop across the driveway from the restaurant or, if it is closed, at the bar. Fishing is good in the area. There's a boat launch if you've brought your own or you can hire a boat and guide.

The access road to the Old Mill leads west from Mex 1 south of Col. Lázaro Cárdenas. It is well- signed at the 1 Km marker. The wide dirt road leads west for 3.3 miles (5.3 km), then you'll see a sign pointing left to the restaurant and RV park. Don't follow signs for Old Pier, that is a different place.

CIELITO LINDO MOTEL AND RV PARK

Address:	Apdo. 7, San Quintín, B.C., México
Telephone:	(619) 222-8955 (U.S. Res.),
	(619) 593-2252 (Voice mail in the U.S.)

GPS Location: N 30° 24' 30.9", W 115° 55' 21.1"

The Cielito Lindo Motel has been around for a long time. It is well-known for its restaurant and fishing charters. At one time it had a large camping area near the beach, that location has been abandoned and is not recommended. There is a second camping area near the hotel which we enjoy. The long and sandy Playa Santa María is a short walk from the campground.

The hotel camping area has 8 back-in slots, they have generator produced electricity with 15-amp outlets, water and sewer. There is a row of pine trees to provide shade and some shelter from the frequent wind in this area. Electricity is produced by an on-site generator so it is available from 7 a.m. to 11 a.m. and from 3 p.m. until the bar closes. The bar also serves as a restaurant, some people come here just because of the food. There is also a small area set aside for tent campers not needing hookups. Restrooms with hot showers are located in a building on the north side of the central courtyard area.

The Cielito Lindo is located near the San Quintín La Pinta Motel. The paved road with lots of potholes leads west from Mex 1 near the Km 11 marker. It is signed for both the La Pinta and the Cielito Lindo. Follow the road west for 2.8 miles (4.5 km) past the La Pinta entrance to the Cielito Lindo entrance.

⊒ EL PABELLÓN RV PARK   [$$] [⛺] [🚰] [🏕] [🚿 HOT]

GPS Location: N 30° 22' 27.3", W 115° 52' 08.7"

Miles of sand dunes and ocean. That's El Pabellón RV park. There really isn't much else. This is a large graded area set in sand dunes close to the ocean. It is being gradually improved. There have been flush toilets and hot showers for some time. There are also six pull through spaces with sewer drains and water and a long line of interesting table-like structures with sinks and barbecues. Everyone just ignores the campsites and parks where they want. Caravans often stop here and circle wagon-train style. Tenters pitch in the dunes in front of the campground or behind rows of trees that provide some shelter if the wind is blowing. There is usually an attendant at the entrance gate.

The turn for El Pabellón is between Km 16 and 17 south of San Quintín. Turn south at the sign and follow the 1.2 mile gravel road to the campground.

Other Camping Possibilities

If you drive the roads around the north side of the Puerto San Quintín estuary you will find primitive camping areas along the bay and on the coast. Do this in small rigs only, the roads can be soft and you can easily get stuck.

South of the San Quintín area and about 5.5 miles (9 km) south of the El Pabellón RV park cutoff is a road to El Socorro beach where free camping is possible.

Side Trips from San Quintín

About 34 miles (55.5 km) north of San Quintín near the Km 141 marker a road goes east to San Telmo, the **Meling Ranch**, and the **Parque Nacional Sierra San Pedro Martír**. The road as far as the Meling ranch at about 32 miles (52 km) is reasonably good and usually OK for smaller RVs. The ranch is about a half-mile off the main road, it has an airstrip and offers overnight accommodations. Beyond the ranch to the park entrance gate at about 51 miles (83 km) the road may not be as good and is sometimes only suitable for pickups and sturdy vans. The road continues to an astronomical observatory at 65 miles (106 km). There are undeveloped campsites in the park and lots of hiking possibilities.

SANTO TOMÁS (SAHN-TOE TOE-MAHS)
Population 200, Elevation 350 ft (105 m)

Tiny Santo Tomás is located in the Santo Tomás Valley some 30 miles (49 km) south of Ensenada. Grapes (for wine) and olives are grown in the valley. The El Palomar resort and balneario is the major attraction of the town. This was a mission village, the grape plantings were by the Dominicans. Today there isn't much left of the mission ruins which are just north of the El Palomar's RV park.

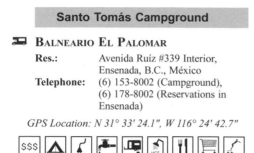

Santo Tomás Campground

🚐 BALNEARIO EL PALOMAR

Res.: Avenida Ruíz #339 Interior,
Ensenada, B.C., México

Telephone: (6) 153-8002 (Campground),
(6) 178-8002 (Reservations in
Ensenada)

GPS Location: N 31° 33' 24.1", W 116° 24' 42.7"

SANTO TOMÁS

Balnearios (swimming resorts) are very popular in Mexico, they often make a good place to camp. This is the best example of such a balneario on the Baja. In 1997 it celebrated its fiftieth anniversary.

The El Palomar has six pull-throughs large enough for big rigs to about 30 feet and about 20 very small back-in spaces. All have 15-amp outlets, sewer, water, patios and barbecues. Many also have picnic tables. Two restroom buildings are clean and in good repair, they have hot water for showers. There are two swimming pools near the camping area and a small lake and water slide about a half-mile away. There's also a small zoo and large areas for picnicking. Across the street in the main building there is a store, a restaurant, and a small gas station. The store has a good collection of Baja books and Mexican handicrafts. Two words of warning are in order. Take a look at the steep entrance before entering and be aware that this is a very popular place with people from Ensenada on weekends during the summer and on holidays. It might be better to avoid the campground during those times since many of the sites are pretty much right in the center of things.

The El Palomar is at the north entrance to the town of Santo Tomás about 30 miles (49 km) south of Ensenada on Mex 1. The office is on the west side of the road and the campground on the east.

Other Camping Possibilities

The coast near La Bocana and Puerto Santo Tomás has several sites suitable for primitive camping. There is also reported to be a formal campground near La Bocana. See the *Side Trips* section below for directions to these spots.

The Malibu Beach RV Park is out on the coast south of Eréndira. It offers full hookups and is next to the beach, unfortunately access would be very difficult for any rig larger than about 24 feet. To get there follow the paved road that leads out to the coast from near Km 78. After about 10 miles (16 km) a temporary-looking road goes left across the dry (hopefully) river bed and climbs the steep bank on the other side. Dirt roads through planted fields then lead you about 3 miles (5 km) south to the campground.

About four miles (6 km) north of Santo Tomás on the main highway is a small picnic and possible camping area. It is associated with the Ejido Uruapan and there is a use fee.

Side Trips from Santo Tomás

There are a couple of roads that lead east to the coast from the vicinity of Santo Tomás. One and nine-tenths miles (3.1 km) north of the El Palomar a gravel road goes along the Santo Tomás valley to **La Bocana** and then north along the coast to **Puerto Santo Tomás**. La Bocana is at the mouth of the Santo Tomás River and is 17.6 miles (28.7 km) from Mex 1. Puerto Santo Tomás is about three miles (5 km) to the north.

South of Santo Tomás near Km 78 (a distance of 16 miles (26 km)) there is a paved road to the coastal town of **Eréndira** at 12 miles (20 km). A smaller road heads north another mile or so to **San Isidro**.

TECATE, BAJA CALIFORNIA (TEH-KAW-TAY)
Population 80,000, Elevation 1,850 ft. (560 m)

Tecate is probably the most relaxed and pleasant border town in Mexico. Besides being a great place to cross into Baja (there is a good road south to Ensenada and a very scenic one east to Mexicali) the town is well worth a short visit.

Tecate is an agricultural center that is gradually turning industrial as the maquiladora industries arrive. The center of town is dominated by the park-like square which is

GREEN ANGEL PROVIDES ASSISTANCE ON MEX 3 NEAR TECATE

just a couple of blocks from the laid-back border crossing. Probably the most famous tourist attraction here is the **Tecate brewery**.

Tecate Campgrounds

⊞ **TECATE KOA, RANCHO OJAI**

Address:	P.O. Box 280, Tecate, CA 91980 (U.S.)
Telephone:	(6) 655-3014 **Fax:** (6) 655-3015
E-mail:	rojai@telnor.net
Web Site:	www.tecatekoa.com

GPS Location: N 32° 33' 32.6", W 116° 26' 09.5"

Rancho Ojai is something a little different in Baja campgrounds. This is a former working ranch located in the rolling hills just east of Tecate off Mex 2. The facilities are brand-new and nicely done. It is now a KOA. This is normally a summer destination, the area is known for its mild summer weather, but winters have an occasional frost.

There are 75 campsites, 41 have full hookups with 30-amp outlets, sewer, and water. The tiled restrooms are brand new and clean with hot water showers. The ranch offers a ranch-style clubhouse, a barbecue area, swimming pool, grocery shop, sports areas

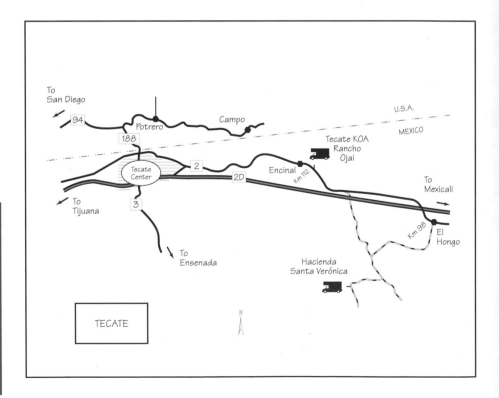

for volley ball and horseshoes, bicycle rentals and a children's playground. The campground is fenced and there is 24-hour security. There's a good restaurant just outside the grounds, just a pleasant stroll through the pasture will take you there.

The Rancho is located about 13 miles (21 km) east of Tecate on the north side of the free highway near the Km 112 marker. It is not accessible from the toll highway. There is a stone arch entrance near the highway and you can see the camping area across the valley.

HACIENDA SANTA VERÓNICA

Address:	Blvd. Agua Caliente No. 4558, Piso No. 1,
	Ofic. 105 Torres de Agua Caliente,
	Tijuana, CP 22420 B.C., México
Telephone:	(6) 681-7428 (Tijuana), (6) 648-5234 (On site)

GPS Location: N 32° 27' 34.3", W 116° 21' 46.6"

Slightly farther east of Tecate than the Tecate KOA is Hacienda Santa Verónica. To get there you must negotiate a partially paved back road but once you've reached the campground you're likely to want to spend some time. This is a 5,000 acre rancho. It is described in its own brochures as rustic, but other than the no-hookup campground it is really surprisingly polished. The rancho is very popular with off-road motorcycle riders and also offers quite a few amenities: rental rooms, a huge swimming pool with a bar in the middle, good tennis courts, a nice restaurant and bar, horseback riding, and occasionally even a bullfight. This is a popular summer destination, in the winter things are pretty quiet except on weekends.

The camping area is a grassy meadow with big oak trees for shade. Spaces are unmarked, you camp where you want to. The restrooms are near the pool, not far from the camping area. In the summer when the pool is in use they have hot water showers. The Santa Veronica also has a nice full-hookup campground that has been closed down because it wasn't getting enough use. Perhaps they'll open it again if enough of us visit!

To find the hacienda head east on Mex 2 from the Tecate KOA to the small town of El Hongo, a distance of 8.7 miles (14 km) from the Tecate KOA. Near the center of town there is a small road heading south through the village, it is marked with an easy-to-miss Hacienda Verónica sign. After 1.1 miles (1.8 km) the road curves right and leaves town. You'll reach a Y after 4.7 miles (7.6 km) take the right fork and you'll reach the gate in another 1.5 miles (2.4 km). Much of this road is rough and unpaved.

Side Trips from Tecate

Laguna Hanson is accessible from the north off Mex 3 but the road is not as good as the one from the south off Mex 3 which is discussed in the *Side Trips from Ensenada* section above. From Tecate go east to Km 72 which is about 36 miles (58.8 km) distant. The road south is not suitable for RVs but OK for smaller rigs with good clearance. The distance to Laguna Hanson is about 40 miles (65 km).

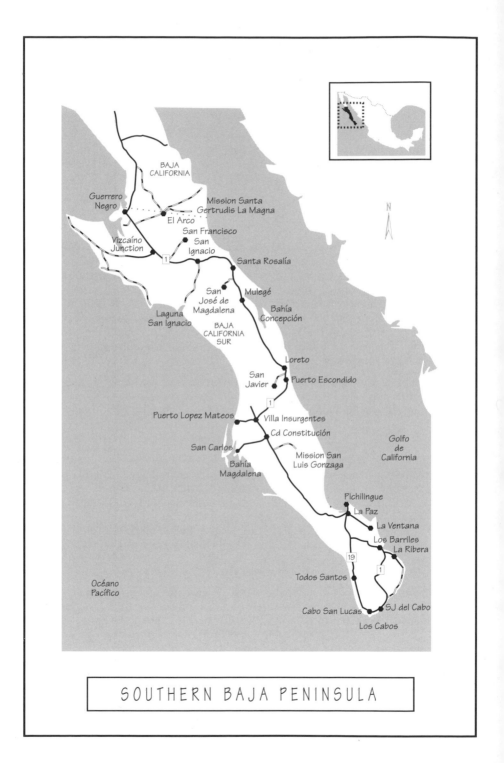

SOUTHERN BAJA PENINSULA

INTRODUCTION

The southern Baja Peninsula, the state of Baja California Sur, extends from the 28th parallel in the north to the tip of the peninsula near Cabo San Lucas, a distance of about 425 air miles (700 km). A range of mountains extends along much of the entire length of this section of Baja near the east coast, just as it does in the north. To the west the land is flat. Often there are large swampy estuaries along the flat west coast while the eastern Gulf Coast is generally rocky. Large areas of desert land have few inhabitants but there are major population centers at La Paz and near the southern tip of the state at San José del Cabo and Cabo San Lucas. The east coast between Santa Rosalía and Loreto has several interesting small towns, often tourist oriented, and farming regions center around Ciudad Constitución and Todos Santos.

ROAD SYSTEM

Just like in the Northern Baja there is one road, Mex 1, that forms the backbone of the transportation routes in Baja Sur. From the north Mex 1 crosses the 28th parallel near Guerrero Negro on the west coast. Then it turns inland and crosses the peninsula to Santa Rosalía on the east coast. Turning south the highway passes Mulegé, Bahía Concepción, Loreto, and Puerto Escondido before climbing into the Sierra de la Giganta and heading southwest for the farming center of Ciudad Constitución. La Paz appears as the highway once again reaches the Sea of Cortez after another desert crossing, then the road circles down the east side of the peninsula to San José del Cabo and Cabo San Lucas. There's also a shortcut between La Paz and Cabo San Lucas, a west coast highway called Mex 19.

Mex 1 is well marked with kilometer signs. In Baja California Sur the signs count from south to north, an order exactly opposite that of the signs in Baja California on the north half of the peninsula. In each section the signs begin at zero. The sections, from south to north, are as follows: Cabo San Lucas to La Paz, 137 miles (224 km); La Paz to Ciudad Insurgentes, 149 miles (240 km); Ciudad Insurgentes to Loreto, 74 miles (120 km); Loreto to Santa Rosalía 122 miles 197 km); Santa Rosalía to Guerrero Negro, 137 miles (221 km).

Opportunities for RVers in larger rigs to get off the main road are limited but available. If you wish to stick to paved roads you can follow the road to the farming area of San Juan de los Planes south of La Paz, drive along the coast to the northeast of La Paz to Pichilingue and the ferry dock (see *Side Trips from La Paz*), drive west from Ciudad Constitución to San Carlos on the Bahía Magdalena or west from Ciudad Insurgentes to Puerto López Mateos (see *Side Trips from Ciudad Constitución*) or go out to see the whales on the road to Ojo de Liebre Lagoon from south of Guerrero Negro (see *Guerrero Negro Campgrounds*).

RVers with smaller rigs have a wider selection of exploration options. A few of them include the road to El Arco (see *Side Trips from Guerrero Negro*), portions of the road system on the Vizcaíno Peninsula west of Vizcaíno and south of Guerrero Negro (see *Side Trips from the Vizcaíno Junction*), and soon perhaps even the road along the east coast of the peninsula between La Ribera and San José del Cabo if it gets completed as planned.

Travelers with high-clearance vehicles who do not mind a lot of washboard surfaces may want to consider the roads east to the coast from El Arco (see *Side Trips from Guerrero Negro*), the poorer roads on the Vizcaíno Peninsula (see *Side Trips from the Vizcaíno Junction*), a short route from south of Santa Rosalía east to the mission town of San José de Magdalena, the road east from Mex 1 south of Ciudad Constitución to Mission San Luis Gonzaga (see *Side Trips from Ciudad Constitución*), the road north along the coast from Los Barriles (see *Side Trips from Los Barriles*), or the road along the east coast of the peninsula between La Ribera and San José del Cabo if it doesn't get improved as planned.

Before the completion of Mex 1 south of Rosario the easiest access to the southern peninsula was by ferry from the mainland. There continue to be three ferry routes from the peninsula to the mainland in operation: Santa Rosalía - Guaymas, Pichilingue (La Paz) - Topolobampo (near Los Mochis), and Pichilingue - Mazatlán. It is possible to make reservations for these ferries and this is recommended but not always necessary. The phone number for reservations is 01-800-6-96-9600 which is a toll-free Mexico number. The Santa Rosalía ferry runs twice weekly and the Pichilingue ones run daily. One inconvenience is that it is usually necessary to pick up your ticket at the local office on the day before sailing. If you are considering using the ferries to reach the mainland remember that you must have your paperwork in order including a vehicle permit for your rig. These are available in La Paz but you might consider getting them at the border when entering Mexico to make sure that you have everything in order before making the long drive south. See the *Ferries* section of Chapter 2 for more information.

HIGHLIGHTS

Fly-in tourists generally head for the cape area and the two towns there: San José del Cabo and Cabo San Lucas. These are also exciting destinations for the camping traveler with every sort of tourist attraction including golf, fishing, beaches, restaurants and many RV parks. The large city of La Paz, about 98 miles (160 km) north, is also an interesting destination because it has tourist facilities but retains a charm reminiscent of the colonial cities on the mainland.

La Paz, San José del Cabo, and Cabo San Lucas are really the only sizable destination cities on the southern peninsula but there are several smaller towns that make interesting stops because of their general ambiance or attractions. These include Todos Santos, Los Barriles, Loreto, Mulegé, Santa Rosalía, San Ignacio, and Guerrero Negro. Each of these towns has at least one RV park and is covered in more detail in this chapter.

One of the most interesting attractions offered in the southern Baja is whale watching. Each winter thousands of gray whales visit the large shallow lagoons on the west side of the peninsula. From January until April they remain in these nursery lagoons where the young are born and grow until they are ready for a long migration north to the Arctic Ocean. Probably the best place to see them is Laguna Ojo de Libre (Scammon's Lagoon) near Guerrero Negro, but they are also present in San Ignacio Lagoon and Magdalena Bay. See the *Guerrero Negro* and *San Ignacio* sections of this chapter for information about visiting the whales.

The Baja Peninsula offers something available almost nowhere else in North America, lots of boondocking or free camping right on the beach. The easiest access to this type of camping, especially for large RVs, is on Bahía Concepción which has a special section in this chapter. There are plenty of other much more remote camping locations. Most require several hours and many miles of driving on rough unimproved roads, but if you have the right rig Baja has some unique offerings. It's hard to think of another place in the would with so many miles of beautiful deserted beaches, and these beaches are in a sunny, warm climate.

EL REQUESÓN BEACH ON BAHÍA CONCEPCÍON

SOUTHERN BAJA PENINSULA

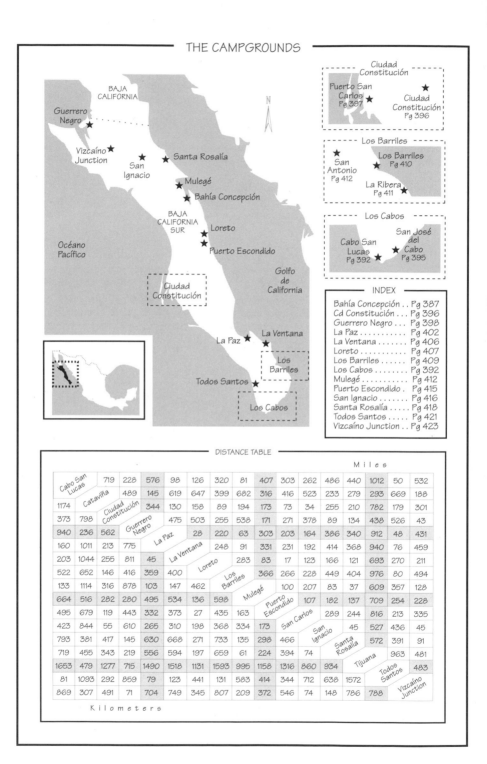

Fishermen will find some excellent sport on the southern Baja. Deep sea fishing is popular out of Cabo San Lucas. Panga charters are available from Mulegé, Loreto, La Paz, and Los Barriles. Campers with their own boats should bring them along, there will be lots of opportunities to use them.

Hikers and tent-campers looking for high pine country like that in the two national parks in the northern Baja have a southern Baja option also. This is the Sierra La Laguna. Located in the middle of the loop that Mex 1 and Mex 19 make between La Paz and Cabo San Lucas these granite mountains rise to 7,000 feet and are accessible only on foot. The easiest-to-find route in is from the west near Todos Santos so you'll find further information in this book under *Side Trips from Todos Santos*.

As you drive along Mex 1 there are several places where you may see government signs pointing down gravel roads where you can find *pinturas rupestres*. These are cave paintings, paintings on the rocks done by Indians long ago. The actual age of most of these paintings is unknown. A side trip to view cave paintings is included in the *San Ignacio* section.

SELECTED CITIES AND THEIR CAMPGROUNDS

BAHÍA CONCEPCIÓN (BAH-HEE-AH KOHN-SEP-SEE-OHN), BAJA CALIFORNIA SUR

For many people, especially RVers, the Bahía Concepción is the ultimate Baja destination. This huge shallow bay offers many beaches where you can park your camping vehicle just feet from the water and spend the winter months soaking in the sunshine. Mex 1 parallels the western shore of the bay for about 20 miles (33 km), you'll see many very attractive spots and undoubtedly decide to stop. The many beaches offer different levels of services. Full hookups are seldom available, but many have toilets, showers, water, and restaurants. Information about the most popular beaches is offered below. While many of these places seem to have no formal organization do not be surprised if someone comes by in the evening to collect a small fee. This usually covers keeping the area picked up, trash removal and pit toilets. Ask one of your fellow campers about arrangements if you have questions. The closest place to get supplies is Mulegé, about 12 miles (20 km) north.

Bahía Concepción Campgrounds

🚐 LOS NARANJOS

GPS Location: N 26° 47' 02.1", W 111° 51' 48.8"

Two camping areas occupy Punta Arena. The one to the north is Los Naranjos.

This campground occupies the actual point. To the north along open beach there is a large open parking area. Along the more protected beach to the south are permanent structures, however there is some space to camp behind them. There is a small restaurant, as well as primitive restrooms with flush toilets and hot showers. There's also a dump station.

The entrance to Playa Los Naranjos is .2 miles (.3 km) south of the Km 118 marker. It

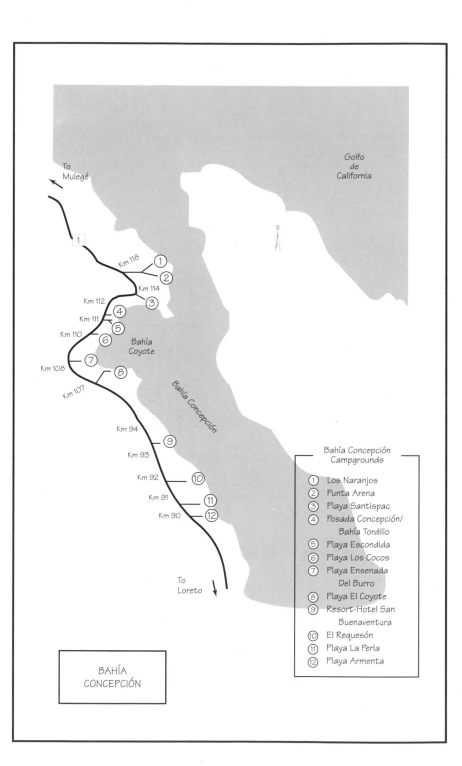

Golfo
de
California

To
Mulegé

1

Km 118   ①
              ②
Km 114
Km 112   ③
Km 111   ④
          ⑤
Km 110   ⑥   Bahía
                   Coyote
Km 108   ⑦
              ⑧
Km 107

Bahía Concepción

Km 94
              ⑨
Km 93
Km 92   ⑩
Km 91   ⑪
Km 90   ⑫

To
Loreto

Bahía Concepción
Campgrounds

① Los Naranjos
② Punta Arena
③ Playa Santispac
④ Posada Concepción/
   Bahía Tordillo
⑤ Playa Escondida
⑥ Playa Los Cocos
⑦ Playa Ensenada
   Del Burro
⑧ Playa El Coyote
⑨ Resort-Hotel San
   Buenaventura
⑩ El Requesón
⑪ Playa La Perla
⑫ Playa Armenta

BAHÍA
CONCEPCIÓN

is marked with a sign to Punta Arena. The road in to the beach is rough but should be negotiable by any RV at very slow speeds. It is 2.1 miles (3.4 km) long, at .4 miles (.7 km) there is a Y where you go left for Playa los Naranjos and right for Playa Punta Arena.

⊞ PUNTA ARENA

GPS Location: N 26° 46' 44.1", W 111° 52' 23.2"

There are actually two different camping area on this large beach: Playa los Naranjos to the north and Playa Punta Arena to the south. The entry road branches not far from the highway and you make your decision there. Punta Arena is the fork to the right.

The beach at Punta Arena is long and not nearly as crowded as the beaches to the south. It is quite easy to find a place along the water most of the time. There are pit toilets. Small palapas are available. In the scrub behind the beach the residents have set up a small sand golf course.

The entrance to Punta Arena is .2 miles (.3 km) south of the Km 118 marker. The road in to the beach is rough but should be negotiable by any RV at very slow speeds. It is two miles (3 km) long, at .4 miles (.7 km) there is a Y where you go left for Playa los Naranjos and right for Playa Punta Arena.

⊞ PLAYA SANTISPAC

GPS Location: N 26° 45' 56.8", W 111° 53' 15.2"

The farthest north beach on sheltered Bahía Coyote is very popular, partly because the entrance road is so short and easy. The fee here is slightly higher than most other beaches in the area.

The long beach offers beachside parking for many, but you will find that the beach sites are often very crowded together and full. There are flush toilets, a dump station, hot and cold showers, and a couple of restaurants. There is also a small muddy hot spring located a short walk to the west just below the highway and at the back of a grove of mangroves.

The entrance to Playa Santispac is midway between the Km 114 and Km 113 markers. The beach is visible from the road. While short and in good shape the entrance road is a little steep, exercise care when leaving the highway. There is a manned entrance station where the fee is collected.

⊞ POSADA CONCEPCIÓN/BAHÍA TORDILLO

Address: Apdo. 14, Mulegé, B.C.S., México

GPS Location: N 26° 45' 11.1", W 111° 53' 56.7"

Posada Concepción is really more subdivision than beachfront camping area, most of the people here live in houses or permanently installed trailers. There are a few spaces for transients, they are nowhere near the water but they do have hookups.

There are ten slots here with full hookups, electrical outlets are 15-amp. The spaces are fine for large rigs. Nice restrooms have flush toilets and hot showers. This beach is well-protected, at low tide the water is very shallow and there are a few hot-water seeps in shallow water. There is also a tennis court.

The entrance to Posada Concepción is just north of the Km 111 marker.

🚐 PLAYA ESCONDIDA

GPS Location: N 26° 44' 42.4", W 111° 53' 44.7"

This small isolated beach is picture-perfect. There is a row of palapas along the water. Outhouses and cold water showers are on the hillside behind.

The road in to this beach is somewhat rough, we recommend it for rigs no longer than 30 feet and not for trailers. The entrance road is just south of Posada Concepción and is shared by the Eco Mundo kayaking operation. At first glance you'll think the road leads to the south side of the same bay occupied by Posada Concepción, but instead it leads .5 miles (.8 km) up over a low saddle to an unexpected beach, hence the name which means hidden beach.

🚐 PLAYA LOS COCOS

GPS Location: N 26° 44' 28.7", W 111° 54' 03.9"

Playa los Cocos is another beautiful beach with minimal facilities. There are palapas, pit toilets, and a dump station. Mangroves are at the rear.

The entrance is at near the Km 110 marker. There is no sign and the entrance road is about .3 miles (.5 km) long. The campground can easily be seen from the highway because it runs very close.

🚐 PLAYA ENSENADA DEL BURRO

GPS Location: N 26° 43' 38.0", W 111° 54' 21.1"

This beach offers the standard pit toilets but also has a restaurant. There's even a small store across the highway. Parking is along the water where there are a number of palapas. Caravans often stay here.

The entrance to Playa Del Burro is at the Km 108 marker. You can easily see the beach from the highway.

🚐 PLAYA EL COYOTE

GPS Location: N 26° 42' 45.2", W 111° 54' 09.6"

Another good beach with few facilities. A tree or two provide shade on this beach and it is not quite as crowded as the spots farther north, perhaps because the road is slightly more difficult. It has bucket-flush toilets and a dump station. There is a hot spring along the rocks to the east. Several guidebooks to the Baja have a picture on the cover of RVs parked on this beach, two palms right next to the water, often with RVs parked beneath, make an enticing shot from above.

The entrance road to El Coyote is near the Km 107 marker. After leaving the highway and driving down to the water turn right and proceed .5 miles (.8 km) along the water below the cliff to the camping area.

SOUTHERN BAJA PENINSULA

RESORT-HOTEL SAN BUENAVENTURA

Address: Km 93 Carr. Transp. Loreto - Mulegé, Playa
Buenaventura, Mulegé, B.C.S., México
Telephone: (1) 153-0408

GPS Location: N 26° 38' 34.4", W 111° 50' 43.5"

Playa Buenaventura has a very nice little hotel, restaurant/sports bar and trailer park, all under the same ownership. English is spoken. The trailer park has 15 slots along the beach with palapas but no hookups. Actually even a few more rigs can be accommodated. There is a flush toilet, hot showers, a launch ramp, and security with lights at night. The bar has U.S. television and there is a mini-market across the highway. Some caravans like this spot but individual campers seem to think the place is too expensive considering the wealth of nearby primitive camping beaches. This well-run operation necessarily has higher overhead than some of the shoestring camping areas on other beaches.

The entrance to San Buenaventura is near Km 93 on Mex 1. The main road is almost at beach level here. There's quite a bit of room out front making this a good turn-around spot if you have missed a turnoff to the north or south.

EL REQUESÓN

GPS Location: N 26° 38' 13.1", W 111° 49' 52.5"

This is the most picturesque of the Bahía Concepción beaches. The beach is a short sand spit which connects a small island to the mainland at low tide. Small, shallow bays border both sides of the spit. There are pit toilets but no other amenities. You can hike along the water to the south as far as Playa La Perla. Someone will come by to collect a small fee each evening.

The entrance to El Requesón is about a half-kilometer north of the Km 91 marker and is signed. The entrance road is rough but should present no problems for most RVs, it is about .2 miles (.3 km) long. You may find that it is easier to enter the road if you are approaching from the north so northbound travelers may drive on less than a mile and turn around in front of Playa Buenaventura.

PLAYA LA PERLA

GPS Location: N 26° 38' 03.6", W 111° 49' 27.1"

This beachside camping area offers pit toilets and many palapas. It is a small sandy cove with a lot of additional camping locations to the north and south of the cove. The cove itself is probably better for tent campers while rigs may prefer the adjoining areas.

The entrance road is between Km 90 and 91. If you enter this way the road is about .4 mile (.6 km) long. You can also use the entrance road to El Requesón, turn right as you reach the beach, and trundle slowly along the shoreline south to Playa La Perla. We find this entrance to be easier with larger rigs, there is less chance of scratching the side of your RV.

PLAYA ARMENTA

GPS Location: N 26° 37' 31.5", W 111° 48' 37.3"

This is an exposed location without a great beach, but it has palapas and pit toilet.

The entrance road is near Km 90. The entrance road is .5 miles long (9 km) and somewhat difficult for big rigs although we've seen 35-foot motorhomes in here.

Other Camping Possibilities

While the most popular beaches are mentioned above you will find that there are others, particularly between Km 89 and 80. The southern shore of the Bahía Concepción is accessible from a road between the Km 76 and 77 markers. There is one of the old government-built RV parks along this road but it is no longer used. There are many campsites along the southern shore of the bay but this area is exposed to weather and not as attractive as the western shore of the Bahía.

Los Cabos, Baja California Sur (loes KAH-bohs)
Population 25,000, Elevation sea level

For many campers headed down the peninsula for the first time Los Cabos (The Capes) is the end of the rainbow, the ultimate destination. While Los Cabos is a world-class resort and very popular destination for folks flying out from the U.S. and Canada you will probably find that you've seen a fine selection of much more desirable stops during your trip south. The truth is that Los Cabos is hectic and oriented toward folks looking for a few days of fun in the sun.

Many old-timers decry the growth and avoid Los Cabos at all costs. That reaction to the Los Cabos area is probably a little extreme. Los Cabos has lots to offer and a good number of decent RV parks provide excellent accommodations. The number of RV parks in the Los Cabos area seems to be declining, however, as land values increase.

The Los Cabos area really covers two major towns: Cabo San Lucas and San José del Cabo which is located about 20 miles (33 km) east. San José del Cabo is the older town and is more relaxed and comfortable. Cabo San Lucas, on the other hand, is chock full of hotels, restaurants, shops, and activity. The area between the two is known as the Cabo Corridor. Most campgrounds are located in the Cabo Corridor just to the east of Cabo San Lucas.

Once you are settled in a good campground you'll be looking for something to do. Los Cabos may not be cheap but it does offer lots of activities. Deep-sea fishing is popular and good, check out a charter or panga rental at the huge marina in the center of Cabo San Lucas. Golf is popular in this area, there are at least six good courses here. If you are looking for a beach you will find several along the road between Cabo San Lucas and San José del Cabo. In the evening head for one of the many restaurants offering good food and music (often rock) in Cabo San Lucas.

Los Cabos Campgrounds

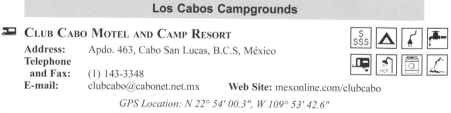

Club Cabo Motel and Camp Resort

Address: Apdo. 463, Cabo San Lucas, B.C.S, México
Telephone and Fax: (1) 143-3348
E-mail: clubcabo@cabonet.net.mx   **Web Site:** mexonline.com/clubcabo

GPS Location: N 22° 54' 00.3", W 109° 53' 42.6"

This campground is different than the others in Cabo. It somehow seems more Euro-

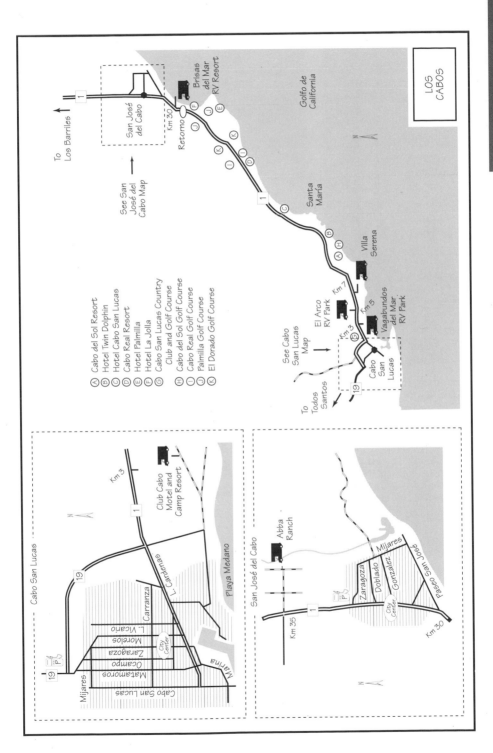

LOS CABOS

To Los Barriles

To Los Barriles

San José del Cabo

See San José del Cabo Map

Km 30

Retorno

Brisas del Mar RV Resort

Golfo de California

Santa María

Villa Serena

Km 7

Km 5

Km 3

El Arco RV Park

Vagabundos del Mar RV Park

See Cabo San Lucas Map

Cabo San Lucas

To Todos Santos

Ⓐ Cabo del Sol Resort
Ⓑ Hotel Twin Dolphin
Ⓒ Hotel Cabo San Lucas
Ⓓ Cabo Real Resort
Ⓔ Hotel Palmilla
Ⓕ Hotel La Jolla
Ⓖ Cabo San Lucas Country Club and Golf Course
Ⓗ Cabo del Sol Golf Course
Ⓘ Cabo Real Golf Course
Ⓙ Palmilla Golf Course
Ⓚ El Dorado Golf Course

Cabo San Lucas

Km 3

Club Cabo Motel and Camp Resort

Playa Medano

Mijares

Matamoros

Ocampo

Zaragoza

Morelos

L. Vicario

Carranza

L. Cárdenas

Marina

City Center

Cabo San Lucas

San José del Cabo

Abba Ranch

Km 35

City Center

Mijares

Zaragoza

Doblado

Gonzalez

Paseo San José

Km 30

pean than Mexican. It is a combination motel and campground and is slightly off the beaten track.

There are 10 campsites, most have 15-amp outlets, sewer, and water. These are all back-in sites. There isn't room for really big rigs, 24 feet is about the maximum length motorhome that can easily enter and park. The bathroom and shower building has a flush toilet and good hot shower. There is a very nice pool and hot tub, coin-operated laundry, hammock lounge area with color TV, barbecue, and kitchen clean-up station. English is spoken and reservations are recommended.

The Club Cabo is located right behind the Vagabundos campground. To get to it you must take a roundabout route. Start from Mex 1 about two miles (3 km) east of downtown Cabo San Lucas where Mex 19 and Mex 1 intersect. Go south from this intersection for .3 miles (.5 km) until it dead-ends. Turn left and drive .2 miles (.3 km) to a Y, the Villa de Palmas is right, go left for Club Cabo. You are now on a small winding road, in .6 mile (1 km) you'll see the Club Cabo on the left.

⛺ VAGABUNDOS DEL MAR RV PARK

Address: Apdo. 197, Cabo San Lucas, B.C.S., México
Telephone: (1) 143-0290 (Mex), 800 474-Baja or
                        707 374-5511 (U.S.)
Fax: (1) 143-0511

GPS Location: N 22° 54' 03.1", W 109° 53' 49.4"

The Vagabundos park probably has the nicest facilities in Cabo. However, it has no view and is not on the beach. It is more convenient to town than most other parks.

There are 85 spaces with 15 or 30-amp outlets, sewer, water, and patios. Many are filled with permanently-located rigs. The roads are paved and the parking spaces are gravel. The restrooms are clean and modern and have hot water showers. There's a swimming pool with a palapa bar and restaurant, a laundry, vehicle washing facilities, and a fence all the way around. English is spoken and reservations are recommended.

The campground is right at the Km 3 marker on Mex 1 east of Cabo San Lucas. It is on the south side of the road.

⛺ EL ARCO RV PARK

Address: Km 5.5, Carr. a San Jose del Cabo,
                        Cabo San Lucas, B.C.S., México
Telephone: (1) 143-1686   **Fax:** (1) 143-3998

GPS Location: N 22° 54' 18.9", W 109° 52' 29.7"

This is a large park located on a hillside overlooking Cabo San Lucas. Many permanents and the bar/restaurant have an outstanding view, but the sites available for travelers really don't have any view at all.

There are 90 camping slots, all have 15-amp outlets, sewer, water, and patios. They are arranged around a semicircular brick driveway or in an area farther up the hill. They are all back-ins. The restrooms are clean and have hot showers. There is a restaurant/bar, swimming pool, and a self-service laundry. English is spoken and reservations are recommended.

The campground is located just east of Cabo San Lucas with the entrance road on the north side of Mex 1 at Km 5.2.

♨ VILLA SERENA

Address: Km 7.5 Carretera Transpeninsular Benito Juárez,
Cabo San Lucas, CP 23410 B.C.S., México

**Telephone
or Fax:**   (1) 143-0509

GPS Location: N 22° 54' 21.9", W 109° 51' 47.7"

This is a new campground with lots of room for big rigs. The facilities are good, but because the place is brand new there is little in the way of landscaping. In fact, there is no shade at all on this large sandy lot. Some trees have been planted but it will take them a while to grow to the point where they are of some use. The campground sits near the highway which is far above the water at this location. Some of the upper sites have a water view.

The campground has 56 very large back-in spaces. Each has electricity, sewer, and water hookups. The outlets are the small 15-amp variety although the breakers are 40 amp. There's a new and very nice facilities building with restrooms with flush toilets and hot showers, a self-service laundry with washers and dryers, and a lounge area. Nearby is the Restaurant Bar Villa Serena, a nice place.

The entrance road goes south from near the Km 7 marker between Cabo San Lucas and San José del Cabo.

♨ BRISA DEL MAR RV RESORT

(Back) *(Front)*

Address: Apdo. 45, San José del Cabo,
CP 23400 B.C.S., México

Telephone: (1) 142-2935

Web Site: www.brisadelmar.com/rvresort/

GPS Location: N 23° 02' 16.2", W 109° 42' 31.5"

The Brisa del Mar is the only beachfront campground left in the Cape region. This is a large popular campground with decent facilities, it is much closer to San José del Cabo than to Cabo San Lucas. The beach is very nice.

This is a large campground, the sites along the beach are pull-in or back-in, the others are mostly pull-throughs. All have 30-amp outlets and water, the beach sites don't have sewer. The sites back from the beach also have patios and some shade. Restrooms are OK but not outstanding, they have hot water showers. There is a bar and restaurant, a pool, and a laundry. There are also some game areas and equipment rentals as well as a small store. English is spoken and reservations are accepted and strongly advised during the winter.

You'll see the campground just south of Mex 1 between the Km 29 and Km 30 markers just west of San José del Cabo. Access heading east is easy, just turn in. If you are heading west on this divided highway you'll have to go another .2 miles west (.3 km) to a retorno and come back to get into the park. There is plenty of room at the turn-around for big rigs.

♨ ABBA RANCH

Address: P.O. Box 206, San José del Cabo, CP 23400 BCS, México

Telephone: (1) 422-3715

GPS Location: N 23° 05' 23.2", W 109° 42' 05.2"

This is a small family-run place located north of San José del Cabo. Despite the small size the facilities are good, and Abba Ranch is definitely a change from the other campgrounds in the area. It is not near the beach, in fact, it is located in a down-scale suburb near the edge of town. The view from some sites and the pool area of the countryside toward the east is very pretty.

There are 14 back-in spaces for rigs to about 35 feet. Spaces have 15-amp outlets, sewer and water. Restrooms are modern and have hot water showers and there is a nice swimming pool. The campground is walled and has lots of trees for shade. There is no swimming or work on Saturdays for religious reasons. The owner will cook vegetarian meals when ordered ahead and also bakes and sells excellent bread.

This campground is located north of San José del Cabo between town and the airport. From town drive north about 1.8 miles (2.9 km). Watch for the sign for Santa Rosa about .1 miles (.2 km) north of the Km 35 marker. The turn for Santa Rosa is at a stop light and goes west, instead turn east on a dirt road. Drive about two blocks, the campground is directly ahead.

CIUDAD CONSTITUCIÓN, BAJA CALIFORNIA SUR
(SEE-OOH-DAHD KOHN-STIH-TOO-SEE-OHN)
Population 45,000

This burgeoning farm town isn't found in most tourist guides. It does have RV parks, supermarkets, and automobile dealerships. Ciudad Constitución's location makes it a handy stop if you're headed north from beyond La Paz (only 130 easy miles (212 km) southeast) or need a base for whale watching in Bahía Magdalena to the west.

The first two campgrounds below are in Ciudad Constitución, the last is 34 miles (55 km) west in Puerto San Carlos.

Ciudad Constitucíon Campgrounds

🚐 **MANFRED'S RV TRAILER PARK**

    Address: Apdo. 120, Cd. Constitución,
                       B.C.S., México
    Telephone: (1) 132-1103

    GPS Location: N 25° 02' 54.4", W 111° 40' 48.9"

$$$ ⛺   🚰   🚐   🚿   🍽   🏊

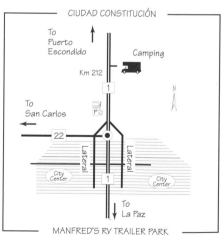

This is a trailer park you just have to appreci-ate. The Austria-born owners are turning a dusty lot into a garden, at last count they had planted 1,600 shrubs and trees.

There are now 34 large pull-throughs with 15-amp outlets, sewer, and water and at least that many smaller back-in spaces with electricity and water. Two spotless restroom build-ings have hot showers. There is a small swimming pool and even an Austrian restau-rant with the food home-cooked by a lady who knows what she's doing.

The campground is very near the northwestern border of Ciudad Constitución and right on Mex 1 at about Km 212.

⊞ CAMPESTRE LA PILA BALNEARIO AND TRAILER PARK

Address: Apdo. 261, Ciudad Constitución, B.C.S., México
Telephone: (1) 132-0582

GPS Location: N 25° 01' 02.0", W 111° 40' 37.1"

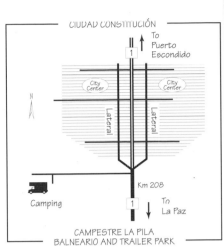

CAMPESTRE LA PILA
BALNEARIO AND TRAILER PARK

This is another balneario RV park. Winter travelers will probably not appreciate the pool quite as much as those passing this way during the really hot months.

There are 18 back-in spaces with 15-amp outlets and water. Sites are separated by grassy areas and the camping area is a very large lot surrounded by palm trees. The nicely landscaped pool area next to the camping area has the bathrooms and there are hot water showers. There is a dump station.

The turnoff from Mex 1 to the campground is near the south end of Ciudad Constitución at the point where the lateral streets begin. Turn west and follow the high tension electrical lines for .7 miles (1.1 km) and turn left into the campground at the sign. The campground is around to the left near the pools, the office in the large building on the right. There is plenty of room to maneuver.

⊞ RV PARK NANCY

Telephone: (1) 136-0195

GPS Location: N 24° 47' 27.6", W 112° 06' 37.4"

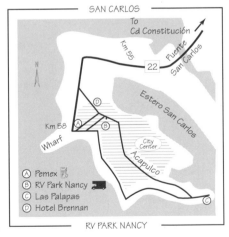

RV PARK NANCY

This is a small new RV park in a town that has needed such a facility for some time.

There are 8 back-in sites with 15-amp outlets and water, also a dump station. The lot where the RV park is located is small, maneuvering room is limited, but by backing the short distance from the street rigs to 40 feet should fit. The restroom has a flush toilet and hot shower.

As you come in to San Carlos you will pass the huge power plant and then cross a slough onto the island. Watch for the sign for San Carlos. The left turn for the RV park is in another .1 mile (.2 km), there is a sign. The RV park is .4 mile (.6 km) down this road on the right.

Other Camping Possibilities

Puerto San Carlos (see *Side Trips from Ciudad Constitución* below) has several location suitable for primitive camping. The town is located on an island accessible by bridge and there are primitive campsites north of town along the water and also through town and near the southeast point of the island where many people camp along the shore near what used to be an RV park called Las Palapas.

Side Trips from Ciudad Constitución

There are two good spots to access the gray whale breeding waters of the **Bahía Magdalena**. One is **Puerto San Carlos** which is accessible on a good, paved 36-mile (50-km) highway that heads west from Ciudad Constitución. The other is **Puerto López Mateos**, also accessible by good paved highway. Drive north on Mex 1 from Ciudad Constitución to Villa Insurgentes and then west to Puerto López Mateos. The distance is 35 miles (56 km). The whales are in the Bahía from January to March, you can arrange tours in both towns. The waters of the Bahía Magdalena are great for small boats, if you have one you can easily find isolated beaches for camping.

Nine miles (15 km) south of Ciudad Constitución on Mex 1 at Km marker 191 a road goes east to **San Luis Gonzaga**. The road is marked for Presa Iguajil and the palms of the San Luis Gonzaga oasis are 25 miles (40 km) down the road which is suitable for small RVs. The mission church has been restored by the Mexican government.

GUERRERO NEGRO, BAJA CALIFORNIA SUR (GEH-REH-row NEH-grow)
Population 8,000, Elevation sea level

The 28th parallel is the dividing line between the states of Baja North and Baja South. You'll know when you pass over the line because it is marked by a huge statue of a stylized Eagle, most people think it looks like a huge tuning fork and it is visible for miles. Two miles (3 km) south of the Eagle the road to Guerrero Negro goes west.

Guerrero Negro is one of the newest towns on the Baja, and it's a company town. Founded in 1955 the town owes its existence to the Exportadora de Sal (ESSA) salt works. Large flats near the town are flooded with sea water which quickly evaporates leaving salt. This is gathered up using heavy equipment and shipped on barges to Isla Cedros offshore where there is enough water to allow cargo ships to dock.

More recently the town has gained fame for the California gray whales that congregate each winter in the nearby Ojo de Liebre or Scammon's Lagoon. There is now a lively tourist industry catering to the many people who come here to visit the whales.

The town itself is small and the places of interest, restaurants and stores, are almost all arranged along the main street. Guerrero Negro has a small supermarket and also two Pemexes. A third one is under construction to the north near the border crossing.

Guerrero Negro Campgrounds

⬛ LA ESPINITA RESTAURANT

GPS Location: N 28° 00' 23.3", W 114° 00' 40.7"

This is a restaurant along the road just north of the border between Baja Norte and Baja Sur. The restaurant has a large fenced parking lot to the side and behind and you can stay for free if you eat in the restaurant. There are restrooms with flush toilets at the rear of the restaurant building, otherwise there are no amenities.

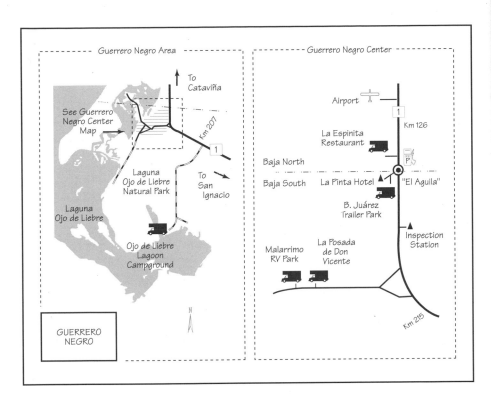

La Espinita is located .2 mile (.3 km) north of the giant eagle that marks the border.

🚐 BENITO JUÁREZ TRAILER PARK

Address: Asunción Morian Canales, Apdo. 188,
Guerrero Negro, B.C.S., México

GPS Location: N 27° 59' 55.6", W 114° 00' 51.6"

The Benito Juárez is another of the government-built trailer parks. It is run by the Ejido Benito Juárez. This one is the only one left on the Baja that offers electrical hookups, however, watch the voltage, it sometimes varies dramatically and can cause damage to your equipment.

This is a large campground. The spaces are pull-throughs with electricity, sewer, and water. Cactus are planted throughout for landscaping, there's a pretty complete collection of the different types you've been seeing along the road on the way south, including boojums. The restrooms are old but work, there are hot showers. The campground is fully fenced and has a manager who speaks some English.

This is an easy campground to find. Just watch for the huge eagle monument at the border between North and South Baja. The campground is just to the west.

MALARRIMO RV PARK

Address: Blvd. Emiliano Zapata S/N, Guerrero Negro,
                 CP 23940 B.C.S., México
Res.:   P.O. Box 284, Chula Vista, CA 91912
Telephone: (1) 157-0100   **Fax:** (1) 157-0100
E-mail: malarimo@telnor.net   **Web Site:** www.malarrimo.com

GPS Location: N 27° 58' 03.7", W 114° 01' 04.3"

The Malarrimo is generally considered the best place to stay in Guerrero Negro. Not only are the campground facilities pretty good, the restaurant is the best in this section of Baja.

There are 36 RV spaces with 15-amp outlets, sewer, and water located behind the restaurant. Guerrero Negro electricity is marginal, watch voltage while hooked up to avoid damage to your rig. Restrooms are modern and clean and have hot water showers. This is a well-run place and English is spoken. They run tours to see the gray whales and cave art, and even have a gift shop. Many people make a special point to overnight in Guerrero Negro so they can eat at the restaurant.

Recently they completed work on a second camping area across the street from the motel so that caravans can be accommodated without displacing independent travelers. There are 16 sites with full hookups in this new section.

To find the campground drive in to Guerrero Negro from the east. Almost immediately after entering town you will see the Malarrimo on the right.

LA POSADA DE DON VICENTE, LAS CAZUELAS RESTAURANT-BAR

Address: Blvd. Emiliano Zapata S/N, Guerrero Negro,
                 CP 23940 B.C.S., México
Telephone: (1) 157-0288

GPS Location: N 27° 58' 05.1", W 114° 01' 31.1"

This place is a motel with an enclosed courtyard and a restaurant out front. It has 8 back-in RV slots with 15-amp electrical outlets and water hookups but no sewer facilities. Guerrero Negro electricity is marginal, watch voltage while hooked up to avoid damage to your rig. There are bathrooms with flush toilets and hot showers. There is limited maneuvering room so rigs over about 30 feet may find things a little tight. This is a fairly new place and it seemed to us that they needed to sort things out a bit, no one was staying here while Malarrimo's just down the street was practically full. Also, the owner was talking about opening another place nearby. Time will tell.

To find the campground just drive in to Guerrero Negro from the east. This facility is well signed, it is on the right about a block before you reach Malarrimo's.

OJO DE LIEBRE LAGOON CAMPGROUND

GPS Location: N 27° 44' 55.9", W 114° 00' 42.2"

One of the top attractions of the Baja Peninsula is a whale-watching trip. One way to do this is to drive across the salt flats to the edge of Laguna Ojo de Liebre (Scammon's Lagoon). It costs a little less to take a tour here than from in town, and camping along the edge of the lagoon is excellent. This place is only accessible during the whale-watching season, approximately the middle of December to the middle of April.

When you arrive at the lagoon there is an entrance kiosk where a $3 fee is collected. There is a large parking lot where visitors on whale-watching trips can park. A large new building is under construction which will house the tour ticket sales as well as a museum and restaurant. Until then kiosks handle ticket sales and there is also a simple restaurant. Camping is beyond the parking lot along a long loop road with pullouts along the beach of the lagoon. Pit toilets are provided.

To reach the lagoon turn westward from Mex 1 at about Km 207. This is 5 miles south of the turnoff for the town of Guerrero Negro. The turn is marked with a large sign for Laguna Ojo de Liebre. The road is graded dirt, it is fine for even the largest rigs. At 4 miles (6 km) you will reach an entrance gate where your name will be recorded as you enter the salt flats working area. You'll probably see heavy equipment collecting the salt from the flats. At 13.8 miles (22.3 km) there is a Y, go right as indicated by the sign. Finally, at 14.9 miles (24 km) you will reach the entrance gate at the lagoon.

Side Trips from Guerrero Negro

The number-one side trip from Guerrero Negro is a visit to see the gray whales at the **Parque Natural de la Ballena Gris** which encompasses **Scammon's Lagoon** or **Laguna Ojo de Liebre** as it is known in Mexico. There are really two ways to do it. You can make arrangements for a tour from town with an operator there, one of the best is offered by the owners of the Malarrimo, also site of a great restaurant and the best RV park in town. Alternately, you can visit the whales in your own vehicle. To do so follow the driving instructions given above for getting to the Ojo de Liebre Lagoon Campground. The whales aren't easy to see from the beach, you'll want to take a boat tour from here. Private boats aren't allowed on the lagoon during whale season.

Before the completion of the new highway the old mining town of **El Arco** was an important way point on the old road. This may explain why there was a decent paved road built in to the town from Mex 1 soon after its completion. There seems to be no other reason for a good road to this small place. Today the road is a mess with only shreds of the original surface remaining but if you take it slowly the 26 mile (42 km) drive into El Arco can even be made in an RV. This road leaves Mex 1 near the 190 Km marker, about 16.4 miles (26.8 km) southeast of the Guerrero Negro cutoff from Mex 1.

From El Arco you can drive on another 23 miles (38 km) east to **Misión Santa Gertrudis La Magna** on a recently improved road suitable for small sturdy RVs and other more maneuverable vehicles. Once San Gertrudis served as the headquarters for Jesuit work in the north. The mission was founded in 1751 and abandoned in 1822, a small chapel continues to be used and is visited by pilgrims, especially on November 16 for the Fiesta de Santa Gertrudis. There is a museum and restoration work underway.

From El Arco it is also possible to reach the coast at **San Francisquito** and then drive on north to **Bahía de los Ángeles**. The distance to San Francisquito is 48 miles (78 km), it is another 81 miles (132 km) on to Bahía de los Ángeles. The road to San Francisquito is poor and really only suitable for high clearance vehicles, preferably with four-wheel-drive. It passes through rugged, empty country and extra caution is advised. See the *Side Trips from Bahia de los Angeles* section for information about the better road from there to San Francisquito.

La Paz, Baja California Sur (law PAHS)
Population 170,000, Elevation sea level

A favorite city on the Baja Peninsula, La Paz has lots of stores for supplies and a number of good campgrounds. Good, not fancy! This is not really a tourist town although it does have tourist amenities like hotels, good restaurants, beaches, and tour operators.

La Paz has been continuously occupied only since 1811. Earlier settlement attempts, including one by Cortés in person, were not successful. The local Indians were not cooperative.

The city feels more like a larger mainland city than any other on the Baja. The waterfront **malecón** is good for strolling and you'll enjoy exploring the older part of town a few blocks back from the water. La Paz's best **beaches** are outside of town toward and past Pichilingue and are virtually empty except on weekends. There's a decent museum, the **Museum of Anthropology**, covering the area's early inhabitants. **Ferries** to the mainland cities of Topolobampo and Mazatlán dock at Pichilingue, see the information about ferries in the *Road System* write-up in the Introduction to this chapter.

La Paz Campgrounds

Oasis RV Park

Address: Km 15 Carr. Transp. al Norte, La Paz, B.C.S, México
Telephone: (1) 124-6090

GPS Location: N 24° 06' 34.3", W 110° 24' 59.8"

This is a very small park located west of La Paz. It is in the small town of El Centenario and is located right on a rather marshy beach.

There are 24 back-in spaces, all with 15-amp outlets, sewer, and water. The restrooms are old but clean, they have tiled floors, white painted walls, and hot water showers. There is a nice swimming pool, a coin-operated laundry, and a restaurant/bar overlooking the beach. Some English is spoken and reservations are taken.

The campground is on the water side of Mex 1 half way between the Km 14 and Km 15 markers. It is in the town of El Centenario which is just west of La Paz.

Casa Blanca RV Park

Address: Carret. Al Norte Km 4.5, Esq. Av. Delfines, Apdo. 681,
                       Fracc. Fidepaz, La Paz, CP 23094 B.C.S., México
**Telephone
and Fax:**   (1) 124-0009

GPS Location: N 24° 07' 53.9", W 110° 20' 29.0"

The Casa Blanca is quite nice, very tidy, easy to find, and usually has lots of room.

There are 43 slots with electricity, sewer, and water. Some sites have 50-amp outlets, others are 15 amp. One is a pull-through, the others are all back-in spaces. The entire area is hard-packed sand and spaces are separated with low concrete curbs. The restrooms are plain but clean and have hot showers. The entire campground is surrounded by a high white concrete wall. It is good for security but seems to keep the

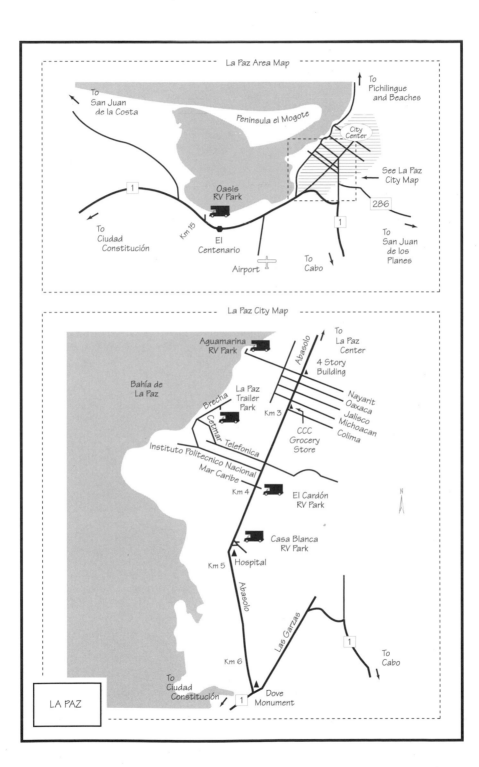

La Paz Area Map

To San Juan de la Costa

Peninsula el Mogote

To Pichilingue and Beaches

City Center

See La Paz City Map

286

To Ciudad Constitución

Km 15

El Centenario

Oasis RV Park

1

To Cabo

Airport

To San Juan de los Planes

1

La Paz City Map

Aguamarina RV Park

Abasolo

To La Paz Center

4 Story Building

Nayarit
Oaxaca
Jalisco
Michoacan
Colima

Bahía de La Paz

Brecha

La Paz Trailer Park

Cetmar

Telefonica

Km 3

CCC Grocery Store

Instituto Politecnico Nacional

Mar Caribe

Km 4

El Cardón RV Park

N

Casa Blanca RV Park

Km 5

Hospital

Abasolo

Las Garzas

1

To Cabo

Km 6

LA PAZ

To Ciudad Constitución

1

Dove Monument

temperature in the campground about 5 degrees higher than anywhere else in town. There is a swimming pool, a decent tennis court, and a palapa meeting/party room. There is often no-one around to collect the fees, particularly in the afternoon, just pull in and park and someone will eventually show up.

The Casa Blanca is right off Mex 1. Zero your odometer at the dove statue (whale's tale) as you come into town, the campground is on the right at 1.2 miles (1.9 km).

EL CARDÓN RV PARK

Address: Km 4 Transpeninsular, Apdo. 104, La Paz,
               CP 23000 B.C.S., México
Telephone: (1) 122-1261

GPS Location: N 24° 08' 08.0", W 110° 20' 16.4"

The El Cardón is an older trailer park, but was being spiffed up a bit last time we visited. There is now an internet access operation located in the building out front, very handy.

There are about 60 usable spaces, most with 15-amp outlets, sewer, and water. Some also have patios and palapas for shade. Many are pull-throughs. The campground has two restroom blocks, one is fine with tile and hot water, the other is best ignored. Water at this campground is slightly salty but they do have a city water tap, ask about the location. This campground also has a swimming pool and a coin-operated laundry. There is a fence around the campground and an night watchman.

A POPULAR RESTAURANT ON THE LA PAZ MALECÓN

The El Cardón is right off Mex 1. Zero your odometer at the dove (whale's tail) statue and you'll see the campground on the right at 1.6 miles (2.6 km).

🚐 AQUAMARINA RV PARK

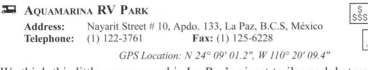

Address: Nayarit Street # 10, Apdo. 133, La Paz, B.C.S, México
Telephone: (1) 122-3761   **Fax:** (1) 125-6228

GPS Location: N 24° 09' 01.2", W 110° 20' 09.4"

We think this little campground is La Paz's nicest trailer park but you can make up your own mind. This is a well-kept park with flowering plants and lots of shade.

There are 19 back-in slots, all have 50 and 30-amp outlets, sewer, water, a patio and shade. Really big rigs might find this campground a little cramped. In the center of the park is a swimming pool and covered patio. Restrooms are well maintained and clean, they have hot water showers. The same owners have a dock in front of the campground where larger yachts tie up, there is a coin-operated laundry in the building they use as an office for both operations. English is spoken and reservations are recommended. This is the La Paz campground most likely to fill up.

The campground is located at the ocean end of Av. Nayarit, which is a dirt street off Absolo as it comes into La Paz. If you zero your odometer at the dove statue (some people see a whale's tail instead) Nayarit goes to the left at 2.5 miles (4 km). There is a small trailer pictogram sign marking the street and a four-story white building with balconies on the right opposite the turn. Follow Nayarit to the end, about .4 mile (.6 km) and you'll find the gate on your right at the beach. You'll pass another gate before reaching this one, it is the night gate and you won't be able to enter here during the day. This park has good security.

🚐 LA PAZ TRAILER PARK

Address: Brecha California #1010, P.O. Box 482,
                         La Paz, B.C.S., México
Telephone: (1) 122-8787   **Fax:** (1) 122-9938

GPS Location: N 24° 08' 42.9", W 110° 20' 31.2"

This large park is a little off the beaten path which is good, less road noise. Unless it is filled by a caravan you can usually find a place to camp here even without reservations.

There are about 40 campsites, both pull-through and back-in. They have 30-amp outlets, sewer, and water. The sites are completely paved over and the few palms provide little shade but there should be plenty of room for slide-outs. The tiled restrooms are clean and modern and have hot showers. There is a swimming pool and coin-operated laundry. Reservations are accepted.

As you enter La Paz zero your odometer at the dove statue (whale's tail). At 1.7 miles (2.8 km) turn left on the first paved road after you pass the El Cardón RV Park, it has a stop light. This is Ave. Telefonica. Drive straight for .4 mile (.6 km) to a Y, take the right fork onto Cetmar and drive another block. Turn right and you will see the RV park on your right.

Other Camping Possibilities

There are primitive campsites along the beach at Tecolote.

Side Trips from La Paz

Ferries from La Paz to the mainland leave from **Pichilingue** which is 14 miles (23 km) northeast of the city along the coast. There are also several beaches up this road, some suitable for primitive camping. The road is paved, after Pichilingue you pass a beach called **Puerto Balandra** and reach **Tecolote** beach in another 4 miles (6.5 km). Tecolote is wide and sandy and has many spots for primitive camping. Unfortunately campers here are often hassled by people from town and the tourist department does not consider camping on Tecolote to be safe.

LA VENTANA
Population 200, Elevation sea level

Highway 286 runs south from a junction with Mex 1 in the southern section of La Paz. It leads about 40 miles (65.3 km) southeast to the farming town of **San Juan de los Planes** and nearby beachside village of **La Ventana**.

La Ventana is a very small village stretched along the west shore of the Bahía La Ventana. The location has become very popular with windsurfers. Actually, the towns of El Teso and El Sargento, both to the north, tend to merge together with La Ventana to form one town. Facilities in the towns are limited to a small store or two and a few restaurants, but new places are appearing to accommodate the visitors.

La Ventana Campground

🚐 **PLAYAS MIRAMAR**

GPS Location: N 24° 03' 17.6", W 109° 59' 24.0"

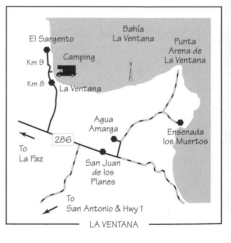

This campground is very popular with windsurfers, in fact, that's why it is here. Winter is the season with reliable winds from the north. Expect to find few RVs, it is usually filled with tents and vans.

The campground is a large flat sandy area directly adjoining the beach. You can park not twenty feet from the water. Watch for soft spots! Facilities consist of a couple of toilet blocks with flush toilets and cold water showers. There are a few water faucets and also some scattered trees providing some shade. The entire area is fenced. There's a mini-super and a restaurant across the street.

As you enter La Ventana you can't miss the camping area and its chain-link fence on the right next to the beach.

Other Camping Possibilities

There are primitive campsites available beyond San Juan de los Planes at **Ensenada los Muertos**. The road as far as San Juan de los Planes and a short distance beyond is paved, access to Bahía de los Muertos is OK for smaller RVs. There is a road along the ocean that leads to Los Barriles but it is only suitable for 4-wheel-drive vehicles due to a bad section called Cuesta de los Muertos (Hill of the Dead) just south of Ensenada los Muertos. Some camping along this road is accessible from Los Barriles to the south.

LORETO, BAJA CALIFORNIA SUR (LOH-RAY-toe)
Population 7,200, Elevation sea level

Loreto is considered to be the oldest continuously occupied town on the Baja having been founded in 1697. This is theoretically true, however the town was virtually abandoned from the time of a major hurricane in 1829 until resettlement in the 1850's. The **Museo de los Misiones** has exhibits explaining the history of the missions throughout the Baja. It is located next to the **Misión Nuestra Señora de Loreto**.

Today the town is part of a FONATUR development scheme like those in Cancún, Huatulco, Ixtapa, and Los Cabos (Cabo San Lucas and San José del Cabo). Most of the infrastructure was put in Nopoló, about 5 miles (8.2 km) south of Loreto. There you'll find an uncrowded but very nice golf course, a tennis center, the Loreto Inn, and a convention center. Even Puerto Escondido is part of the scheme, it is now supposed to be called Puerto Loreto. See the *Puerto Escondido* section below for more information.

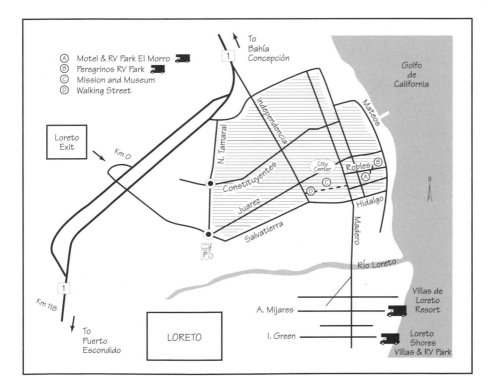

Fishing and boating are popular activities in Loreto. You can arrange a trip in a panga or larger fishing cruiser. Just offshore from Loreto is Isla Carmen, the island has beaches and sheltered anchorages. Many experienced kayakers visit the island or you can arrange a panga for the trip.

Loreto Campgrounds

LORETO SHORES VILLAS AND RV PARK

Address:	Apdo. 219, Loreto, CP 23880 B.C.S., México
Telephone:	(1) 135-0629
E-mail:	shores@loretoweb.com.mx

GPS Location: N 25° 59' 57.8", W 111° 20' 15.2"

This is the largest RV park in Loreto and a good place to stop for the night if you're traveling. It has plenty of room for big rigs on entry roads and inside the park. The spaces look a lot like those in the government parks, perhaps this was one of them. If so it has an unusually good waterfront location. Unfortunately the waterfront is now blocked by permanent structures. In fact, much of this campground has been used for permanents, the remaining free spaces seem to be managed as an afterthought.

There are about 35 pull-through spaces remaining here, all with 30-amp outlets, sewer, water and patios. The restrooms are clean and have hot water showers. A few small trees have been planted but will have to grow to provide much shade. The campground is fenced in the rear but the beach side is open.

Zero your odometer at the Loreto turnoff from Mex 1. This will take you toward the ocean through a traffic circle and then a stop light. Take the turn to the right at 1.4 miles (2.3 km) onto Francisco Madero at another light. You'll cross a dry arroyo and continue straight. When you are .8 miles (1.3 km) from the turn make a left turn onto Ildefonso Green, the RV park is directly ahead.

VILLAS DE LORETO RESORT

Address:	Antonio Mijares y Playa, Apdo. 132, Loreto, CP 23880 B.C.S., México
Telephone:	(1) 135-0586
Web Site:	www.villasdeloreto.com

GPS Location: N 26° 00' 03.0", W 111° 20' 19.9"

This is a cute little hotel on the waterfront in Loreto, it has some RV slots in the rear. Eventually the trailer park may disappear as more permanent structures are built in the area, meanwhile this is probably the nicest RV park in Loreto.

There are about 11 sites with 15-amp outlets and water hookups and quite a bit of shade. There is a dump station. The restrooms are modern and very spiffy, they have hot showers of course. There's also a coin-operated laundry in the building. The resort has a swimming pool out front overlooking the water.

Zero your odometer at the Loreto turnoff from Mex 1. This will take you toward the ocean through a traffic circle and then a stop light. Take the turn to the right at 1.4 miles (2.3 km) onto Francisco Madero at another light. You'll cross a dry arroyo and continue straight. When you are .6 miles (1.22 km) from the turn make a left turn onto Antonio Mijares and you'll see the resort on the right as you reach the beach. Big rigs will want to enter at the back entrance which is usually closed, just park outside while you walk in to register.

MOTEL & RV PARK EL MORO

Address: Rosendo Robles No. 8, Col. Centro, Loreto,
              CP 23880 B.C.S., México
**Telephone
and Fax:** (1) 135-0542

GPS Location: N 26° 00' 41.0", W 111° 20' 27.7"

The El Moro doesn't have a lot of extras in the way of facilities, just hookups and restrooms. There is also a motel on the property.

There are 12 spaces, all are large back-in slots with 30-amp outlets, sewer, and water. The restrooms are simple but clean and have hot water showers. Maneuvering room for both driving to the campground and parking would be tight for bigger rigs.

Zero your odometer at the Loreto turnoff from Mex 1. Drive straight into and through town until you reach the waterfront malecón at 1.6 miles (2.6 km). Turn left and take the second left turn on Rosendo Robles at odometer 1.7 miles (2.7 km). The RV park is on the left at odometer 1.8 miles (2.9 km).

PEREGRINOS RV PARK

Address: Rosendo Robles S/N, Colonia Centro, ,
              CP 23880 Loreto B.C.S., México
Telephone: (1) 135-1267

GPS Location: N 26° 00' 43.4", W 111° 20' 26.7"

Just across the road from the El Moro and a few feet closer to the ocean is a very small new RV park. It has already started to fill with permanently located units but a few spaces remain for tent campers and smaller RVs.

The RV park has 7 spaces, all are back-ins with 15-amp outlets, sewer and water. Showers with hot water and flush toilets are provided.

Zero your odometer at the Loreto turnoff from Mex 1. Drive straight into and through town until you reach the waterfront malecón at 1.6 miles (2.6 km). Turn left and take the second left turn on Rosendo Robles at odometer 1.7 miles (2.7 km). The RV park is on the right at odometer 1.8 miles (2.9 km).

Side Trips from Loreto

One of the most interesting missions on the Baja, **San Javier**, makes a good day trip if you have a vehicle with good ground clearance. The road heads west from Mex 1 at Km 118 about a mile south of the Loreto intersection. The road in to the mission and surrounding village is 21.5 miles (35.1 km) long, very scenic, and often in poor shape. Check in Loreto for information about the road condition when you visit. The mission was built in 1720 and is constructed of volcanic rock. December 3 is the day of the mission's patron saint, if you visit then you will have company in the form of many pilgrims. The week leading up to the saint's day is the small town's fiesta week.

LOS BARRILES, BAJA CALIFORNIA SUR (LOES BAR-EEL-ACE)
Population 1,000, Elevation sea level

Los Barriles and nearby Buena Vista and La Ribera are enjoying a surge of RVer popularity as development overtakes the campgrounds farther south near Cabo. This is an excellent area for windsurfing. You'll find a number of restaurants, some small hotels, trailer parks, an airstrip, and a few shops in Los Barriles. Fishing is quite good because deep water is just offshore, campers keep their car-top boats on the beach. Trucks are used for launching boats, there is no ramp.

Los Barriles Campgrounds

MARTIN VERDUGO'S BEACH RESORT

Address: Apdo. 17, Los Barriles, CP 23501 B.C.S., México
Telephone: (1) 141-0054
E-mail: martinv@lapaz.cromwell.com.mx

GPS Location: N 23° 40' 55.9", W 109° 41' 56.1"

This Los Barriles campgrounds is a very popular place. It's located on an beautiful beach although there are two large motel buildings between the camping area and the water. There is a swimming pool and palapa bar overlooking the beach. The resort offers fishing expeditions on its own cruisers and room to keep your own small boat on the beach.

The campground has 65 RV spaces with 10 and 30-amp outlets, sewer, and water. The RVs seem a little crowded but plenty of big rigs find room. There are also 25 tent spaces with water and electric hookups. Restrooms are clean and modern, they have hot water showers. There is a coin-operated laundry, a library in the office, a restaurant atop one of the two hotel buildings, and of course the pool and palapa bar over-

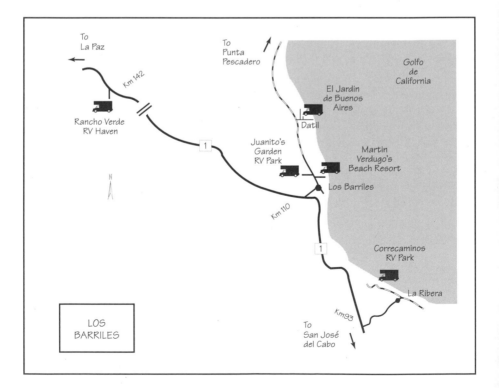

SOUTHERN BAJA PENINSULA

looking the beach. English is spoken and reservations are recommended. They require a $50 deposit.

Take the Los Barriles exit from Mex 1 between La Paz and Cabo San Lucas near the Km 110 marker. You'll reach a T in .3 miles (.5 km). Turn left and you'll see the RV park on the right in .2 miles (.3 km).

🚐 JUANITO'S GARDEN RV PARK

Address:	Apdo. 50, Los Barriles, CP 23501 B.C.S., México
Telephone and Fax:	(1) 141-0024
E-mail:	hotellosbarriles@cabonet.net.mx

GPS Location: N 23° 41' 00.7", W 109° 41' 56.9"

This smaller Los Barriles RV park is almost entirely filled with permanently-located units, but continues to be an acceptable alternative if you can get in.

The RV park has only three open spaces remaining, all with 30-amp outlets, sewer, and water. Restrooms are clean and modern and have hot water showers. There is a coin-operated laundry. A motel with the same management as the RV park is located on the property, it has a beautiful swimming pool that can be used by guests at the RV park. English is spoken and telephone reservations are recommended.

Take the Los Barriles exit from Mex 1 between La Paz and Cabo San Lucas near the Km 110 marker. You'll reach a T in .3 miles (.5 km). Turn left and you'll see the RV park on the left in .3 miles (.5 km).

🚐 EL JARDÍN DE BUENOS AIRES

GPS Location: N 23° 41' 54.5", W 109° 42' 05.3"

This is a new place gradually being built in a residential area to the north of the other Los Barriles campgrounds.

There are 10 sites with 30-amp outlets, sewer and water. There are currently no other facilities so the place is only suitable for self-contained rigs. Each site is separately fenced and has a patio. They are nice, the owner is aiming at folks who stay the season. He says he's planning more sites as well as bathrooms, a laundry, and a pool.

Take the Los Barriles exit from Mex 1 between La Paz and Cabo San Lucas near the Km 110 marker. You'll reach a T in .3 miles (.5 km). Turn left and drive 1.5 miles (1.5/.62 km). You will pass the end of the pavement and be on a sand and dirt road. Make a right turn onto Datil, just after the turn you will see the campground on the left.

🚐 CORRECAMINOS RV PARK

GPS Location: N 23° 36' 00.4", W 109° 35' 15.7"

If you are looking for an out of the way, slow-moving, friendly place to spend some time this is it. Located near the quiet little town of La Ribera, Correcaminos RV Park might seem like a little piece of paradise. The people we met there certainly think so.

Correcaminos is nothing fancy. There are 10 spaces with electricity, sewer and water. If you don't need hookups there's lots more space, including an area near the beach. The bathrooms are rustic and have hot water showers. There's also a washing machine. The wide beach is about a quarter-mile away along the sandy road that runs through the campground. Light boats can be launched across the sand.

To find the campground turn east on the paved road near Km 93 south of Las Barriles. The excellent road runs 7.3 miles (11.8 km) to the small village of La Ribera. Drive through town, and at the T just after the pavement ends and down a hill turn left. You'll see the campground entrance on the right .2 miles (.3 km) after the turn.

🚐 RANCHO VERDE RV HAVEN

Address:	7975 Dahlberg Siding, Eureka, MT 59917 USA (Reservations)	
Telephone:	(406) 882-4887 (U.S.)	**Fax:** (406) 882-4987 (U.S.)
Internet:	www.rancho-verde.com	

GPS Location: N 23° 45' 45.6", W 109° 58' 46.2"

This is a newer campground located in the mountains west of Los Barriles. The green high wooded country is a nice change from flat desert and sandy seashore.

There are 29 widely separated back-in spaces. Each one has water and sewer hook-ups, there is no electricity. The restrooms are in a simple palapa roof building but are extremely clean and have hot water for showers. This is ranch country and there are miles of trails for hiking and bird-watching. Lots are for sale but you need not fear high pressure sales tactics. You may fall in love with the owner's open-air living area and RV shelter next to the campground.

Rancho Verde is located in the mountains about 20 miles (33 km) west of Los Barriles near San Bartolo. The entrance road is off Mex 1 near Km 142.

Side Trips from Los Barriles

From Los Barriles an unpaved road goes up the coast to resorts at **Punta Pescadero** (9 miles (14.7 km)) and **El Cardonal** (14 miles (22.9 km)). There is resort with RV parking at El Cardonal. Beyond there the road becomes much worse and is not recommended although its condition varies. It actually goes all the way north to where it meets a paved road from La Paz near **San Juan de los Planes**.

From near La Ribera a road heads south along the coast. It actually goes all the way to San José del Cabo, but heavy storms often cut it making the whole trip uncertain. There are plans to upgrade this road and pave it but last time we checked it was only paved and upgraded to a dead end about 8 miles (13.1 km) south of La Ribera. Small RVs and others use a different entrance that is actually in La Ribera to reach primitive campsites at **Cabo Pulmo** and other beaches but the road is really not suitable for RVs and should be scouted in a smaller vehicle. Campers with capable vehicles will find lots of good places to pitch a tent along this 70 mile (113 km) road and will be in no hurry to see it become a paved highway route.

About 17 miles (28 km) south of the Los Barriles cutoff a road goes east 2.5 miles (4.1 km) to the small but historic town of **Santiago**. Founded as a mission town in 1724 there is no trace of the mission today, but there is a small zoo.

MULEGÉ, BAJA CALIFORNIA SUR (MOO-LAY-HAY)
Population 6,000, Elevation sea level

Situated near the mouth of the palm and mangrove-lined Río Mulegé, Mulegé is a

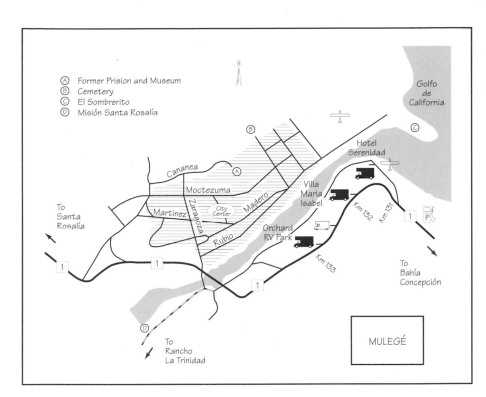

Ⓐ Former Prision and Museum
Ⓑ Cemetery
Ⓒ El Sombrerito
Ⓓ Misión Santa Rosalía

Golfo
de
California

Ⓑ

Hotel
Serenidad

Ⓒ

Cananea

Ⓐ

Moctezuma

Villa
Maria
Isabel

To
Santa
Rosalía

Martinez

Zaragoza

City
Center

Madero

Km 132

Km 131

1

P

Rubio

Orchard
RV Park

Km 133

1

1

1

To
Bahía
Concepción

Ⓓ

To
Rancho
La Trinidad

MULEGÉ

welcome tropical paradise after the long drive across desert country to the north. In many ways Mulegé may remind you of San Ignacio, both have a definite desert oasis ambiance. Mulegé is a popular RVer destination, many people make their seasonal home here, there are three decent RV parks, and the beaches and coves of the Bahía Concepción begin only 12 miles (19.6 km) to the south.

Fishing, diving, and kayaking are all popular here. Yellowtail are often thick during the winter and summer anglers go offshore for deep water fish. The nearby Santa Inés Islands are popular diving destinations, dive shops in Mulegé offer trips to the islands and other sites. Kayakers love Bahía Concepción and the coastline north and south.

Sights in Mulegé itself are limited. The **Misión Santa Rosalía** is located about 2 miles (3.3 km) upstream from the bridge on the right bank (facing downstream). It is usually locked except during services but the excursion offers excellent views of the town and river. Mulegé is also known for its **prison**. Now closed the prison building houses a museum and you can take a look at the cells. You can drive out to the mouth of the river (if you have a smaller rig) on the north shore, there you'll find a rock formation known as El Sombrerito, you can't miss it.

Mulegé is accustomed to visitors and takes them in stride, there's a large norteamericano population. There are quite a few good restaurants and some small grocery shops. Street-side phones are available. A few miles south of town is a self-service Pemex, it has lots of room for big rigs and is an excellent place to fill up.

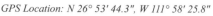

Mulegé Campgrounds

THE ORCHARD RV PARK

Address: Apdo. 24, Mulegé, CP 23900 B.C.S., México
Telephone: (1) 153-0568

GPS Location: N 26° 53' 44.3", W 111° 58' 25.8"

The Orchard is an attractive park set under date palms near the Mulegé River.

There are now about 30 spaces with 30-amp outlets, sewer, and water with parking on gravel or packed dirt. Some have palapas. The campground seems to be gradually filling with attractive permanent-type units. Restrooms are modern and have hot water showers. Rental canoes are available for boating on the estuary at the back of the property. Caravans often use this campground so it is sometimes full.

The Orchard is located .5 miles (.8 km) south of the Mulegé bridge off Mex 1.

VILLA MARIA ISABEL RECREATIONAL PARK

Address: Apdo. 5, Mulegé, CP 23900 B.C.S., México
**Telephone
and Fax:** (1) 153-0246

GPS Location: N 26° 53' 49.0", W 111° 57' 50.8"

This is an excellent place to stay if you are looking for an RV park with full hookups in Mulegé. Like the other Mulegé campgrounds it sits near the south shore of the Mulegé River. Although there are a lot of permanents here there also is a special grass-covered area set aside for travelers. There is a very popular little bakery, a great swimming pool, and a laundromat.

The campground has 18 pull-through spaces with 30-amp outlets, sewer, and water. Parking is on grass and the slots will accommodate larger rigs. There is also an area for tent campers with a shared palapa. The restrooms have hot water showers. The swimming pool is a big attraction, especially during hot summer weather and the bakery draws people from well outside the campground. There is a boat ramp and a dry long-term storage area.

The campground is 1.3 miles (2.1 km) south of the Mulegé bridge off Mex 1.

HOTEL SERENIDAD

Address: Apdo. 9, Mulegé, CP 23900 B.C.S., México
Telephone: (1) 153-0530   **Fax:** (1) 153-0311
Web Site: www.serenidad.com

GPS Location: N 26° 53' 49.6", W 111° 57' 32.0"

The Serenidad is a hotel located on the south bank of the Mulegé River near the mouth. It has its own airstrip and was a popular fly-in fishing destination even before the Transpeninsular Highway was built.

The hotel has 8 RV spaces along a wall at the back of the property. The location is hot and unappealing considering the nearby alternatives, but there are full hookups with 15-amp outlets. Restrooms are available with hot showers. The hotel has nice facilities, there is a swimming pool and restaurant, a pig roast draws people from around the area on Saturday nights.

The entrance to the Serenidad is the farthest south along Mex 1 of all the Mulegé campgrounds. If you zero your odometer at the bridge you'll see the entrance road at 2.2 miles (3.5 km). There's a half-mile gravel entrance road leading along the side of the airstrip to the hotel.

PUERTO ESCONDIDO (PWER-TOE ESS-KOHN-DEE-DOE)
Population 100, Elevation sea level

Long popular as a camping and yachting destination, Puerto Escondido is now a part of the FONATUR plan to turn the Loreto area into a world-class resort. You'll be amazed at the paved but deteriorating boulevards, quay, and abandoned half-built hotel sitting next to this beautiful hurricane hole. Yachts are thick in the bay but campers are nowhere to be seen, boondocking is not allowed at the port. There's a boat ramp here so fishermen like to use Puerto Escondido as a base for accessing the off-shore waters and long stretch of coast to the south toward La Paz which has little road access. Kayakers put in here for trips down the coast to La Paz.

Puerto Escondido Campgrounds

🚐 **TRIPUI RV PARK-HOTEL RESORT**

Address: Apdo. 100, Loreto, CP 23880
                  B.C.S., México
Telephone: (1) 133-0818   **Fax:** (1) 133-0828

GPS Location: N 25° 48' 21.7", W 111° 19' 10.1"

This RV park has lots of permanents and nice facilities, unfortunately traveling rigs are relegated to a somewhat barren gravel parking lot. Some small palm trees have been planted to help make the place more attractive. Still, full hookup campgrounds with lots of amenities are scarce in this area so the Tripui is well-used. Another reason the Tripui is popular is the boat-launch ramp a short distance away at the port.

There are 31 back-in spaces in a fenced gravel lot with 30 and 50-amp outlets, sewer, and water. Cement curbs separate the sites. The sites are short but no problem for big rigs since you can project far into the central area without really getting in anyone's way. The restrooms are fine, they have hot showers and flush toilets and are in good repair. This resort also has a lot of permanent rigs in a separate area, there's a small store, a gift shop, and a laundry as well as a nice pool area and a restaurant.

Take the Puerto Escondido cutoff from Mex 1 near Km 94 about 16 miles (26 km) south of Loreto. Drive .6 miles (1 km) on the paved road and you'll see the campground on the right. You'll first pass the transient camping area and then see the sign

for the office. Big rigs may want to pull into
the camping area if there appears to be empty
spaces and then walk over to sign in.

 JUNCALITO BEACH

   GPS Location: N 25° 49' 10.3", W 111° 18' 58.7"

This little beach has nothing in the way of
amenities, not even pit toilets. However, it is a
nice beach, close to the road, and excellent for
self-contained campers. The road in is pretty
good, better than a lot of the roads up at Bahía
Concepción, and is only .7 mile (1.1 km) long.

The road to the beach is just north of the Km
97 marker, that's 1.7 miles (2.7 km) north of the road out to Puerto Escondido.

SAN IGNACIO, BAJA CALIFORNIA SUR (SAHN EEG-NAH-CYOH)
Population 4,000, Elevation 510 ft (155 m)

San Ignacio is a date-palm oasis built around lagoons formed by damning a river
which emerges from the earth nearby. The town is located just south of Mex 1. The
road into town is paved and big rigs should have no problems since they can drive
around the main square to turn around. The main square is also the location of the
mission church of San Ignacio, one of the easiest to find and most impressive mission churches on the Baja. This one is built of lava rock and has four foot thick walls.

From San Ignacio it is possible to take a guided tour to see rock paintings in the
surrounding hills. You should visit the rock art museum located just south of the
church, next door is where you register to visit rock-art sites. It is also possible to
follow the thirty mile long unpaved road to **Laguna San Ignacio** to see gray whales
from January through March. Tours to do this are available in San Ignacio.

San Ignacio Camping

 **RICE AND BEANS OASIS**
   Telephone: (1) 154-0283

         GPS Location: N27° 17' 54.7", W112° 54' 20.1"

San Ignacio has a brand new RV park, something to celebrate. The campground also
boasts a new restaurant, arguably the best place to eat in San Ignacio. Both the RV
park and associated restaurant are owned and operated by the same family that has the
popular Rice and Beans Restaurant up in San Felipe.

There are 29 spaces all with full hookups with 15-amp outlets. They are located on
two terraces overlooking San Ignacio's date palm forest. Since this is a brand new
place there is not any shade, hopefully that will come. Restrooms are separate rooms
with flush toilets and hot showers. The restaurant is at the entrance, we found the food
to be excellent.

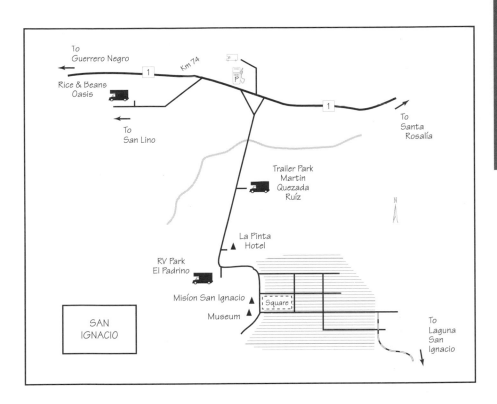

The campground is not located on the main road into San Ignacio like the other two mentioned here. Instead it is in the neighboring village of San Lino. The paved road to the campground leaves Mex 1 some .3 miles (.5 km) west of the main road in to San Ignacio. The campground is .4 miles (.6 km) from the highway on the right.

⛺ RV PARK EL PADRINO

Telephone: (1) 154-0089

GPS Location: N 27° 17' 06.2", W 112° 54' 01.2"

The El Padrino is the closest RV park to town, you can easily stroll in to the zócalo or over to the nearby La Pinta Hotel for dinner.

There are about 9 back-in spaces with electric and water and the campground has a dump station. There are also large areas for camping without hookups. The restrooms have flush toilets but are in poor condition, they do have hot water showers. A centrally located restaurant also serves as an office. The campground offers gray whale watching tours to San Ignacio Lagoon which is about two hours away.

Take the San Ignacio cutoff near the Pemex. The campground is just past the La Pinta, 1.3 miles (2.1 km) from the cutoff.

⛺ TRAILER PARK MARTIN QUEZADA RUÍZ

GPS Location: N 27° 17' 22.6", W 112° 54' 20.1"

This is a grass-covered clearing in the trees with a pit toilet and dribbling cold water shower. There is room for a rig of any size, tent camping is pleasant. You'll probably find dates drying on platforms near the front of the property.

To find Martin's zero your odometer at the exit from Mex 1 and head toward town. The campground entrance is on the left at 1.1 miles (1.8 km). If no one is around don't worry, someone will be around to collect.

Other Camping Possibilities

There is a trailer park, sometimes called the San Ignacio Trailer Park, located behind the Pemex at the San Ignacio junction. This is one of the old government trailer parks, there are now about 20 spaces. Last time we stopped there was no one around and no working hookups but this could easily change at any time. Even if it is closed this would be a place to spend the night if you don't need hookups.

Side Trips from San Ignacio

The **Laguna San Ignacio** is one of three places along the west coast of the peninsula where gray whales calve from January to March of each winter, there is a 40 mile road to the lagoon from San Ignacio. This road is not great but smaller RVs can usually negotiate it. Watch for soft sand and be aware that it is sometimes difficult to pick out the proper track. Once at the lagoon you can probably find a boat and guide at one of the fish camps. It is also possible to arrange trips from San Ignacio, ask at the El Padrino RV Park.

The town **San Francisco de la Sierra** serves as the headquarters for excursions to view rock paintings in the area. Guides must be used to visit the rock painting caves. The easiest to reach is **Cueva del Ratón**, you reach it about a mile before entering town but must go on into town to get a guide before visiting. You can also arrange day trips from San Ignacio to see Cueva del Ratón. Longer mule trips that last several days can also be arranged in San Francisco de la Sierra or in San Ignacio. The town is reached by driving east on a cutoff that leaves Mex 1 about 28 miles (46 km) west of San Ignacio. This road is suitable for pickups and sturdy vans and is about 22 miles (36 km) long.

SANTA ROSALÍA, BAJA CALIFORNIA SUR (SAHN-TAH ROH-SAH-LEE-AH)
Population 15,000, Elevation sea level

Don't pass through Santa Rosalía without stopping. This old mining town is unlike any other town on the Baja. Located at the point where Mex 1 finally reaches the Gulf of California, Santa Rosalía was founded in the 1880's by a French company to extract the large amounts of copper ore located here. The mining operation lasted until the 1950's. Now the town is a fishing and ferry port, it serves as a hub for the surrounding area. The ferries run from here to Guaymas on Mexico's west coast.

Much of the town is constructed of wood imported from the Pacific Northwest, the building designs are French colonial. **Santa Rosalía's church** is unique, it was designed by A.G. Eiffel who is better known for his tower in Paris. It was prefabricated in France and shipped by boat around Cape Horn. The town also has a well-known **French-style bakery**.

It is best not to drive a large rig in to town, although the town is built on a grid plan the roads are fairly constricted. It is better to park along the road north of town and then walk in.

Santa Rosalía Campgrounds

🚐 LAS PALMAS RV PARK

$$$ 🏕️ 🔌 🚰 🔲 🚿 HOT 🧺

Address: Apdo. 123, Santa Rosalía, B.C.S., México
Telephone: (1) 152-2070

GPS Location: N 27° 18' 52.9", W 112° 14' 35.0"

The Las Palmas is the most convenient place to stay if you want to be close to Santa Rosalía. It's a well-done full-hookup facility, but suffers from being away from the water.

There are 30 grassy spaces separated by concrete curbs arranged around the edge of the campground. All have electricity with 15-amp outlets, sewer, and water. The restrooms are decently maintained, they have hot water showers. There is a coin-operated laundry. When we visited the owner did not stay on site, he stopped by in the evening to collect.

The Las Palmas is just off Mex 1 about 2 miles (3.2 km) south of Santa Rosalía on the east side of the highway.

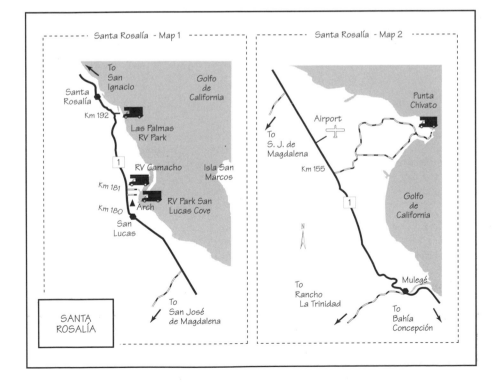

RV Camacho

GPS Location: N 27° 13' 16.3", W 112° 12' 50.3"

This is a small campground just north of the much larger RV Park San Lucas Cove. There are 10 waterfront sites with palapas. A large area behind the waterfront sites provides lots of room for additional parking. There are hot water showers and flush toilets as well as a dump station. The campground is fenced and there is small office at the entrance gate which is usually manned.

To reach the campground watch for the sign at Km 181 south of Santa Rosalía. The .6 mile (1 km) dirt road east to the campground is fine for any size rig.

RV Park San Lucas Cove

Address: Apdo. 50, Santa Rosalía, B.C.S., México

GPS Location: N 27° 13' 07.4", W 112° 12' 49.4"

This is a waterfront campground that may remind you of those farther south on Bahía Concepción. It is not quite a scenic as those but has a similar ambiance. The fishing in this area is excellent and most of the campers in this park are here for the fishing.

There are about 20 parking sites along the beach and at least 40 more on a large hard-packed sandy area behind. The campground now has flush toilets and a hot water shower as well as a dump station, so it is possible to make an extended visit. Folks either pull their boats up on the beach or anchor them out front.

The campground entrance is .2 miles (.3 km) south of the Km 181 mark south of Santa Rosalía. This is about 8 miles (13.1 km) south of Santa Rosalía. The road in to the campground is packed sand and is about .5 miles (.8 km) long. Big rigs will have no problems negotiating it.

Punta Chivato

GPS Location: N 27° 04' 27.4", W 111° 56' 52.4"

The beach at Punta Chivato has long been a popular beachside camping spot with few amenities, a good trade-off for having the ocean just outside your front door. This area is associated with a nearby hotel which has been a fly-in fishing destination for years. Many homes have been built along the coast, mostly to the east of the hotel between it and the camping area. The hotel has been purchased by a new owner and is being refurbished. The future of the camping area is uncertain at this time. It appears that the new owner may intend to upgrade the facility and continue to offer it as a camping destination.

Camping is in a large parking area behind a sandy beach. A small spit provides enough protection for small fishing skiffs. Restrooms were being built at the time we visited, workers said they would have flush toilets and showers. Water is available at the camping area and there is a dump station back near the hotel and airport.

Access to the resort and camping area is via a long dirt road. It too has been upgraded recently and now takes a more direct route to the resort than in former years. The access road leaves Mex 1 just south of Km 155 between Santa Rosalía and Mulegé. The distance from Mex 1 to the camping area is 11.2 miles (18.1 km). We found the road solid and fine for any vehicle, however, conditions undoubtedly vary and you should check with someone who has driven the road lately before attempting it in your rig. After 2.1 miles (3.4 km) there is a fork in the road, take the right fork for the new road. The road nears the shoreline at 5.4 miles (8.7 km) and turns left to parallel the shoreline some quarter mile back from the beach. At about 8.5 miles (13.7 km) from the highway the road turns inland and rounds the end of a runway, then returns toward the beach reaching the resort at 10.5 miles (16.9 km). Turn left here following signs for Playa Camping and proceed another .7 mile (1.1 km) eastward to the camping area. En route you will pass through a row of houses which overlooks the beach and campground.

TODOS SANTOS (TOE-does SAHN-toes)
Population 4,000, Elevation 100 ft (30 m)

Todos Santos is the Baja's art colony. This is an old mission and sugar cane town but today it is better known for the many norteamericanos who have arrived in search of a simple small-town ambiance. There are galleries, crafts stores, and restaurants, as well as a bookstore called El Tecolote. The town is only a mile or so from the coast, there are decent beaches near town but the one at the San Pedrito RV park is one of the best in the area. You're just south of the Tropic of Cancer in Todos Santos, that means you're in the Tropics!

Todos Santos Campgrounds

TODOS SANTOS

To La Paz · 19
(A) Hotel California
(B) Juarez Statue
(C) Supermercado

To Cabo San Lucas · 19

EL LITRO

🚐 EL LITRO

GPS Location: N 23° 26' 25.4", W 110° 13' 37.1"

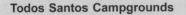

This is a small campground on a dusty back road in the village of Todos Santos. The entrance road is a little tight but passable, once inside there's room for the largest rigs to maneuver. There's a definite small village Mexican ambiance to this campground.

The campground has 16 back-in spaces with 15-amp outlets, sewer, and water hookups. There is also a shaded area under a large tree for tent campers. Several of the spaces have patios, some are even shaded by palapas. A small building has two restrooms with flush toilets and hot water showers. The attendant is not always there but he'll be by in the evening to collect.

To find the campground turn west on Carillo near the southern entrance to Todos Santos. The turn is marked by a campground sign. The campground is directly ahead .2 miles (.4 km) from the turn.

🚐 SAN PEDRITO RV PARK

    Address: Apdo. 15, Todos Santos, B.C.S., México
    Telephone: (1) 127-9909   **Fax:** (1) 123-4643

GPS Location: N 23° 23' 29.3", W 110° 11' 17.2"

San Pedrito is located on a beautiful beach some 4 miles (6.5 km) south of Todos

Santos. There's a sandy but decent road leading the 1.8 miles (2.9 km) from Mex 19 out to the campground. One there you have a choice, there's an RV park with full hookups and a camping area next to the beach with no hookups. This is a popular surfing beach and many van and tent campers use the less expensive no-hookup area. The full-hookup area is just as popular with RVers.

The RV campground has 71 pull-through spaces with 15-amp outlets, sewer, and water. Exercise caution about straying off well-used roadways, this is a sandy area and there are soft spots. Restrooms for the RV area are clean and in good repair, they have hot showers. The San Pedrito has a restaurant/bar with satellite TV, a

pool, and a laundry. There are even a few cabañas for rent. English is spoken and reservations are accepted.

The cutoff for the campground is near the Km 59 marker about 4 miles (6.5 km) south of Todos Santos. It is well marked with a large sign. The sandy road to the campground has a Y at 1.4 miles (2.3 km), go left. You'll reach the campground gate at 1.7 miles (2.7 km).

🚐 LOS CERRITOS CAMPGROUND

GPS Location: N 23° 20' 49.2", W 110° 09' 43.2"

This is another of the old government campgrounds. It is located just above a beautiful beach, a very popular surfing location.

Campers park either in the campground or in front above the beach. The front fence to the government campground is gone so there is little difference. The hookups other than sewer are non-functional anyway. There are no restrooms other than pit toilets.

The road out to the campground is .1 mile (.2 km) south of the Km 65 marker. The road is usually unmarked. It is a rough dusty road but can be traveled by any size rig. Driving toward the beach you'll reach a Y in 1.3 miles (2.1 km). The right fork takes you directly to a beach parking area, the left to the camping area in .3 miles (.5 km).

Side Trips from Todos Santos

The central **Sierra de la Laguna** are most easily entered from near Todos Santos. These granite mountains have pine forests and a large flat meadow at 5,600 feet known as **La Laguna** that is a popular hiking and tent camping destination. These mountains are unlike others on the peninsula in that the eastern slopes are the most gradual with

SOUTHERN BAJA PENINSULA

the western ones being much steeper. Unfortunately, access from the east is confusing and the trails hard to follow, unless you plan to use a guide the western access near Todos Santos is preferable.

There are three trails that cross the area, the northern-most which follows the Cañon San Dionisio is the most popular and the only one passing through La Laguna. Plan on at least two days for this hike, three would be better. You will need detailed topographical maps and warm clothes since the nights will be cold at high altitudes.

VIZCAÍNO JUNCTION, BAJA CALIFORNIA SUR (BIS-KAW-EEN-OH)

This junction is near the Km 144 marker of Mex 1 about 45 miles (73 km) southeast of Guerrero Negro and the border between North and South Baja. There's little at the junction except the Motel Kadekamaan and a Pemex station. If you follow the intersecting road toward the west you will eventually reach the ocean at Bahía Tortugas and Punta Eugenia.

Vizcaíno Junction Campground

🚐 MOTEL KAADEKAMÁN

Address: Carretera Transpeninsular Km 143,
                  Vizcaíno, B.C.S., México
Telephone: (1) 154-0812

GPS Location: N 27° 38' 46.1", W 113° 23' 05.8"

If you find yourself on the road east of Guerrero Negro when night falls you have no problem, the Motel Kaadekamán makes a convenient place to pull off the road and spend the night with electricity and water hookups.

This is a very small motel with five RV sites next door. Fifteen-amp outlets and water are available to the sites. The motel has no restroom facilities set aside for RVers but will put a room with hot shower at your disposal if you need them. Home-cooked meals are available.

The campground is located near the Km 143 marker on Mex 1 in the town of Vizcaíno. It is .4 miles (.6 km) east of the Pemex station.

Side Trips from the Vizcaíno Junction

The Vizcaíno Desert fills a huge sparsely-populated peninsula south of the Guerrero Negro lagoon. Long roads of varying quality cross it to reach the coast which has several decent sized towns including **Bahía Tortugas** and **Bahía Asunción**. Both towns can be reached by small RVs but the roads are long and rough. From the Vizcaíno Junction it is 111 miles (179 km) to Bahía Tortugas and 85 miles (139 km) to Bahía Asunción. The coast near both towns offers boondocking opportunities and there is even an access road to the fabled beachcombing at **Malarrimo Beach**. Any excursions off the two main roads requires suitable vehicles (often 4-wheel-drive) and a caravan of several vehicles would be a safer way of visiting this remote area.

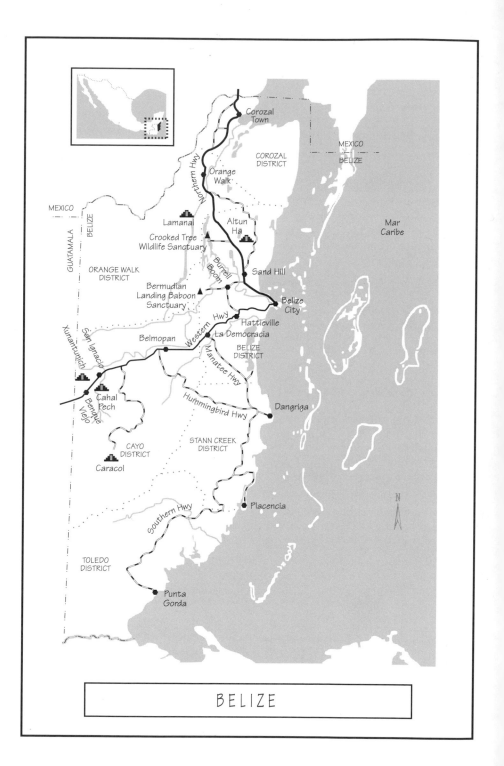

BELIZE

CHAPTER 14

BELIZE

INTRODUCTION

If you happen to be in the Yucatán with your RV you might consider a sidetrip to Belize. The country makes an interesting contrast to Mexico. It also has it's own unique set of attractions, many very different than anything you will find in Mexico. There are difficulties too, mostly involving the border crossing. You'll want to take a careful look at the *Crossing the Border* section below before making your go, or no-go, decision.

The most noticeable difference between Belize and Mexico is probably the language. Belize is English speaking. But the differences are deeper than just language. You'll notice that most of the houses in Belize are made of wood, not concrete. There are few Catholic churches, instead you'll find Protestant ones. The closest ties to Europe in Belize are to Great Britain, not Spain. In fact, Britain has done a lot over the years to keep Belize from becoming part of Guatemala. Even today you are likely to see British troops driving along the roads, particularly in the western part of the country.

Although English is the official language you'll find quite a bit of Spanish spoken, particularly in the north. You'll also find a language called Creole, a combination English, Spanish, and African dialects. The people in the country are a true variety with Mayas, Creoles, Guatemalans, Mexicans, Indians (from India) and even Mennonites.

Belize has an area of 8,867 square miles, it's about 175 miles from north to south and 70 miles from east to west. The total population is only about 240,000 people. All of the northern and eastern part of the country is very flat. The coast is very low-lying and is covered with mangroves. It's not a place where you'll find beautiful beaches. Off-shore, however, is a water playground. The offshore islands, known as cayes, are popular places for fishing, scuba diving, and boating. Mountains do rise in the west, at least mountains by Belize standards. Mountain Pine Ridge and the Maya Mountains rise to a height of around 3,000 feet and are covered by pine forests.

In Belize the political subdivisions we would call states are known as Districts. From north to south these are the **Corozal**, **Orange Walk**, **Cayo**, **Belize**, **Stann Creek**, and **Toledo** Districts. Large towns are scarce, the largest is **Belize City** on the coast with a population of 56,000. The capital is **Belmopan** which is about 55 miles (89 km) inland from Belize City and has a population of around 7,000. Other major towns are **Corozal Town**, **Orange Walk**, **San Ignacio**, **Dangriga**, and **Punta Gorda**.

Industries in Belize include fishing, logging, and growing sugar, bananas and citrus, Since there are no deep-water harbors it is difficult and expensive to ship products out of the country. Most products are grown or produced for the local economy. The Mennonites grow a great deal of the agricultural items sold in the stores including eggs, dairy products, and vegetables. Unemployment and underemployment are a problem here. It is hoped that tourism will help and in fact tourism has been becoming more and more important during the past few years. Most tourism is centered around the offshore cayes but there is also tourist interest in the inland Mayan sites and eco-logical destinations.

The currency in Belize is the Belize dollar. It is valued at two Belize dollars for one U.S. dollar. We find that the use of Belize dollars is not necessary if you have U.S. dollars, in fact everyone we did business with preferred U.S. dollars. Mexican pesos are more difficult to use, you will want to go to a bank to buy Belize dollars if you have only pesos.

ROAD SYSTEM

There are two modern paved highways in Belize. They're both two-lane highways built to good standards. The New Northern Highway leads from the border near Chetumal south to Belize city, a distance of 105 miles (169 km). The Western High-way leads west from Belize City a distance of 85 miles (137 km) past Belmopan, San Ignacio and Benque Viejo to the Guatemala border and the road onward to Tikal.

These two highways provide access to all of the camping areas described in this book. A short gravel road, which is being improved, provides a shortcut well outside Belize City between the two highways so that it is not necessary to drive into the city. Head-ing south from the Mexico border the short-cut goes west near mile marker 14, that's the distance from Belize City. It is signed for the Community Baboon Sanctuary. On the Western Highway the short-cut goes north near mile marker 15, that's also the distance from Belize City.

There are other roads, of course. Probably the most notable is the Hummingbird High-way leading south from near Belmopan to Dangriga. It connects with the Southern Highway which continues on to Punta Gorda near the southern border. There's also the Manatee Highway which also connects with the Southern Highway. None of these highways are considered suitable for most RVs but they can certainly be explored in a tow car, pickup, or van.

HIGHLIGHTS

For RVers the attractions of Belize are for the most part not along the seacoast. Road access there is limited and most tourist facilities are actually on islands. Inland, how-ever, there is plenty to do. Most attractions probably fall into the categories of archeo-logical sites and eco-destinations.

Belize, like the Yucatán Peninsula to the north, was an important Maya area. There are many important sites, some can be visited easily. The best include **Lamanai**, **Altun Ha**, **Cahal Pech**, **Xunantunich**, and **Caracol**. There's more information in the individual district write-ups below.

The Maya city of **Tikal** is actually in Guatemala, but many folks come to Belize to visit the site. Tikal is one of the most impressive of the Maya sites, you can easily take a tour into Guatemala to the site from San Ignacio or the border.

There are many ecological attractions in Belize, and more every year. This is the growth industry in this country. Some of these include **New River Lagoon**, **Crooked Tree Wildlife Sanctuary**, the **Bermudian Landing Baboon Sanctuary**, and the **Belize Zoo**.

A note about **Belize City**. The largest city in Belize is not really considered much of a tourist attraction by most people. Crime is a problem and the sights are limited. The city is a gateway to the islands and we'll talk about it briefly in the Belize District section below.

CROSSING THE BORDER

The border crossing is just a few miles west of the city of Chetumal, you'll see the turnoff as you approach the city. The crossing is open from 6 a.m. to 5 p.m. seven days a week. However, crossing on Sunday is difficult since you can't buy required liability insurance at the border on that day. Office hours at the border insurance office are 6 a.m. to 5 p.m. Monday through Friday, 6 a.m. to 2 p.m. on Saturday. You would have to buy it ahead of time in Chetumal or visit the border ahead of time just to buy the insurance.

There are two main reasons that few people take RVs into Belize from Mexico. Tourist card problems and insurance.

Mexican border officials at the Belize border usually want to take your tourist card away from you when you leave and issue you a new one when you return to the country. The new card they give you is a Transmigrante visa, it is designed to travel through the country to the U.S. and only gives you 15 days. This is a problem for most RVers since they plan to stay much longer in Mexico. The border officials do nothing with your vehicle permit so it remains as it was originally.

During the winter of 2000/2001 a new procedure was in effect. For a fee of 50 pesos (approximately $5 U.S.) the Mexican border officials would stamp your tourist card *Double Entrada* when you went into Belize and let you keep it so that you could return and continue your travels as before. This is despite the fact that the tourist cards are already multiple-entry cards and that at the U.S. border you are allowed to leave and come back without surrendering your card.

This procedure is unusual and doesn't seem to be in accordance with the policies and procedures we have become accustomed to at the U.S. border. It is difficult to say what will be happening when you visit.

The second problem is the insurance situation in Belize. Only liability insurance seems to be available, not comprehensive. That means that you are taking the entire risk for any damage to or loss of your own rig while in Belize. That's enough to keep most folks from crossing the border in their RVs.

BELIZE

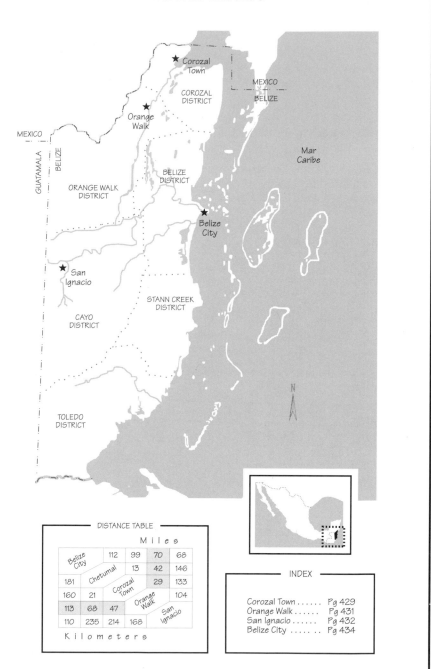

THE CAMPGROUNDS

★ Corozal Town

COROZAL DISTRICT

MEXICO
BELIZE

★ Orange Walk

MEXICO

GUATAMALA

BELIZE

ORANGE WALK DISTRICT

BELIZE DISTRICT

Mar Caribe

★ Belize City

★ San Ignacio

CAYO DISTRICT

STANN CREEK DISTRICT

TOLEDO DISTRICT

N

DISTANCE TABLE

Miles

Belize City	112	99	70	68
	Chetumal	13	42	146
181		Corozal Town	29	133
160	21		Orange Walk	104
113	68	47		San Ignacio
110	235	214	168	

Kilometers

The crossing procedure goes as follows. You are stopped at the Mexican border station going in and, hopefully, are able to get your tourist cards stamped *Double Entrada*. As you enter Belize you will see a small white building on your right. This is where you buy your insurance, it is not open on Sunday so if you plan on entering on Sunday you'll have to have previously purchased Belize liability insurance in Chetumal. The insurance is inexpensive, the rate based upon the number of cylinders in your engine. We paid $29 Belize dollars ($14.50 U.S.) for a week for our eight-cylinder van. You must have insurance before you will be allowed to bring in your RV. You'll be given a sticker by the insurance company to post on your window.

Next you go into the customs building on your left. Your first stop is to get a tourist card, this cost is $2 Belize dollars per person (or $1 U.S.). U.S. and Canadian citizens will need a passport. Then you go to another station to take care of getting a permit to bring in your auto and any other vehicles. These are logged in a hand-written ledger, they'll be crossed off when you leave. There's one further stop, you will be stopped just past the border station to have your vehicle fumigated (just the wheels, you stay in the rig), the cost is $8.50 Belize dollars or $4.25 U.S.

When you return to the border you have to pay a departure tax of $20 Belize dollars ($10 U.S.) per person and an ecology fee of $7.50 Belize dollars ($3.75 U.S.) per person. You also must visit the vehicle station inside the customs building to check out. Going in to Mexico you'll have your paper checked but under the Double Entry stamp procedure you should enter with no further paperwork.

As always, border procedures change often, they may very well be different when you visit.

Henry Menzies, a guide and the manager of the Caribbean Village RV park in Corozal Town, sometimes assists RVers when they cross the border. You can give him a call if would like to be escorted through the crossing. He provides this service for a fee. His phone number is 501-4-22725, his Fax 501-4-23414.

SELECTED CITIES AND THEIR CAMPGROUNDS

COROZOL TOWN AND THE COROZOL DISTRICT
Population of town 8,000

The northernmost district in Belize is called the Corozol District, the main town is Corozol Town. This is a very flat region, near the coast it is swampy while inland it is farming land. In the past this was a sugar cane farming area, now there is a great deal of clothing manufacture, particularly in Corozol Town.

Corozol Town sits in the coastline, which makes it vulnerable to the frequent hurricanes that hit this coast. Although there are many wooden buildings here today, there were many more before the town was almost destroyed by Hurricane Janet in 1955. You'll find a bank, stores, gas stations and restaurants in the town.

Sights in this northernmost district are few. There are a few Maya ruins including **Santa Rita**, a very small one on the northern outskirts of Corozol Town. There's another site, **Cerros**, just across the bay. You can hire a water taxi in Corozol Town to get there or, during the dry winter season, drive there in a tow car or small rig. You also might want to drive northeast from central Corozol Town about seven miles to Consejo Shore, where some of the nicer homes are located. RV campers will find that Corozol's campgrounds make a good base for exploring some of the sights a little farther south since distances are so short in Belize.

Corozal District Campgrounds

🚐 LAGOON CAMPGROUND

Address: Bill Dixon, General Delivery, Corozal Town, Belize

GPS Location: N 18° 28' 14.0", W 088° 23' 47.5"

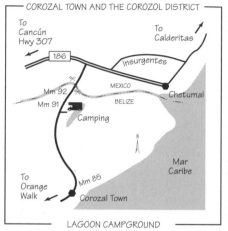

COROZAL TOWN AND THE COROZOL DISTRICT — LAGOON CAMPGROUND

The first campground you'll see as you enter Belize is actually one of the nicest . It's not in a town so it's quiet but not terribly convenient for getting acquainted with the people of a new country. It's on the shore of Four-mile Lagoon, a large lake that opens into the Rio Hondo. A large grassy area fronts the camping area next to the lake.

Campsites are back-in spaces set in trees, much like a national park campground in the states. They're all back-in sites, most are suitable for big rigs. There are nine with full hookups (15-amp outlets) and there is also a dump station. Restrooms are simple, they have flush toilets and cold water showers. There's also a picnic table with a palapa shade.

The campground is on the east side of the road near Mile 91. That's about 1.5 miles (2.4 km) south of the border. There's a large sign out front.

🚐 CARIBBEAN VILLAGE

Address: P.O. Box 210, Corozal Town, Belize
Telephone: 501-4-22725   **Fax:** 501-4-23414

GPS Location: N 18° 22' 59.3", W 088° 23' 43.9"

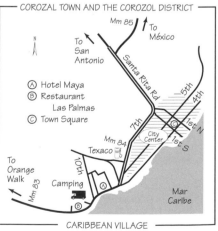

COROZAL TOWN AND THE COROZOL DISTRICT — CARIBBEAN VILLAGE

Located at the southern edge of the town of Corozol this campground makes an excellent place to stay on your first day in Belize. The manager, Henry Menzies, probably knows more about RVing in Belize than anyone else in the country. He acts as a guide for many of the caravan companies. They often park in Chetumal and have Henry guide them into Belize on bus tours.

From the campground it's easy to stroll into town to check out the Belize lifestyle and the prices in the grocery stores.

The campground is located in a grassy field across the highway from the ocean. Eight back-in sites have electricity (15-amp outlets) and sewer, some also have water. Large rigs will fit. The restrooms are basic but have flush toilets and cold showers. There's a restaurant on the property.

To find the campground just follow the main road south through town until it meets and runs south along the ocean. Watch for the Hotel Maya on the right, the campground is just beyond. The restaurant Las Palmas sits on the campground property, the first turn into the campground is north of the restaurant and there is another to the south.

ORANGE WALK AND THE ORANGE WALK DISTRICT
Population of town 16,000

Orange Walk District is definitely sugarcane country. You'll likely encounter many heavily loaded trucks along the cane-littered highway. It's also Mennonite country, you're bound to notice their horse-drawn buggies.

The major town is Orange Walk, Belize's second largest town. It's an active town with much more street life than in Corozol Town. Still, it's small and offers little more than restaurants, banks, and a few stores.

Undoubtedly the most popular tourist attraction in the district is **Lamanai**. These Maya ruins are set in the jungle, there are more than 60 structures. One of the best parts of a visit is the hour and a half boat trip up the **New River** and across the **New River Lagoon** to get there. You'll see a variety of bird life and probably a crocodile or two as well. Boats leave from the Tower Hill toll bridge which is along the Northern highway about .3 miles (7 km) south of Orange Walk Town. Contact Jungle River Tours at the landing or by calling (3) 23749. Boats leave about 9 a.m.

Four miles (6 km) south of Orange Walk the highway splits with the paved New Northern Highway going right and the Old Northern Highway to the left. If you continue on the old highway you'll reach **Altun Ha**, another large Maya site. It's actually in the Belize District but is easier to visit from campgrounds in the north

Orange Walk District Campground

🚐 VICTOR'S INN

GPS Location: N 18° 05' 01.4", W 088° 32' 26.9"

$$ ⛺ 🚐 🚿 🍽️

Victor's Inn is actually a restaurant located a mile or so outside Orange Walk, not on the main Northern Highway but on a side road running out of town to the east. The restaurant has a large cleared field in the rear and additional room for parking near the front. There are no hookups but a dump station is being installed and there is a restroom with flush toilet and cold shower.

ORANGE WALK AND
THE ORANGE WALK DISTRICT

THE QUIET STREETS OF ORANGE WALK

If you are entering Orange Walk from the north watch for the hospital on your right. Zero your odometer here and in .4 miles (.6 km) you should spot a road going left that crosses a bridge just .1 mile (.2 km) from the highway. You want to follow this road across the bridge, then 1 mile (1.6 km) from the bridge at a Y take the right fork which is marked for Honey Camp Beach. In another .2 miles (.3 km) you'll see Victor's on the right.

San Ignacio and the Cayo District
Population of town 11,570

As you approach Santa Elena (sometimes called Cayo), about 70 miles (113 km) west of Belize City, the land begins to rise and you actually find yourself in an area of very scenic rolling hills. Best of all, the temperature drops several degrees from what it is in the flatlands to the east.

Probably for these reasons San Ignacio and a string of small towns that stretch eastward including Georgeville and Santa Elena are favorites of expatriate Americans and Canadians. They're also an excellent place to base yourself to explore the attractions of the region.

San Ignacio sits along the Macal River. On the far bank is Santa Elena and joining the two are two bridges, a scenic old suspension bridge and the new bridge. San Ignacio and Santa Elena together offer pretty much everything you will need including good restaurants, tour information and tour guides, and the necessary places to buy the supplies you need. You actually may find that you do your shopping in the nearby Mennonite town of Spanish Lookout, locals say the offerings are better there.

Although there is a government information office in San Ignacio the real info center is Eva's Restaurant in central San Ignacio. Tourists and locals congregate there and information is readily exchanged.

You'll find that there is lots to do in the Cayo District. One attraction is the Pine Mountain Ridge, a hilly region that stretches from east to west south of San Ignacio. Dirt roads suitable for tow cars penetrate the area and there are a number of interesting destinations including the **Rio On Pools and Falls**, the **Rio Frio Caves**, and **Hidden Valley Falls**. Get a local map before heading out because the road system in the hills can be confusing.

There are a variety of Maya sites in the Cayo District. The easiest to see is on the outskirts of San Ignacio. This is **Cahal Pech**. Just follow Buena Vista Road up the hill from the vicinity of the old suspension bridge, you'll see the sign sending you to the left in about .6 mile (1 km). It's a small site but some of the structures have been stuccoed, just as they were in ancient times. A larger site west of San Ignacio, **Xunantunich**, is fun to visit because of the way you get there. Drive westward about 8 miles (13 km) from San Ignacio to the town of San Jose Succotz. From there you must cross the river on a small ferry, the site is up the hill on the far side. More difficult to visit and much more impressive is **Caracol**. This is a huge 88-square-mile site located near the southern edges of the Pine Mountain Ridge area. It's difficult to visit in just one day and is best done in a four-wheel-drive rig. If you want to visit it's easiest to book a tour in San Ignacio and let them take care of transportation.

Cayo District Campgrounds

⎙ CAESAR'S PLACE GUEST HOUSE

    Address: P.O. Box 48, San Ignacio, Belize
    Telephone: 501-9-22341   **Fax:** 501-9-23449

   GPS Location: N 17° 12' 17.1", W 088° 57' 11.3"

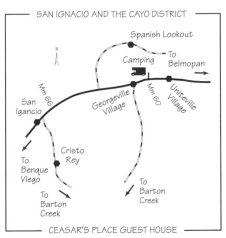

SAN IGNACIO AND THE CAYO DISTRICT
CEASAR'S PLACE GUEST HOUSE

Caesar's Place is an excellent location to use as a base for exploring Santa Elena and the Mountain Pine Ridge. In addition to the camping area there are guest rooms and a restaurant and bar as well as a gift shop.

There are only four spaces here, two are back-ins and two are parallel parking along the driveway. Spaces have electric (15-amp outlets), water, and sewer hookups. There's a restroom with flush toilets and cold showers. Internet access is available at the gift shop. An Airstream caravan stayed here shortly before we visited, they were able to park (for a fee) in a large field next door that is owned by the guest house.

Caesar's is on the north side of the highway near Mile 60. Watch for a Shell gasoline station on the right, the guest house is on the right 1.1 miles (1.8 km) after the station.

INGLEWOOD CAMPING GROUNDS

Address: Mile 68 1/4 Cayo, Benque Viejo
                 Rd., Belize

**Telephone
and Fax:**   501-9-23555

GPS Location: N 17° 08' 20.7", W 089° 05' 15.5"

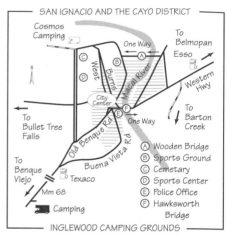

This is a new campground located on the far (west) side of San Ignacio. There is lots of room for big rigs and the owner is very accommodating. Tents are allowed.

The campground has four back-in sites with electricity (15-amp outlets) and water. More electric hookups are planned. There is also room for perhaps 50 rigs to boondock here in a large grassy field. There is also a dump station. A new restroom building has flush toilets and hot showers. Several palapas are provided for shade.

The campground is along the Western Highway just outside San Ignacio to the west very near the Mile 68 marker. This is a distance of perhaps 1.5 miles (2.4 km) from central San Ignacio.

Other Camping Possibilities

Tent campers have a couple more possibilities in San Ignacio. Both **Cosmos** and **Midas Resort**, along the river a short walk northwest of town offer a place to pitch a tent.

Side Trip from San Ignacio

Many visitors to Belize come because they want to visit **Tikal**. Tikal is actually in Guatemala. The road from the Belize border to Tikal is now mostly paved so it is actually possible to make the visit as a day trip so that you don't have to worry about accommodations in Guatemala. Van tours are readily available, one good place to check for tours is Eva's Restaurant.

BELIZE CITY AND THE BELIZE DISTRICT
Population of city 80,000

Belize City is the largest and, while no longer the capital, certainly the most important city in the country. Small by most standards, the place is a little intimidating due to its poverty, garbage, and aggressive panhandlers, con men and dope salesmen. However, reports are that it has improved in recent years and a visit should be interesting. It's also the place to catch a boat out to the cayes. The best way to visit is to leave your rig at a secure campground outside the city and use the bus system, if you do drive in make sure to park your vehicle only in a guarded parking lot.

For a walking tour of the town start at the **Swing Bridge** which bridges **Haulover Creek** near its mouth. Follow **Regent Street** on the south bank and it will lead you through the business district. One block to your left will put you on the waterfront, a popular tourist destination is the **Bliss Institute**. Most stores are along **Albert Street** which is one block inland from Regent Street.

If you go northward instead from the Swing Bridge you're in an area with hotels and older residences. You can make your way to the waterfront to see the **Baron Bliss Memorial** and **Memorial Park**.

The docks for small boats out to the cayes are just inland from the Swing Bridge. Most boats leave in the morning before 10. The fares are generally pretty reasonable.

There are a number of interesting sites in Belize District to the east of Belize city. The **Belize Zoo** has an excellent collection of local wildlife, it is at Mile 28.5 on the Western Highway. The **Monkey Bay Wildlife Sanctuary**, at Mile 31.5 of the Western Highway, is a protected natural area with trails and a river. **Guanacaste National Park**, near the intersection of the Western Highway with the Hummingbird Highway, is a small protected rainforest area featuring a 100-year-old guanacaste tree and nature trails. The **Community Baboon Sanctuary** at Bermudian Landing is located off the road that connects the Western and Northern Highways west of Belize City. It protects over 1000 black howler monkeys, called baboons here. There's a wildlife museum and there are trails and river trips available to see wildlife, excellent for bird watching.

Belize District Campground

🚐 **JB's WATERING HOLE**

Address:	P.O. Box 290, Belmopan, Belize
Telephone:	501-8-13026 **Fax:** 501-8-13026
E-mail:	neesermgm@btl.net
Web Site:	www.jbbelize.com

GPS Location: N 17° 19' 03.6", W 088° 34' 22.2"

$$ \boxed{\text{\$\$}} \quad \boxed{⌂} \quad \boxed{↟} \quad \boxed{\text{🍴}} \quad \boxed{\text{C}} \quad \boxed{💻} $$

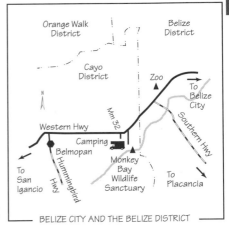

BELIZE CITY AND THE BELIZE DISTRICT

JB's is really a bar and restaurant. The most reliable customers are the many British and U.S. troops stationed or on training maneuvers in western Belize. This is a friendly and fun place, and also a pretty good place to park your rig if you are going in to Belize City, you can catch a bus on the road out front. Also, the food is excellent.

There are a couple of spaces where you can string an electrical line and no other hookups. There is room, however, for about 10 large rigs to boondock in the parking lot here. There is also a nice lawn on the far side for tent campers. The restaurant has a restroom with flush toilet but no shower. Phone and internet services are available.

JB's is on the south side of the Western Highway near Mile 32. This is 2.7 (.3 km) miles west of the Belize Zoo. You've probably noticed that this campground is not in Belize City at all, but it's a good place to leave your rig while you visit the city by bus.

Other Camping Possibilities

The **Monkey Bay Wildlife Sanctuary** at Mile 31.5 of the Western Highway offers tent camping and a dormitory.

Side Trip from Belize District

The southern half of Belize has much poorer roads than the north, but they can easily be explored in any smaller vehicle, not a large RV. The best road south is the mostly-paved Hummingbird Highway which heads south from Mile 48 of the Western Highway near Belmopan.

The coastal town of **Dangriga** is about 55 miles (89 km) from the intersection with the Western Highway. This town is southern Belize's largest with a population of 10,000. It is best known for each year's November 19 celebration of Garifuna Settlement Day.

From not far inland of Dangriga another highway, the Southern Highway extends on to **Placencia** and Punta Gorda. Placencia is a laid-back coastal town that is much like the towns on the cayes, but this one is connected to the road system. It's on a peninsula and offers sandy beaches (hard to find in Belize) and small restaurants and bars. Tent camping is possible at the northern edge of town along the beach. The drive from Dangriga to Placencia is about 30 miles (49 km)

Much farther south at the end of the road is **Punta Gorda**. From here small boats go south to Guatemala. Excursions can be arranged in town to visit tourist sites in the surrounding Toledo District. These include the village of **San Pedro Columbia**, and the **Lubaantun** and **Nim Li Punit** Maya sites. Punta Gorda is 80 miles (130 km) south of Placencia.

INDEX

TERRI AND MIKE AT PARACUTÍN

ABOUT THE AUTHORS

For the last nine years Terri and Mike Church have traveled in Mexico, Alaska, Europe, Canada, and the western U.S. Most of this travel has been in RVs, a form of travel they love. It's affordable and comfortable, the perfect way to see the places that interest them.

During the course of their travels they noticed that few guidebooks were available with the essential day-to-day information that camping travelers need when they are in unfamiliar surroundings. *Traveler's Guide to European Camping, Traveler's Guide to Mexican Camping, Traveler's Guide to Camping Mexico's Baja, Traveler's Guide to Alaskan Camping,* and *RV Adventures in the Pacific Northwest* are designed to be the guidebooks that the authors tried to find when they first traveled to these places.

Terri and Mike now live full-time in an RV traveling, writing new books, and working to keep these guidebooks as up-to-date as possible. The books are written and prepared for printing using laptop computers while on the road.

Traveler's Guide To Camping Mexico's Baja
6" x 9" Paperback, 224 Pages, Over 65 Maps
ISBN 0-9652968-5-7

Sun, Sand, and clear blue water are just three of the many reasons more and more RVers are choosing Mexico's Baja as a winter destination. The Baja is fun, easy, and the perfect RVing getaway.

With the right information crossing the border onto the Baja is a snap. Only a few miles south you'll find many camping opportunities-some on beaches where you'll park your vehicle just feet from the water.

The Transpeninsular Highway 1 extends south for 1,061 miles, all the way to the tip of the peninsula in Cabo San Lucas. This two-lane paved highway gives access to some of the most remote and interesting country in the world, including lots of desert and miles and miles of deserted beaches. RVers love this country for boating, fishing, beachcombing, and just plain enjoying the sunshine.

Traveler's Guide To Camping Mexico's Baja starts by giving you the Baja-related infromation from our popular book *Traveler's Guide To Mexican Camping*. It also covers nearby Puerto Peñasco. We've added more campgrounds, expanded the border crossing section, and given even more information about towns, roads, and recreational opportunities. Like all our books, this one features easy-to-follow maps showing exactly how to find every campground listed. If you're planning to visit the Baja or Puerto Peñasco this book is a great economical alternative to our Mexican camping guide which covers Mexico's mainland as well as the Baja.

Traveler's Guide To European Camping
6" x 9" Paperback, 448 Pages, Over 250 Maps
ISBN 0-9652968-3-0

Does the map on the side of your camping rig show you've visited most of the 48 contiguous states, Alaska, or even Mexico? You've shopped the biggest mall in America, wintered in the Florida Keys, camped in the desert outside Quartzsite, Arizona, seen the color in the Northeast in the fall? What next?

If you're looking for a new camping experience, try Europe. *Traveler's Guide To European Camping* makes touring the European continent as easy and as affordable as traveling in North America. The guide gives you complete information for planning your trip as well as cost data and specific instructions on how to ship your camping vehicle from North America to Europe, buy a camping vehicle in Europe, or rent a camping vehicle in Europe.

The guide covers almost 250 campgrounds including several in each important European city. Both driving directions and maps are provided to make finding the campgrounds in these foreign cities as easy as finding those in America. The book features campgrounds in:

* Paris	* Munich	* The Romantic Road
* London	* Madrid	* The Loire Valley
* Rome	* Athens	* The Swiss Alps
* Lisbon	* Istanbul	* The Greek Islands
* Amsterdam	* Oslo	* And Many More!

In addition to planning and campground information, *Traveler's Guide To European Camping* gives you invaluable details about the history and sights you will encounter. This information will help you plan your itinerary and enjoy yourself when you are on the road.

Go for a week, a month, or a year. Europe could fill your RVing seasons for years to come!

Traveler's Guide To Alaskan Camping
6" x 9" Paperback, 416 Pages, Over 100 Maps
ISBN 0-9652968-2-2

Alaska, the dream trip of a lifetime! Be prepared for something spectacular. Alaska is one-fifth the size of the entire United States, it has 17 of the 20 highest peaks in the U.S., 33,904 miles of shoreline, and has more active glaciers and ice fields than the rest of the inhabited world.

In addition to some of the most magnificent scenery the world has to offer, Alaska is chock full of an amazing variety of wildlife. You are likely to see bald eagles, Dall sheep, moose, bison, brown bears, caribou, beavers, black bears, a wide variety of marine birds and waterfowl, whales, porpoises, sea lions, sea otters, and more. Some of these animals may even pay you a visit at your campsite.

Alaska is an outdoor enthusiast's paradise. Fishing, hiking, canoeing, rafting, hunting, and wildlife viewing are only a few of the many activities which will keep you outside during the long summer days.

Traveler's Guide To Alaskan Camping makes this dream trip to Alaska as easy as camping in the "lower 48". It provides details on:

❑ Over 400 campgrounds throughout Alaska and on the roads north in Canada with campground descriptions and maps showing the exact location of each campground.

❑ Complete coverage of the routes north, including the Alaska Highway, the Cassiar Highway, and the Alaska Marine Highway.

❑ RV rental information for both Alaska and Canada.

❑ Things to do and see throughout your trip, including suggested fishing holes, hiking trails, canoe trips, wildlife viewing opportunities, and much more.

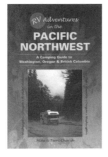

RV Adventures in the Pacific Northwest
6" x 9" Paperback, 224 Pages, Over 75 Maps
ISBN 0-9652968-4-9

There are many reasons why the Pacific Northwest is considered an RVers paradise. It offers everything an RV vacationer could desire: seashores, snow-topped mountains, old-growth forests, visitor-friendly cities, and national parks. In fact, the Pacific Northwest is one of the most popular RVing destinations in North America.

RV Adventures in the Pacific Northwest provides exciting and interesting 1-week itineraries from the Northwest gateway cities of Seattle, Portland, and Vancouver. Maps and written descriptions guide you along scenic easy-to-negotiate tours. Each day's drive leads to an interesting destination. The book includes descriptions of the local attractions and activities as well as maps showing good local RV campgrounds.

So come and join us for a tour of the Northwest. Go for a week or spend the entire summer, the choice is yours. Here are a few of the well known destinations we'll visit:

* The Olympic Peninsula
* Mount St. Helens
* The Oregon Coast
* The Columbia Gorge
* Victoria
* Banff and Lake Louise

* Mount Rainier
* The North Cascades
* The Oregon Trail
* Hell's Canyon
* Vancouver Island
* And Lots More!!

To order complete the following and send to:

Rolling Homes Press
161 Rainbow Dr., #6157
Livingston, TX 77399-1061

Name_____

Address_____

City_____State_____Zip_____

Telephone_____

Description	Qty	Price	Subtotal
Traveler's Guide To Alaskan Camping	____	$19.95	_____
Traveler's Guide To Mexican Camping	____	$19.95	_____
Traveler's Guide To Camping Mexico's Baja	____	$12.95	_____
Traveler's Guide To European Camping	____	$19.95	_____
RV Adventures in the Pacific Northwest	____	$14.95	_____

Subtract - Multiple Title Discounts

3 Book Set (3 Different Titles Shown Above)	**-10.00**	_____
4 Book Set (4 Different Titles Shown Above)	**-15.00**	_____
5 Book Set (5 Different Titles Shown Above)	**-20.00**	_____

Method of Payment
- ❑ Check
- ❑ Visa
- ❑ Mastercard

Order total: _____
Shipping: 5.00 *
Total: _____

Credit Card # _____ Exp. date _____

Signature _____

To order by phone call toll free from the U.S. or Canada 1-888-265-6555
Outside the U.S. or Canada call (425) 822-7846
Have your VISA or MC ready

U.S. Dollars or MC/VISA only for non-U.S. orders

Rolling Homes Press is not responsible for taxes or duty on books shipped outside the U.S.

*$5 shipping regardless of quantity ordered for all orders sent to the same address

Visit our web site at **www.rollinghomes.com**